I0446073

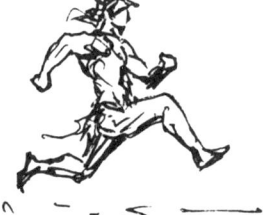

THE FANTASTIC ART OF
Roy G. Krenkel

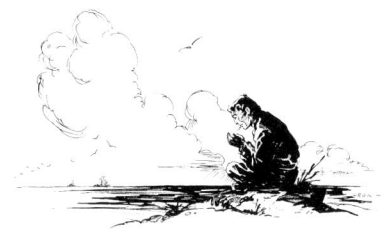

CURATED BY CRAIG YOE
PRODUCED BY CLIZIA GUSSONI

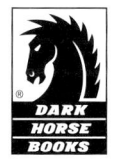 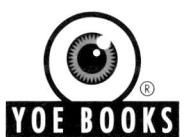 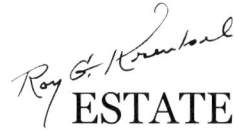

MIKE RICHARDSON
president and publisher, Dark Horse Books

CRAIG YOE and CLIZIA GUSSONI
co-editors, designers, and publishers, Yoe Books

BARRY KLUGERMAN
trustee of the Estate of Roy G. Krenkel

ANDREW STEVEN DAMSITS
associate editor, Yoe Books, and executive project developer, the Estate of Roy G. Krenkel

a very special thank you to TOPPER HELMERS,
a great artist who knows a great artist when he sees one

Special thanks to Sara Frazetta and Michael Wm. Kaluta for their support of this project and generous foreword pieces. Special thanks to Cary Grazzini.

PHILIP R. SIMON
senior editor, Dark Horse Books

ROSE WEITZ
associate editor, Dark Horse Books

ADAM PRUETT
digital art technician, Dark Horse Books

THE FANTASTIC ART OF ROY G. KRENKEL

© 2025 Gussoni-Yoe Studio, Inc. All rights reserved. ART Copyright © 2025 THE ESTATE OF ROY G. KRENKEL. ALL RIGHTS RESERVED. Dark Horse Books® and the Dark Horse logo are registered trademarks of Dark Horse Comics LLC, registered in various categories and countries. All rights reserved. Dark Horse is part of Embracer Group. Yoe Books and the Yoe Books logo are registered trademarks of Gussoni-Yoe Studio, Inc. All rights reserved. No portion of this publication may be reproduced or transmitted, in any form or by any means, without the express written permission of Dark Horse Comics LLC.

Dark Horse Books
A division of Dark Horse Comics LLC
10956 SE Main Street
Milwaukie, OR 97222

Represented in the EU by Authorised Rep Compliance Ltd.
Ground Floor, 71 Lower Baggot Street | Dublin, D02 P593, Ireland
ARCCompliance.com

DarkHorse.com

YoeBooks.com

Comic Shop Locator Service: ComicShopLocator.com

Library of Congress Control Number 2024051484

First edition: September 2025
Ebook ISBN 978-1-50674-826-9
Hardcover ISBN 978-1-50674-530-5
Limited Edition Hardcover ISBN 978-1-50675-020-0

10 9 8 7 6 5 4 3 2 1
Printed in China

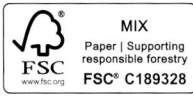

ROY KRENKEL
Friend and Mentor

Roy G. Krenkel (July 11, 1918 - February 24 1983) born in The Bronx, was an American illustrator who specialized in fantasy and historical drawings and paintings for books, magazines, and comic books. Krenkel was an avid collector and a lifelong student, constantly seeking inspiration from the greats which came before him, such as J. Allen St. John, Norman Lindsay, and Franklin Booth. He left behind a considerable legacy, reviving the writing of Edgar Rice Burroughs with his gorgeous paperback covers, and influenced at least three generations of fantasy and science fiction artists, including his dear friend, Frank Frazetta.

Before serving as a private in the U.S. Army in the Philippines in World War II, Krenkel studied at the Art Students League of New York under George Bridgman. After World War II, he attended Burne Hogarth's classes at the Cartoonists and Illustrators School, which became the School of Visual Arts. Professionally, Krenkel first drew comics for EC and other houses. It was through this schooling and comic work he met and worked with Al Williamson, Frank Frazetta, Ernie Bache, John Severin, Wally Wood, and others. Krenkel met Frazetta for the first time through their mutual friend, Al Williamson. He and Al drove to Frazetta's Brooklyn home in the early 1950s. Krenkel remarked, "He wasn't called 'The Great Frazetta' in

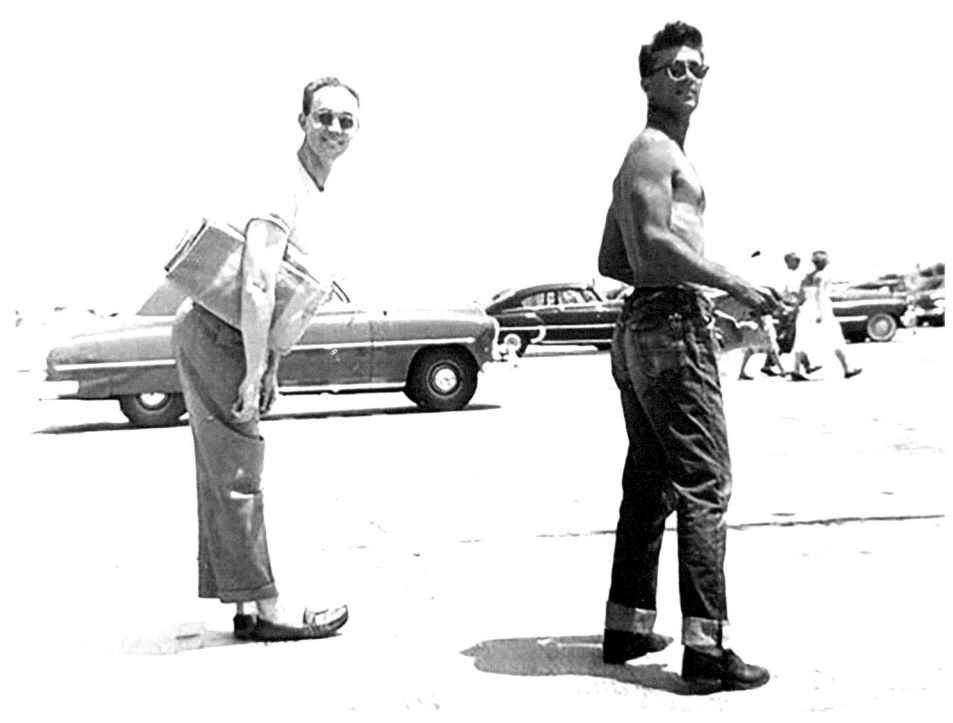

Above: Roy G. Krenkel [left] and Frank Frazetta [right] were mutual admirers, sometimes collaborators, and fast friends.

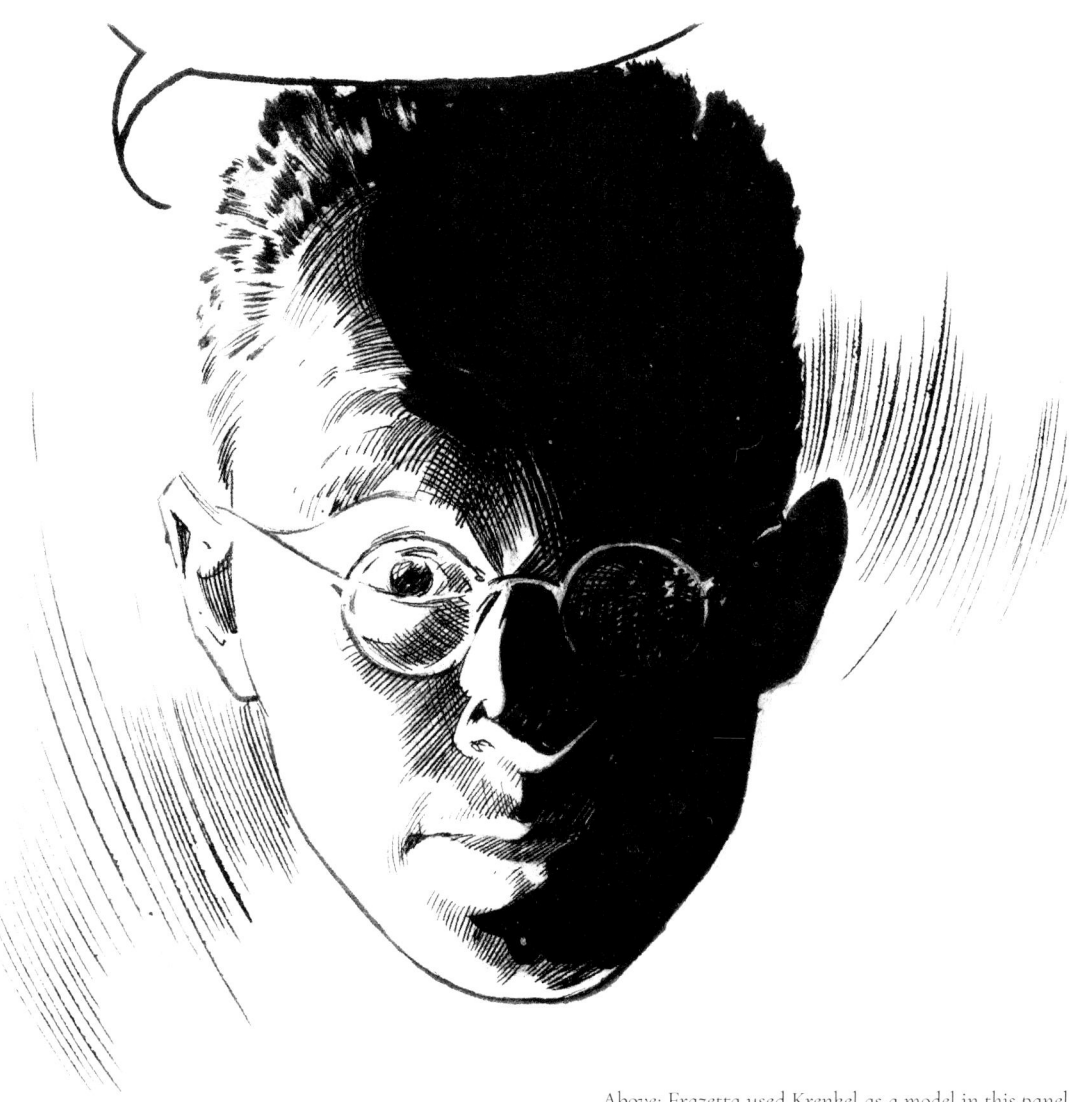

Above: Frazetta used Krenkel as a model in this panel art from an unpublished EC sci-fi comic book story.

those days...but we were all awed by his talent. He could do anything! And we knew him for a couple of years before we knew about his background, and of little things like the 'Snowman' and the funny little animals that he did in comic books. We knew that he was doing 'Dan Brand'...at the time we met, he was just starting to futz around with Dan Brand. Of course, he was influenced by Foster then, and at times he was the equal of Foster. We were impressed!"

Krenkel, Williamson, and Frazetta became close friends fairly quickly after their meeting. Together, they enjoyed each other's unique perspectives, talent, and sense of humor. They had fun when they worked and never really felt like they were working. Williamson called it, "a labor of love." A notable collaboration for the group, nicknamed, "The Fleagle Gang," was a 7-page story in *Weird Fantasy* #20, "I Rocket" (EC, 1953). Williamson, Frazetta, and Krenkel teamed up to illustrate the classic tale adapted from a story by sci-fi legend, Ray Bradbury. The pages, pencilled by Williamson, inked by Frazetta, and detailed by Krenkel, were absolutely stunning, like all of the artwork they collaborated on.

Krenkel went on to illustrate for SF magazines, paperback covers for historical novels, and most notably, set a new standard for excellence for fantasy art with his covers he painted for Ace Books. Don Wollheim, author and editor in the paperback field, discovered Roy from his work in the fanzine *AMRA*, and tapped him to illustrate the new line of ACE Edgar Rice Burroughs paperbacks. Krenkel knocked it out of the park with his cover for ERB *At The Earth's Core* (Ace books, 1962).

Krenkel's success with ACE led to more work than he wished to handle, so he called his good friend Frank Frazetta for assistance. Frazetta assisted him on the *Tarzan the Invincible, Back To The Stone Age,* and *The Mastermind of Mars* ACE paperback covers. After a series of well received collaborative paperback covers, Krenkel suggested that Don Wollheim hire Frazetta. Wollheim was reluctant, but Krenkel convinced him, "You gotta get this guy, Frazetta. He is different!"

"I did the first few covers by myself, and then somewhere down the line, maybe the fourth one, if memory serves, I dragged Frank in to helping me with the difficult areas. Not so much with the idea, but the painting, which Frank could do and I couldn't. When he would help me, Frank's problem was to try and make it look like mine. It was very difficult for him to attempt to confine himself to my rigid, dull style at that time. Frank would paint the hair, and work out how lighting would go across a face, or a hand, he picked up the color...little details, highlights. He knew just how to 'pop it.' When I would get to an area that I was unsure of, and didn't want to kill the thing at that point, I'd say, 'you'd better take it, Frank.' And, he would dutifully try to keep it as rigid as the rest of the damn stuff. I didn't know, for instance, how an eye would go when the head was tipped down. I couldn't figure out where it would be dark and where it would be light. Frank knew all this, and he had great control, which I didn't have. I was pretty sloppy in those days, and am getting sloppier now."

A few years later, Krenkel and Frazetta once again joined forces. Krenkel created preliminary roughs for Frazetta's *Dracula vs. Wolfman* and *Gargoyle*, which would be published on the covers of *Creepy* and *Eerie* (Warren Publishing). Krenkel and Frazetta remained colleagues and lifelong friends until Krenkel passed away from cancer in 1983. In an interview conducted shortly after Krenkel's death, Frazetta remembered his old friend this way: "I thought of Roy as just a wonderful inspiration, a lot of fun, a lot of laughs. Certainly, he made me go. There are a few people that made me go in my career, but he was certainly a major factor. Roy really introduced me to books and showed me art and showed me just how far you could really go. I was awfully casual about it; I just did my thing my way, and really didn't make any pretensions of going to high places or anything quite like that. And Roy said: 'You must do this, Frank. Look at these guys, look at these guys.' And he'd show me this wonderful art that really got me fired up. Not that I wanted to be like them, but it just amazed me as to the kind of talent that really was out there that I wasn't aware of. Whether they were alive or dead, you know? And it really got me fired, just like it seems I inspire younger artists. These guys inspired the hell out of me, forced me to look! It was great. It was great conversation about the many, many nuances of art. What makes it work, what doesn't make it work, and it was quite an education."

—Sara Frazetta
Sara Frazetta is the granddaughter of legendary fantasy artist Frank Frazetta, and she carries on his legacy as the co-founder and CEO of Frazetta Girls. Dedicated to preserving and expanding her grandfather's iconic work, Sara curates exclusive merchandise, collaborations, and media content that honor his artistic vision. Through her YouTube series "Frazetta Fridays," she delves into Frank Frazetta's inspirations, artistic process, and lasting impact on pop culture. Sara's passion and dedication have solidified her as a pivotal figure in the fantasy art community, bridging past and future generations of Frazetta fans with a modern, high-end aesthetic.

ROY KRENKEL

AMRA

Unlike the work by the championed Robert E. Howard artists, all known for creating definitive or near-definitive single images that sum up one or another of REH's iconic characterizations, each small, jewel-like piece of Roy G. Krenkel's artwork appearing here is as one pure pen stroke among the thousand others set toward an ever-evolving delineation of the entire REH universe. Every presented barbarian, warrior, princess, king, god, goddess, vizier, satrap, throng, animal, city, and scene combines with every previously viewed RGK image, creating in each's imagination detailed visions that grow, stroke by stroke, leading us into the fully realized world that is Robert E. Howard's Domain of Dreams.

Most of Roy's *AMRA* published drawings matched against the Art of the Ages could appear to be of little consequence, each drawing being a brief fantasy gesture frozen in time... but, although a reader might gloss past dozens of Roy's gems while absorbing the contents of each *AMRA*, the images were prone to reappear in the reader's mind once every little while, enhancing any random REH or ERB thought... as they may have been intended to do. In gathering together the wealth of sketches and drawings, the word "plethora" lights up the stage. There's little need to study any of these seemingly off-hand 'doodles' (as Roy would name them) except to be rather stunned if one suddenly totaled up the vast number of the small, appropriate gifts Roy gave us and the world.

Picture if you will, a taller, ganglier, most likely happier Doc Emmitt Brown (as seen in the *Back To The Future* movies), high-water pants, penny loafers, Roy bouncing on his toes, chuckling, amused with himself and the world. In his cataloging of his surroundings, most everything meets with his approval, or is passed over as having nothing to do with Life As We Know It.

Roy claimed, and there never was reason to doubt his claim, to keep his cat schooled in its natural attitudes and graces. Come feeding time, he'd set the cat's food bowl on the left waist high kitchen countertop... there was a countertop of equal height and depth on the right-hand side, the two counters being bisected by the kitchen door to the outside... a span of at least three feet, or perhaps as many as four. Between the two countertops, Roy would securely set a house broom, a tall pole handle, and the fan of sweeper straw on the other end. That delta of bound straw would, laid onto the right-hand counter, firm up the broom as a viable 'bridge' with no chance of it tipping or rotating. That right-hand counter top was easily cat-accessible, Roy having set a chair with a healthy stack of books up against the drawers, making, in fact, a ladder from the kitchen floor to that countertop. Hence the only access the cat had to the food bowl was across a round broom handle of between 3 and 4 feet.

Roy would preamble this story with the admonition, or perhaps schooled information, that a cat needed to be challenged... and that one should endeavor to challenge one's cat at every opportunity. There were natural feats any cat could accomplish should it deign to care to, and, even against the feigned recalcitrance often noted in house cat behavior, a cat would take on all challenges of balance and dexterity if so challenged with firm authority.

To eat that evening, Roy's cat would have to 'tightrope' from one countertop to the other in Indian Trail across the length of round broom handle... And Roy's cat would, not caring to note Roy's absolute delight in the performance. On rare occasions, when his cat felt he was not to be trivialized, the cat would take one spring leap from kitchen floor to the countertop on which his meal was waiting.... This was, of course, something that delighted Roy even more, and, could he figure a way where the challenge was always to leap from floor to food, Roy would have definitely set forward that challenge.

Roy's cat bowl story was spurred into the telling by his astounded noting that Bernie, 'owner' of Pancho T. Gizzbazz (T for Thudpaw: Gizzy was a polydactyl Tom) had left Gizzy's bowl empty. With his accustomed bark of laughter, Roy would disclaim: "Don't EVER leave the cat's bowl empty!!! You can grow a cat (gestures with hands held big fish length apart) THIS BIG!!!"

Other cat teases would follow: Roy said, given a really wide and 'loose' rubber band (like one cut from a car innertube) set around a cat's middle (loose, understand) and then one of the cat's rear legs brought forward through the loop around the belly, a cat would be 'driven' to either flop around, as we humans might, or, in one of those "Did you see THAT" gestures, walk out of the band as if it'd not really been there. The Point Being, it was up to the titular cat's 'owner' to do as much as possible to have the cat remind us he or she was the apex of mammalian cleverness and dexterity, while staying as cool as a breeze throughout.

As a cap to all the afore-noted, my memory wakes to a favorite remembered REH passage (from Almuric), a sentence that encompasses both the work of Robert E. Howard as accentuated, pictured, enhanced, illuminated by Roy's *AMRA* images:

"My mind peopled the distance with nightmare shapes..."

—*Michael Wm. Kaluta*
Michael Wm. Kaluta, born in Guatemala in 1947 but raised in Virginia and attended Richmond Professional Institute there, has since 1969 lived and worked in New York City. Finding fame first with his adaptations of *Carson of Venus* and *The Shadow* for DC Comics, in the late 1970s as a member of The Studio, and in the years since with the release of a steady stream of prints, portfolios, the 1994 J.R.R. Tolkien calendar, and book illustrations.
While Michael continues to provide covers and stories to publishers in the comics field his most ambitious work, in collaboration with Elaine Lee since the 1980s, are the ongoing *Starstruck* sagas.

A young Wm. Kaluta used this envelope to submit art to the Amra fanzine.

RGK

The Deftest of Doodlers

Every undaunted caveman, valorous Roman, and courageous apeman Roy G. Krenkel drew had some self-portraiture in it—in my adoring fanboy mind, anyway. My hero!

When I met Roy at a New York comic con hosted by Phil Seuling in the early seventies, the master artist physically stood out—and above—the crowd. The silver-haired artist was the "oldest guy in the room," by far. He was taller than most of the convention attendees. He embodied the idea of an "elder statesman". He was downright regal to me. But the king had a jester side to him: he trucked across the convention floor with red high-topped tennis shoes! This was way before running shoes of all stripes and colors.

The hook-up happened after a talk in a tiny room by a young Jeff Jones (not yet Jeffrey Catherine Jones). I had sat in the front row next to one of the rare female convention-goers during that caveman sausage party era. She was a ringer for Jones's sensuous, full-bodied comic character, Idyl. I assumed she was Jones's model/muse. But what really caught my eye was the presence of Krenkel a couple of rows back

After the talk and slide show, when we exited the room, I made a point of walking alongside Krenkel and asked about the small portfolio he held. Roy sat down with me at a little table covered with a red cloth in the hall and displayed to me the treasures therein. I eagerly, for a modest sum, purchased a page with a handful of Tarzan-like images and he autographed it with an "RGK" for me. Then he paused and added "after St. John." If Krenkel was a king for me, J. Allen St. John, the pioneering *Tarzan* artist, was a saint to him. (Roy loved and shared with fellow artists many past greats. RGK saw himself as much of an art book collector and art advocate as an artist).

Possessing these "doodles," as Roy modestly deemed his commanding drawings, only whetted my appetite for more. When I returned to Ohio, I penned him a letter. I told him I had a zaftig friend who modeled for me every morning, and I found her enticing to draw because of the corpulent women he delineated. I wondered if he would pen an "ultimate Krenkel Girl" for me.

Roy immediately wrote back, "I can't believe you found such a girl to model for you! If you spot a diet Tab-drinking, lettuce-chomping girl on the bus and ask her if she might someday model for you, she'll tear off her clothes and strike a pose then and there. If you do the same with a girl with meat on her bones, she'll be outraged and yell for a cop!"

Roy, having found a Big Beautiful Woman appreciator, enthusiastically agreed to accept my commission and, within days, I received a package and tore it open to find his ideal. She was a striking woman, her face in that unique Krenkel female profile and her figure in a rear view, adorned with only a few bracelets. She was in no way vulnerable. The dark-haired goddess was almost as wide as she was tall. Roy captioned this highly rendered doodle, "A Woman of Substance."

No woman had as much substance in the work Roy sent to the *Amra* fanzine. However in the pages ahead, you will find women with the qualities RGK always imbued into all his females: strength, boldness, fearlessness. Without exception, they are forces to be reckoned with.

There are an abundance of manly-men here, too, cave and tree-dwellers, spear-and-sword carriers.

These women and men rarely used their weapons in the art of RGK. Krenkel's world was a realm where these implements were more a symbol of strength than a harmer of humans or beasts. More than not, the spear-carriers, swordsmen, and the few with guns in Krenkel art stood in repose, or even sat on the ground, seemingly pondering life, or even just enjoying the view of Roy's wistful landscapes. His barbarians weren't usually barbaric, but appeared admirably at peace with their fellow man. Saber-tooths and dinosaurs and lions, oh my!, were often companions, fellow adventurers rather than adversaries.

When I stayed in poster, record cover, and underground comix artist Rick Griffin's home in San Clemente, CA, he showed me a notebook he had assembled of Krenkel's art for inspiration. This touchstone included an original piece of art done for the *Amra* fanzine. We discussed, both of us hippie-Christians, that Krenkel's work had a spiritual quality to it. I'm not saying that Roy's art will likely be hung in Sunday school classrooms, but there was an ethereal aspect to the worlds Krenkel's graceful characters inhabited.

The Fantastic Art of Roy G. Krenkel collects every single drawing done for the fanzine *Amra: The Journal of The Hyborian Legion*. The high quality edited and printed *Amra* ran from 1959 to 1982. George Scithers, recipient of the World Fantasy Award for Lifetime Achievement, was *Amra*'s editor and publisher, and focused the "pro-zine" on the genre of Sword and Sorcery. Scithers stated, "*Amra* is about various heroic heroes, mostly of swordplay-&-sorcery stories set in fantasy worlds."

As shared in Zin Wiki, the pages of the twice Hugo-winning periodical included essays on fantasy characters, especially Robert E. Howard's Conan, plus Fritz Leiber's Fafhrd and the Grey Mouser, Fletcher Pratt and L. Sprague de Camp's Harold Shea, Michael Moorcock's Elric, and Edgar Rice Burroughs's John Carter.

Amra's writers included professional fantasy and science fiction writers such as Frank Herbert, Jerry Pournelle, Leigh Brackett, L. Sprague de Camp, Poul Anderson, Harry Harrison, and Fritz Leiber. Leiber, de Camp, Moorcock, Dick Eney, Katherine MacLean, and John Pocsik once wrote "story vignettes" based on a Krenkel work of centerfold art.

Though obviously highly esteemed by Scithers, Krenkel wasn't the only incredible artist who sent art to *Amra*. For context, this book shows samples of other notable artists, who occasionally contributed work. But plenty of Krenkel illustrations profusely filled the pages and defined the look of the zine. The art in *Amra* wasn't "illustration" in the sense that it was done for specific writings, but came from the artists' imagination around the modern heroic fantasy genre.

Without question there was a vast quantity of Roy's art in *Amra*, of which the sheer quality you will witness for yourself. Some were small spots, others magnificently appeared as covers or spanned across two pages. Some were deftly loose, other pieces were highly detailed. On occasion, RGK made a diversion from his dancing pen lines and introduced what appears to be some bold brushwork, with rich blacks as part of the shading on his subjects and in his scenes. Sometimes Roy picked up a pencil to render tone to great effect.

Pen, brush, or pencil, Krenkel's art for *Amra* was created in black and white. To me this added an other-worldly feel, since ours is a world of color. Actually, Roy had doubts about his own color work, which is why he eventually enlisted his friend Frank Frazetta to assist him on Edgar Rice Burroughs's paperback covers. Frazetta, as we well know, went on to thrill the world as he took over the work on that line. As much as we all love Frazetta's astounding work, I wish Krenkel had worked more on painting because his color pieces matched the quality of any other artist. Nonetheless, you'll get lost in the skilled monotone and magical lines of Roy's *Amra* body of work.

I place RGK's imagination, compositions, and figure work on par with resoundly extolled, much more well known artists throughout history. Roy's art deserves considerably more acclaim.

Roy G. Krenkel, An Artist of Substance.

—*Craig Yoe*

RGK's Amra Artist Associates

For context, we present other artists, some friends of Roy's,
who graced the fanzine's pages…

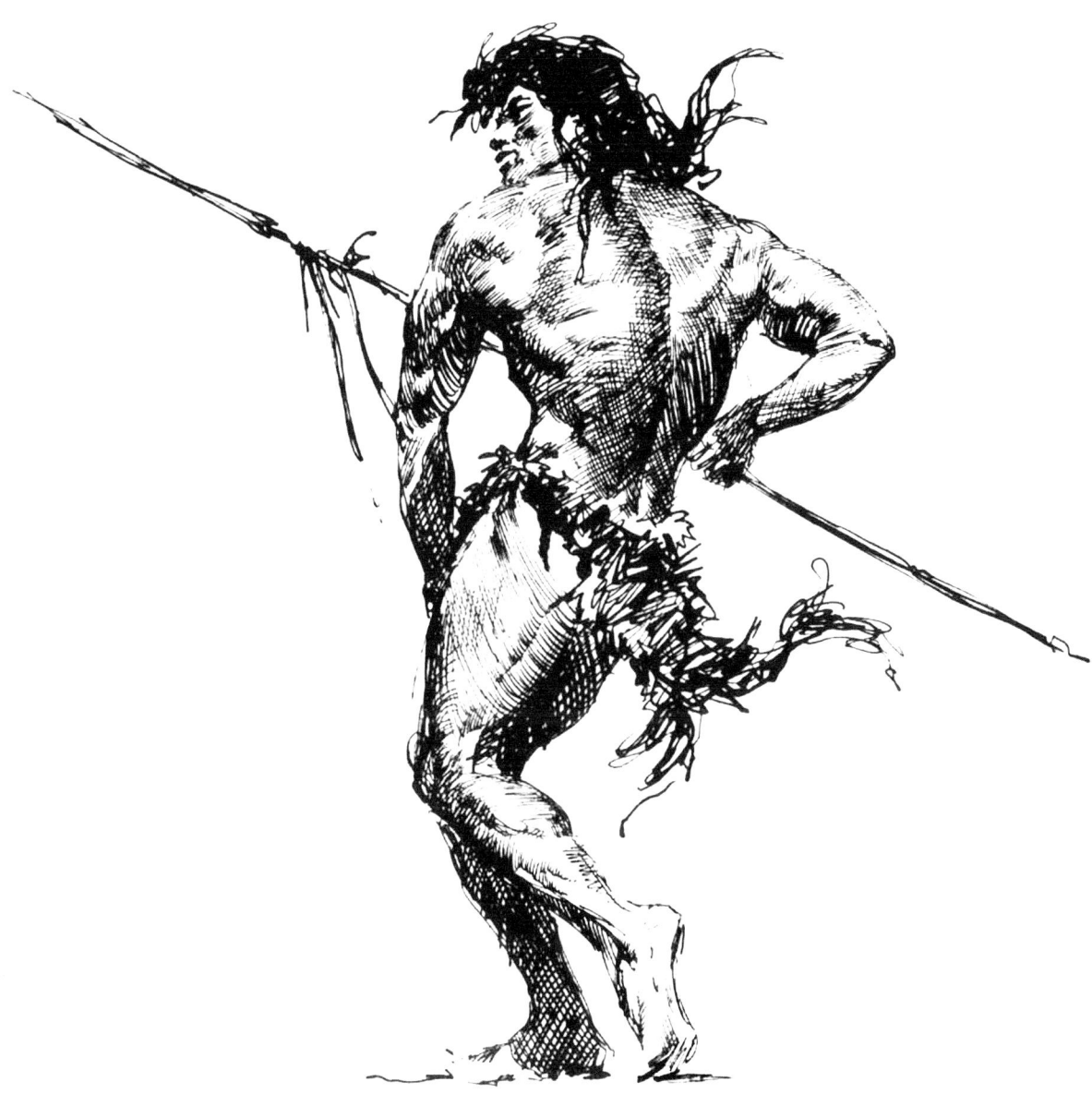

Frank Frazetta (1928–2010), the recognized master fantasy
artist, couldn't resist briefly joining his pal and mentor Roy in
the pages of *Amra*, and even seemed to channel Krenkel in this
particular piece from #22 (July 1962).

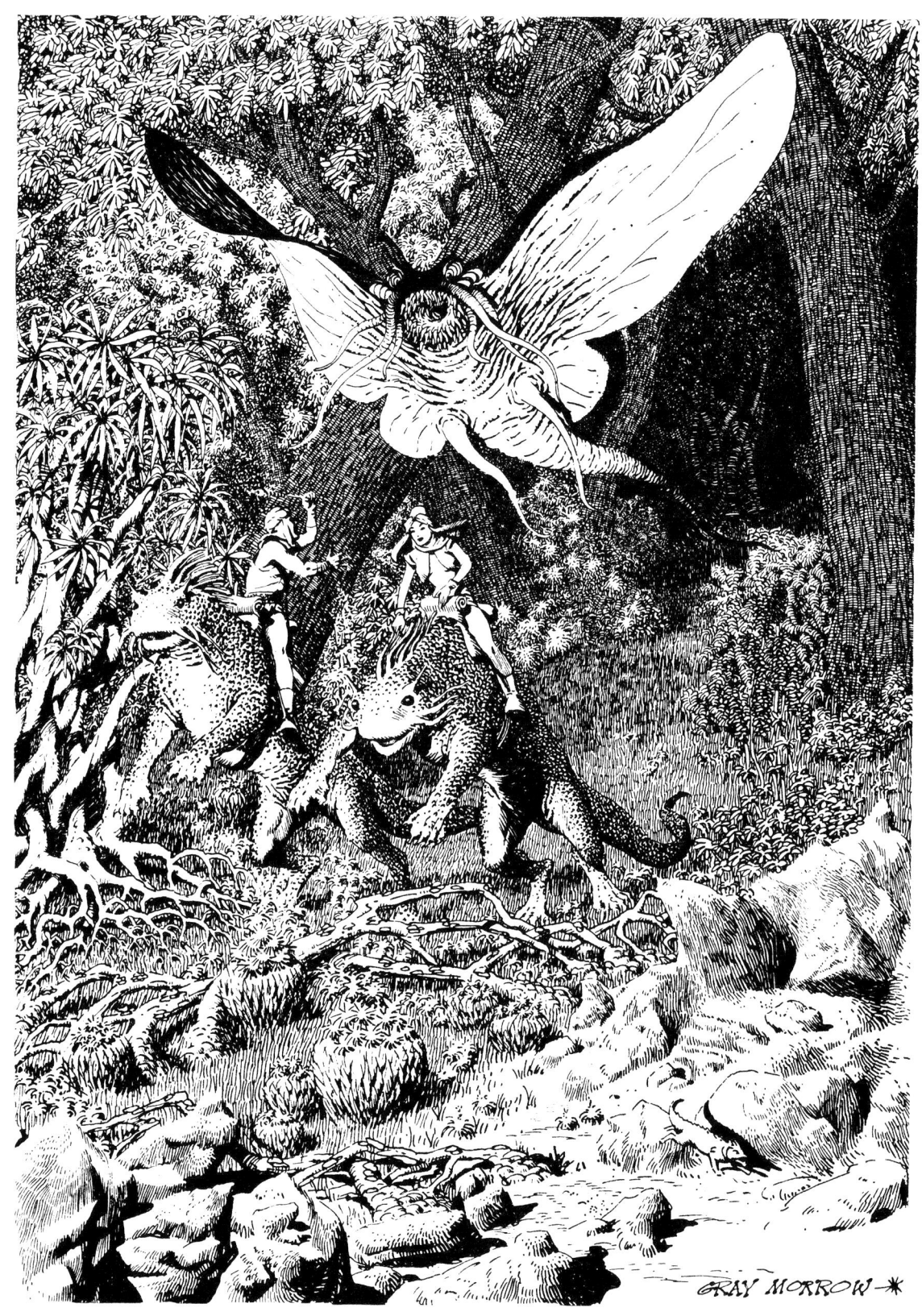

Gray Morrow (1934–2001) drew in a classic illustrative style
and submitted this highly-detailed piece first to *Amra*, then to
Wally Wood's magazine *Witzend*. *Amra* #26, October 1963

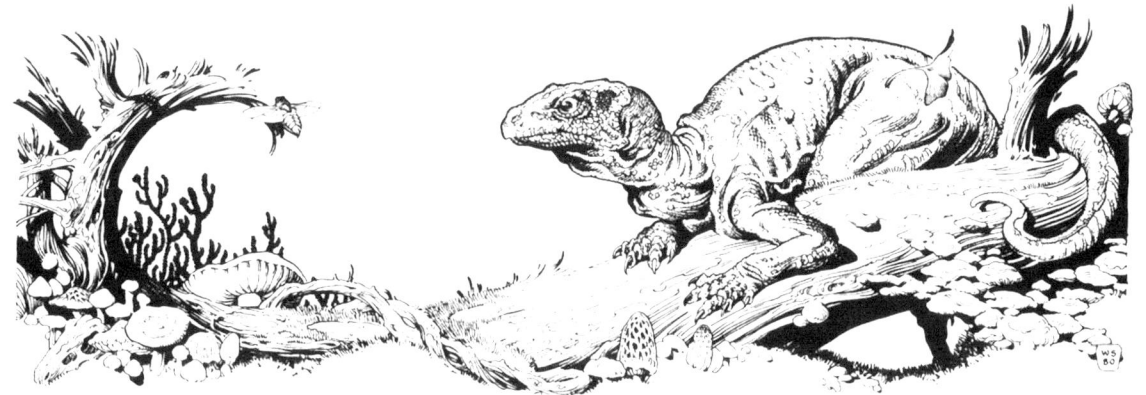

William Stout (b. 1949) stands as one of fantasy's finest practitioners and his stellar talents have distinguished books, album covers, comic books, and movie posters. Plus, he is a lauded film story-board artist. *Amra #72, July 1982*

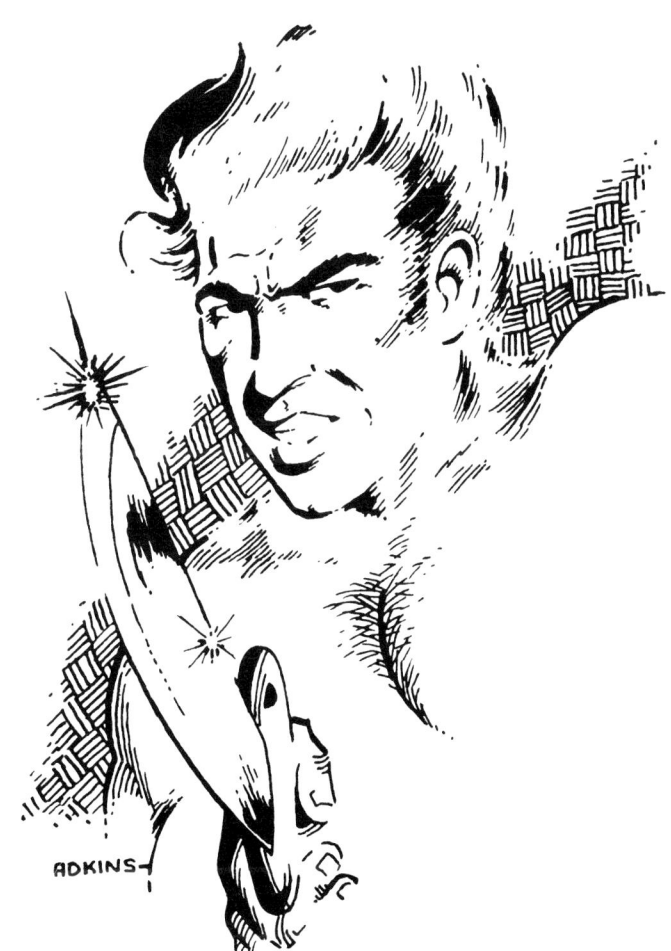

A prodigious inker as well as penciler and writer for publishers DC and Marvel, Dan Adkins (1937–2013) got his start in science fiction fanzines, including his self-published *Sata. Amra #19, February 1962*

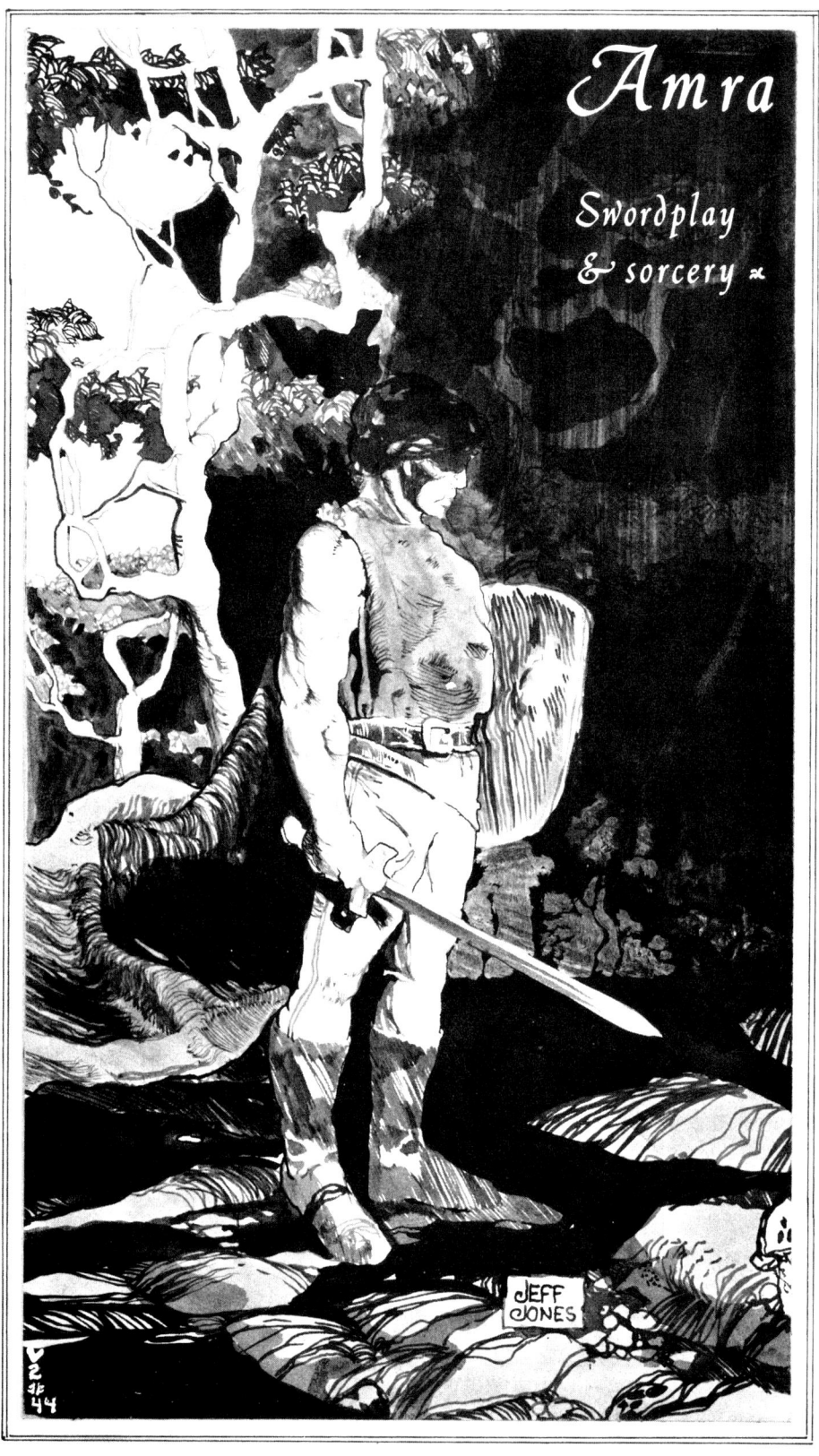

Krenkel, by far, drew the most *Amra* covers, but Jeff Jones (later
Jeffrey Catherine Jones), created this striking offering in skillful
pen and wash. *Amra* #44, October 1967

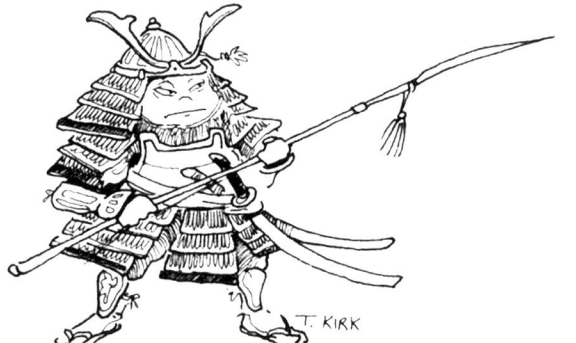

Tim Kirk's (b. 1947) imaginative art is often full of delight and whimsy, an innate skill that has served him well in his work as an illustrator for J.R.R. Tolkien's books and as a Disney Imagineer, designing theme parks. *Amra #52, April 1970*

Bernie Wrightson (1948–2017) found inspiration as a young man from EC Comics artists like Frazetta and Graham Ingles, but grew to become the eminent horror delineator. *Amra #45, December 1967*

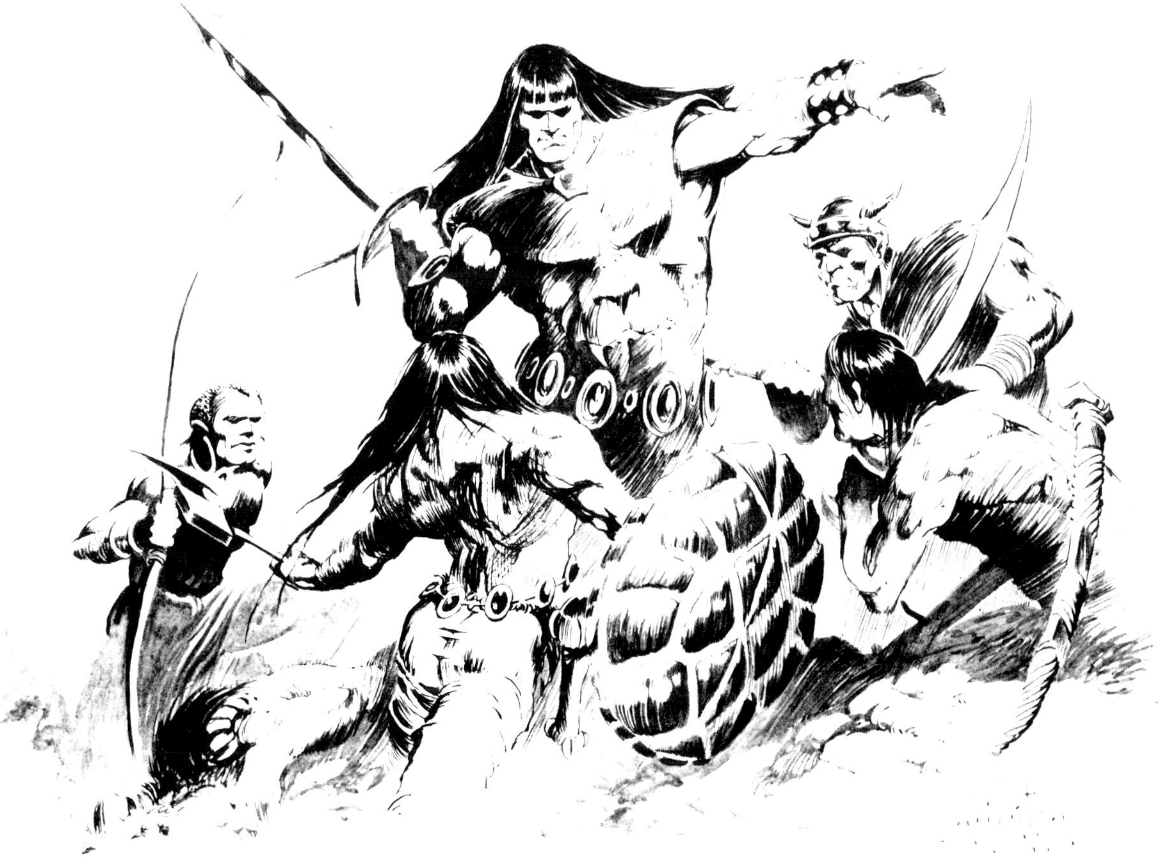

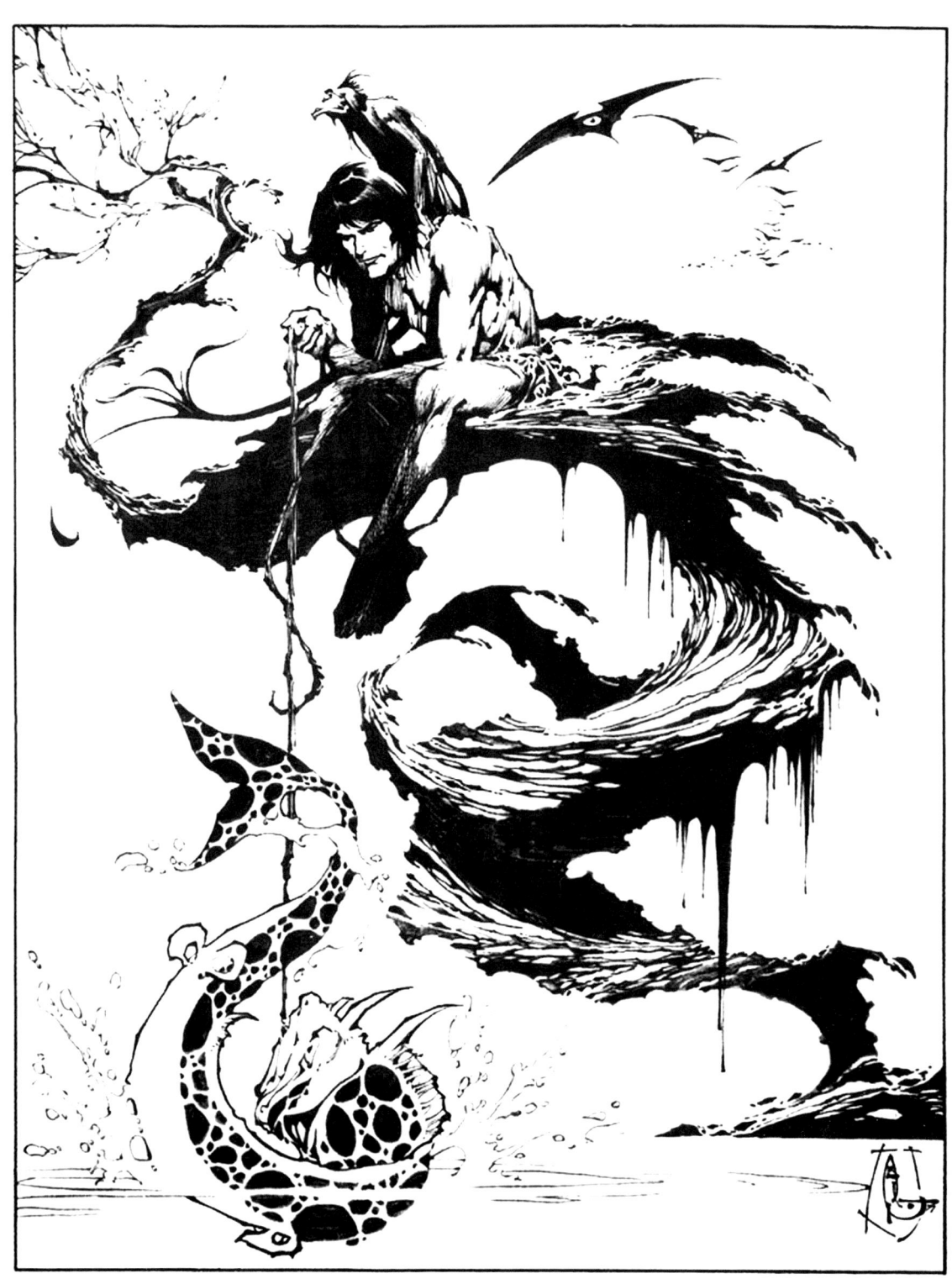

The Philippines-born superlative artist Alex Nino (b.1940) has become one of the most innovative and acclaimed comic book and illustration creators in the world. *Amra* #63, April 1975

The Fantastic Art of
Roy G. Krenkel

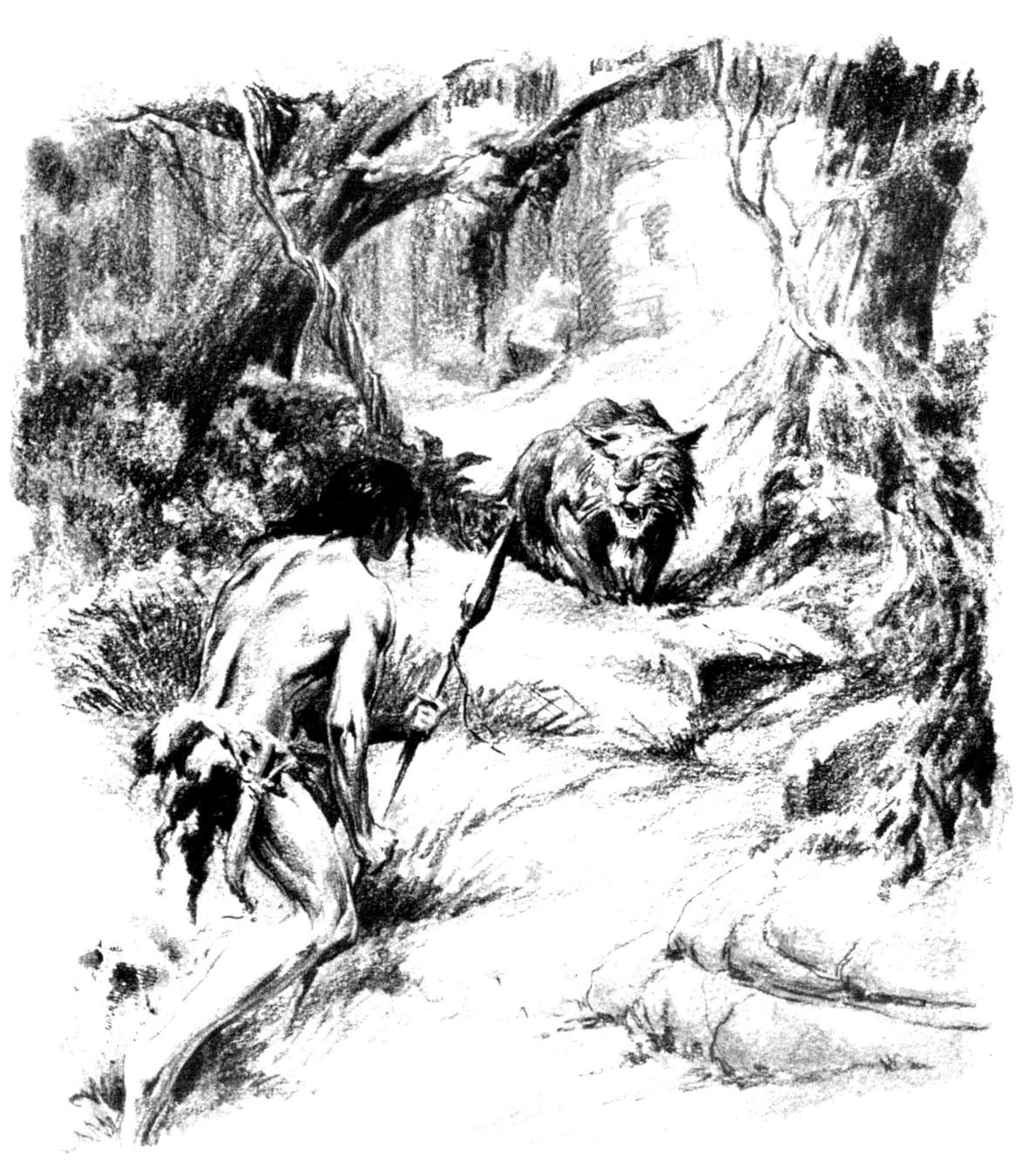

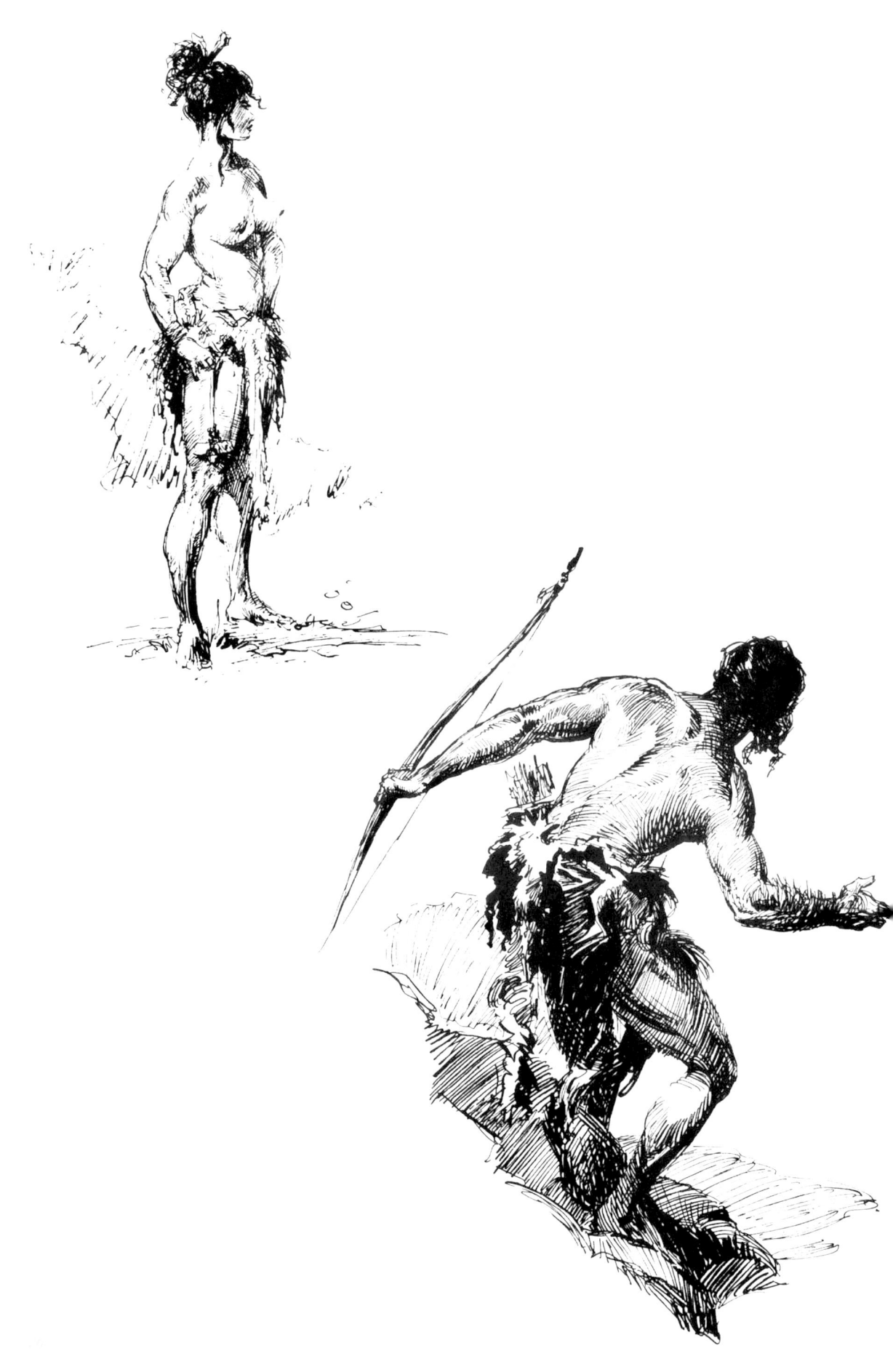

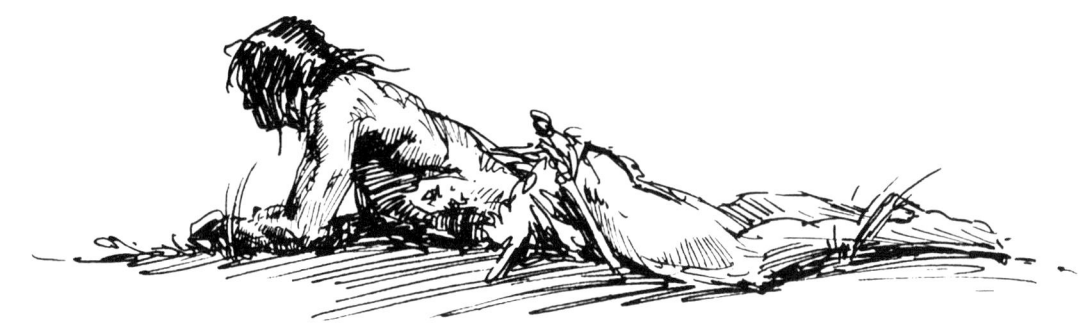

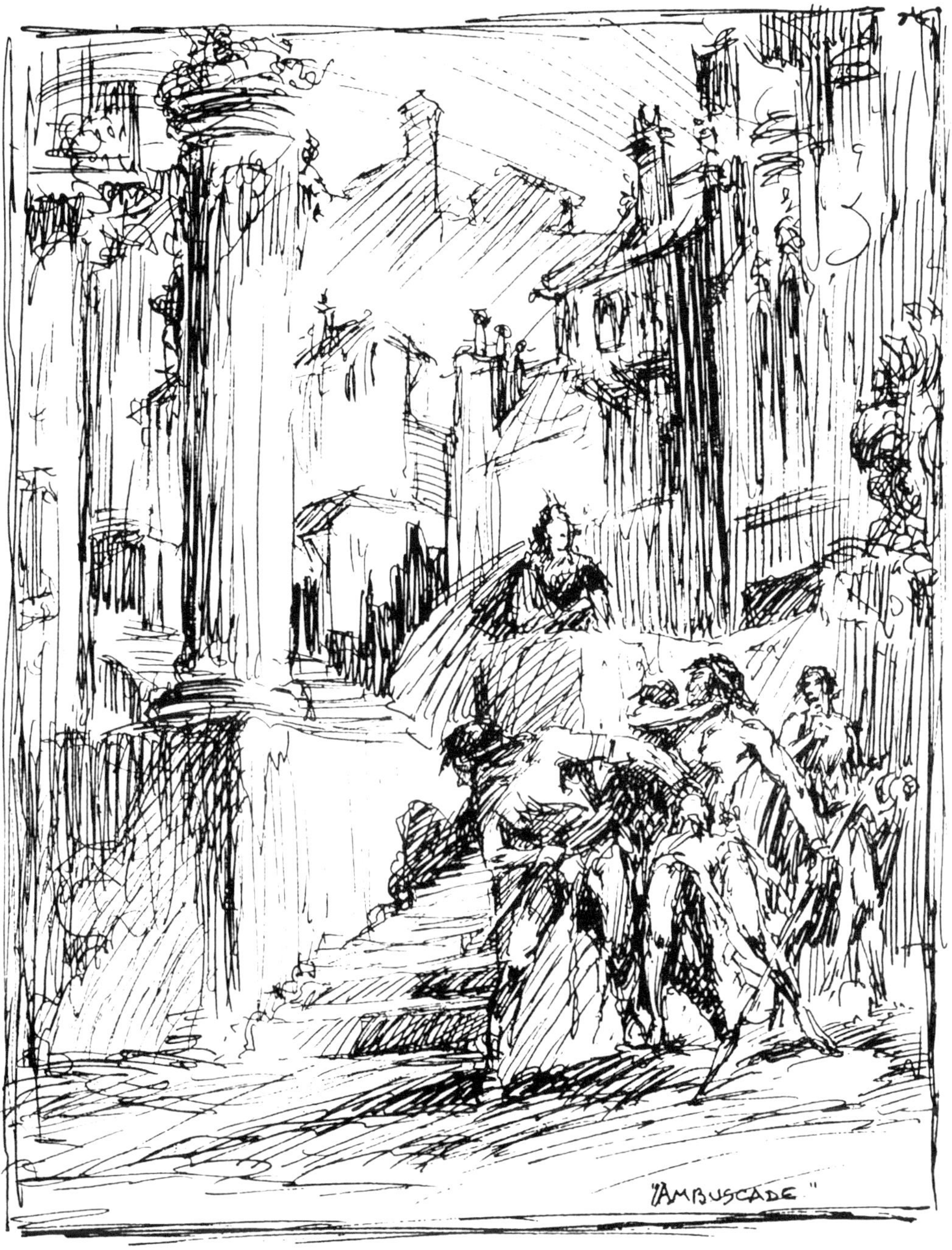

"AMBUSCADE"

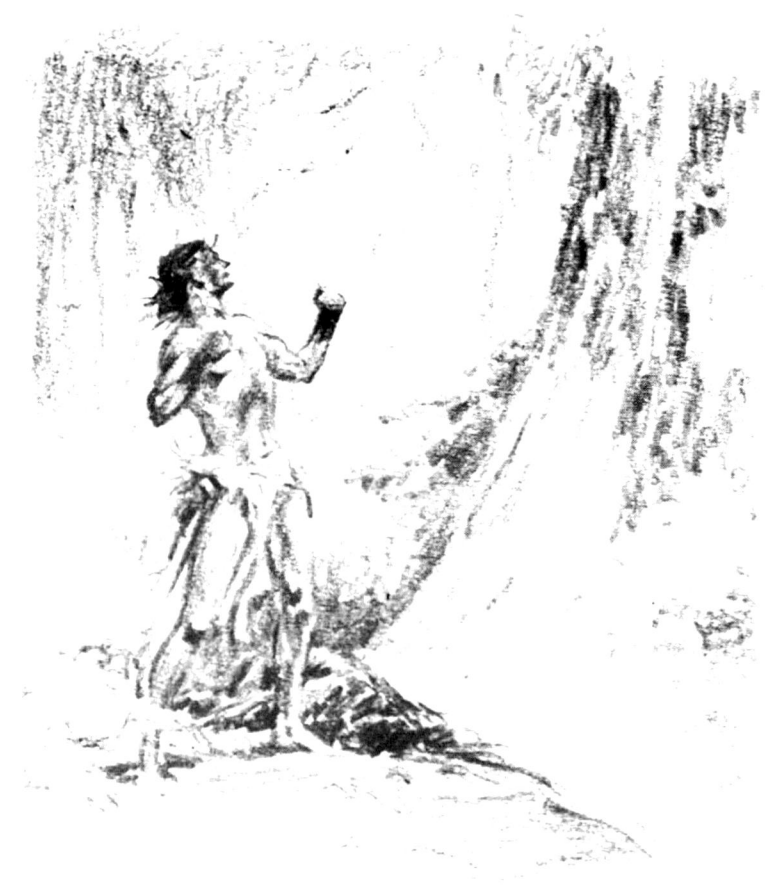

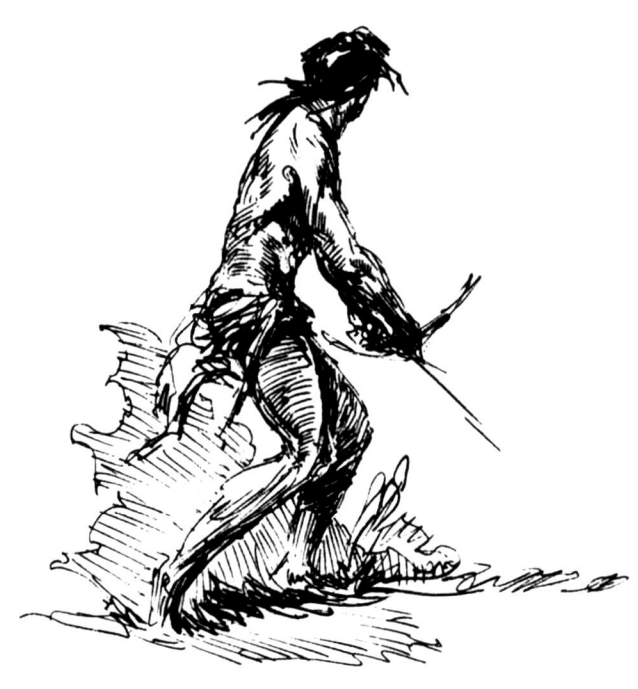

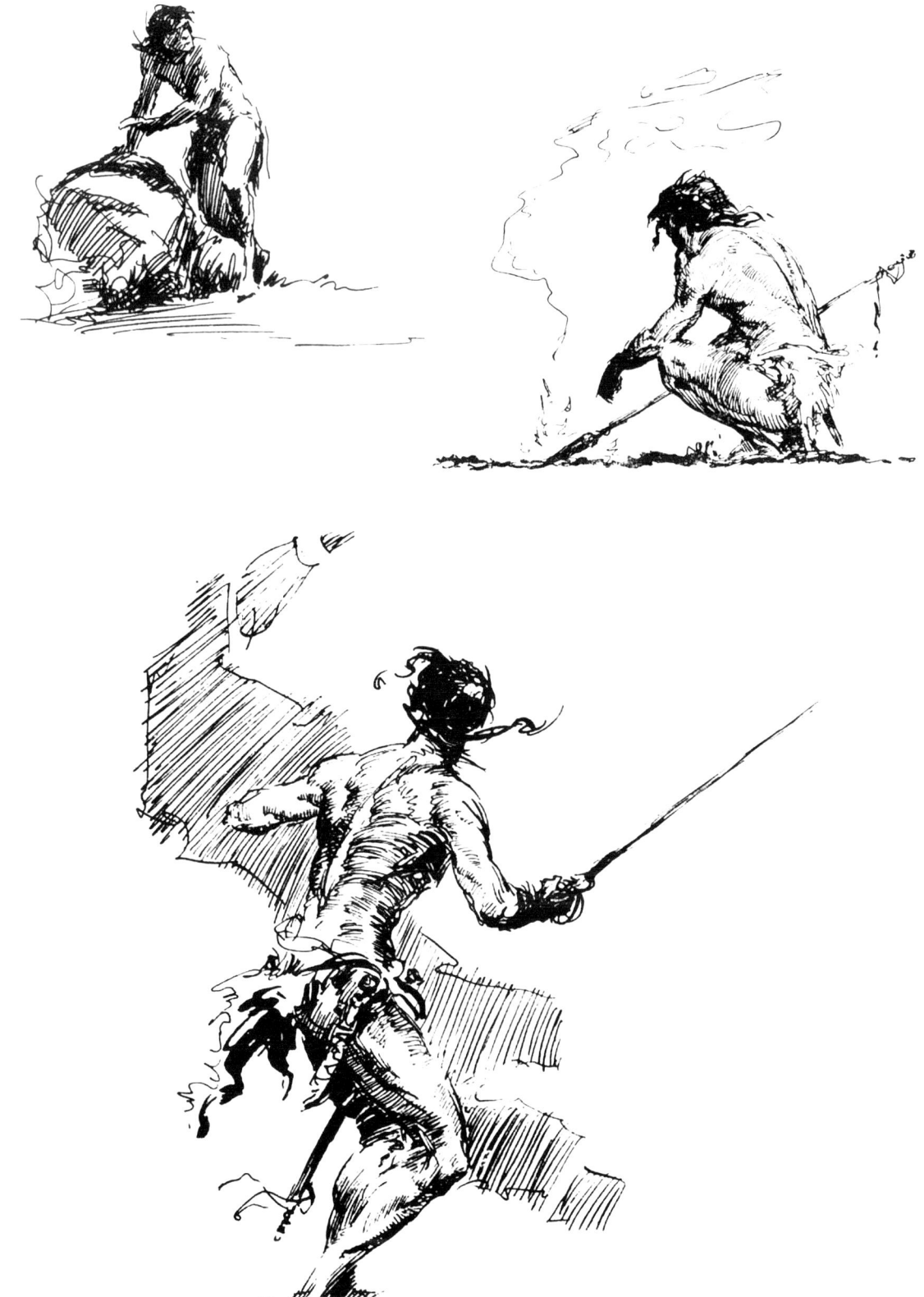

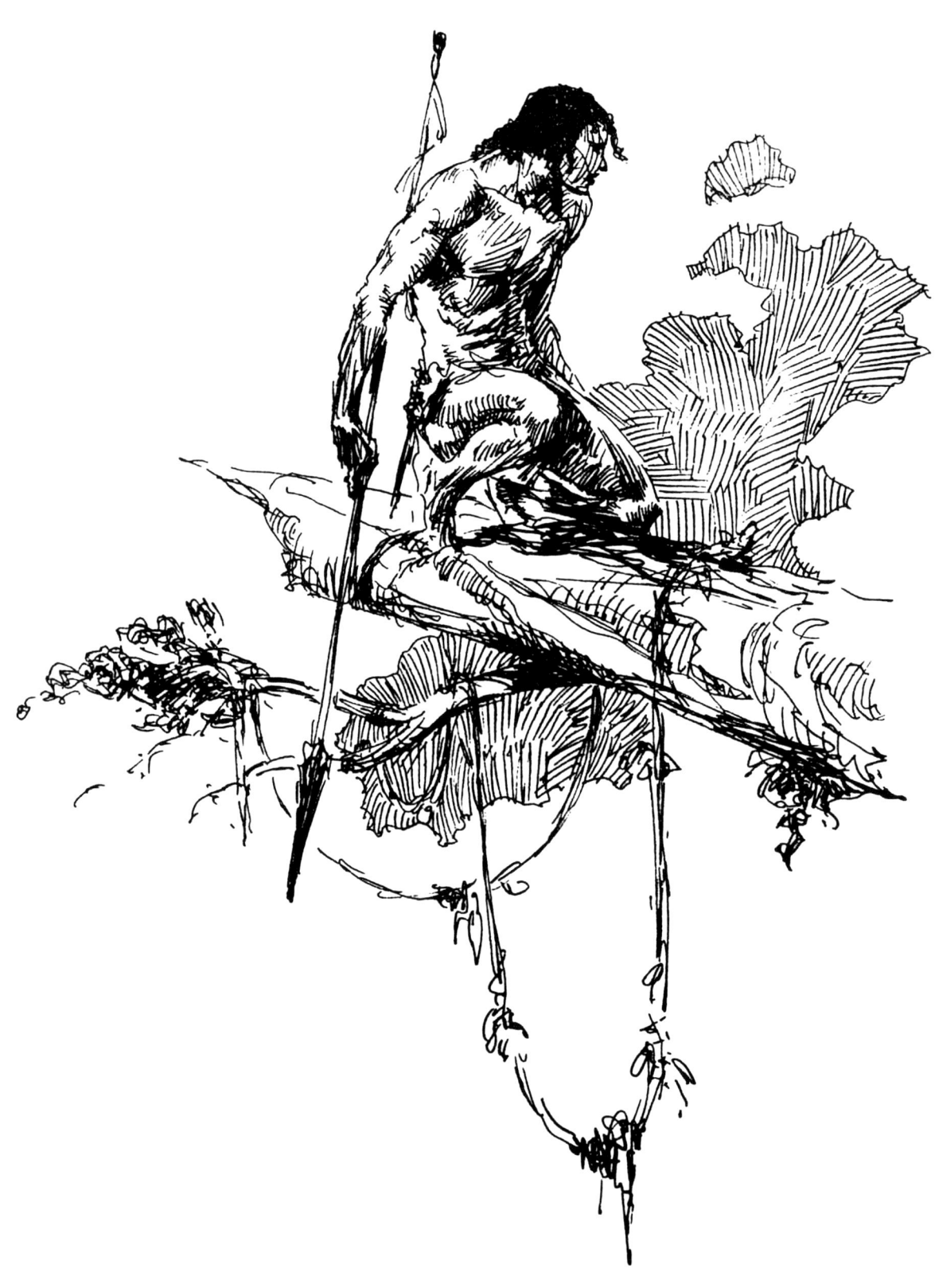

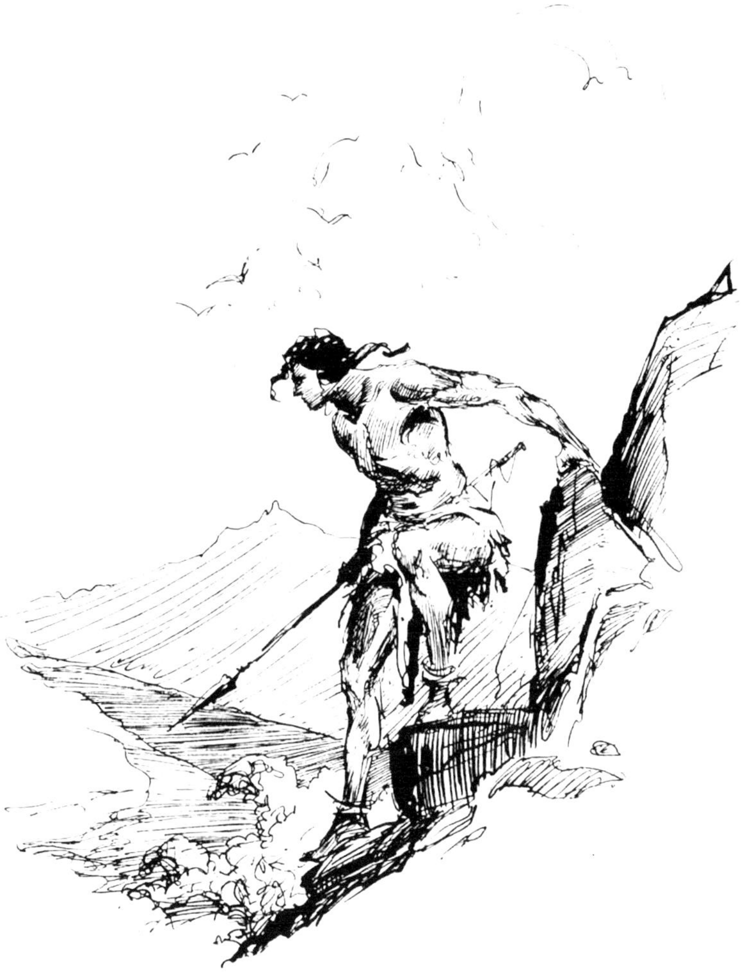

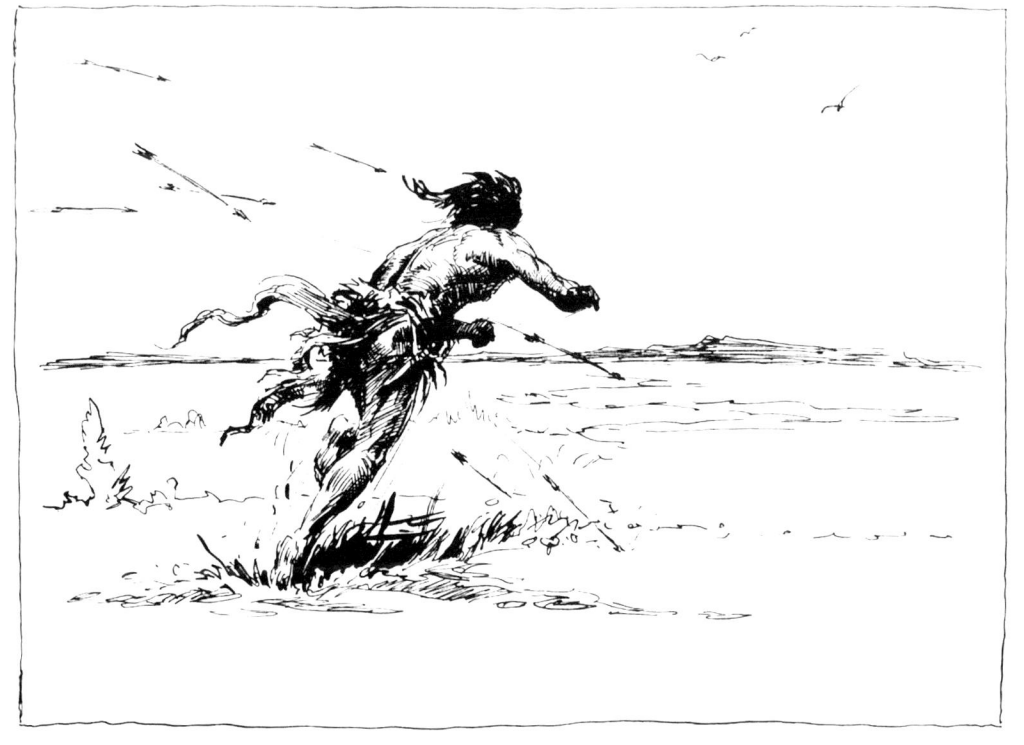

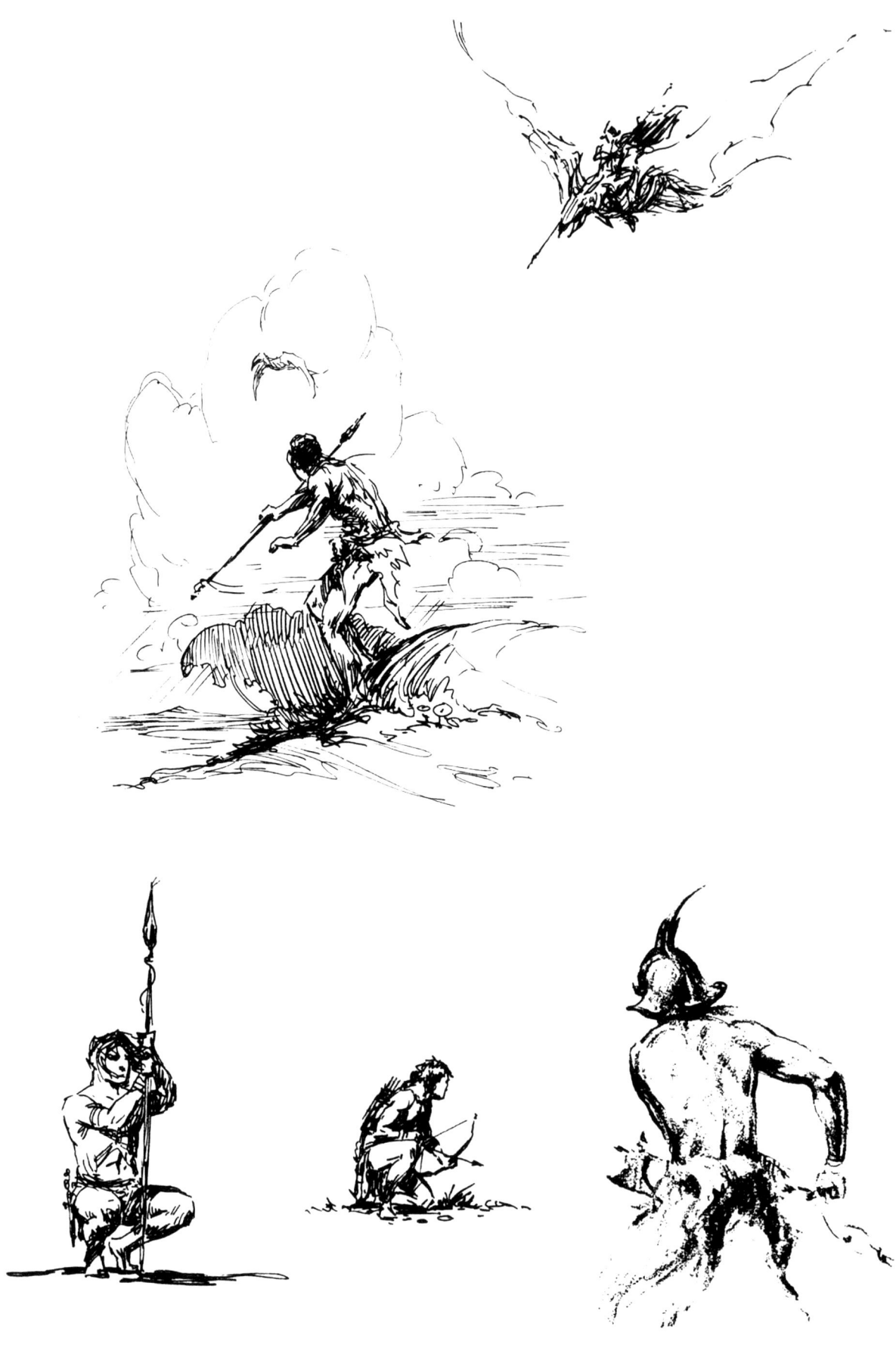

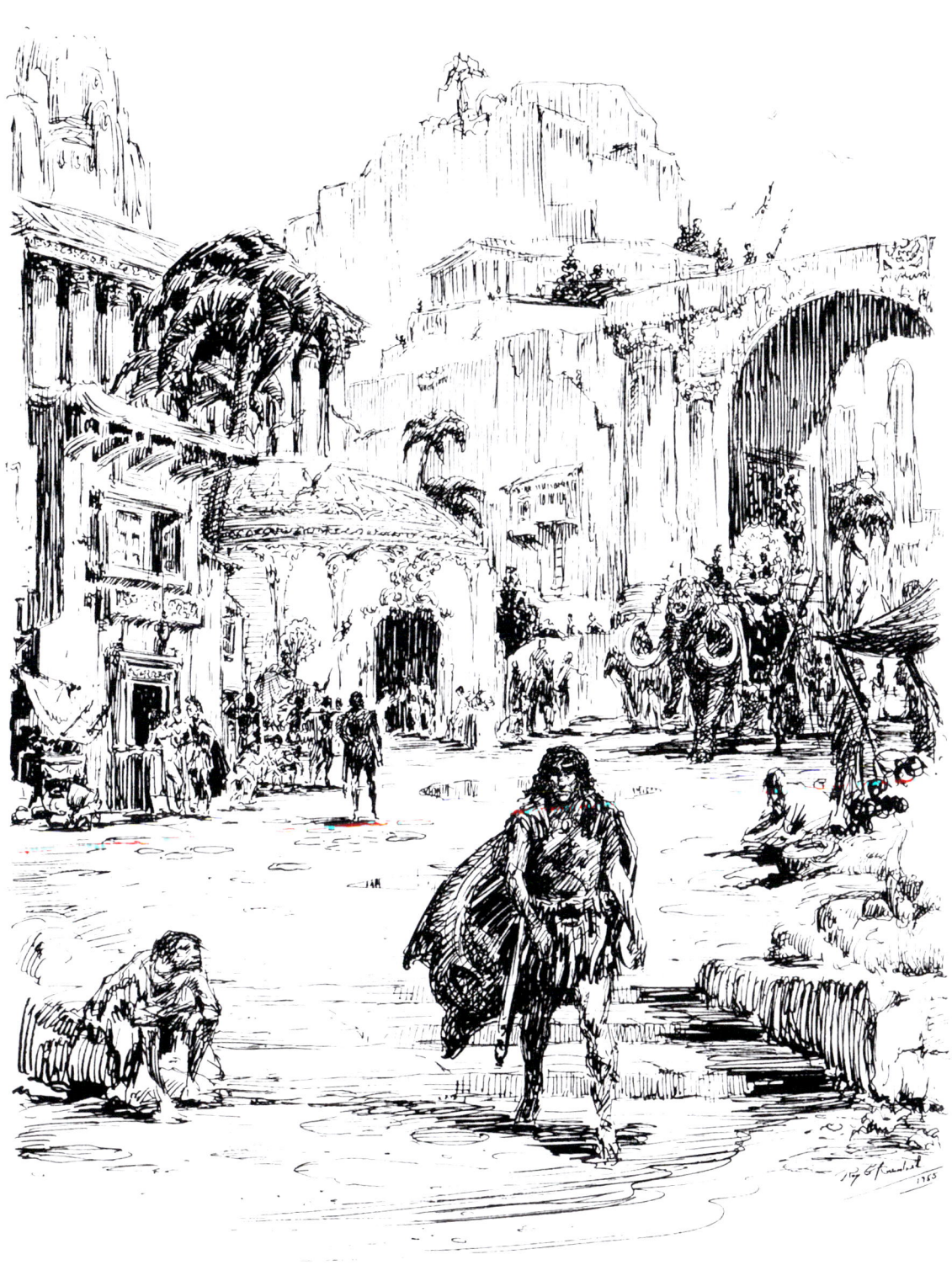

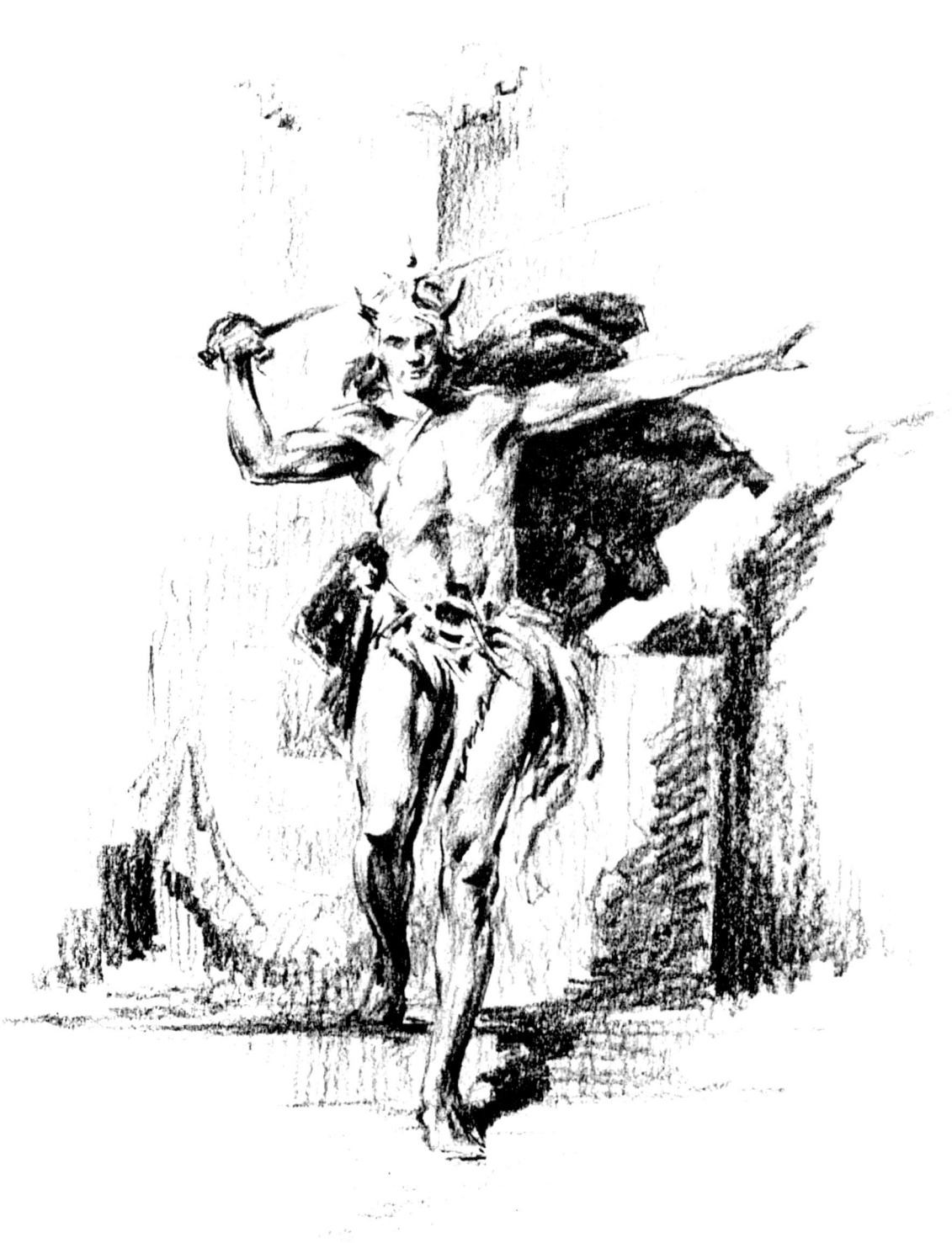

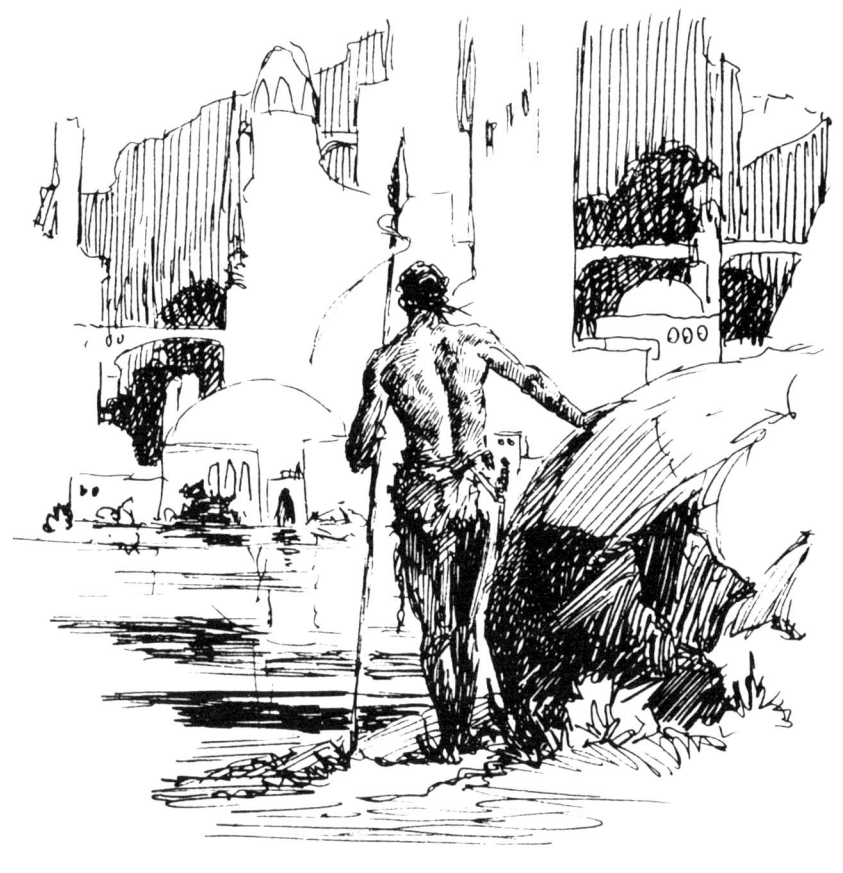

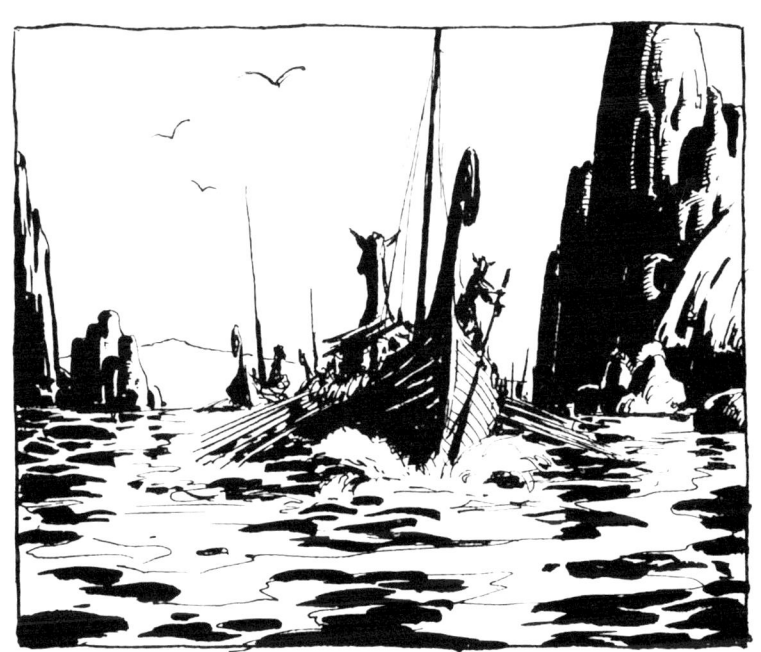

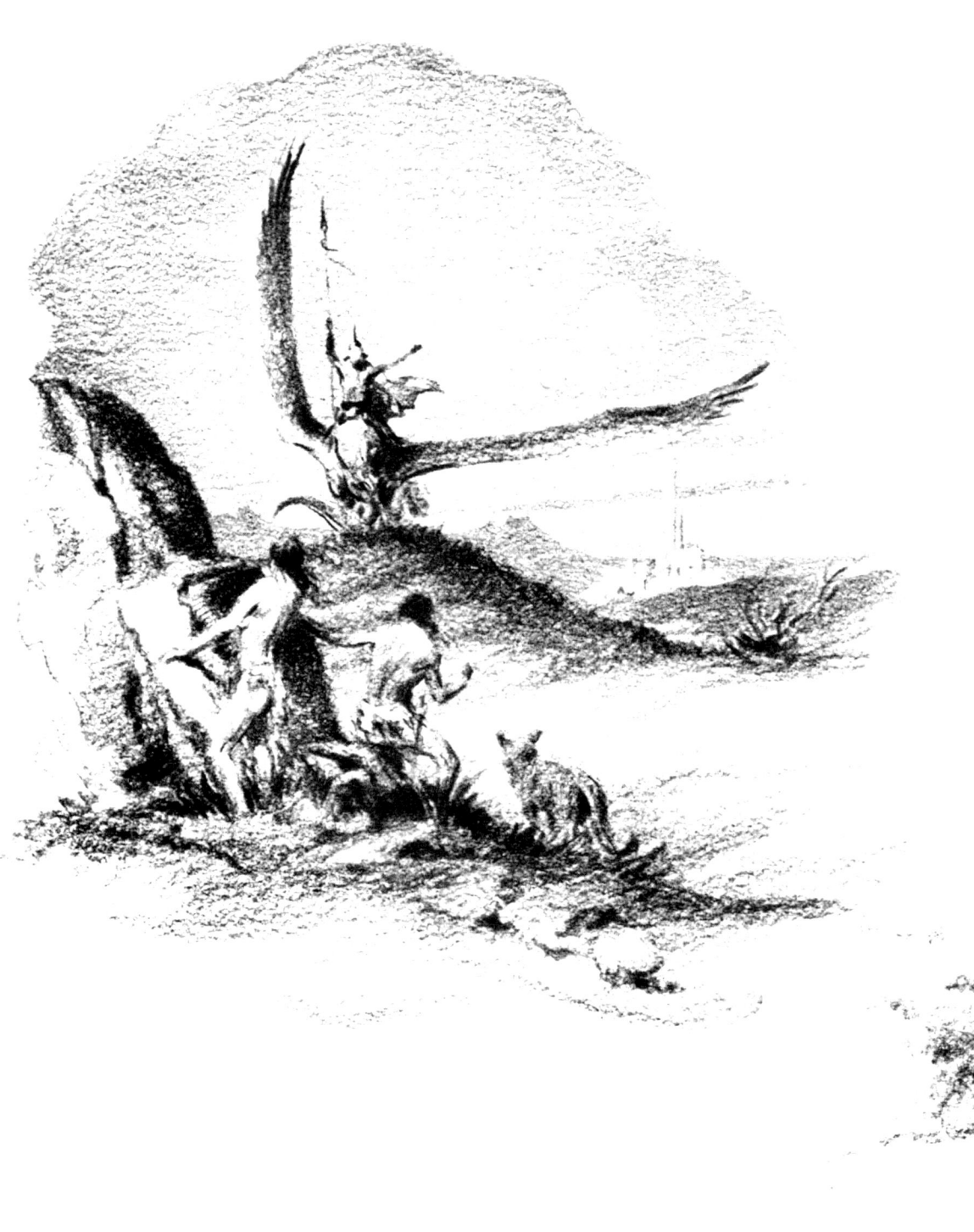

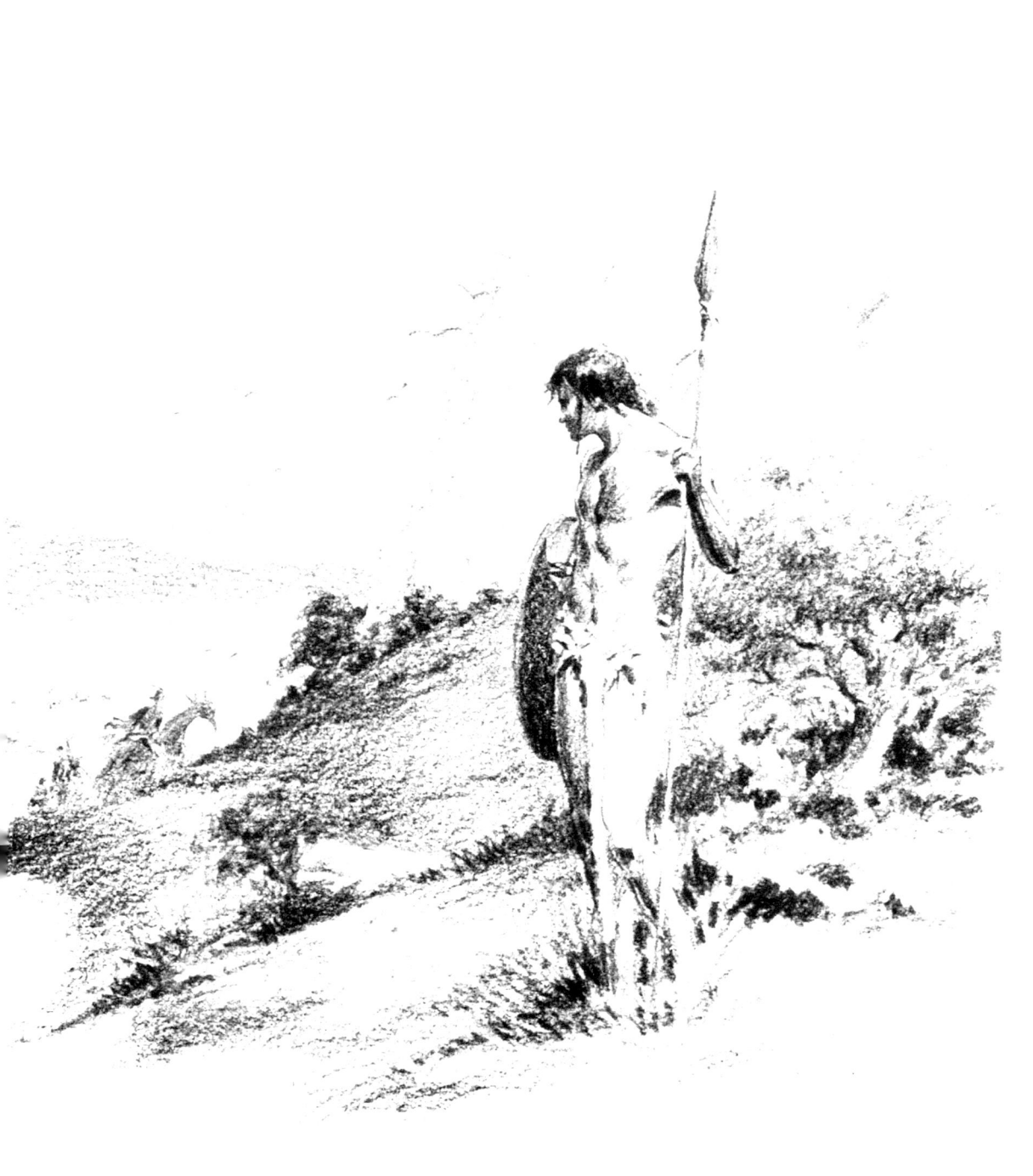

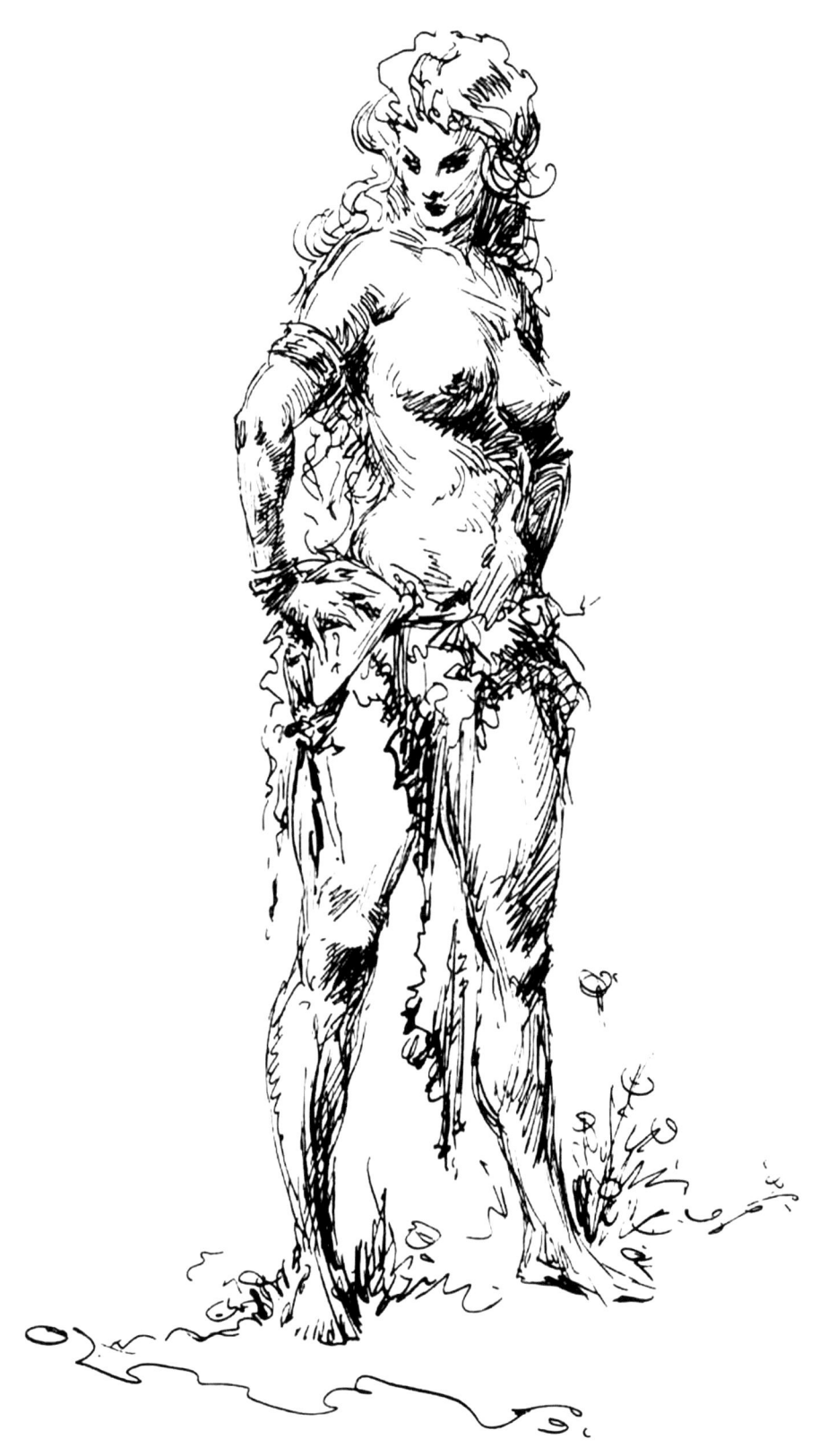

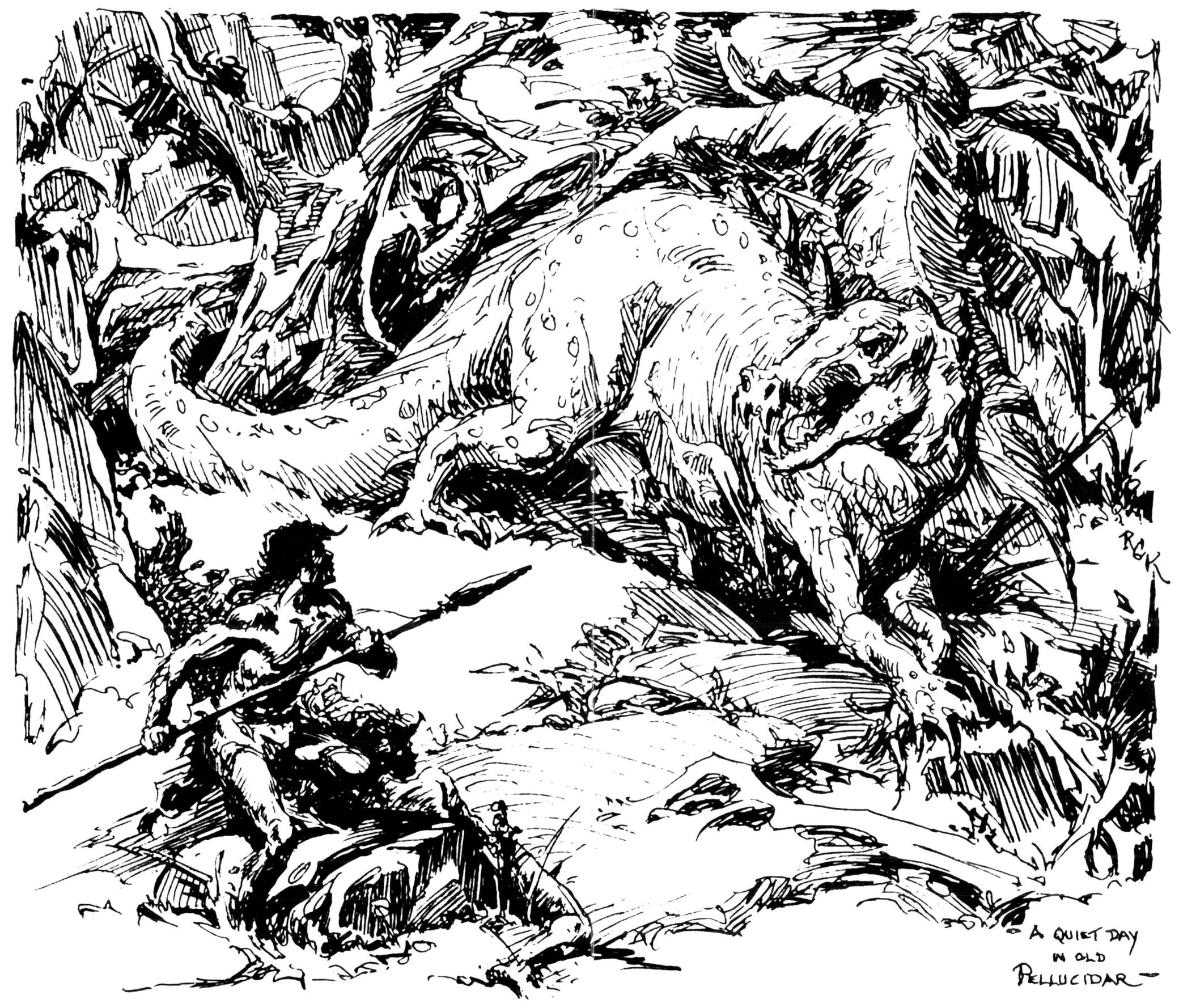

A QUIET DAY IN OLD PELLUCIDAR

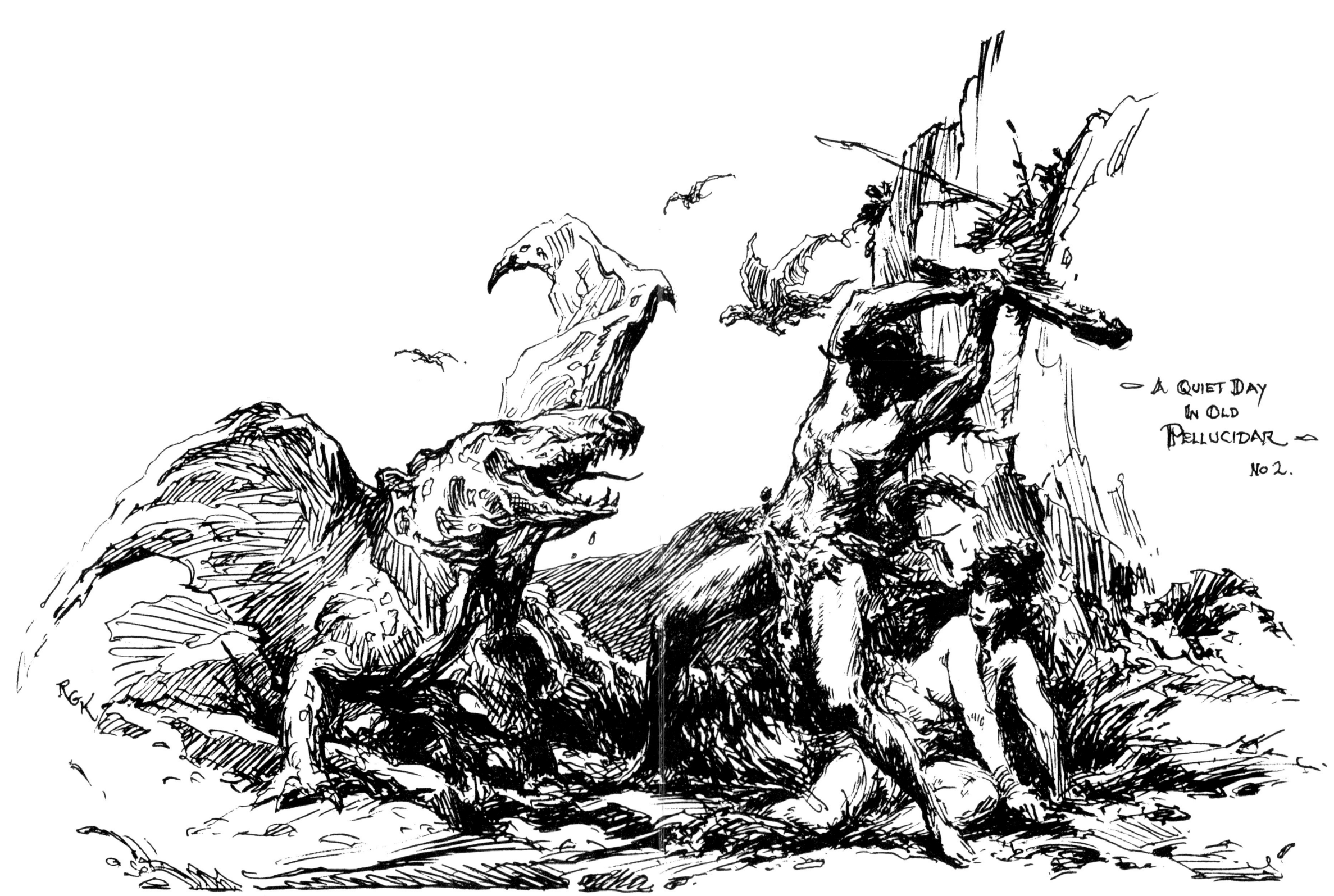

A QUIET DAY IN OLD PELLUCIDAR No 2.

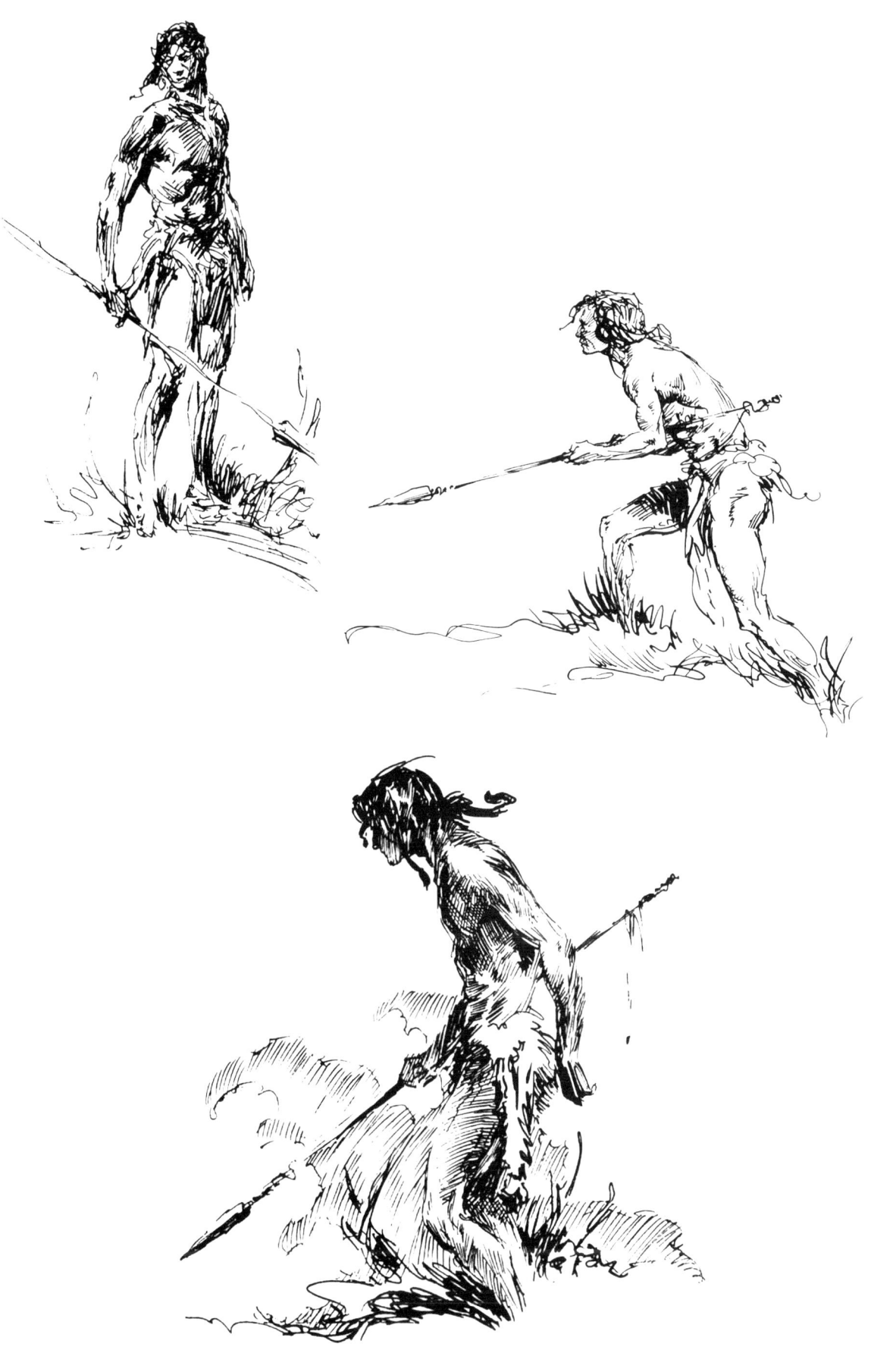

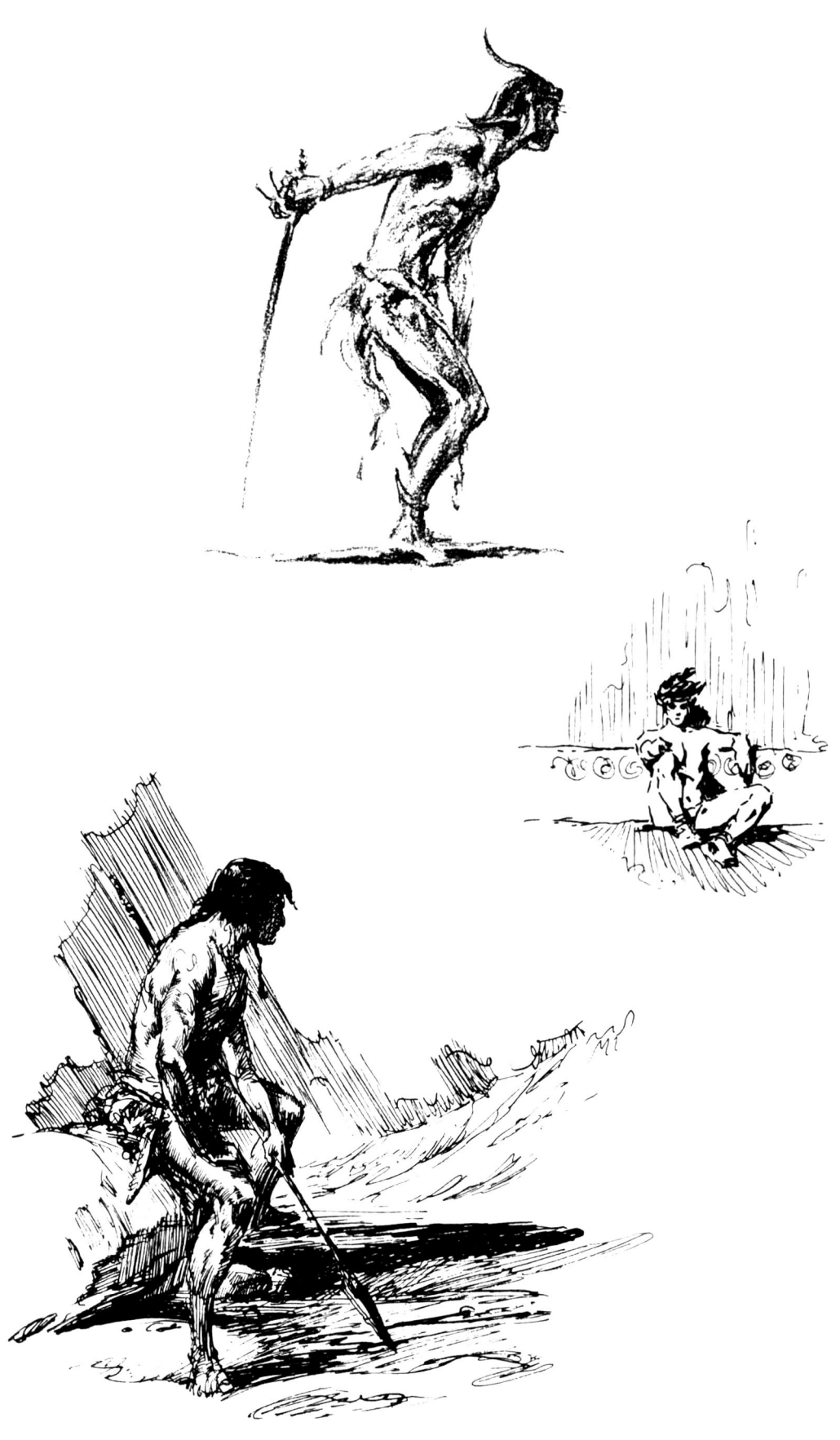

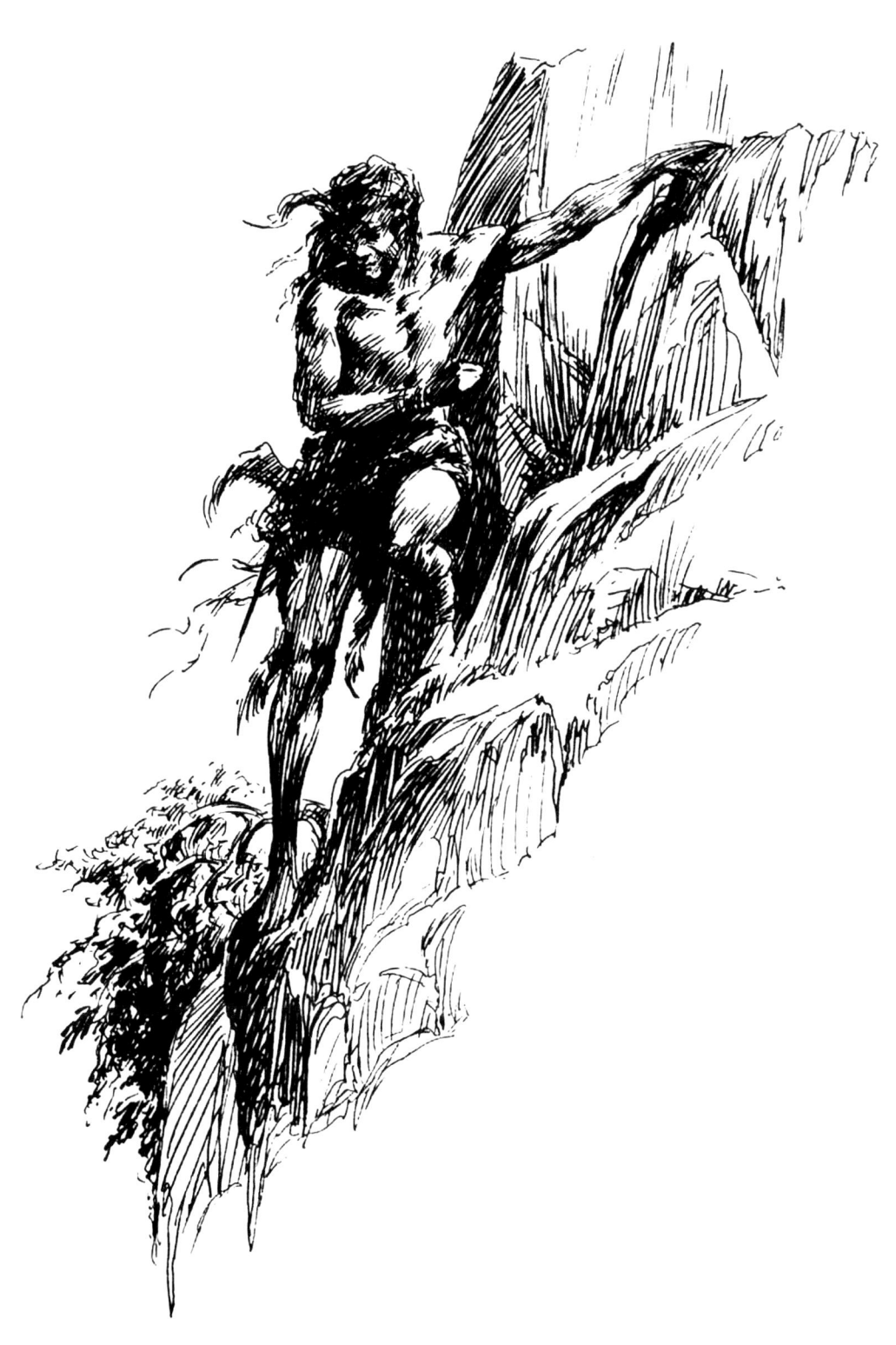

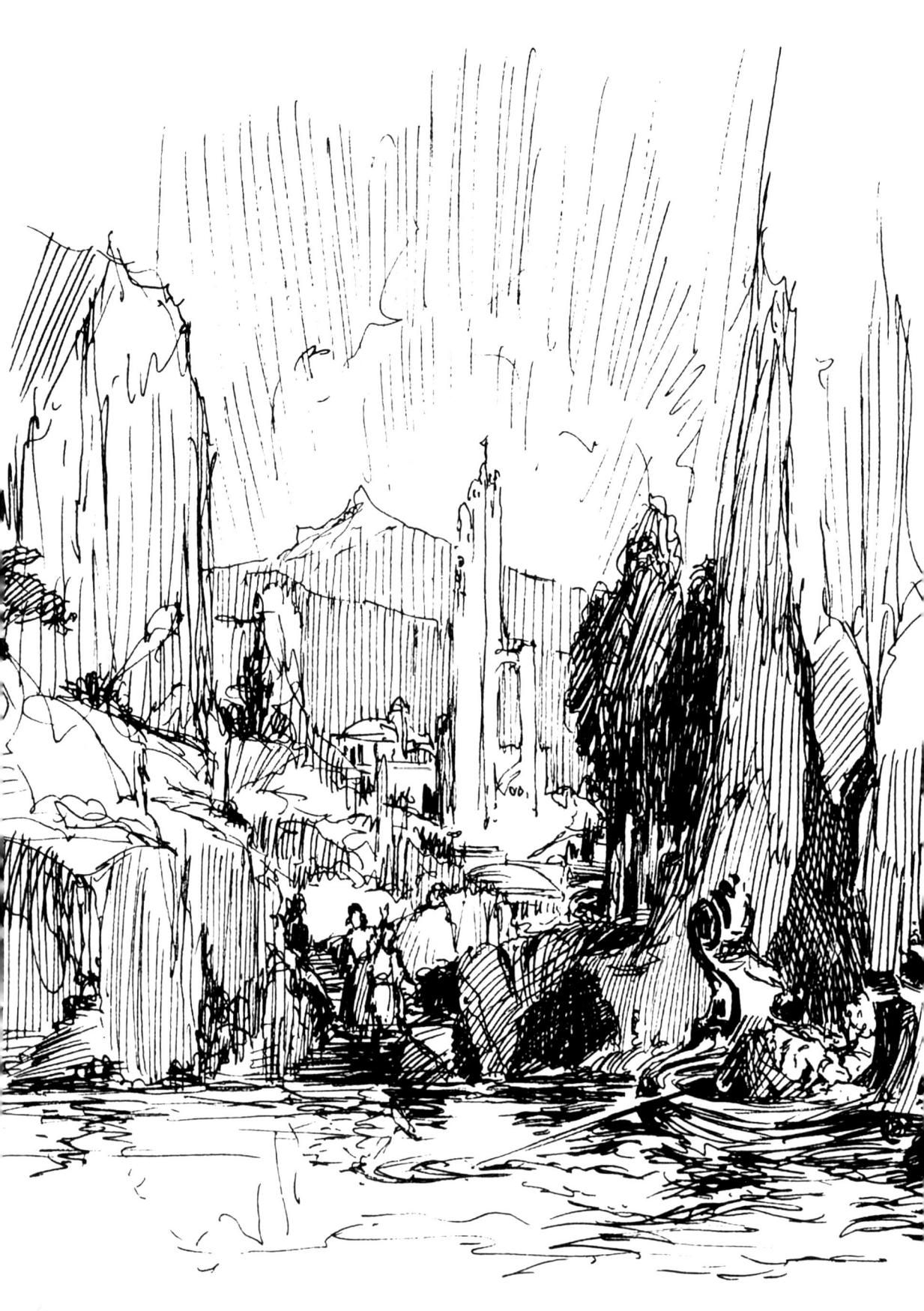

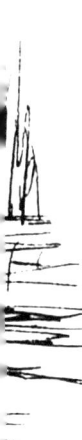

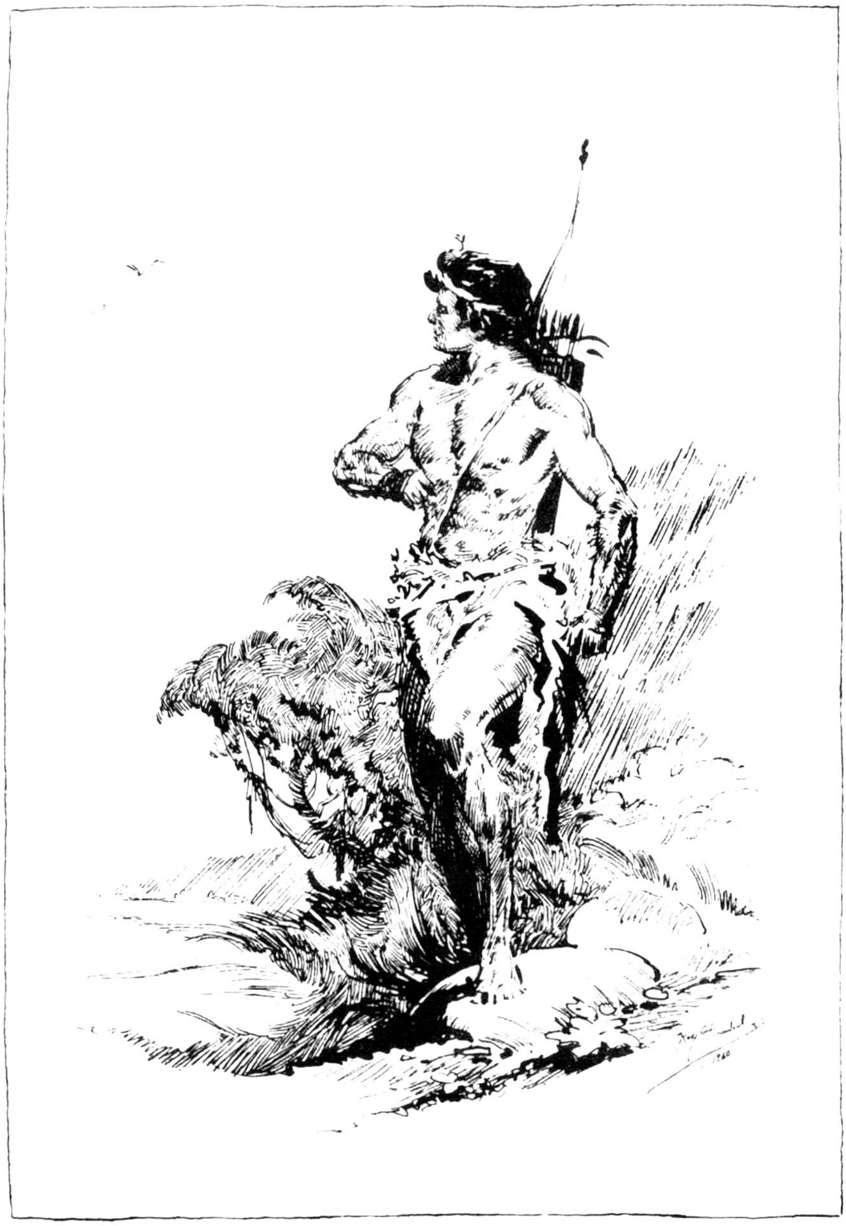

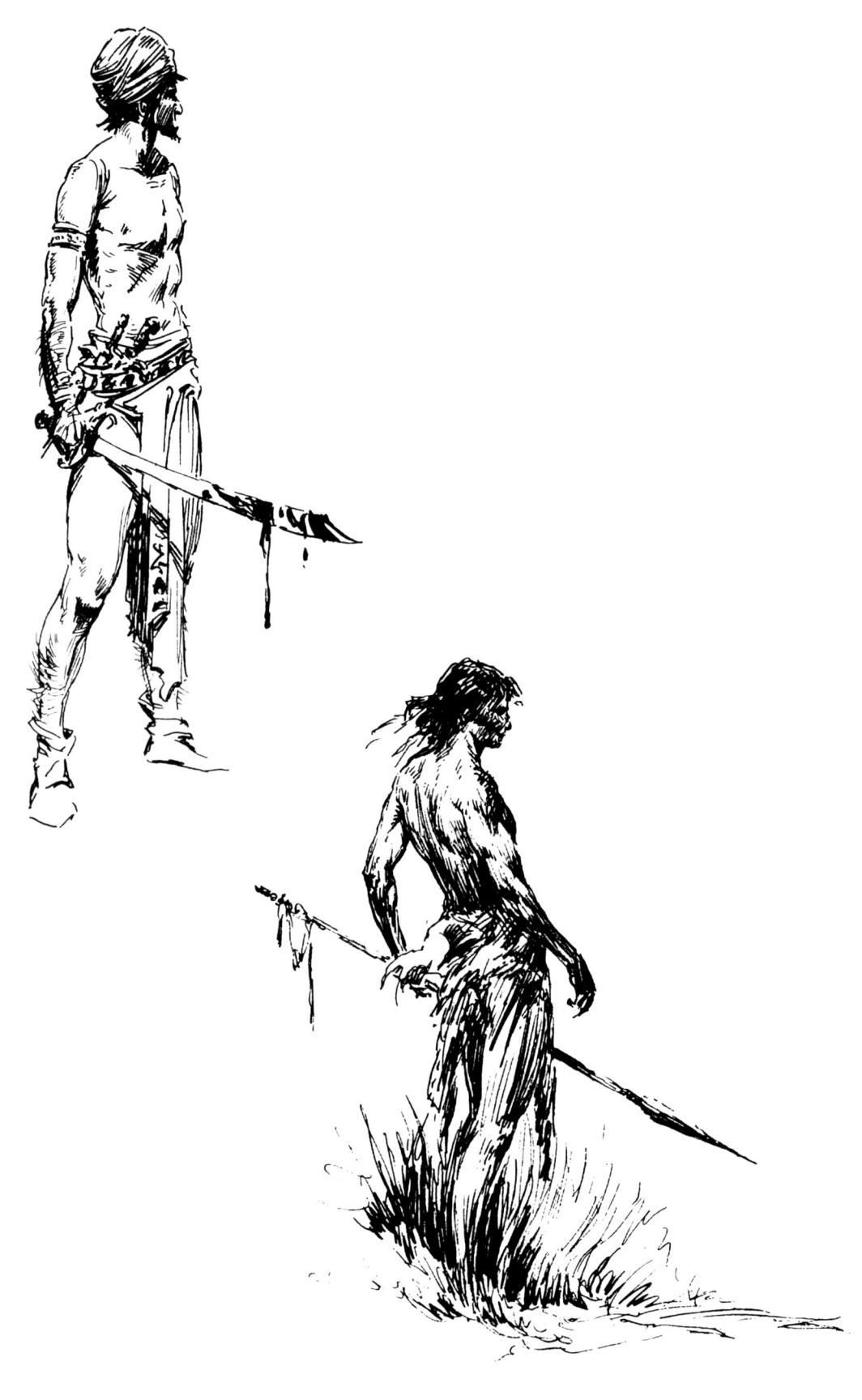

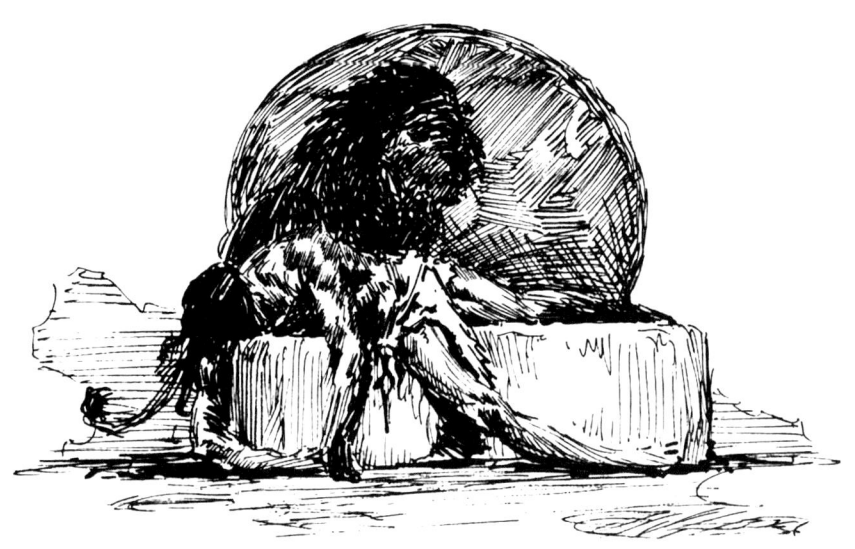

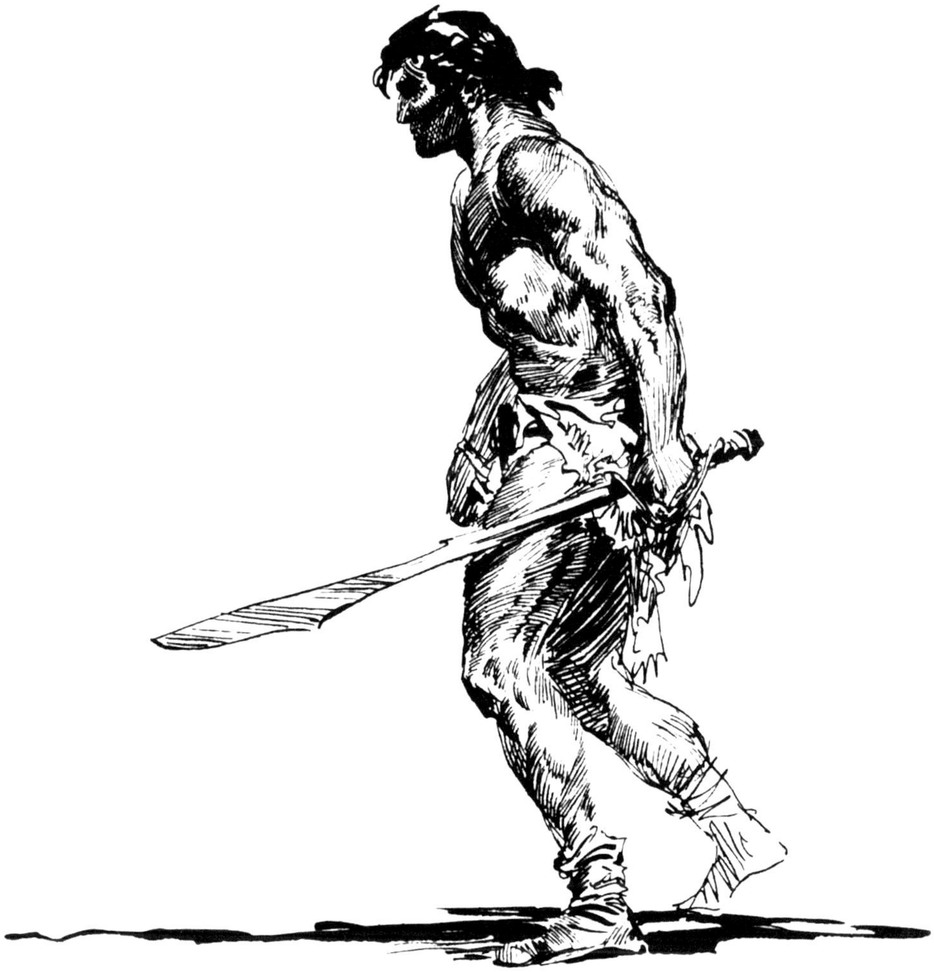

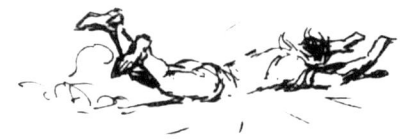

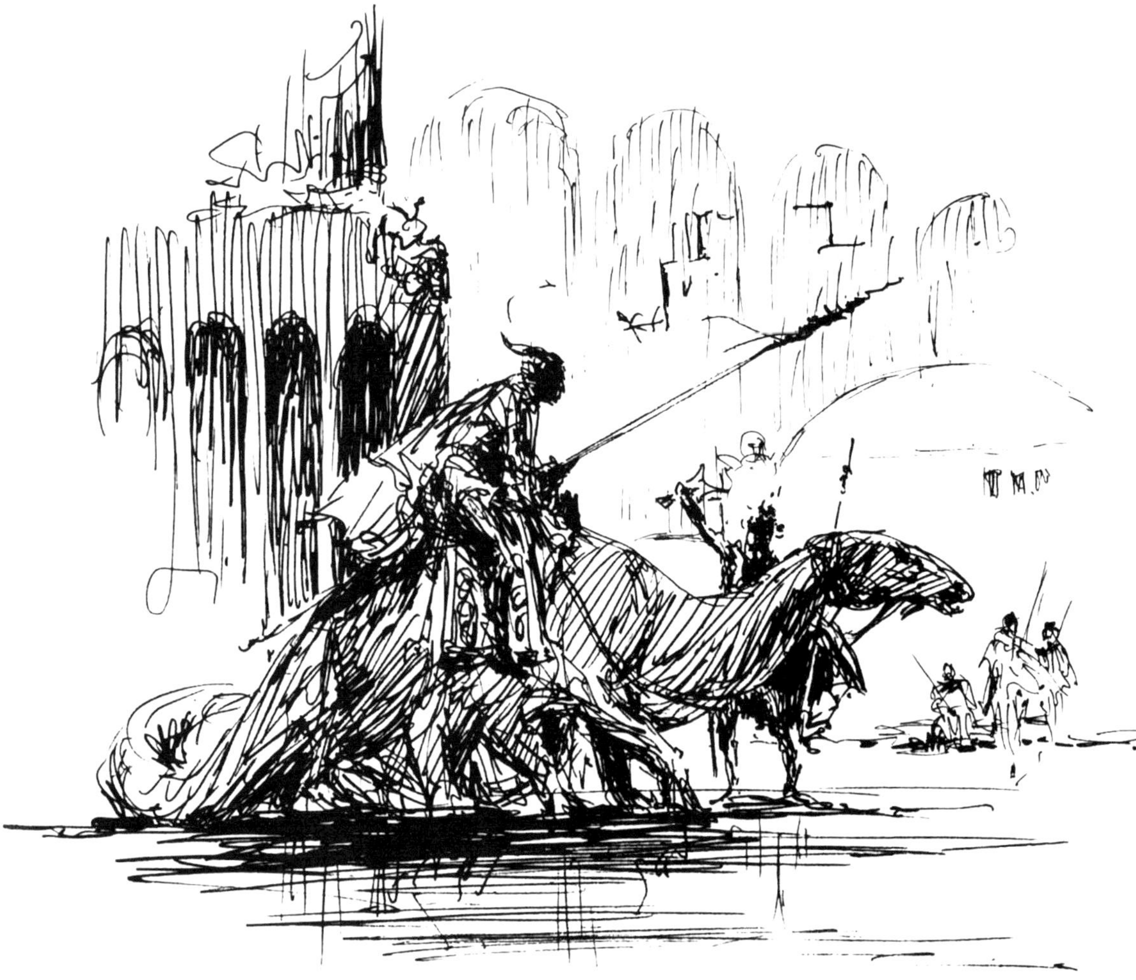

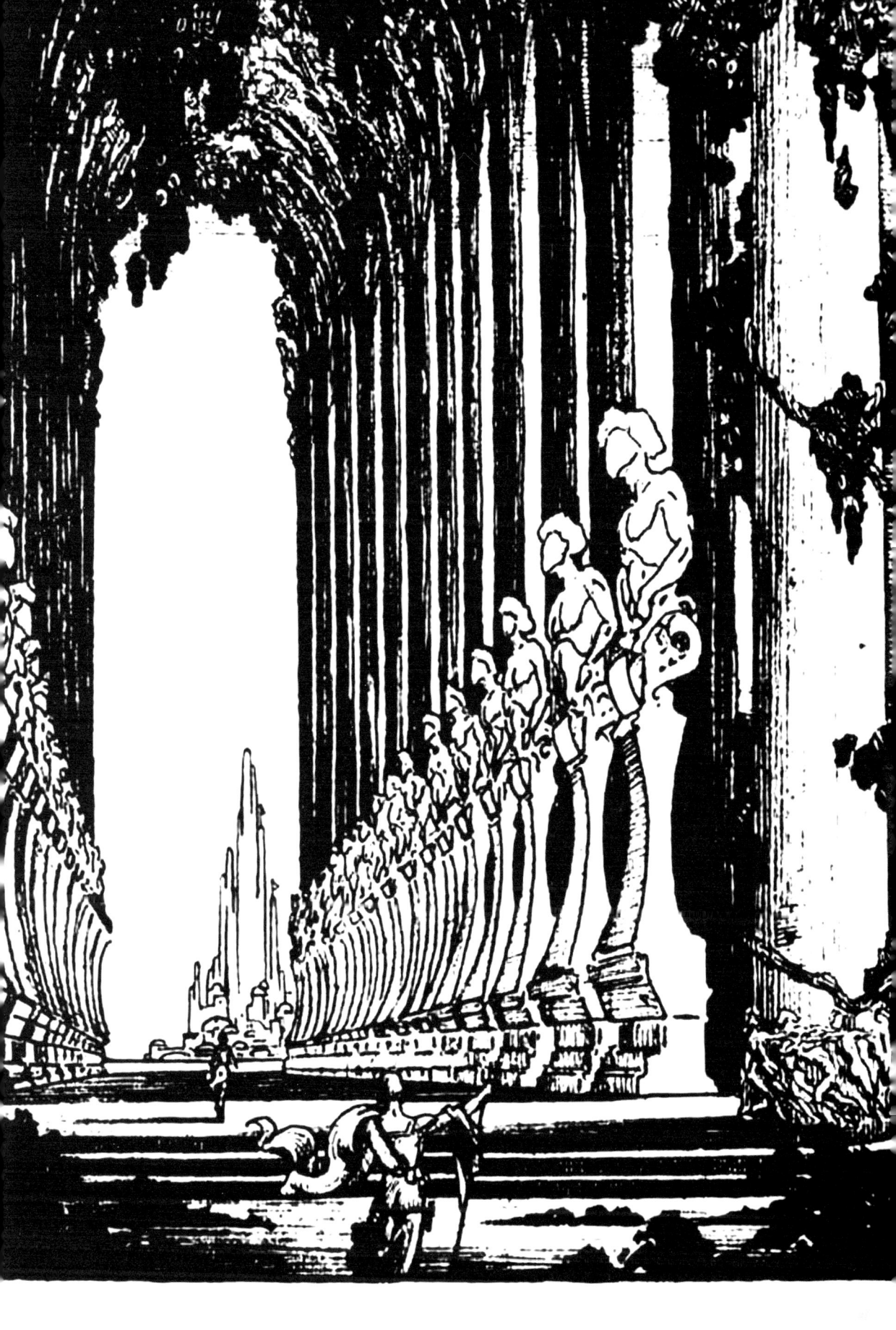

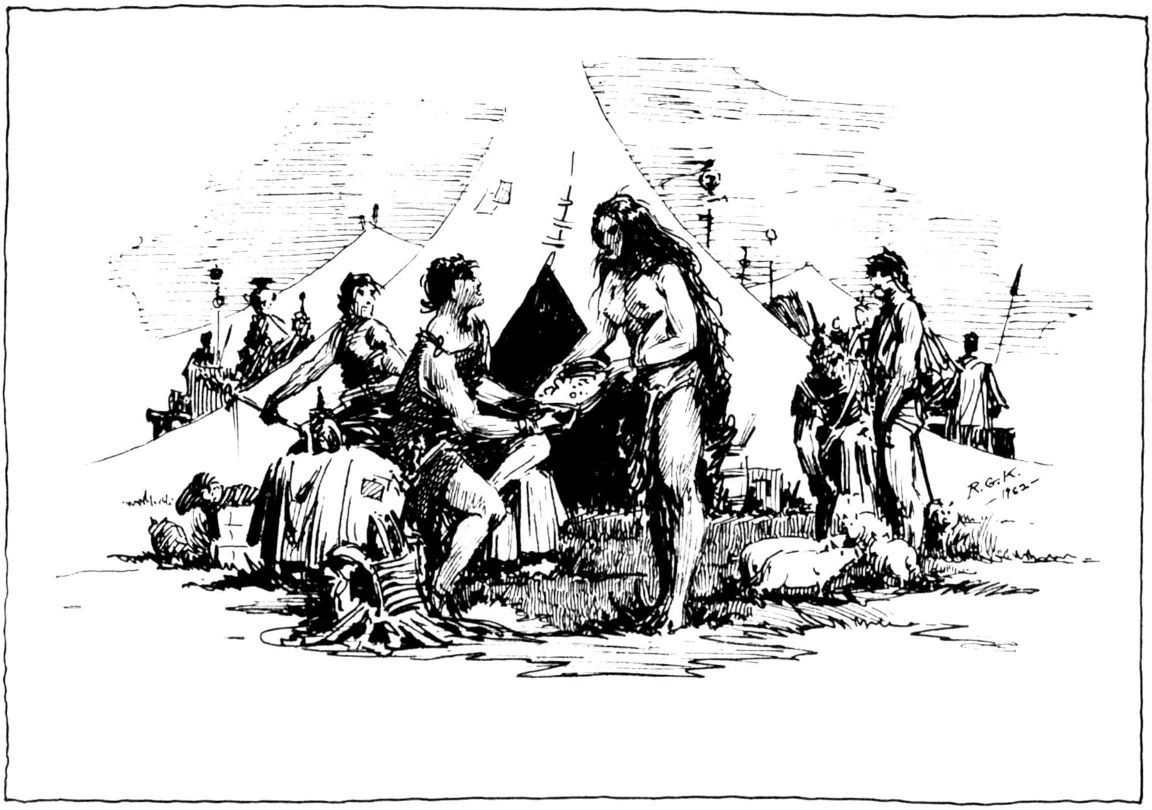

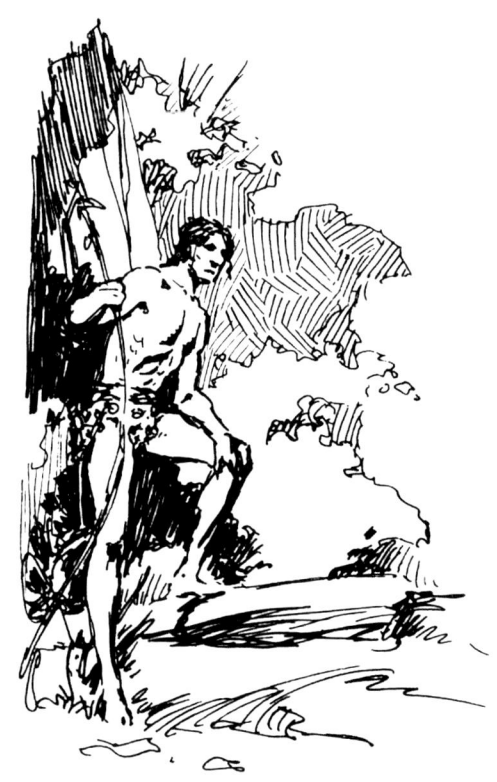

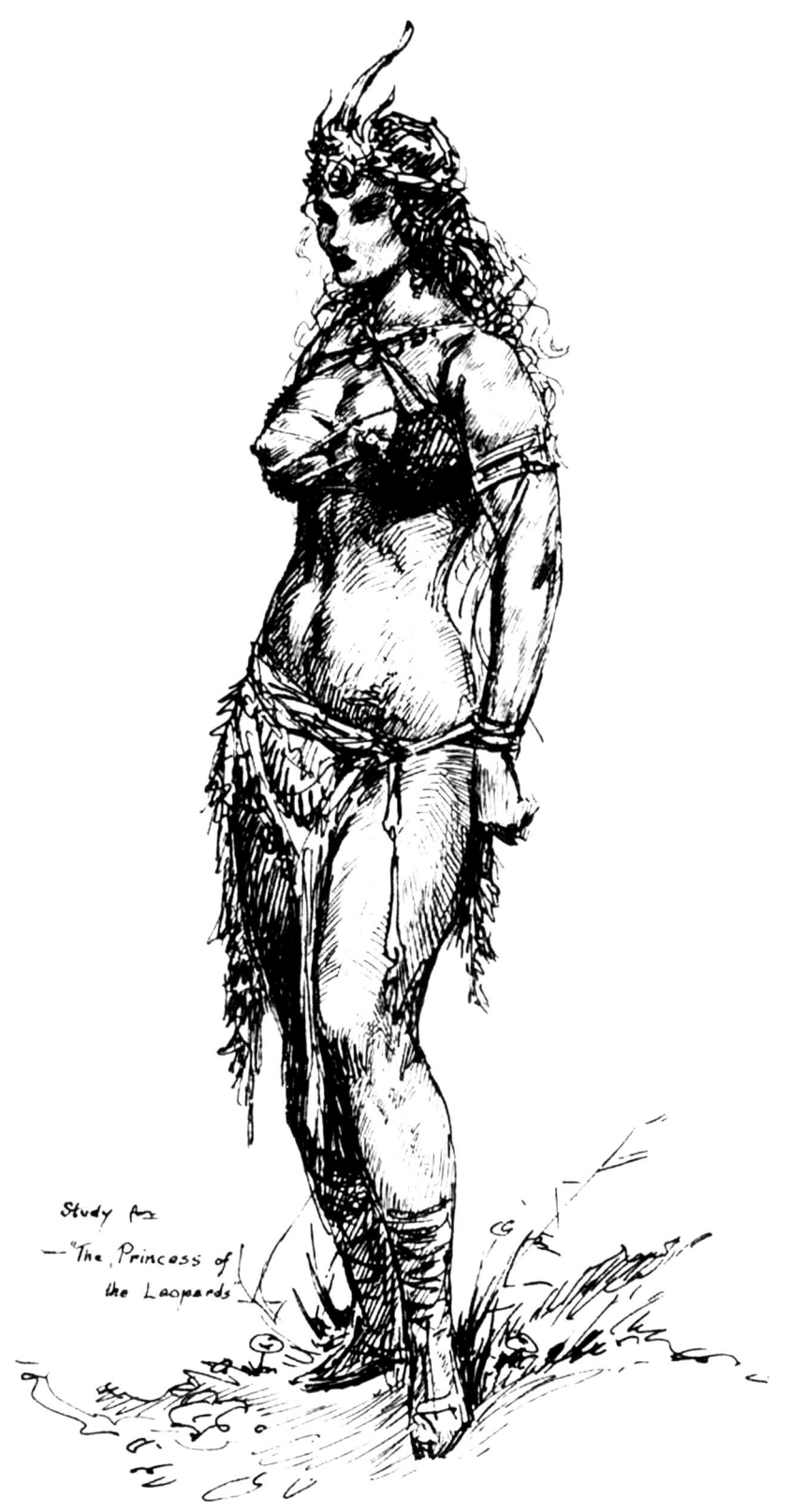

Study for
— "The Princess of
the Leopards"

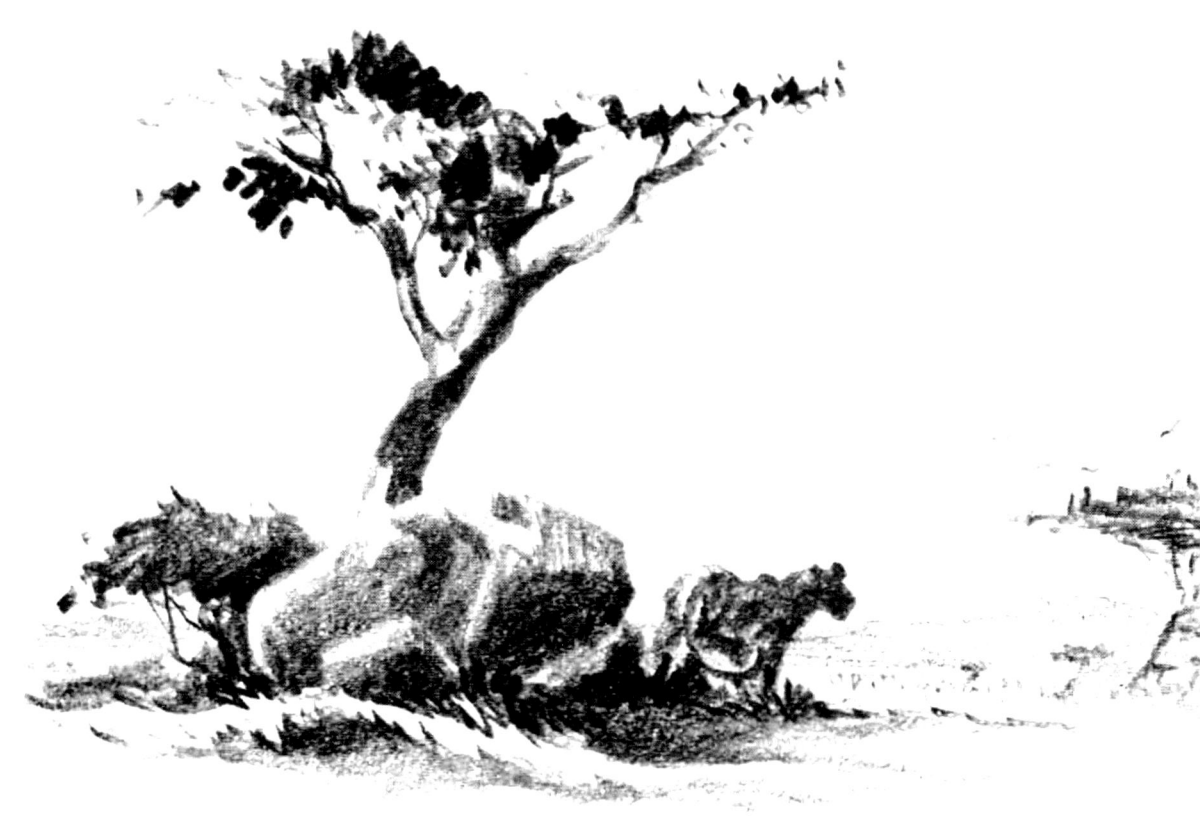

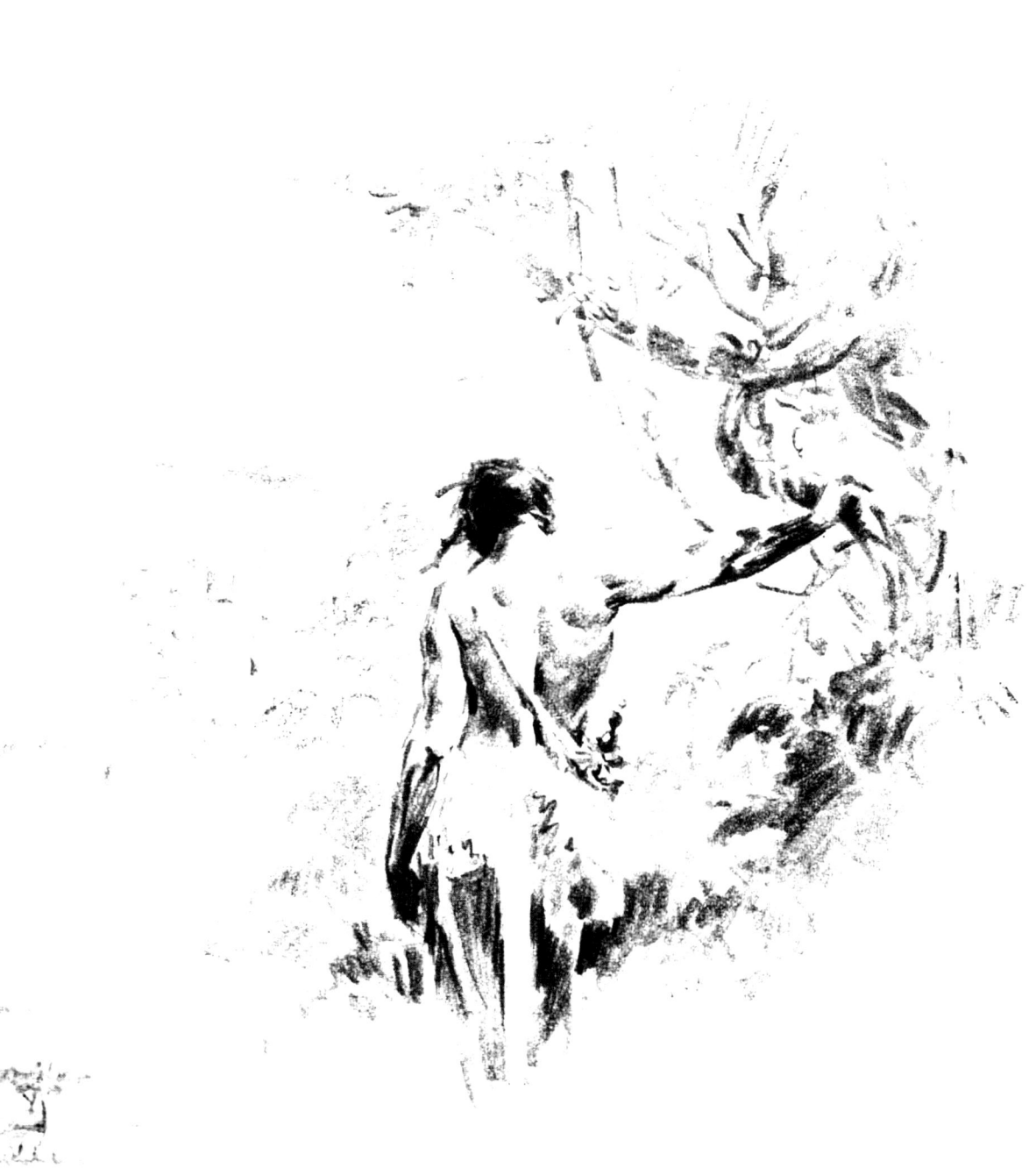

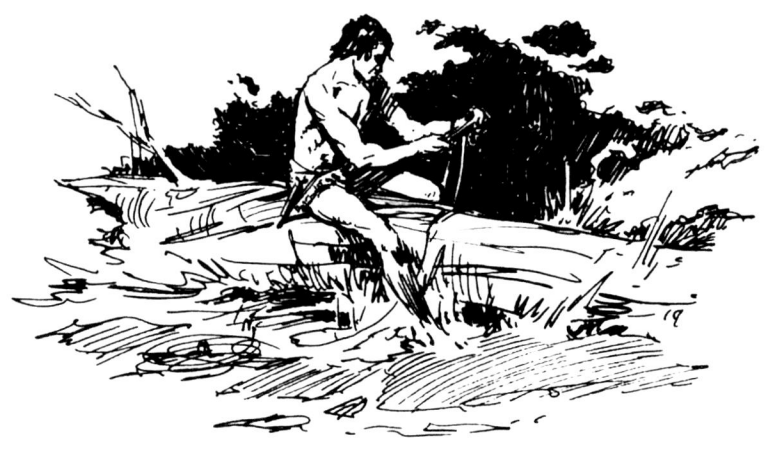

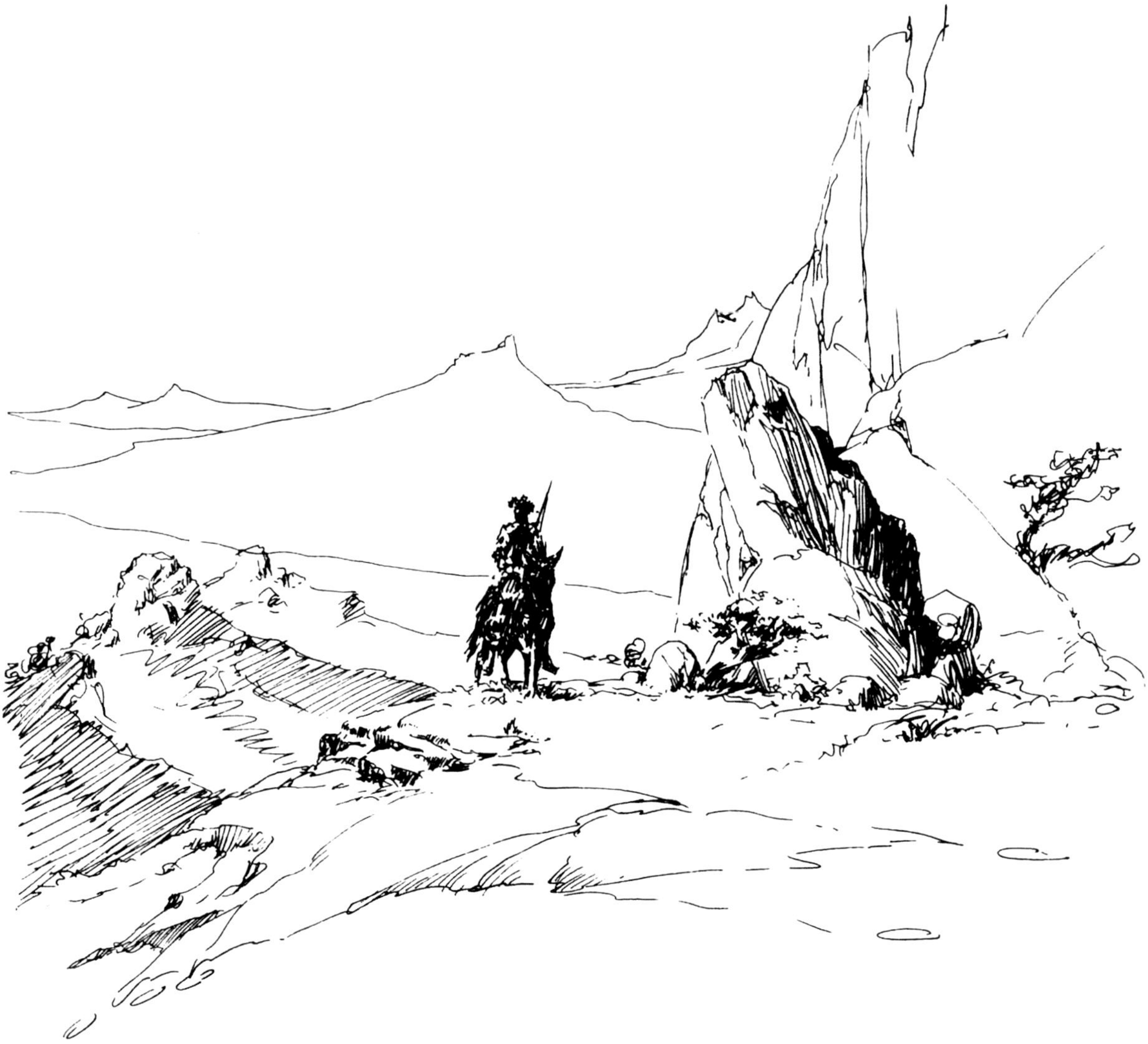

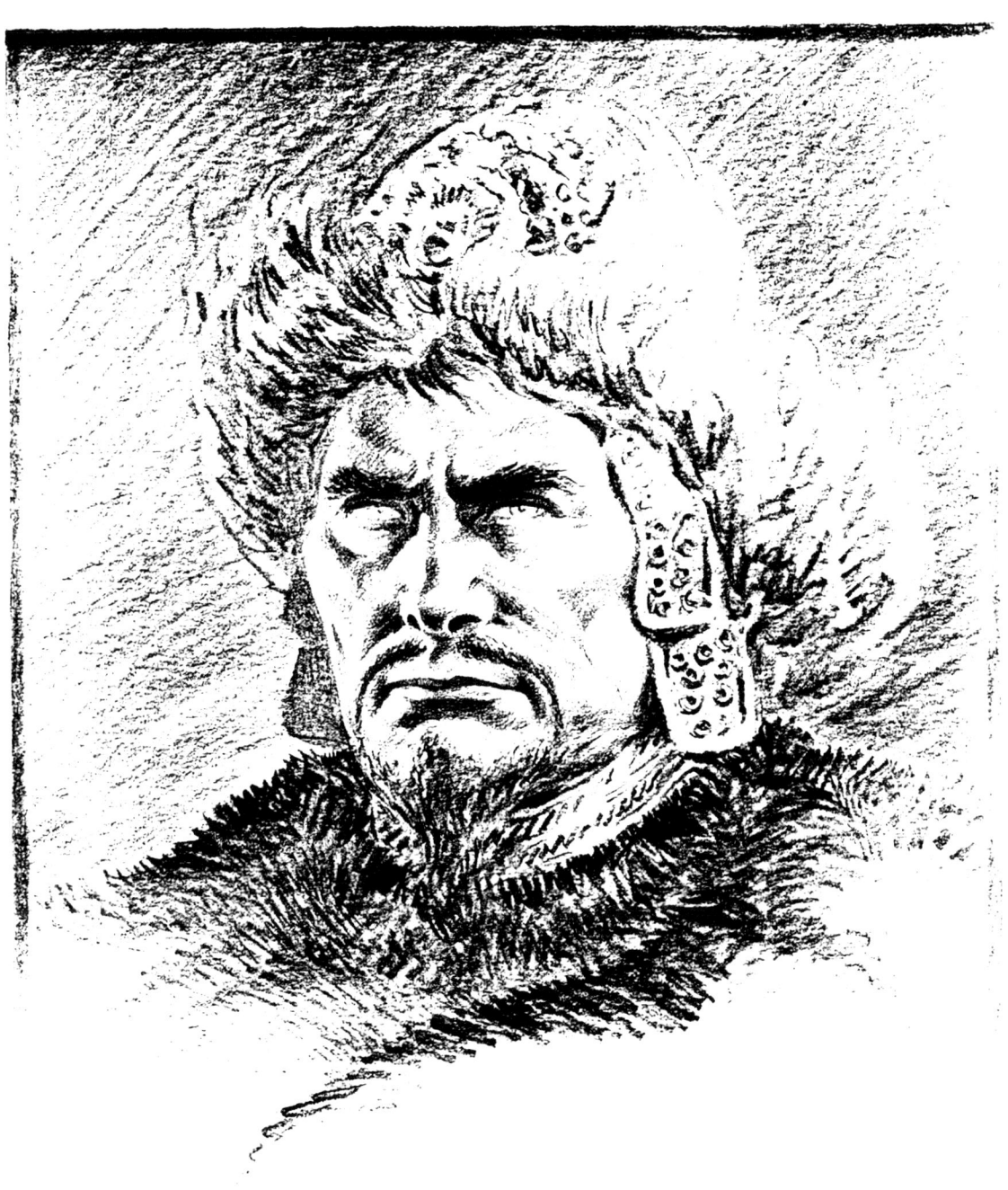

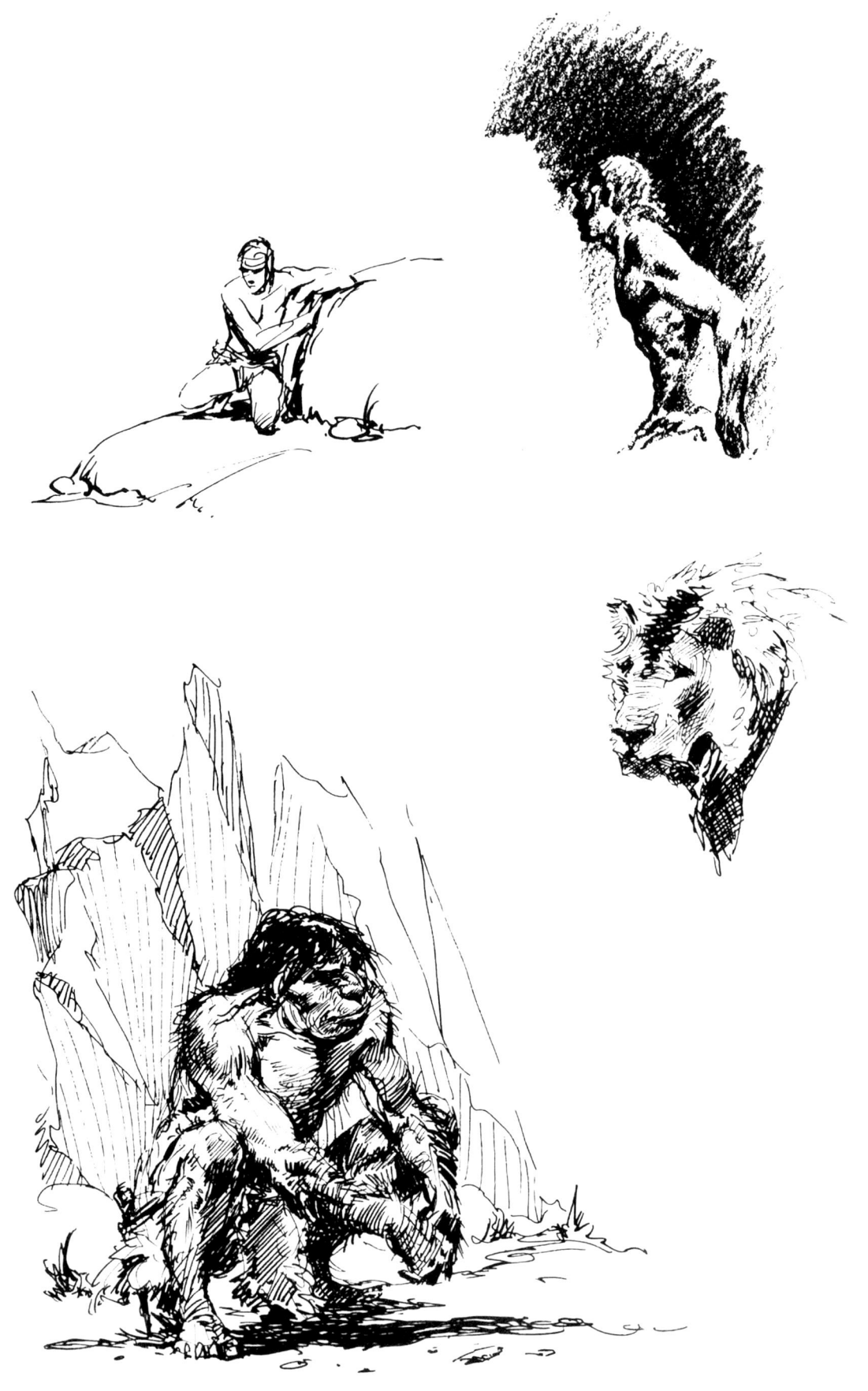

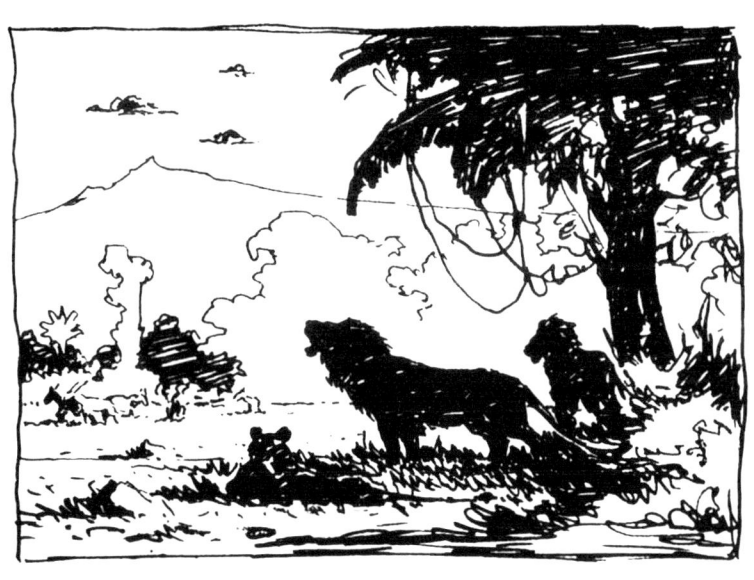

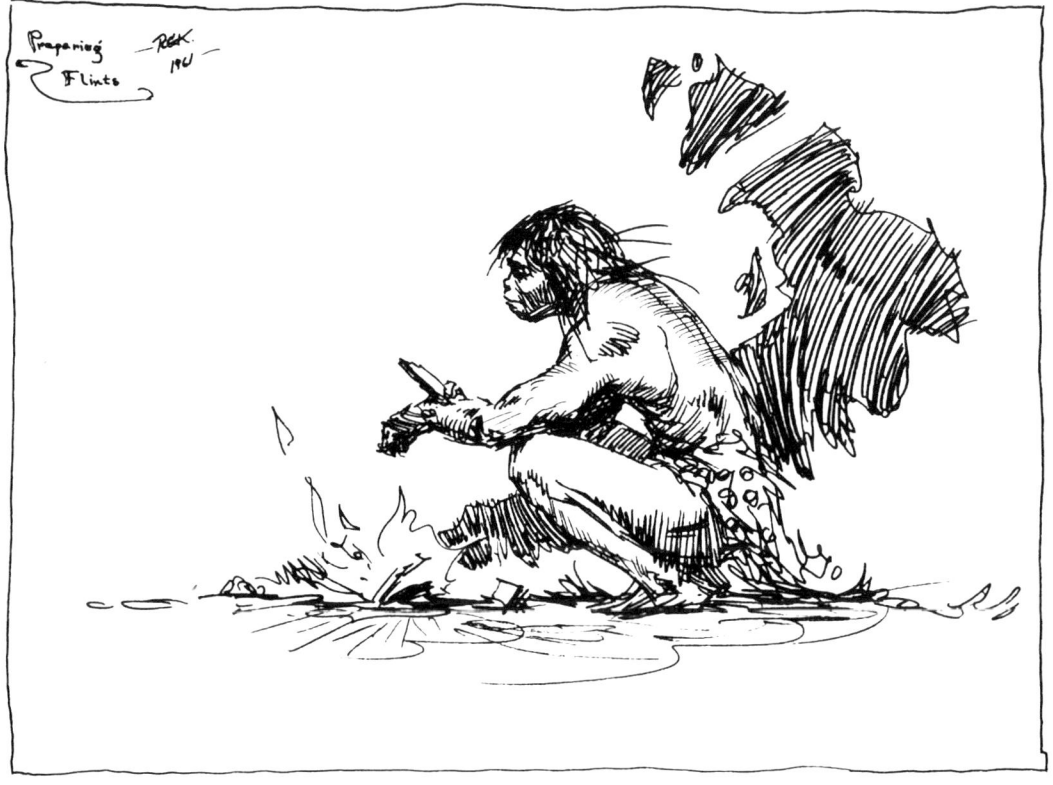

Preparing
Flints

RGK.
1961

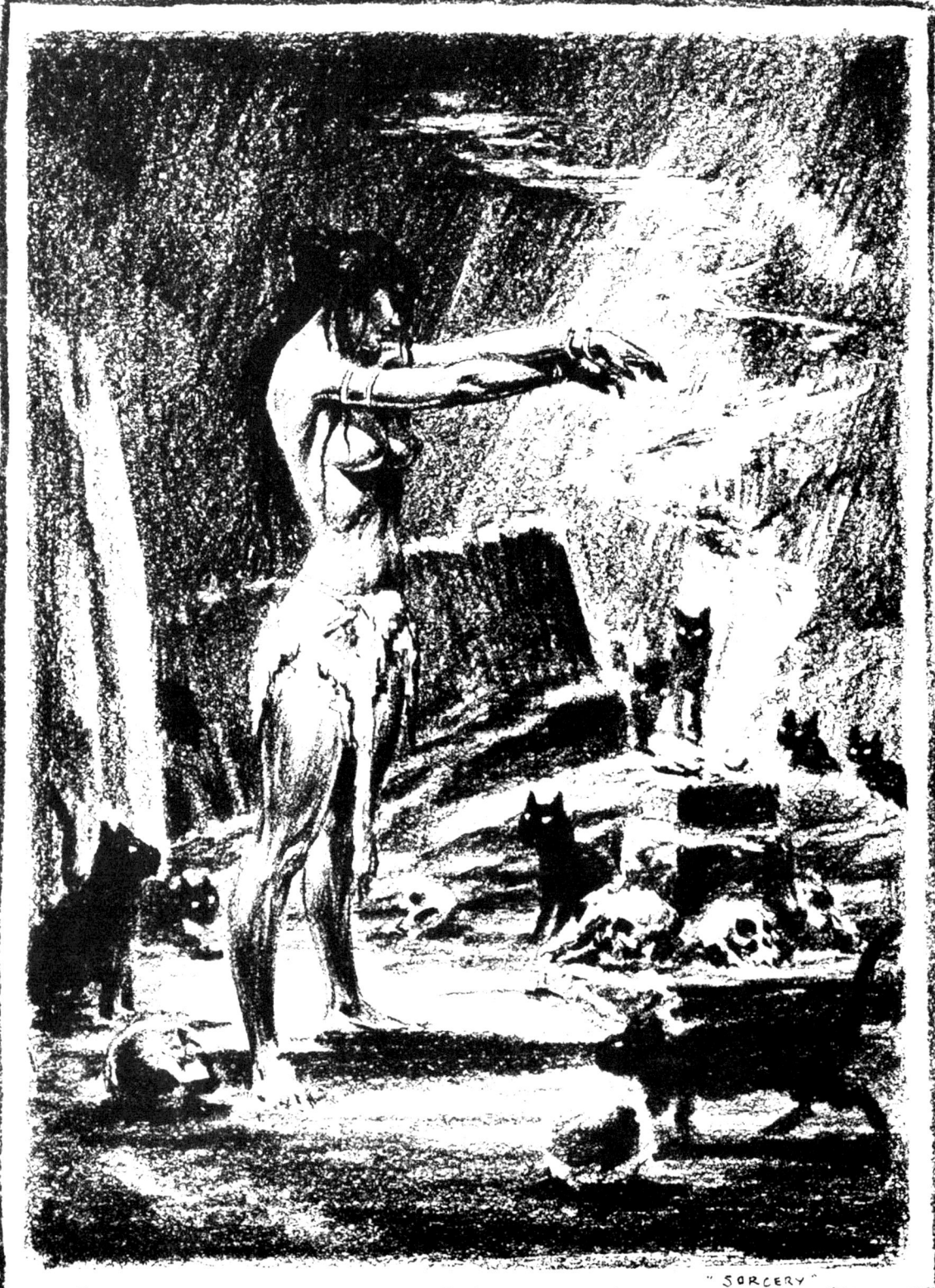

"SORCERY"

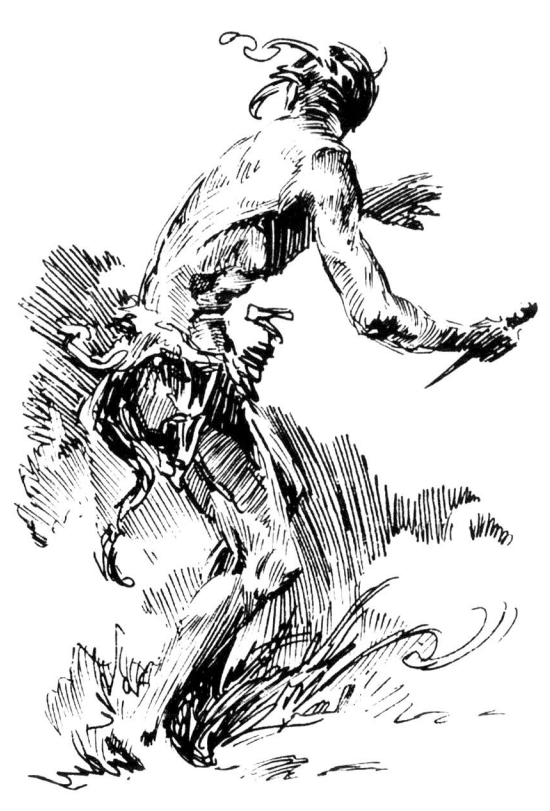

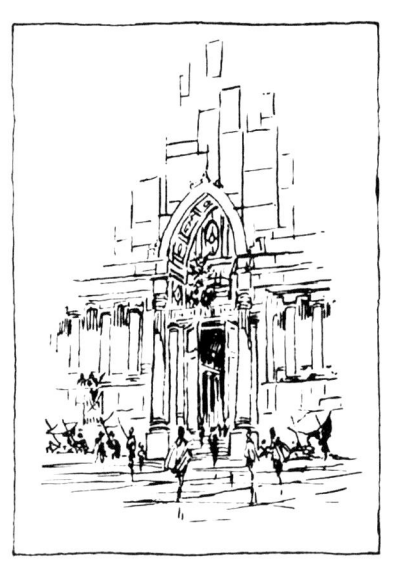

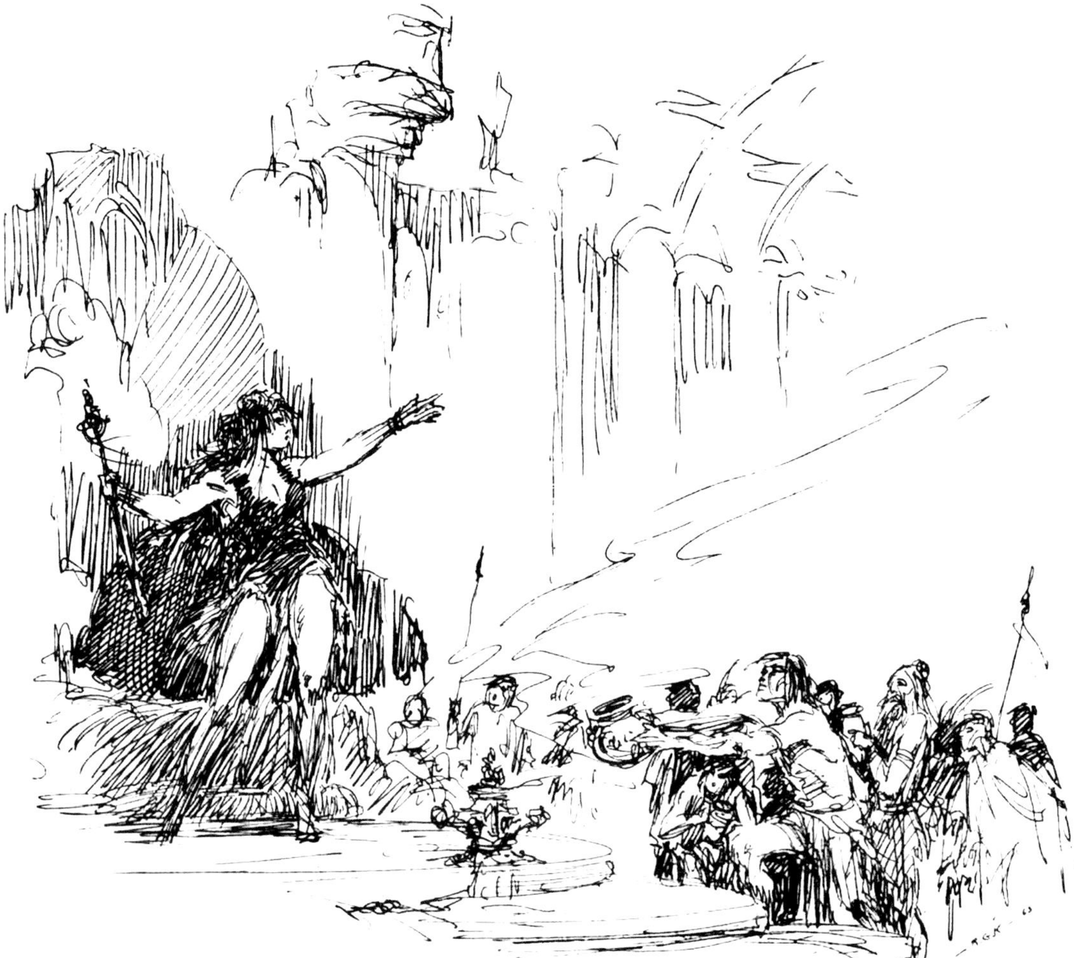

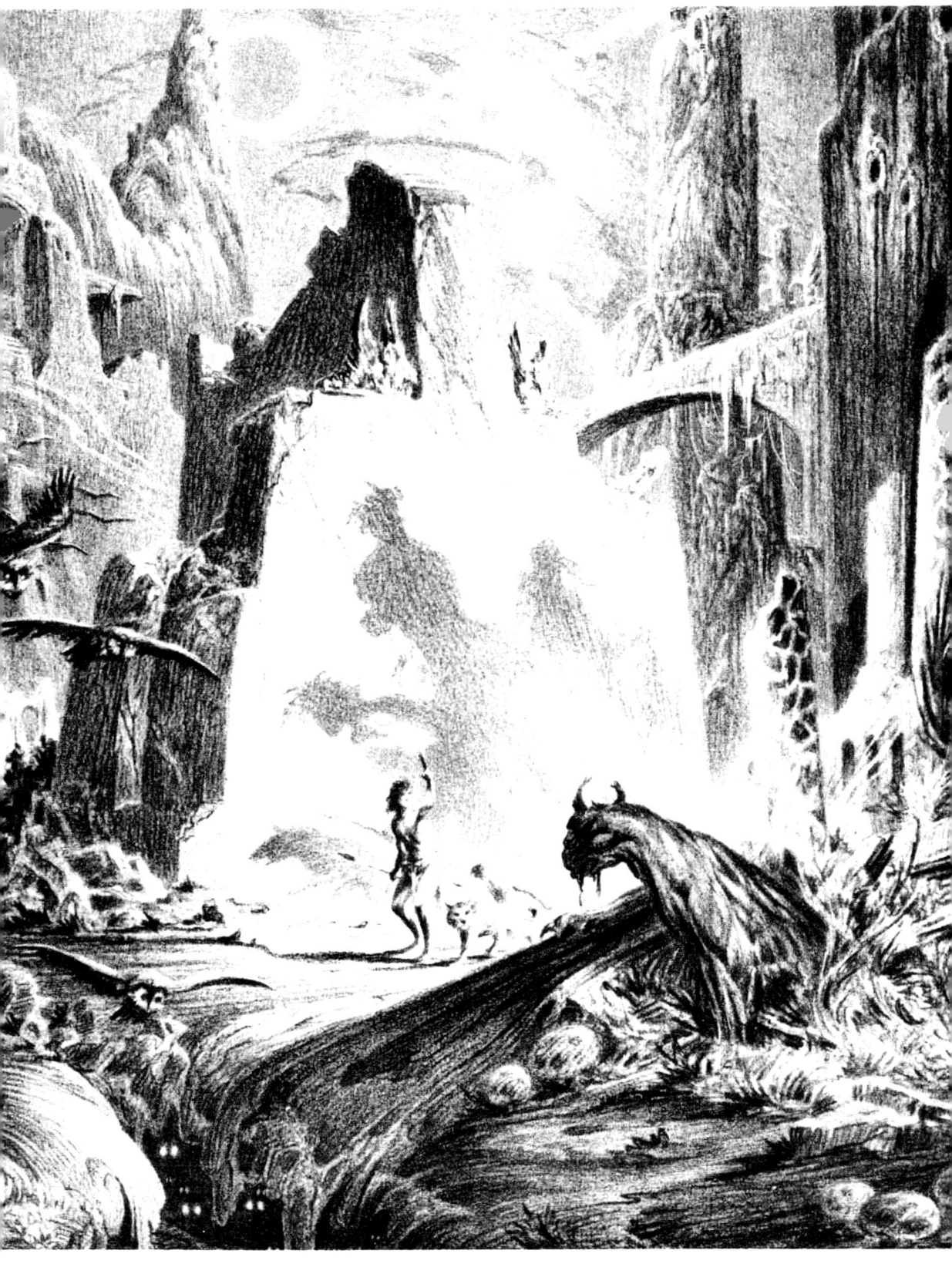

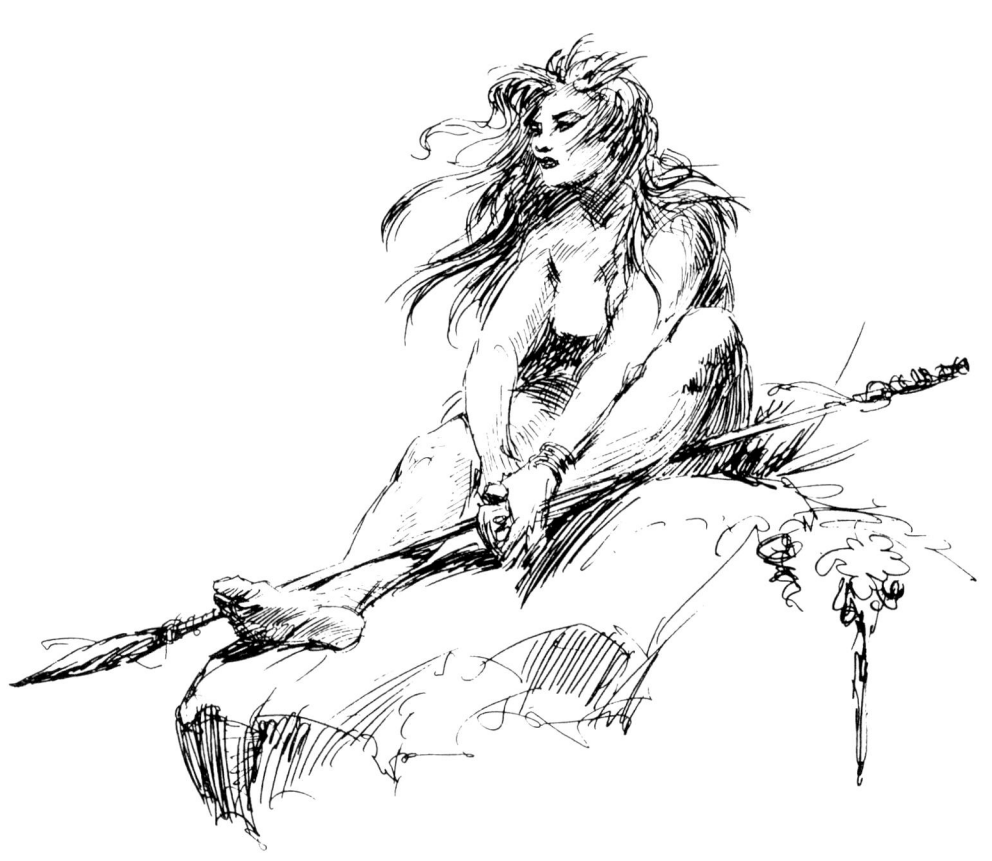

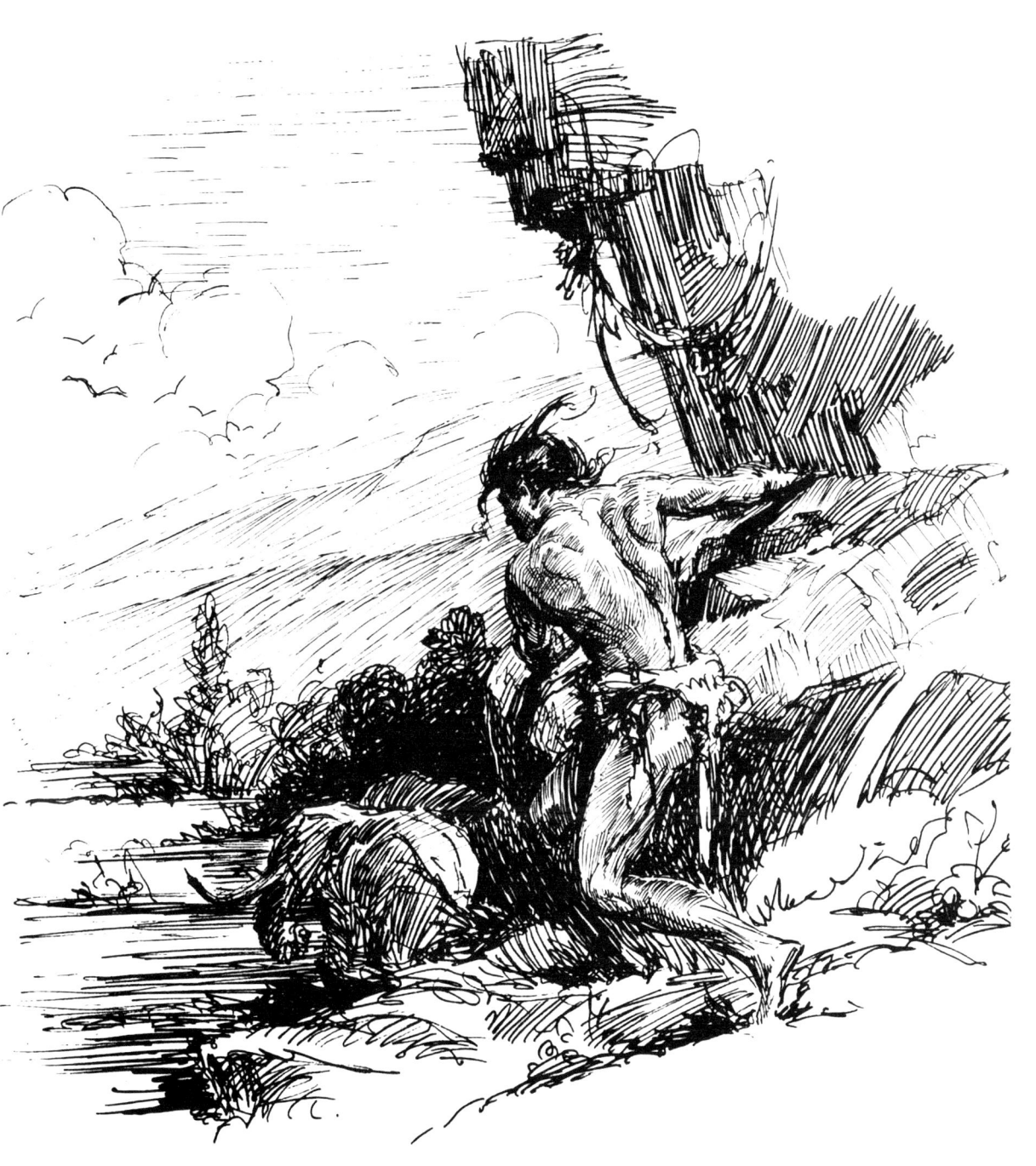

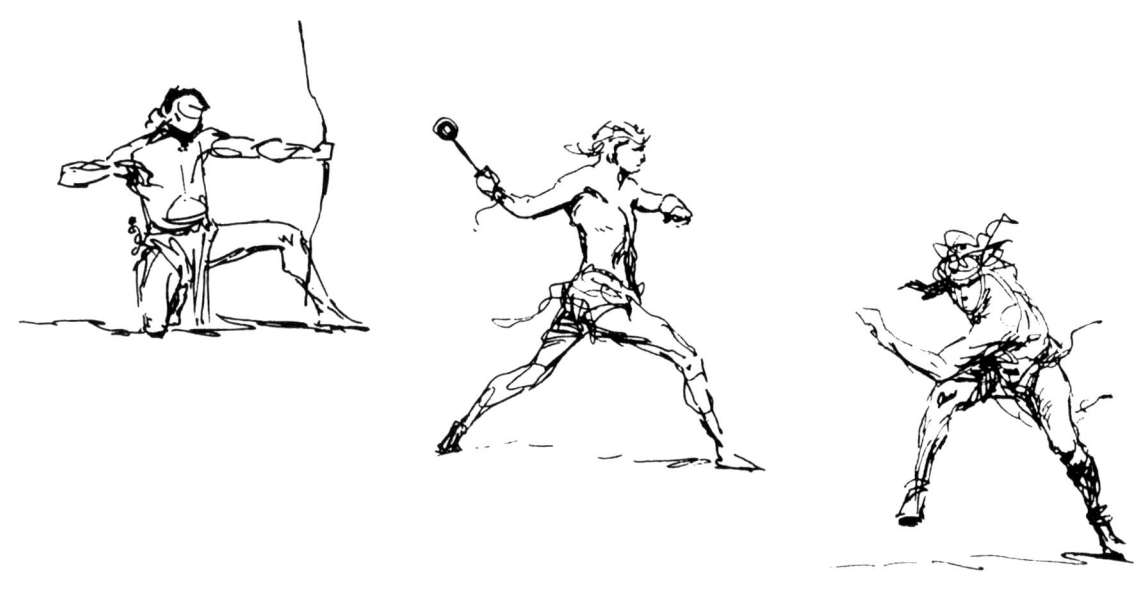

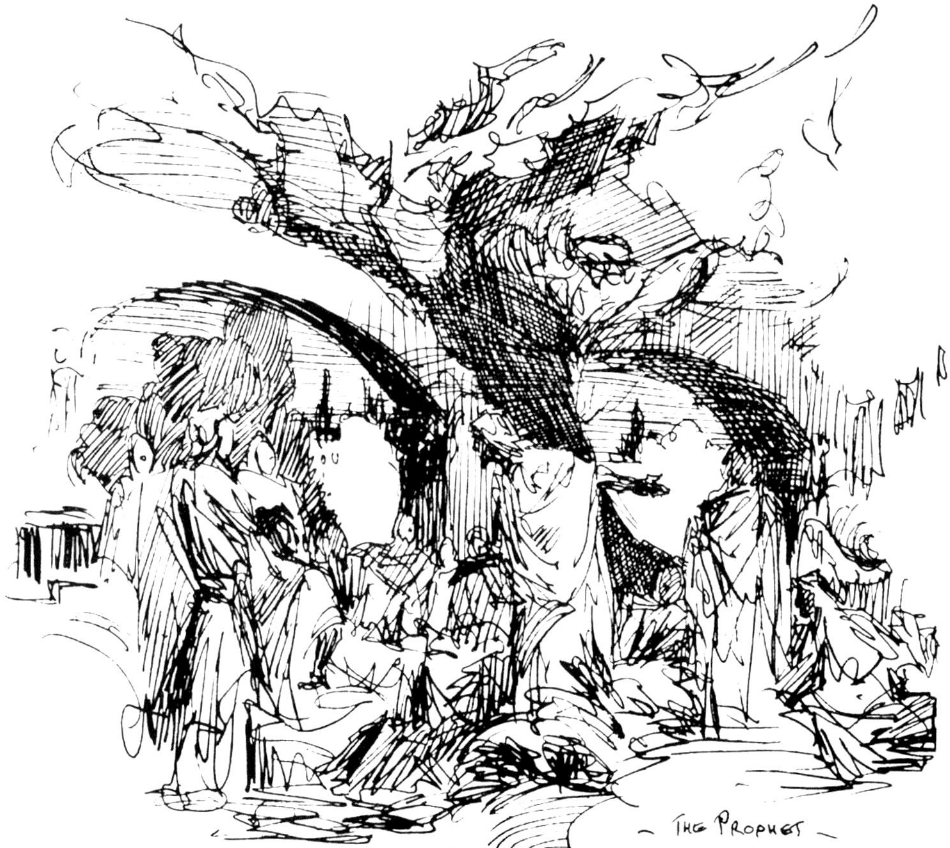

— THE PROPHET —

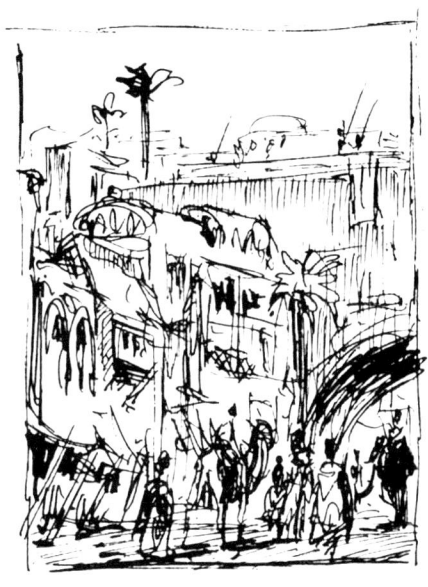
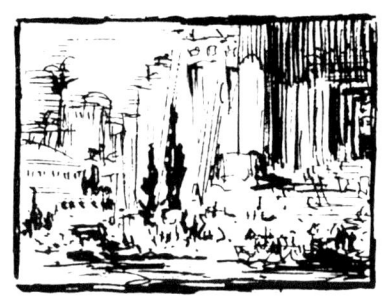
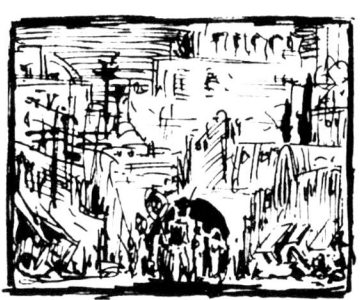
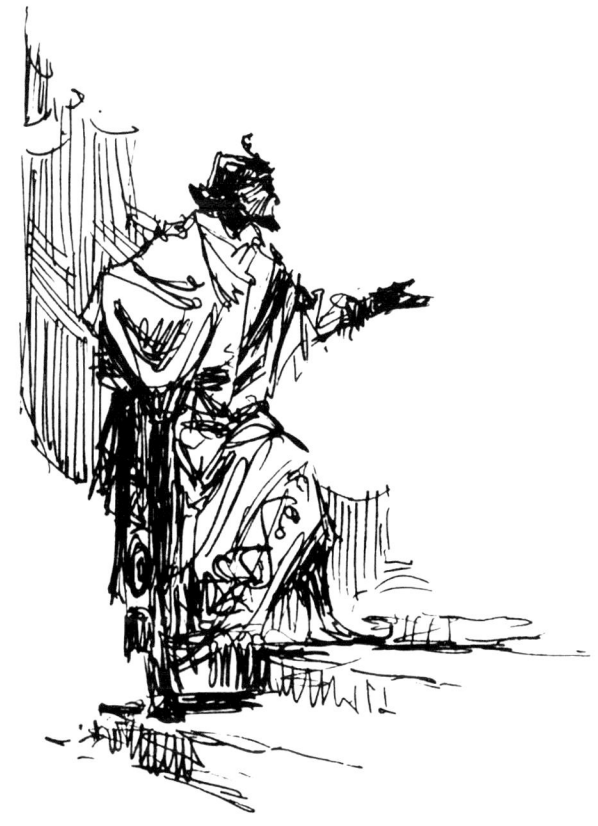

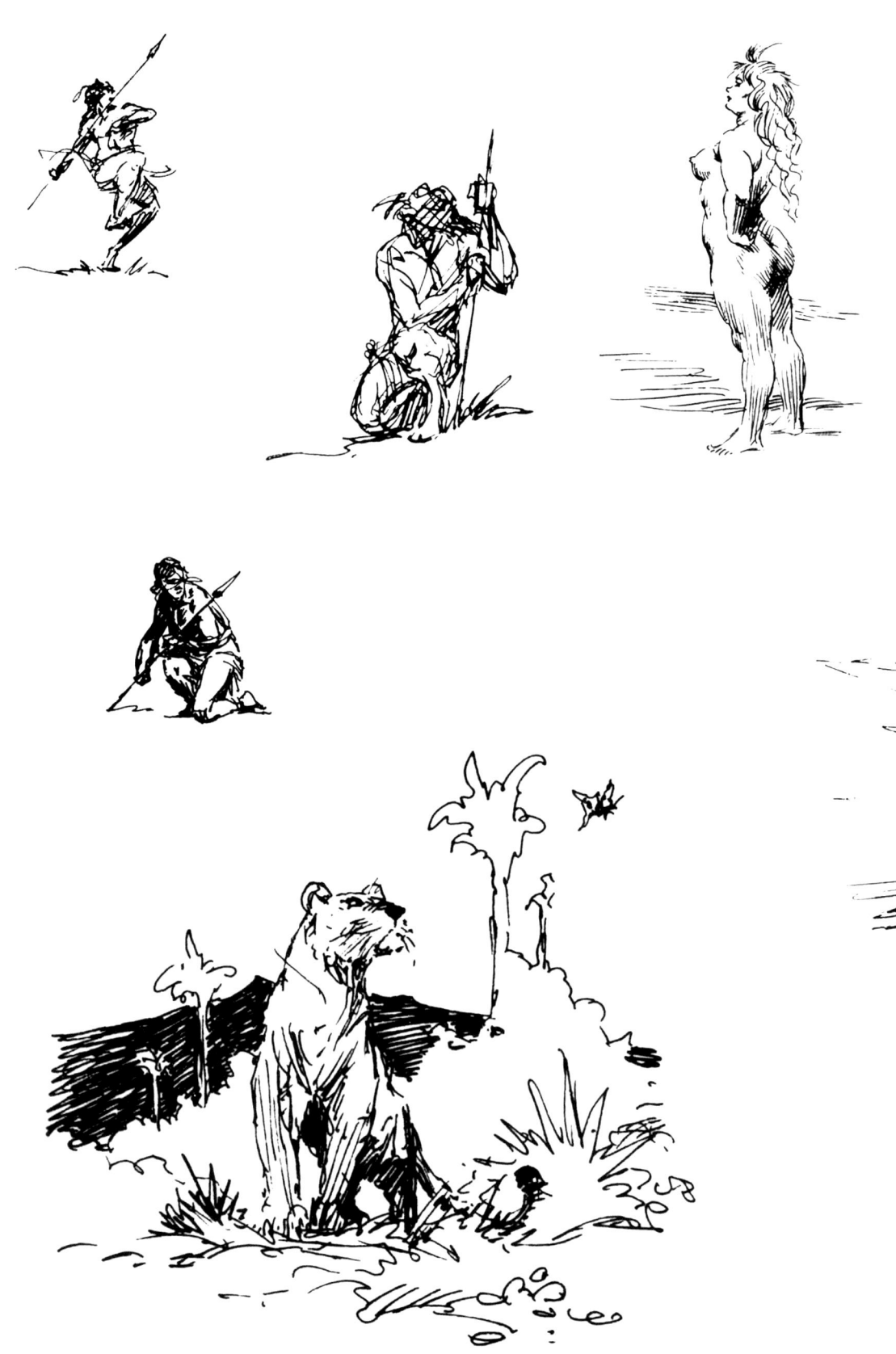

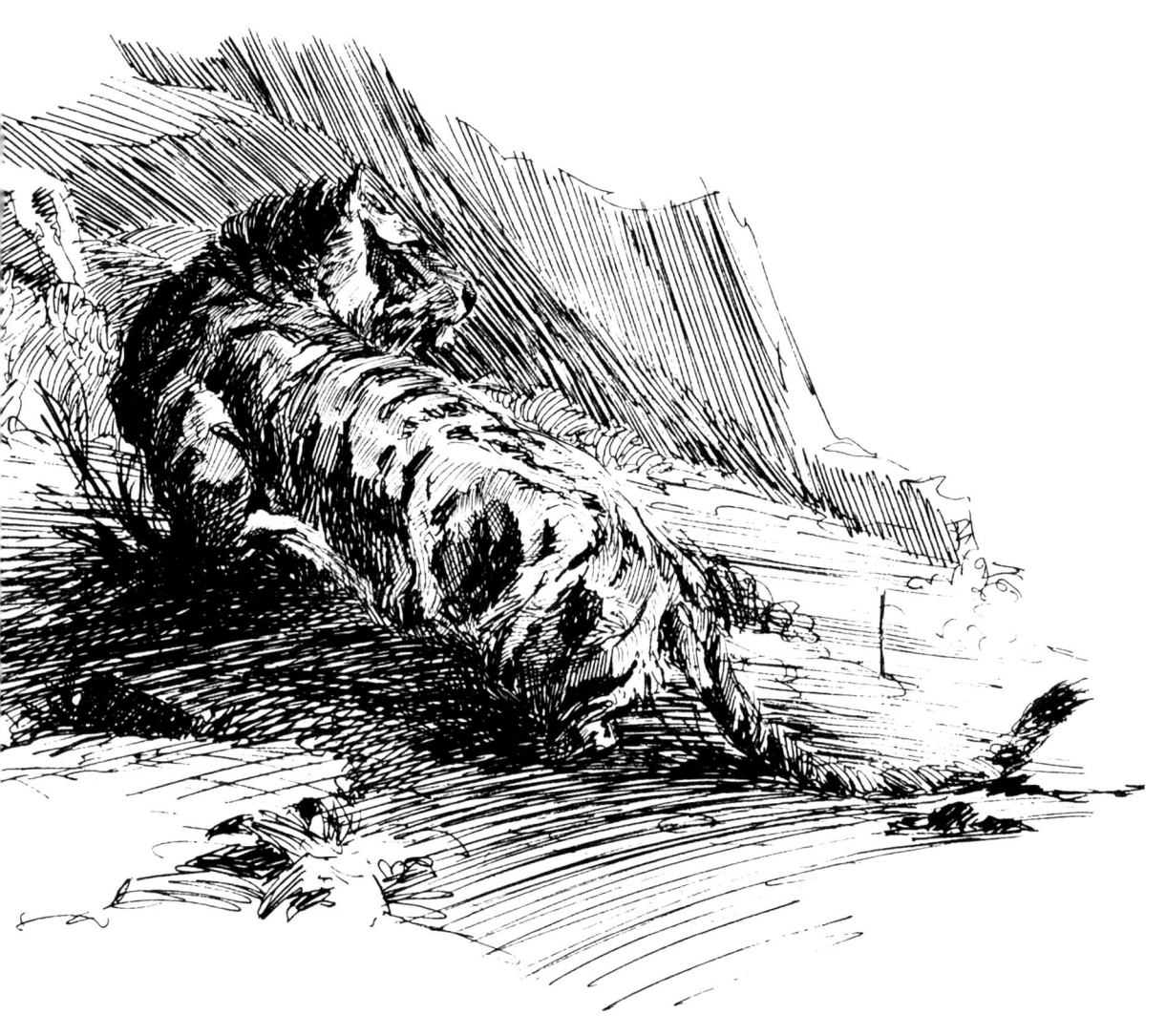

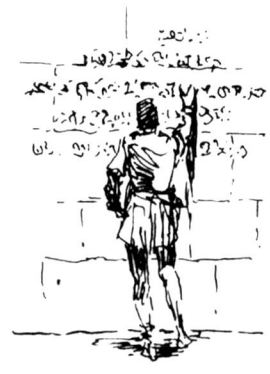

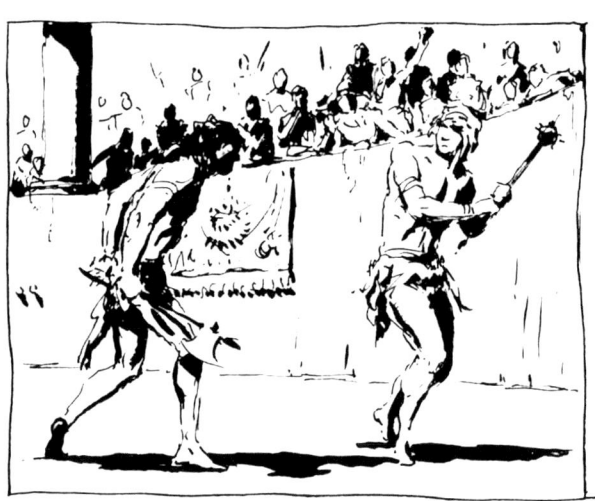

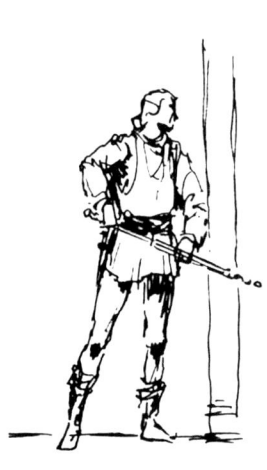

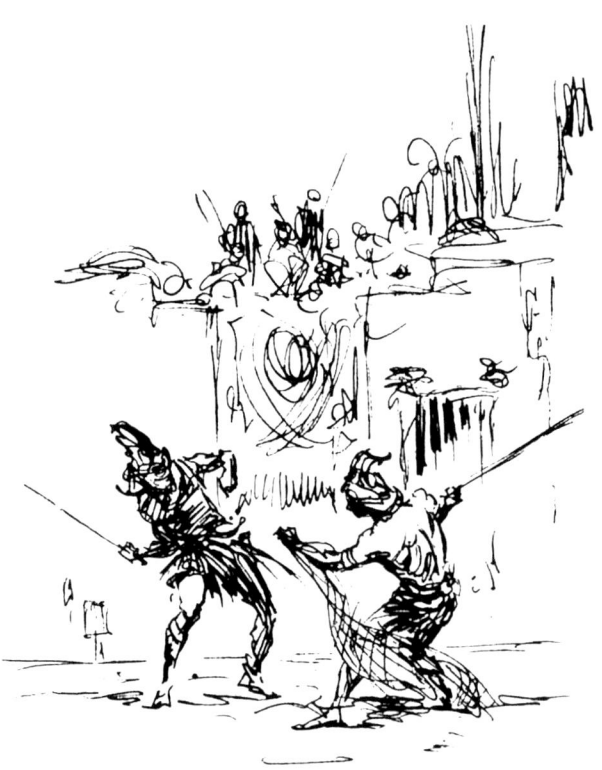

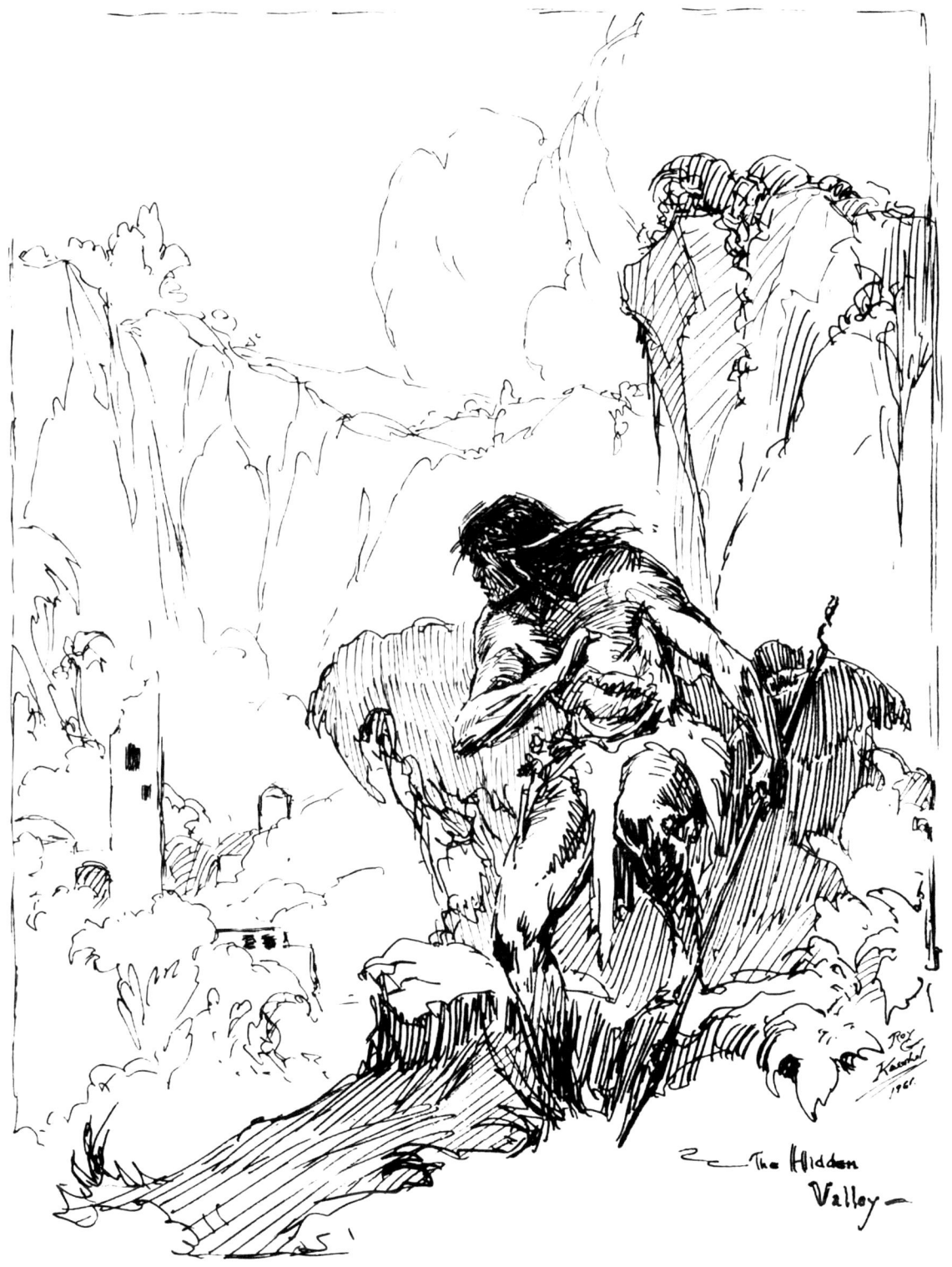

The Hidden Valley

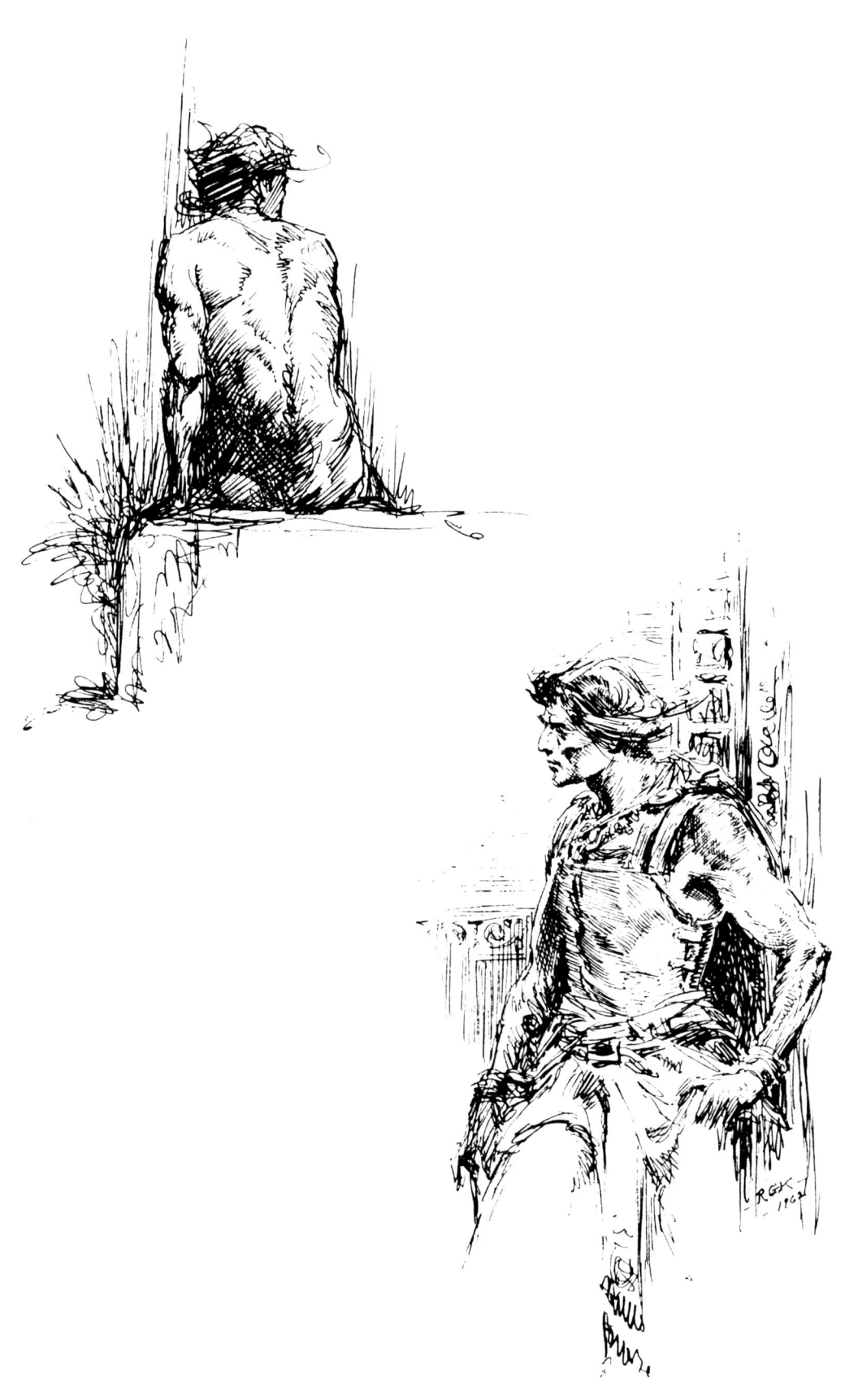

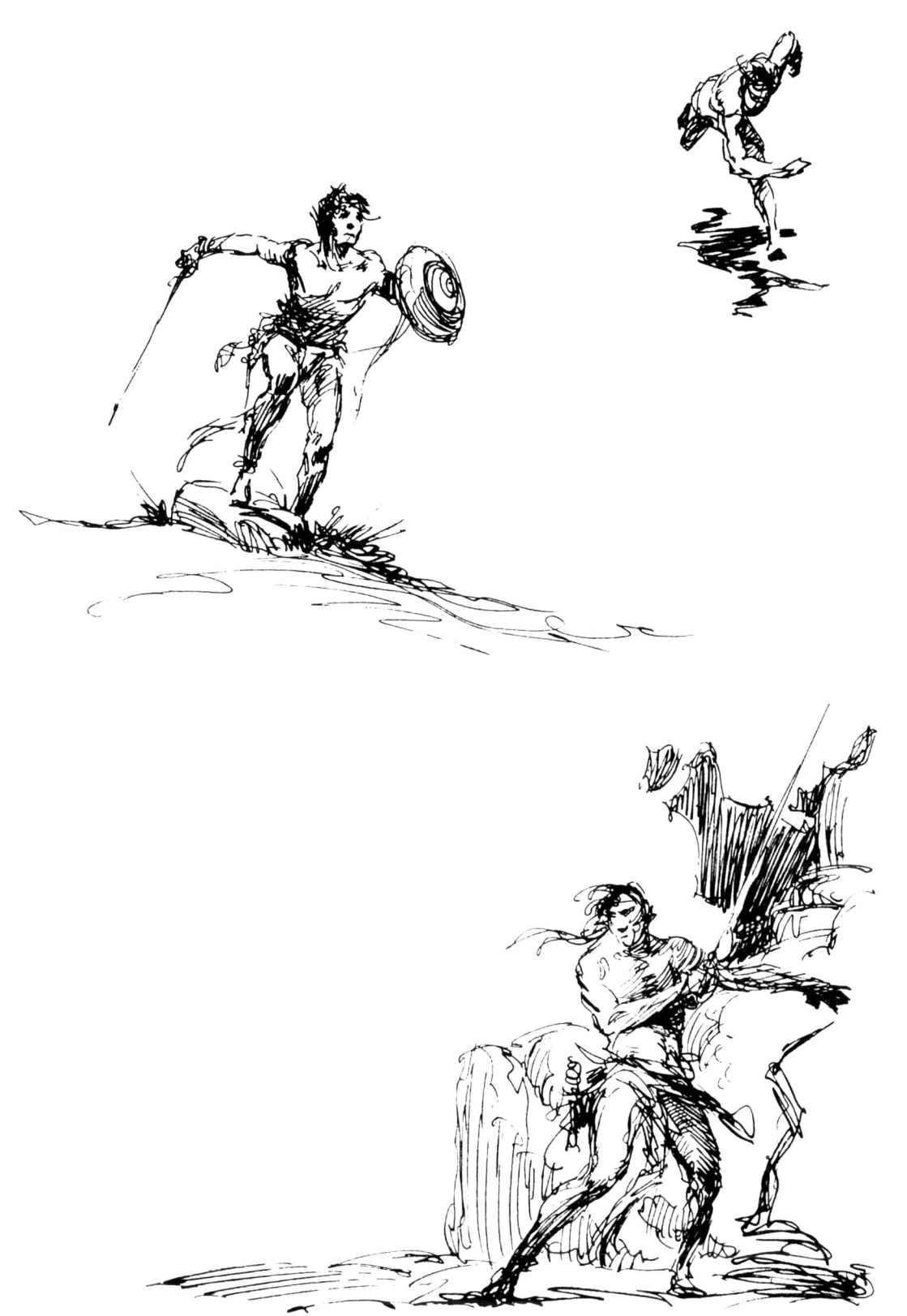

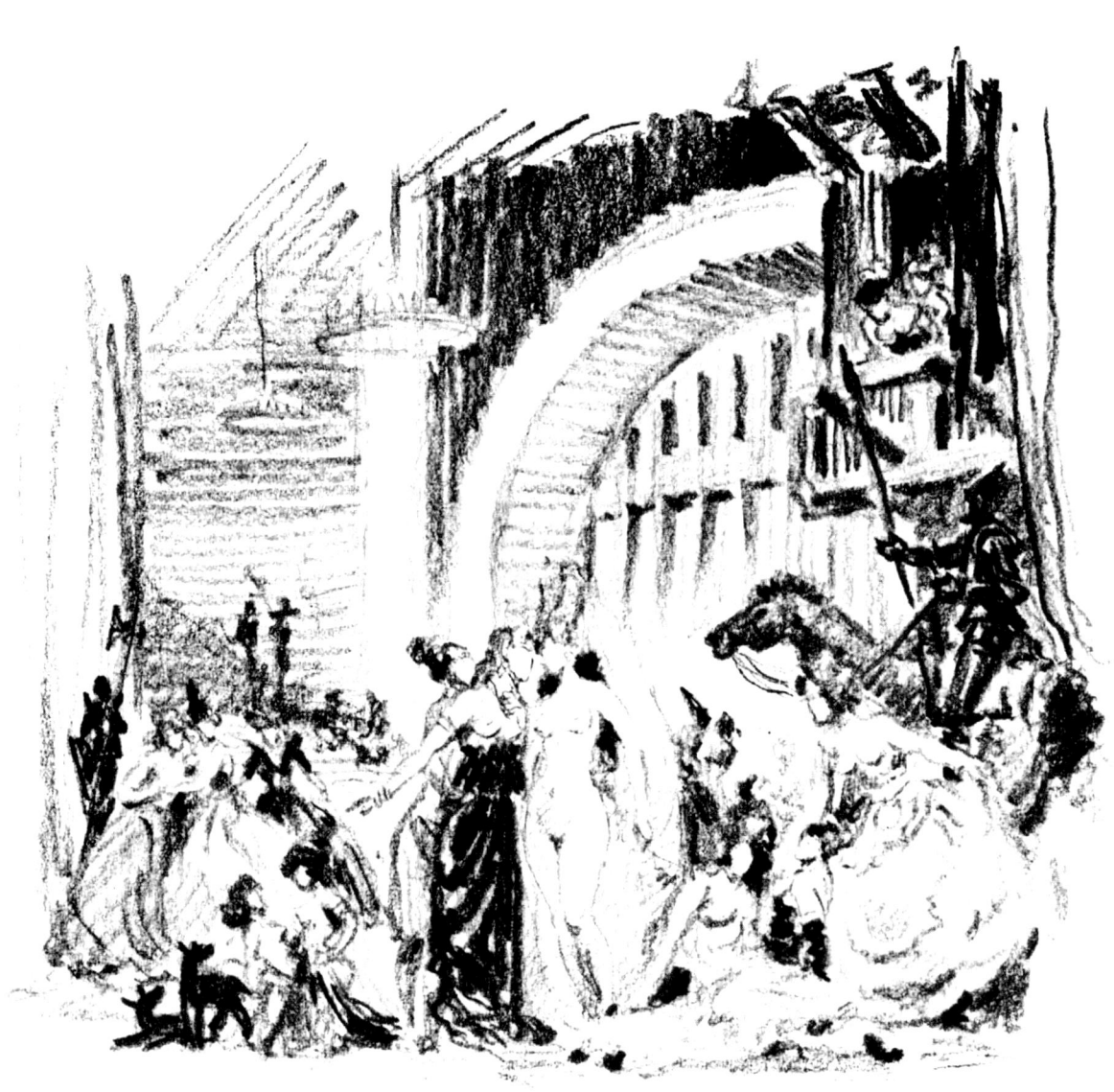

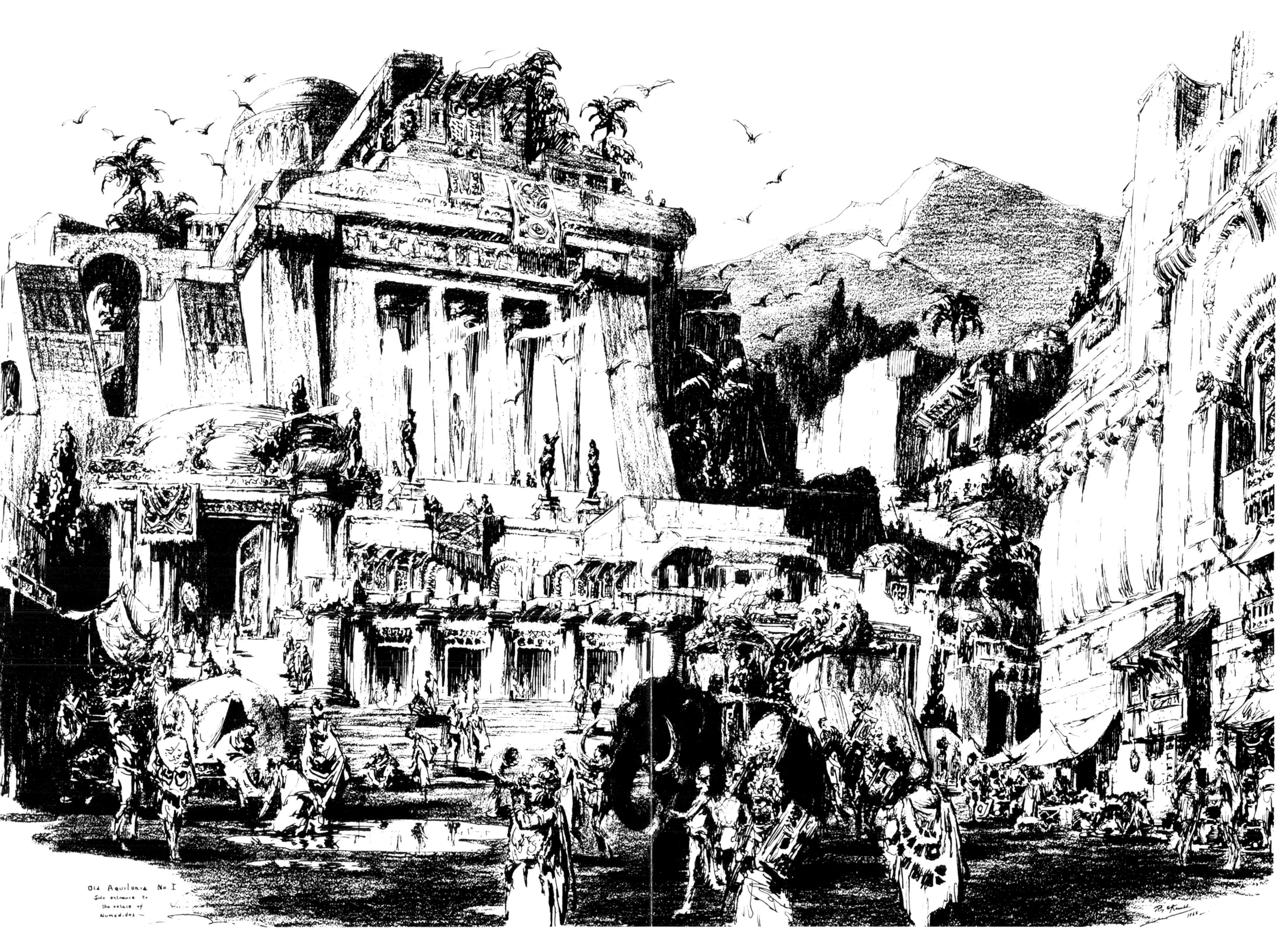

Old Aquilonia No. I
Side entrance to
the palace of
Numedides ~

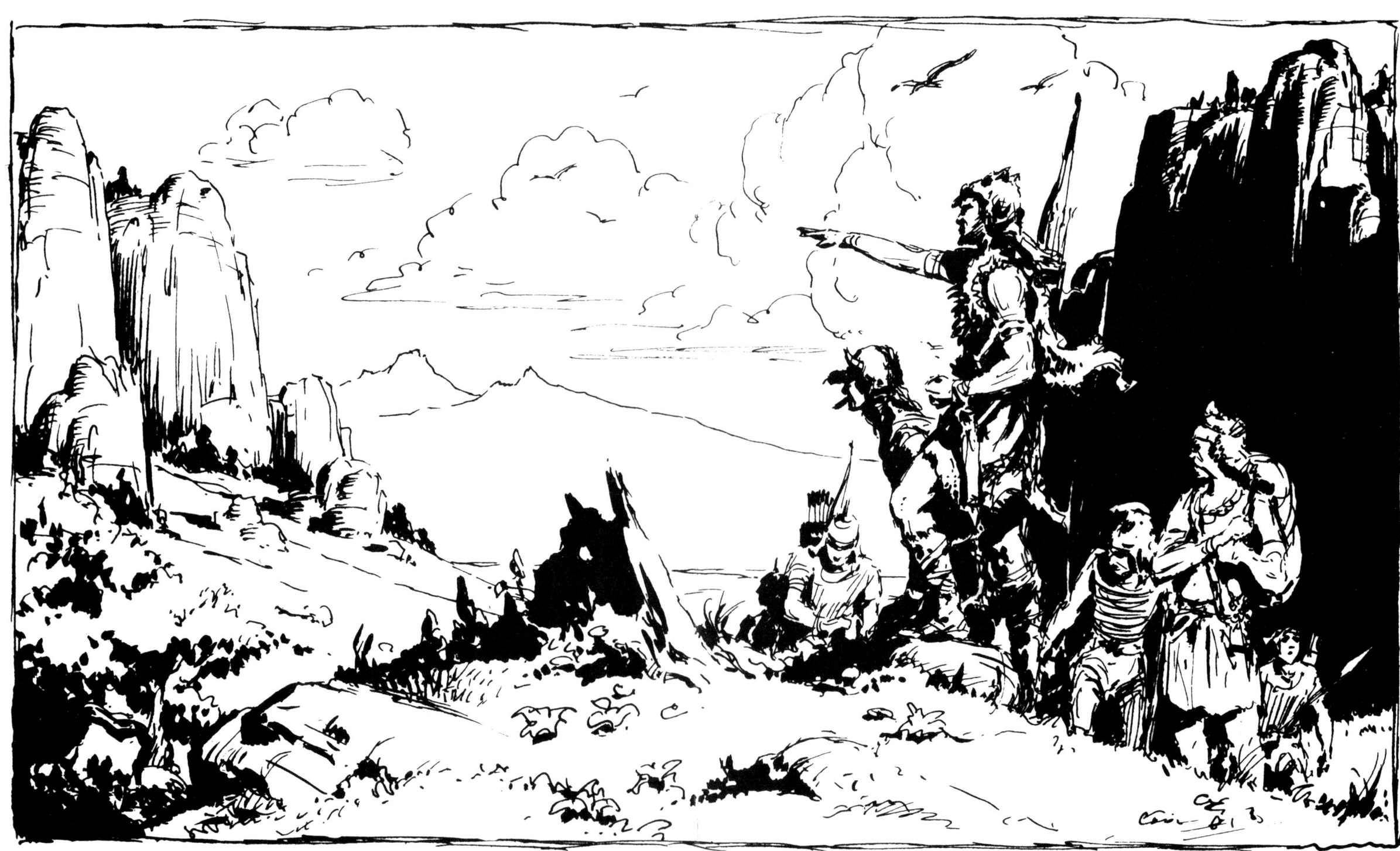

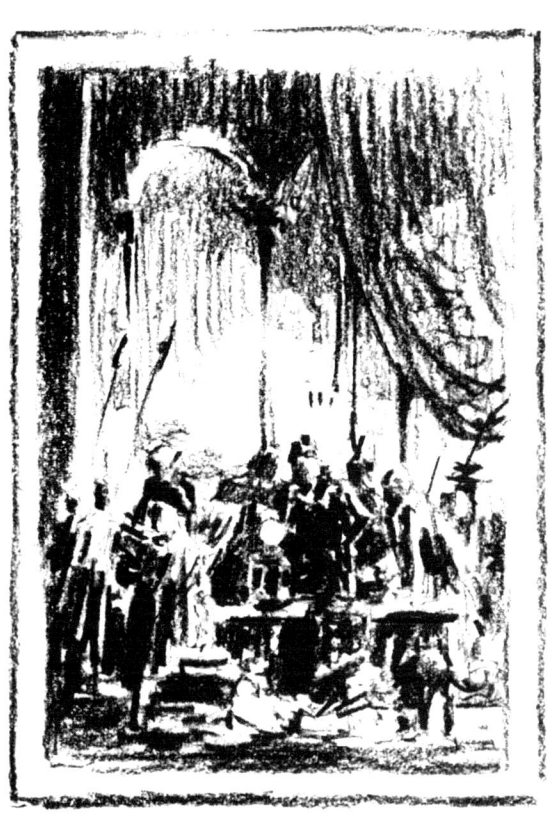

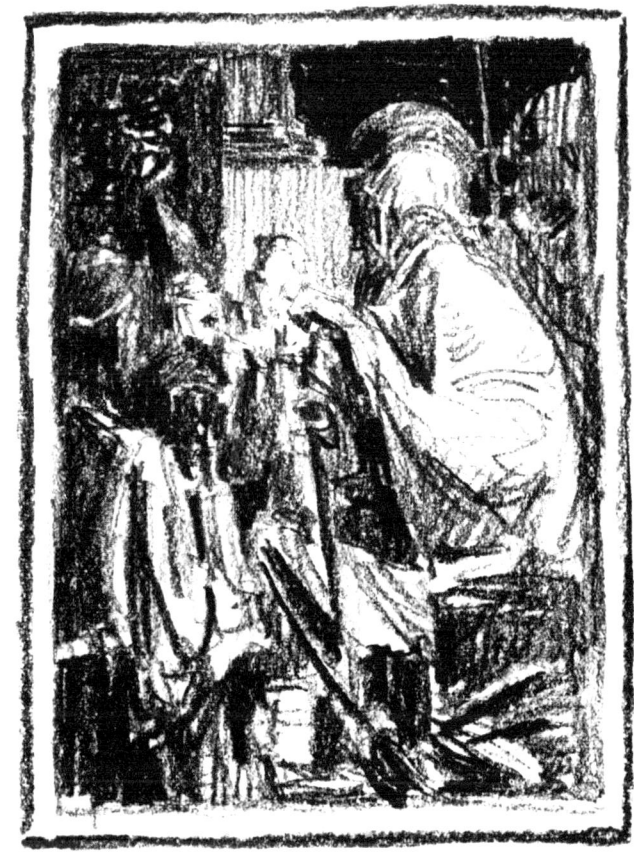

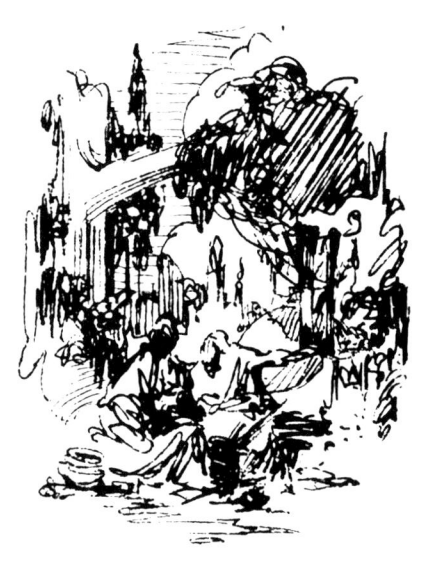

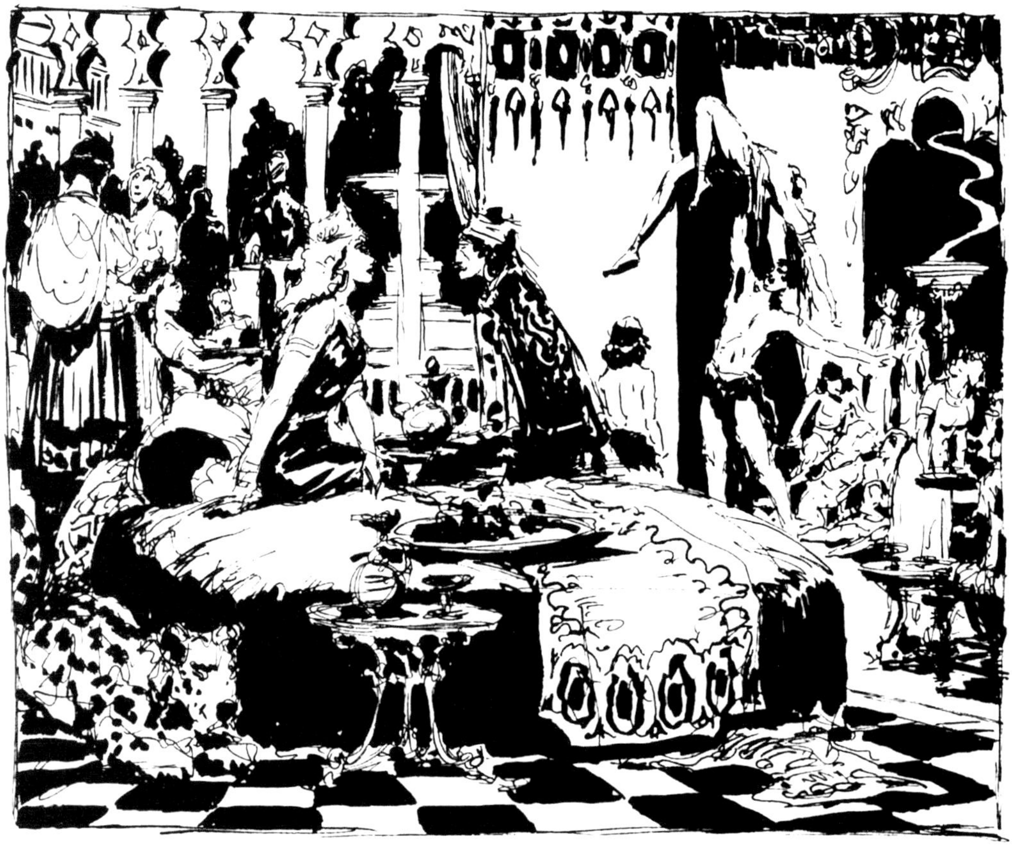

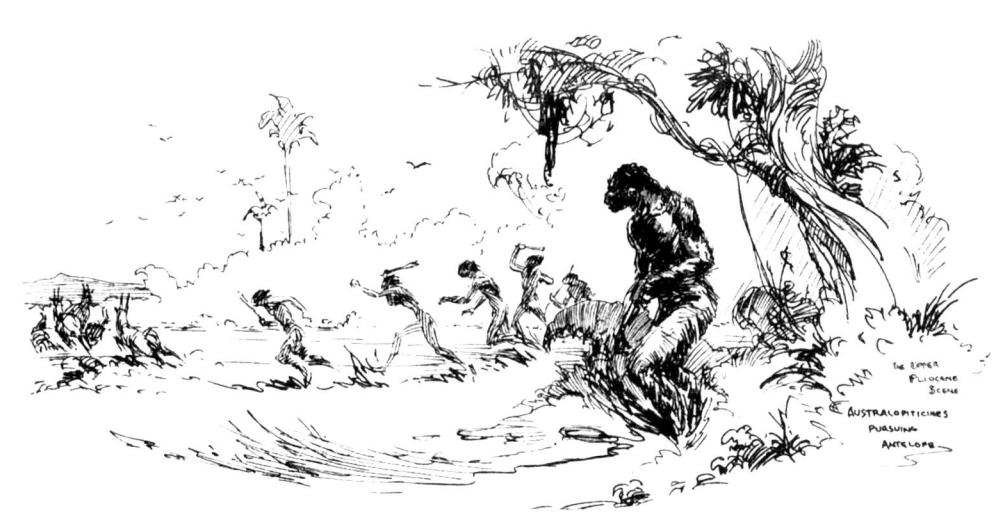

The latter
Pliocene
Scene
Australopithicines
pursuing
Antelope

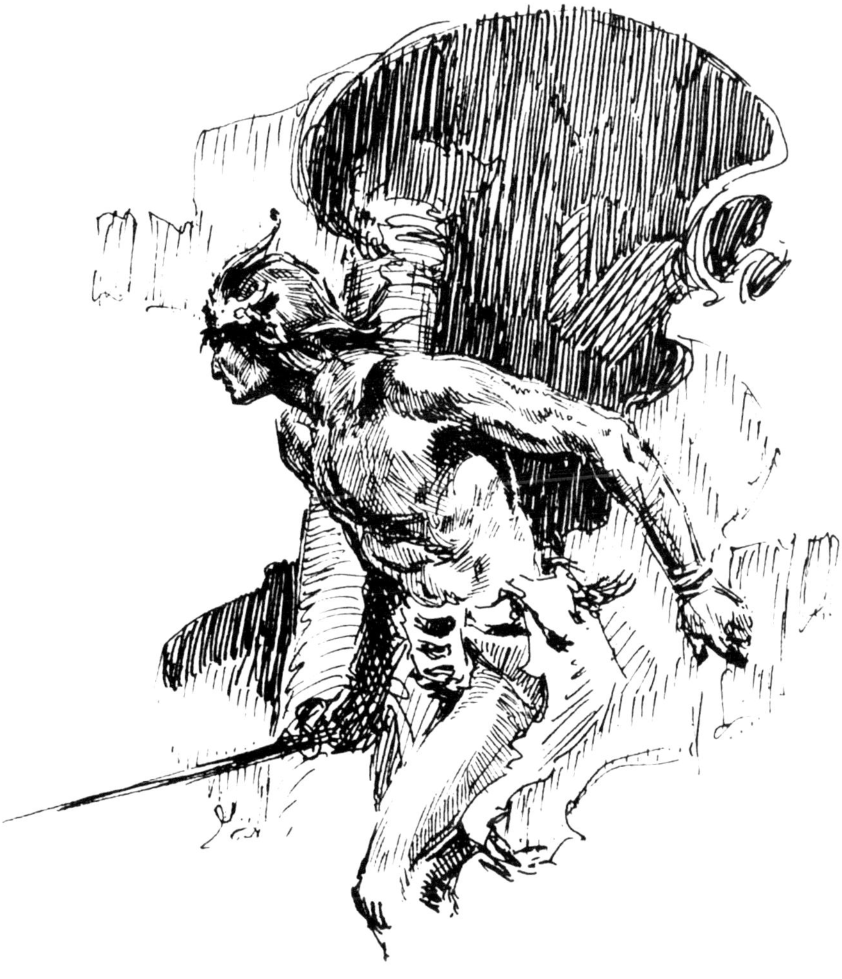

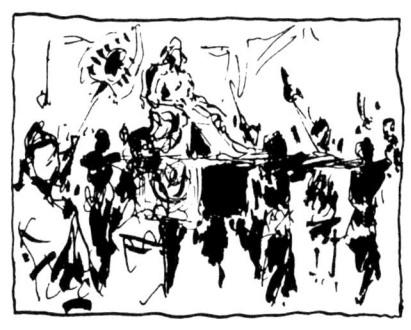

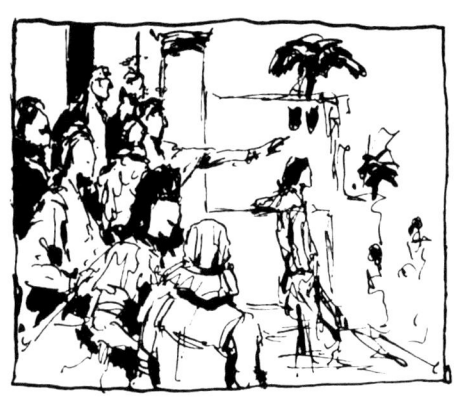

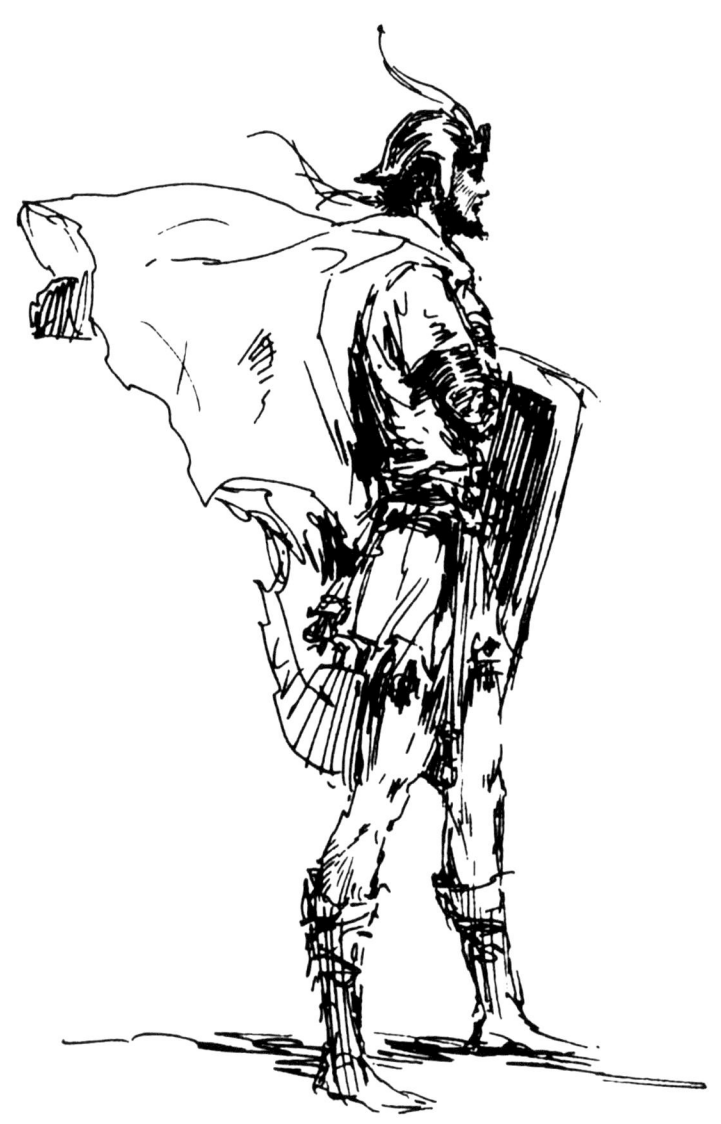

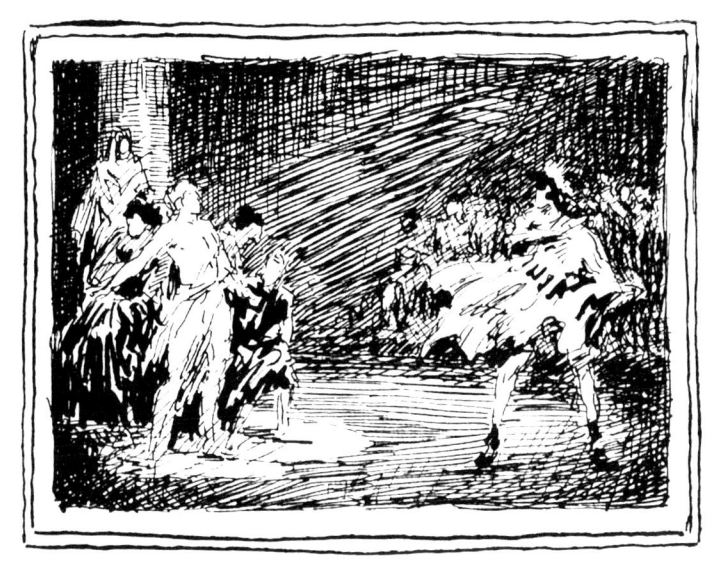

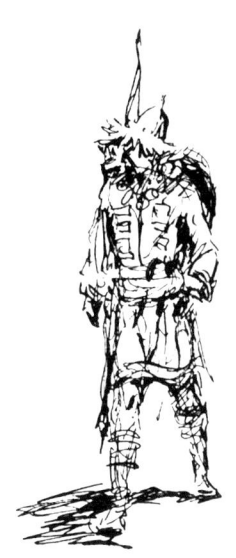

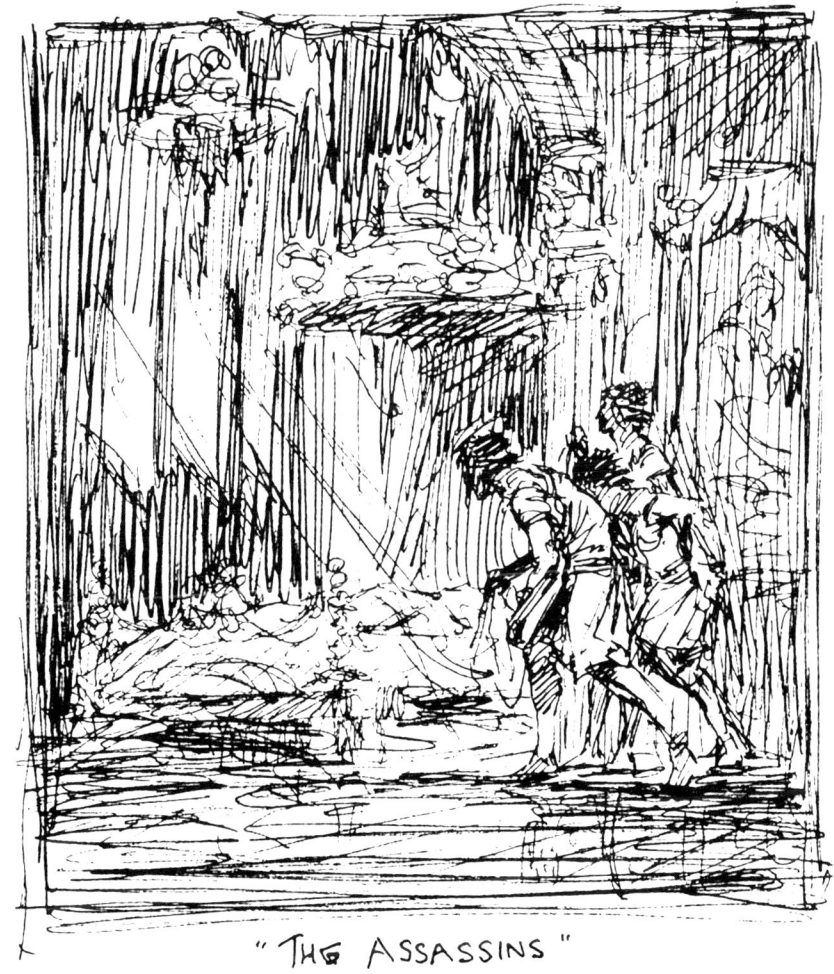

"The Assassins"

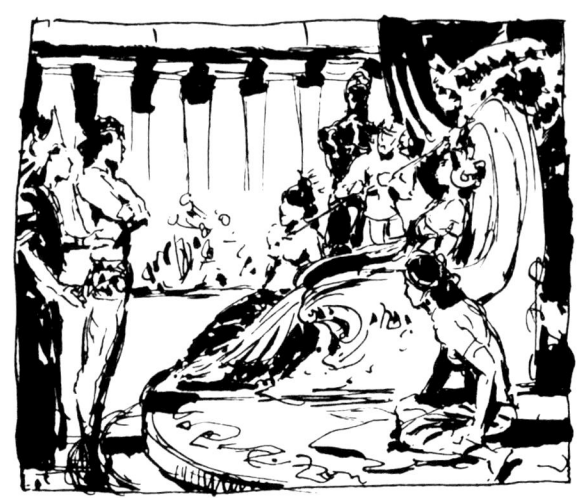

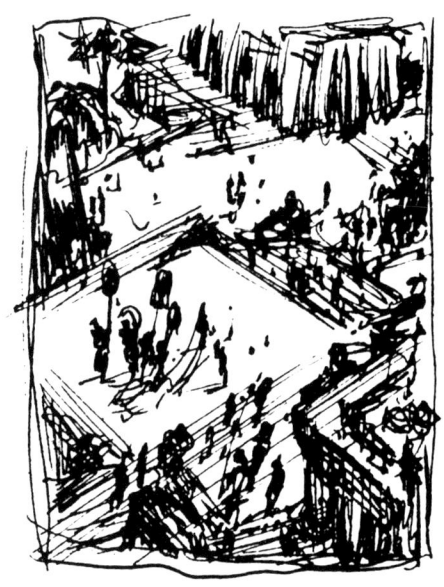

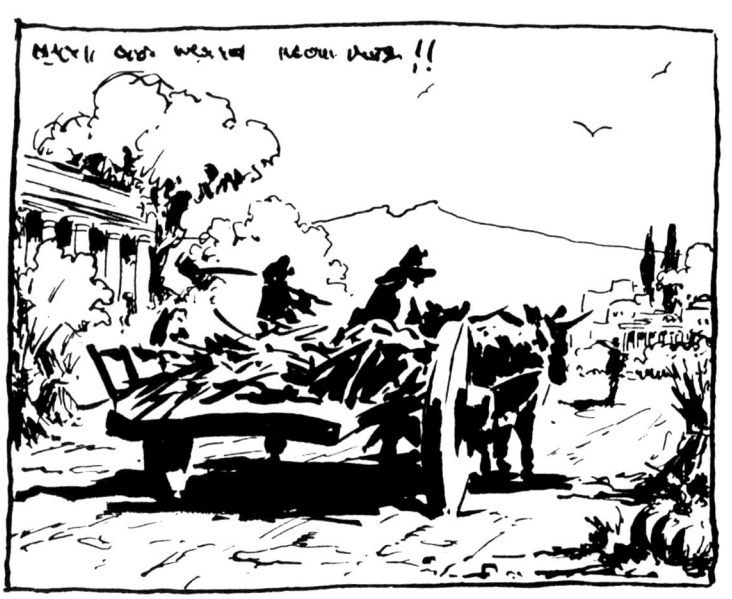

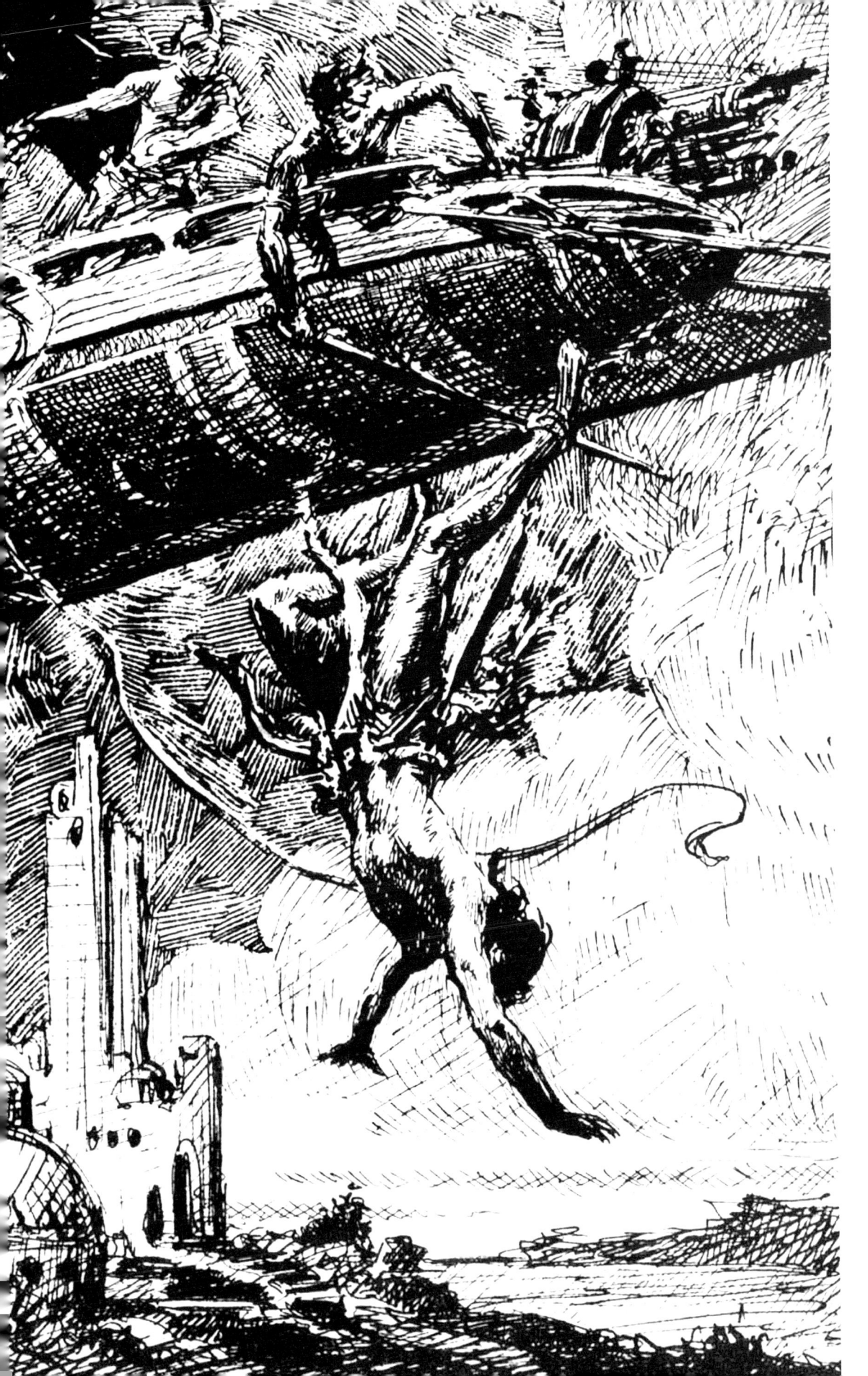

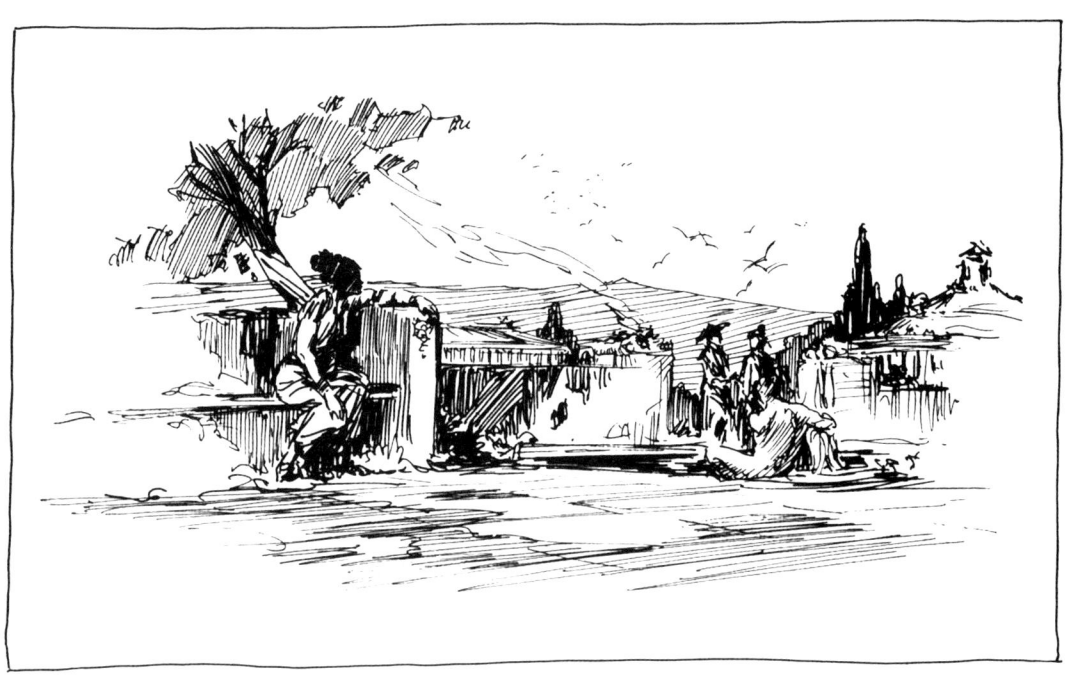

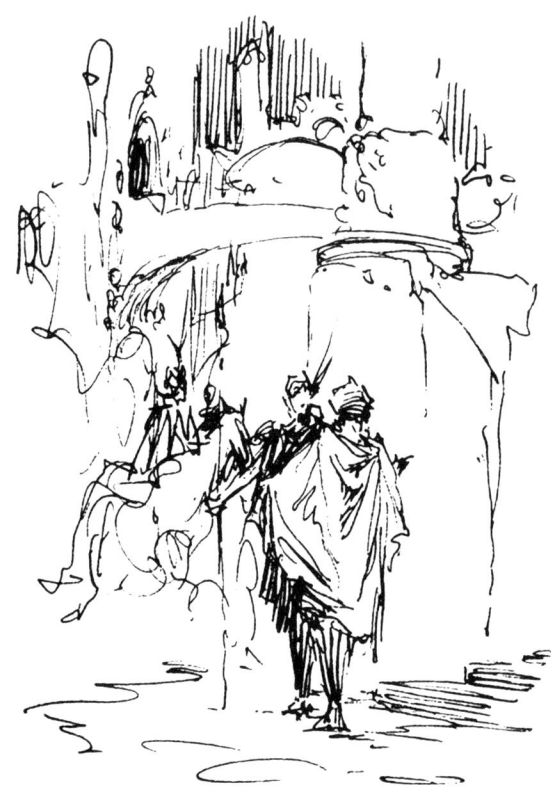

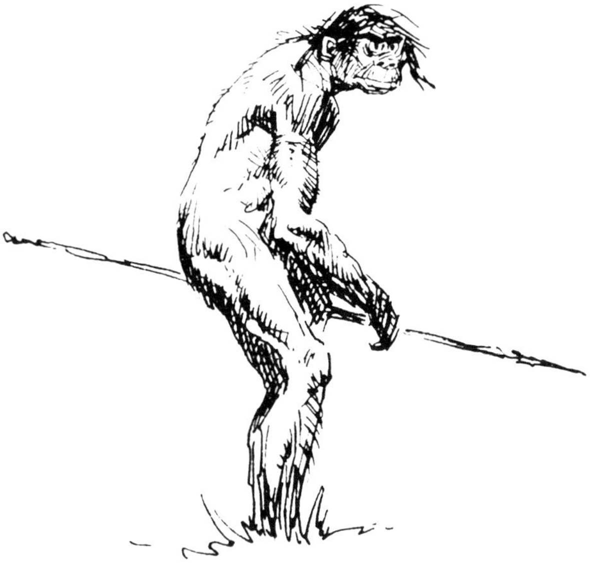

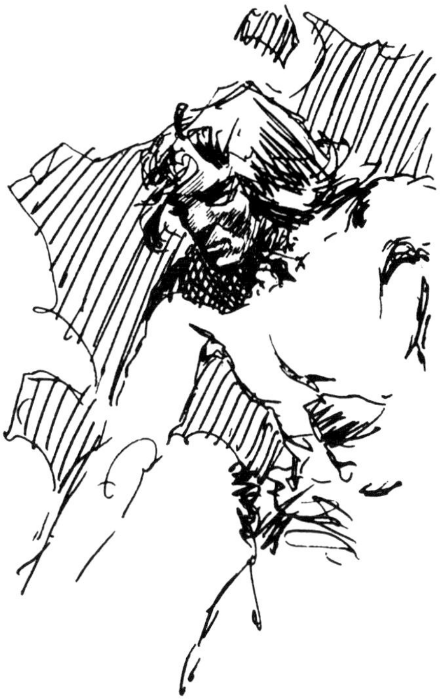

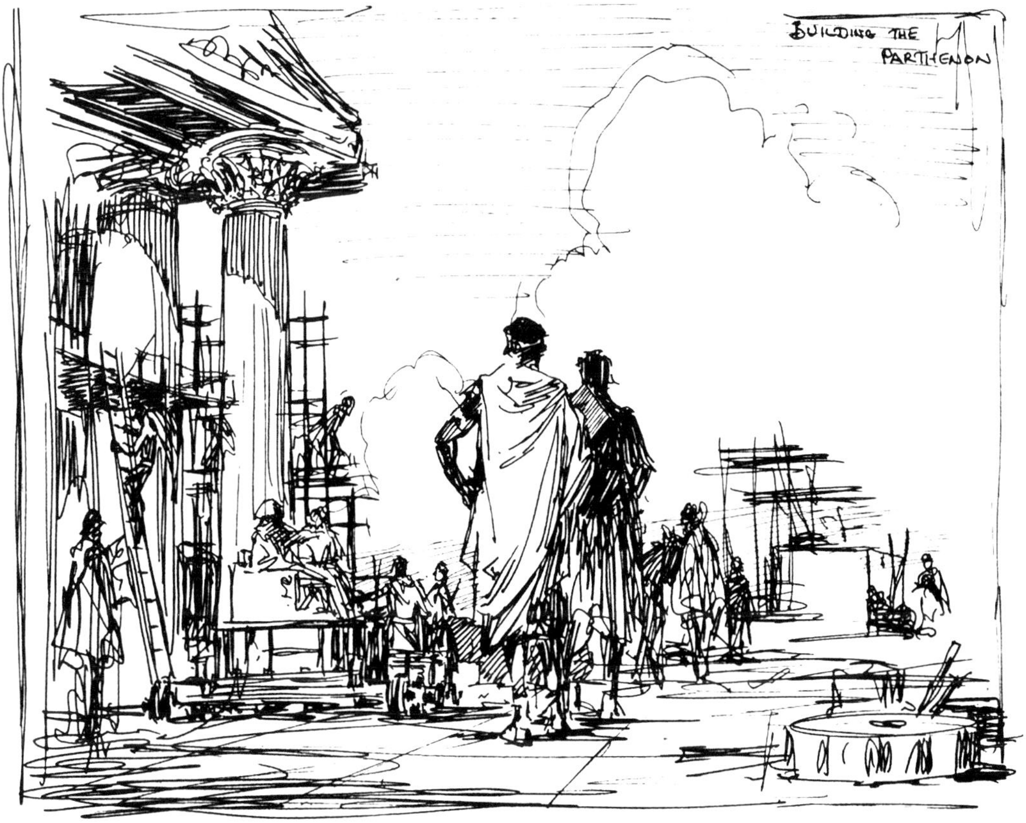

BUILDING THE PARTHENON

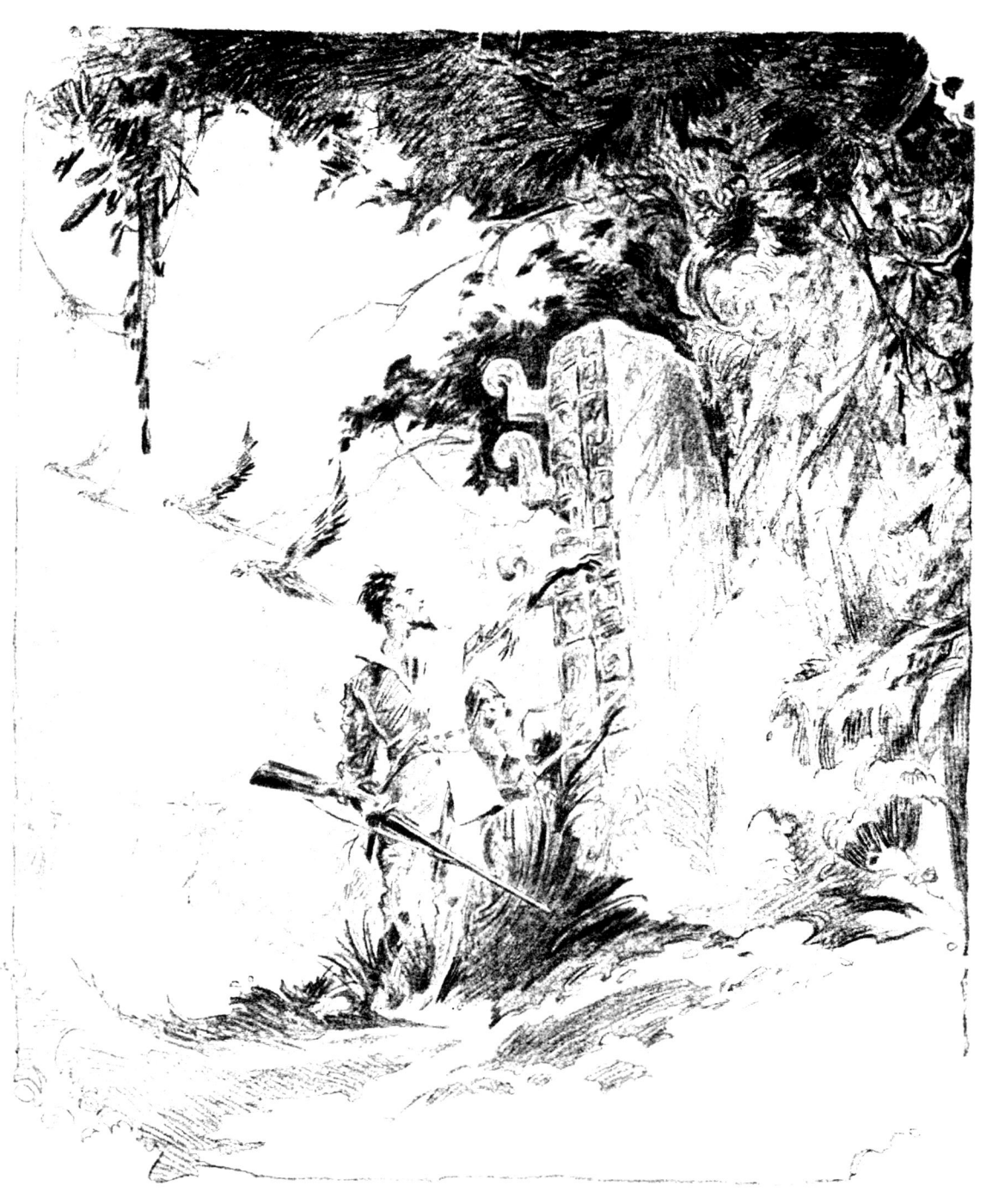

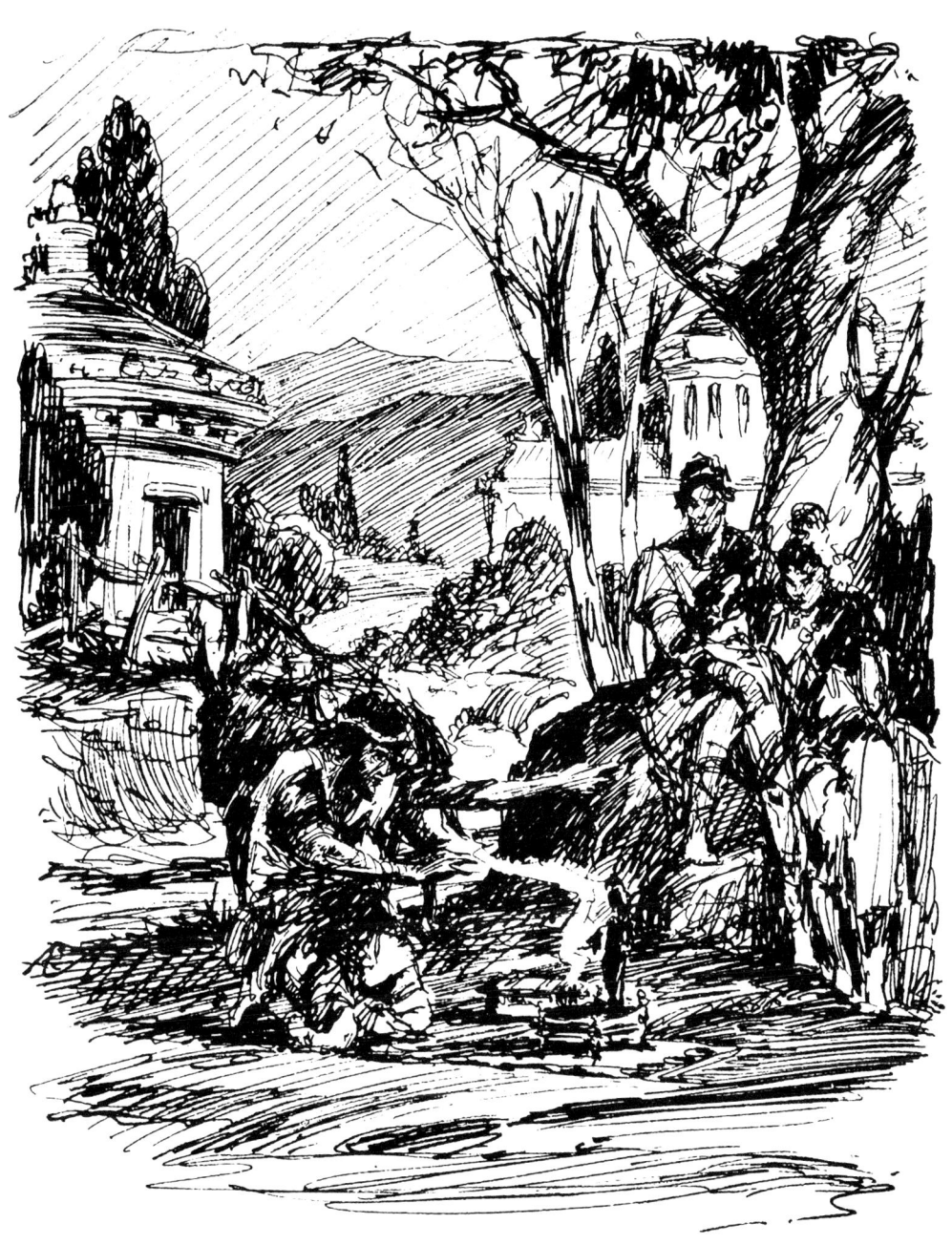

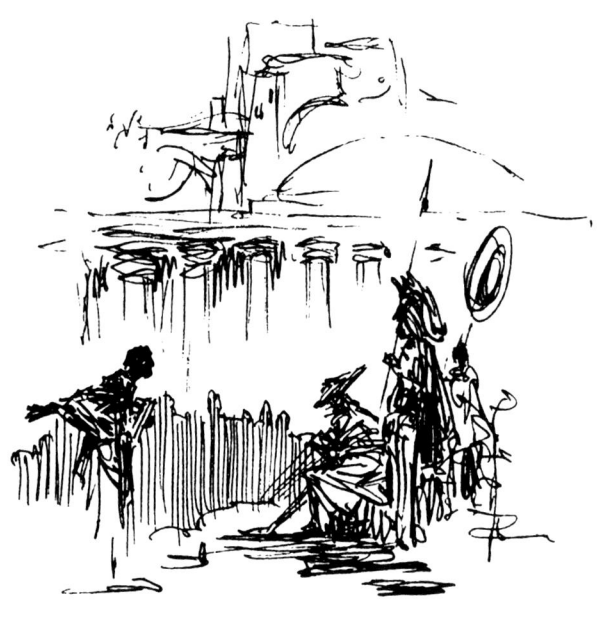

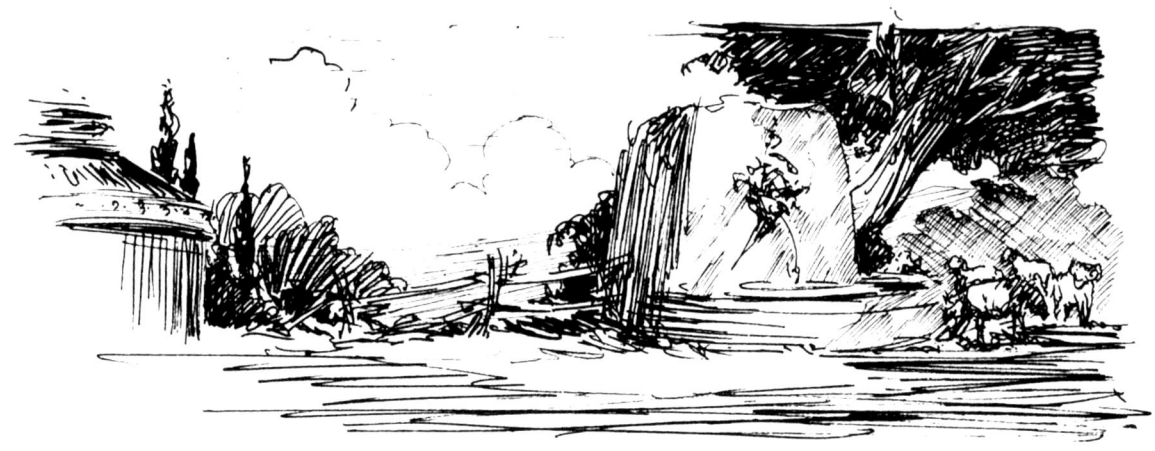

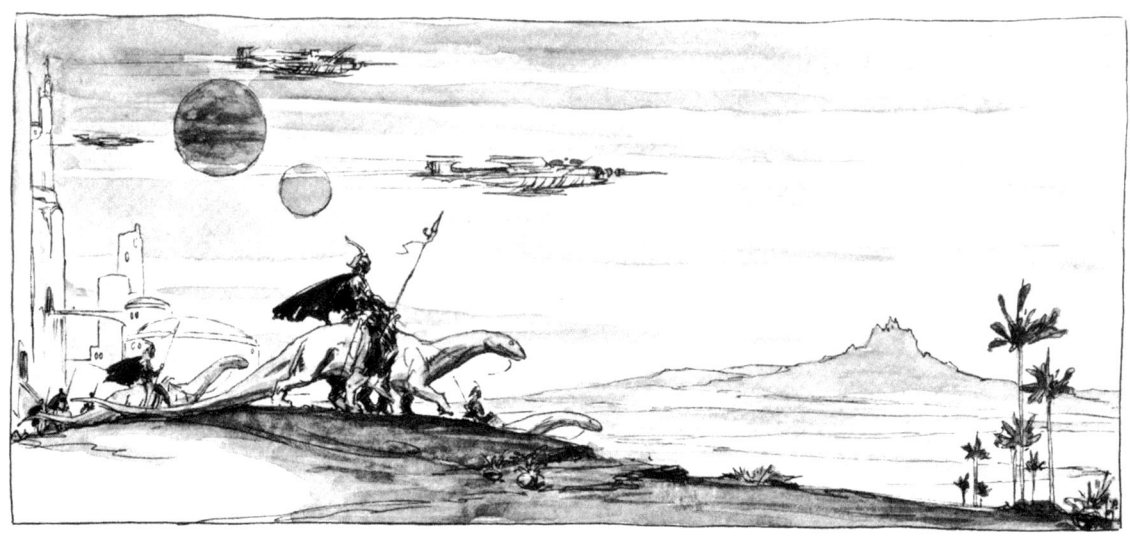

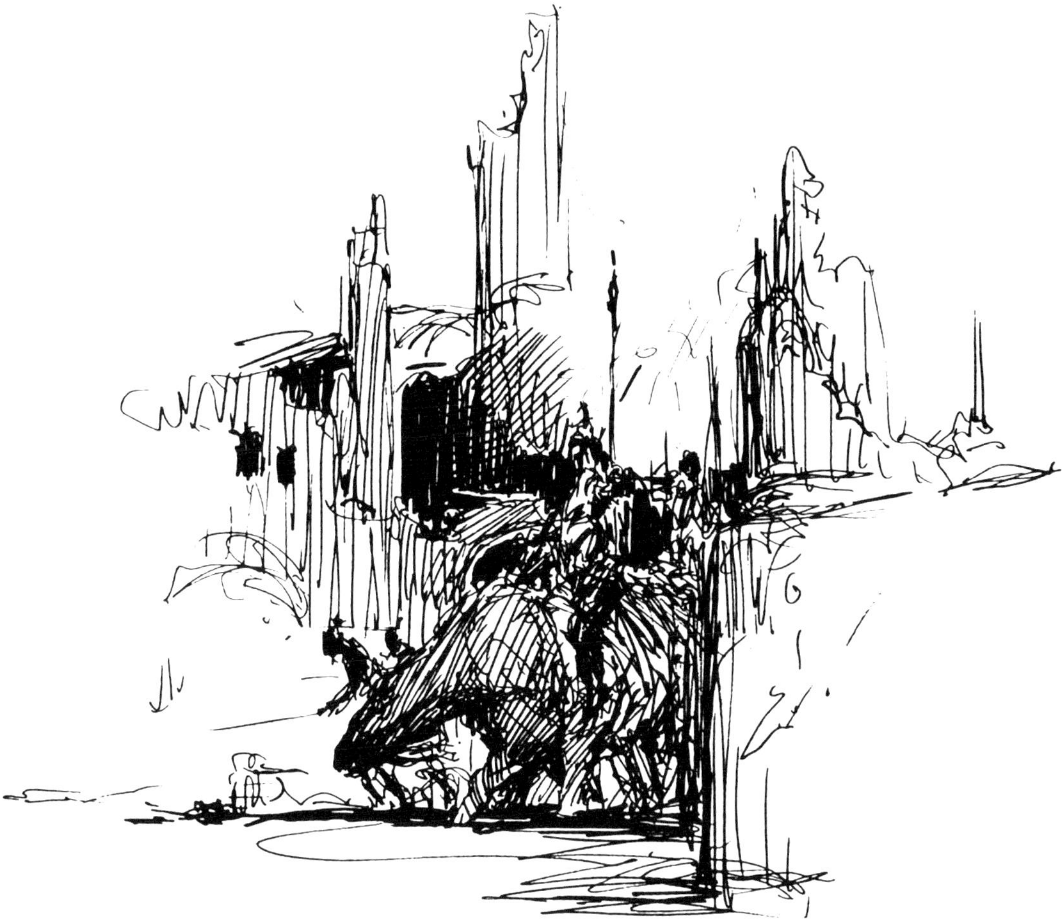

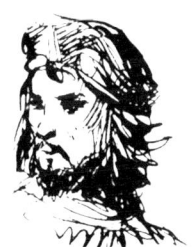
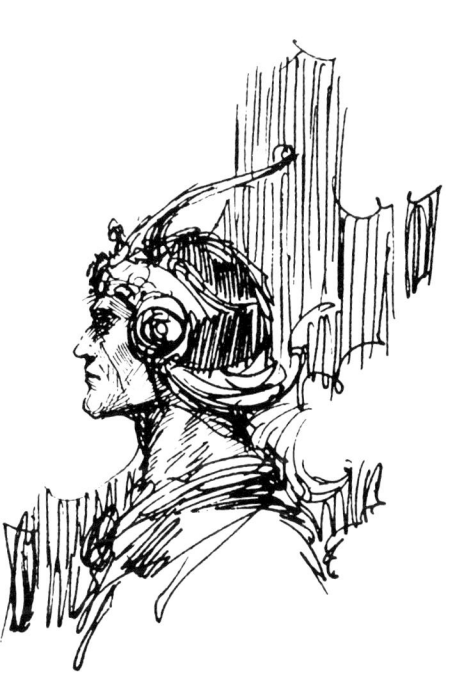

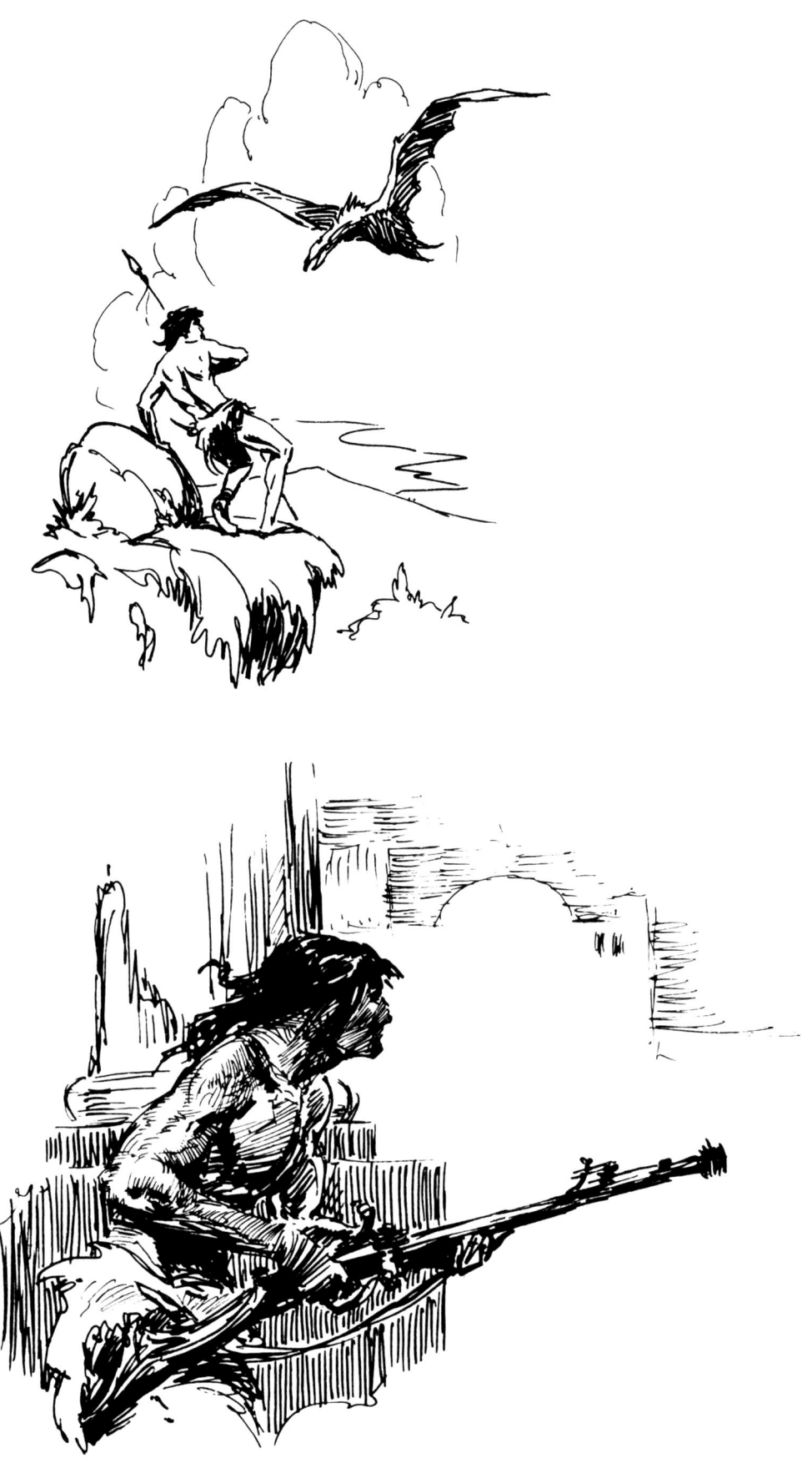

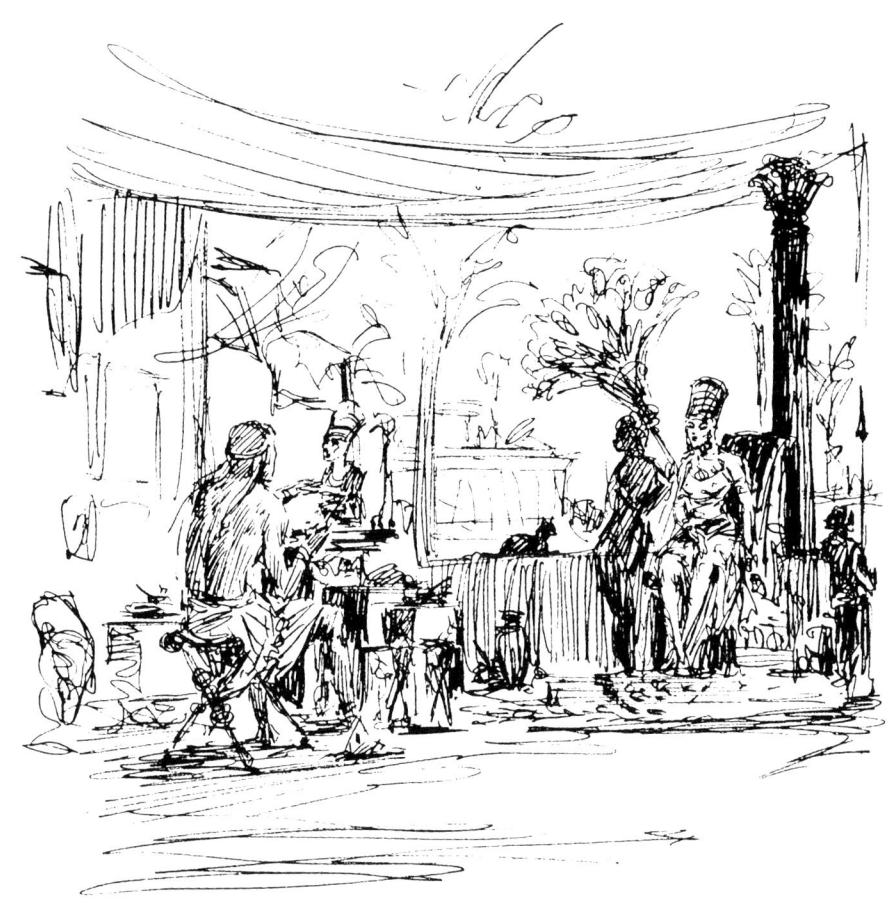

"Neferetiti"

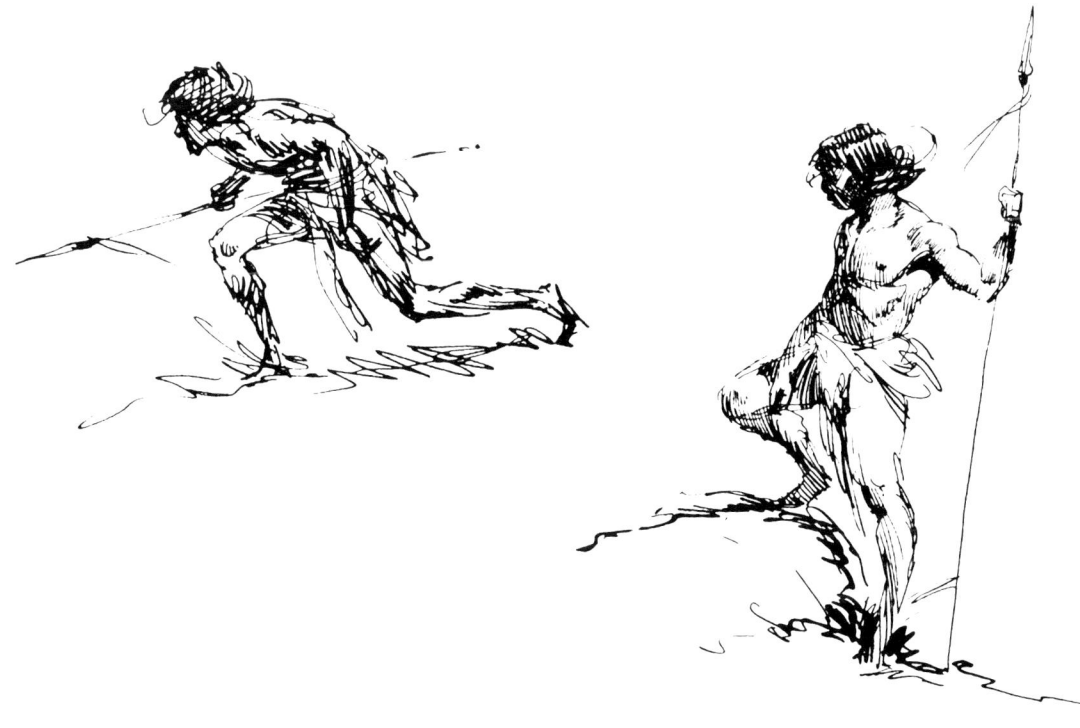

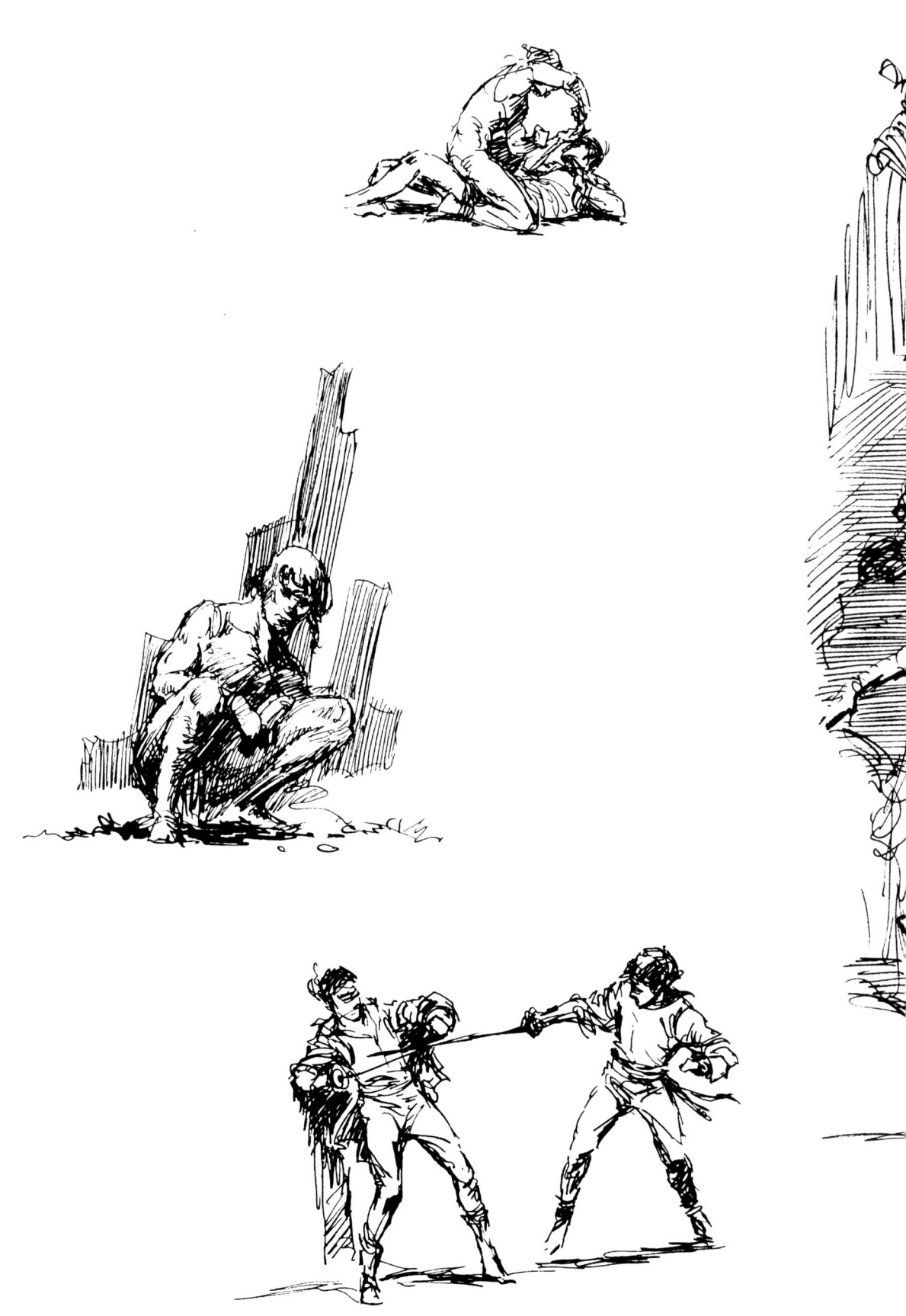

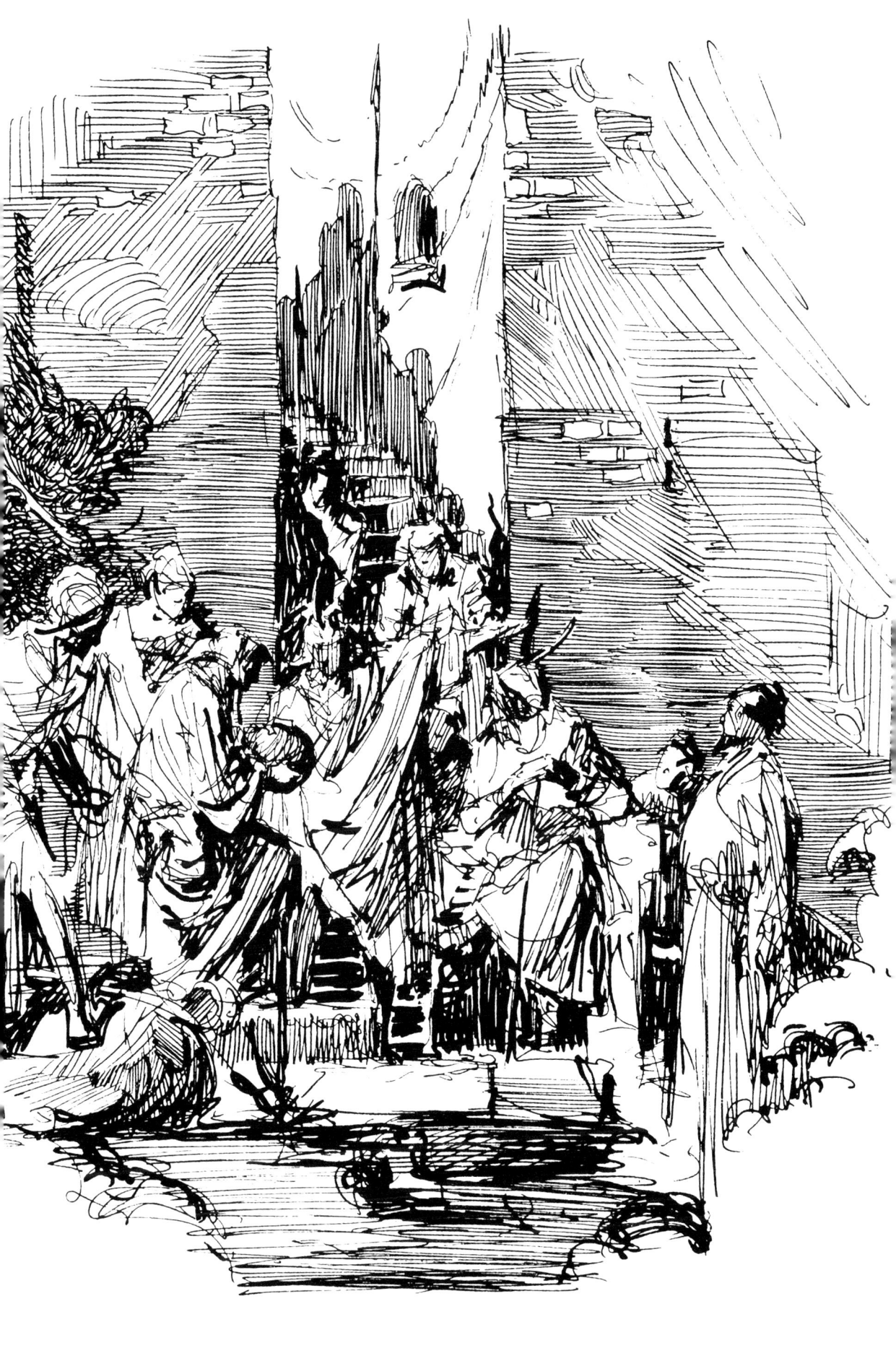

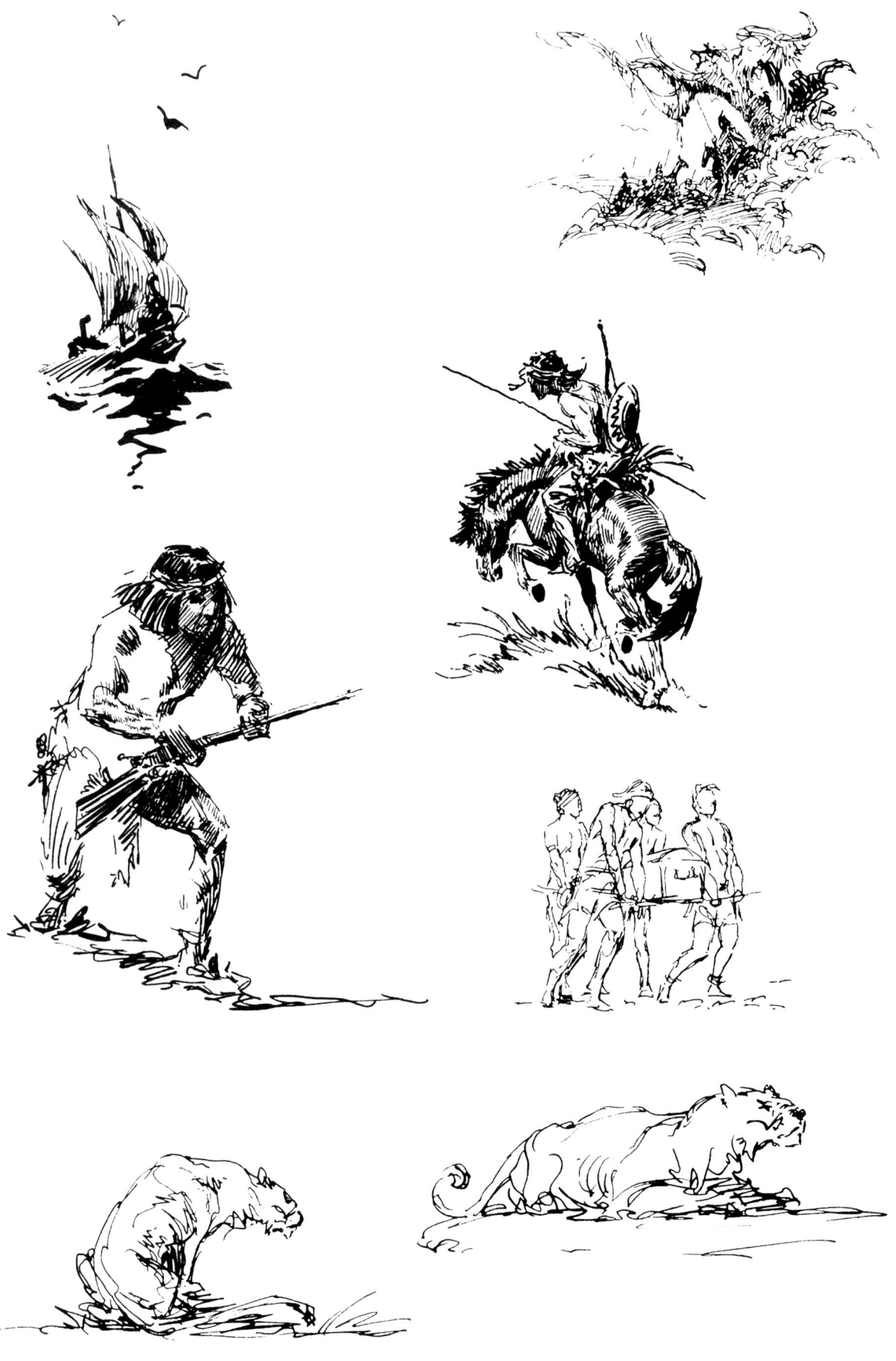

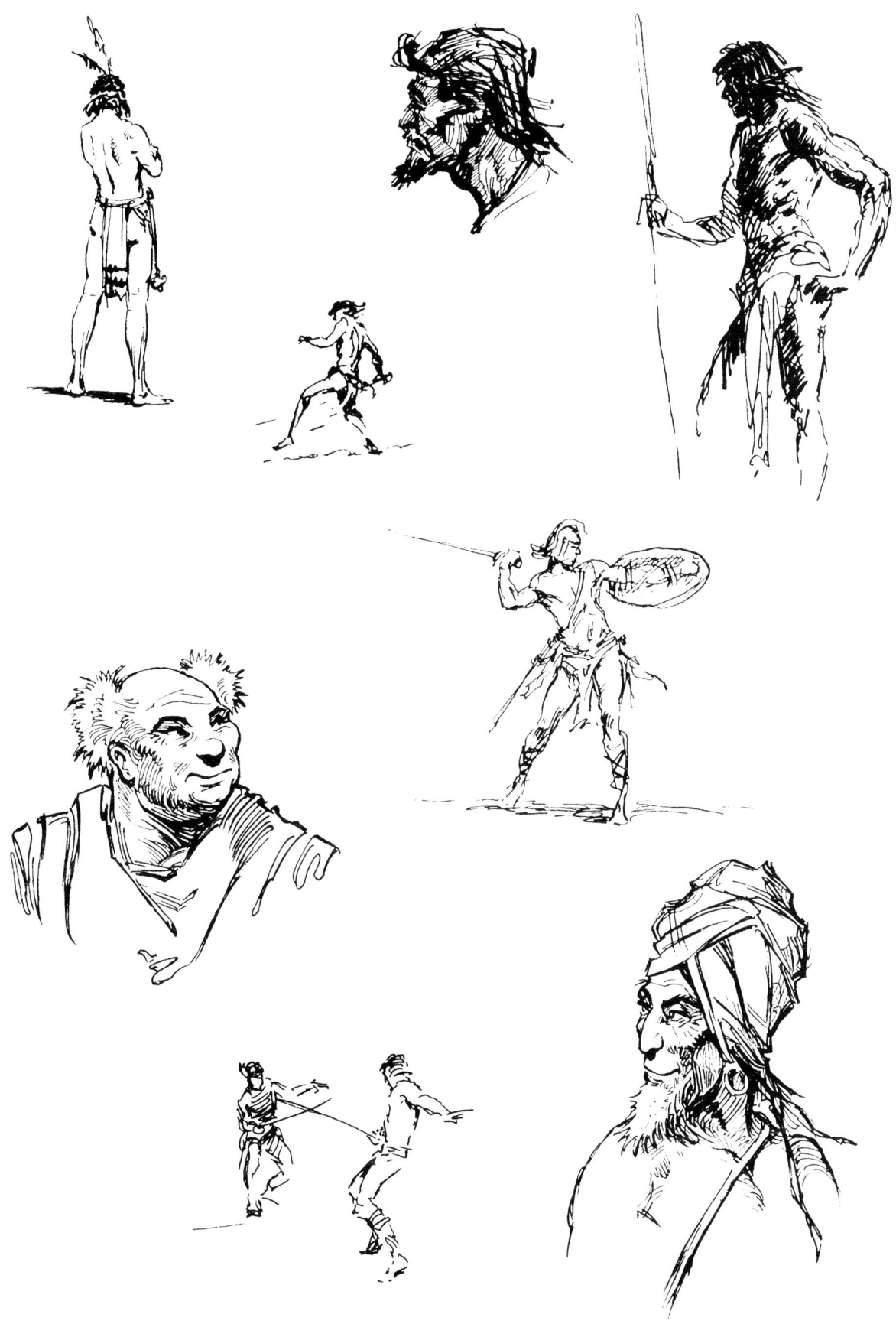

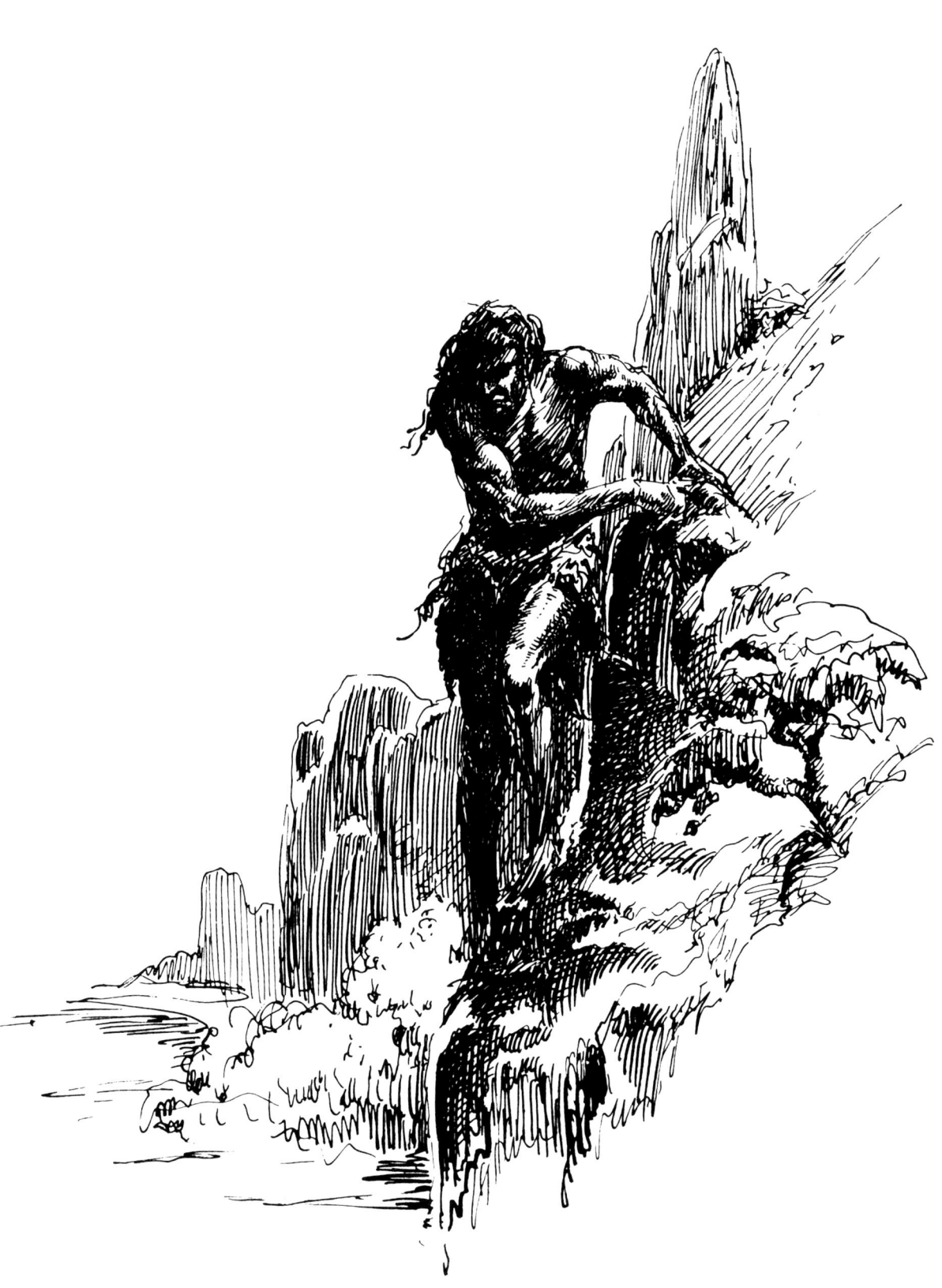

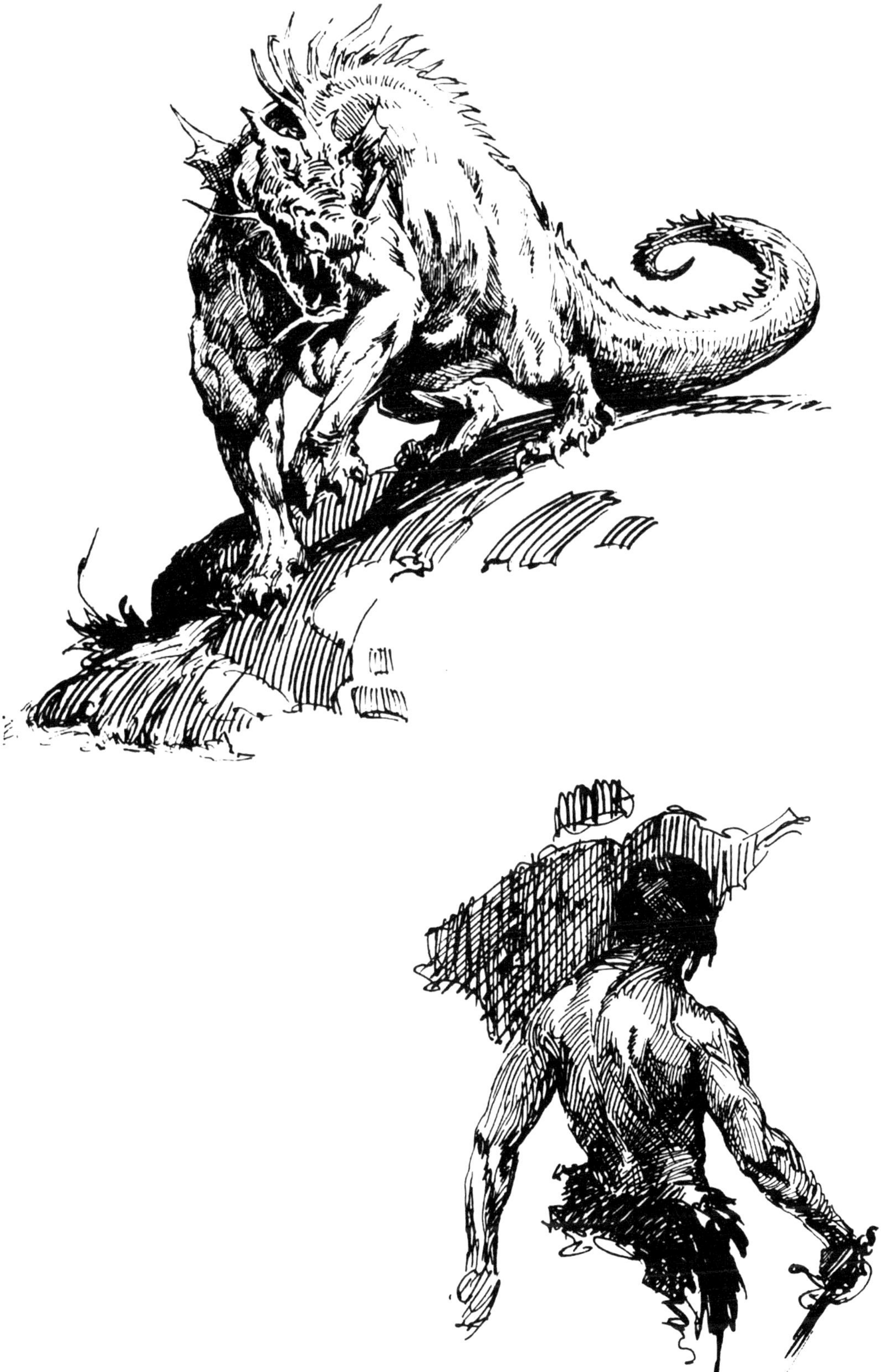

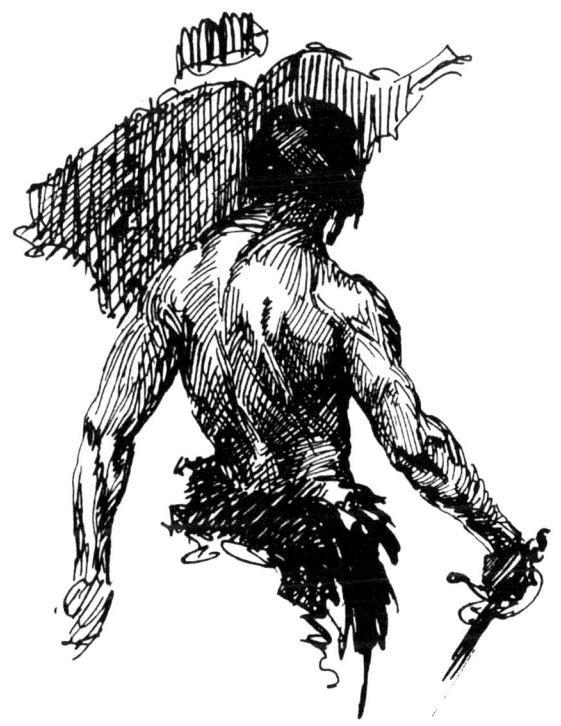

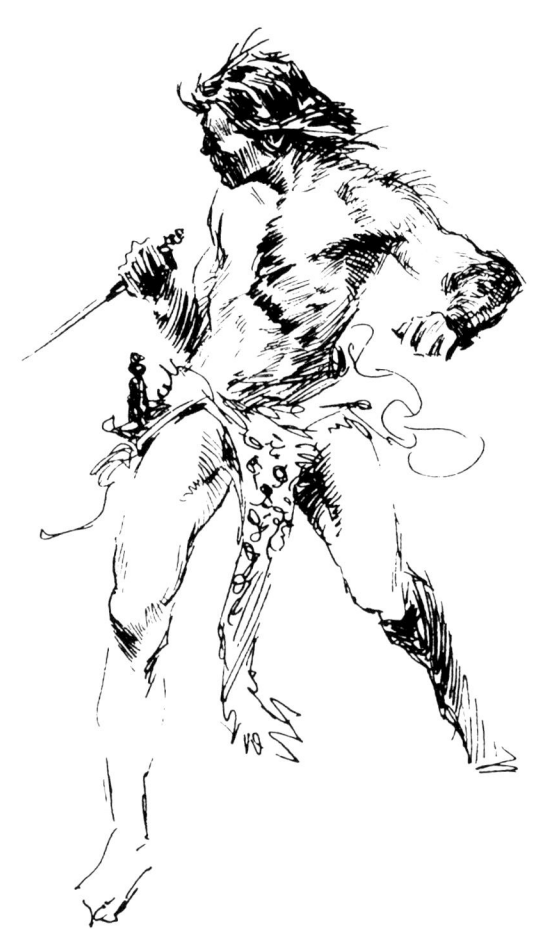

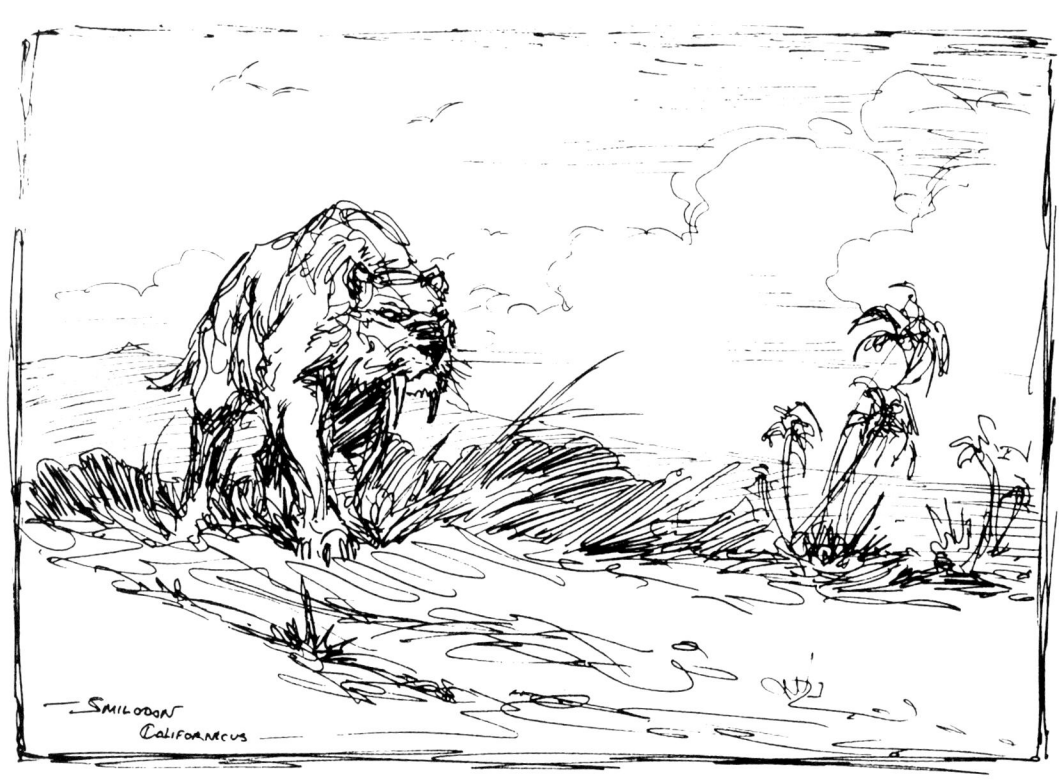

SMILODON
CALIFORNICUS

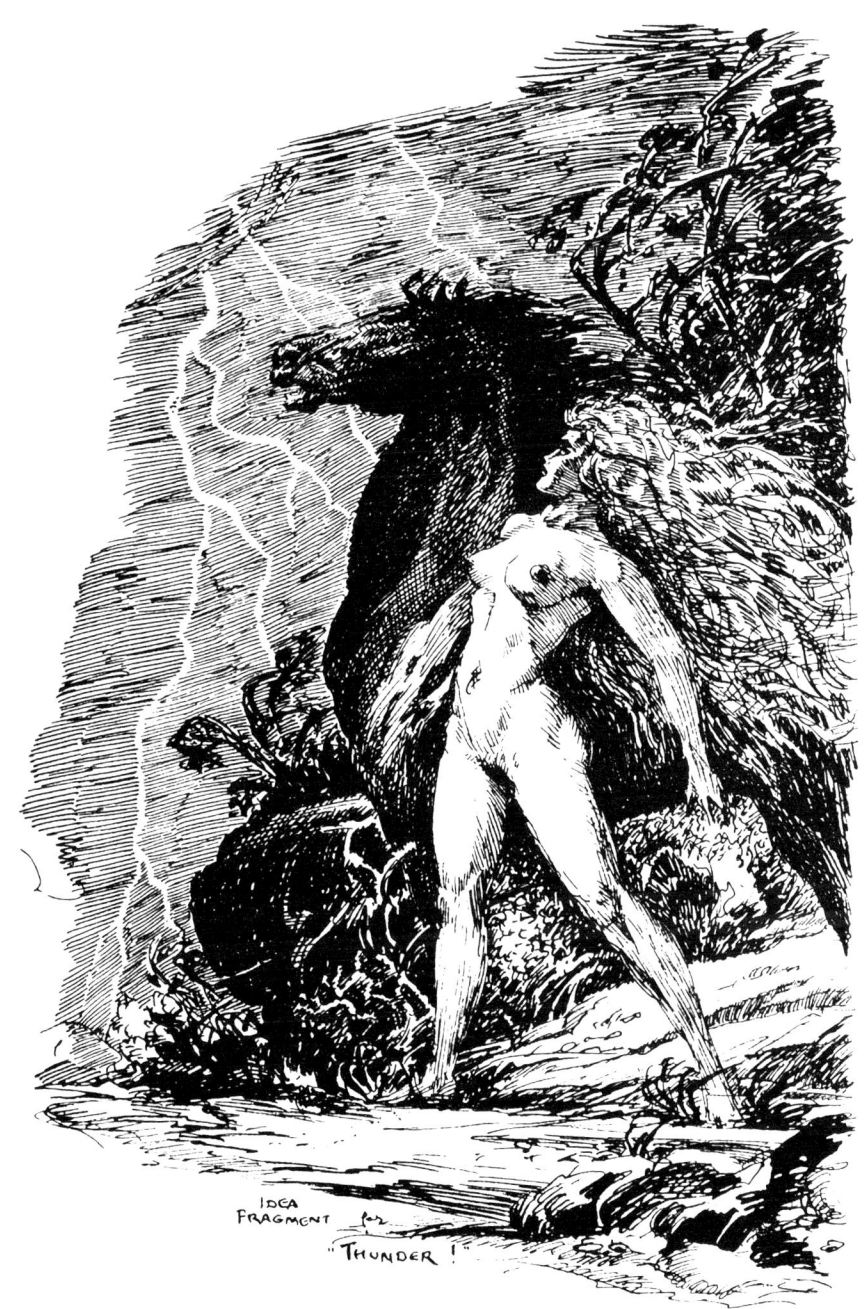

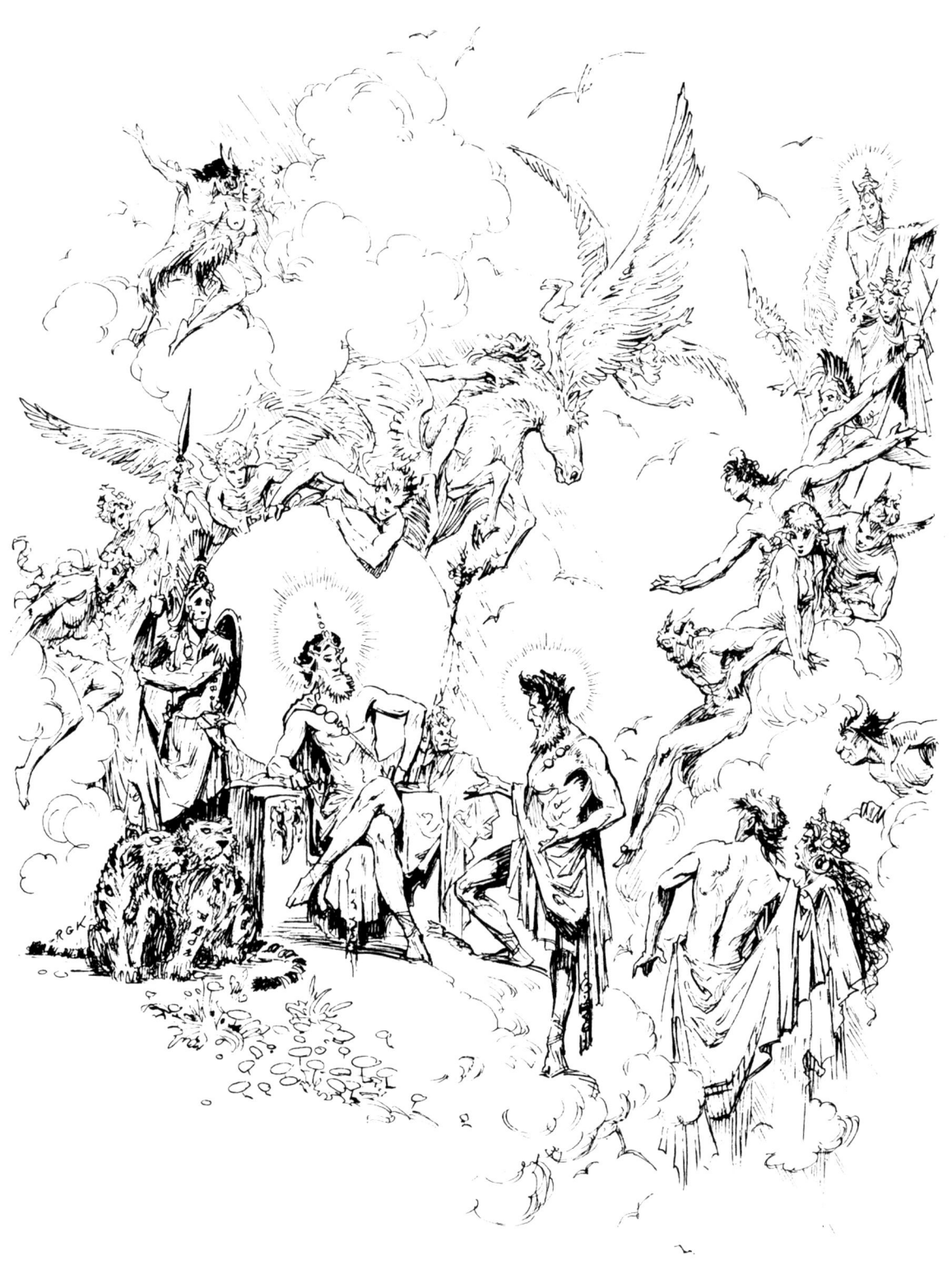

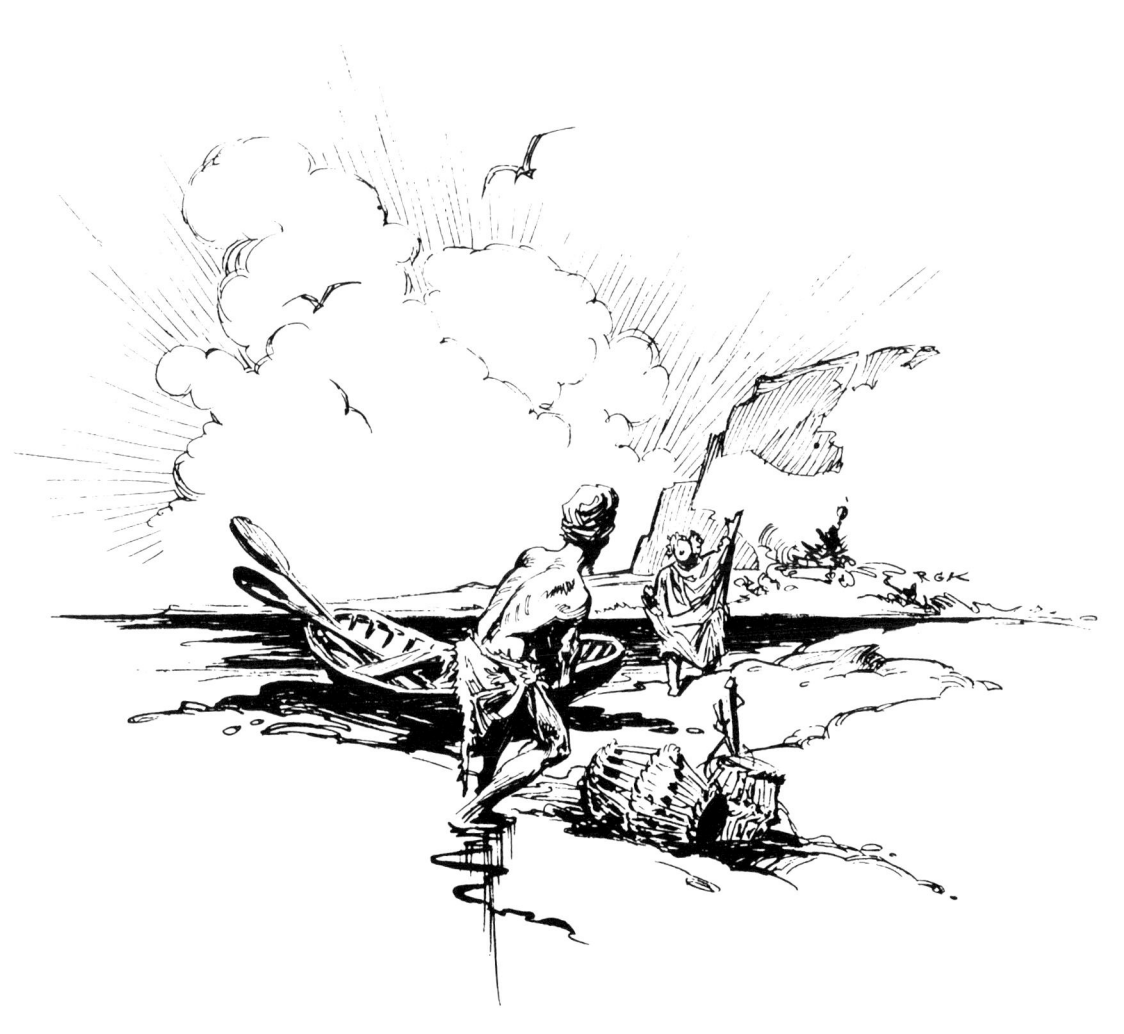

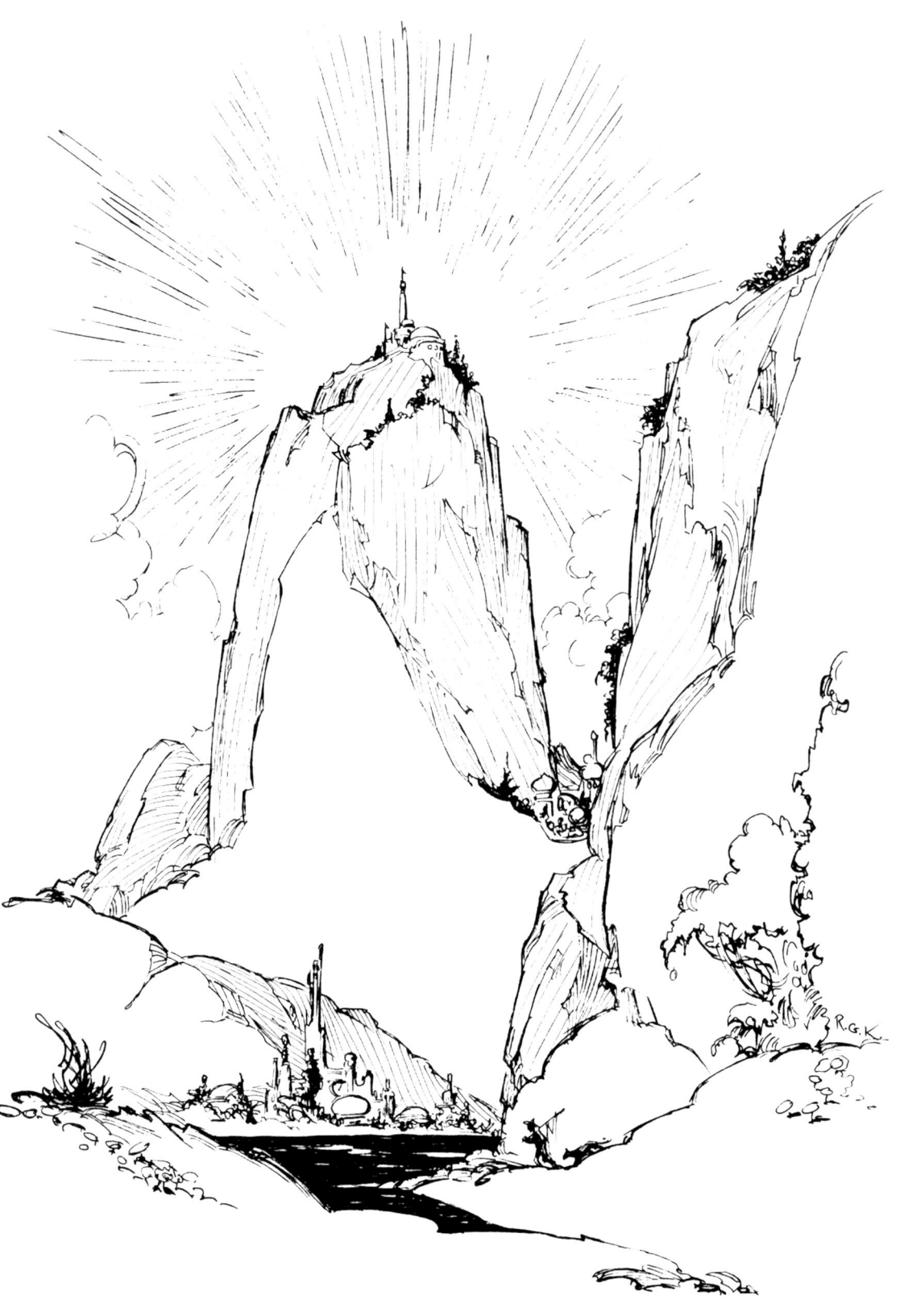

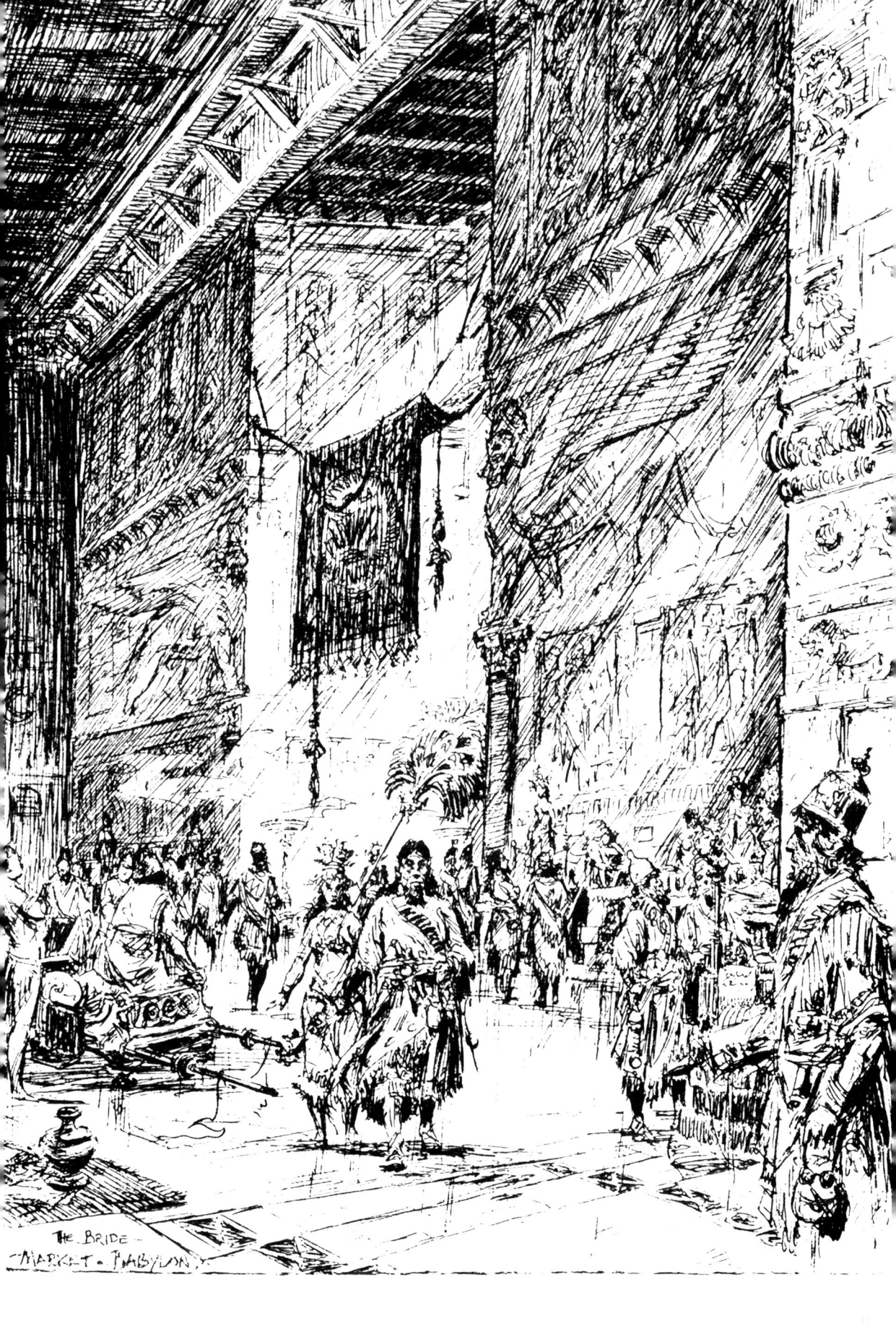

THE BRIDE
MARKET · BABYLON

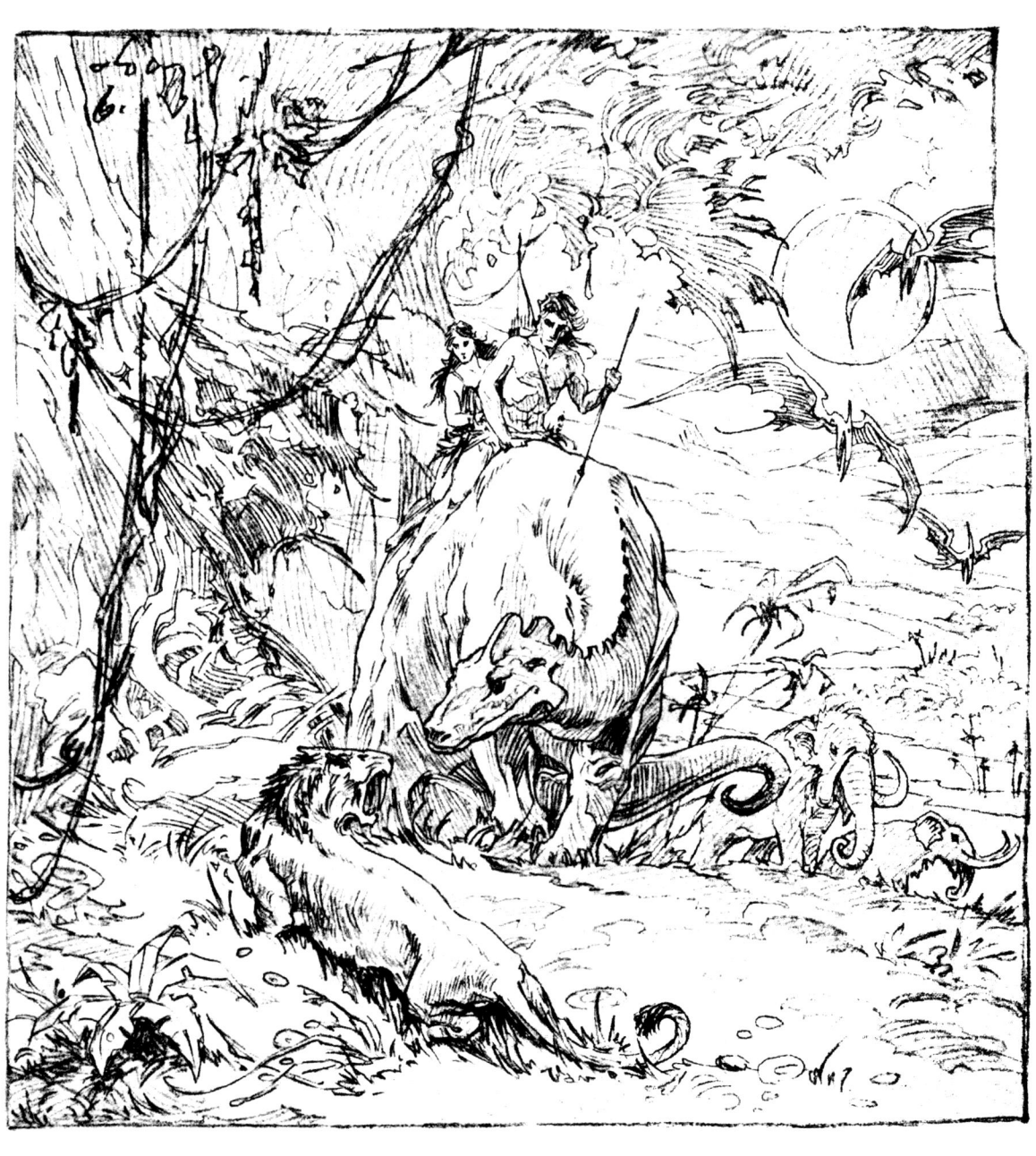

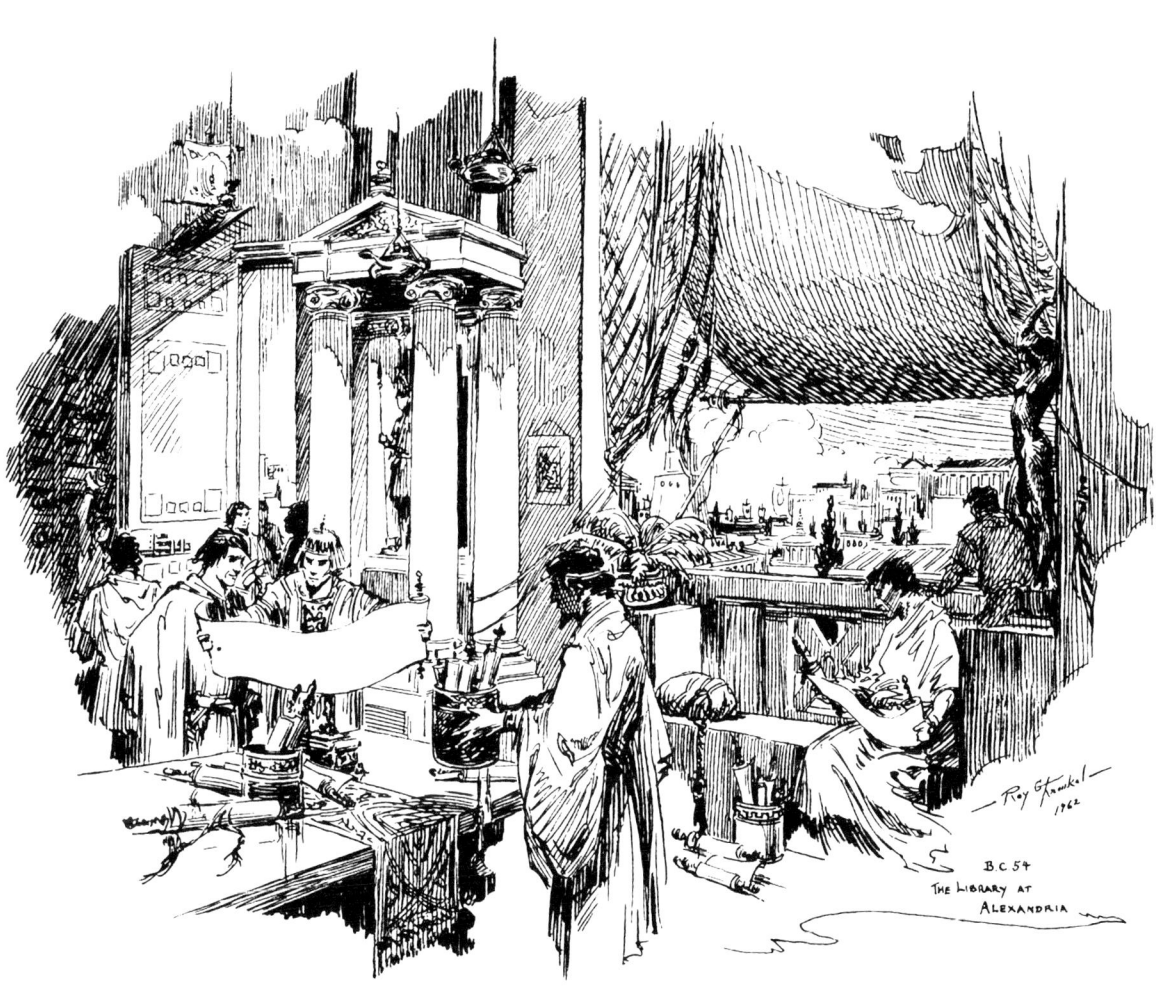

B.C 54
THE LIBRARY AT
ALEXANDRIA

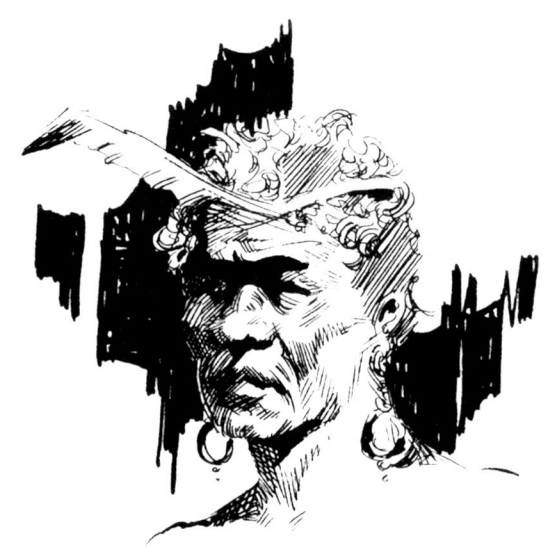

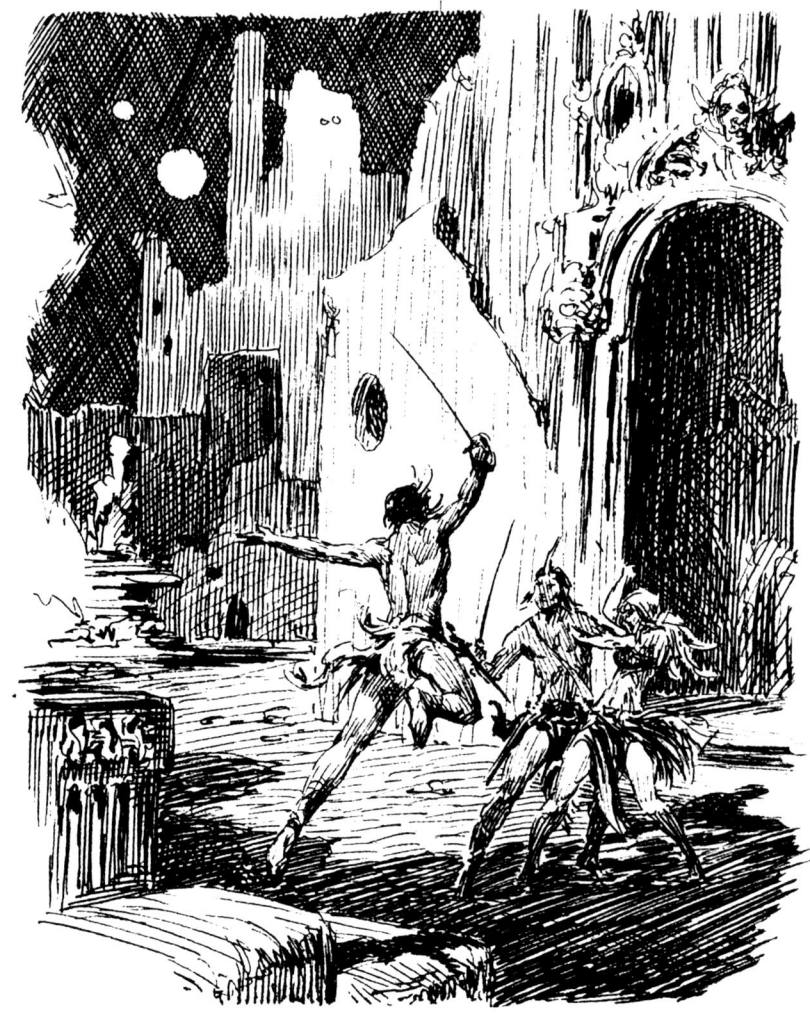

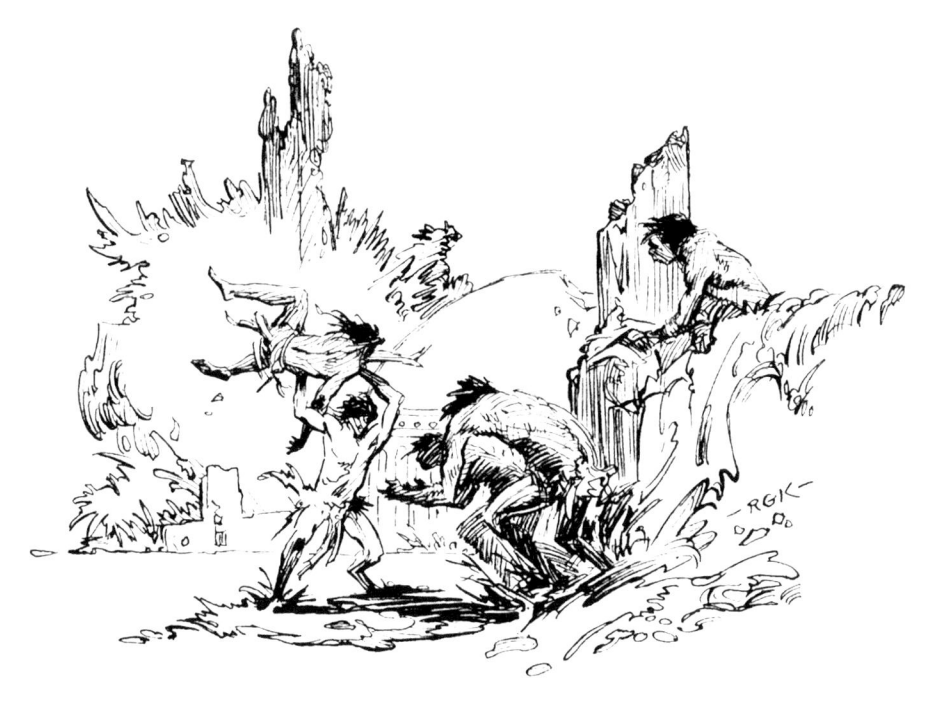

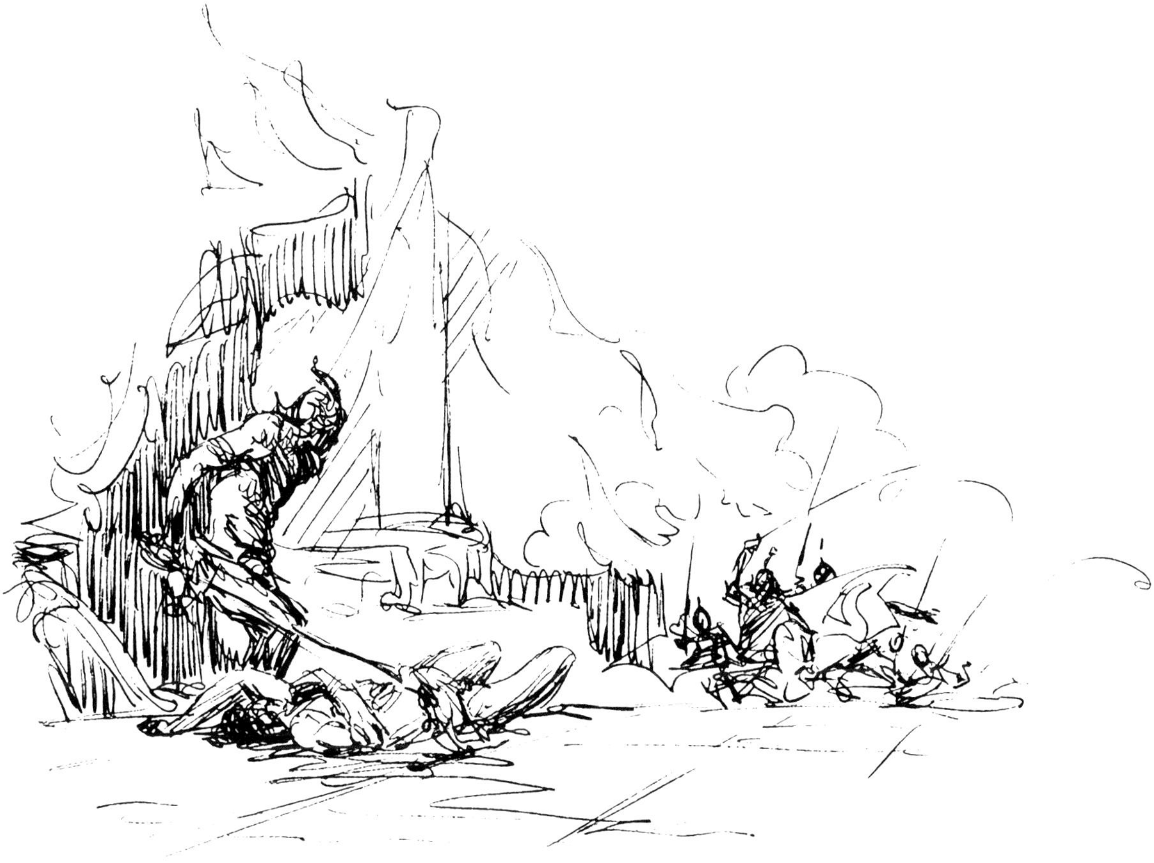

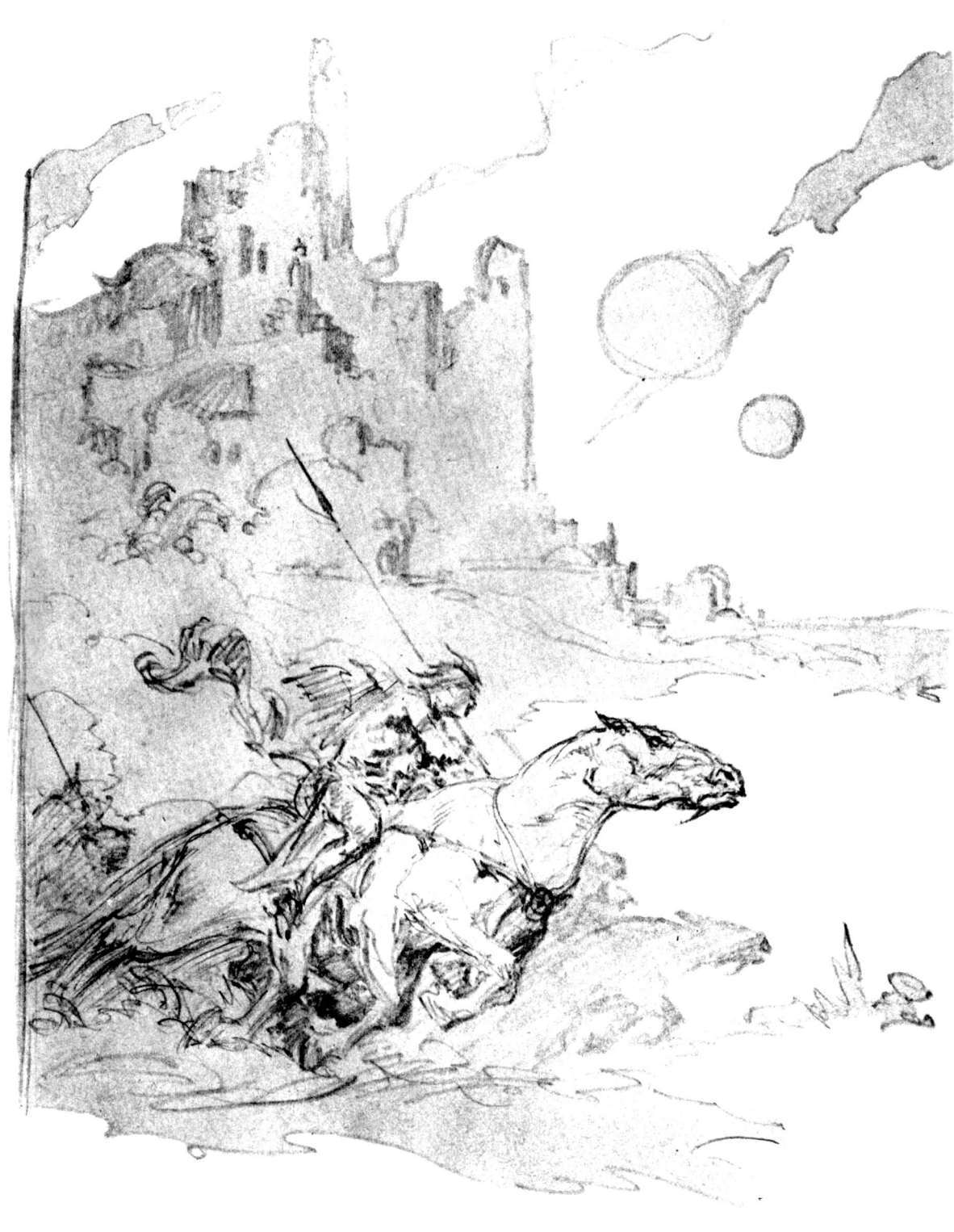

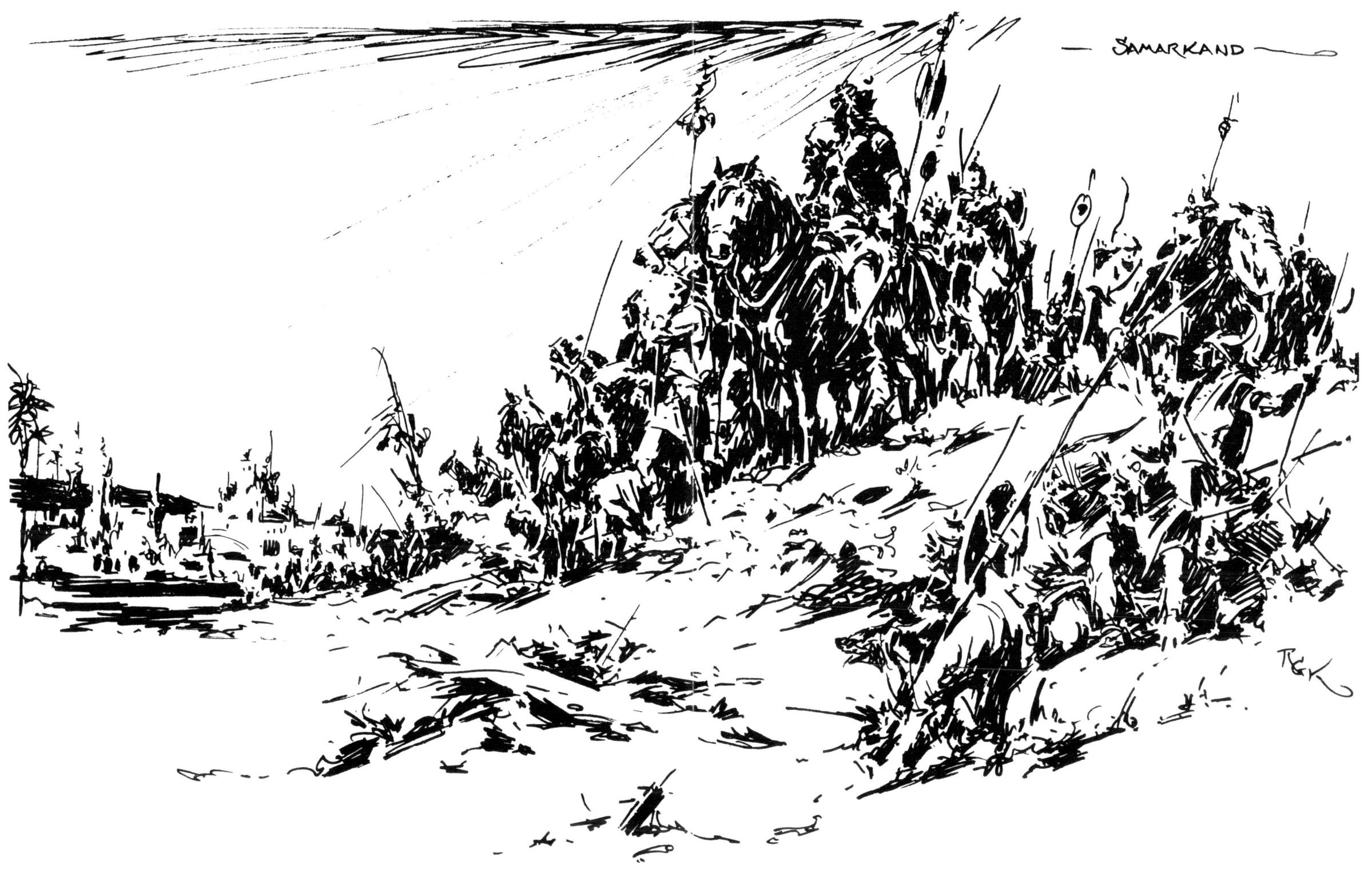

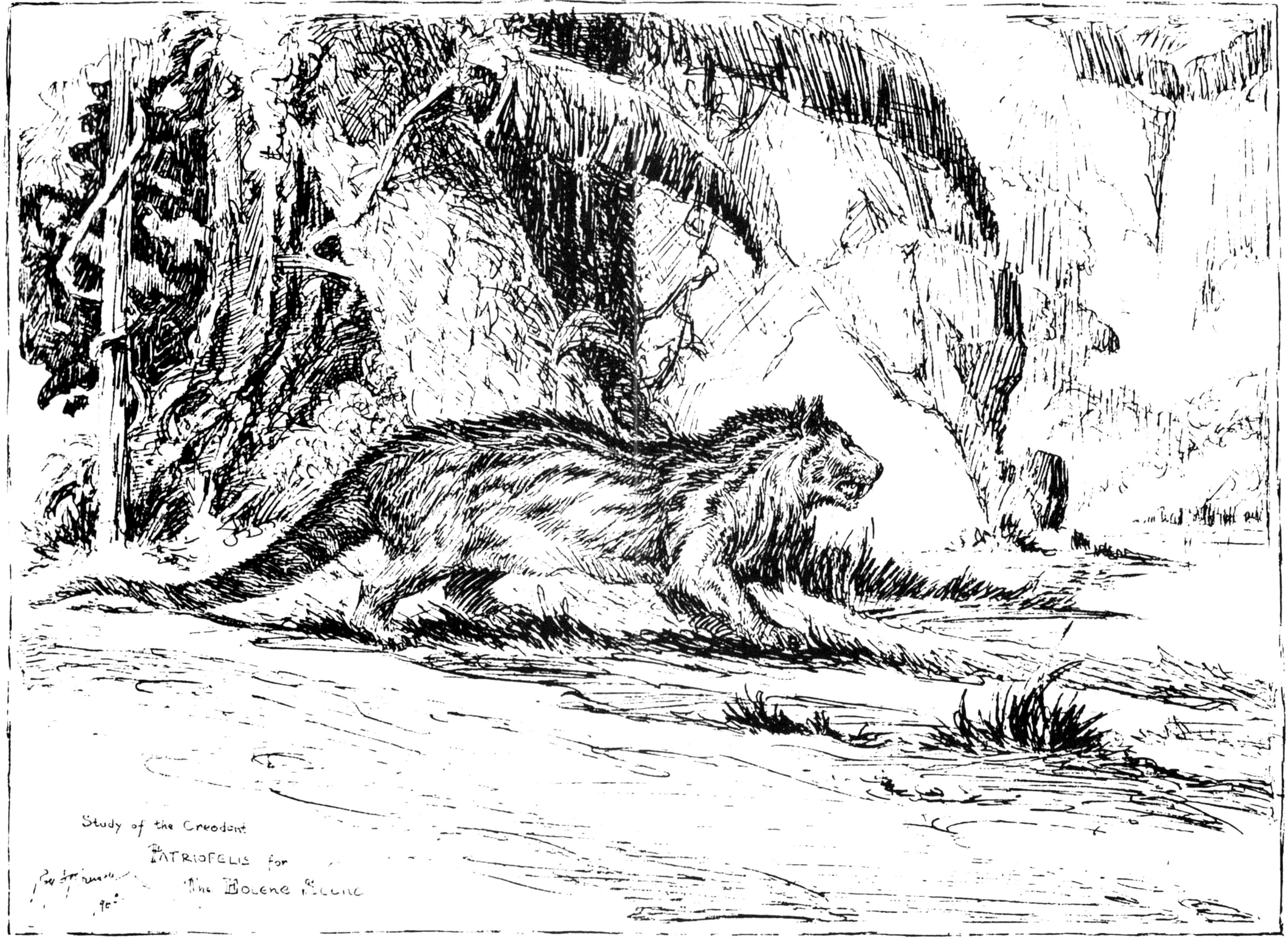

Study of the Creodont
PATRIOFELIS for
The Eocene Scene

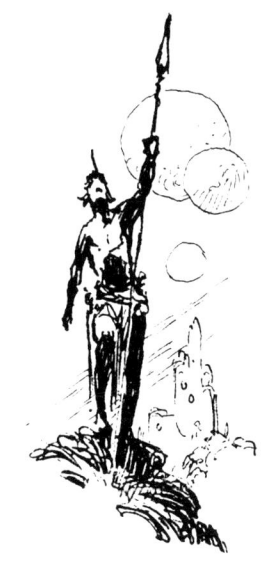

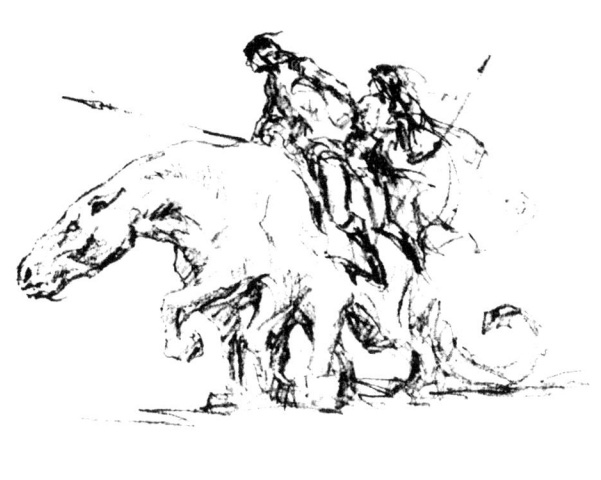

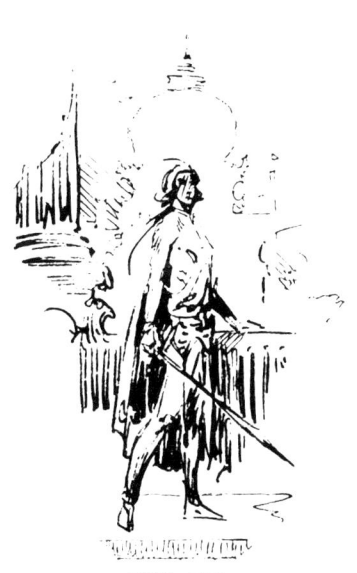

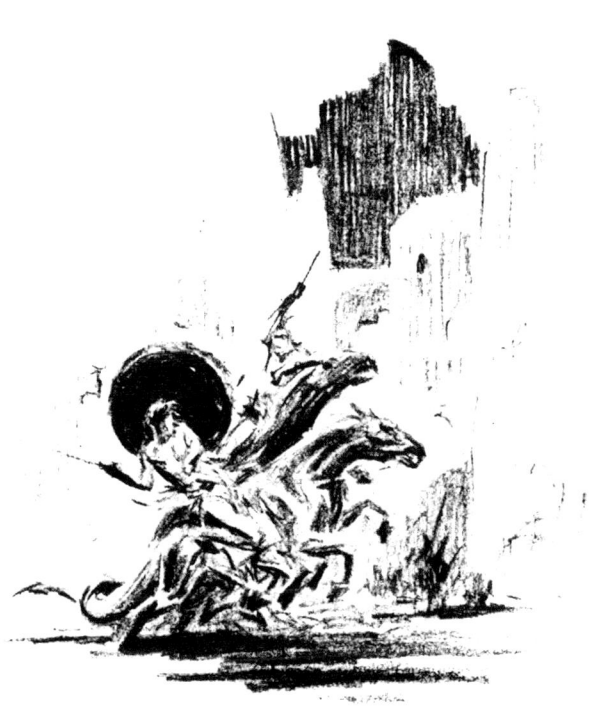

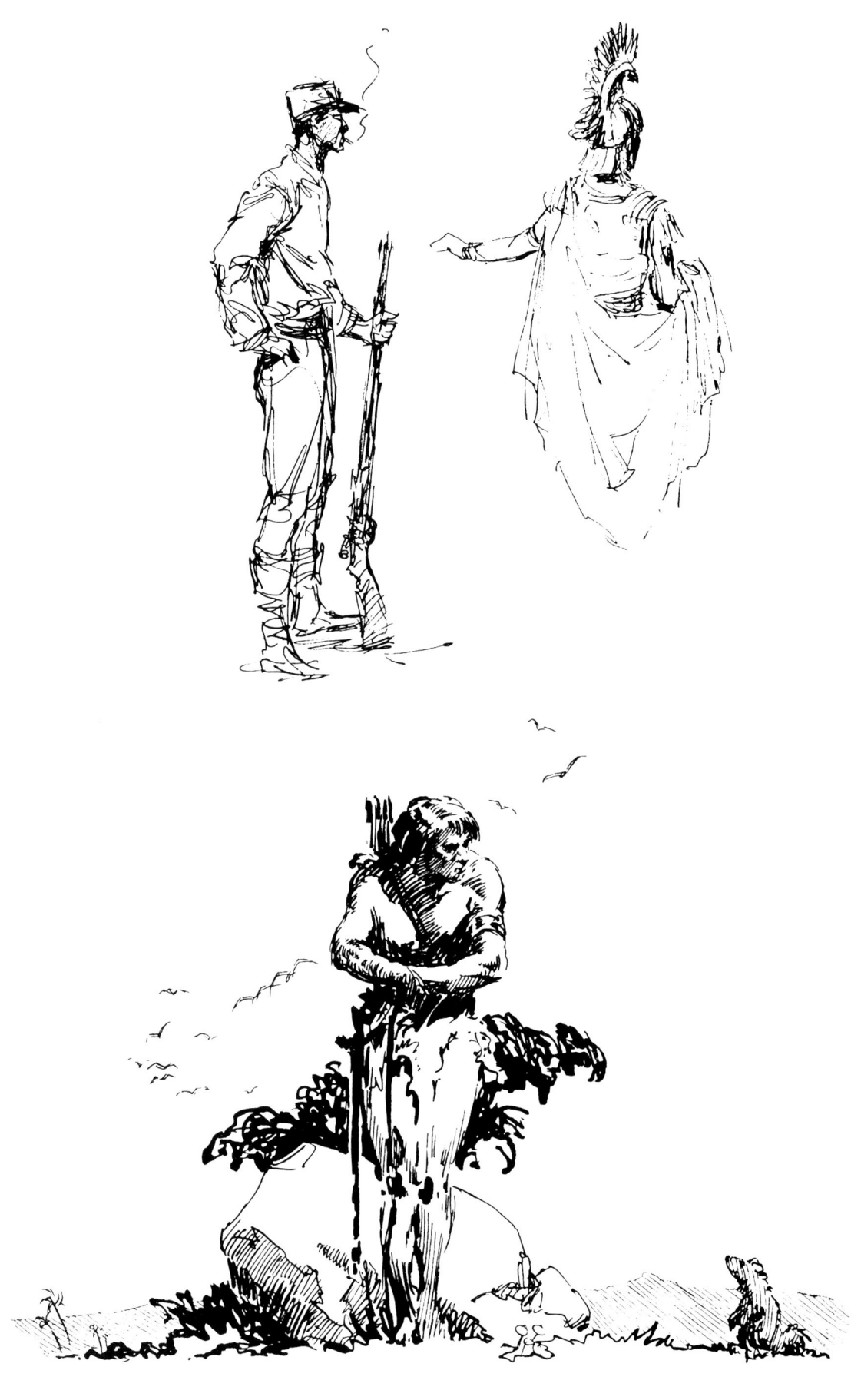

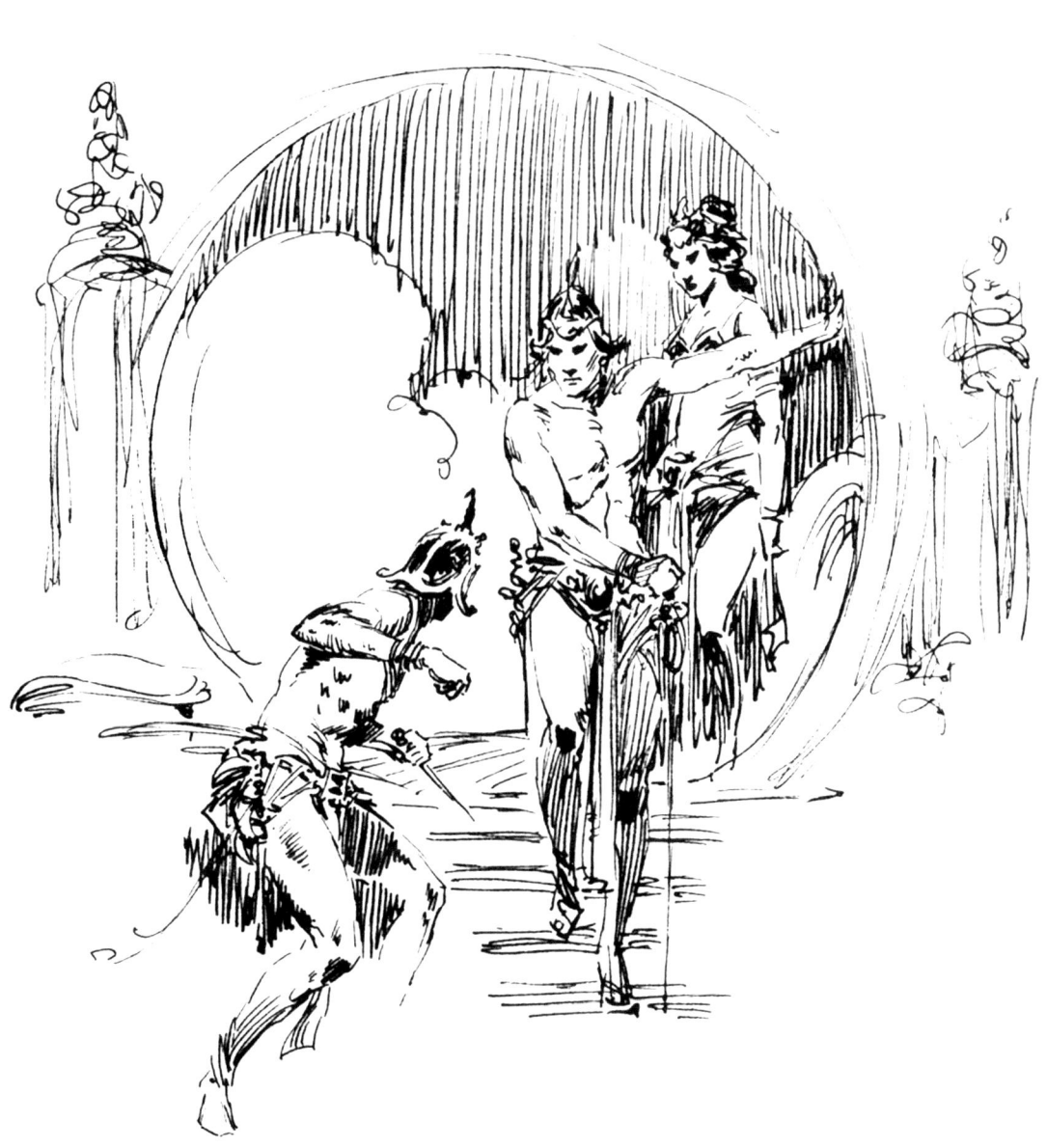

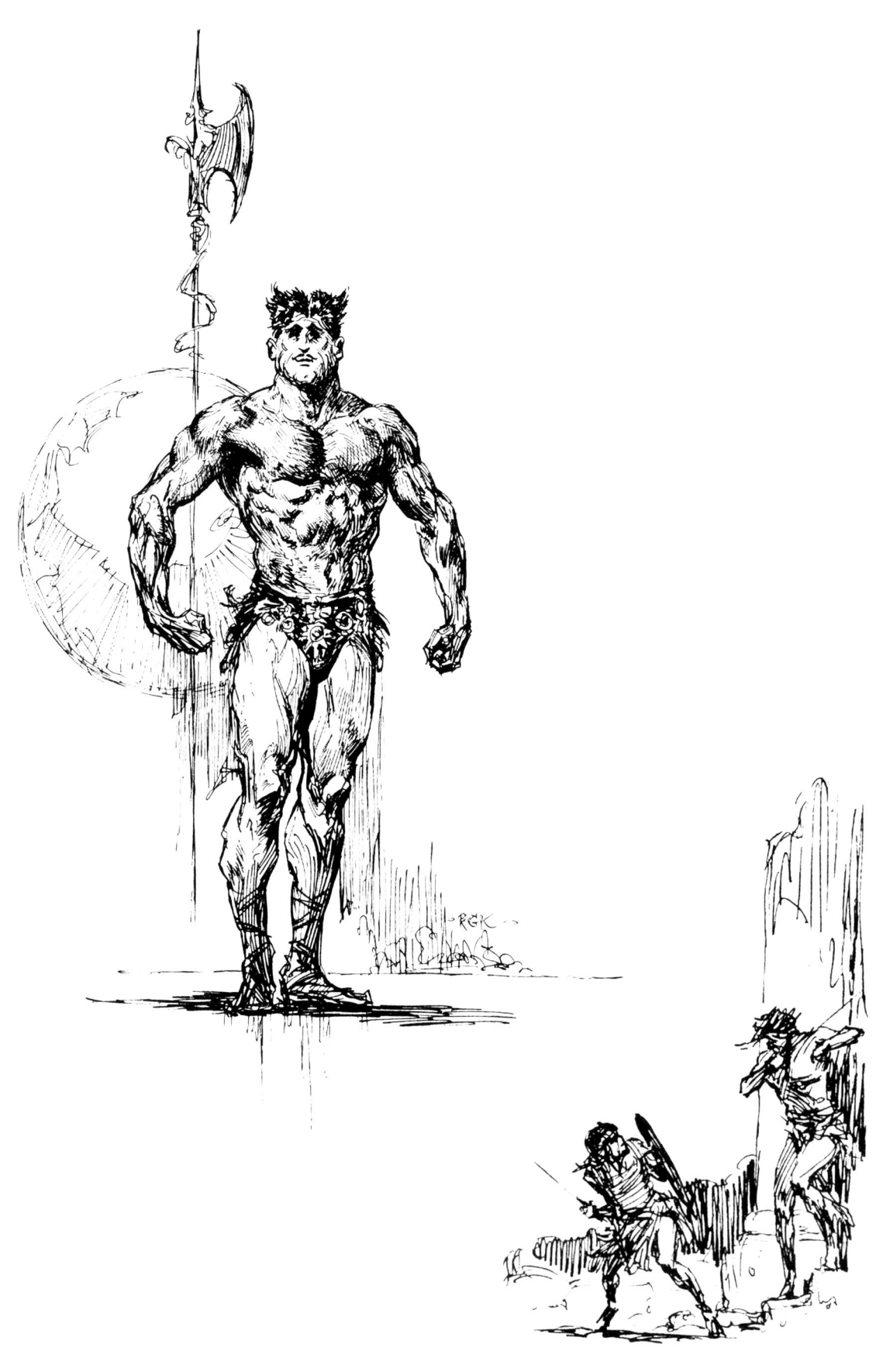

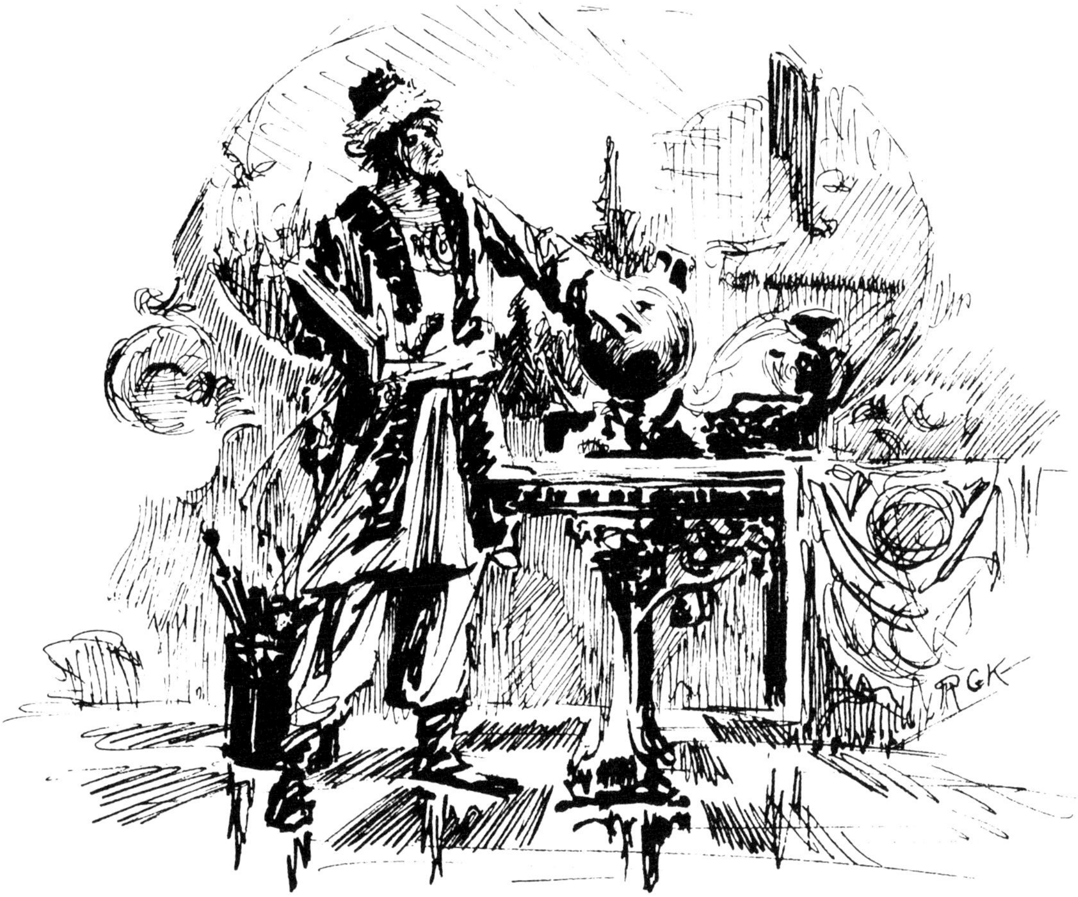

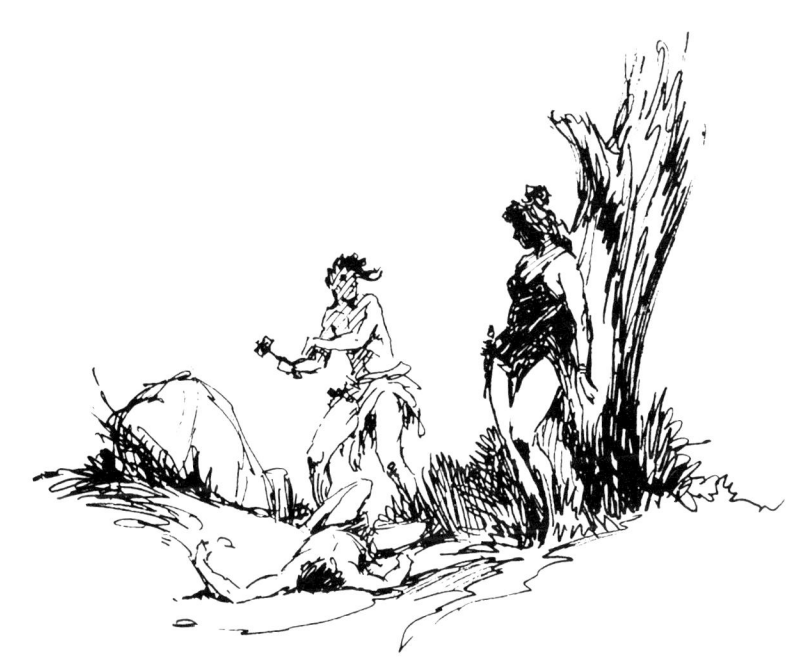

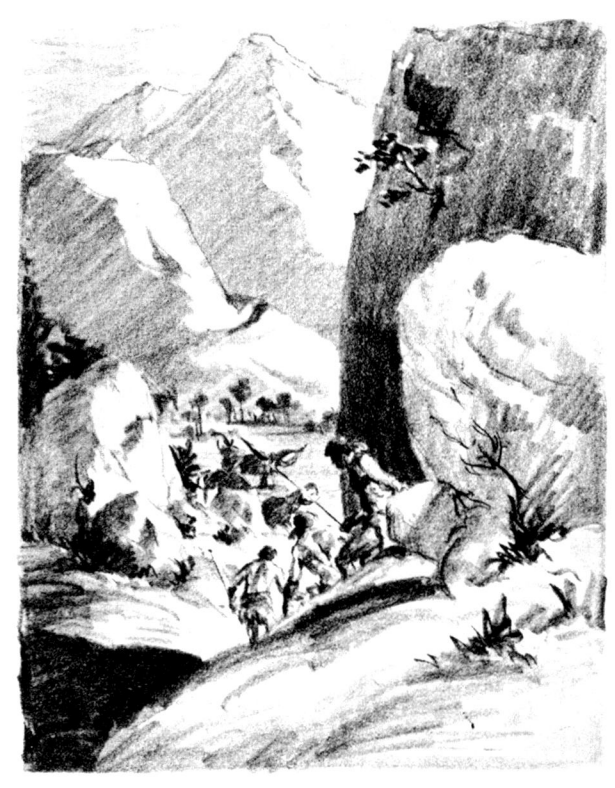

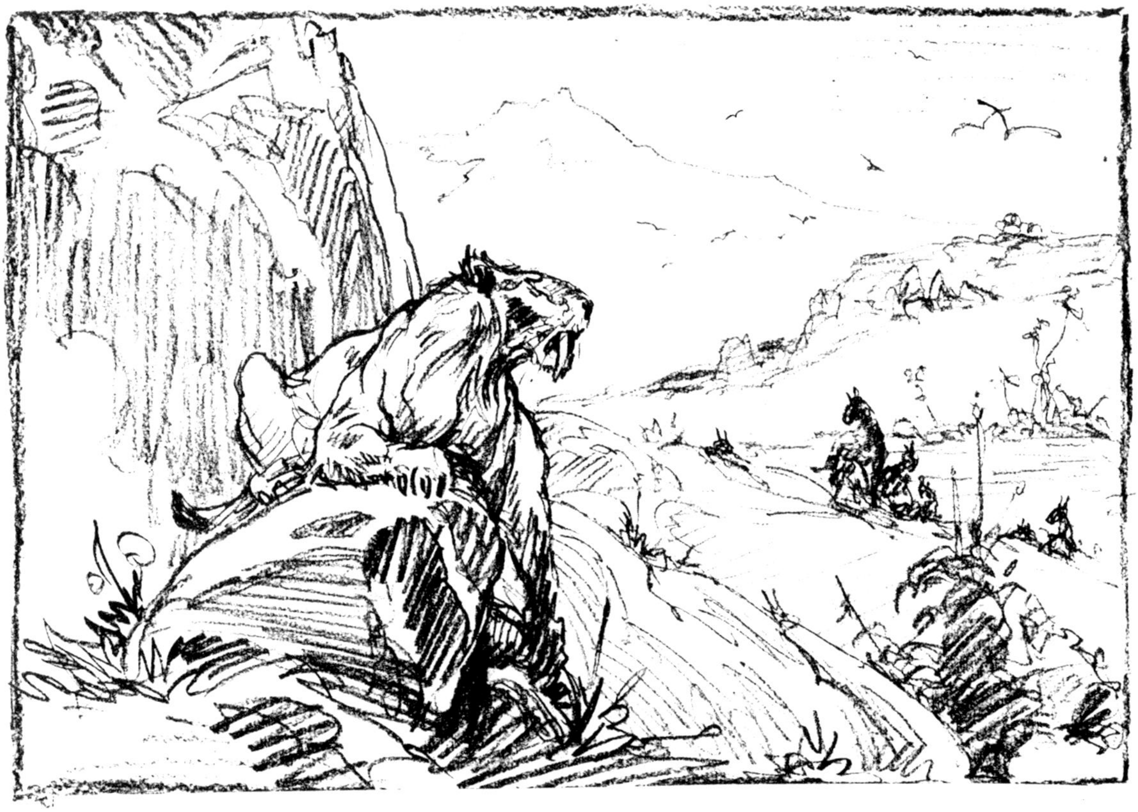

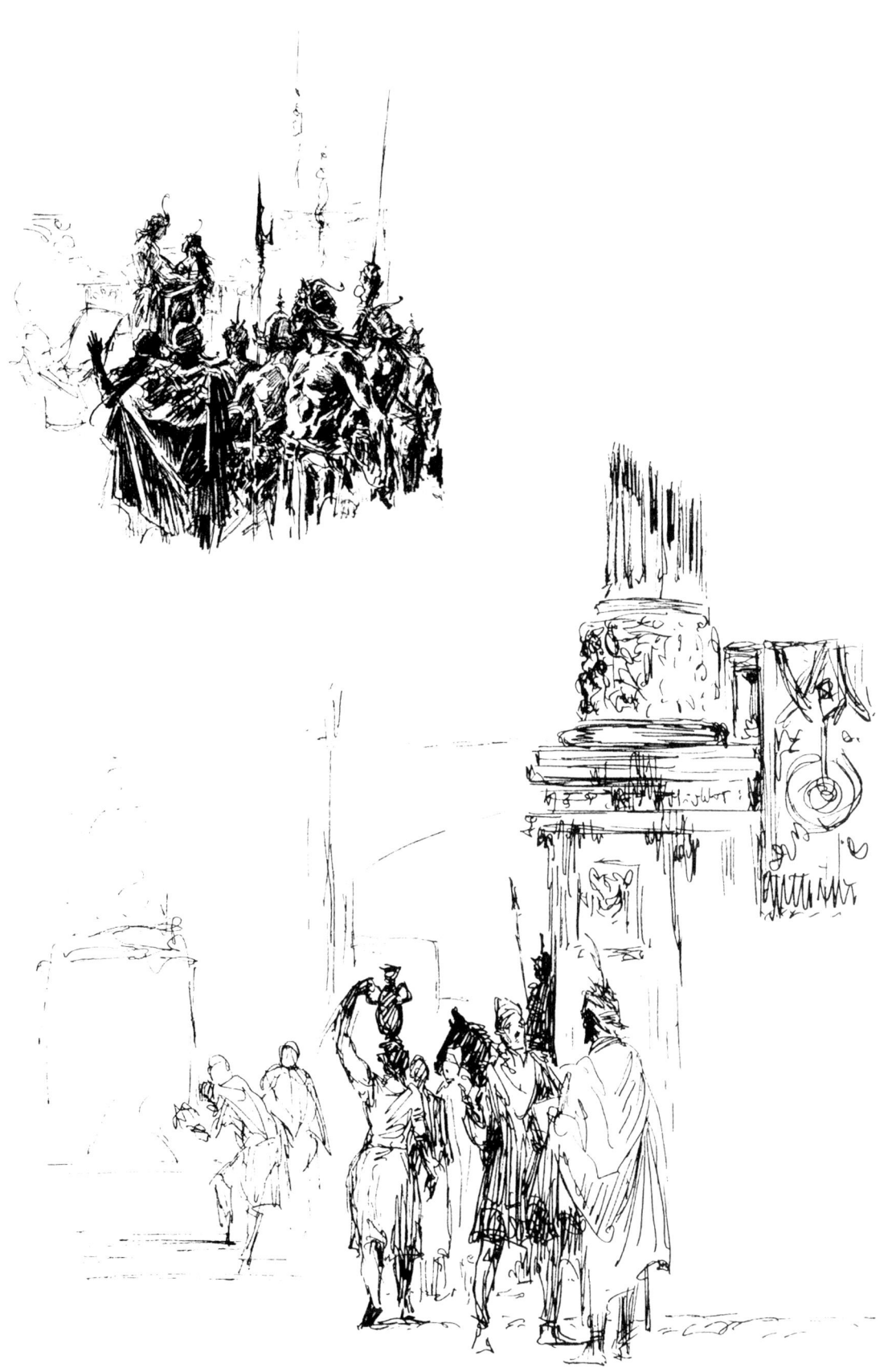

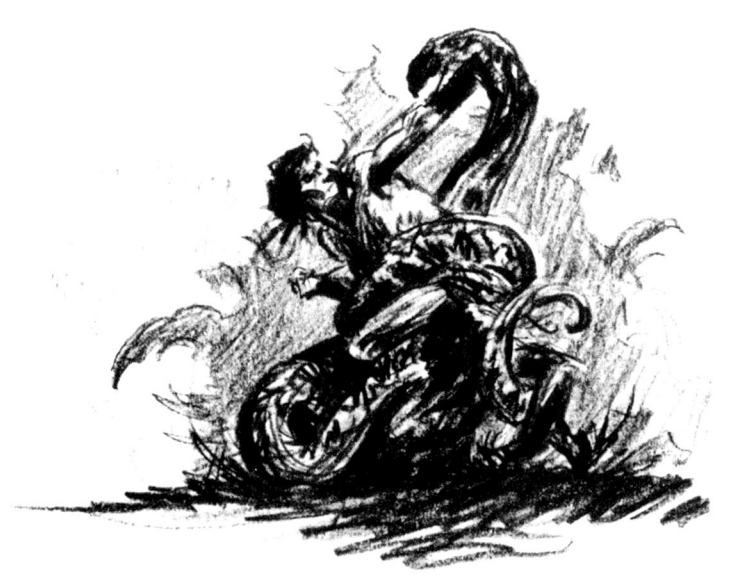

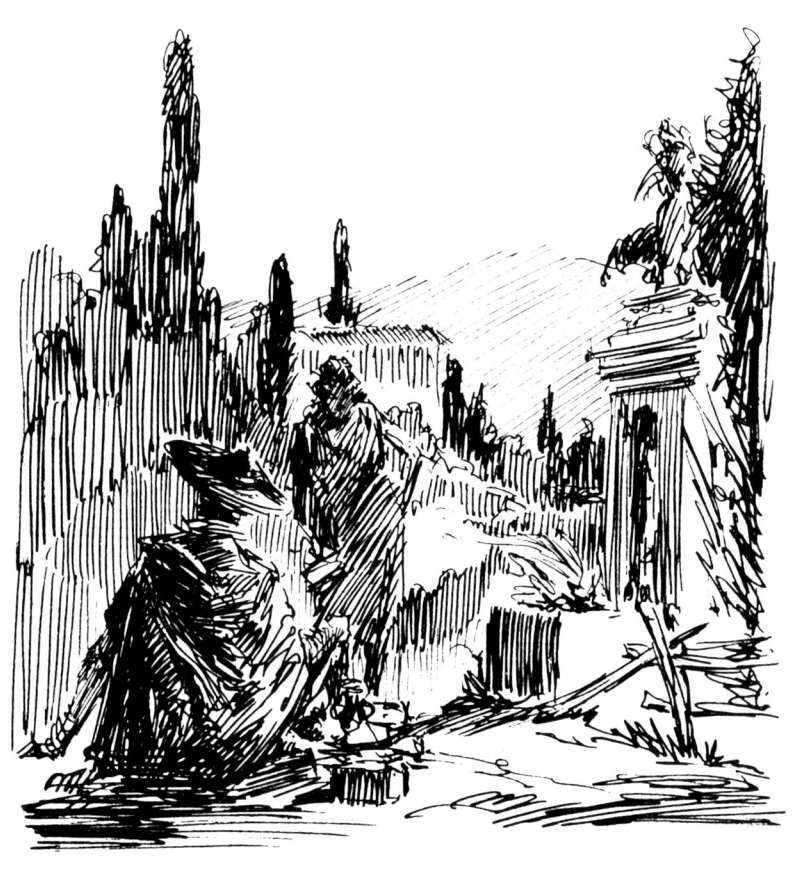

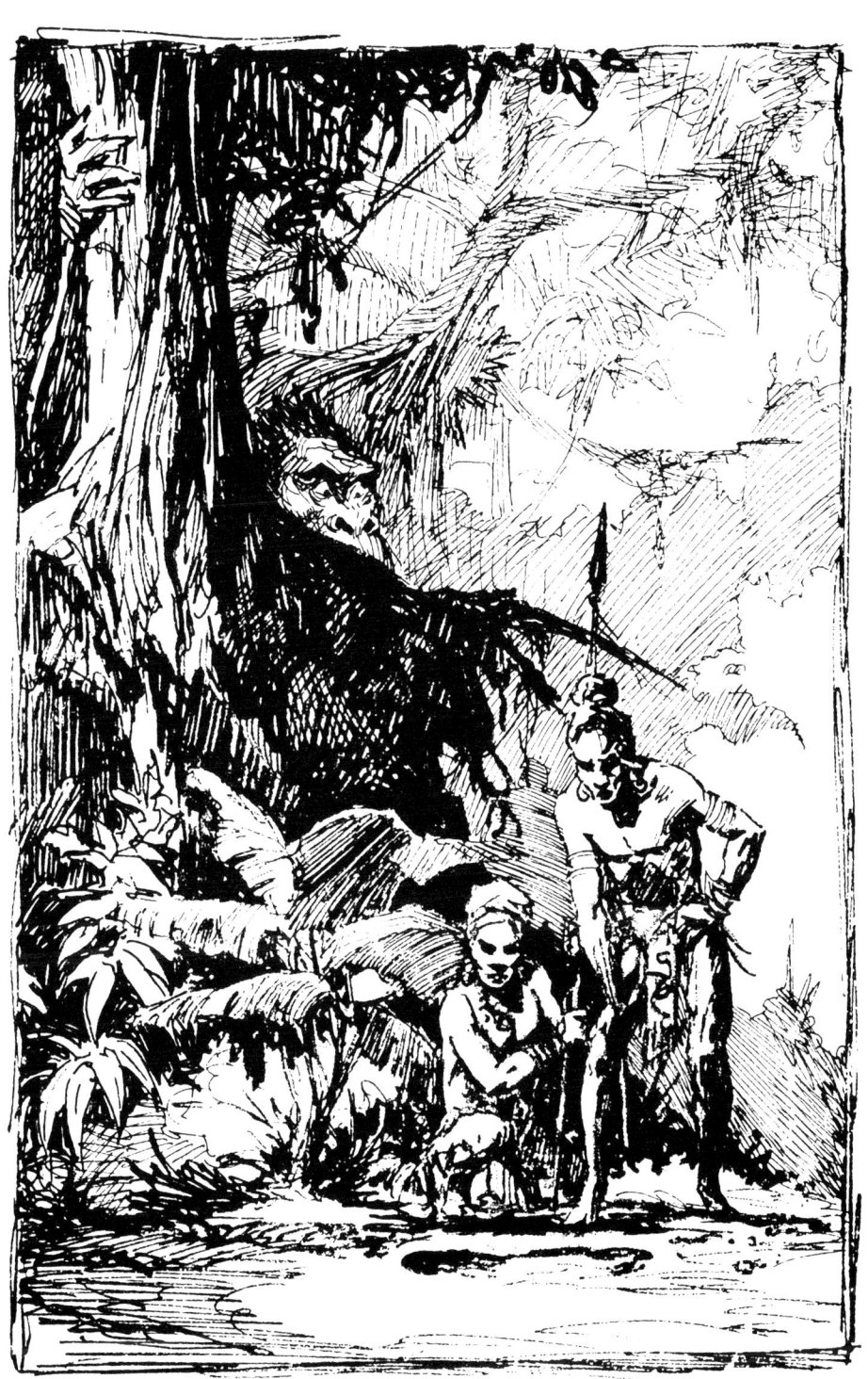

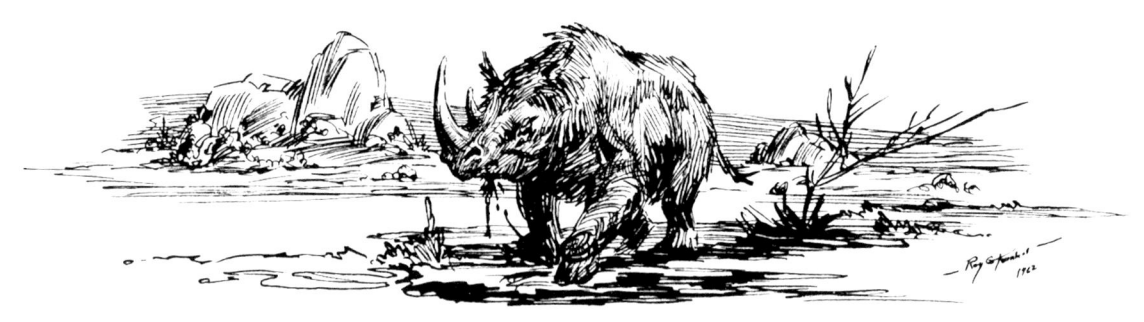

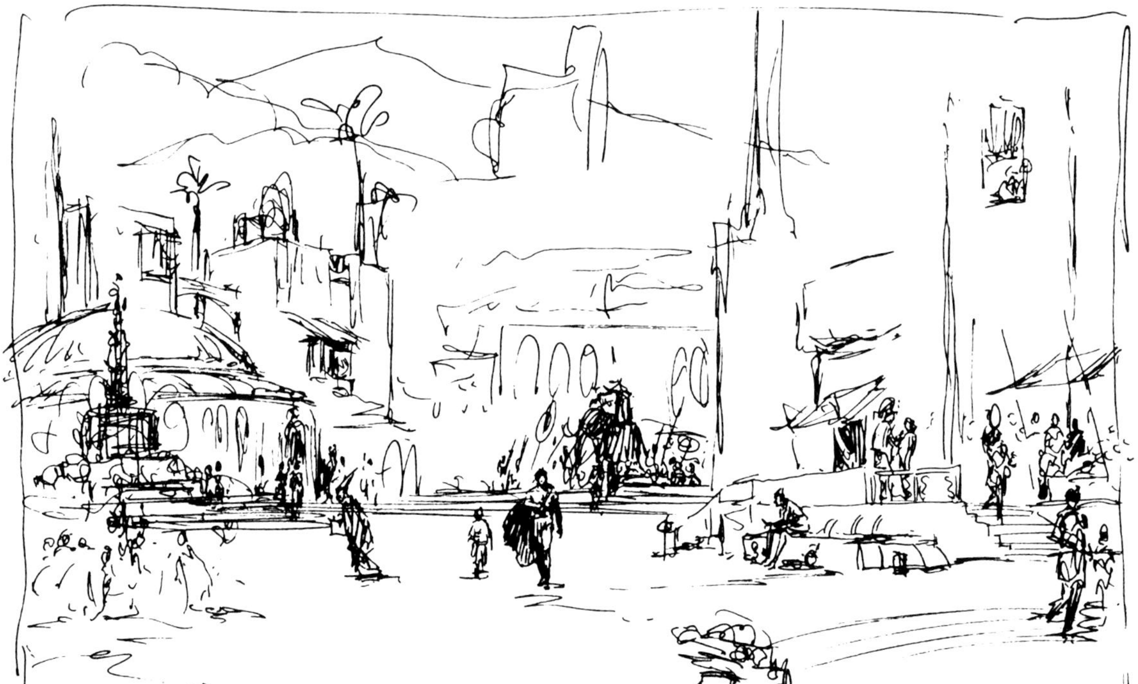

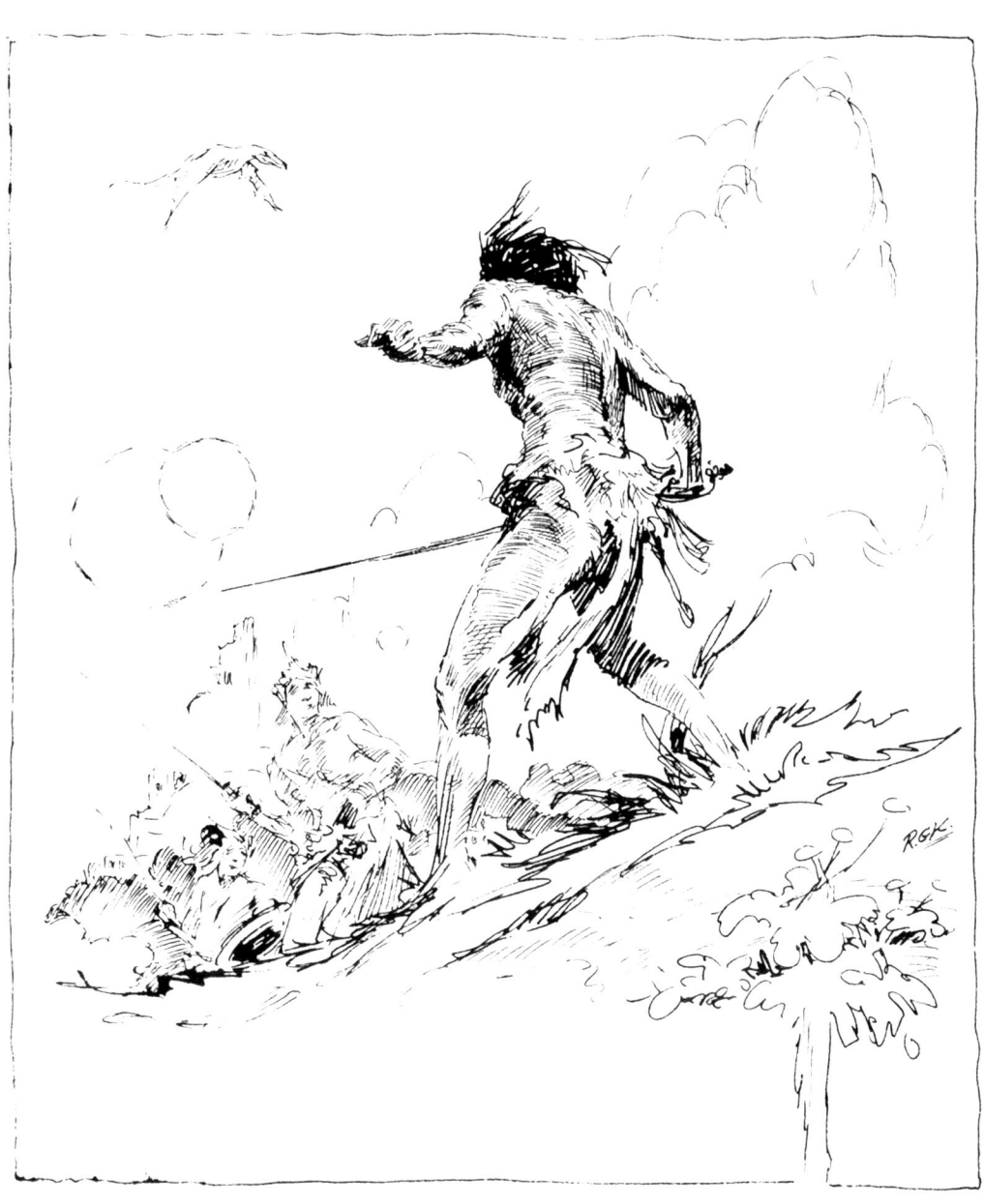

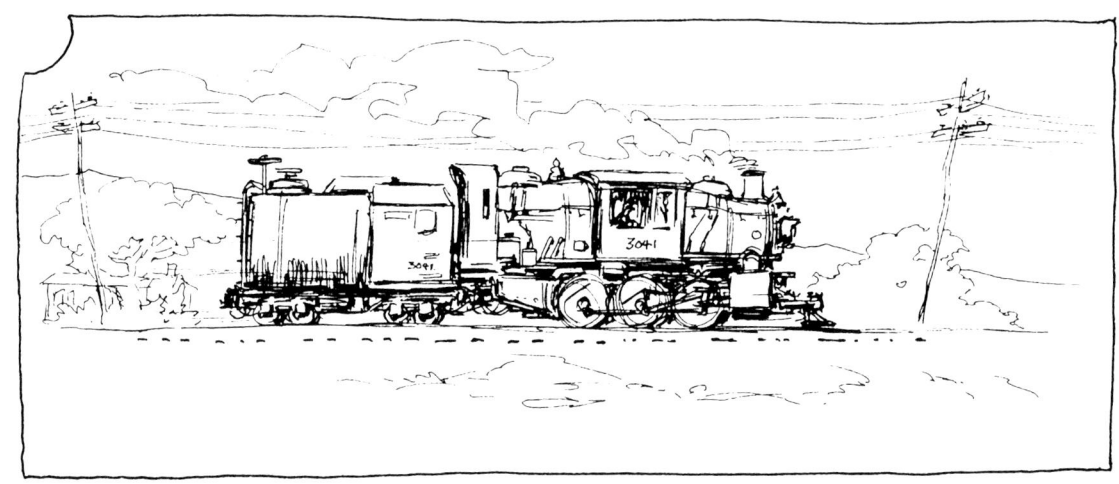

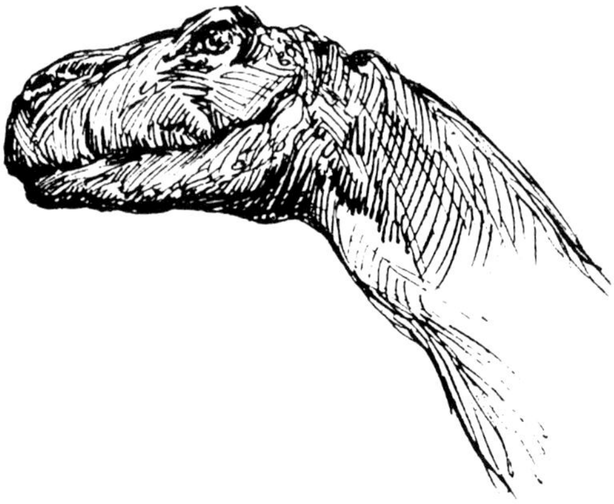

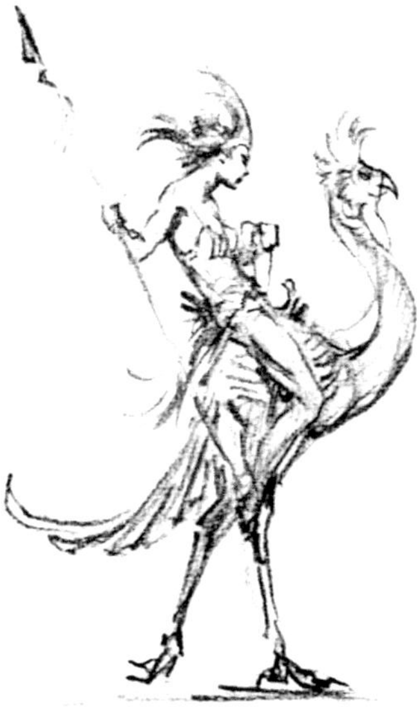

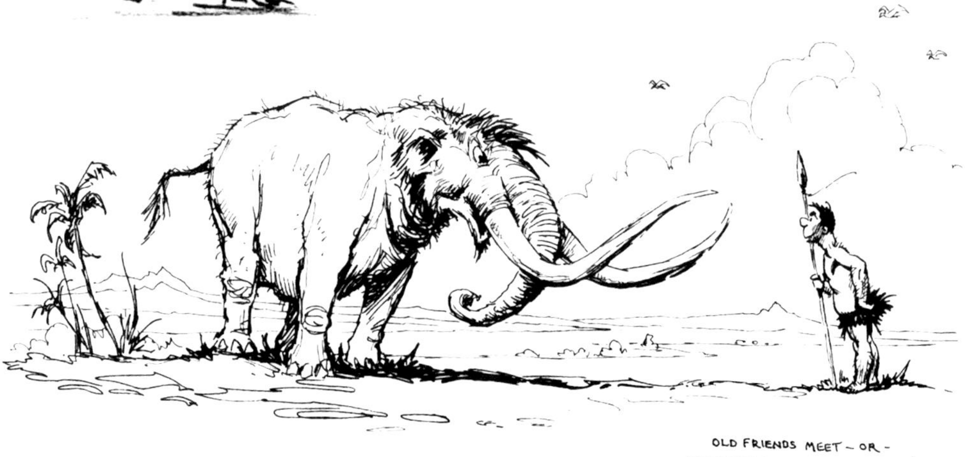

OLD FRIENDS MEET — OR —
IRRELEVANT NEVER FORGETS!

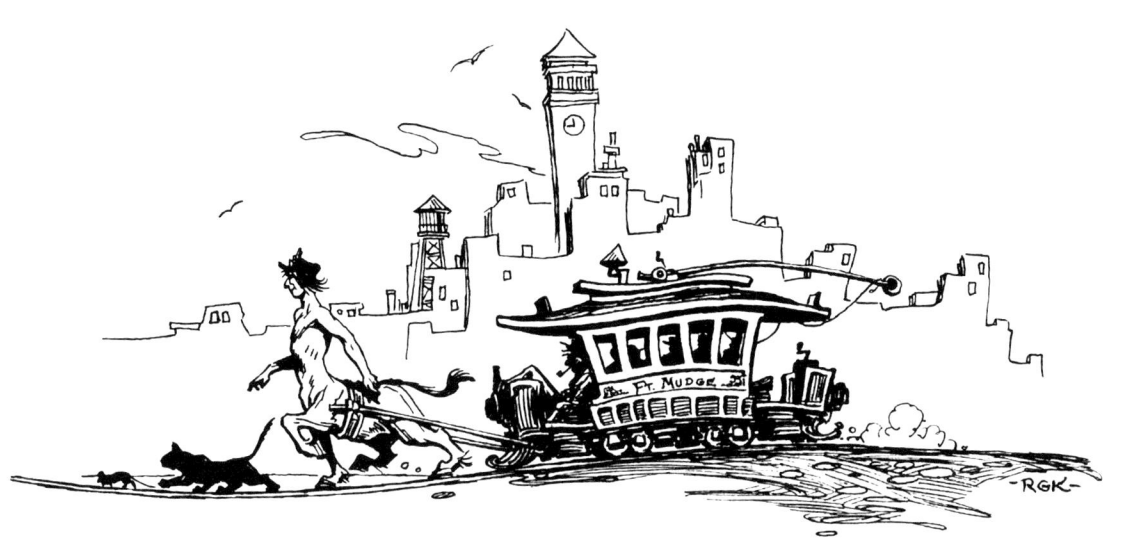

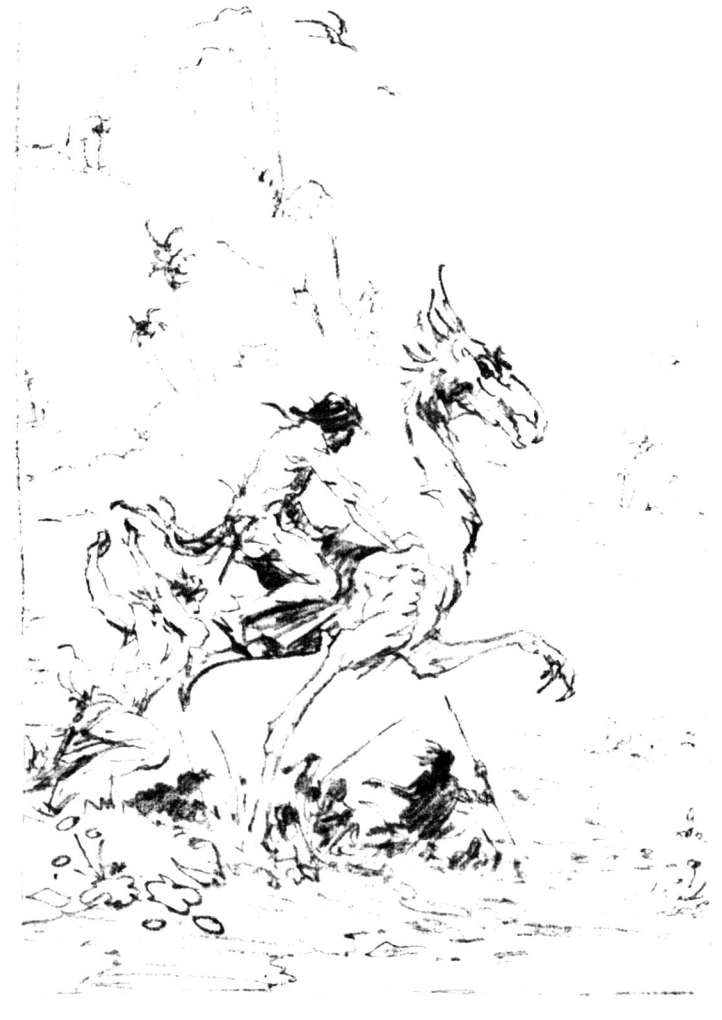

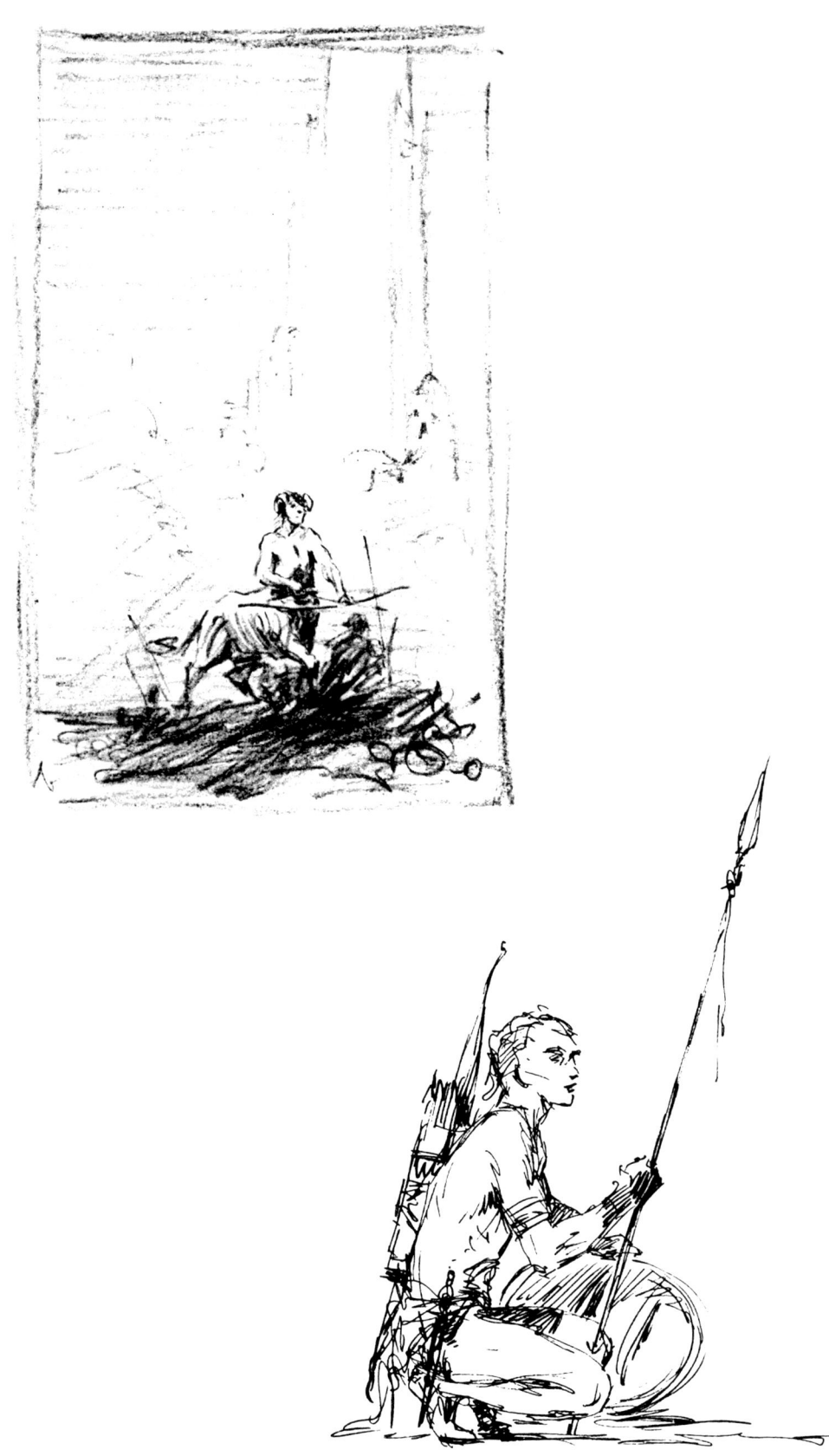

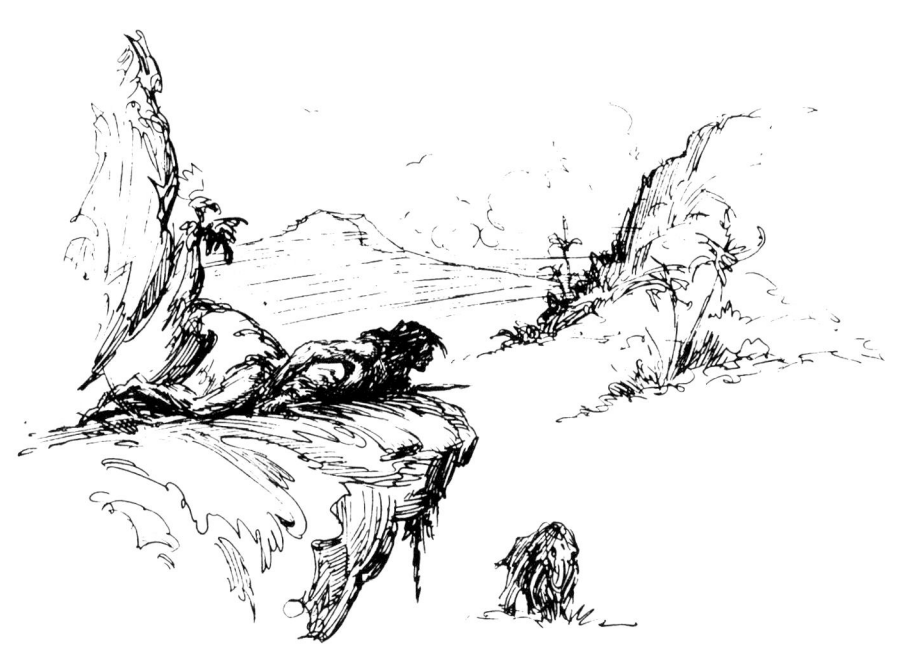

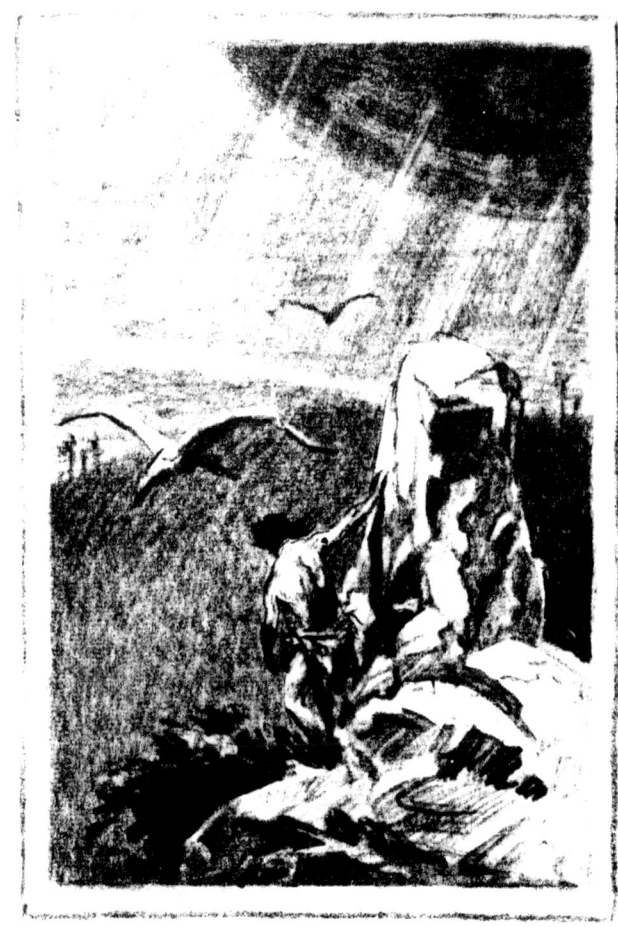

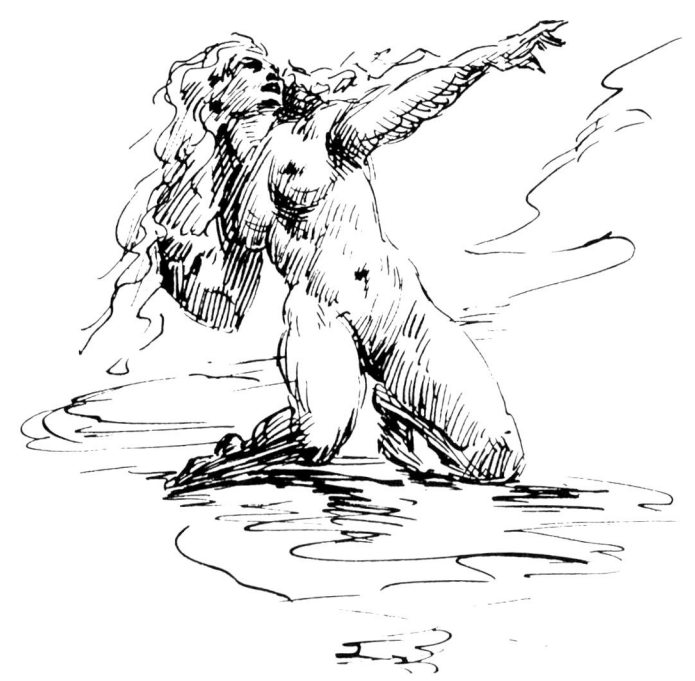

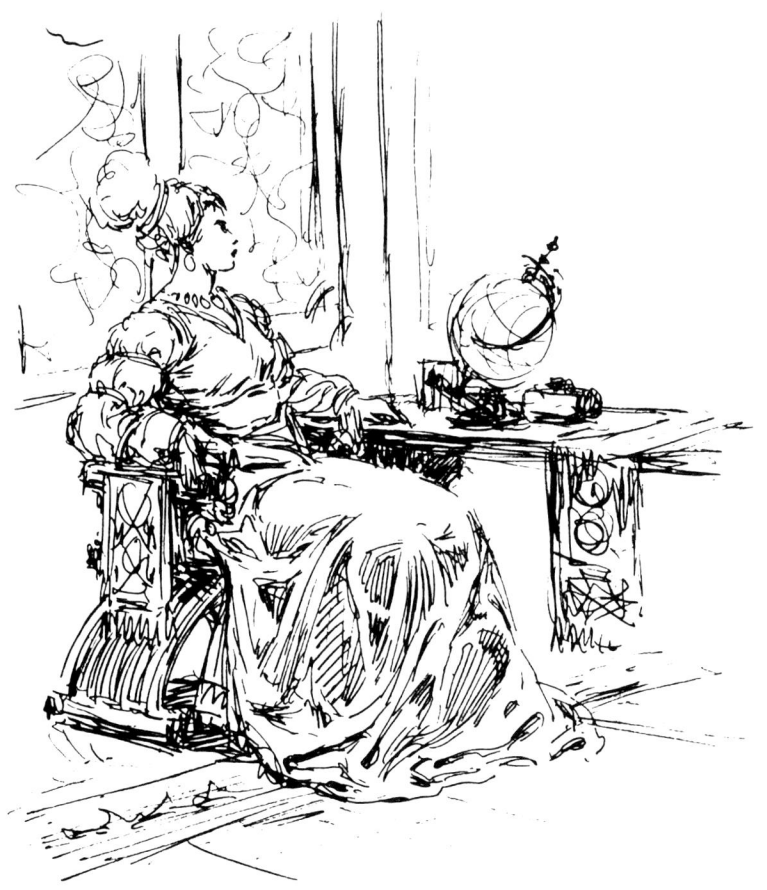

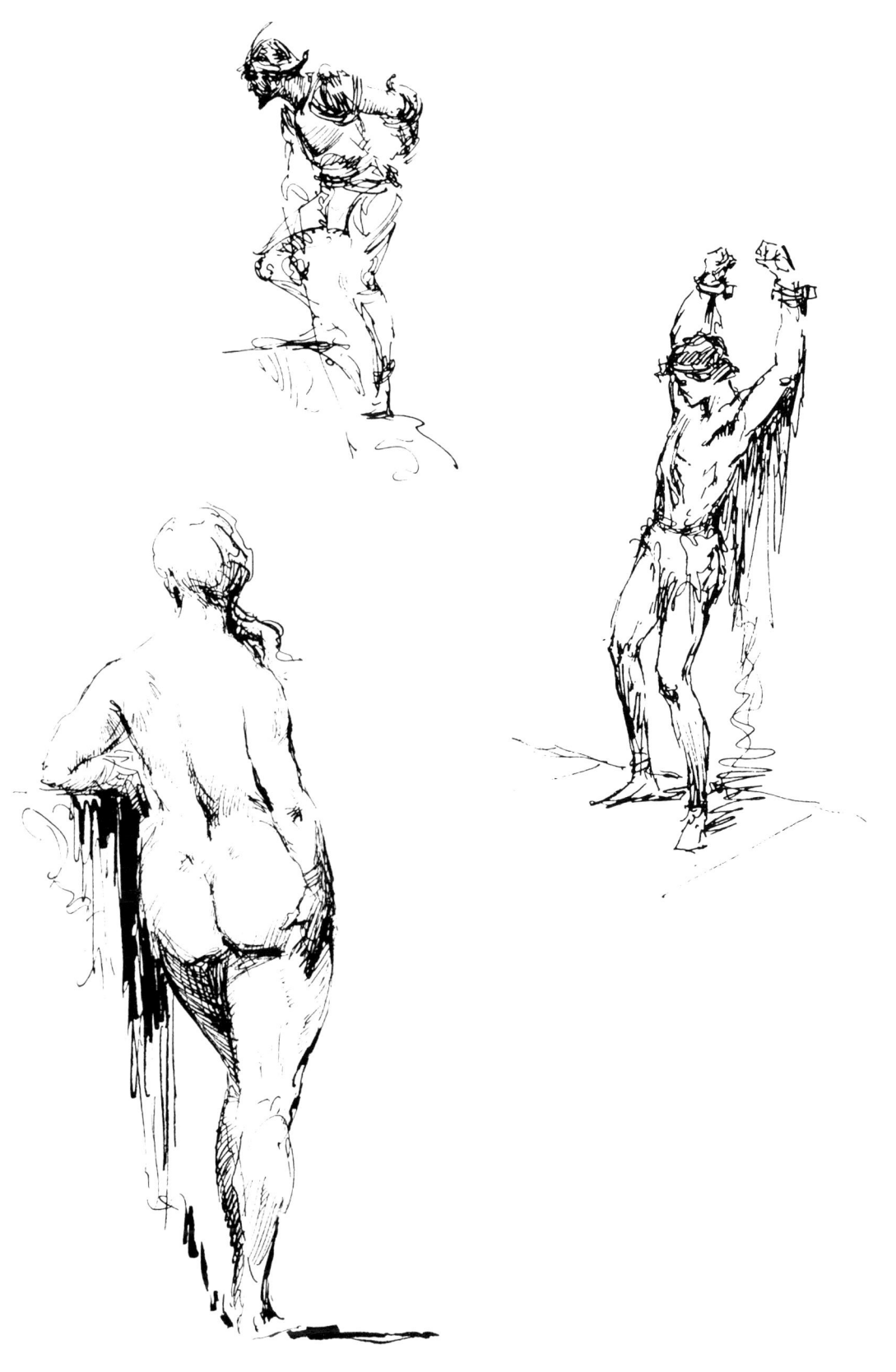

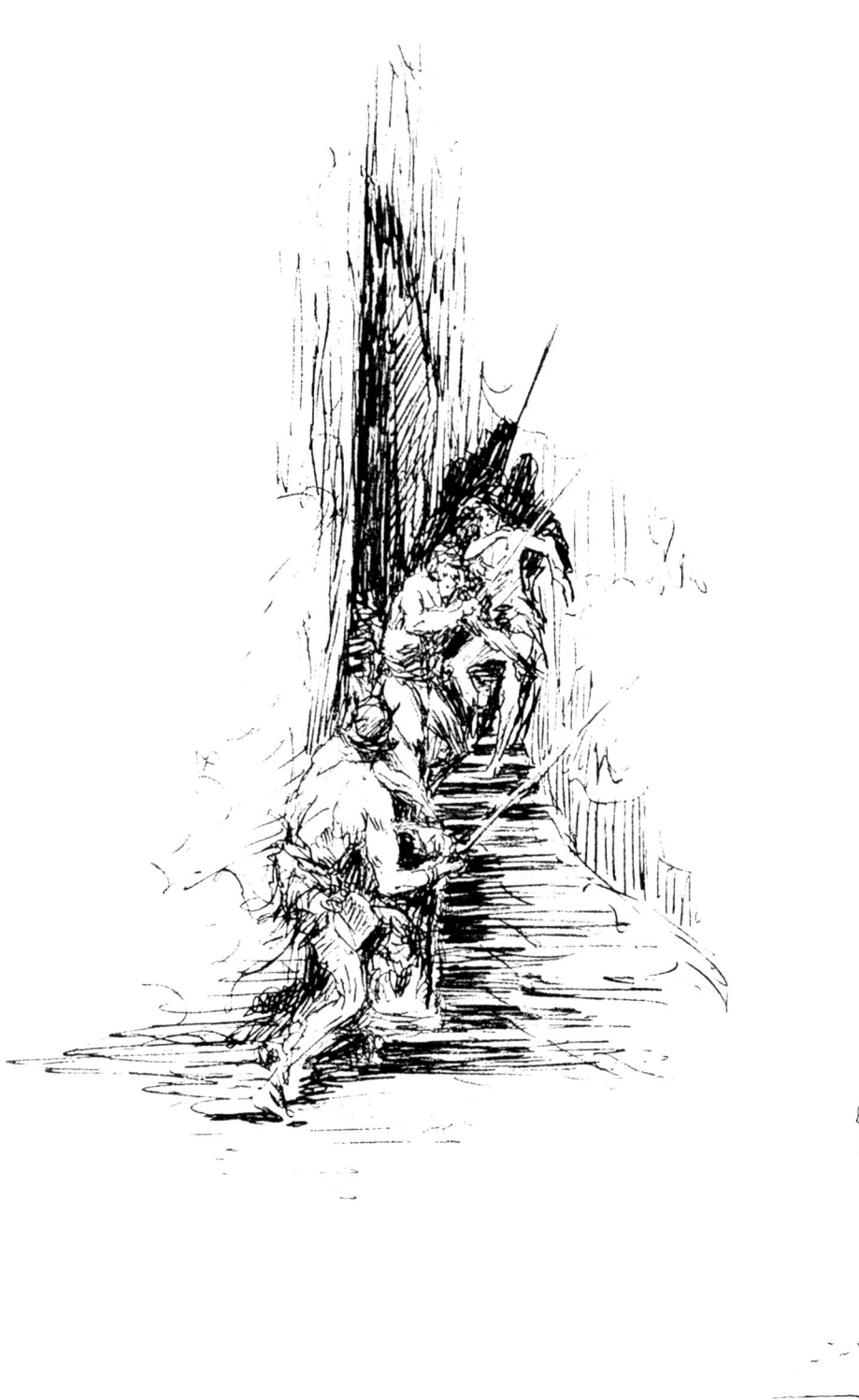

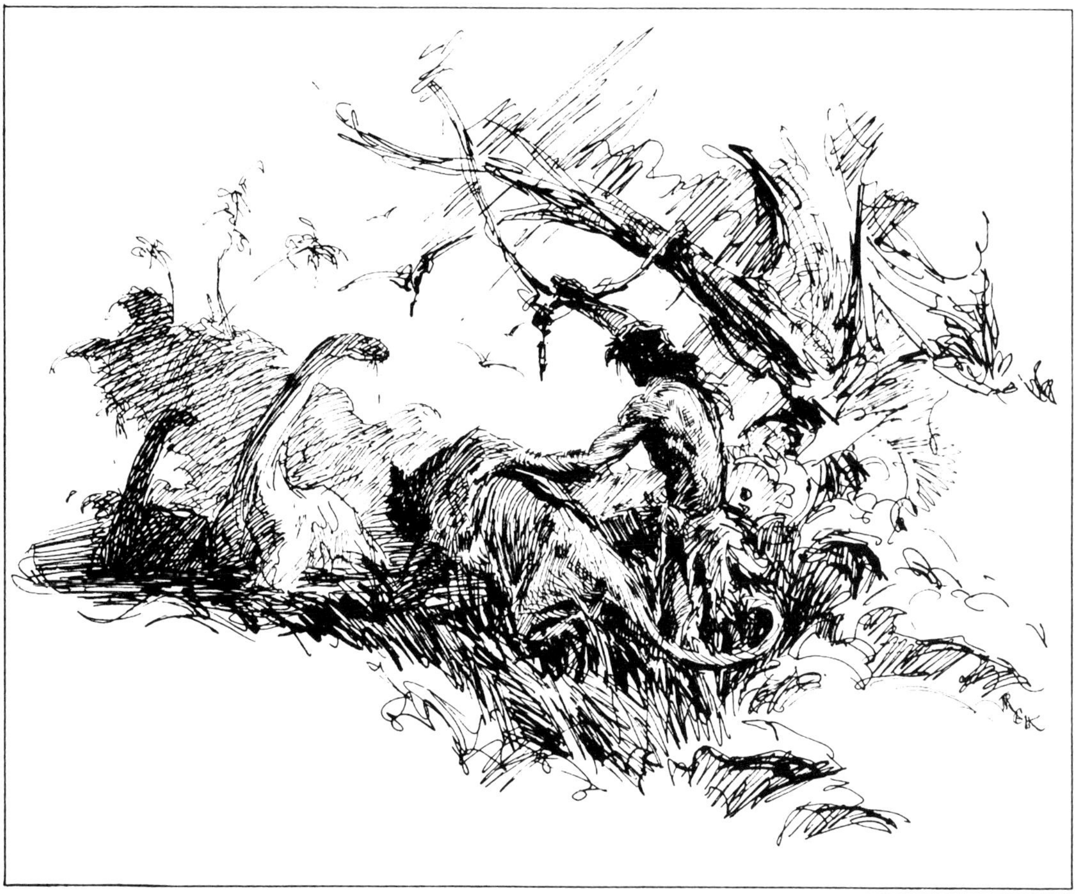

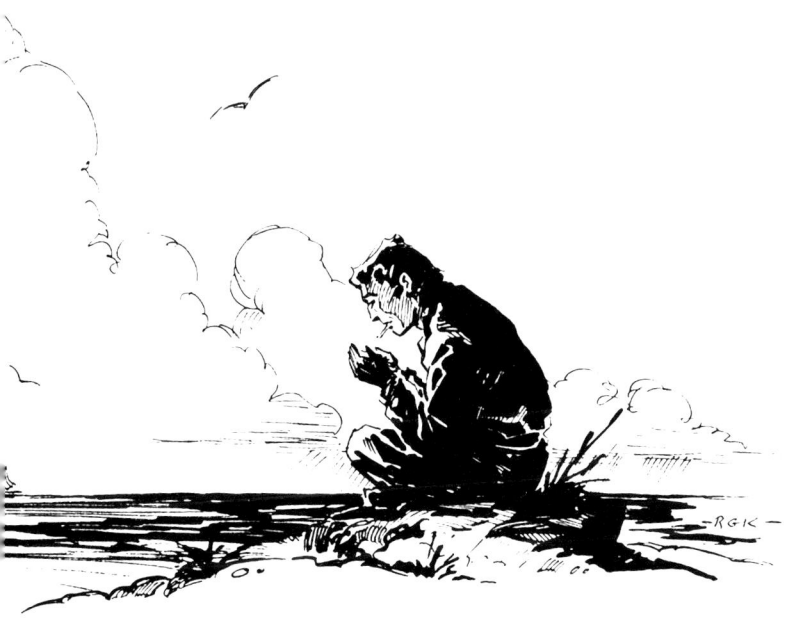

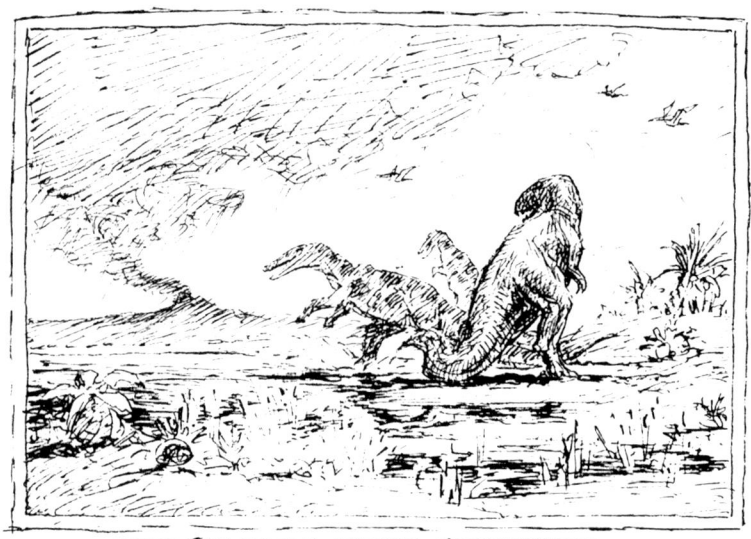

— TYRANOSAURUS ATTACKING TRACHODON —

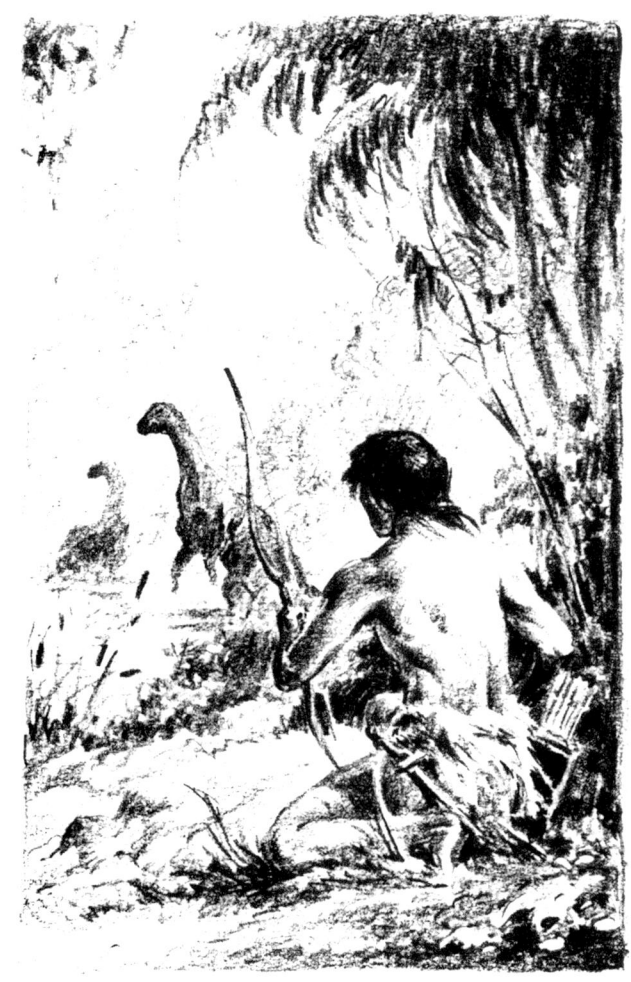

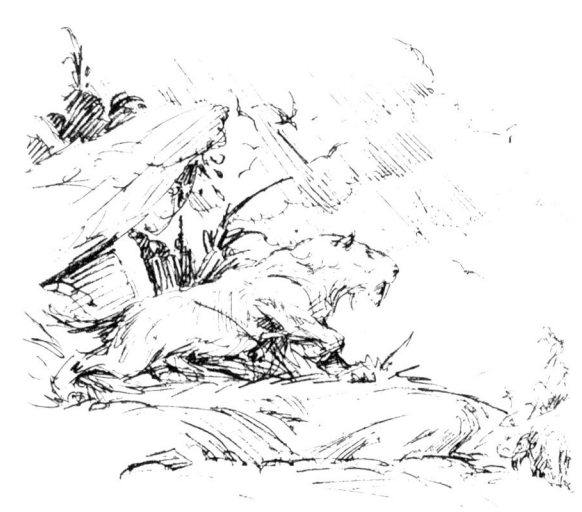

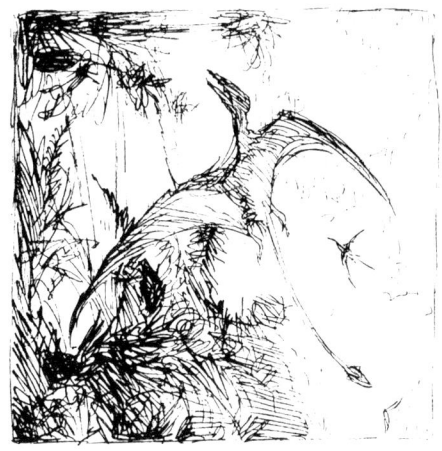

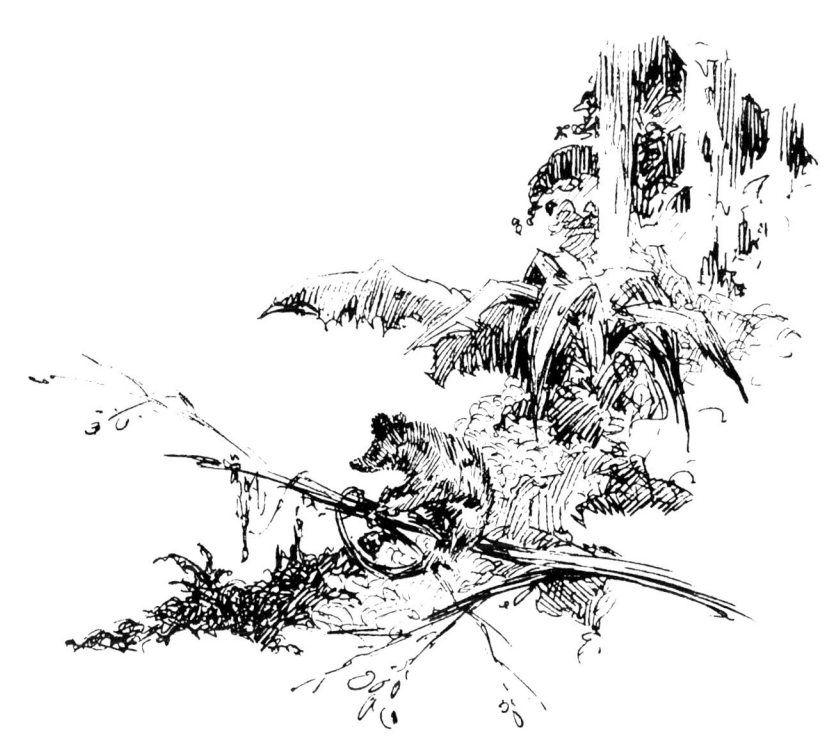

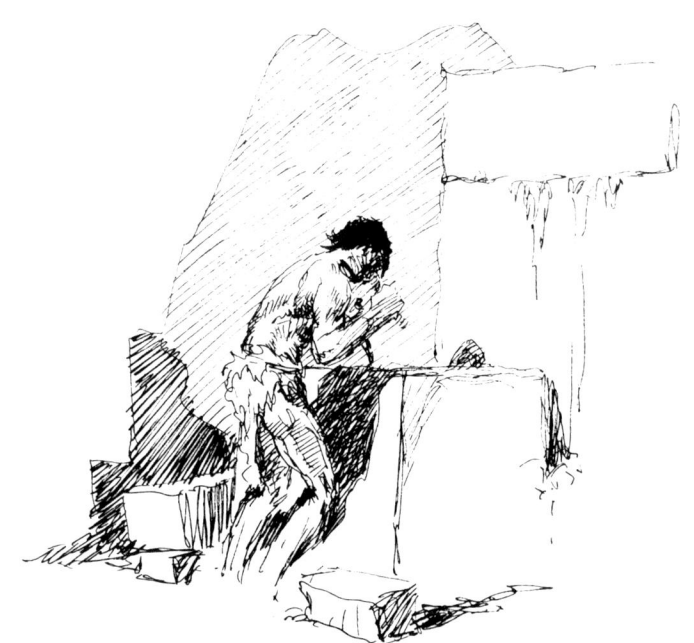

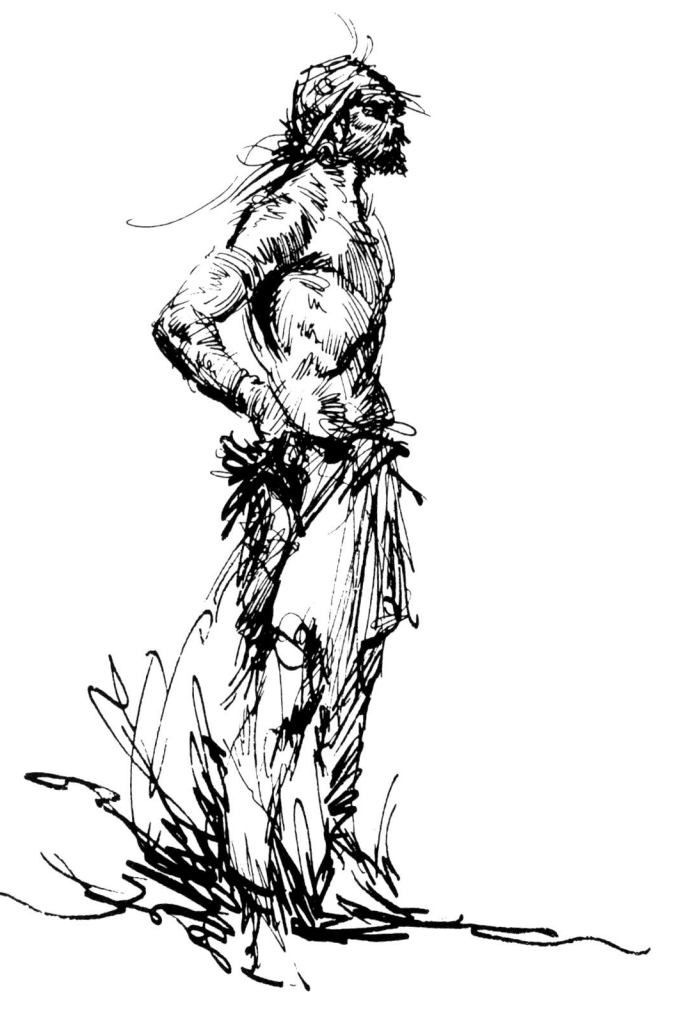

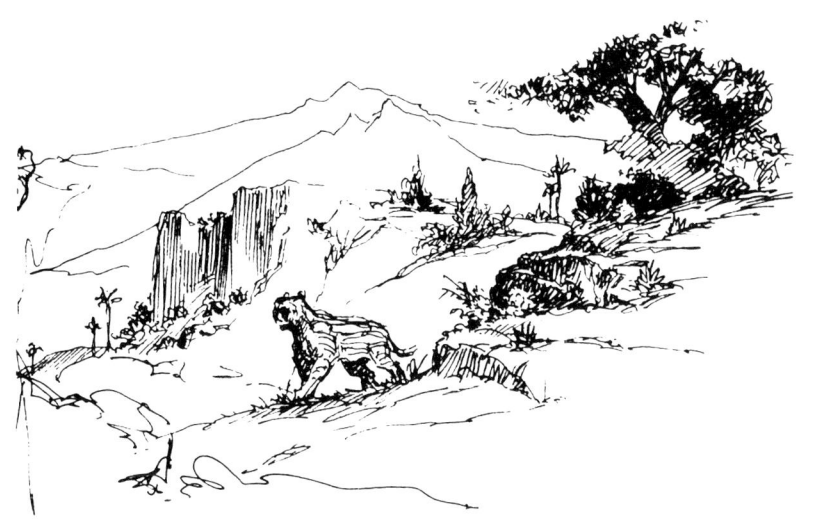

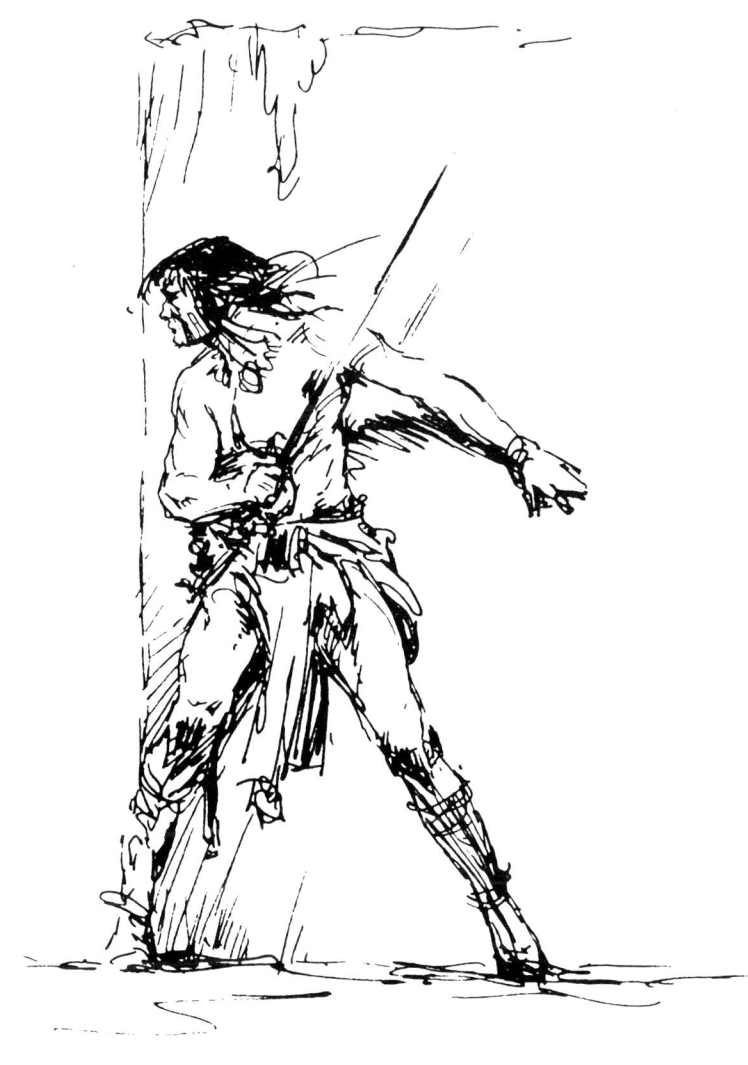

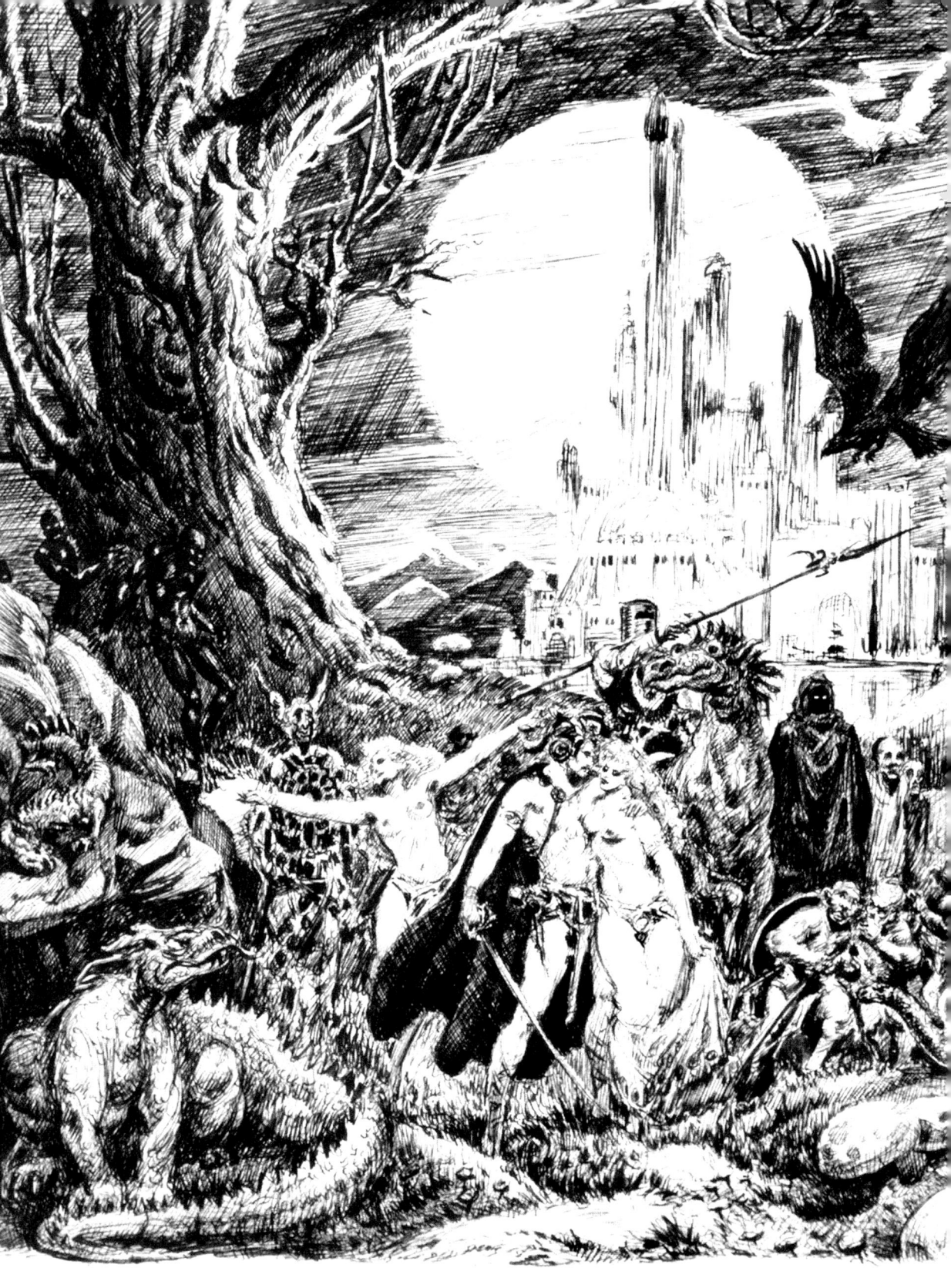

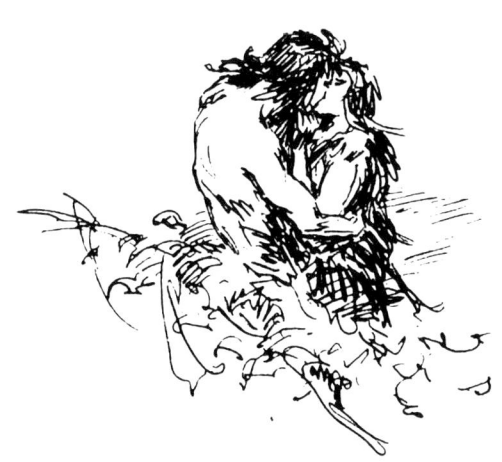

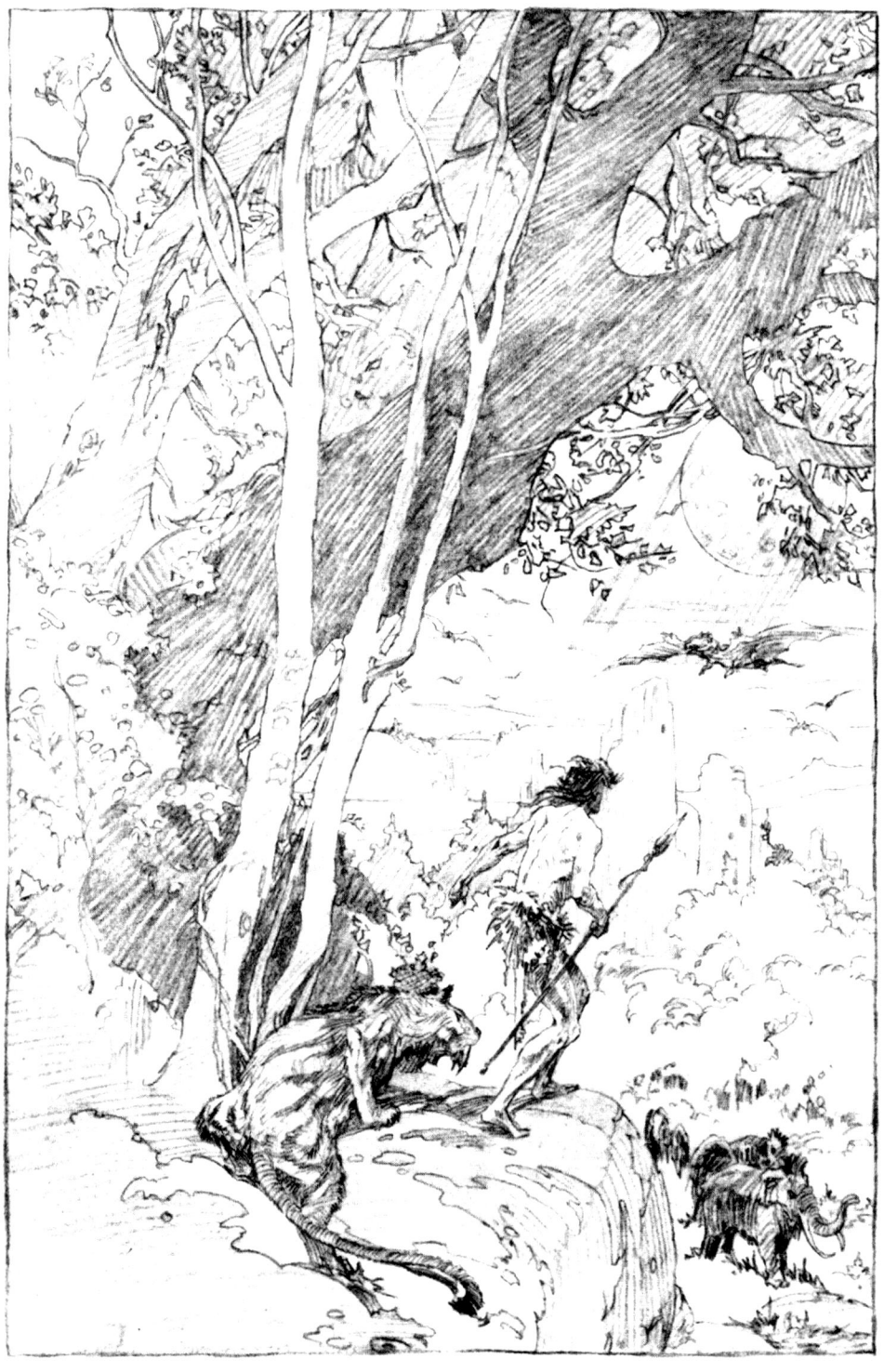

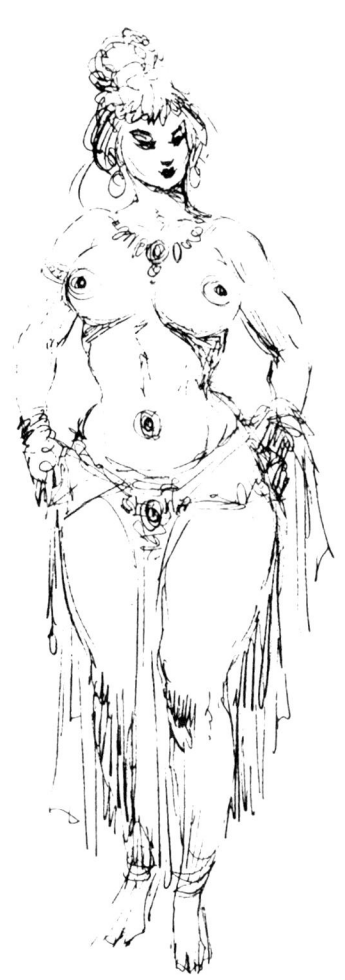

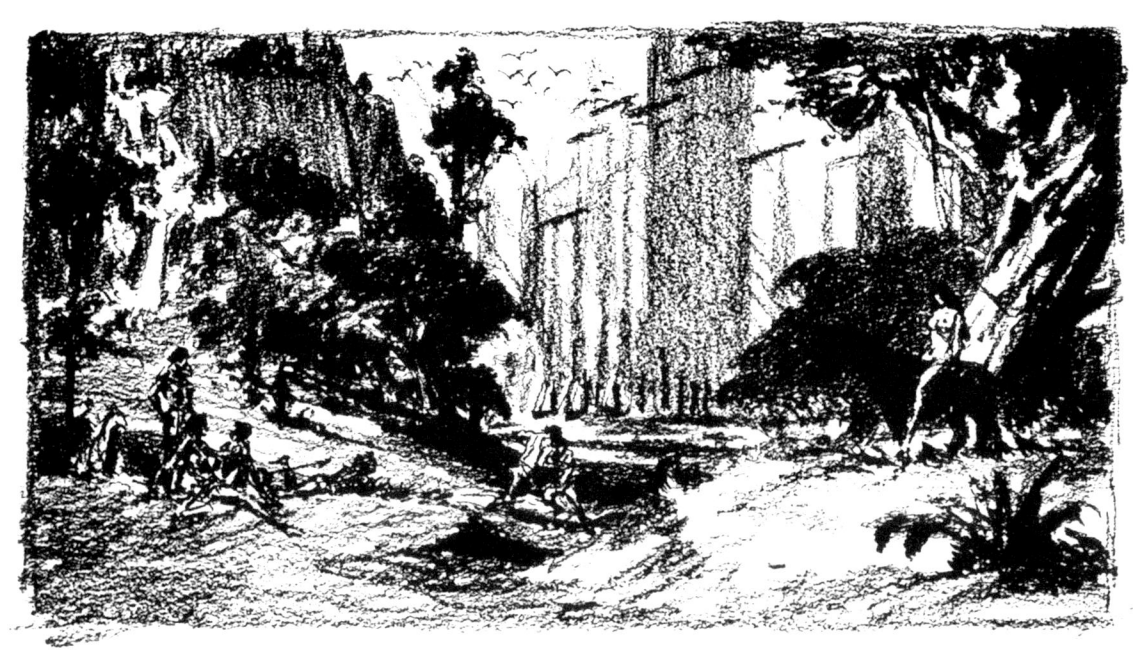

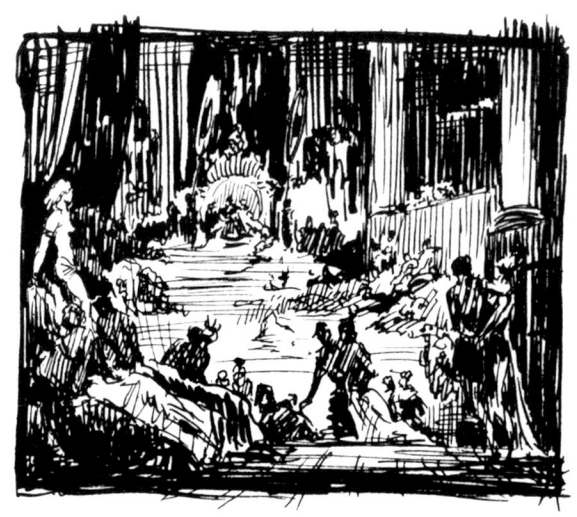

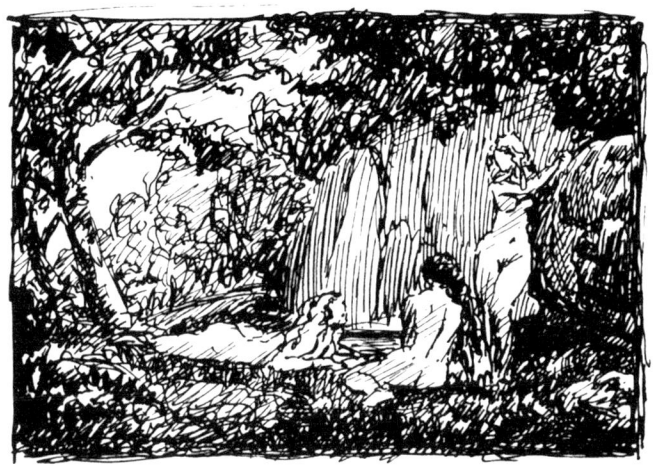

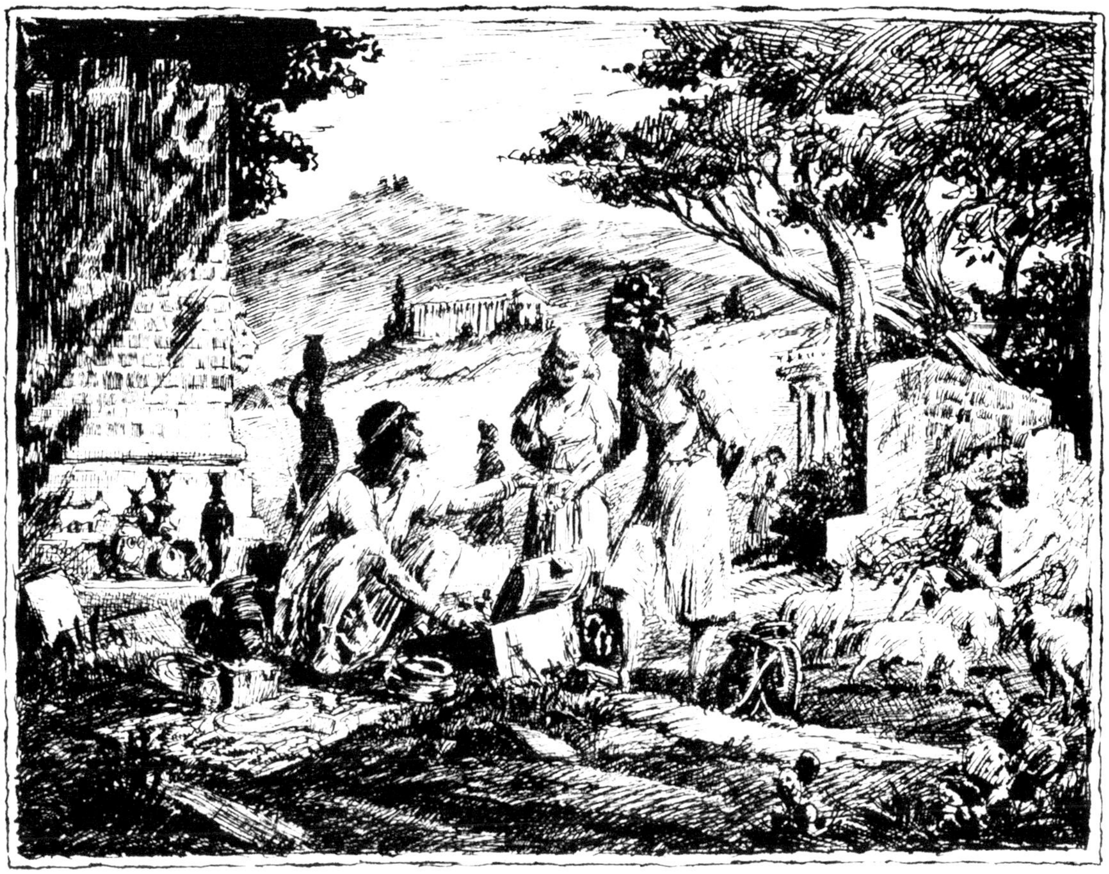

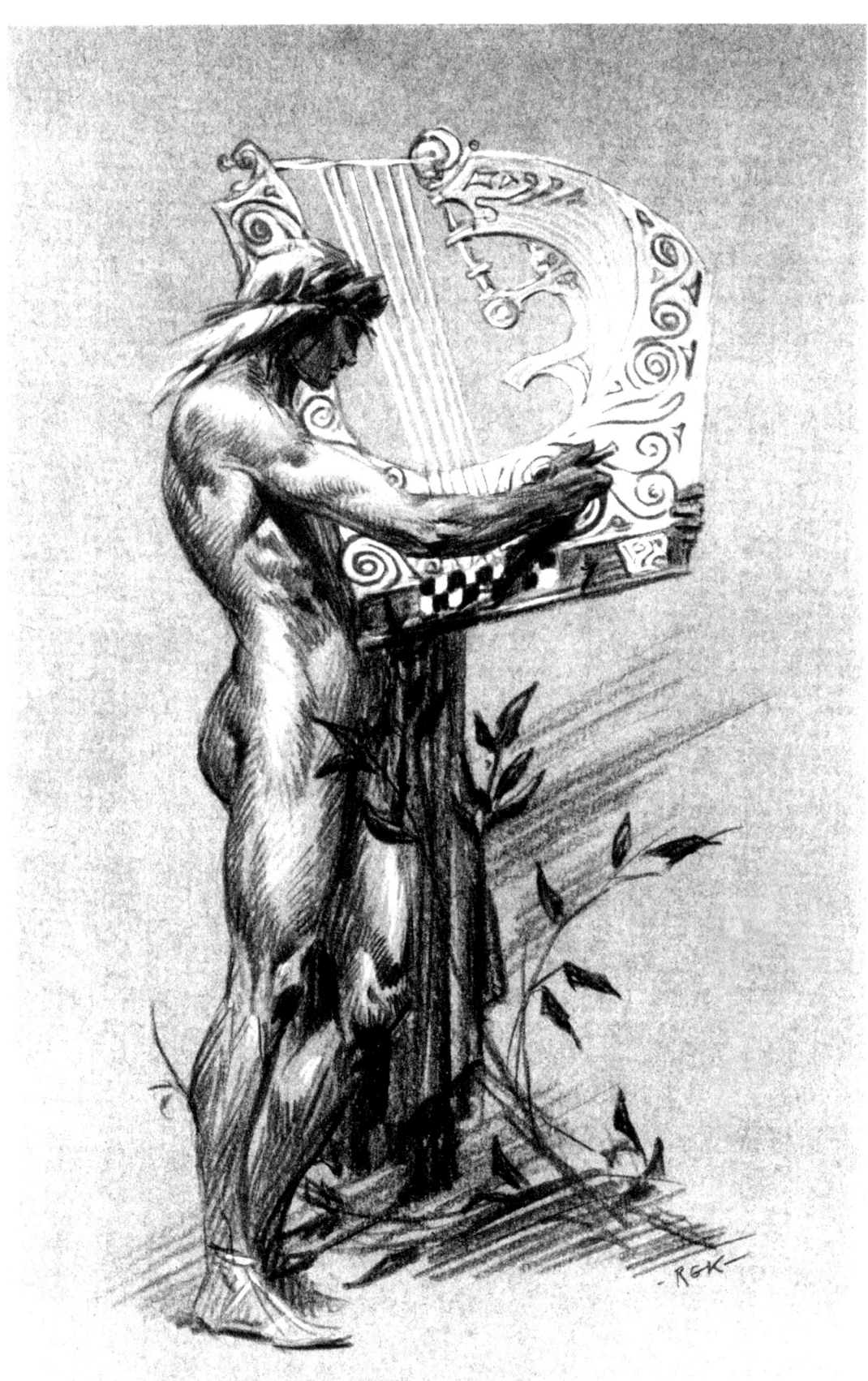

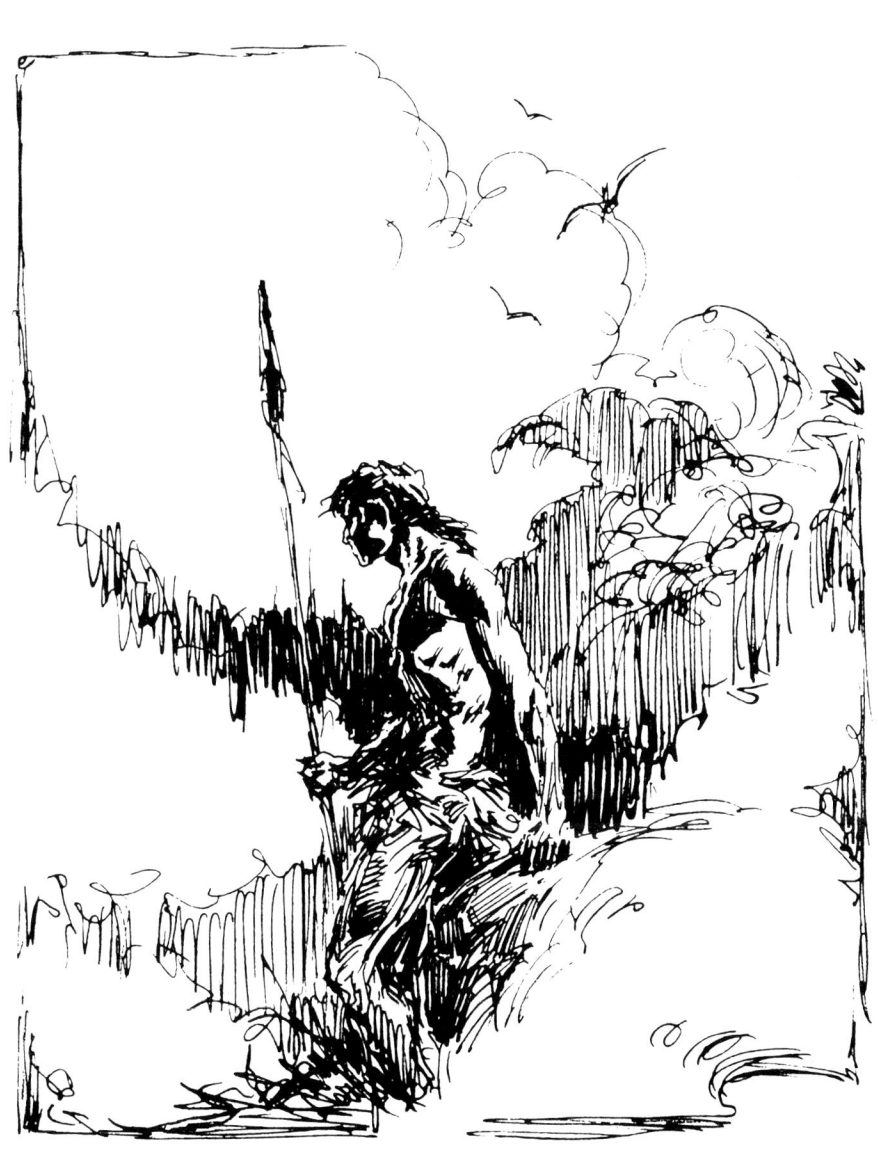

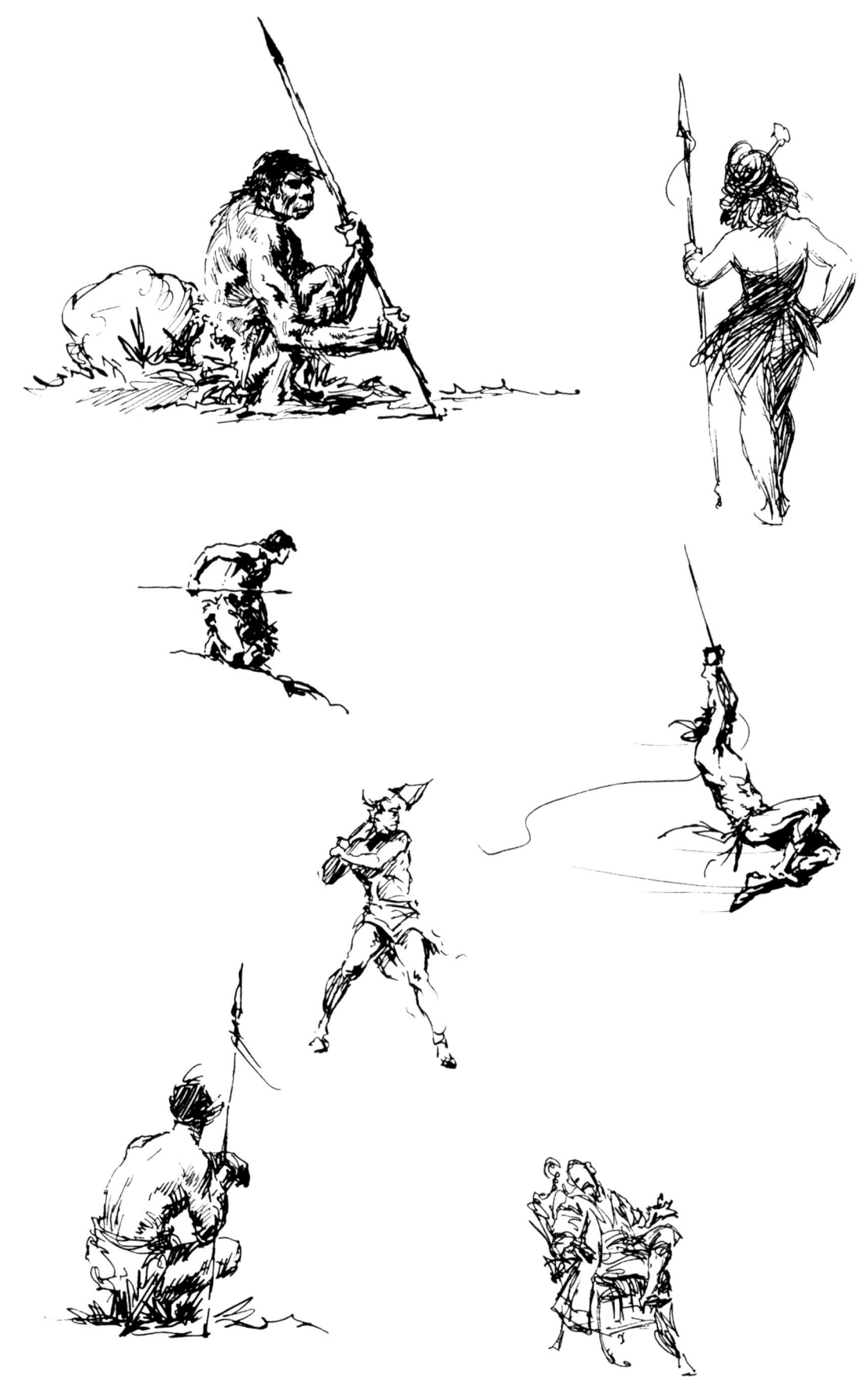

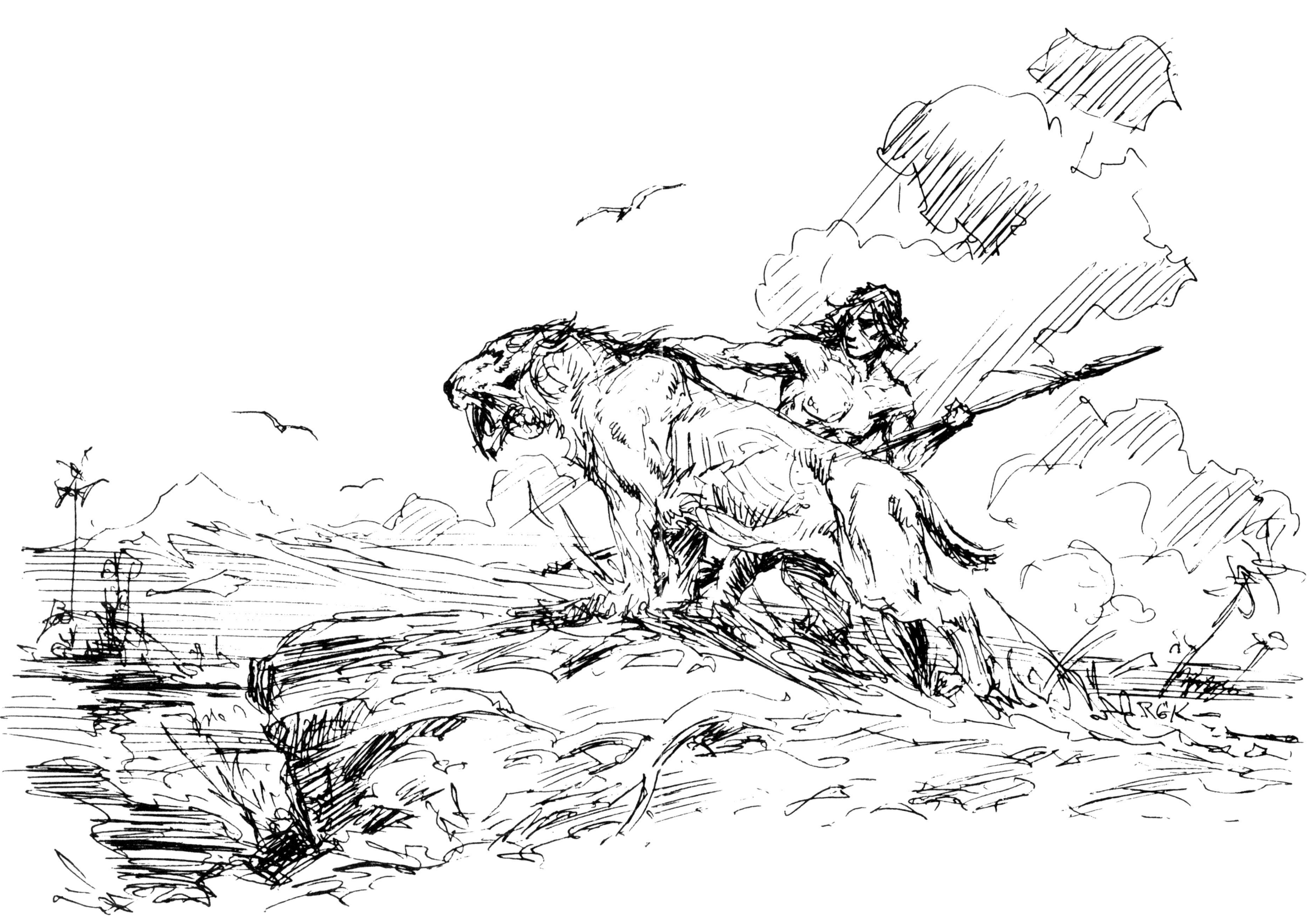

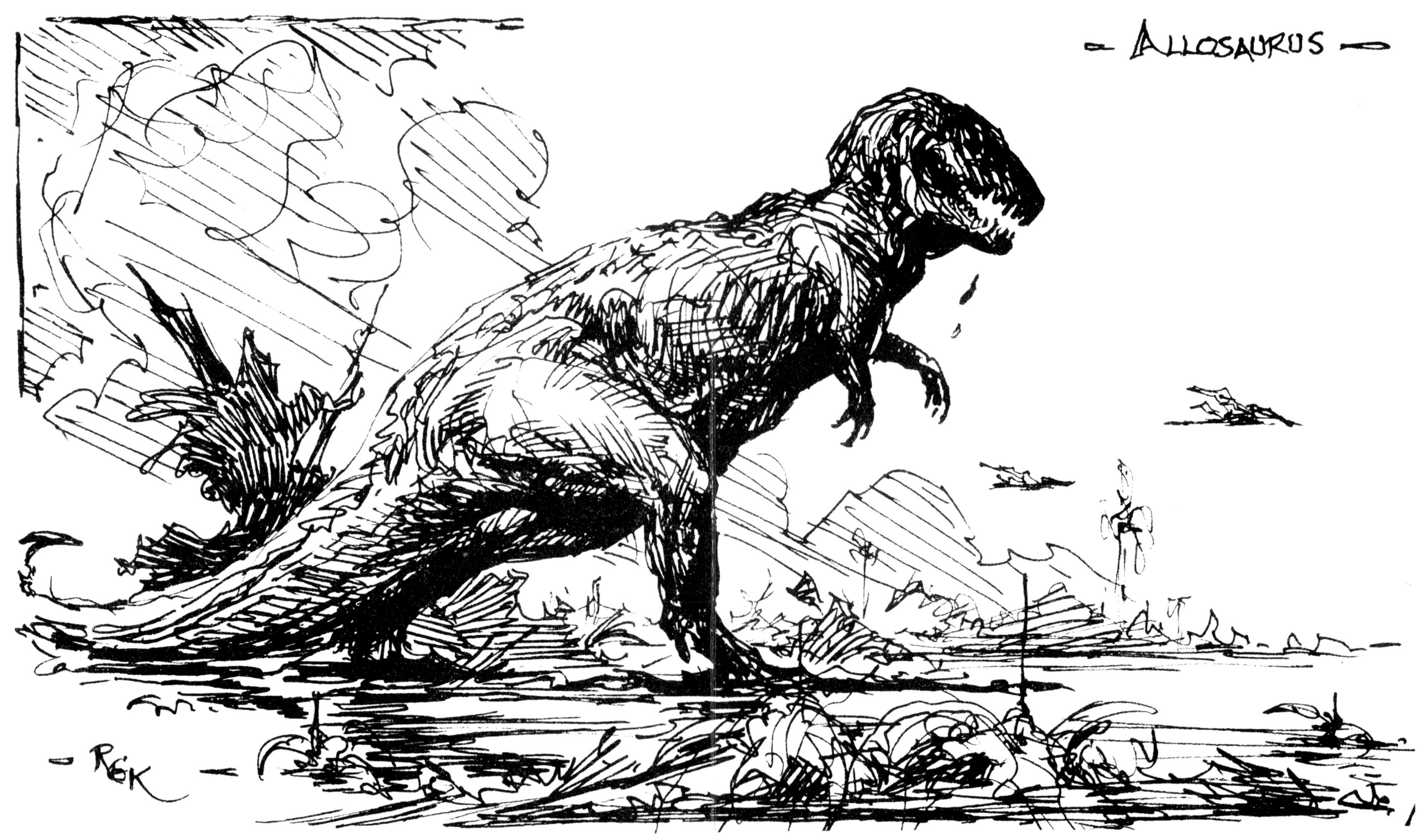

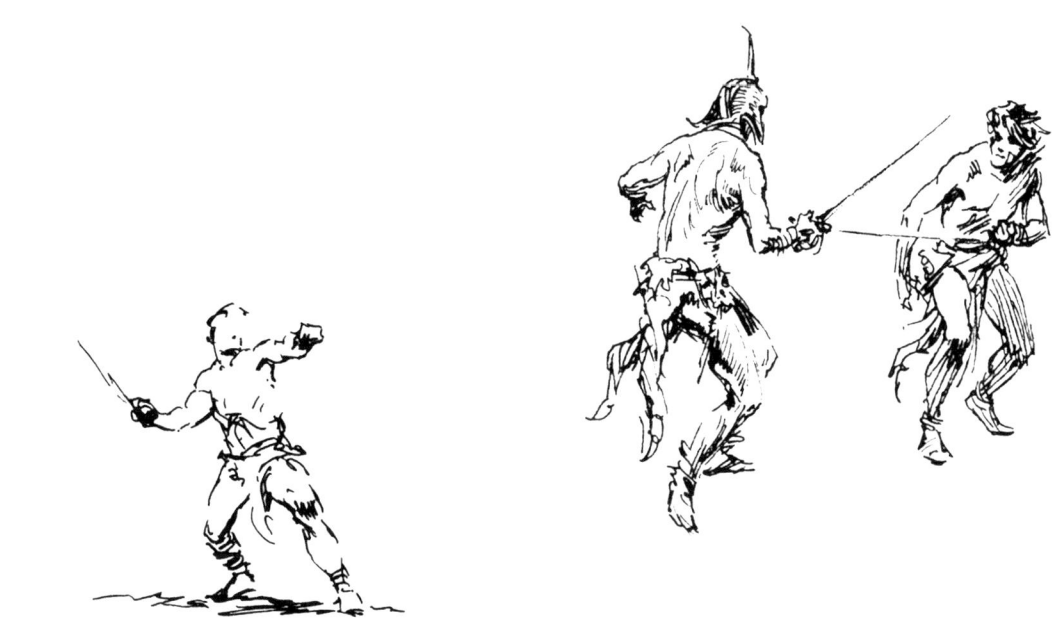

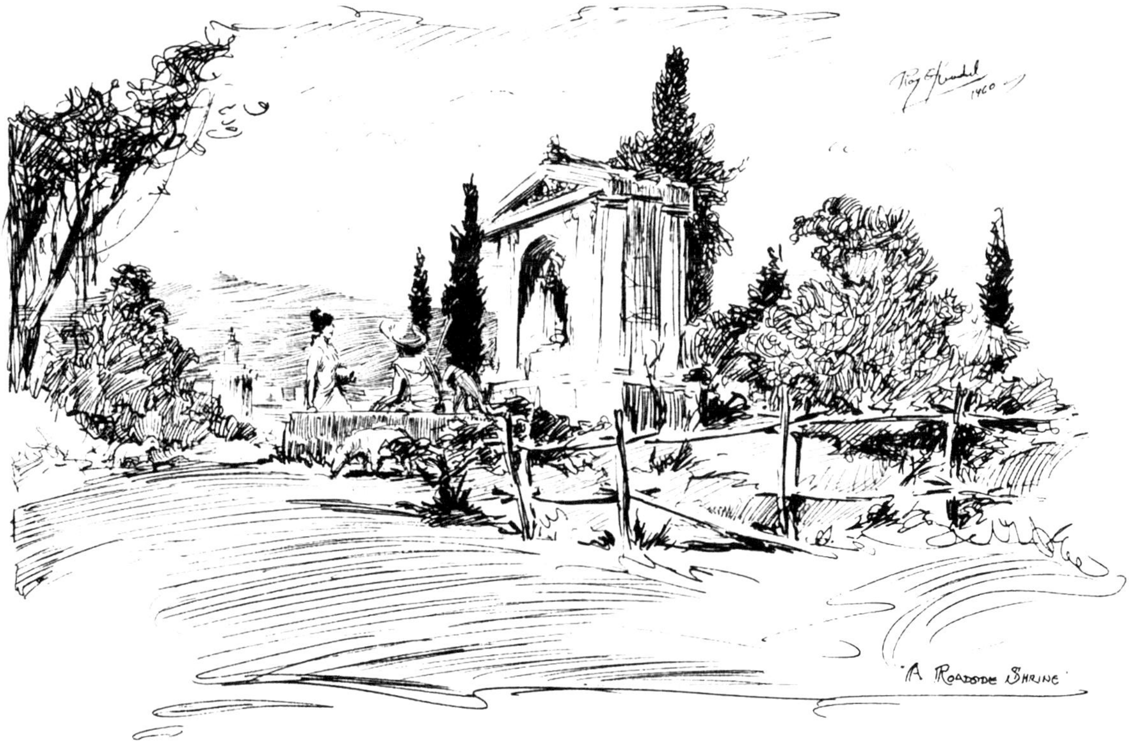

"A Roadside Shrine"

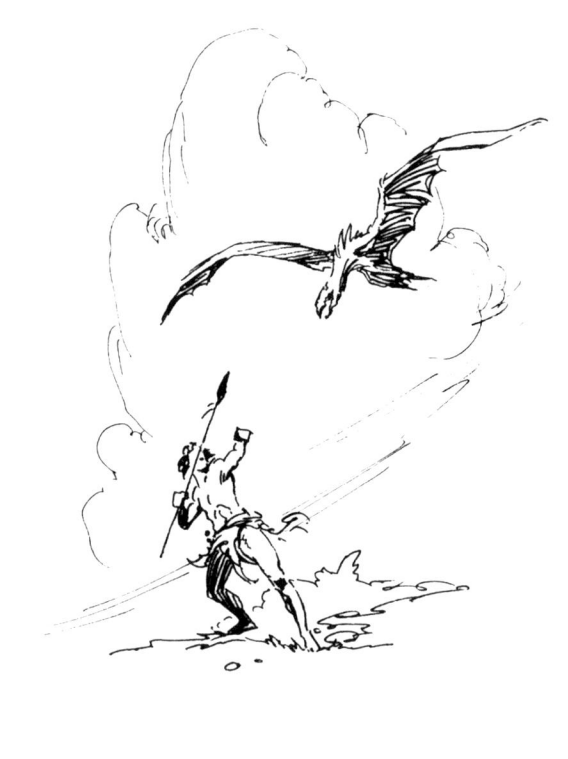

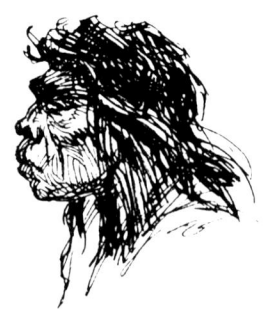

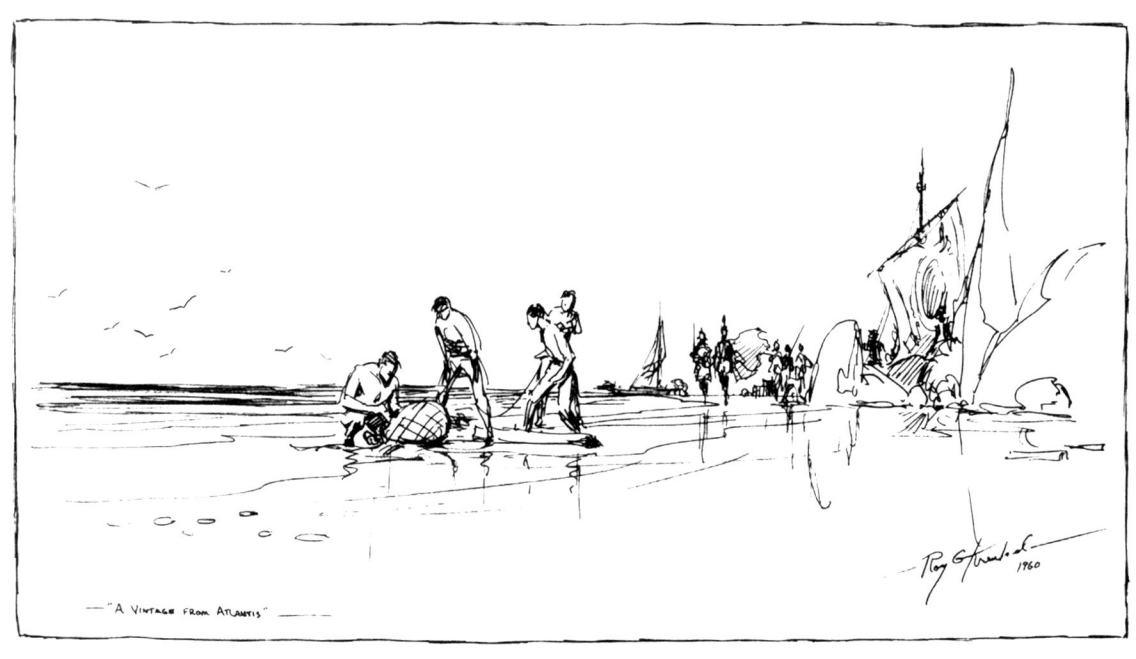

"A Vintage from Atlantis"

Roy G. Krenkel
1960

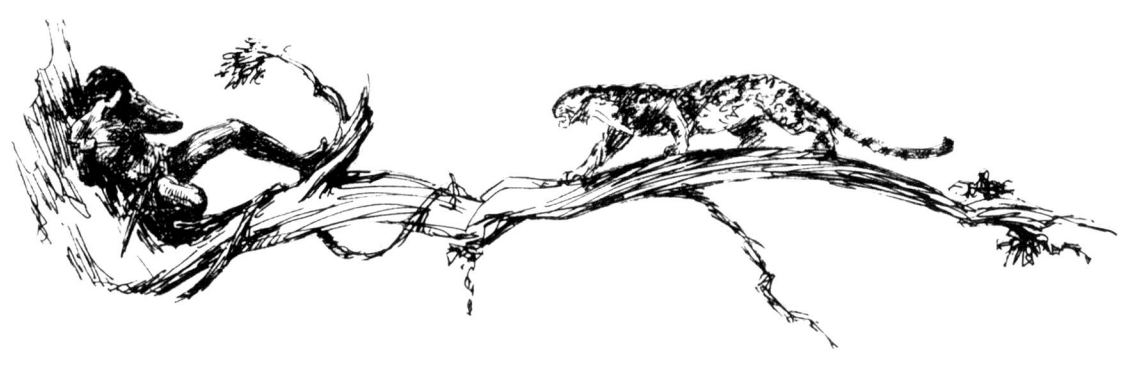

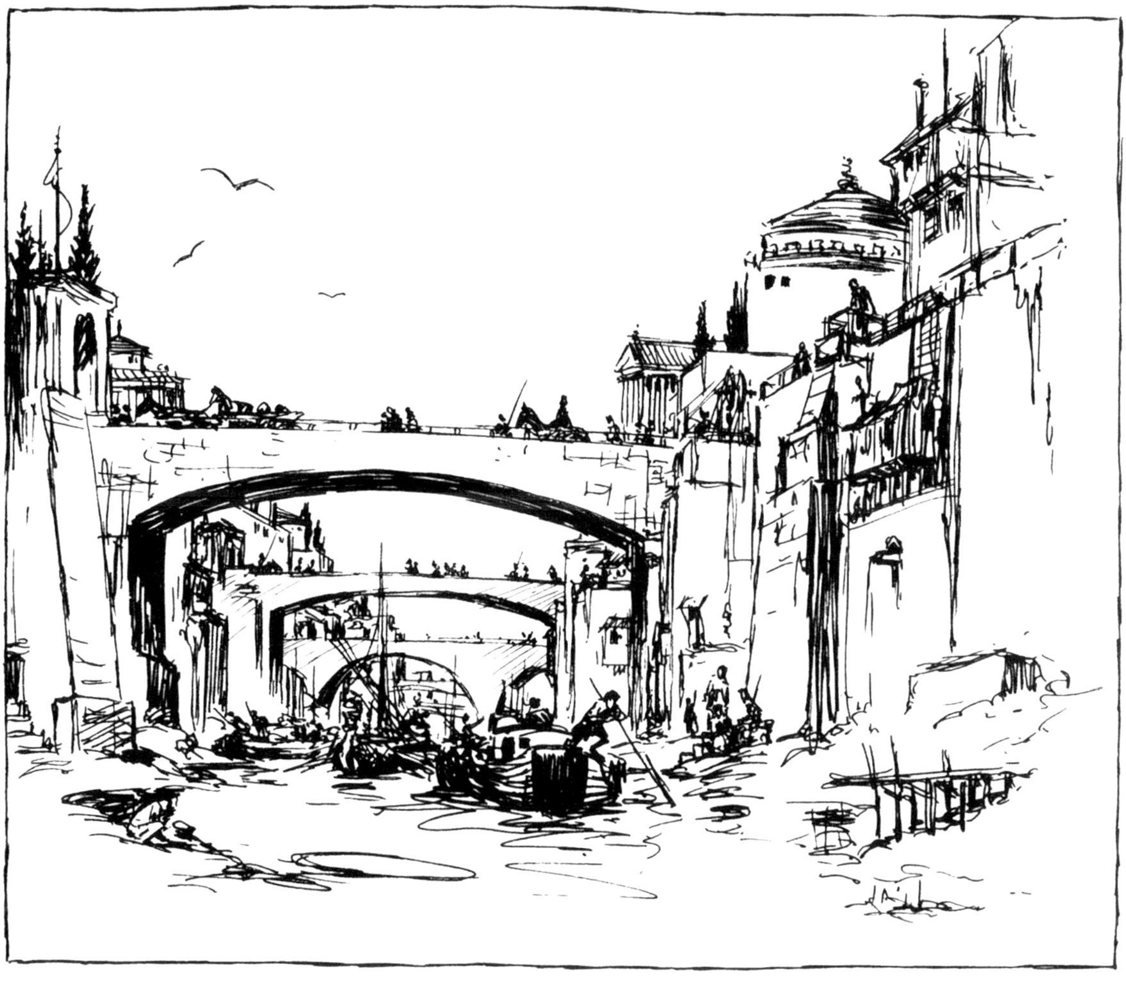

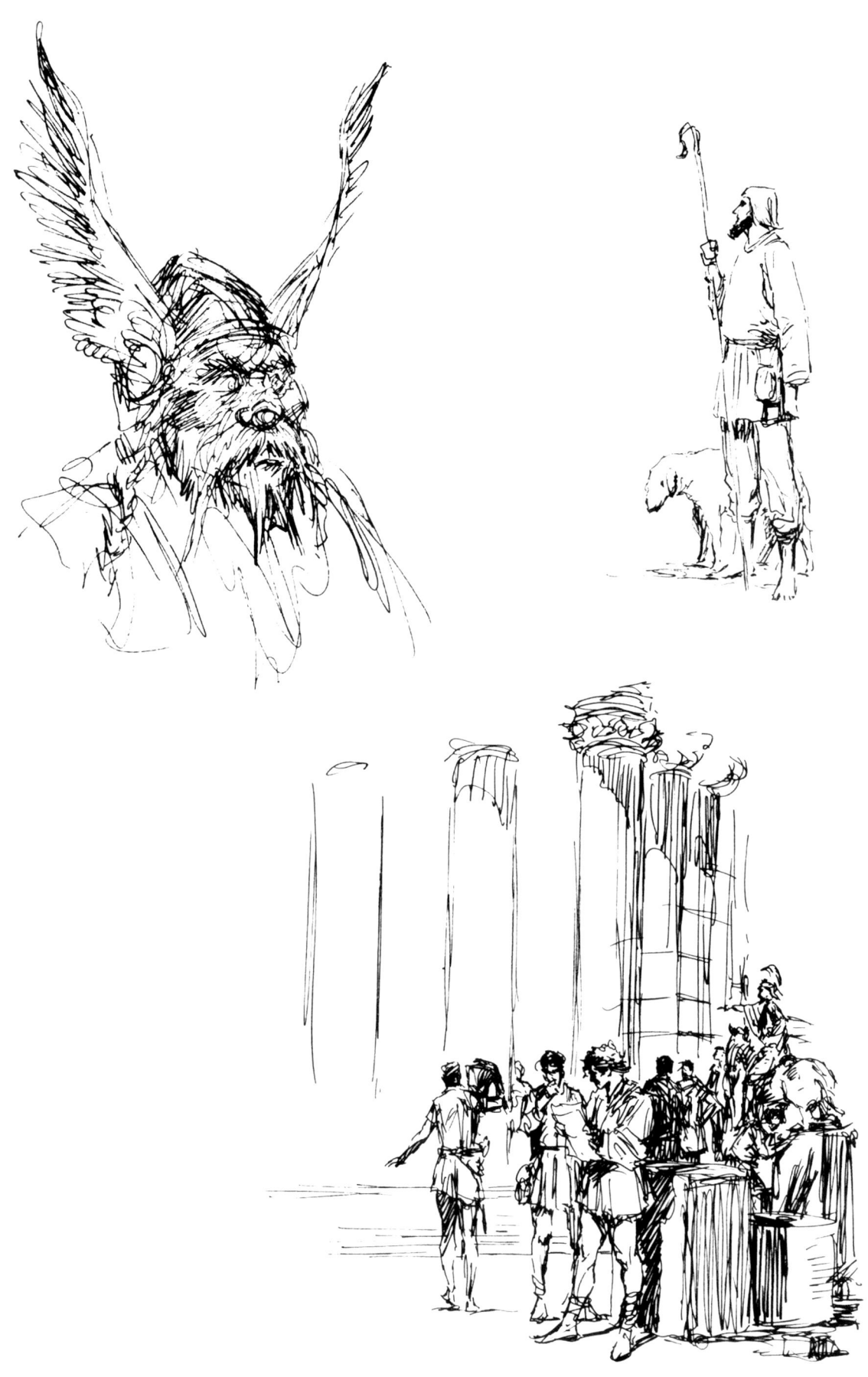

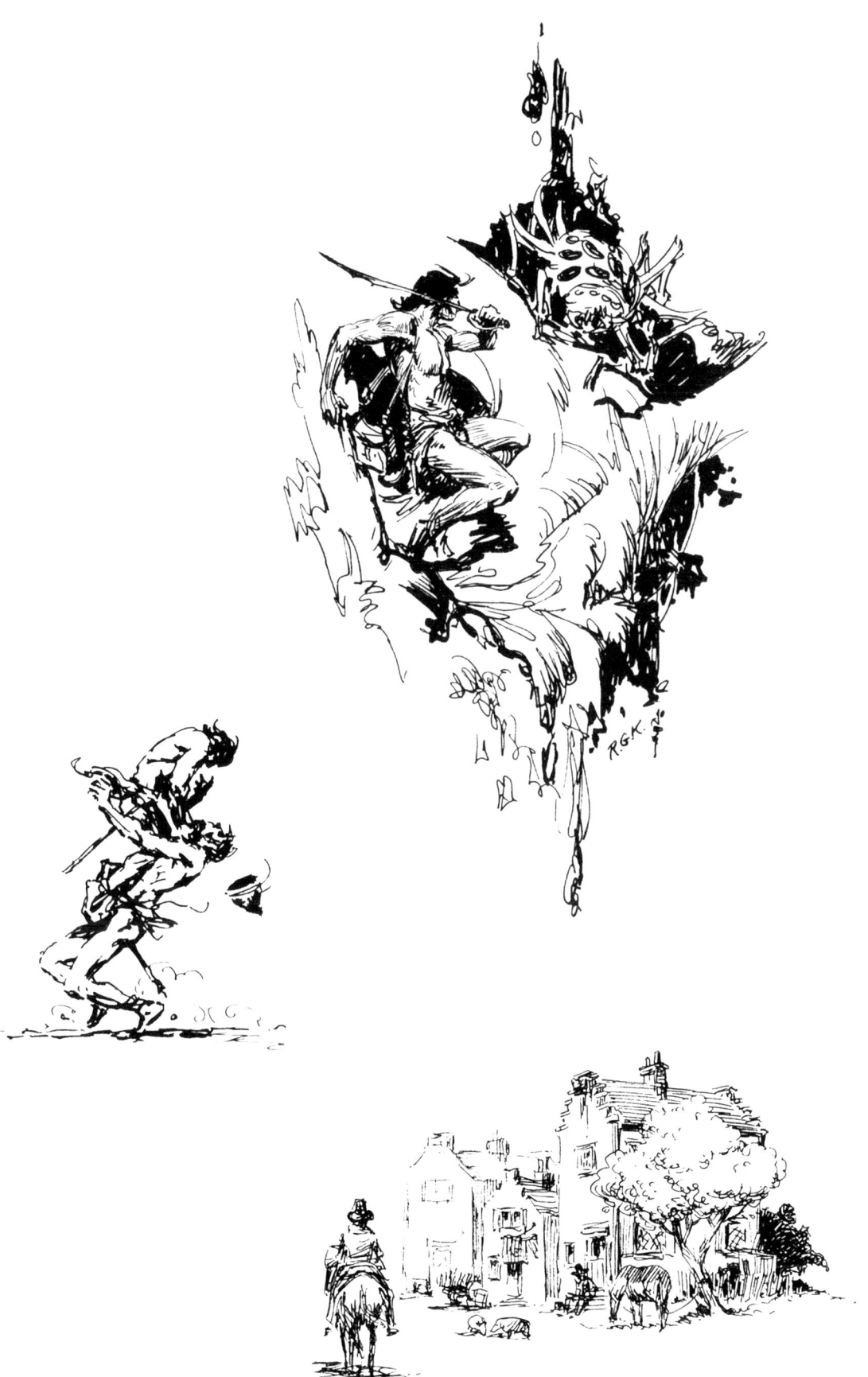

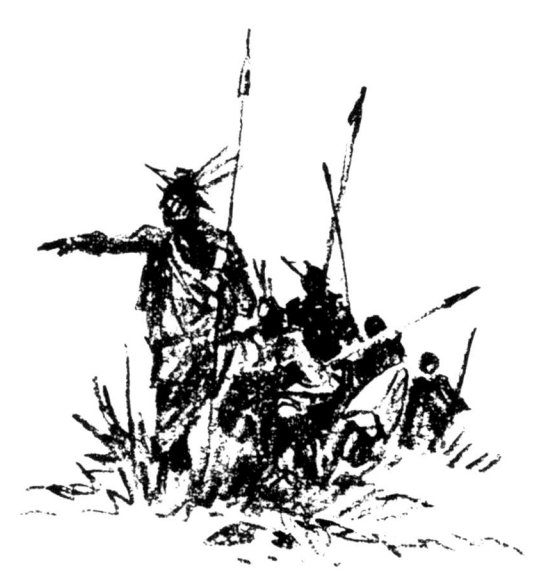

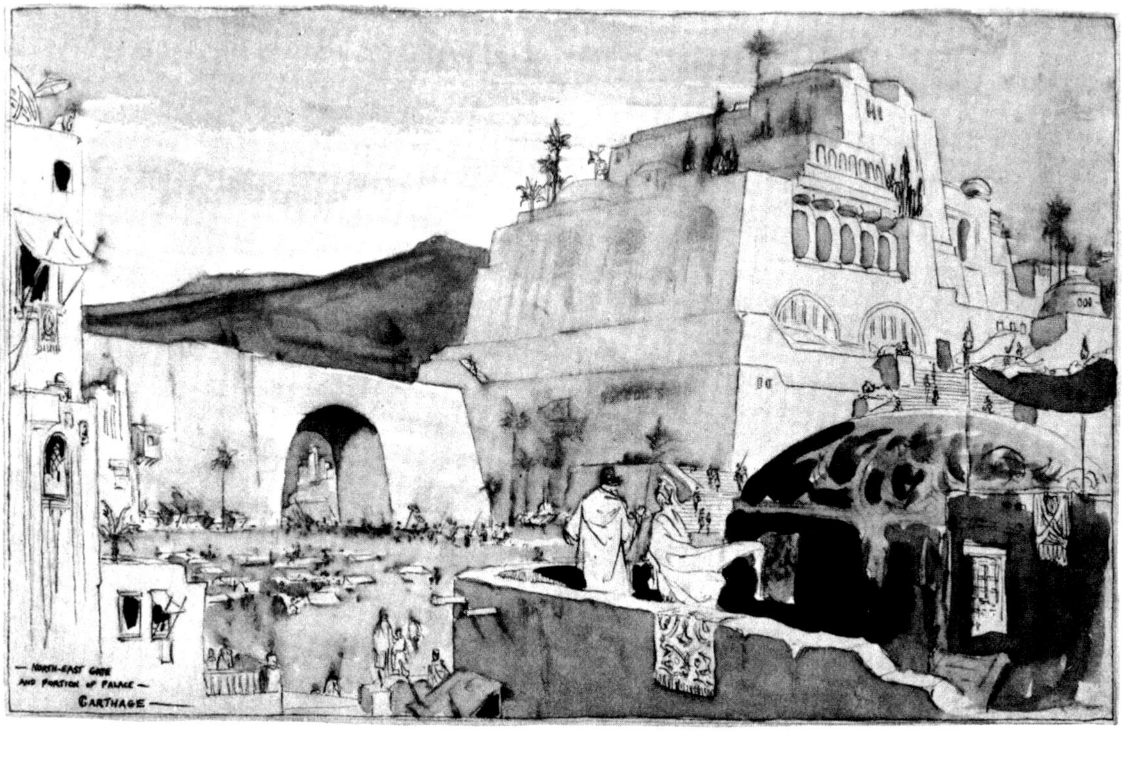

NORTH-EAST GATE
AND PORTION OF PALACE —
CARTHAGE —

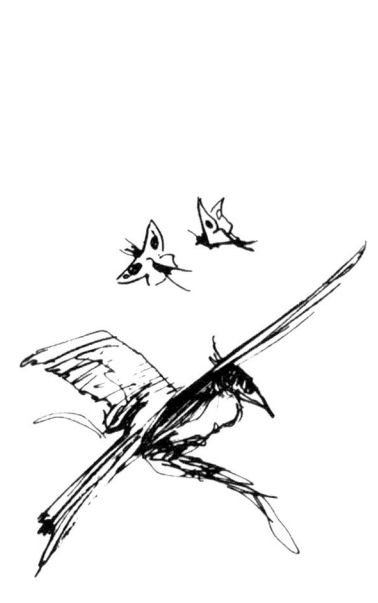

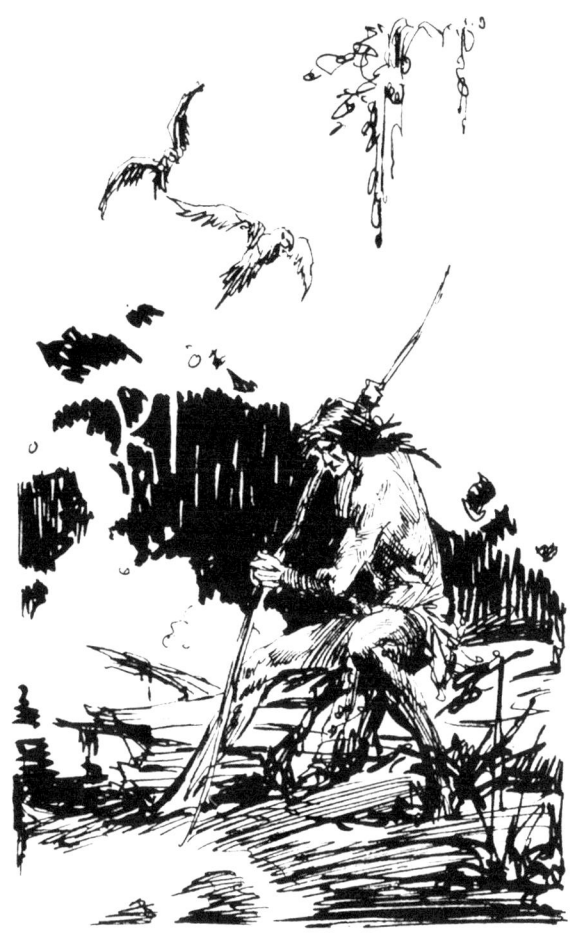

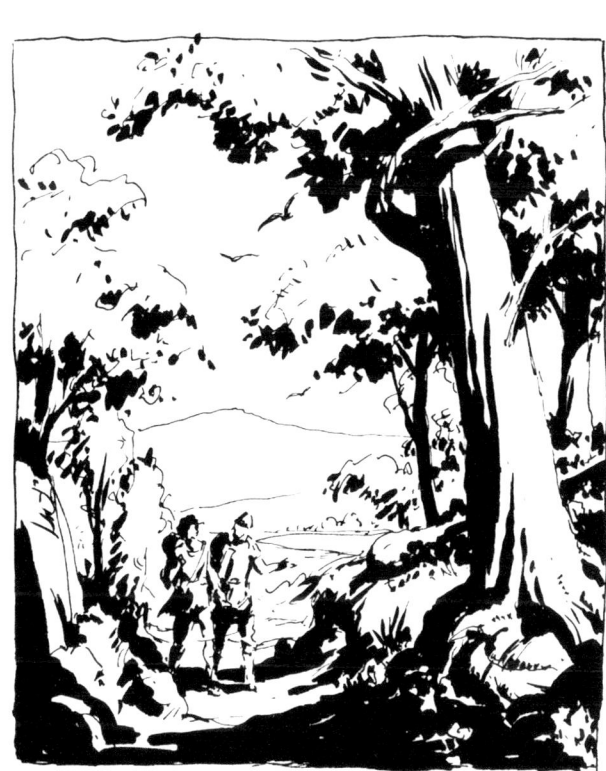

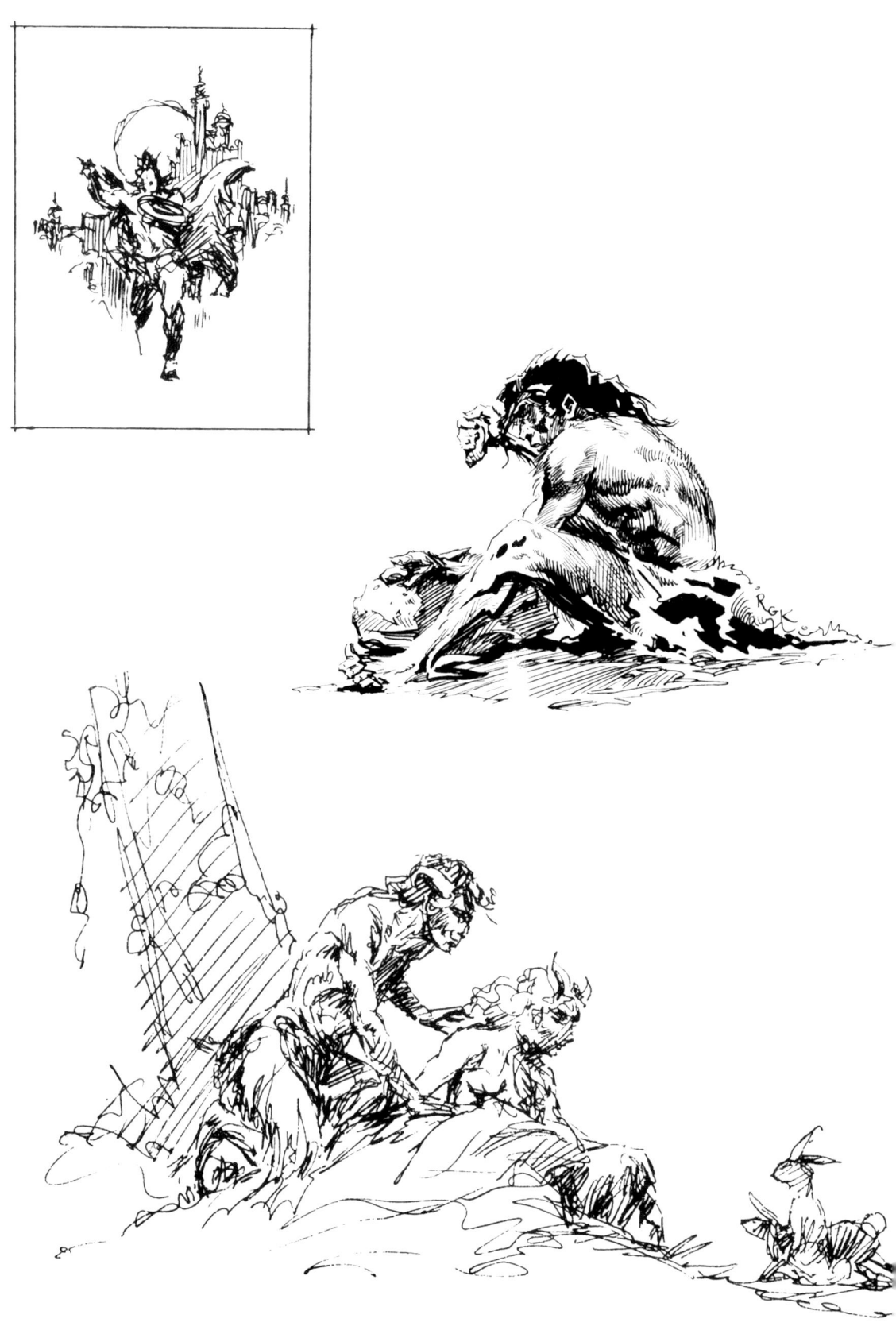

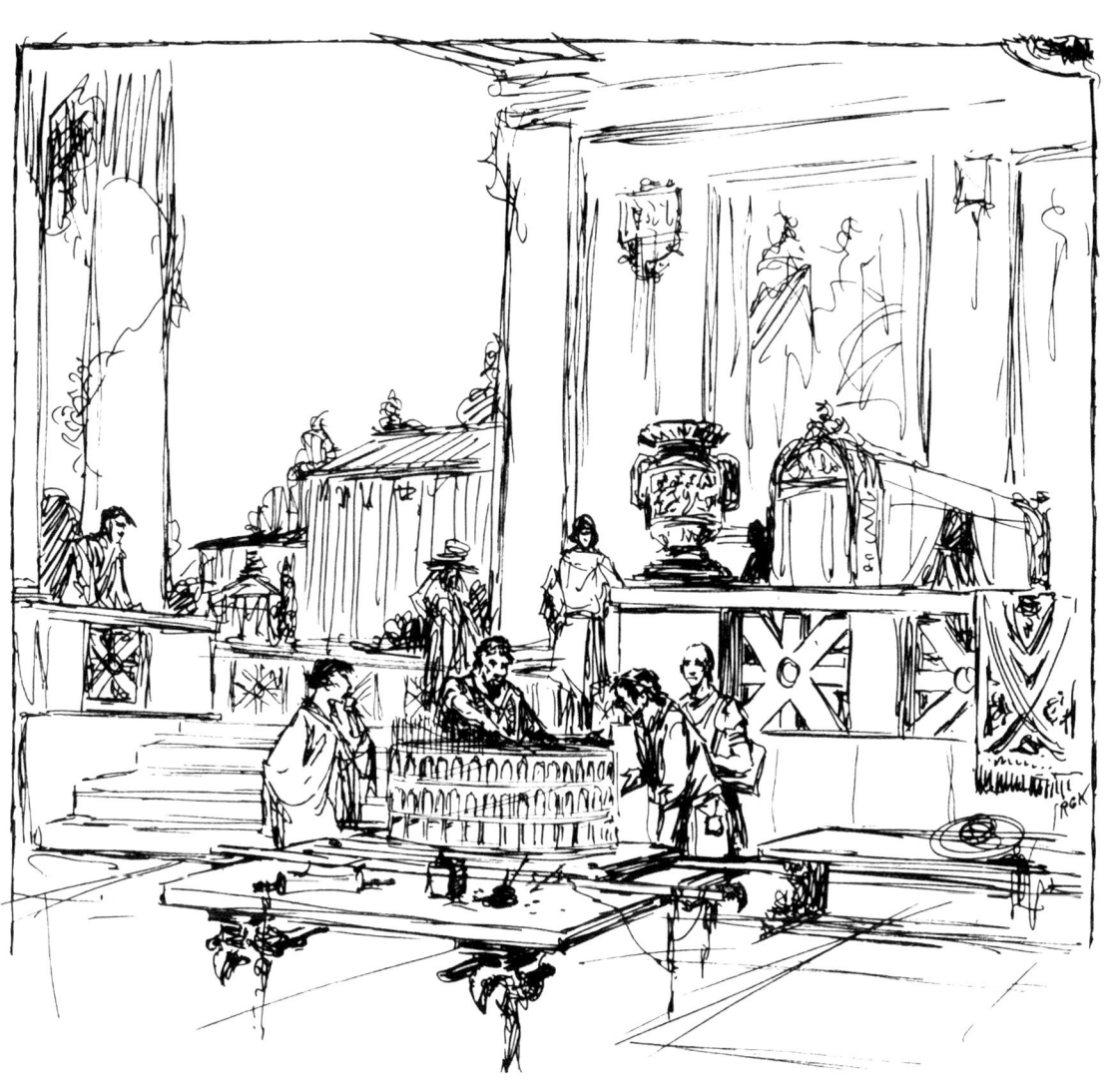

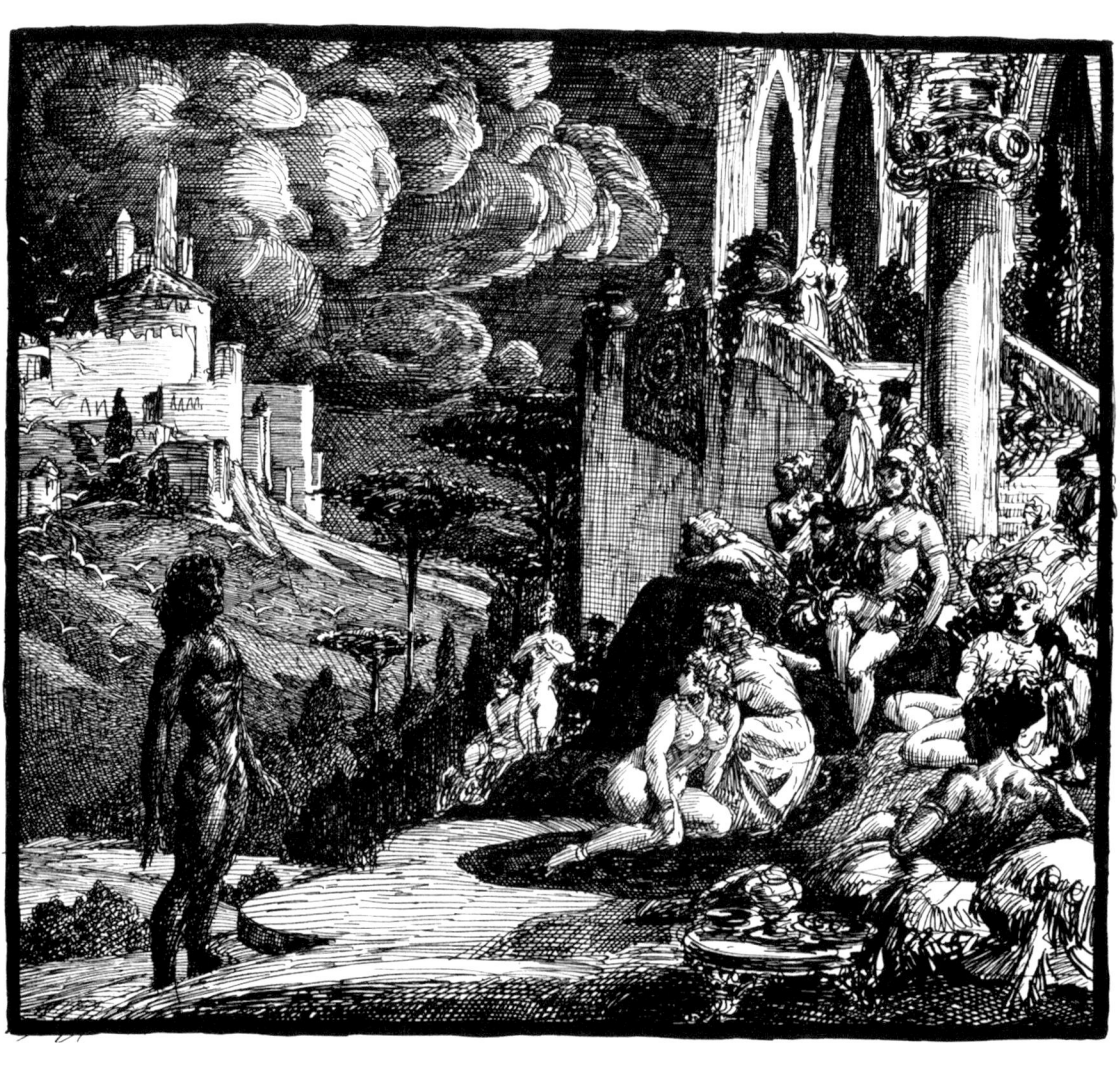

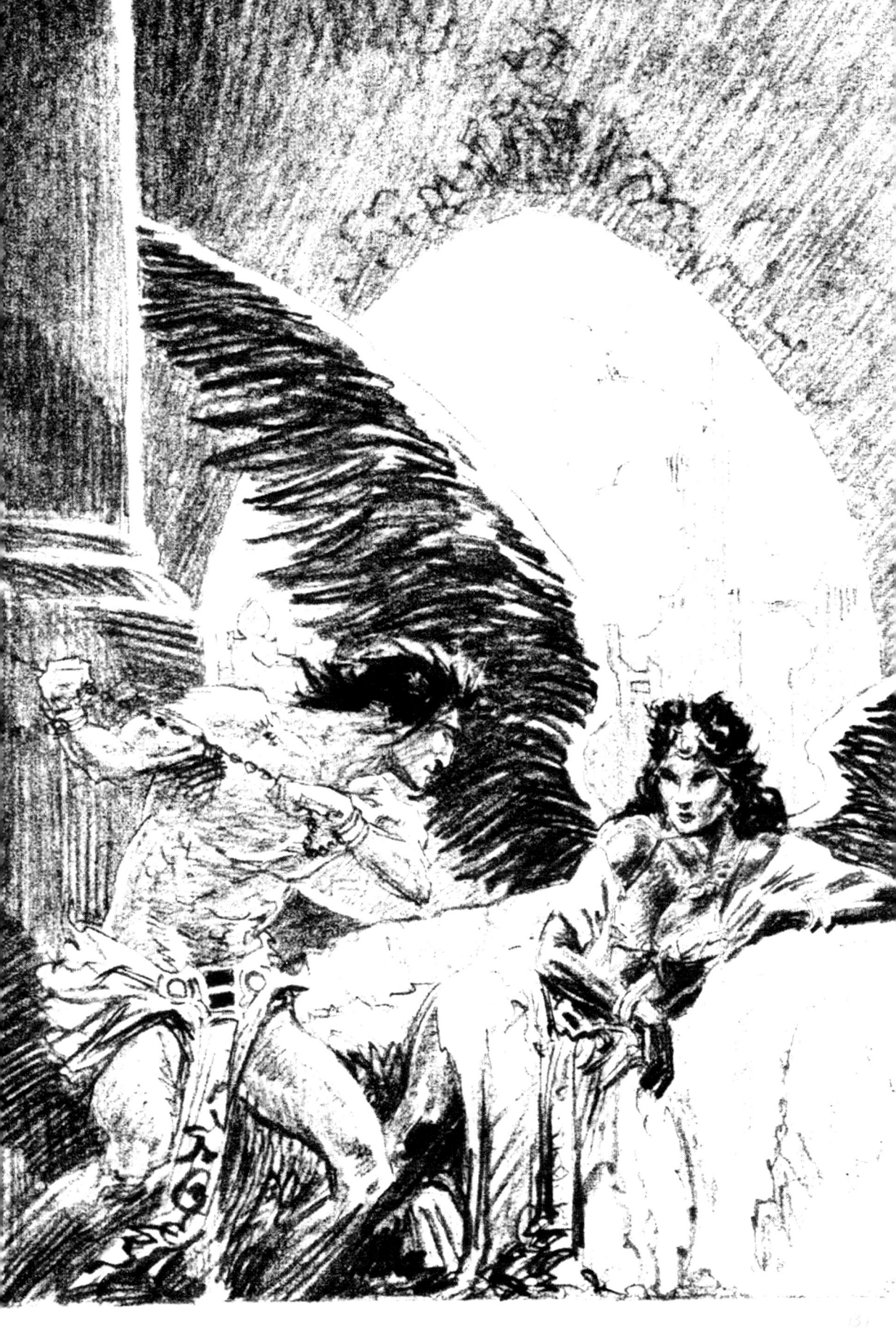

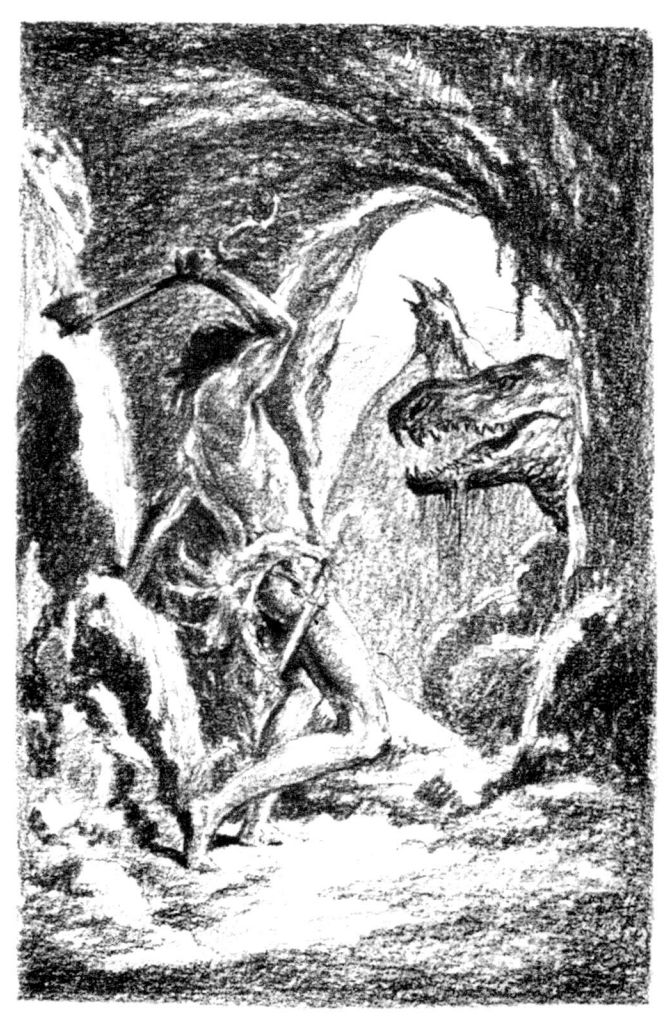

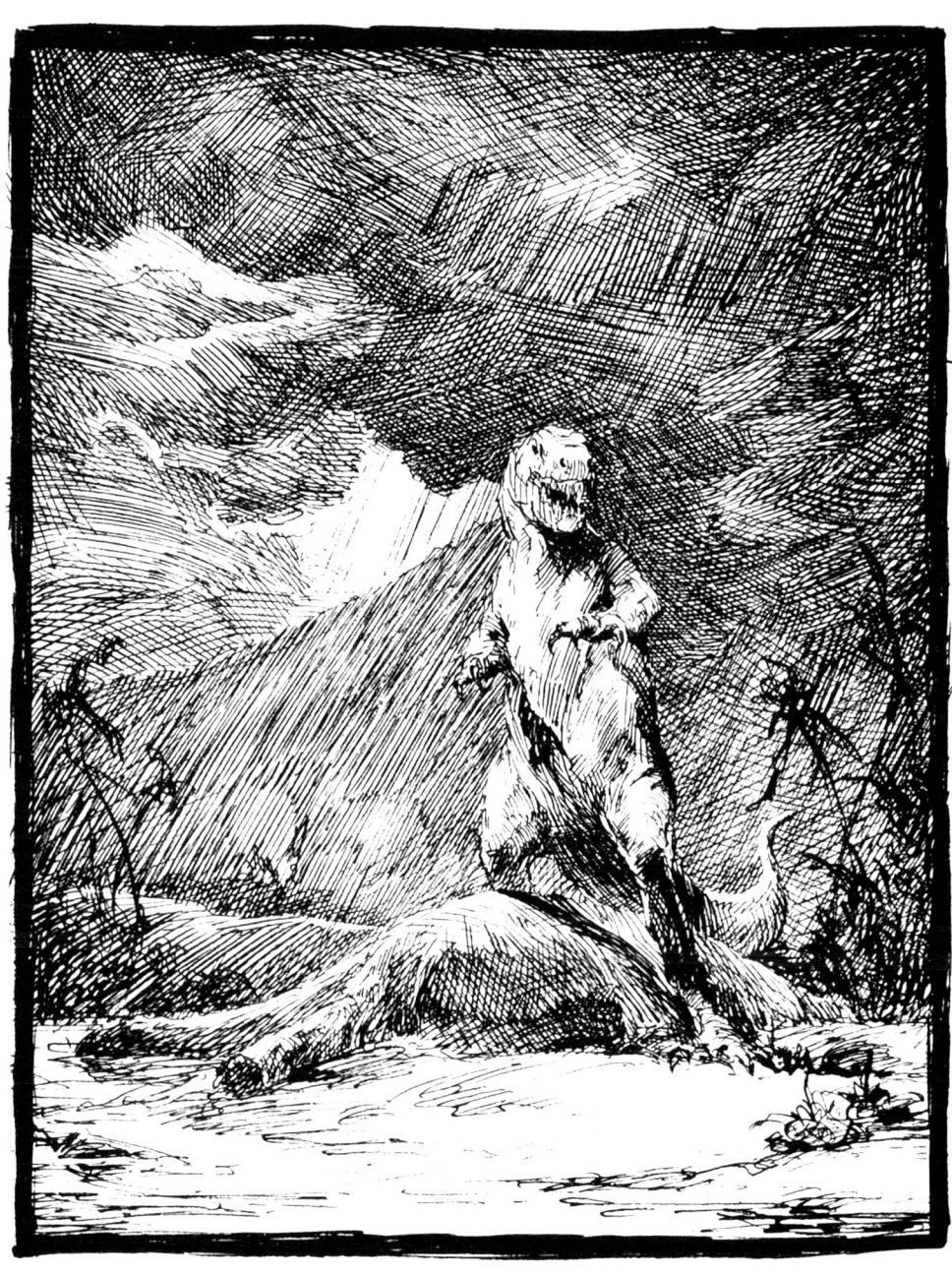

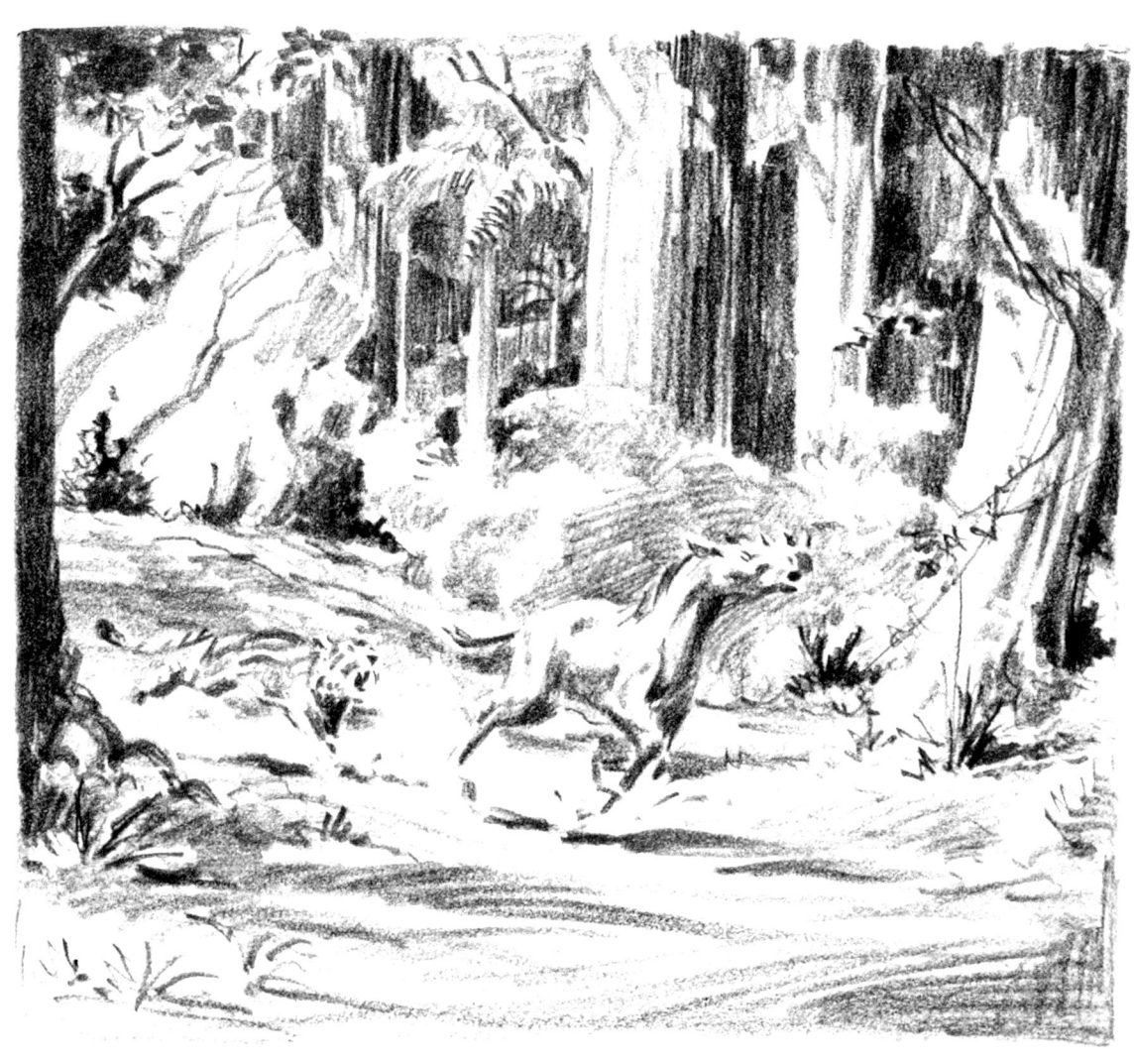

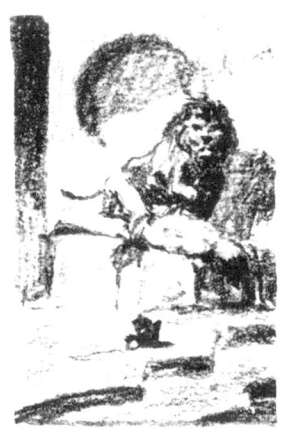

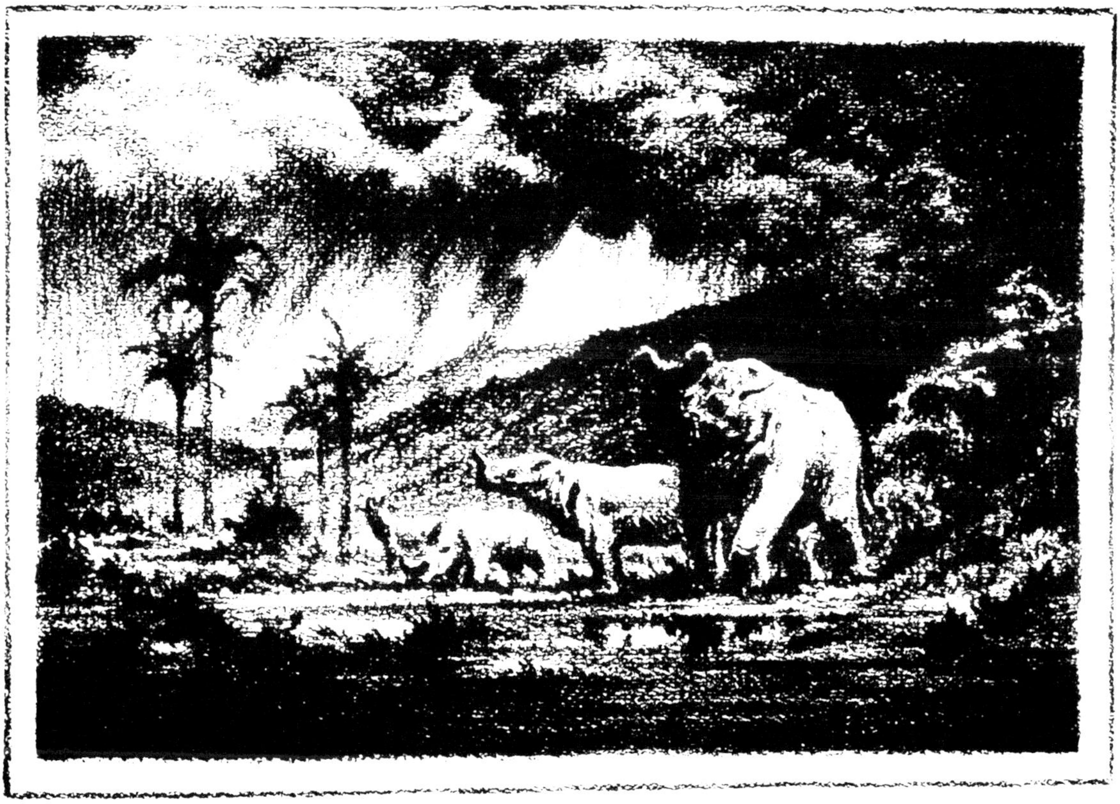

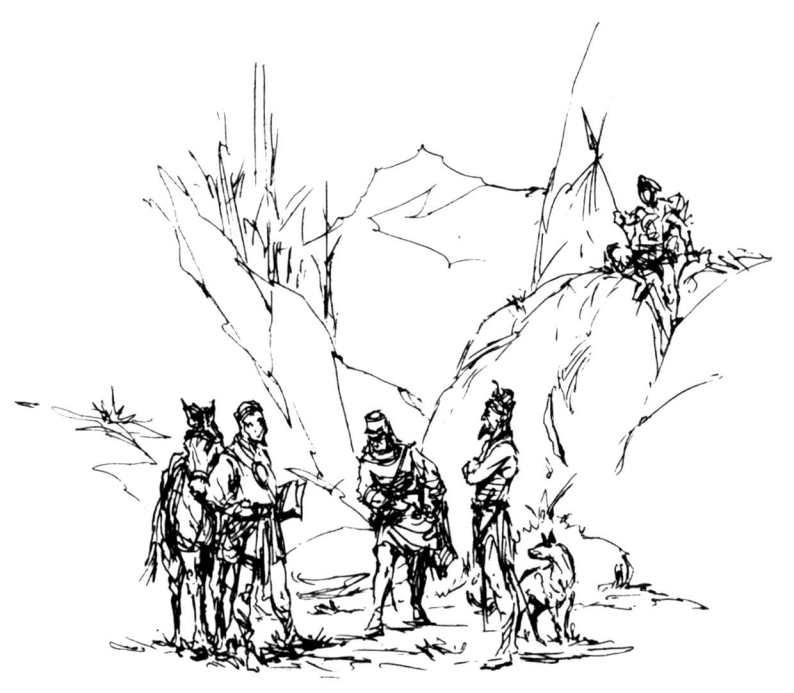

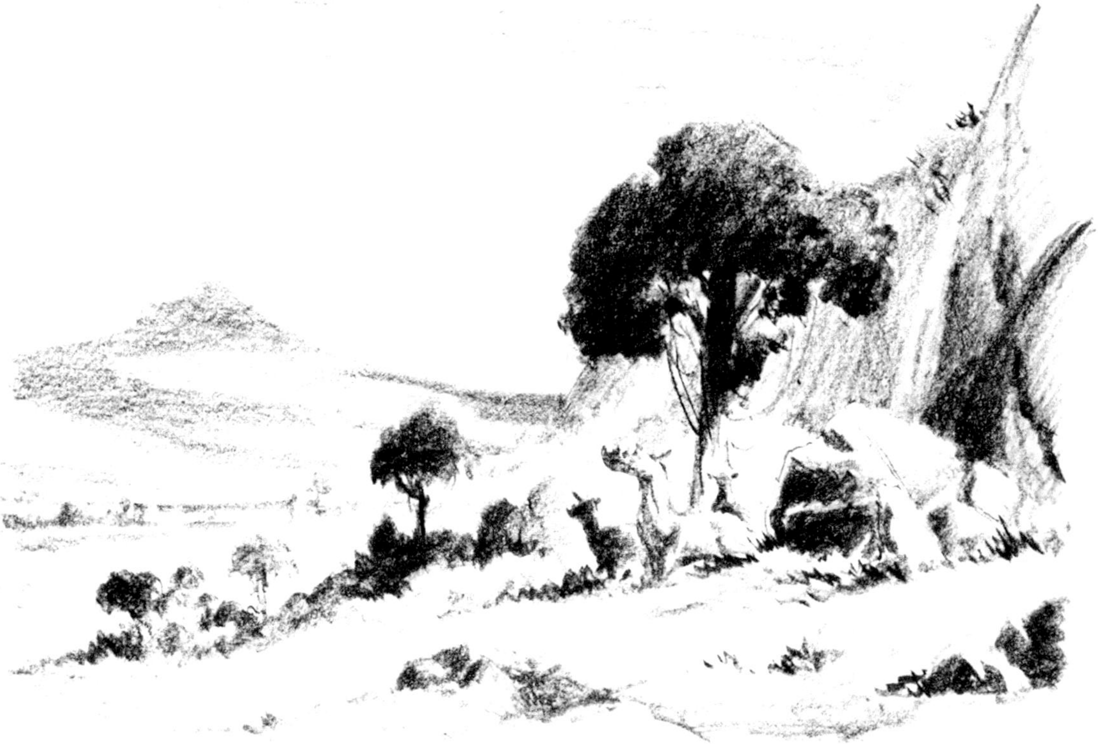

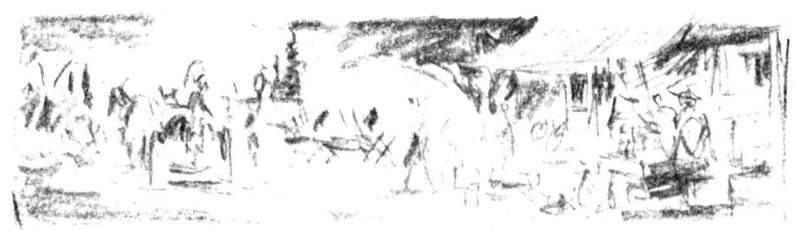

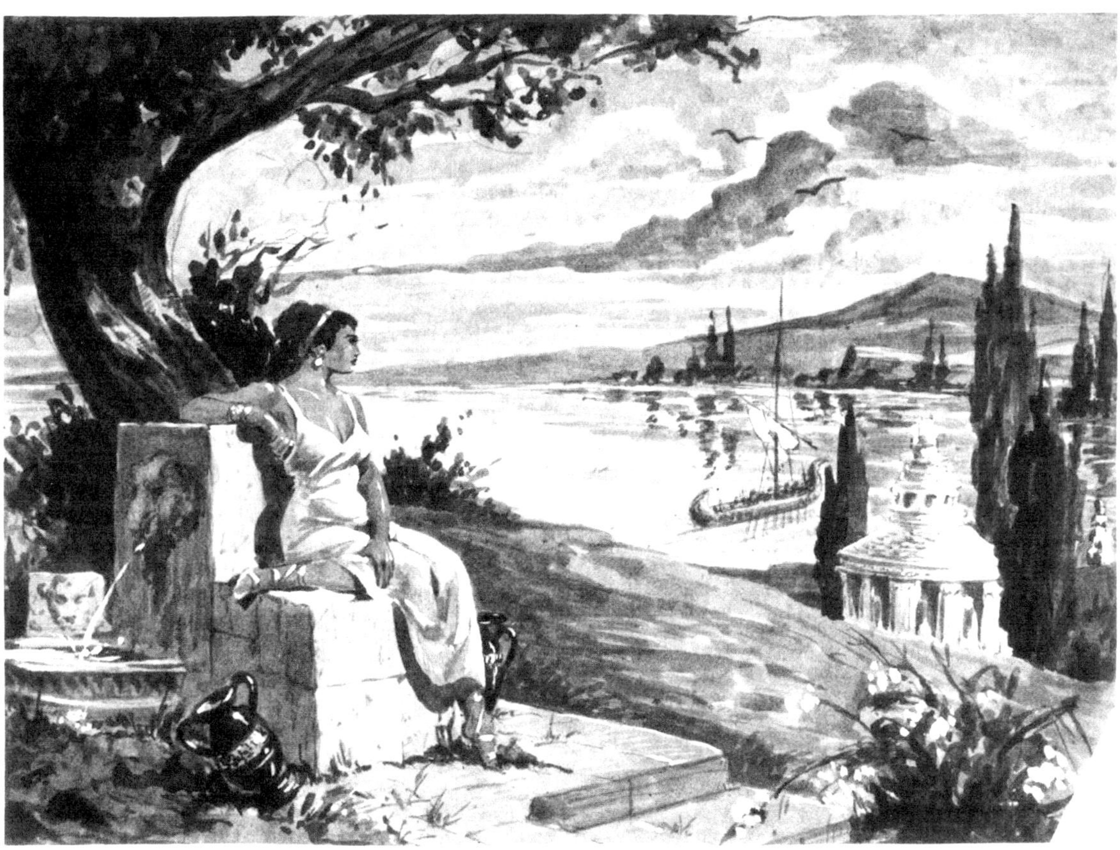

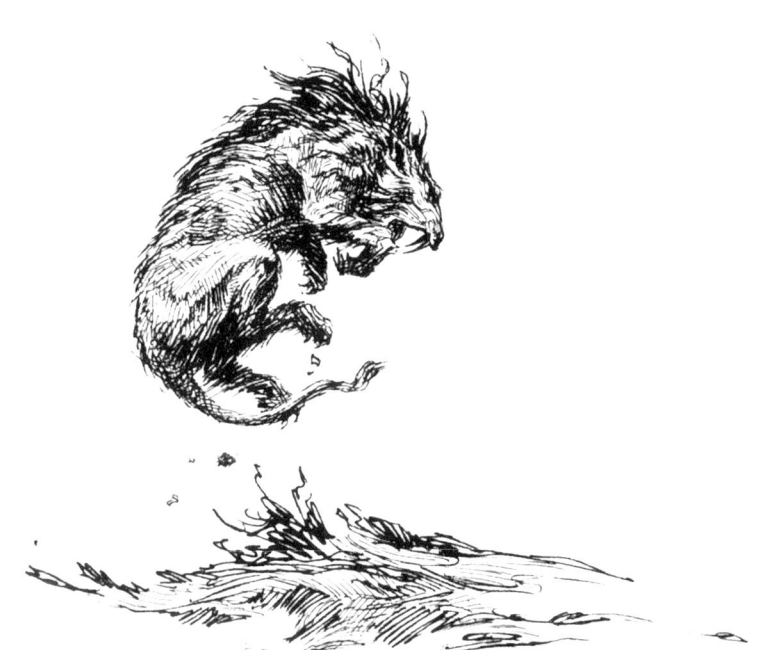

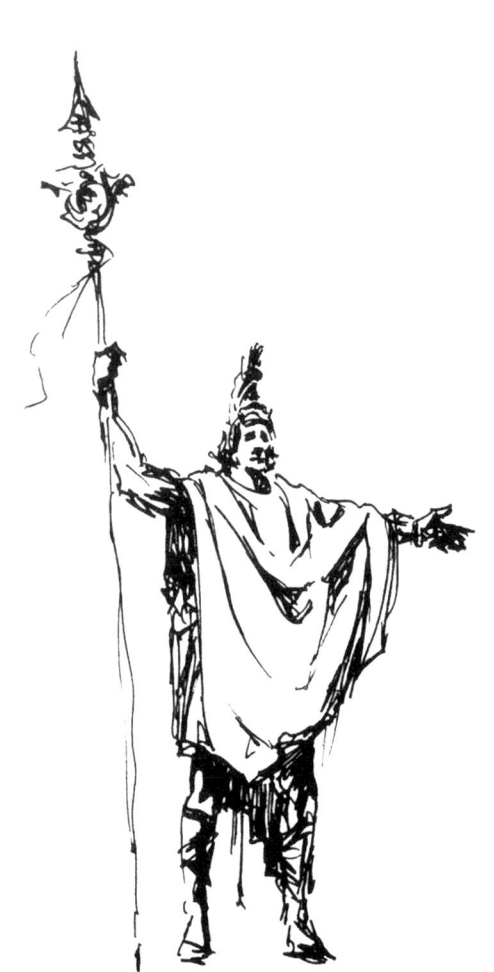

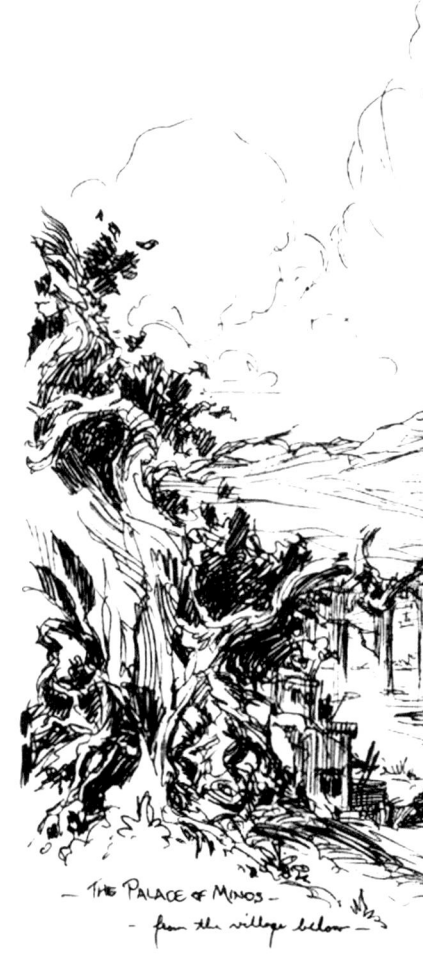

— THE PALACE OF MINOS —
— from the village below —

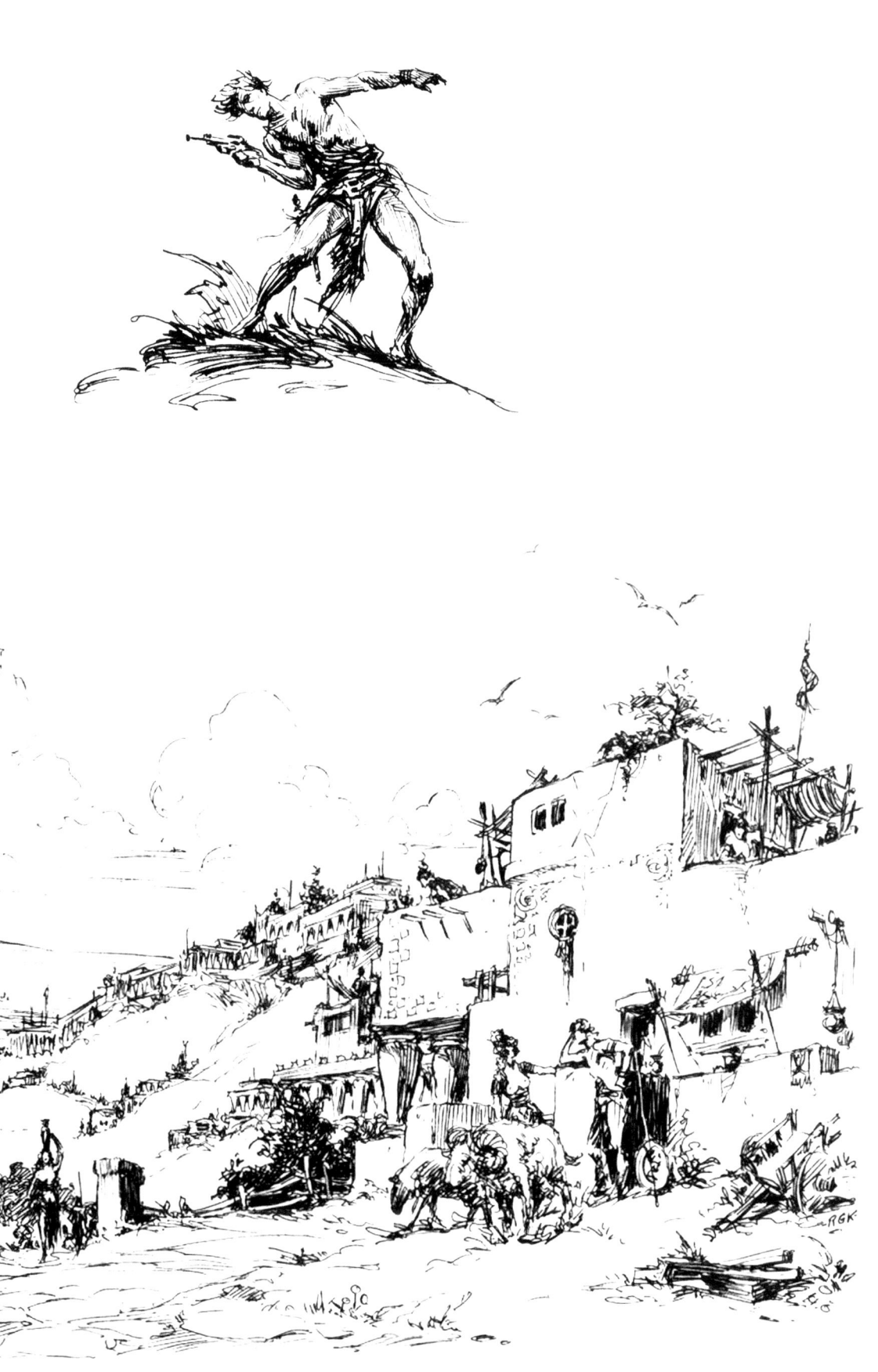

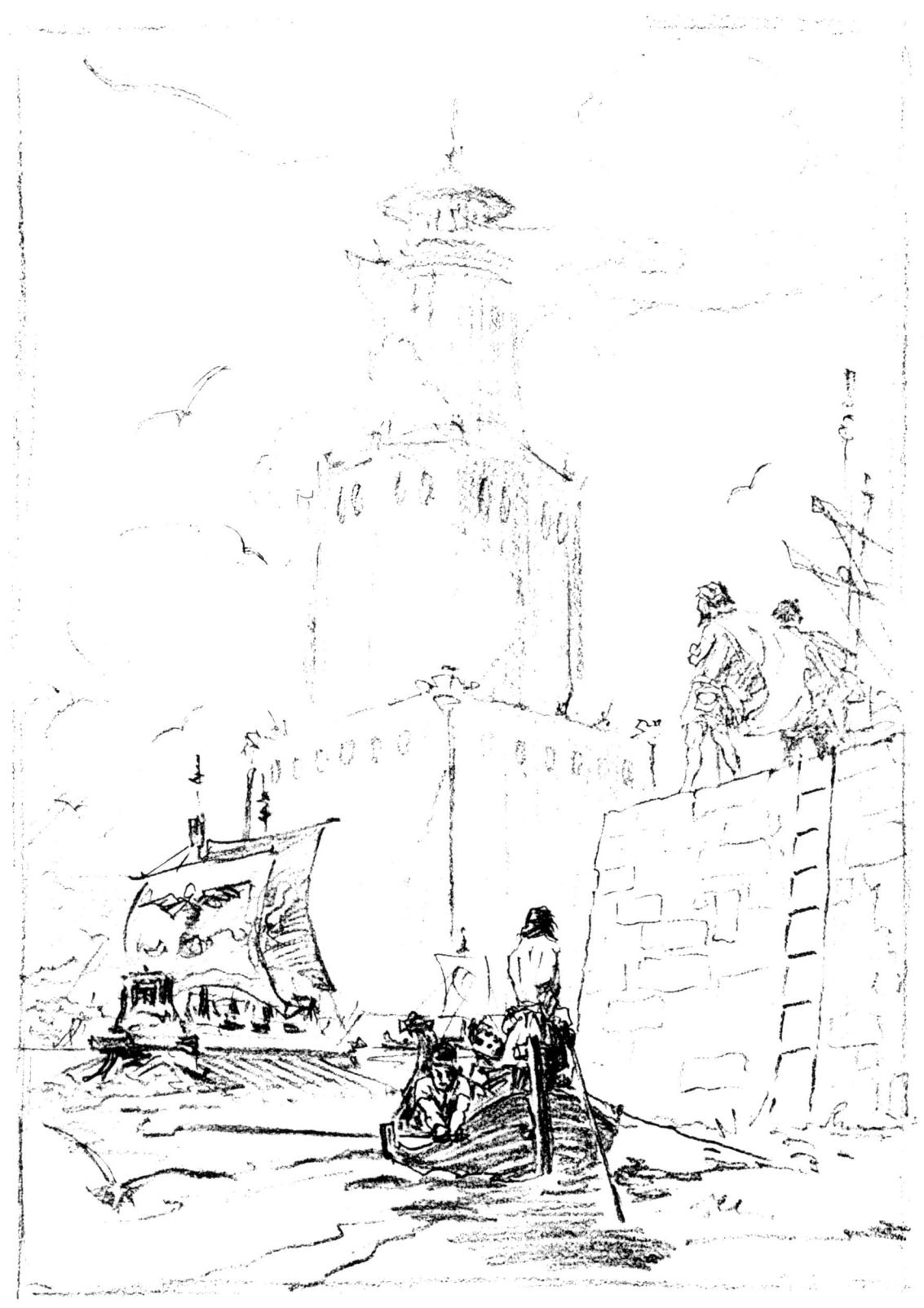

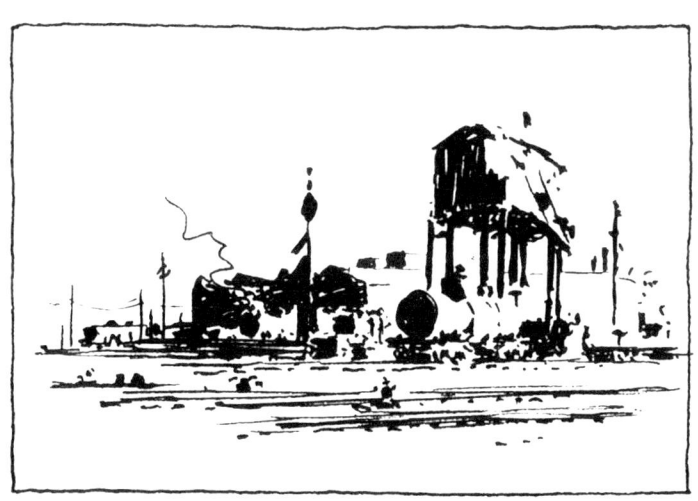

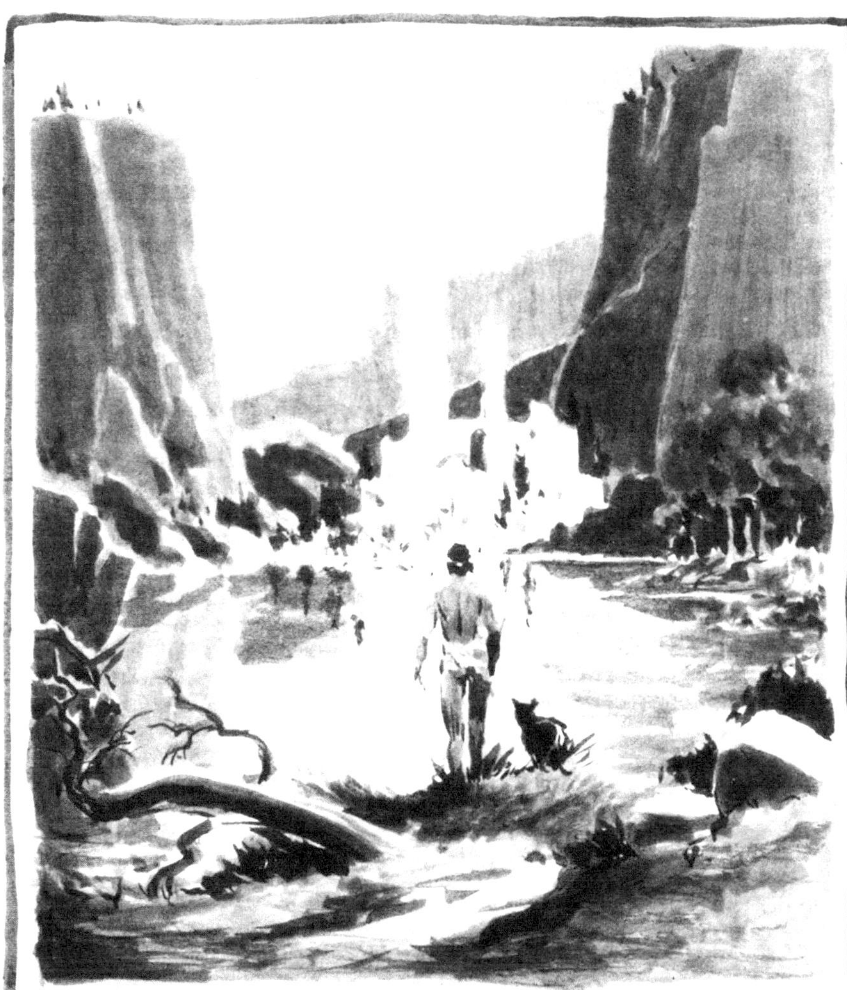

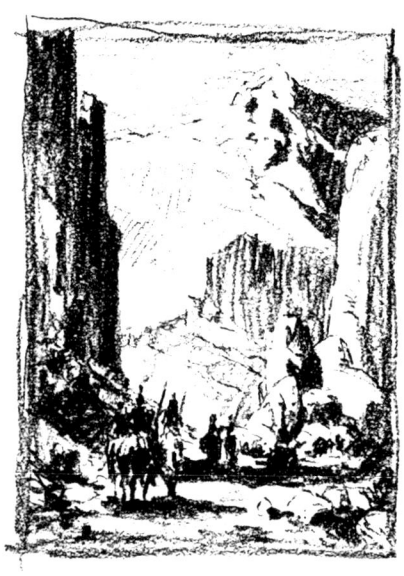

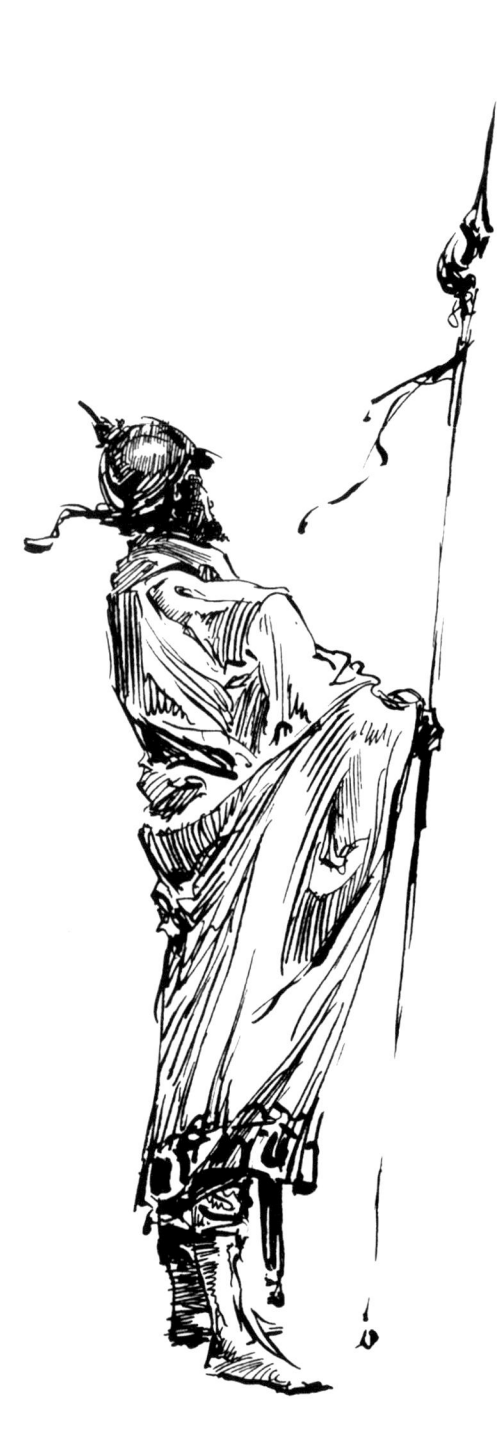

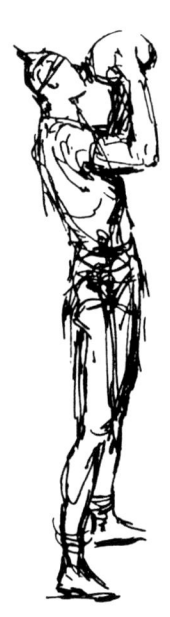

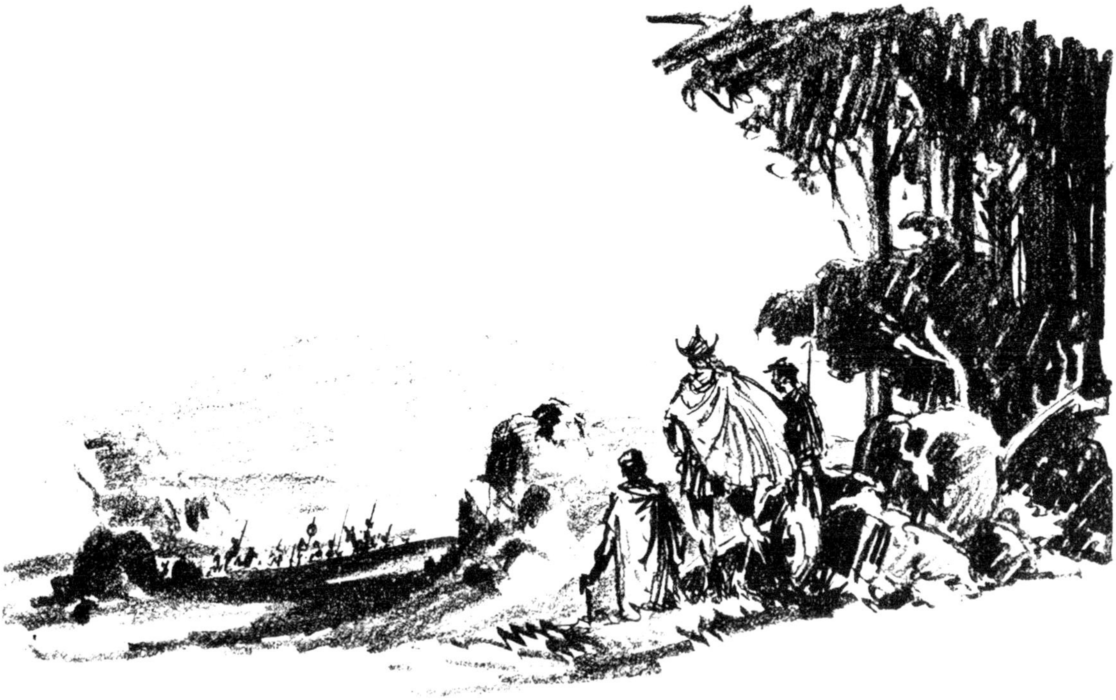

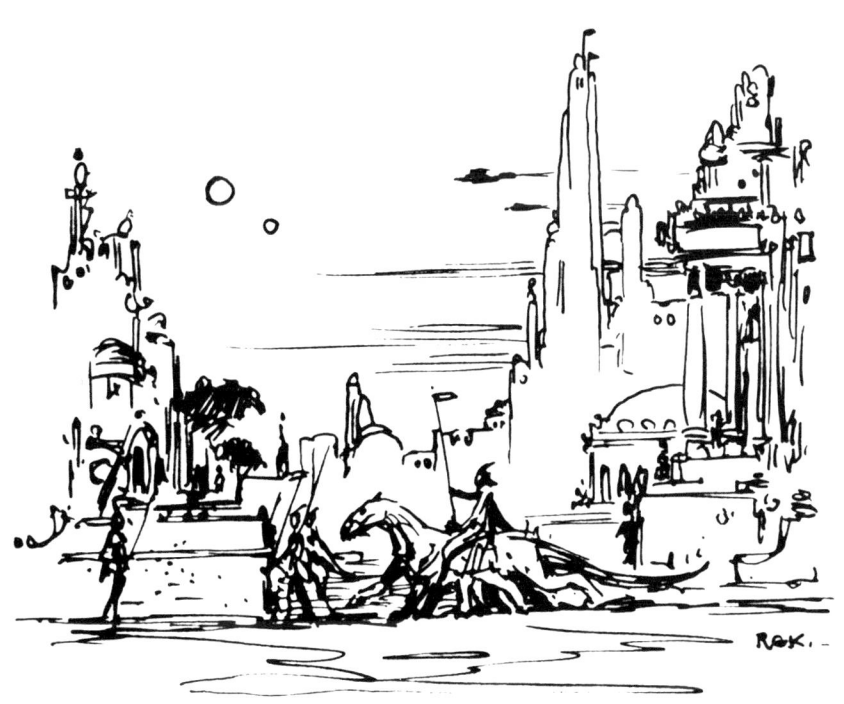

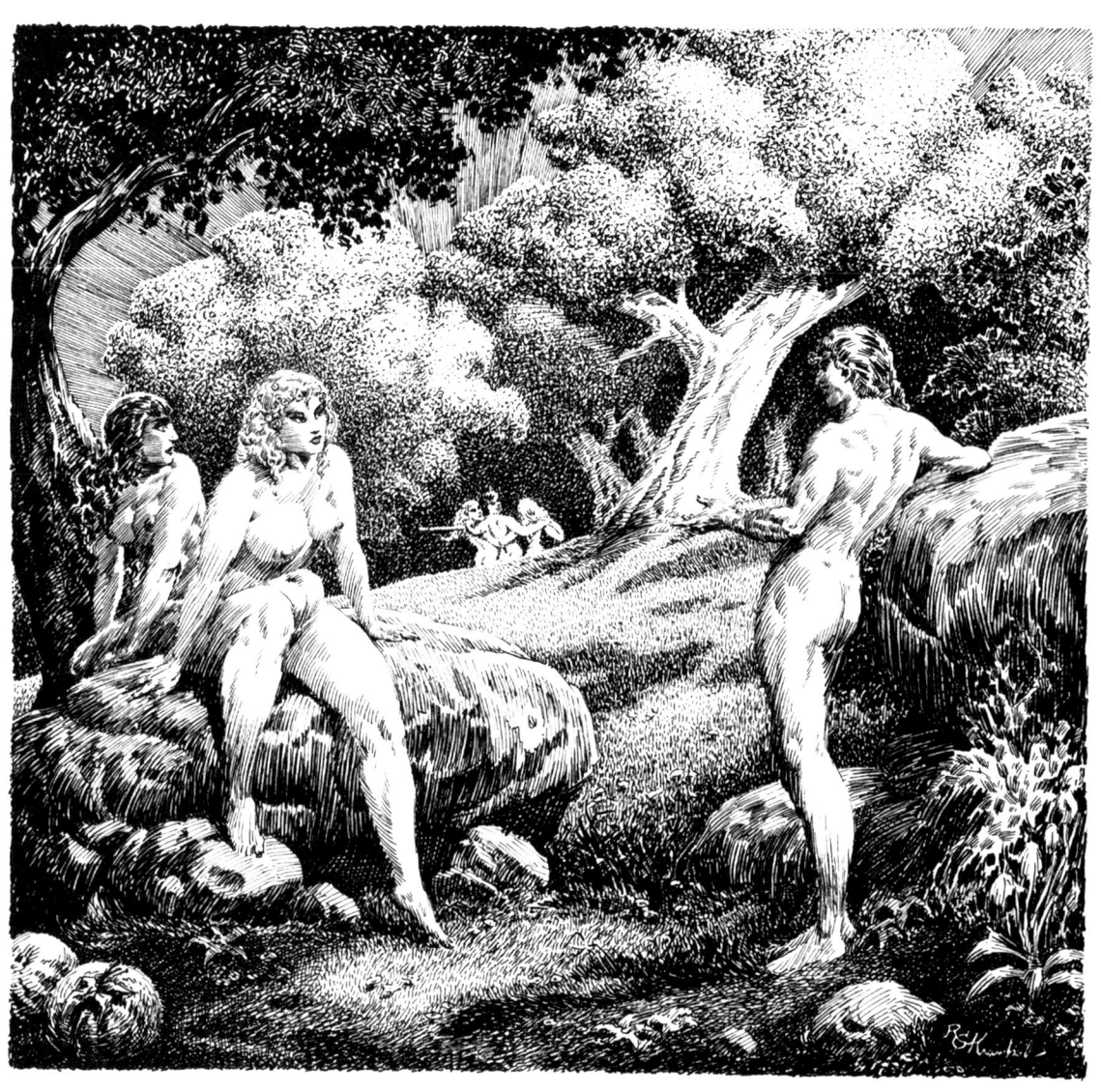

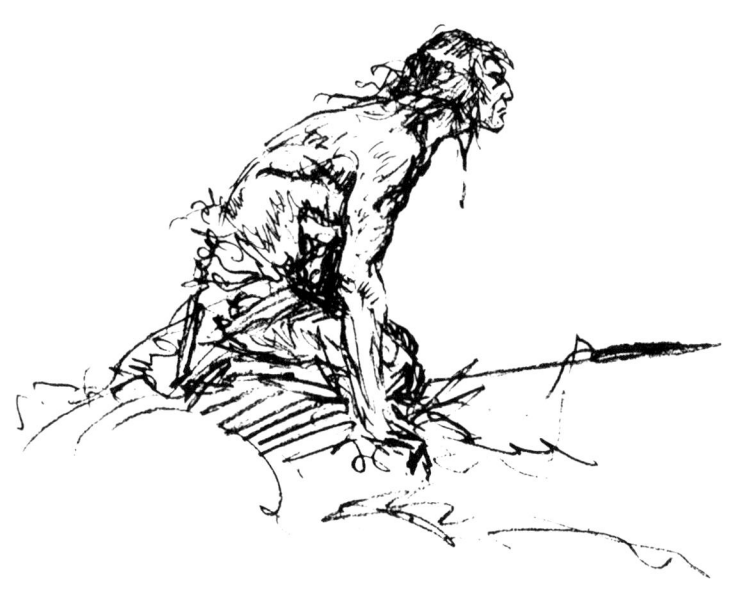

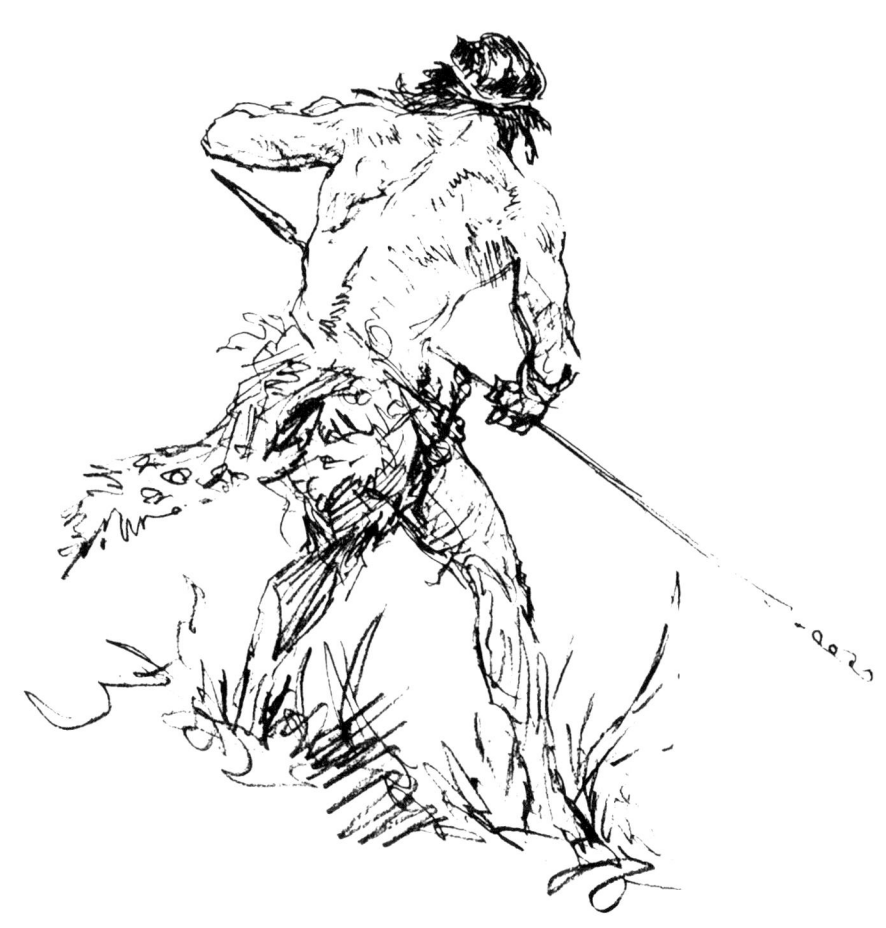

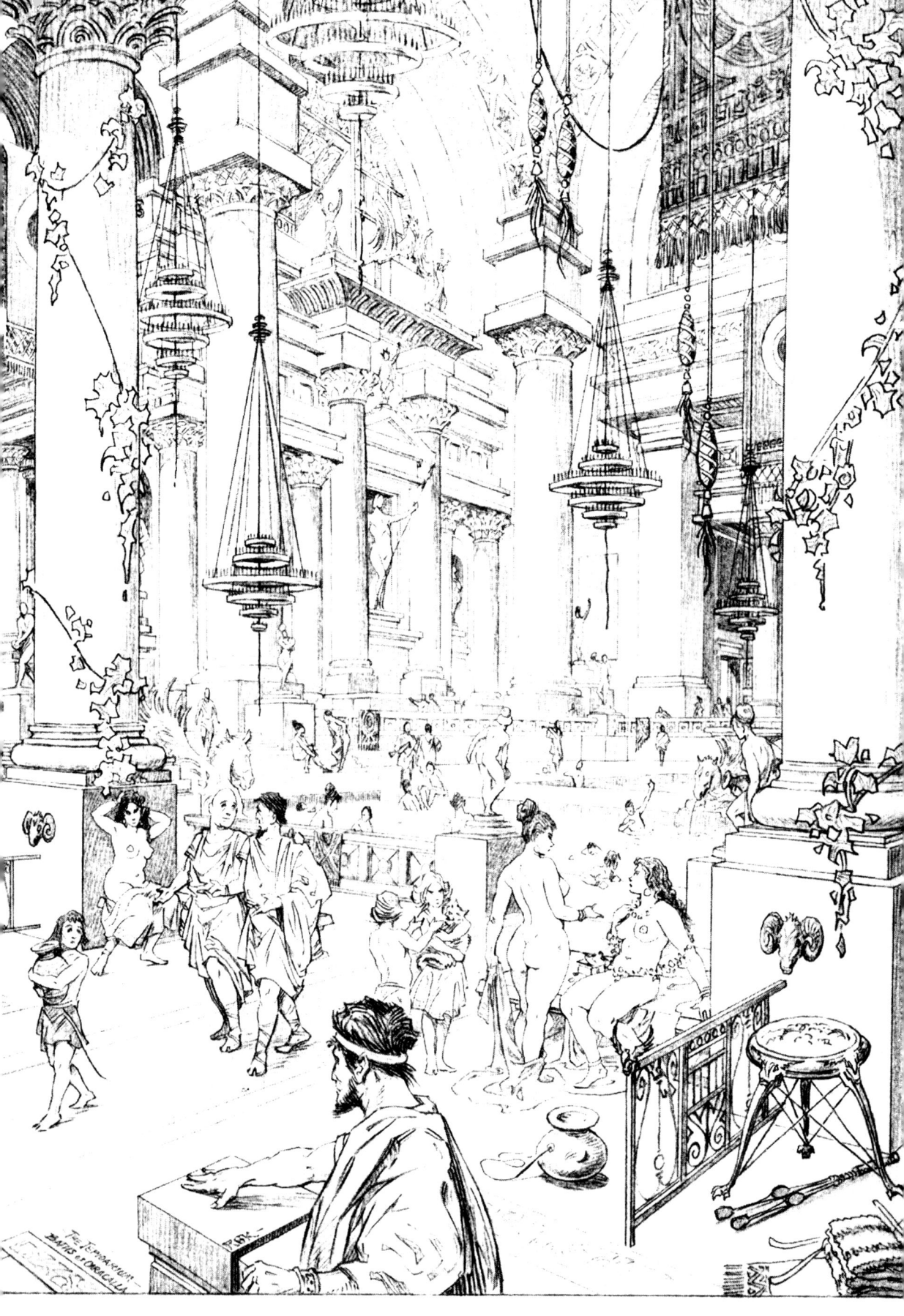

THE EMPORIUM
BATHS of CARACALLA

154

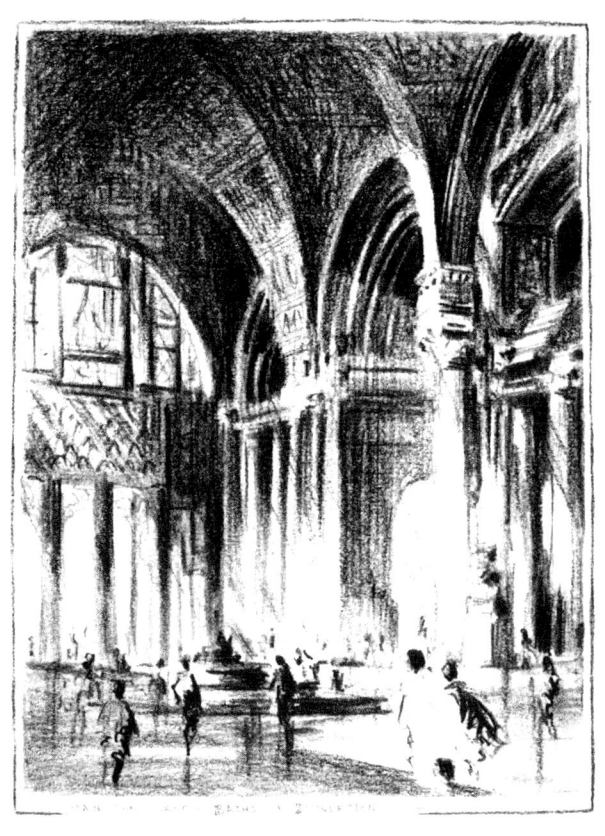

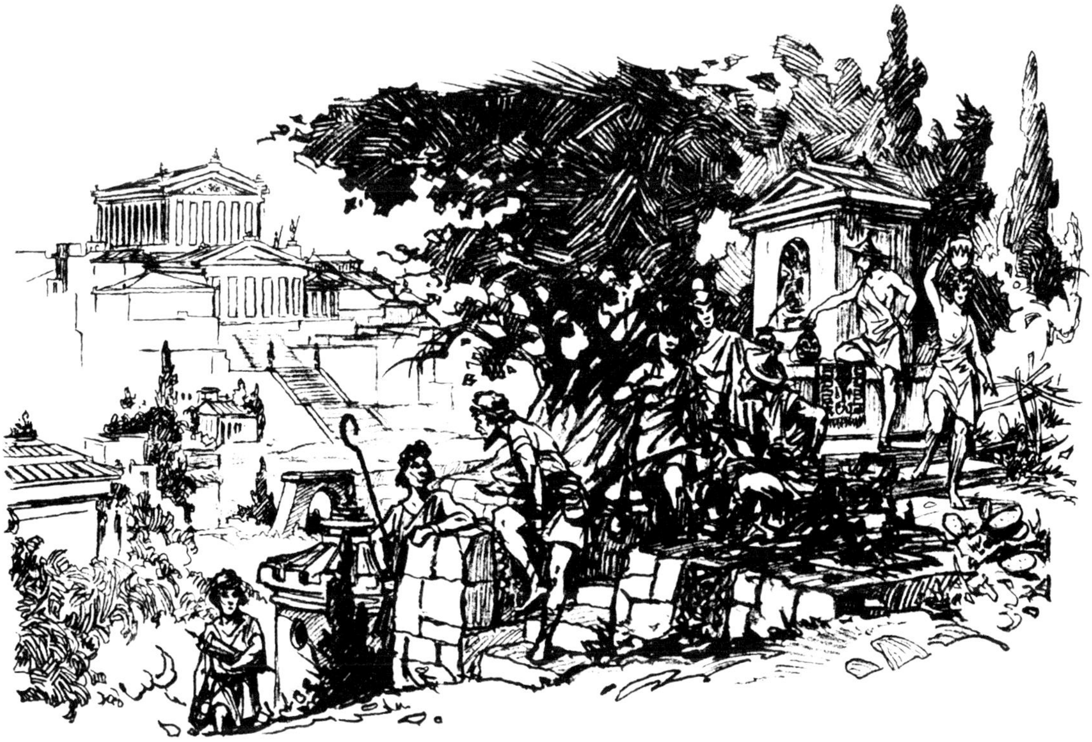

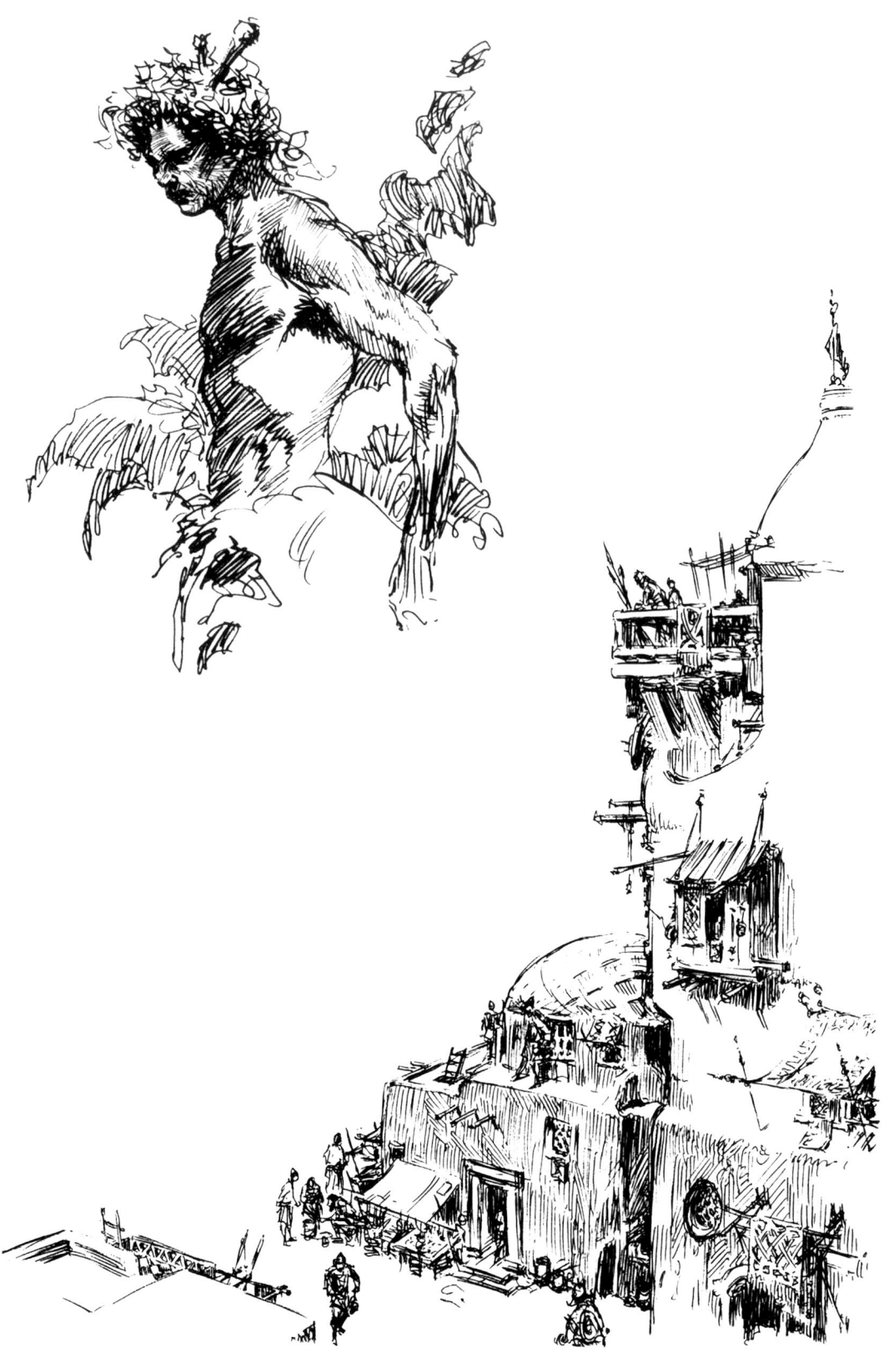

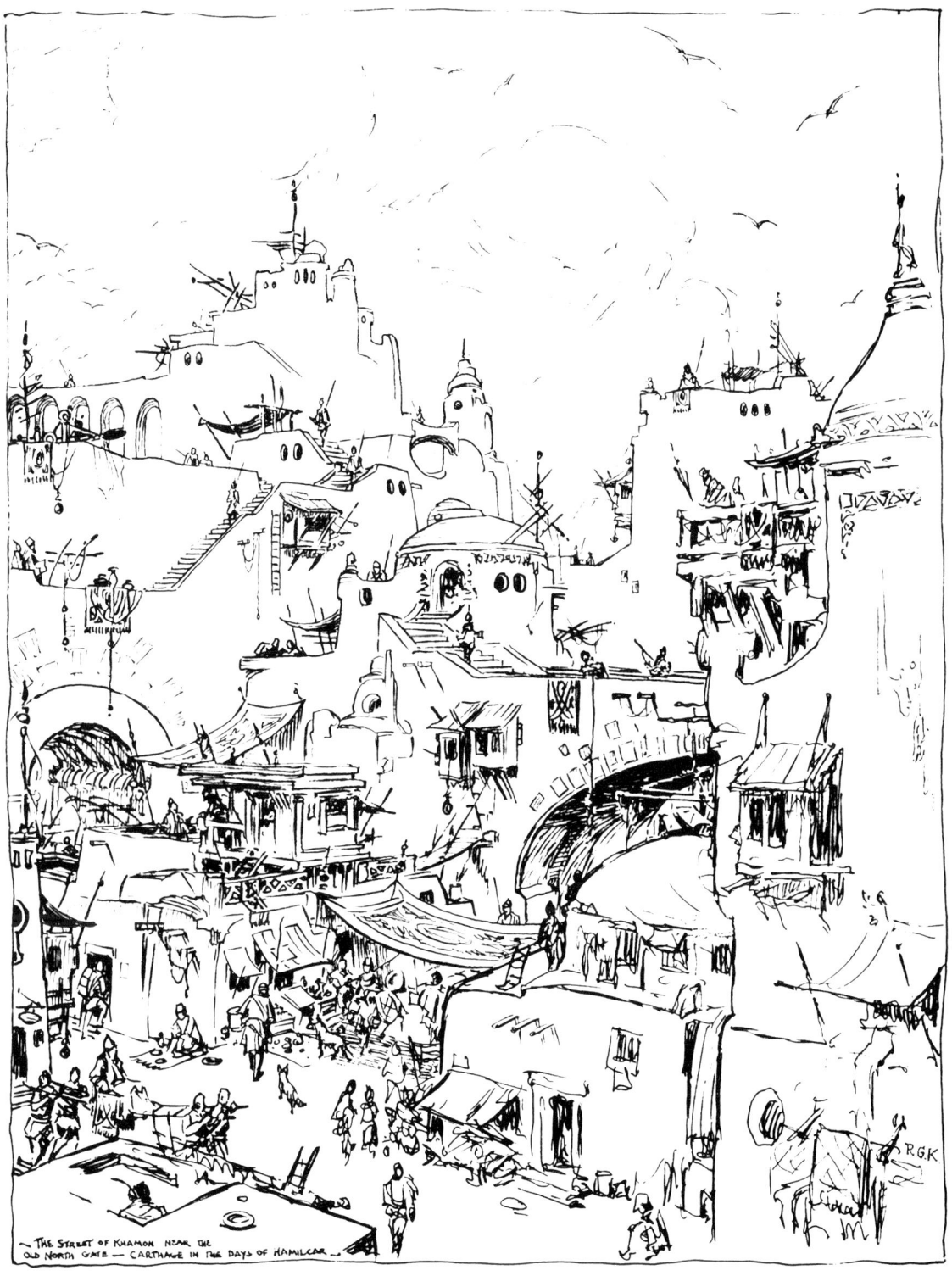

~ THE STREET OF KHAMON NEAR THE
OLD NORTH GATE — CARTHAGE IN THE DAYS OF HAMILCAR ~

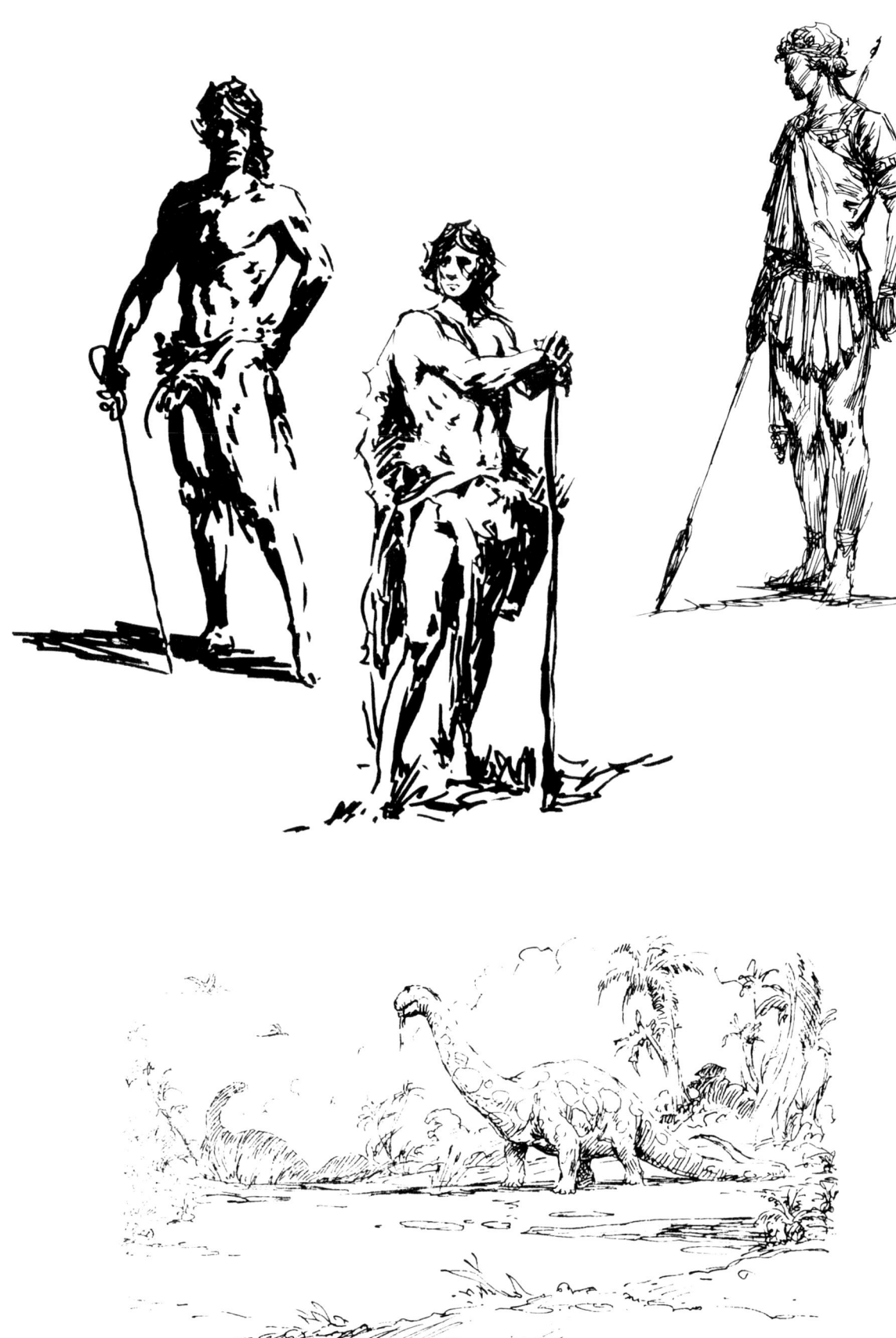

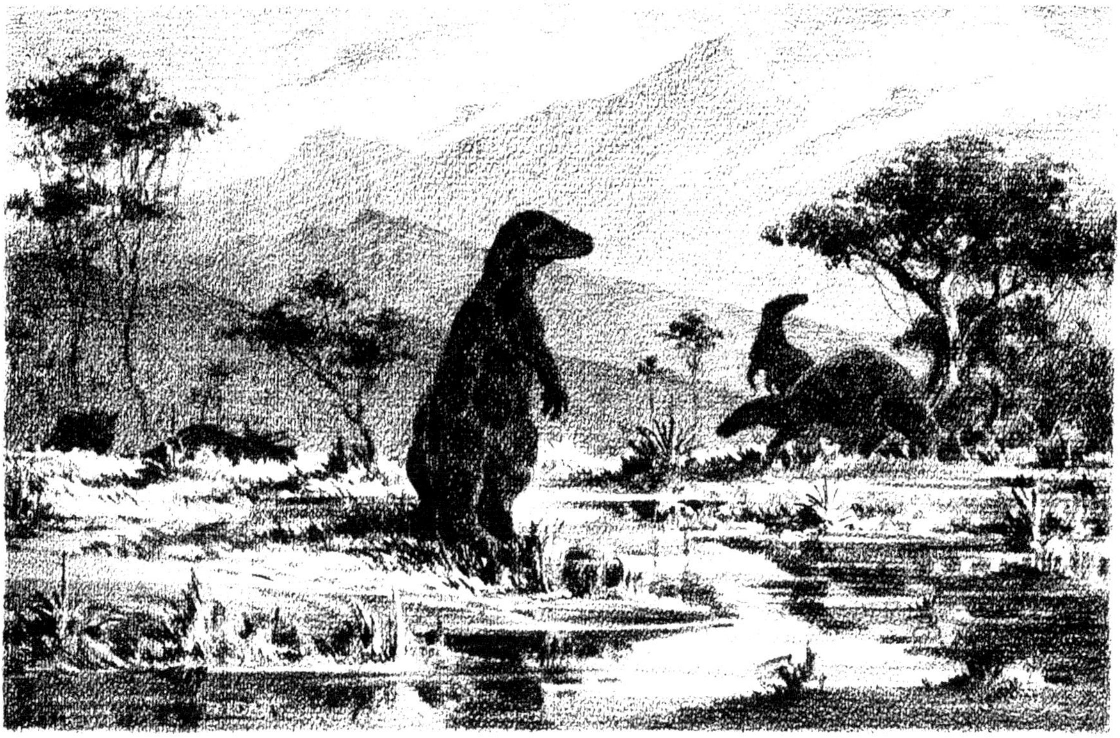

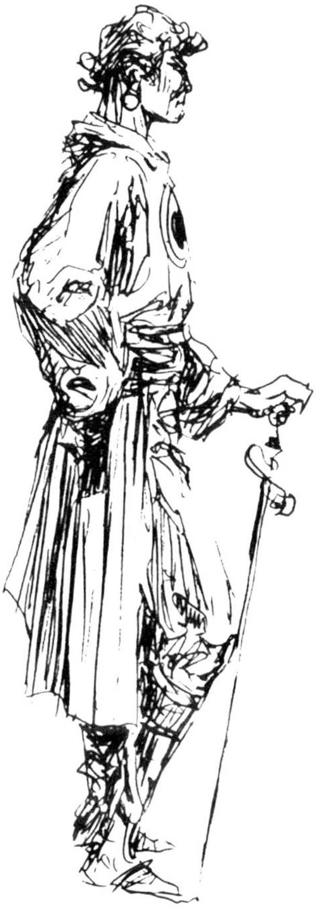

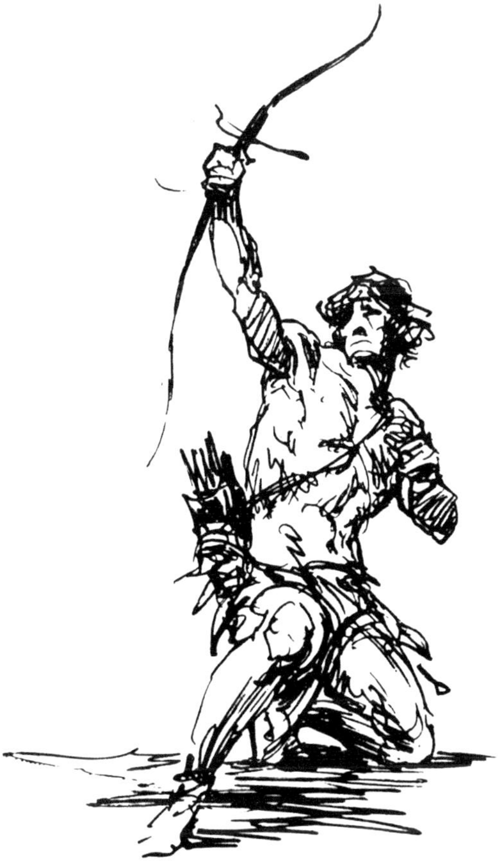

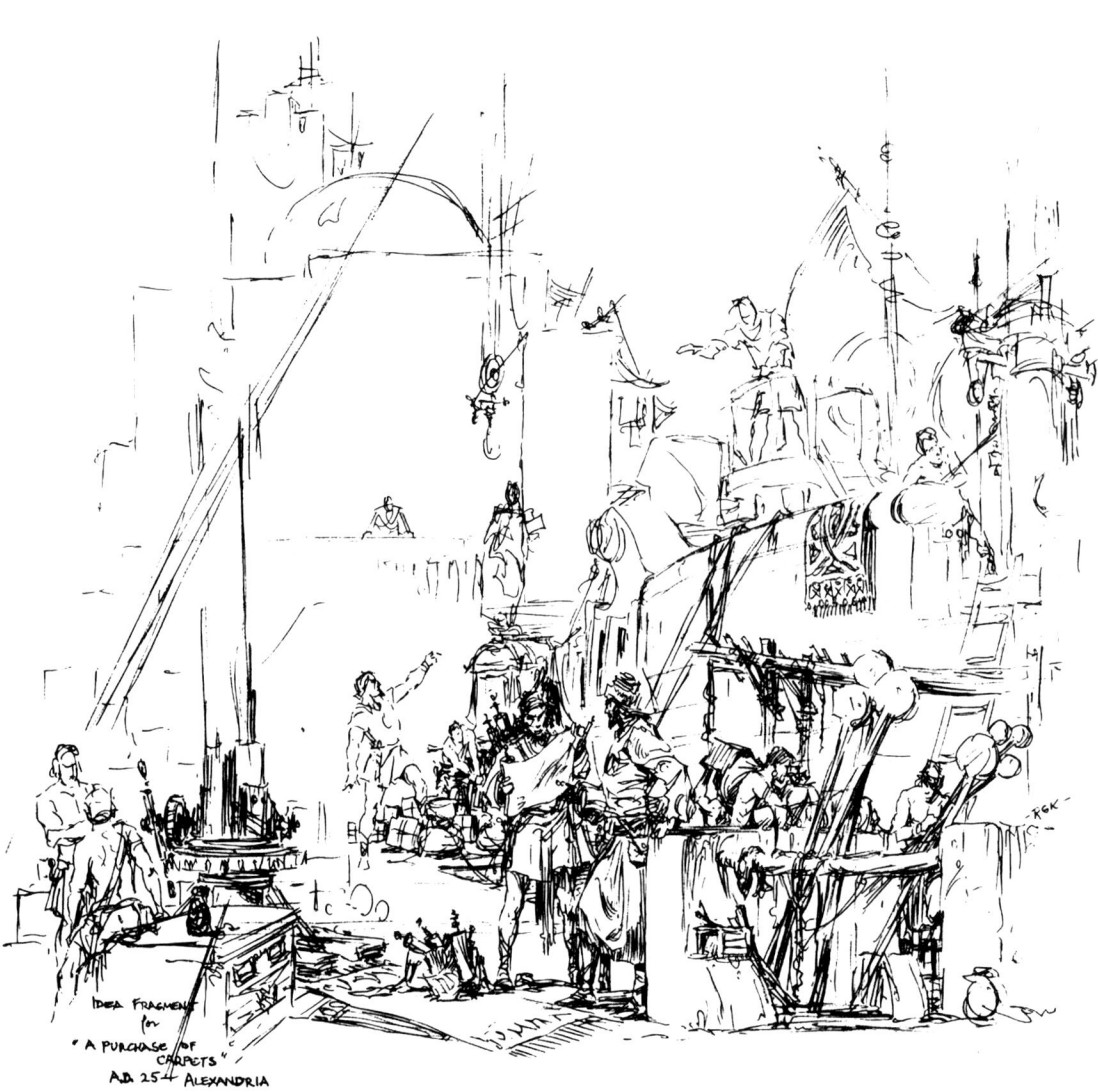

IDEA FRAGMENT for
"A PURCHASE of
CARPETS"
A.D. 254 ALEXANDRIA

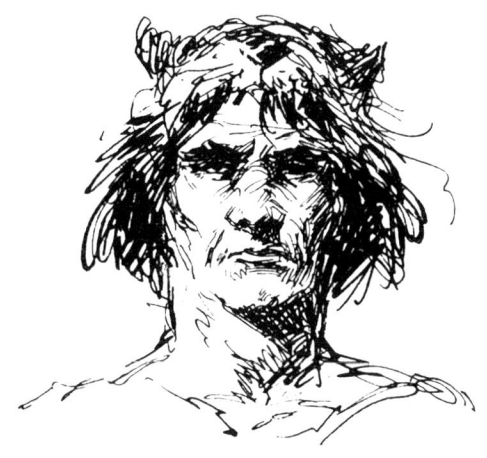

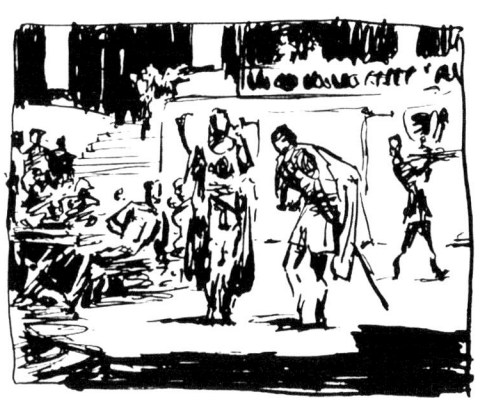

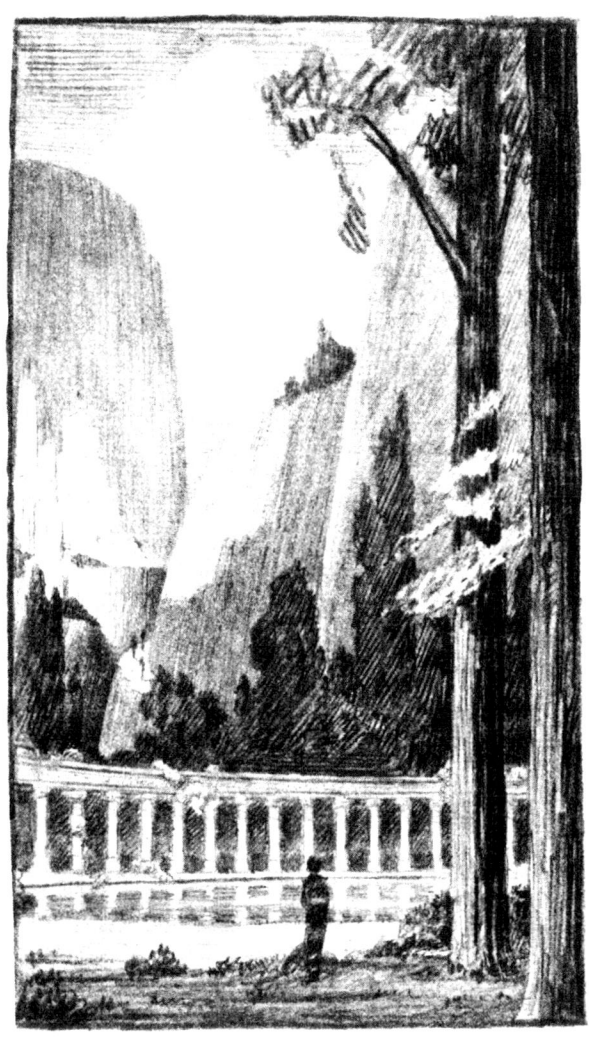

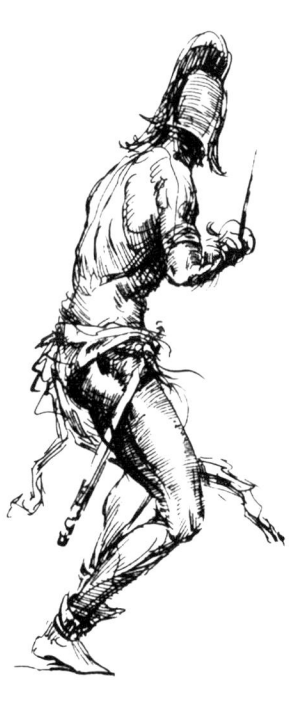

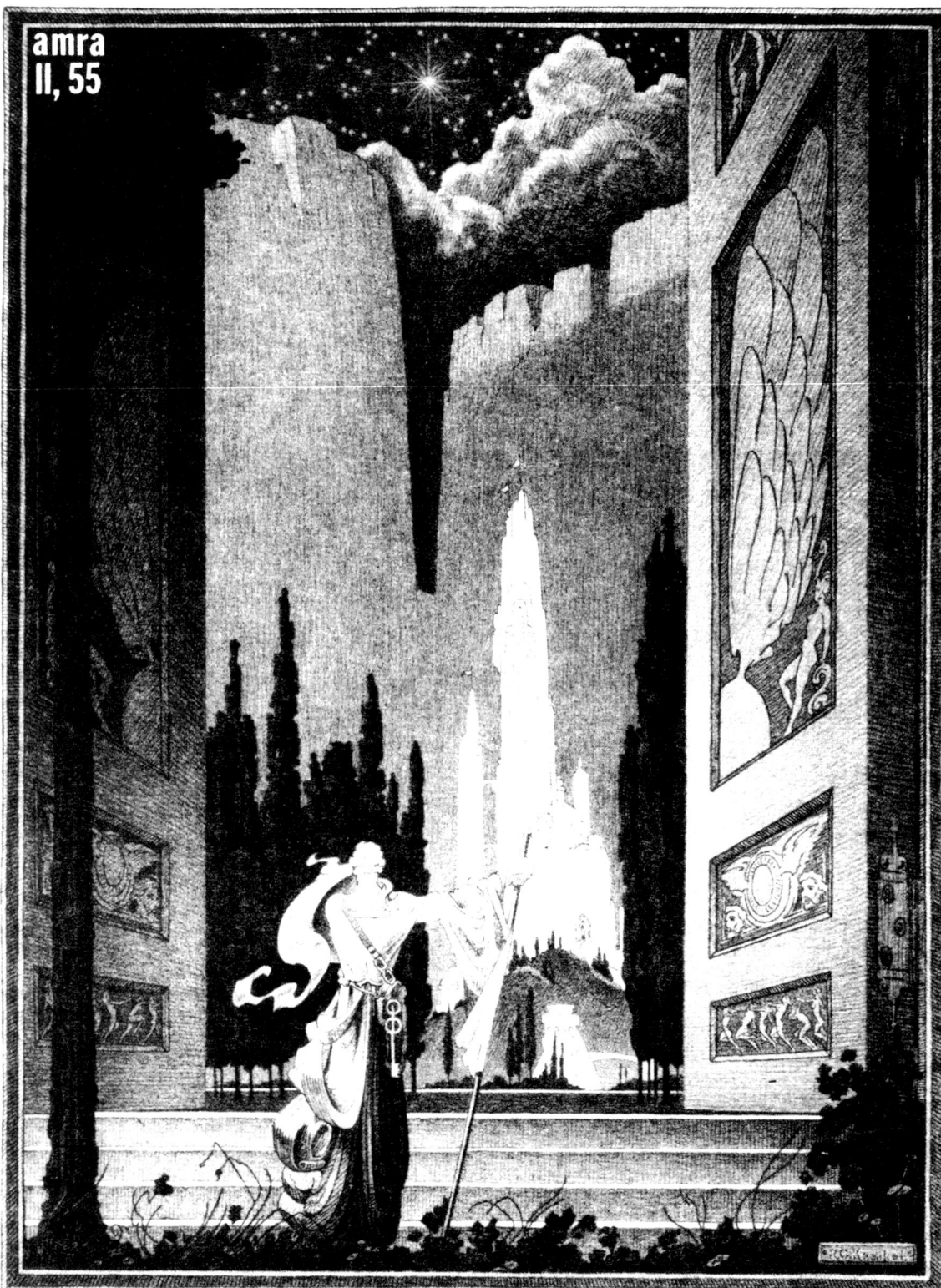

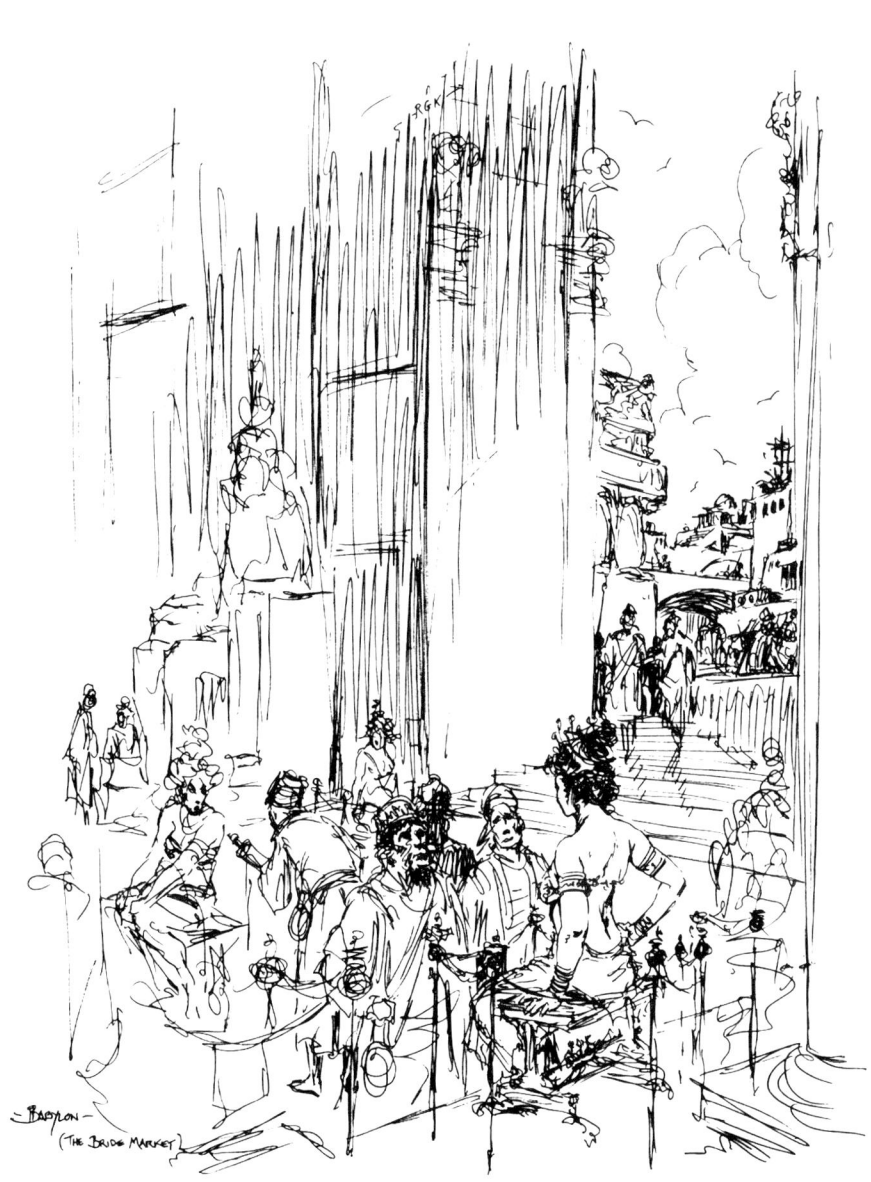

BABYLON
(THE BRIDE MARKET)

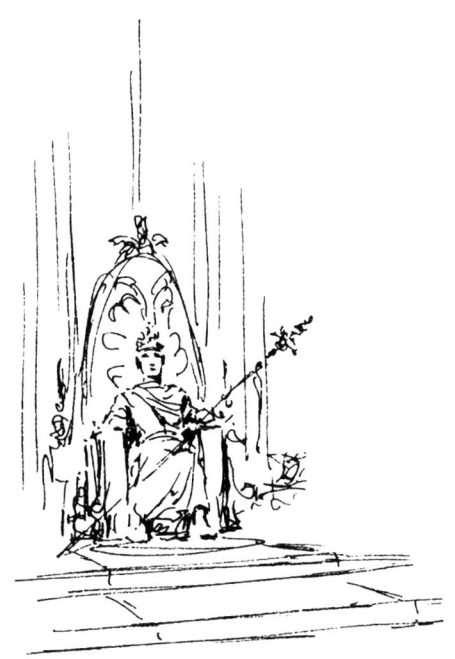
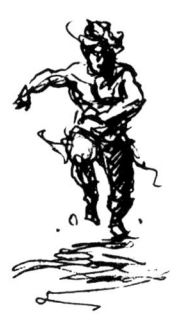
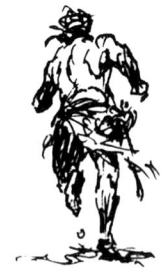
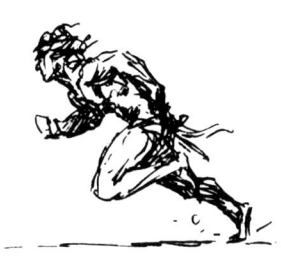
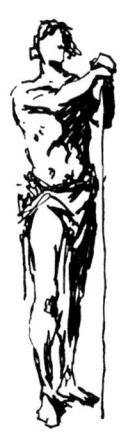
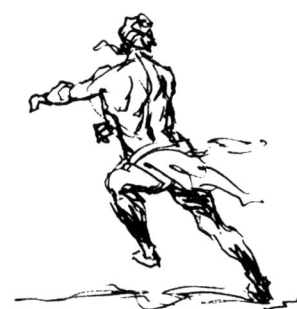

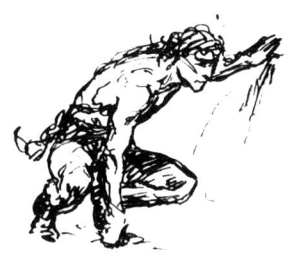
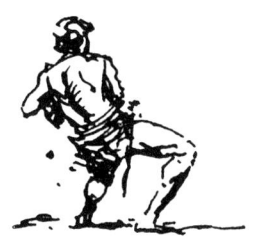
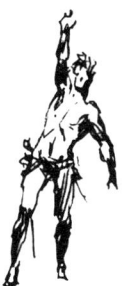
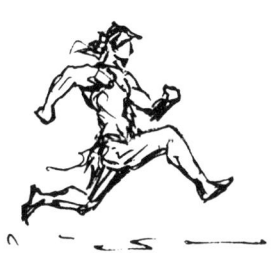
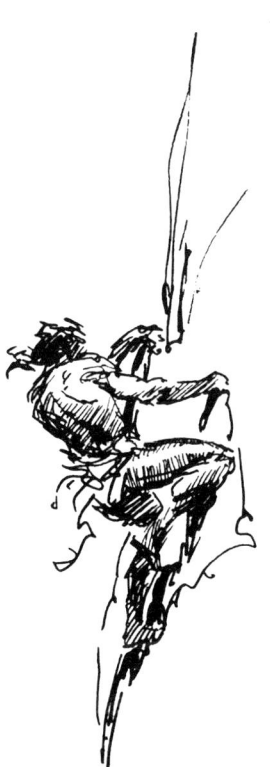
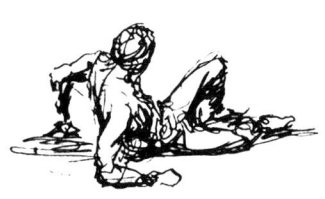

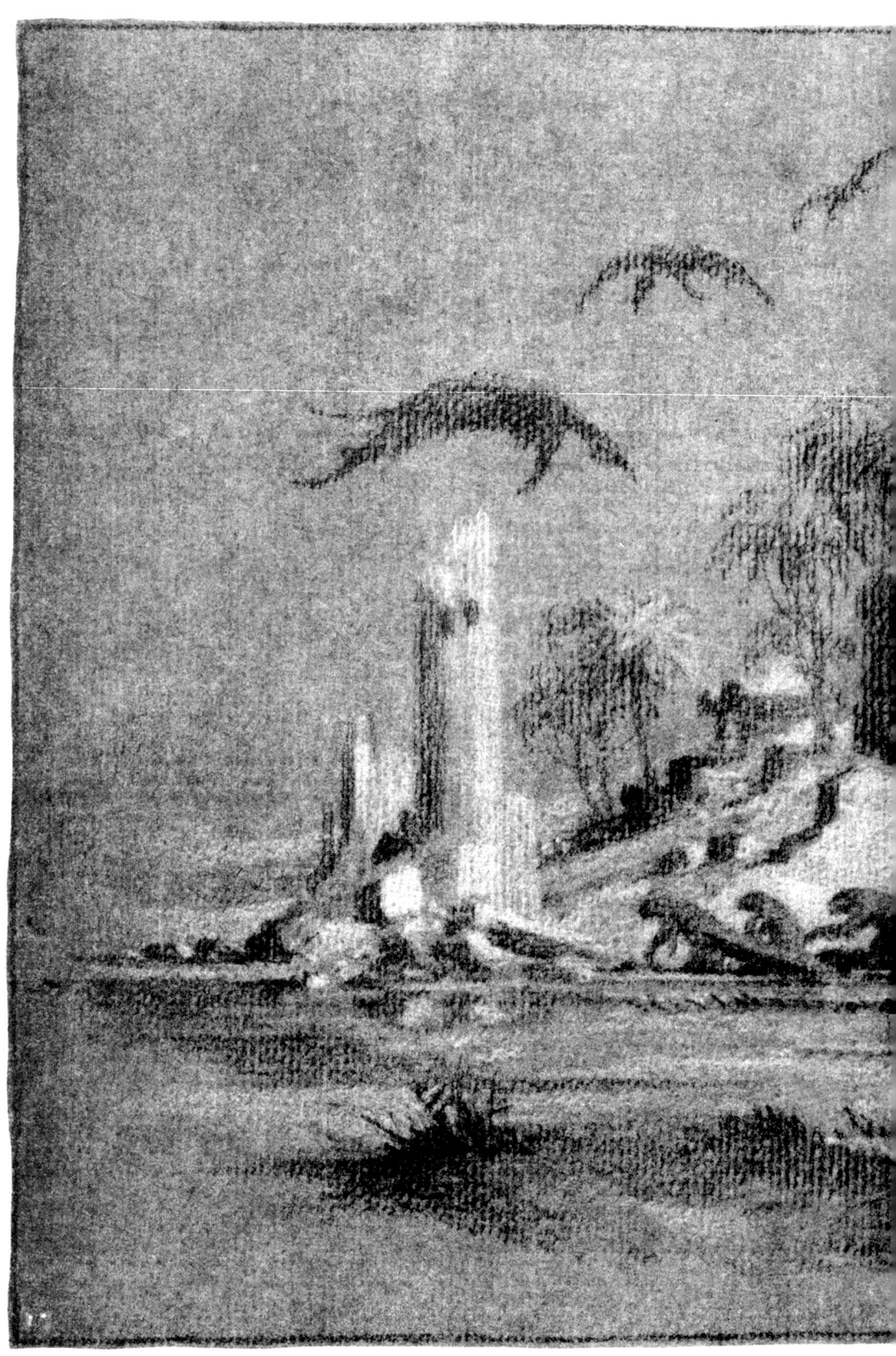

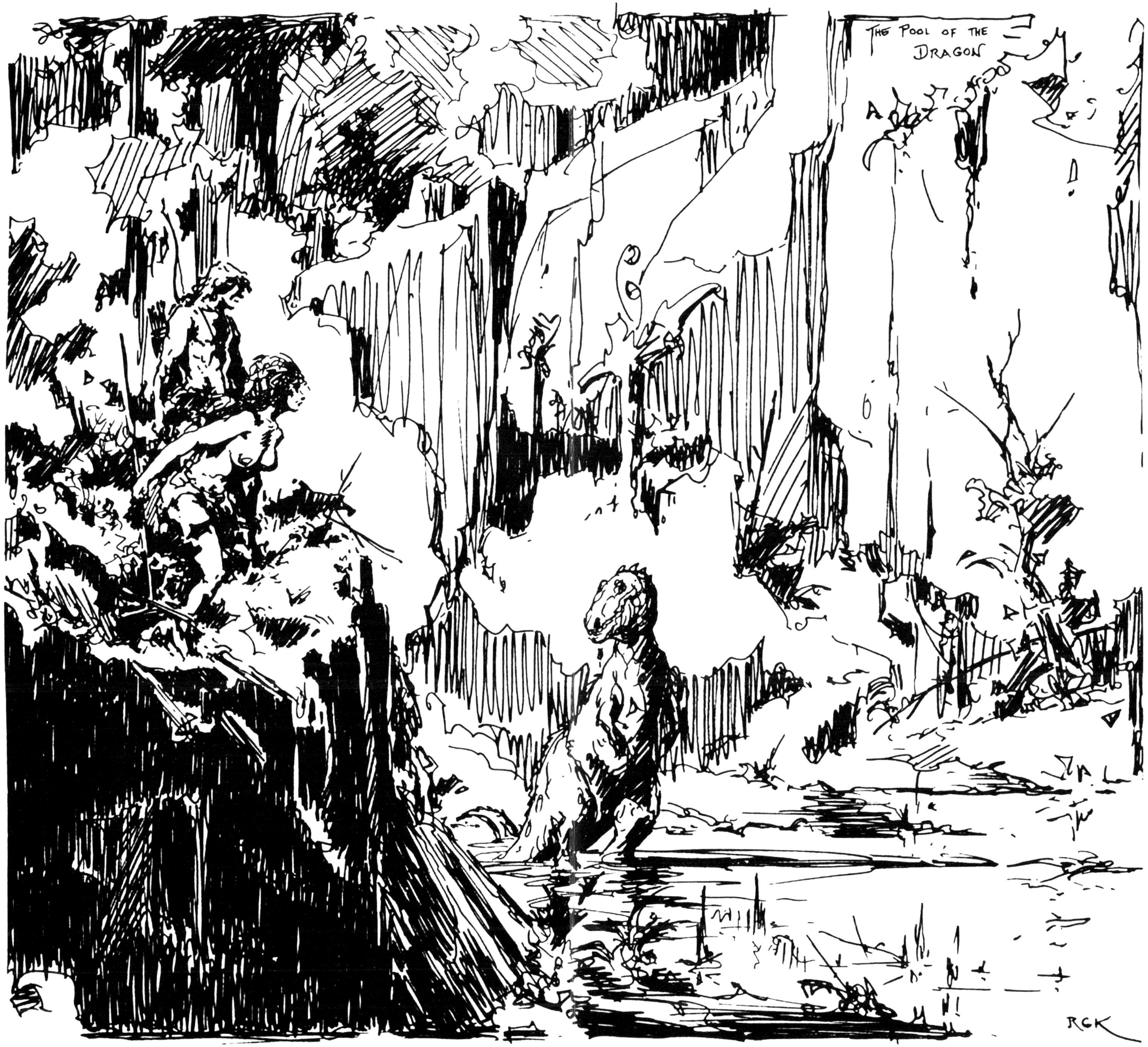

THE POOL OF THE DRAGON

RCK

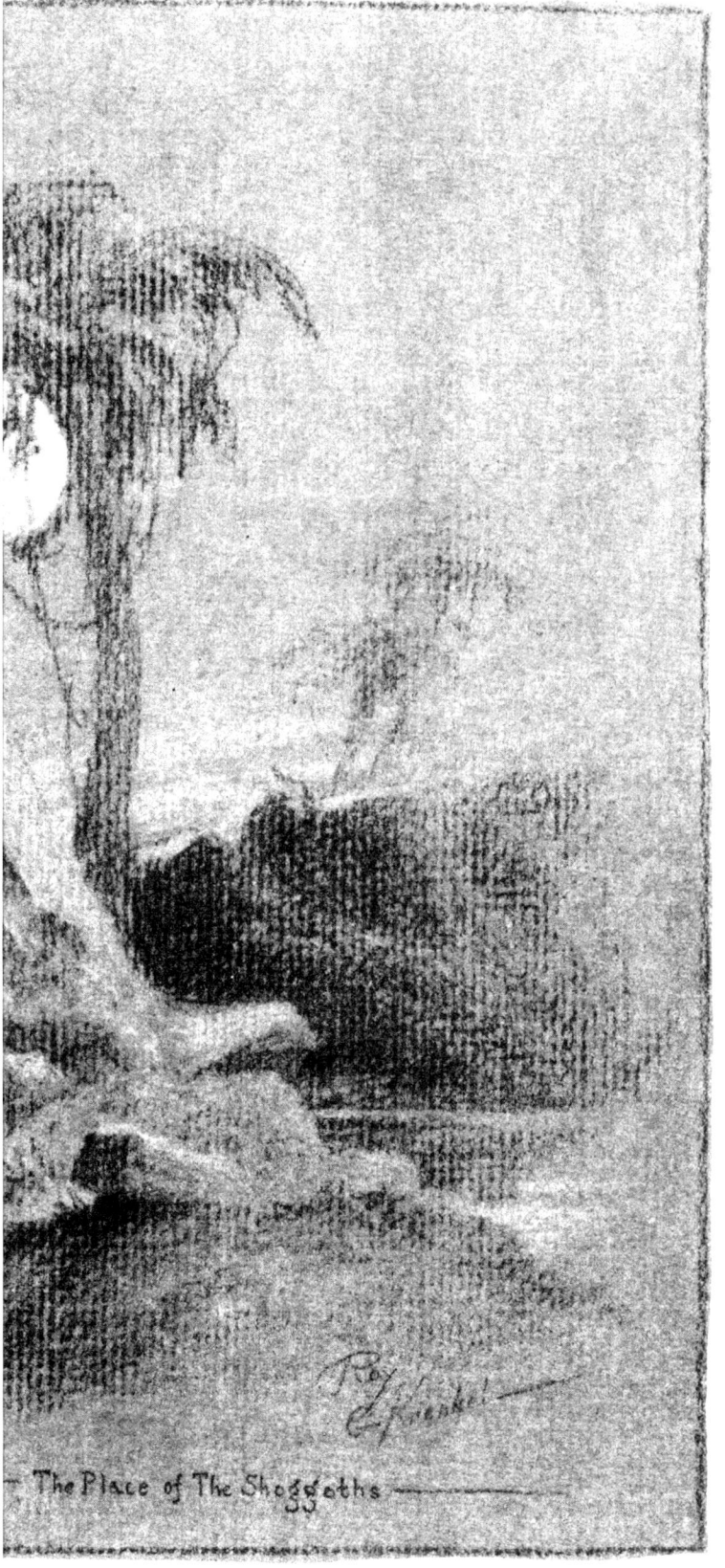

The Place of The Shoggoths

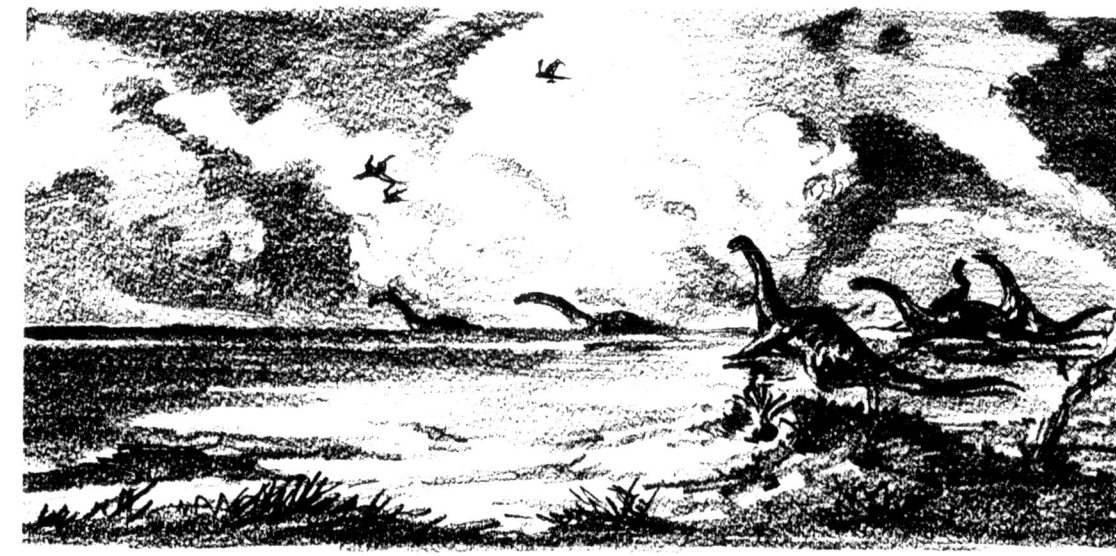

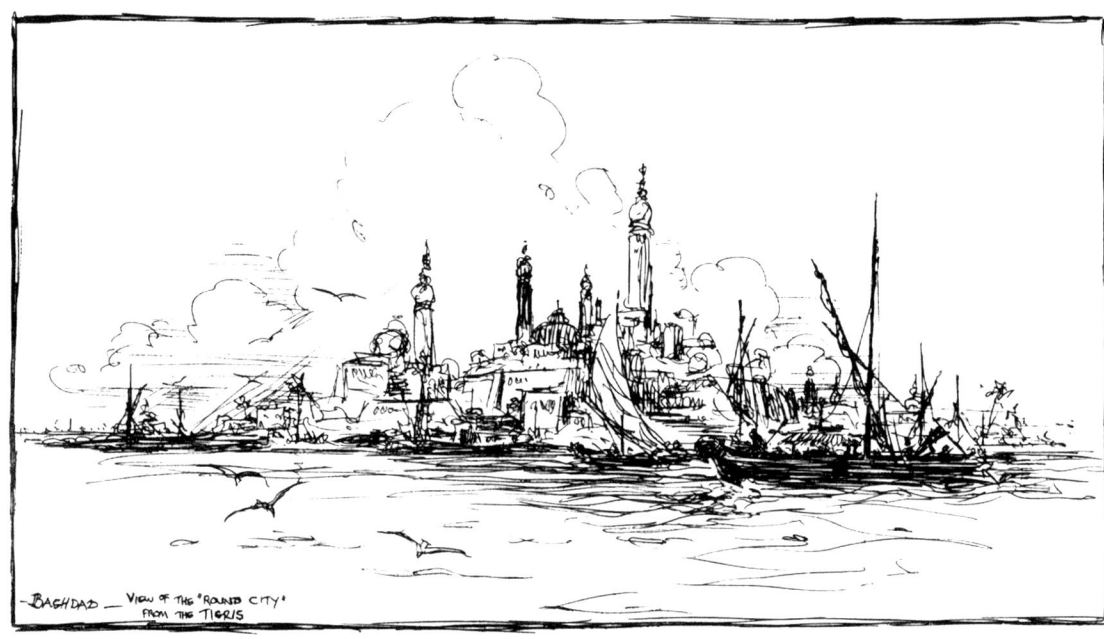

BAGHDAD — VIEW OF THE "ROUND CITY" FROM THE TIGRIS

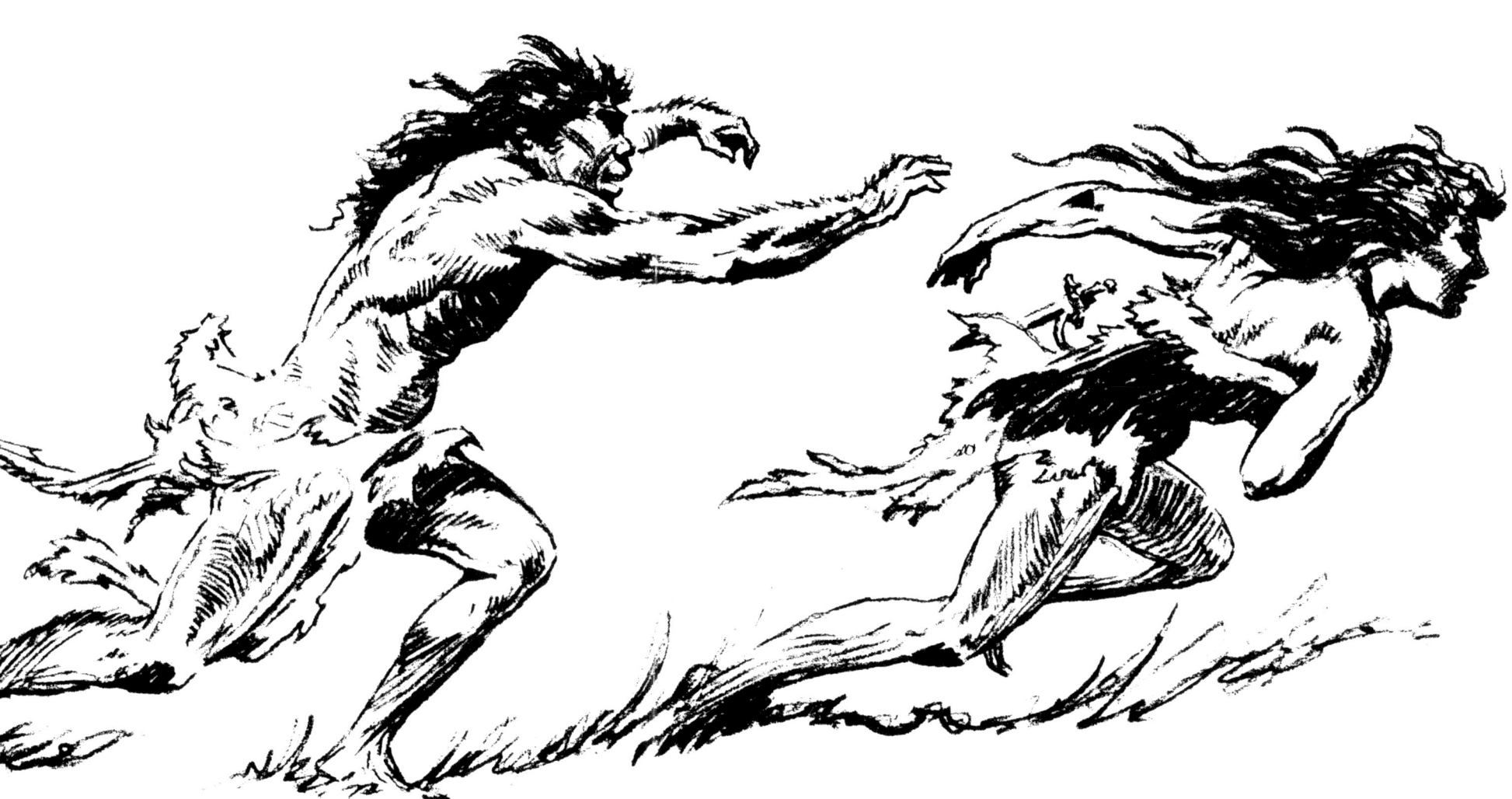

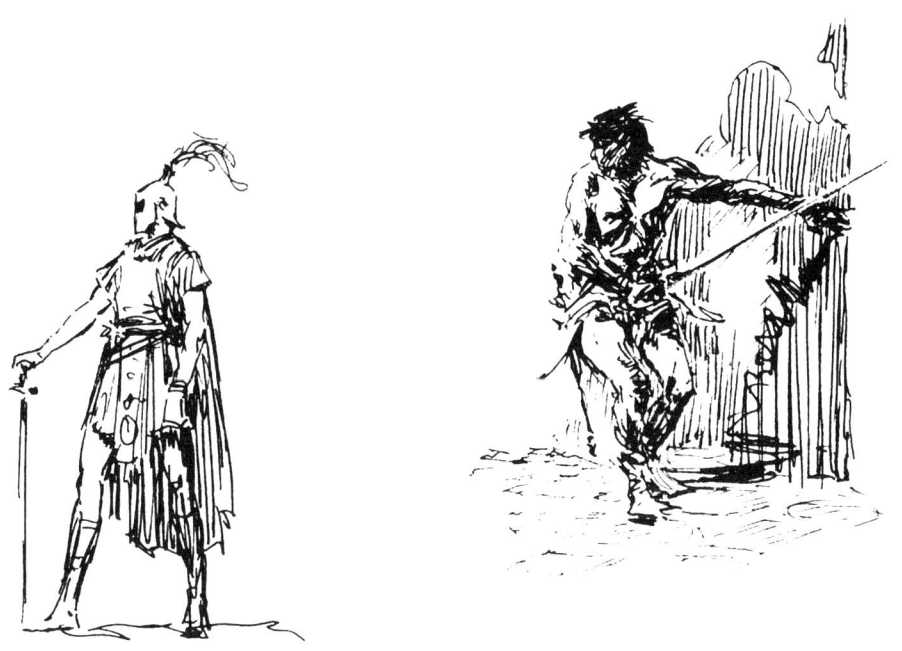

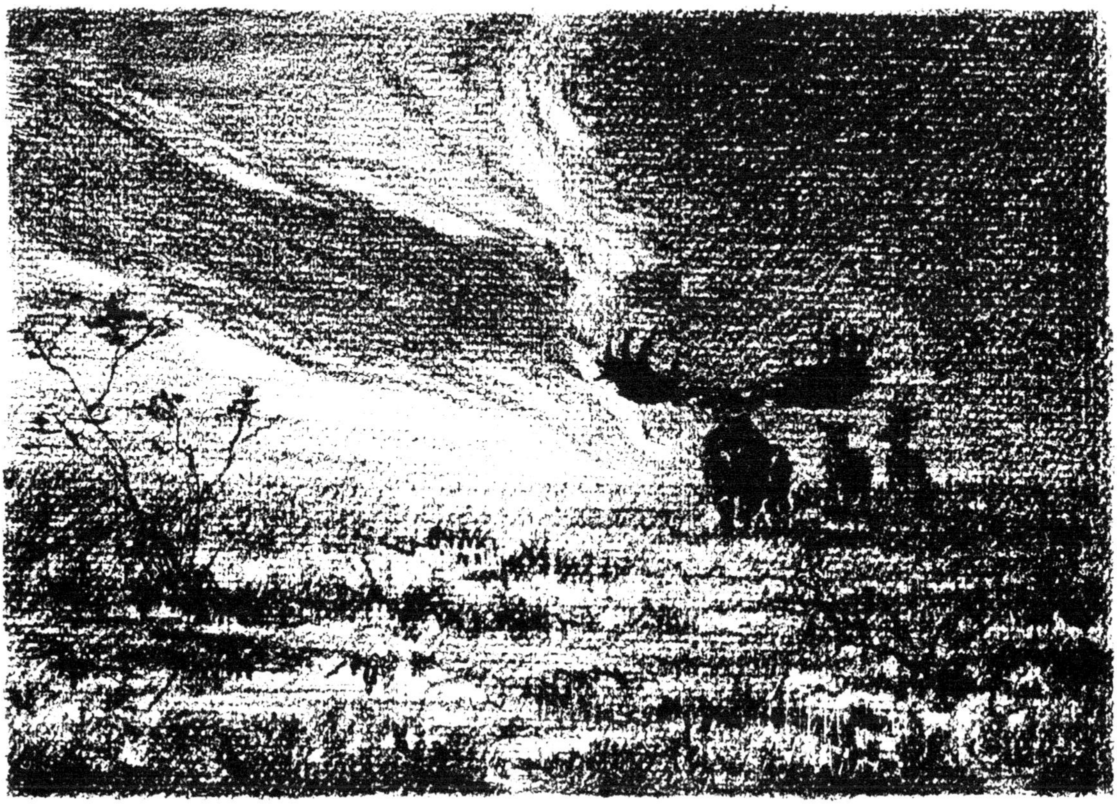

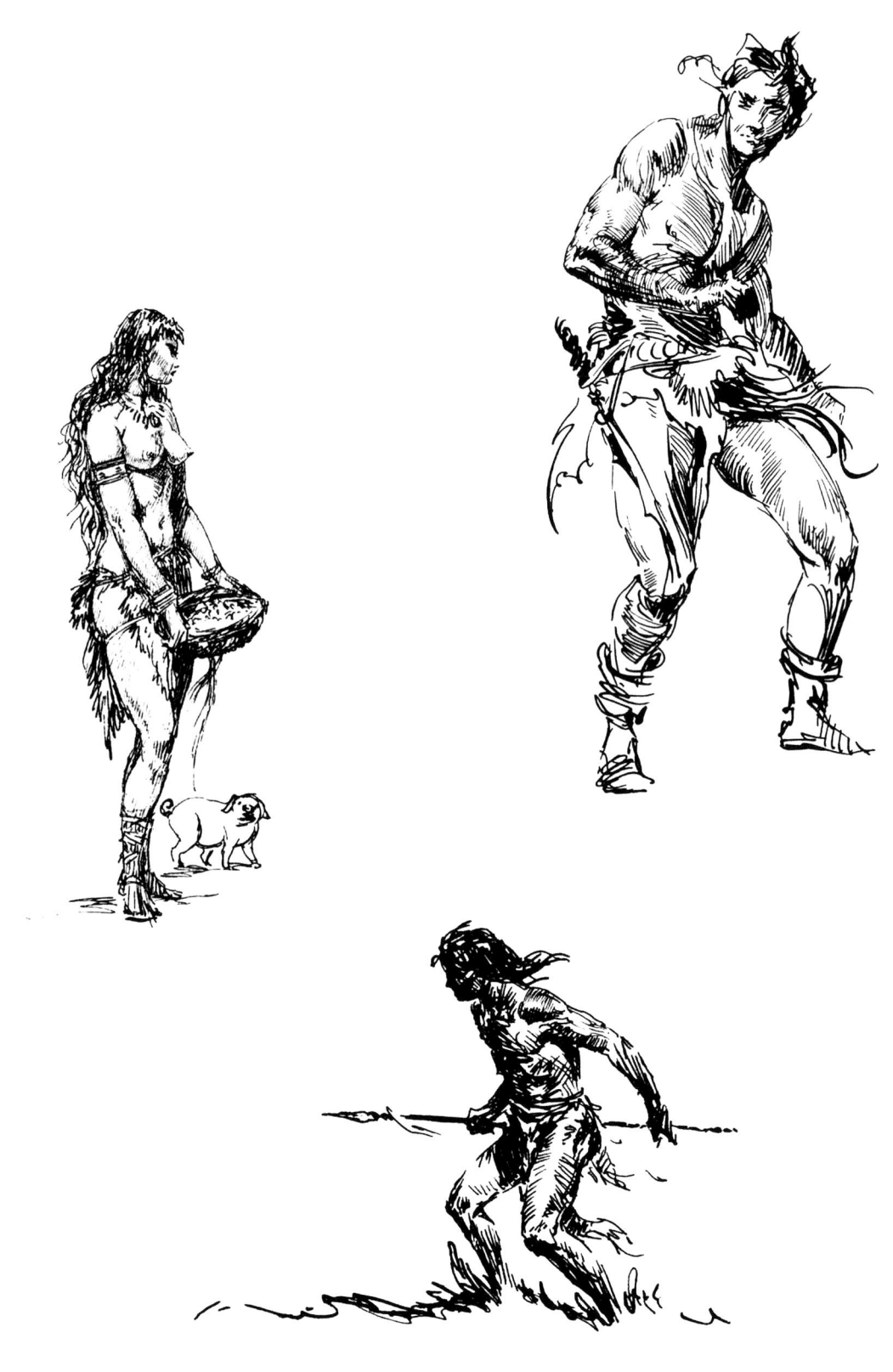

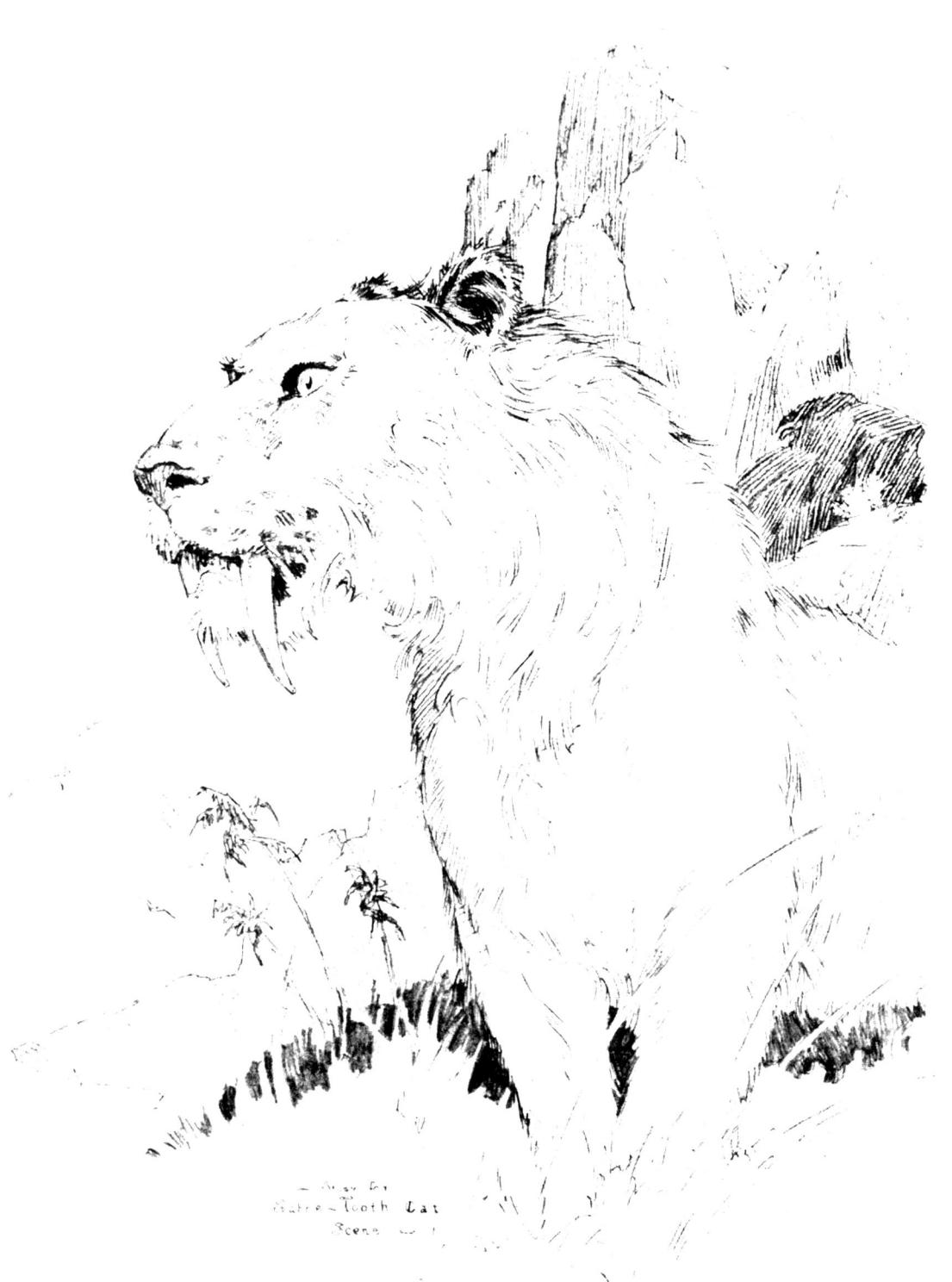

Saber-Tooth Cat
Scene

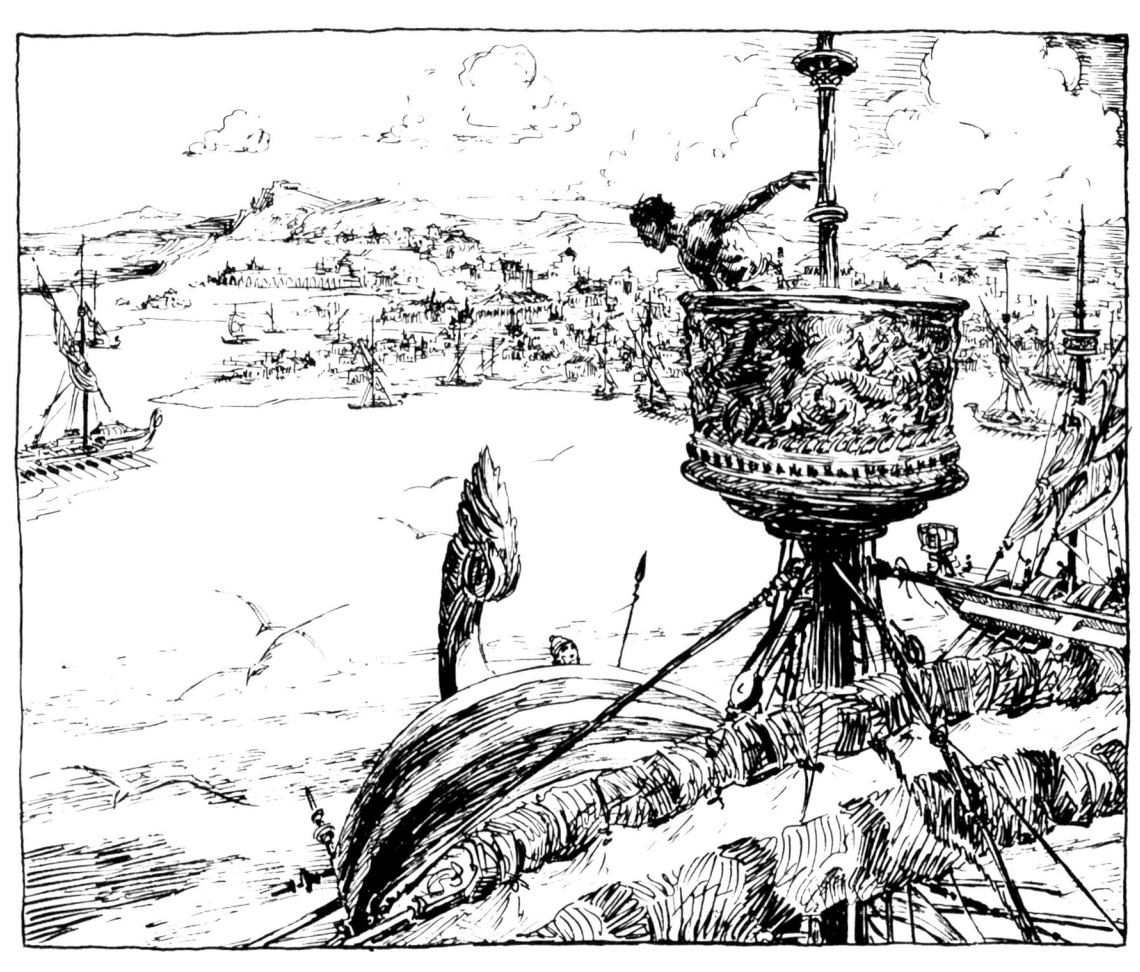

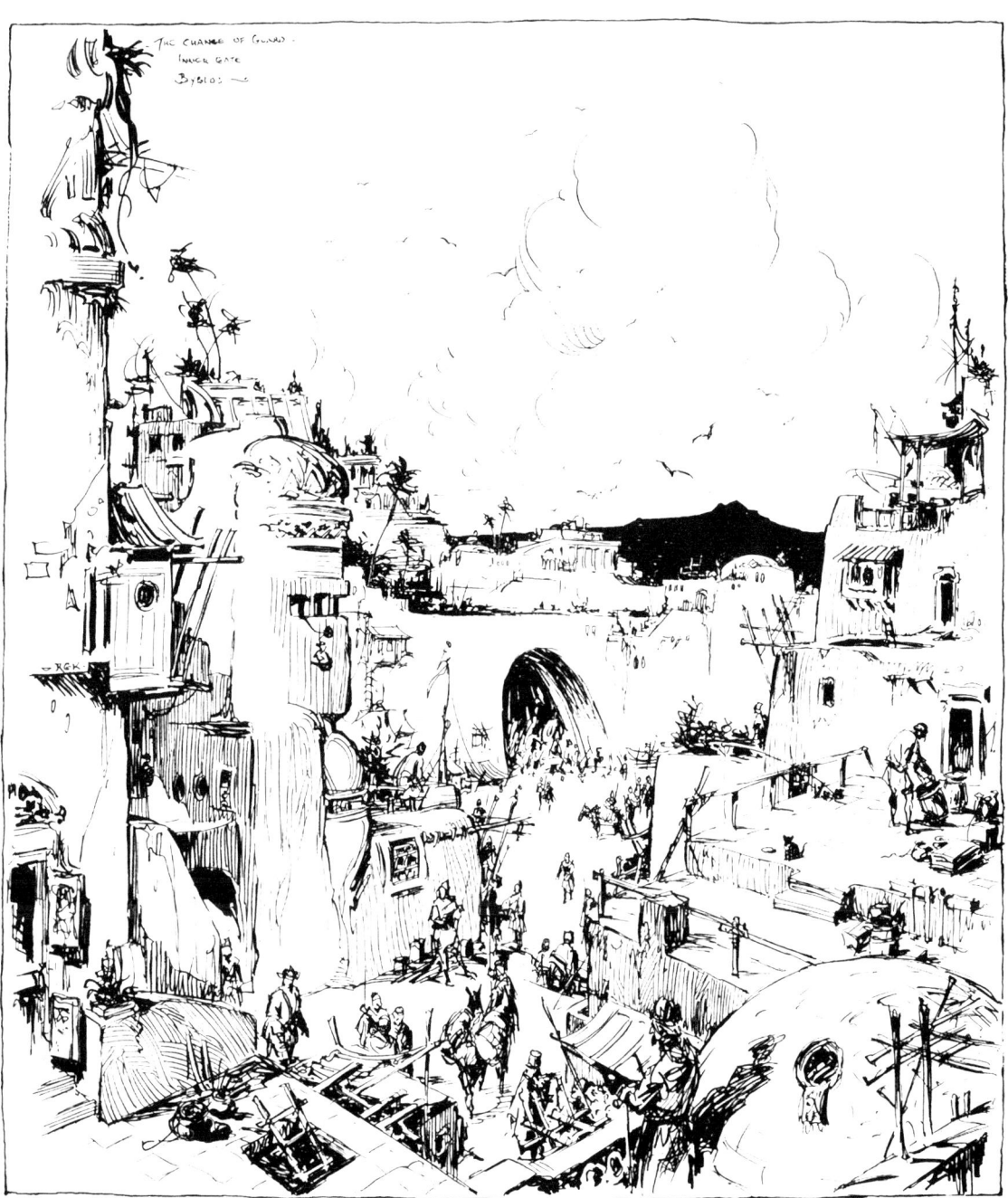

THE CHANGE OF GUARD.
INNER GATE
BYBLOS

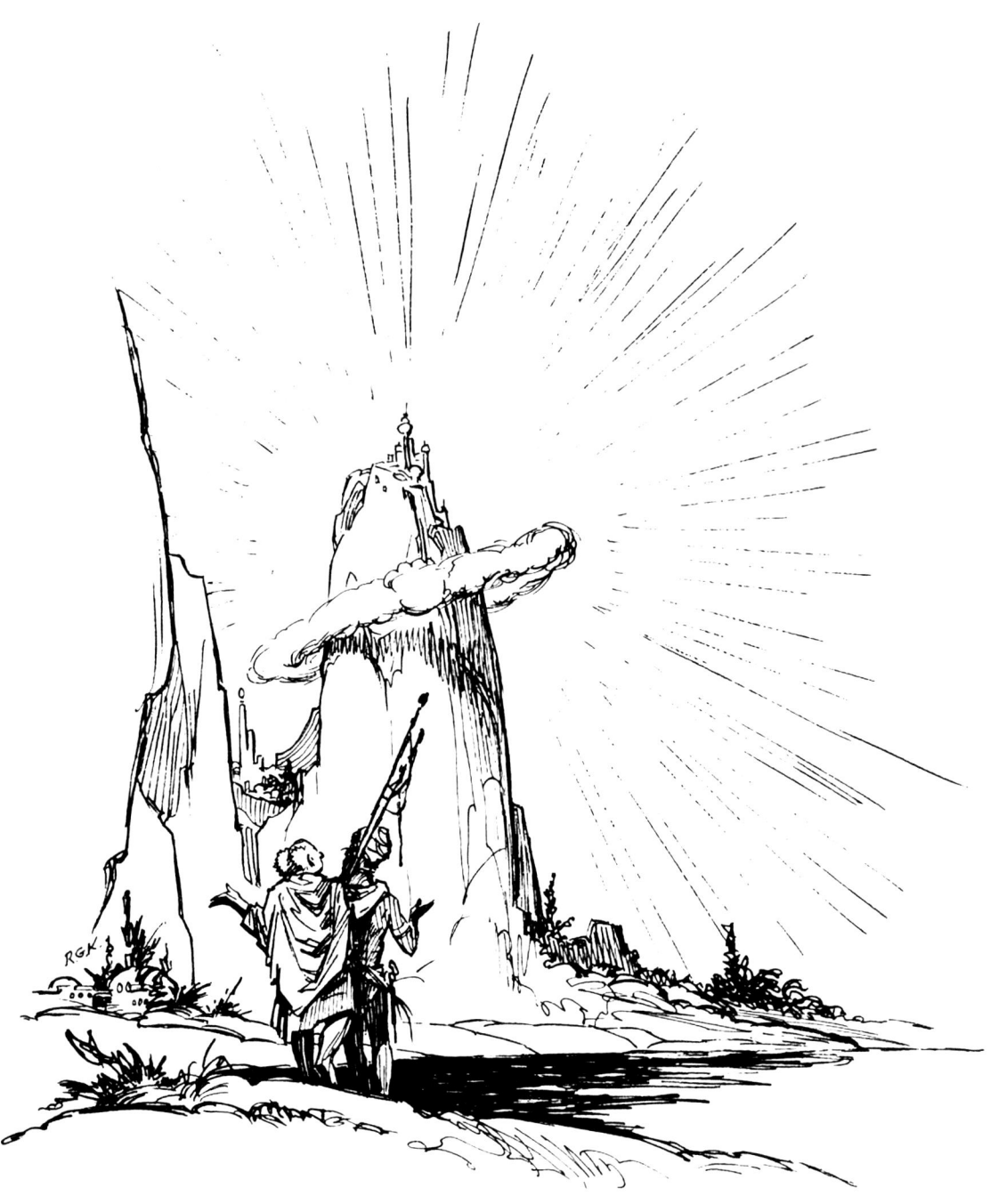

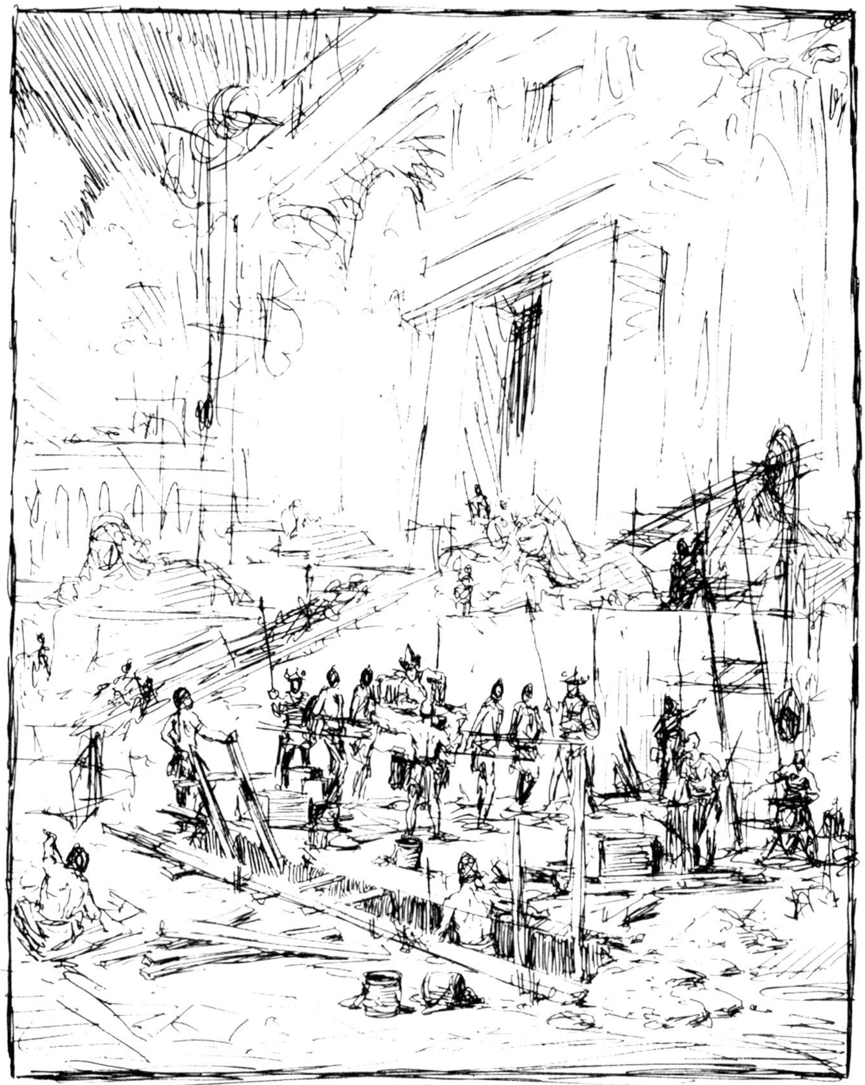

Construction of a Temple — Karnak

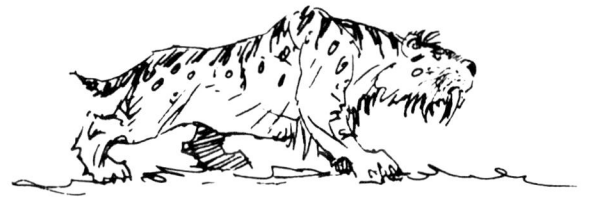

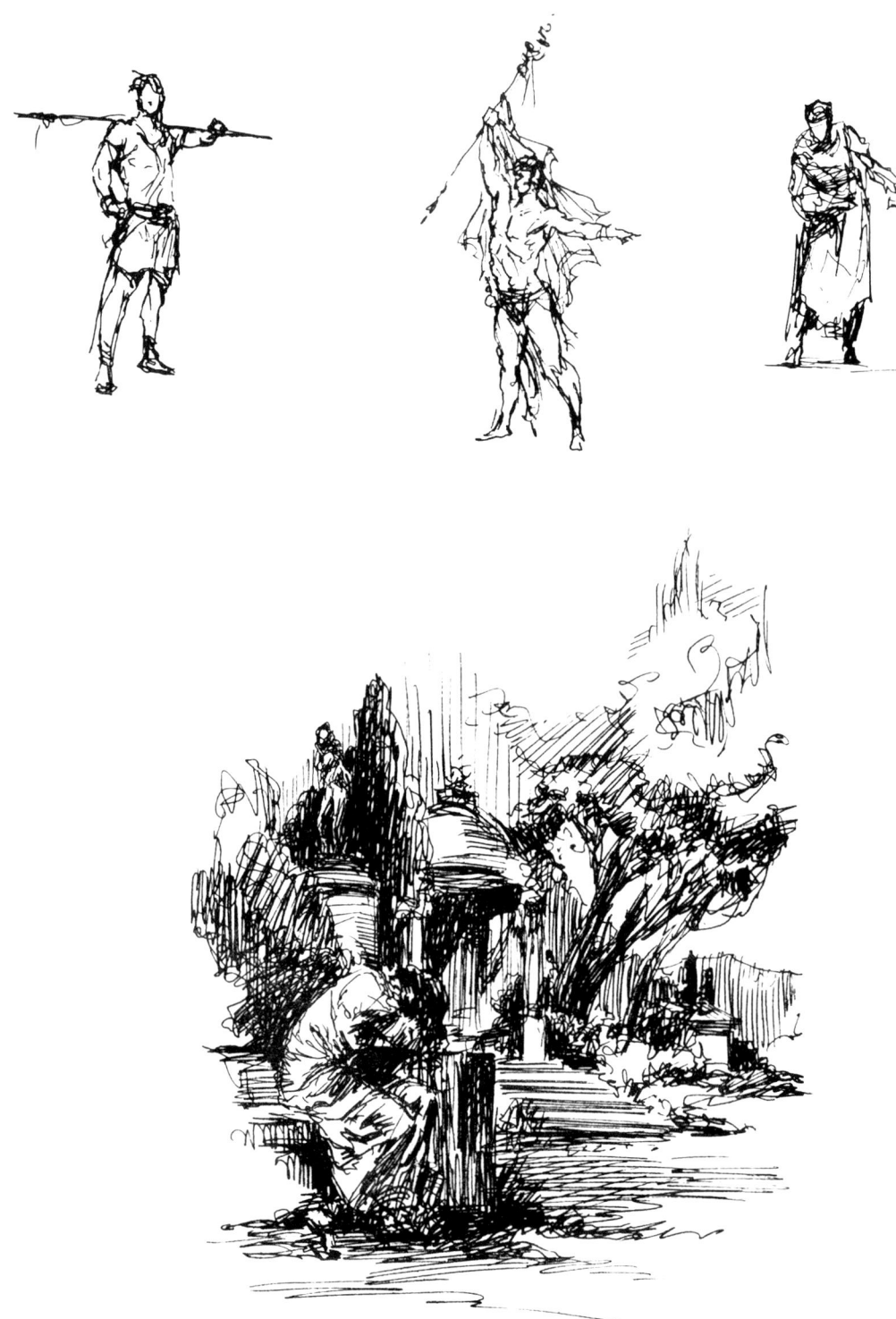

IDEA for – "The Forsaken Bower"

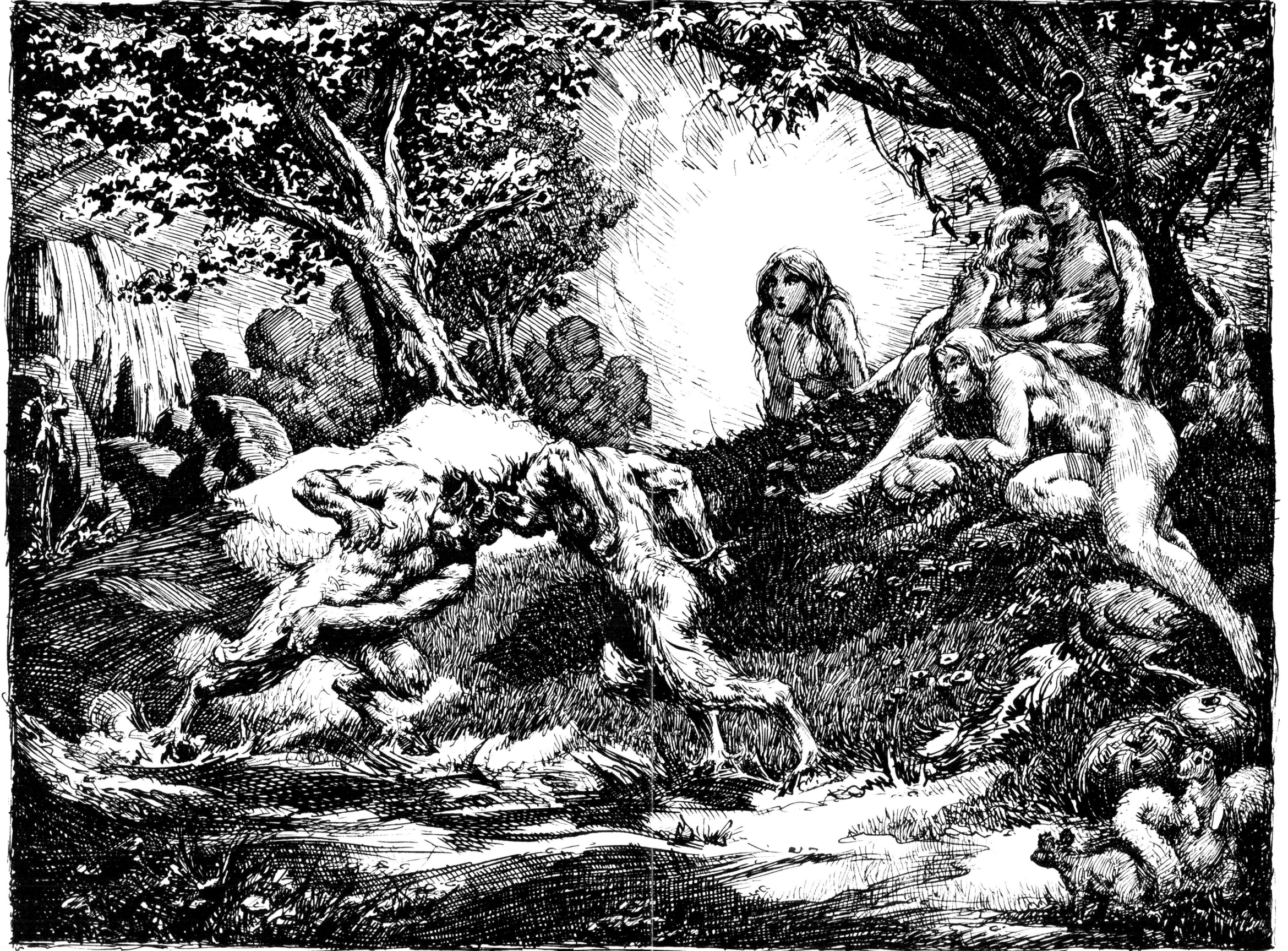

Satyrs Fighting

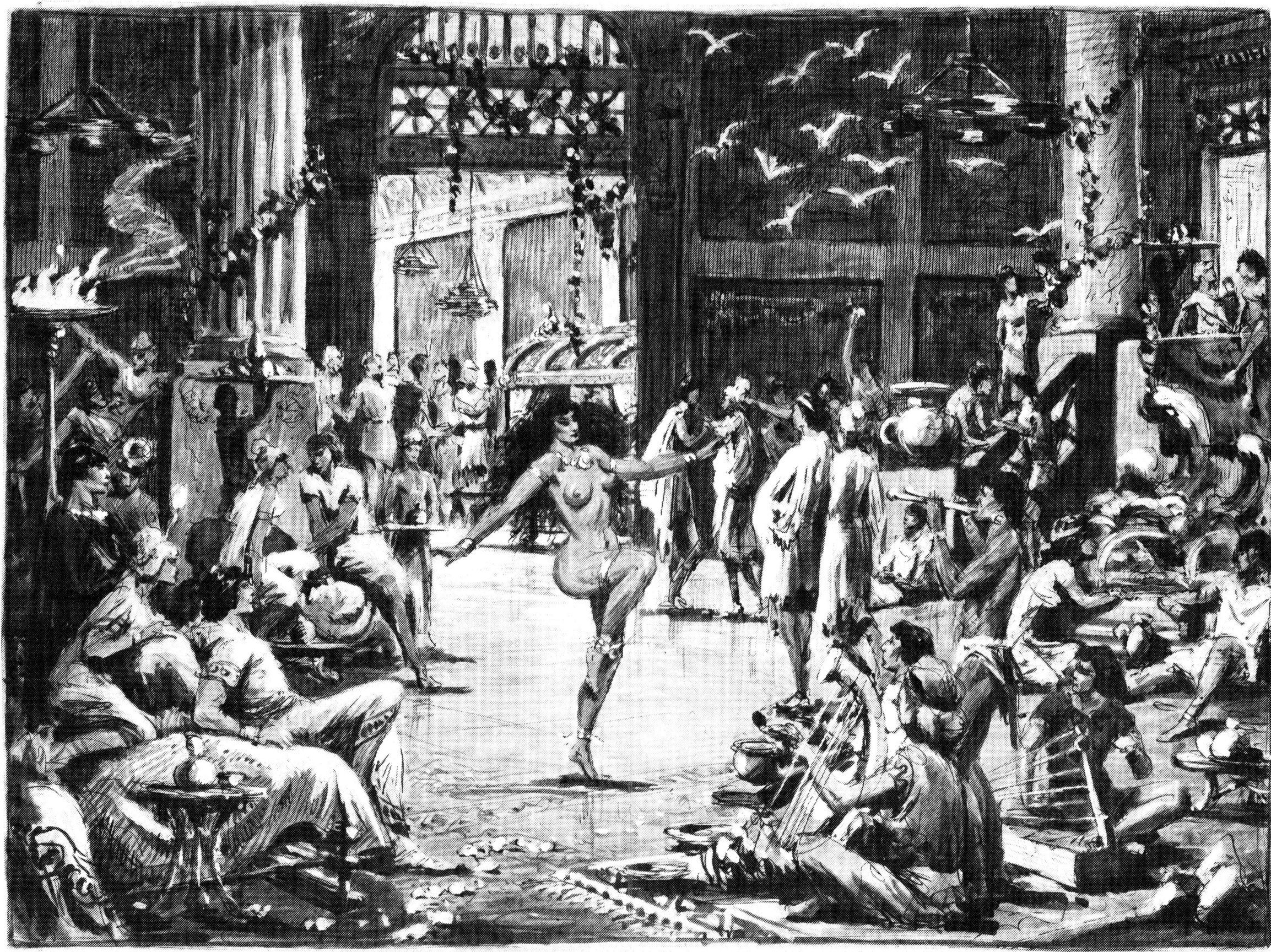

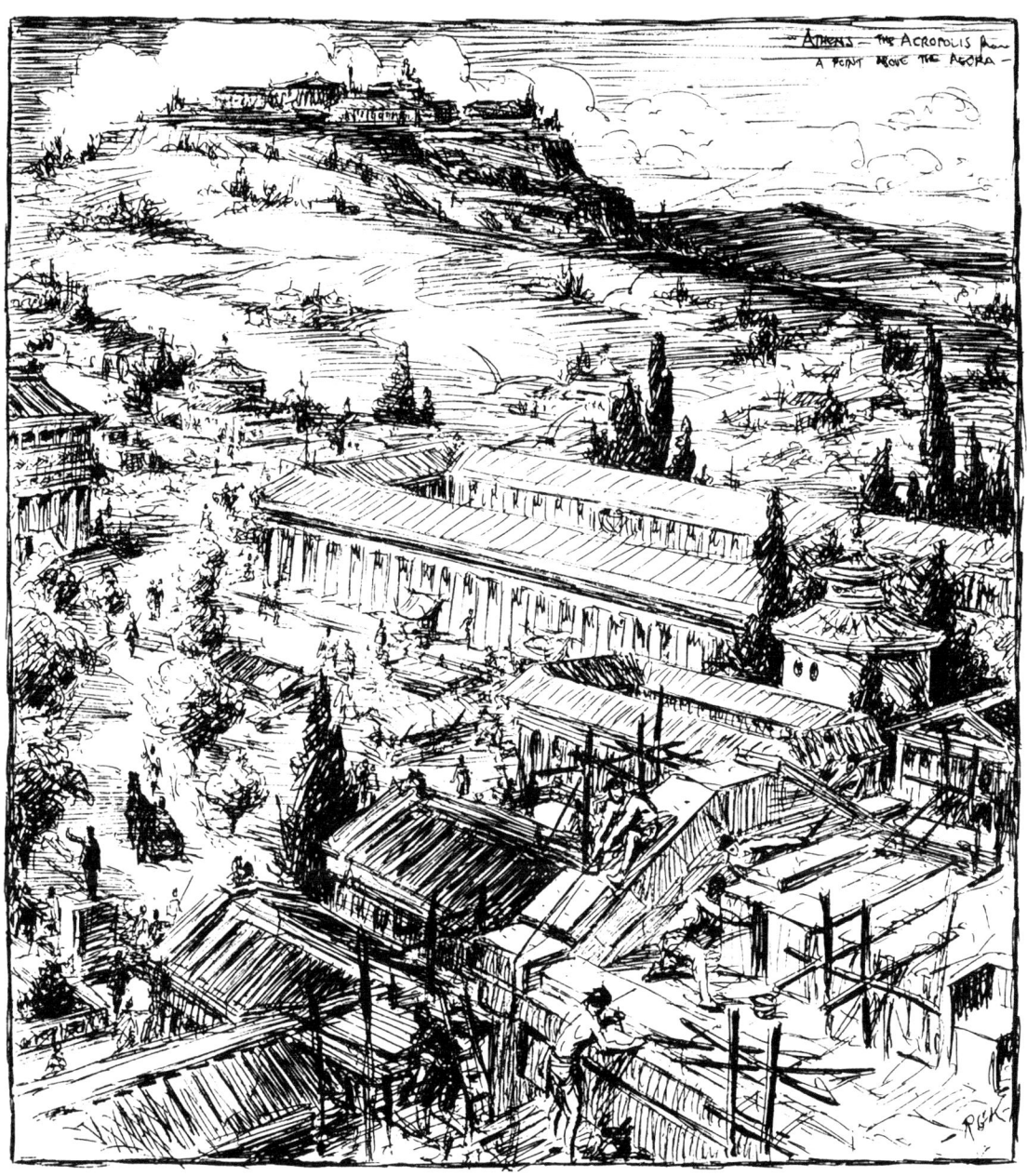

ATHENS — THE ACROPOLIS from
A POINT ABOVE THE AGORA —

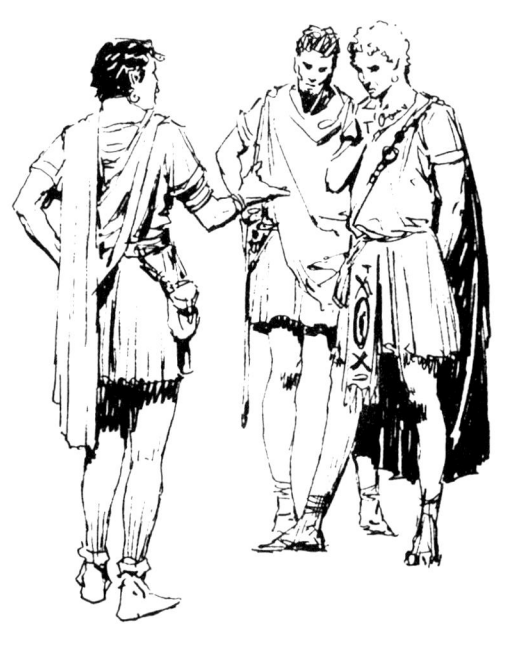

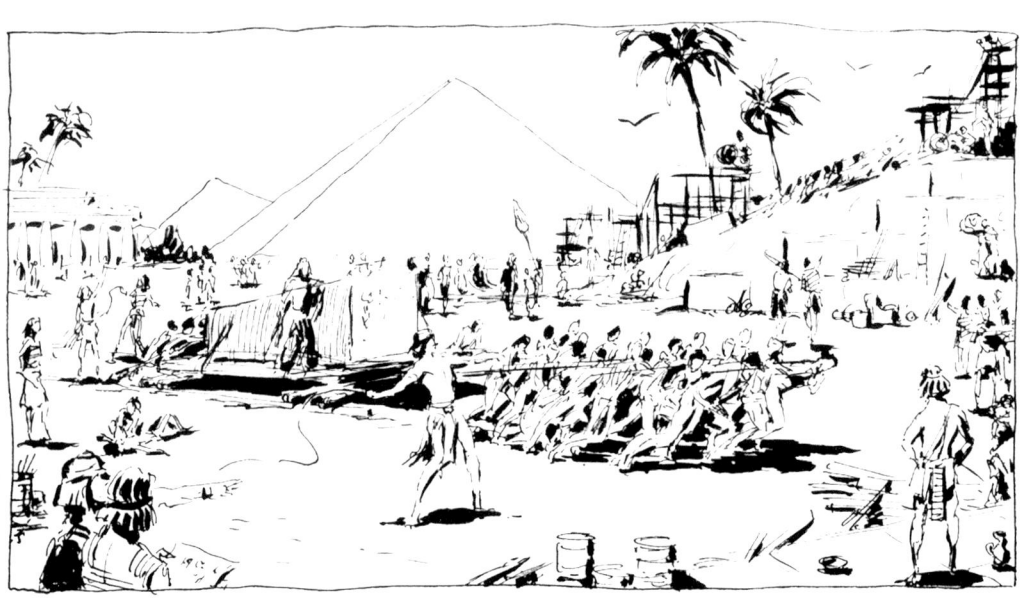

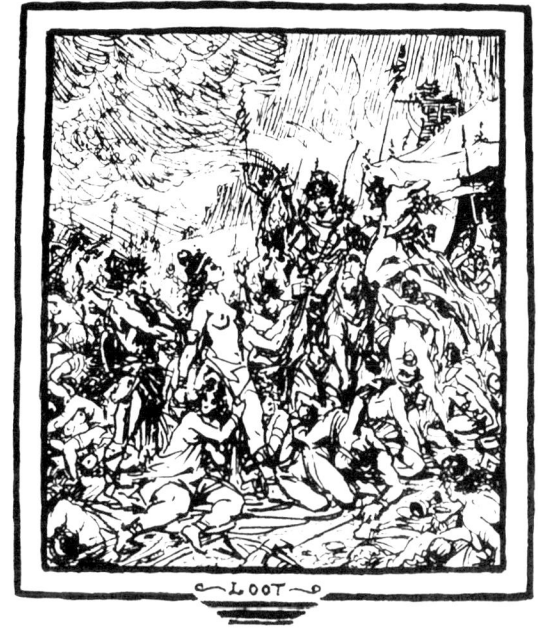

LOOT

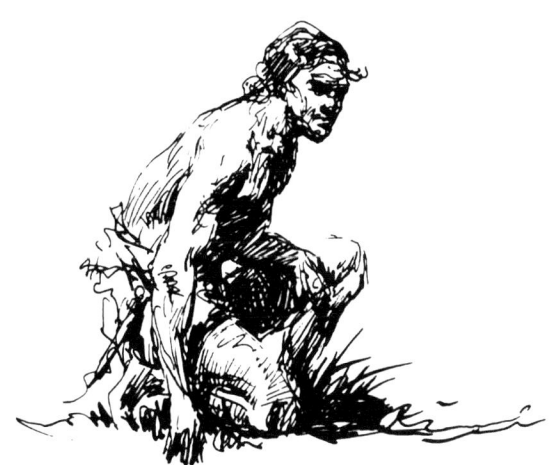

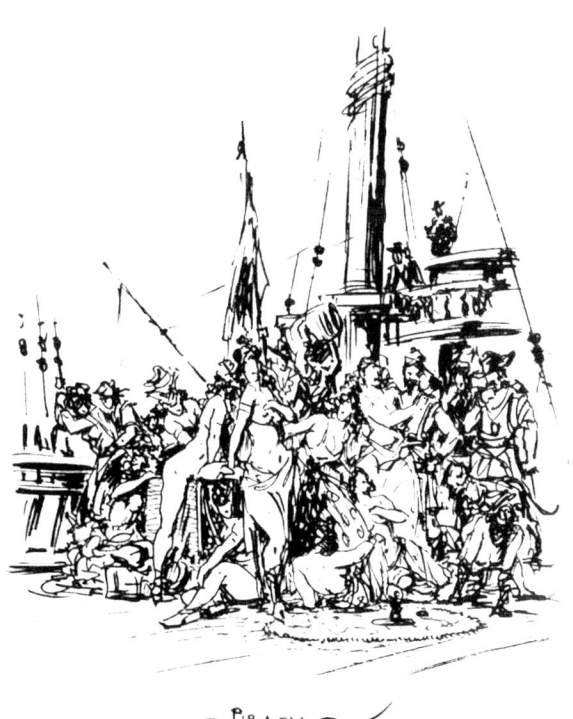

PIRACY

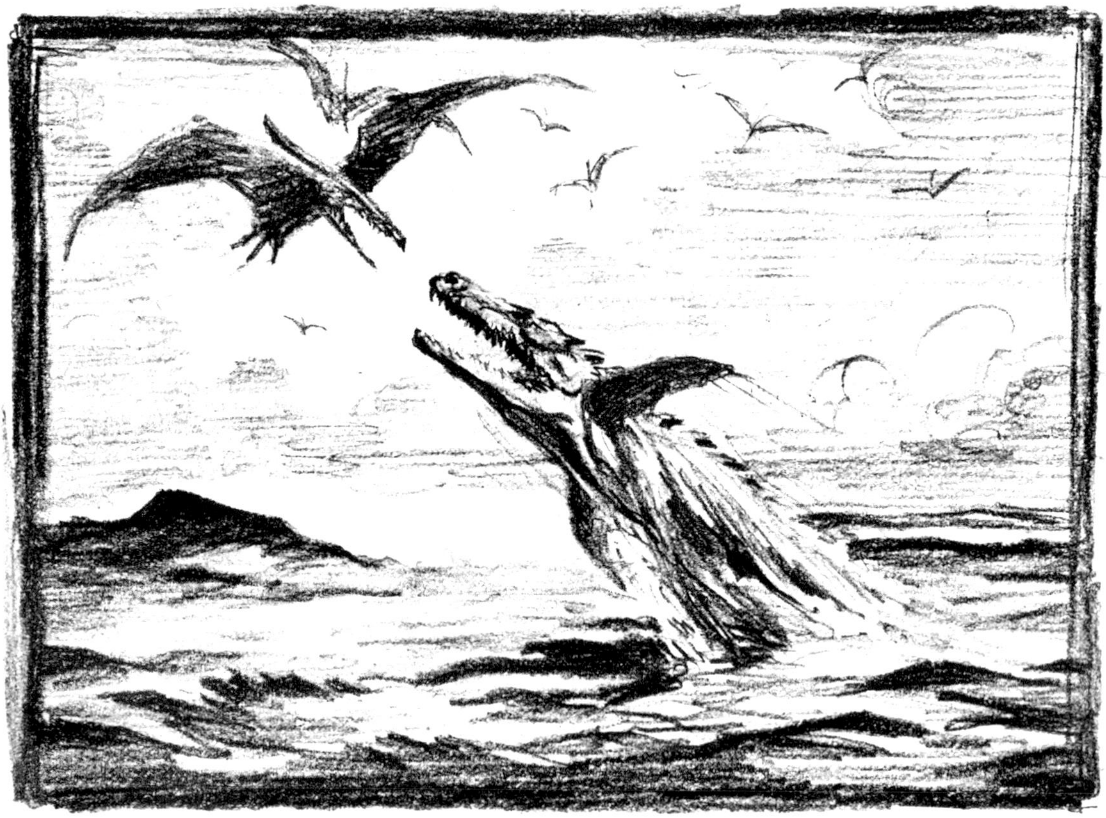

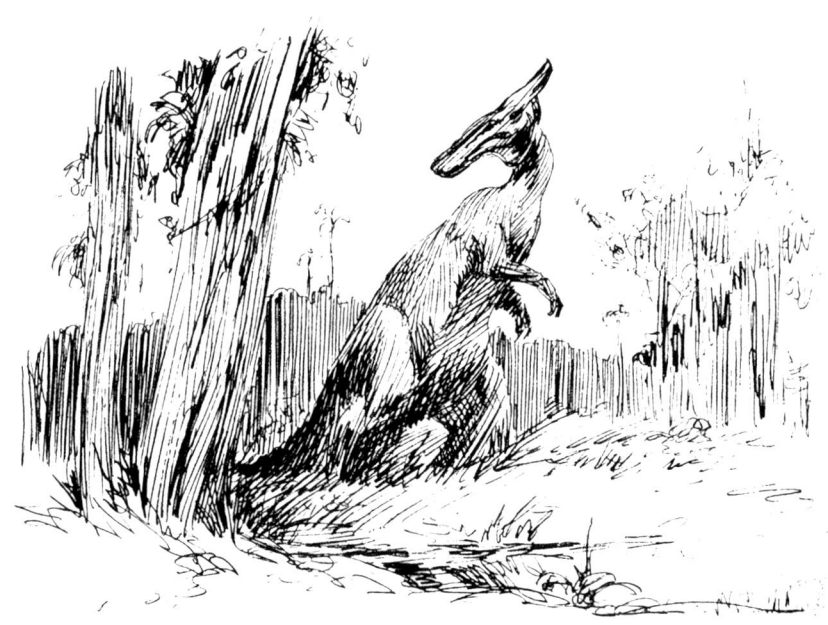

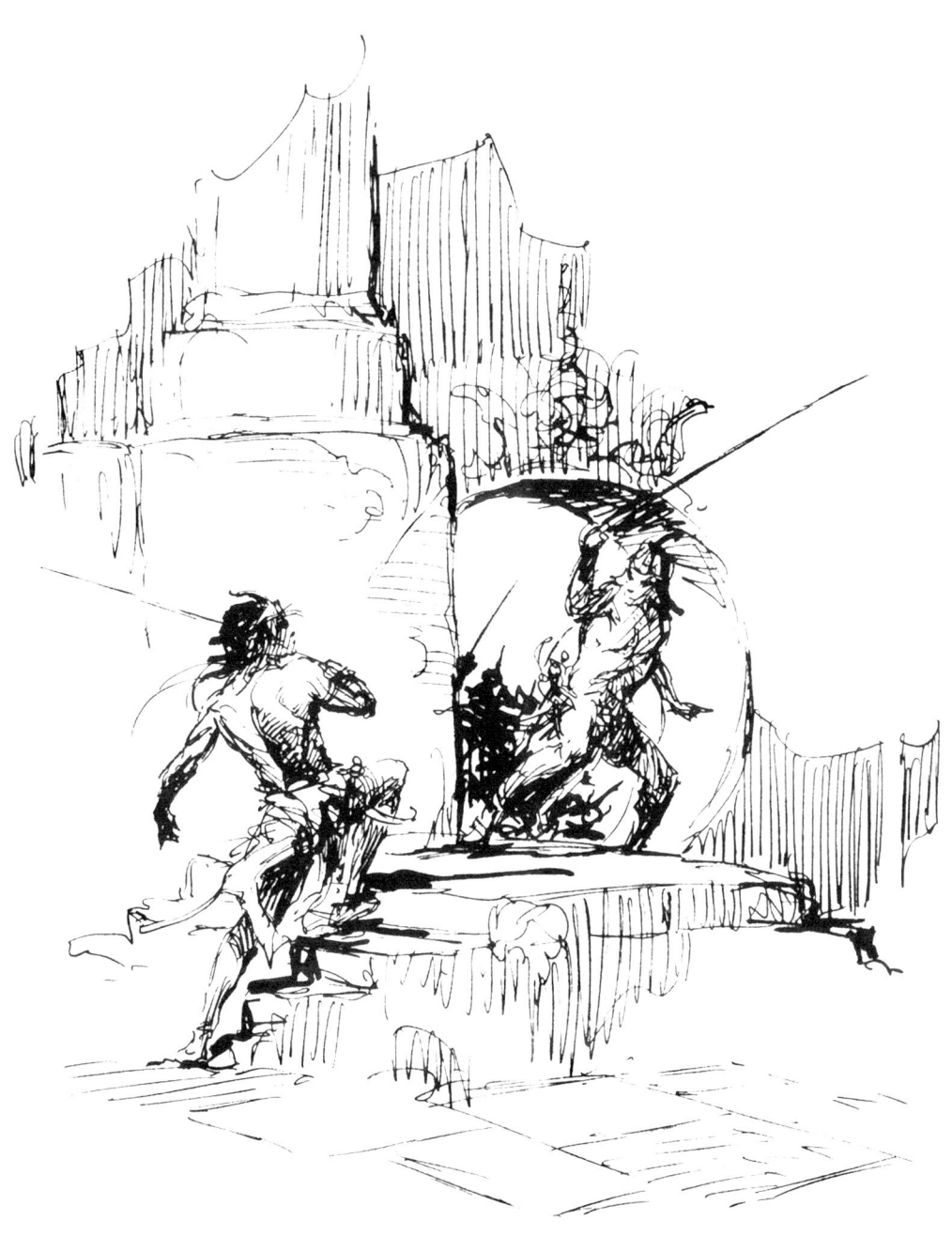

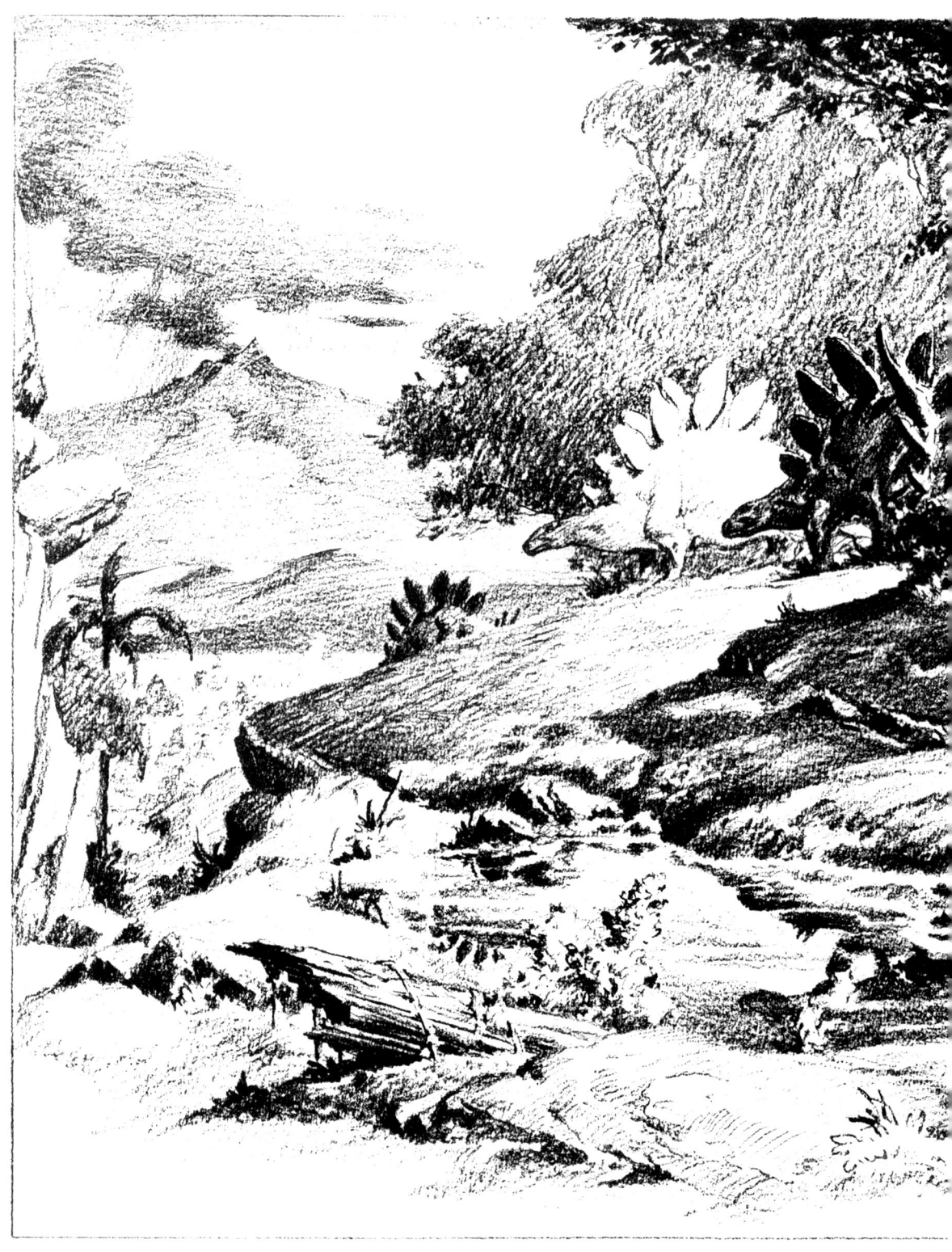

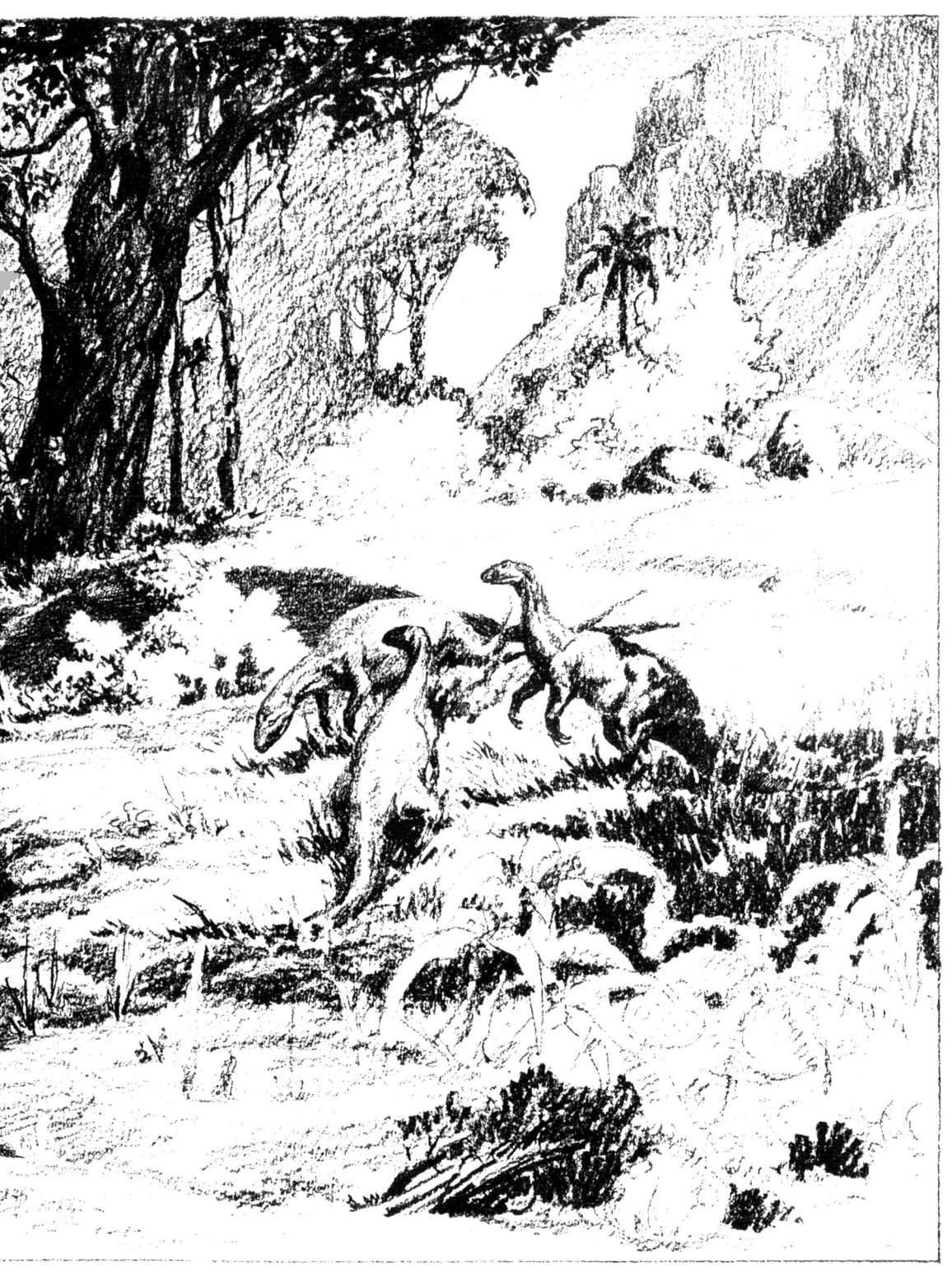

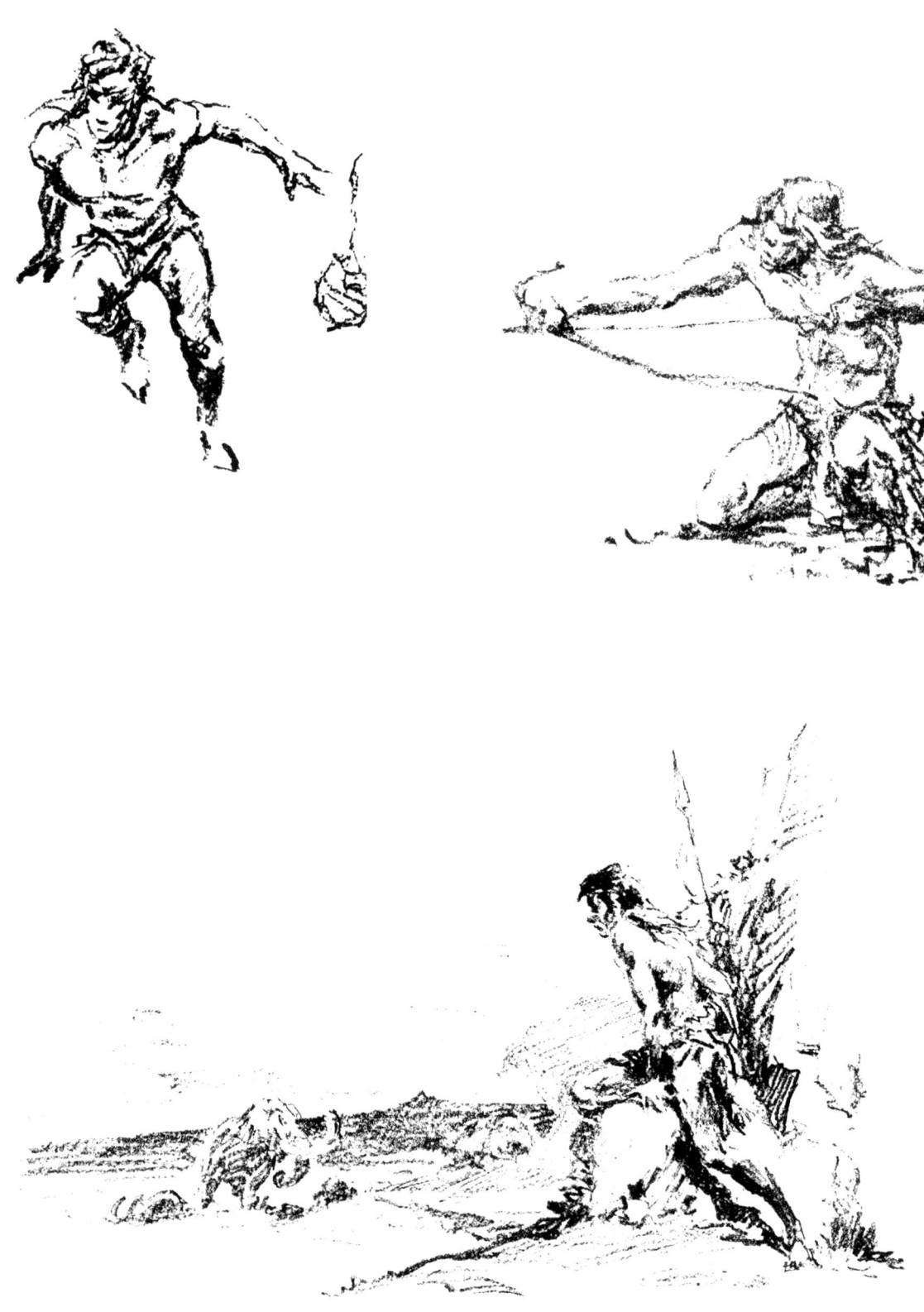

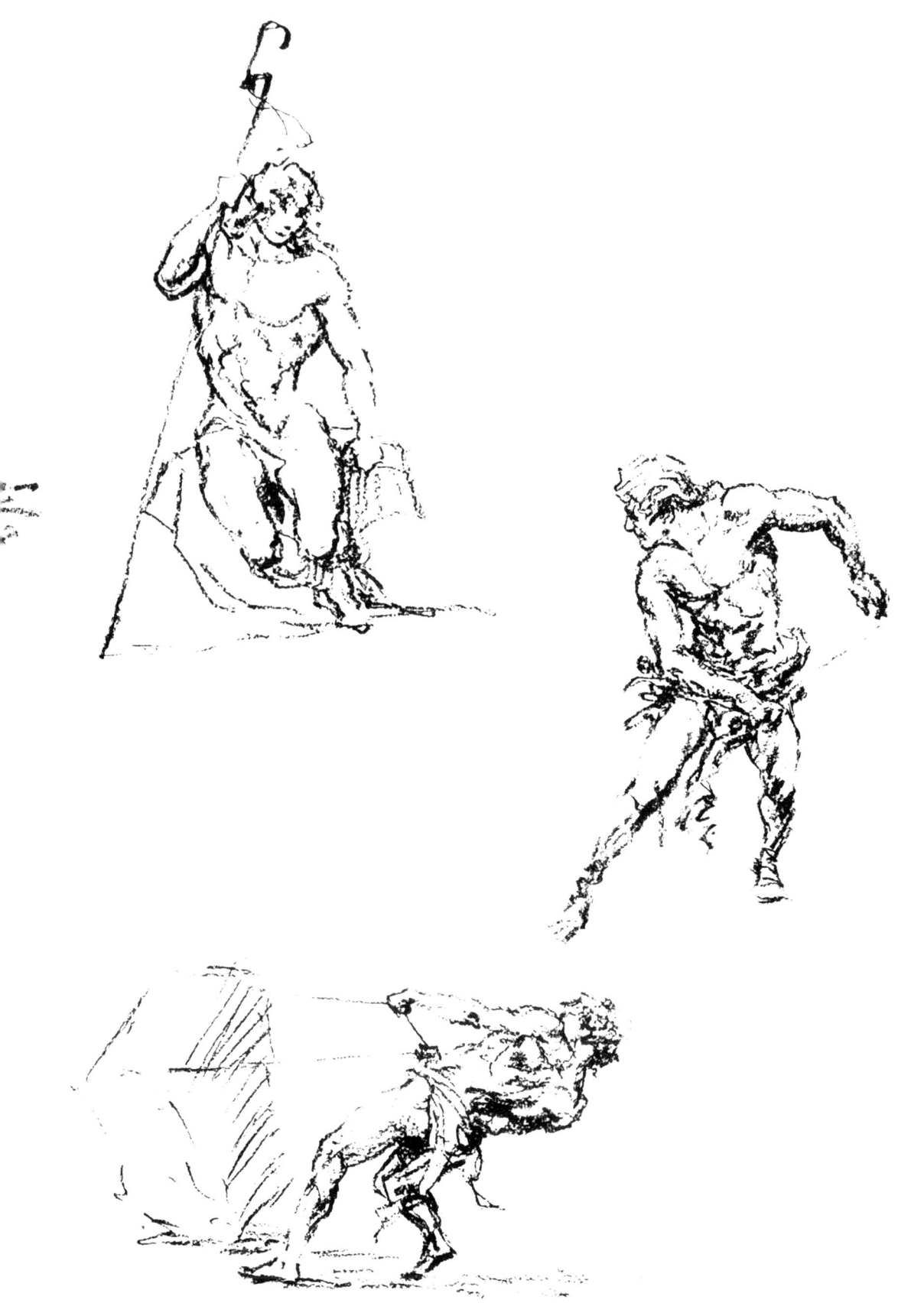

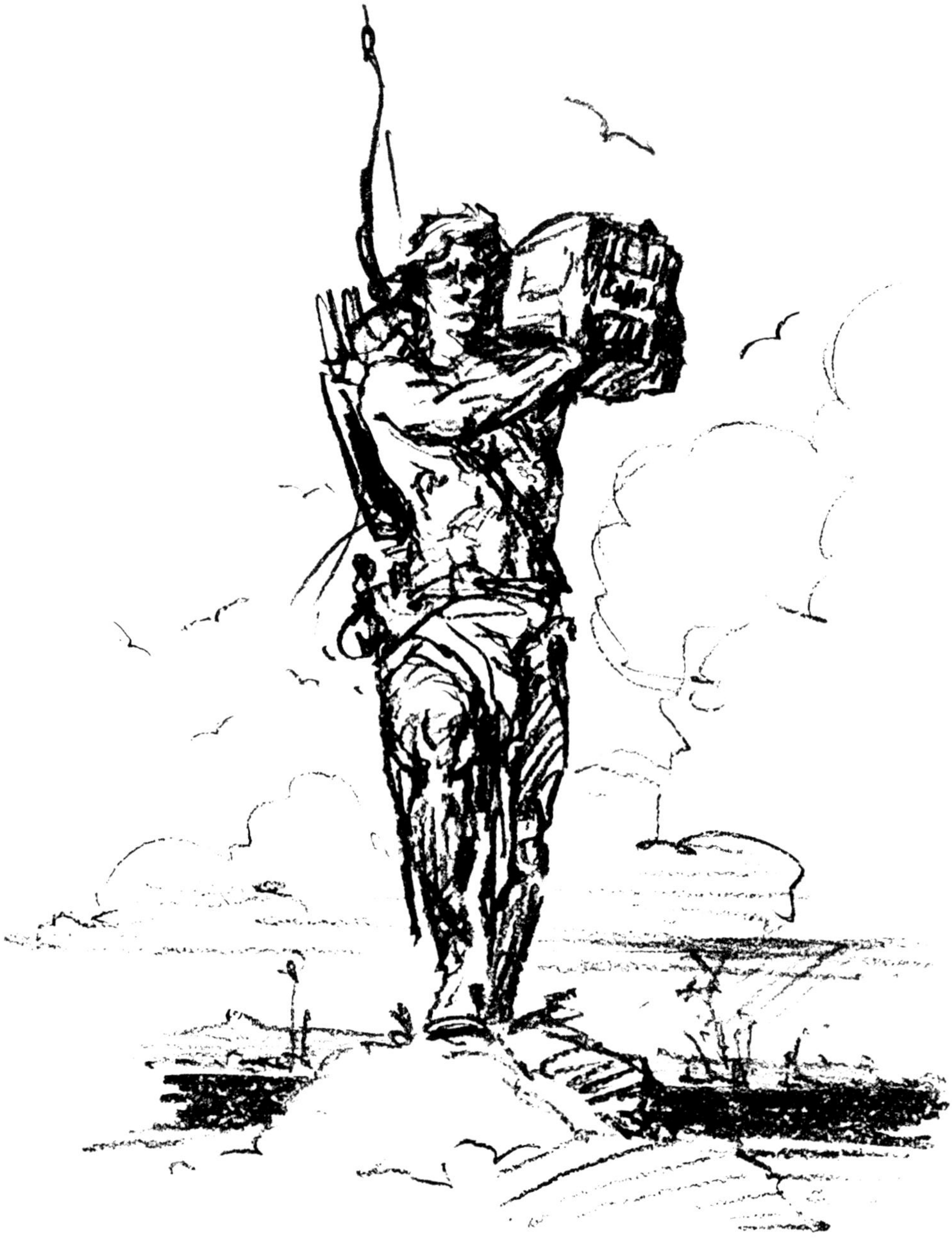

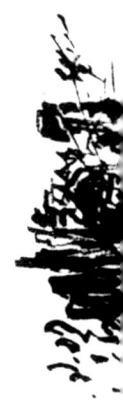

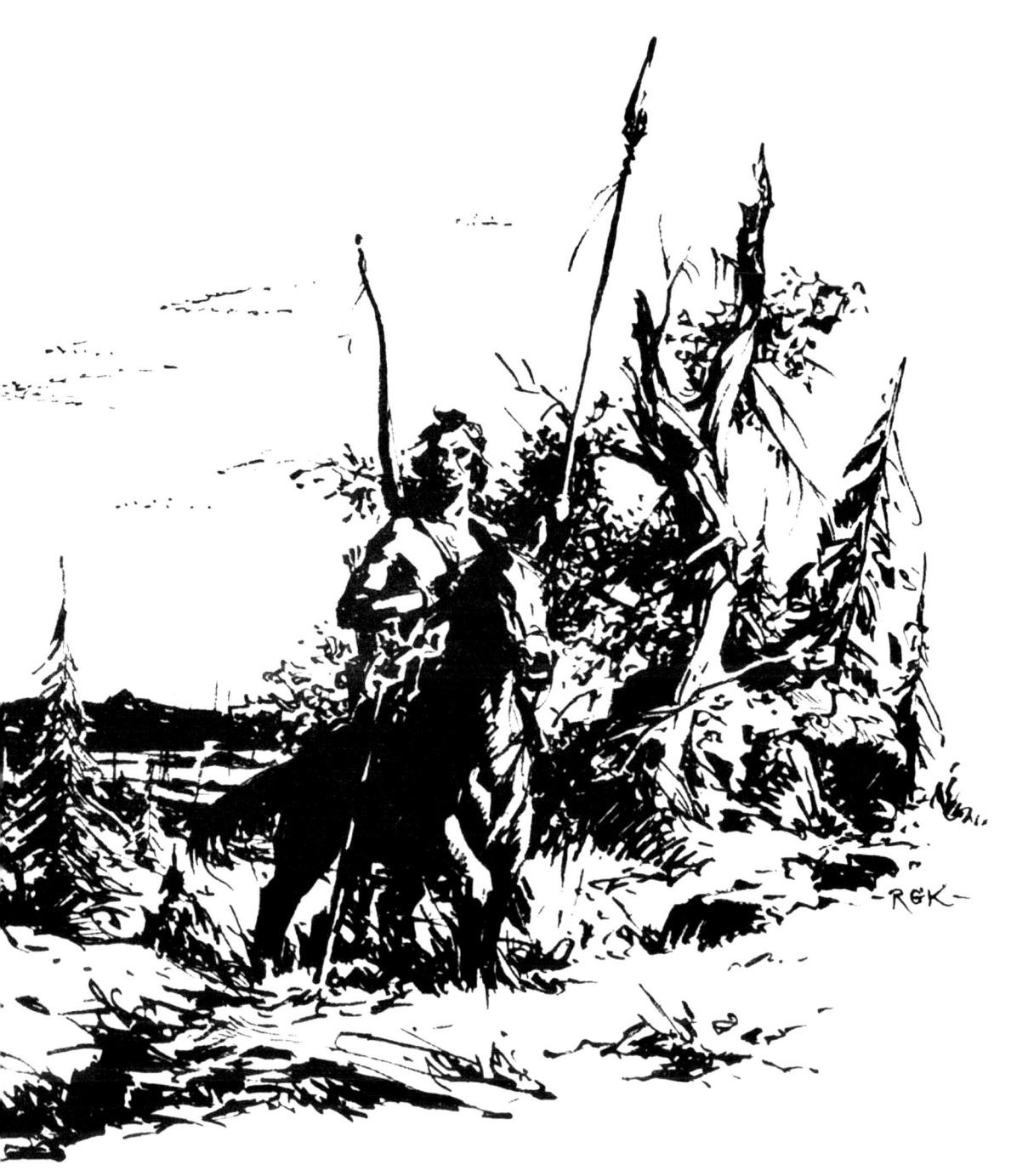

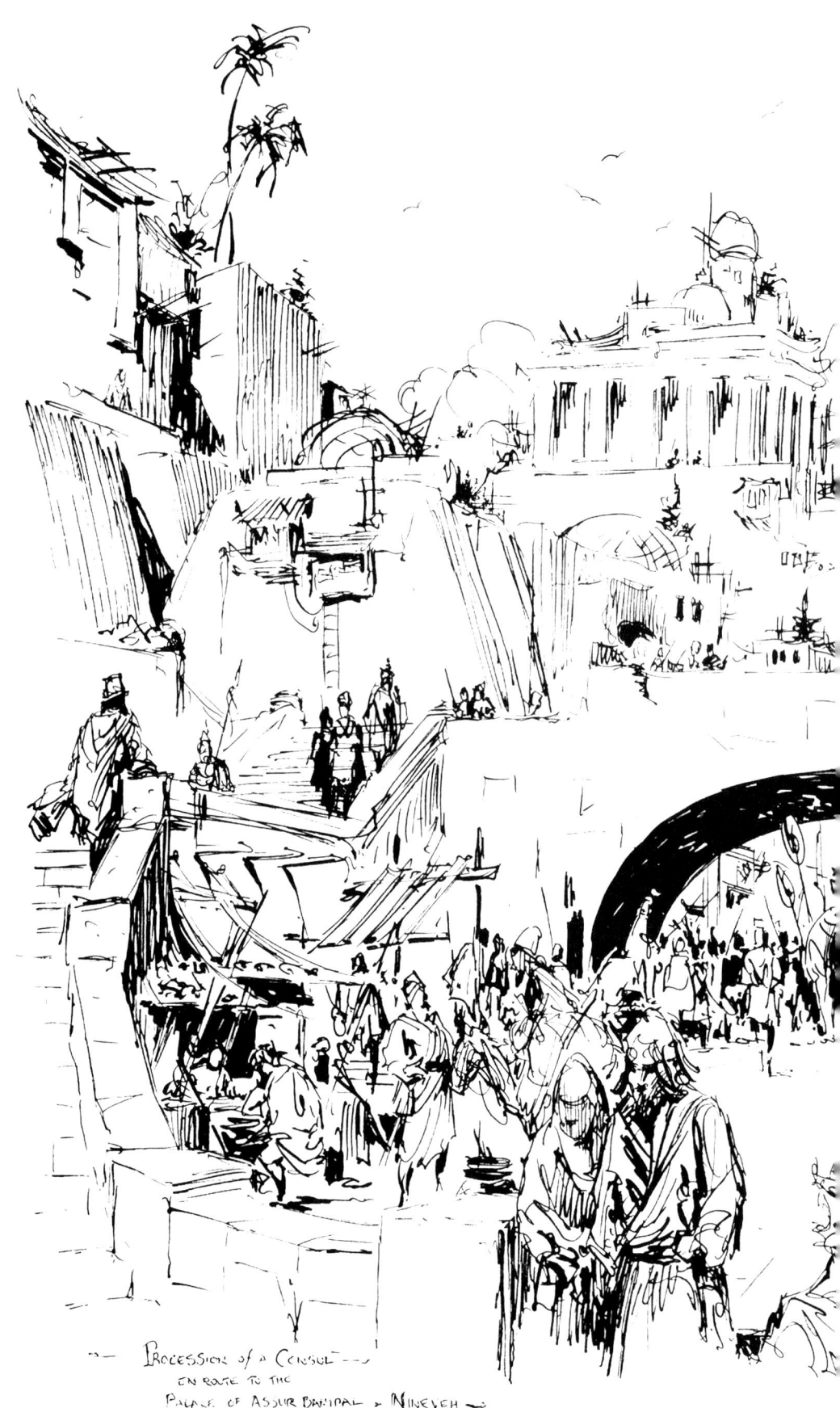

PROCESSION OF A CONSUL ⸻
EN ROUTE TO THE
PALACE OF ASSUR BANIPAL ⸱ NINEVEH ⸱

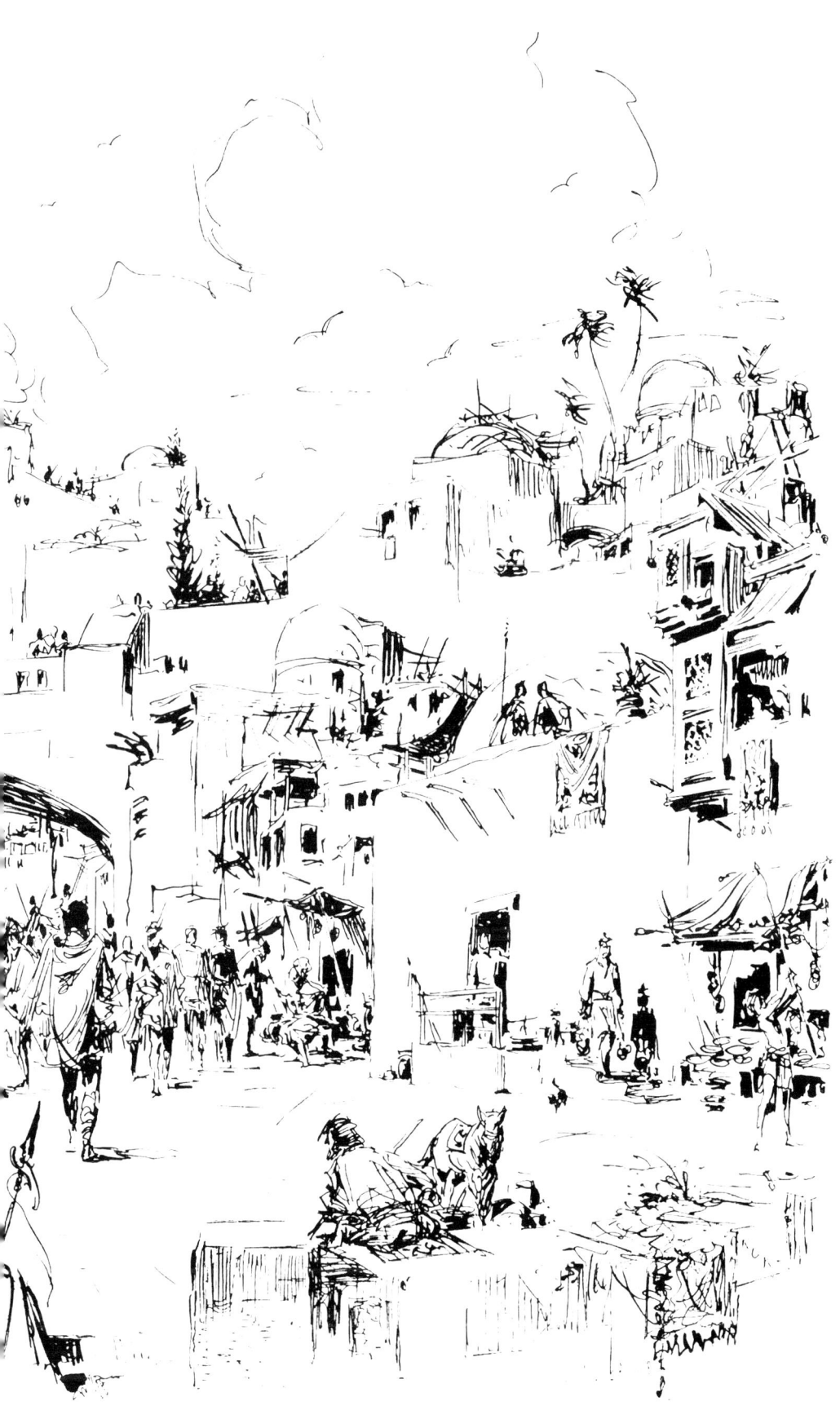

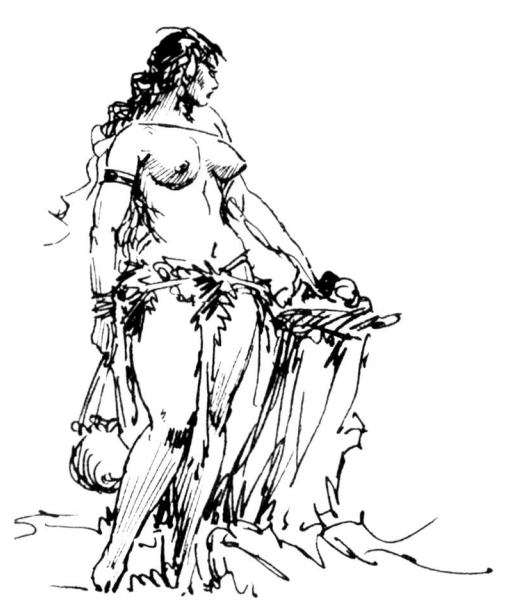

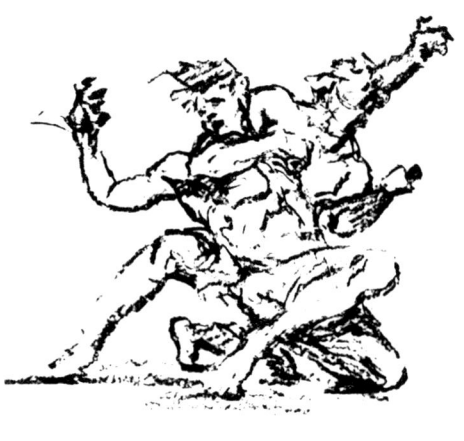

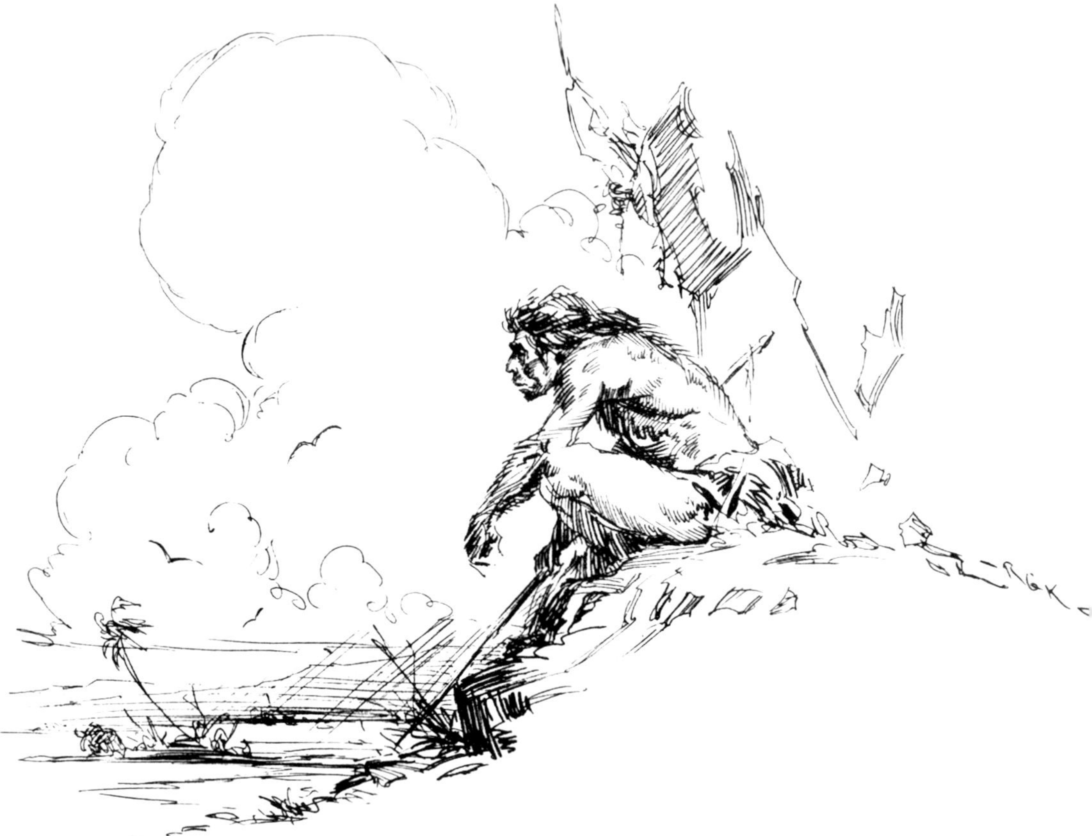

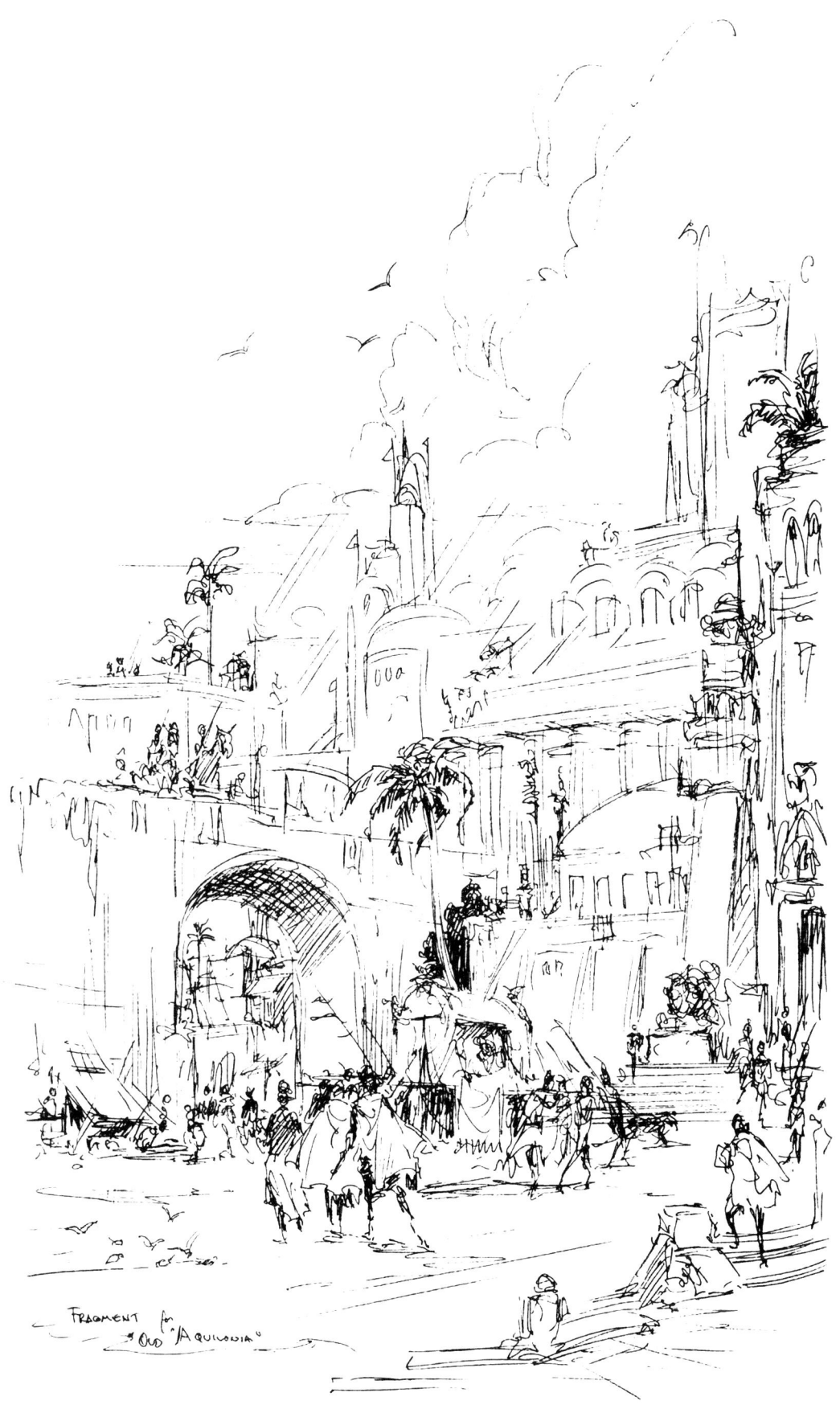

FRAGMENT for OLD "AQUILONIA"

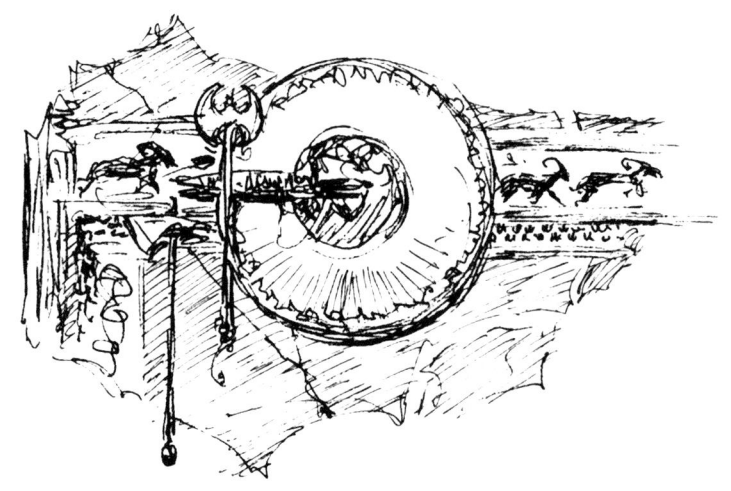

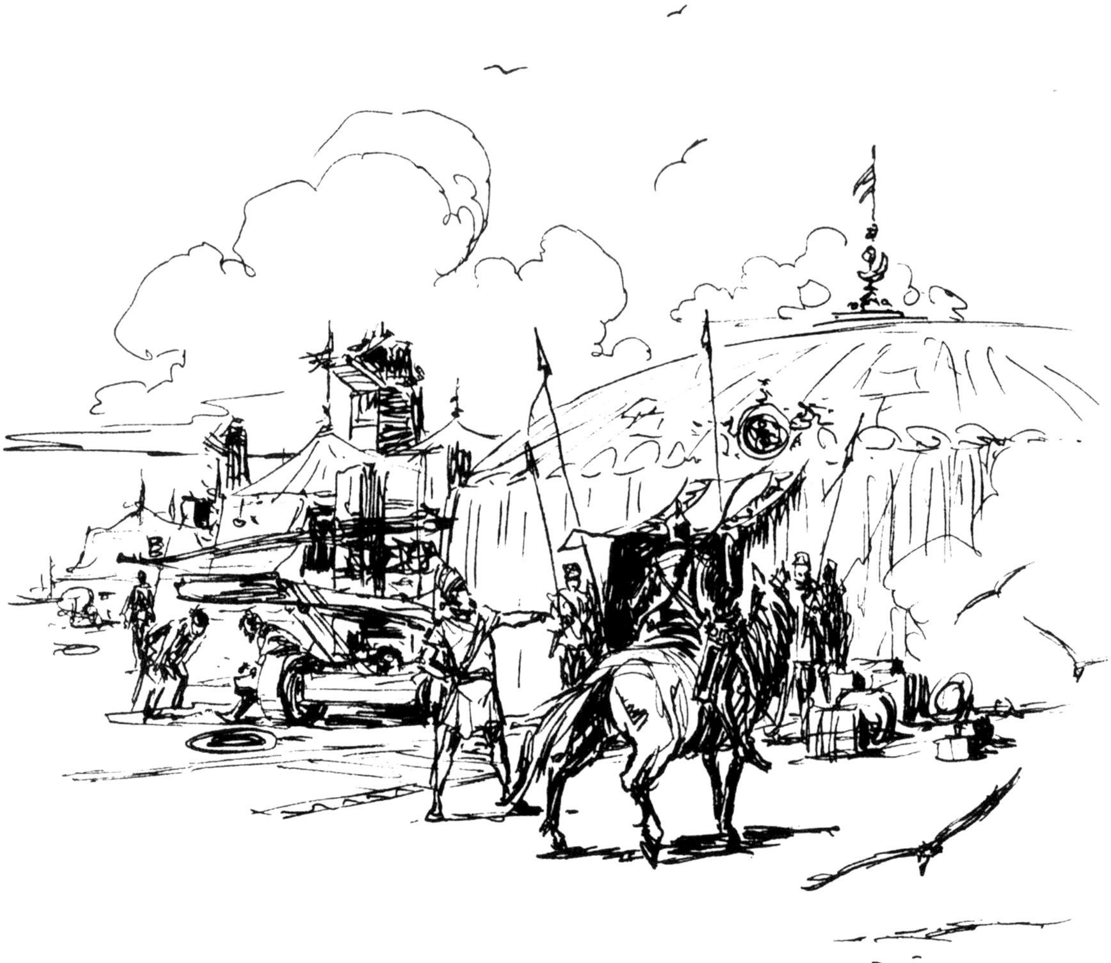

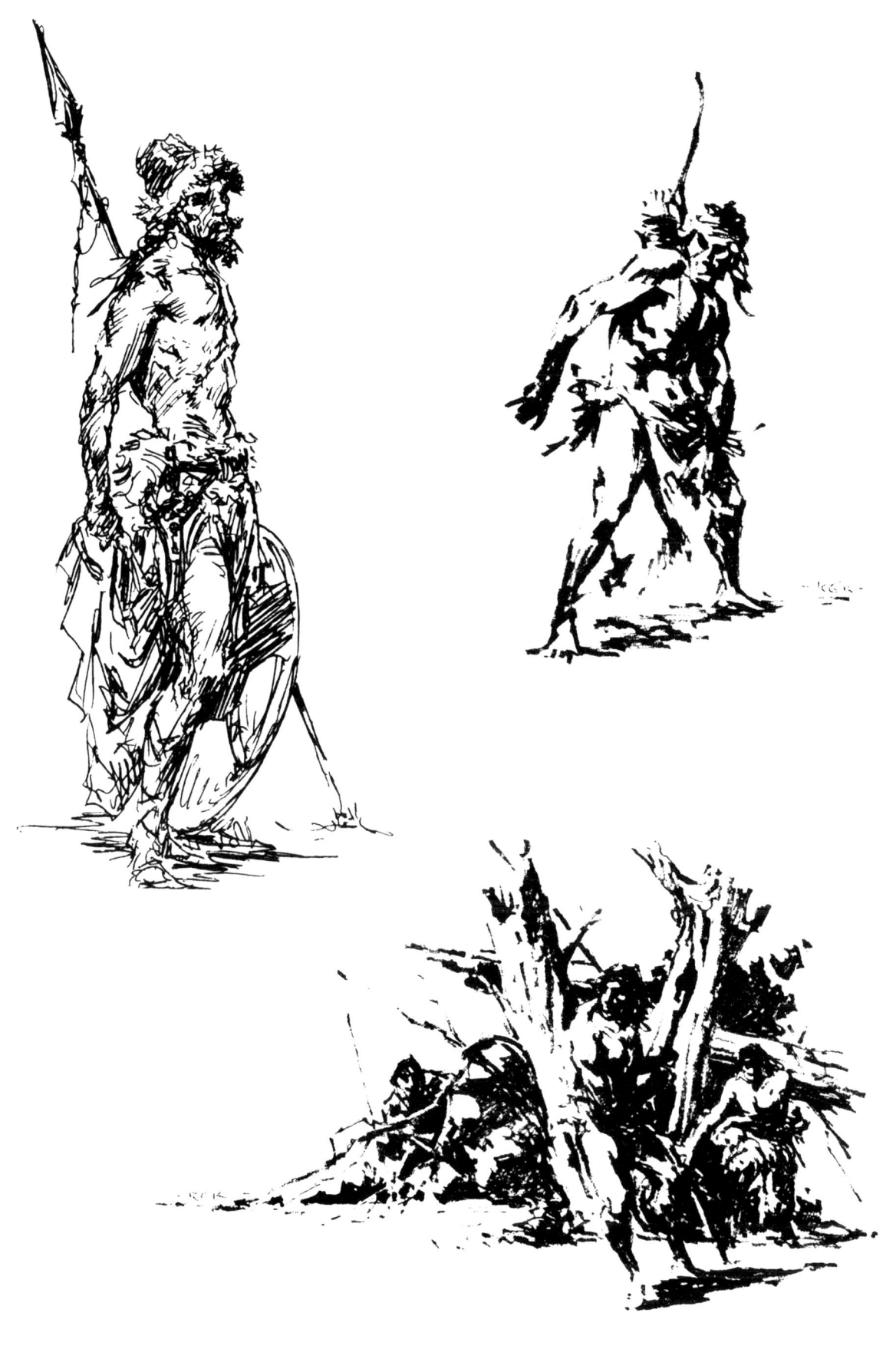

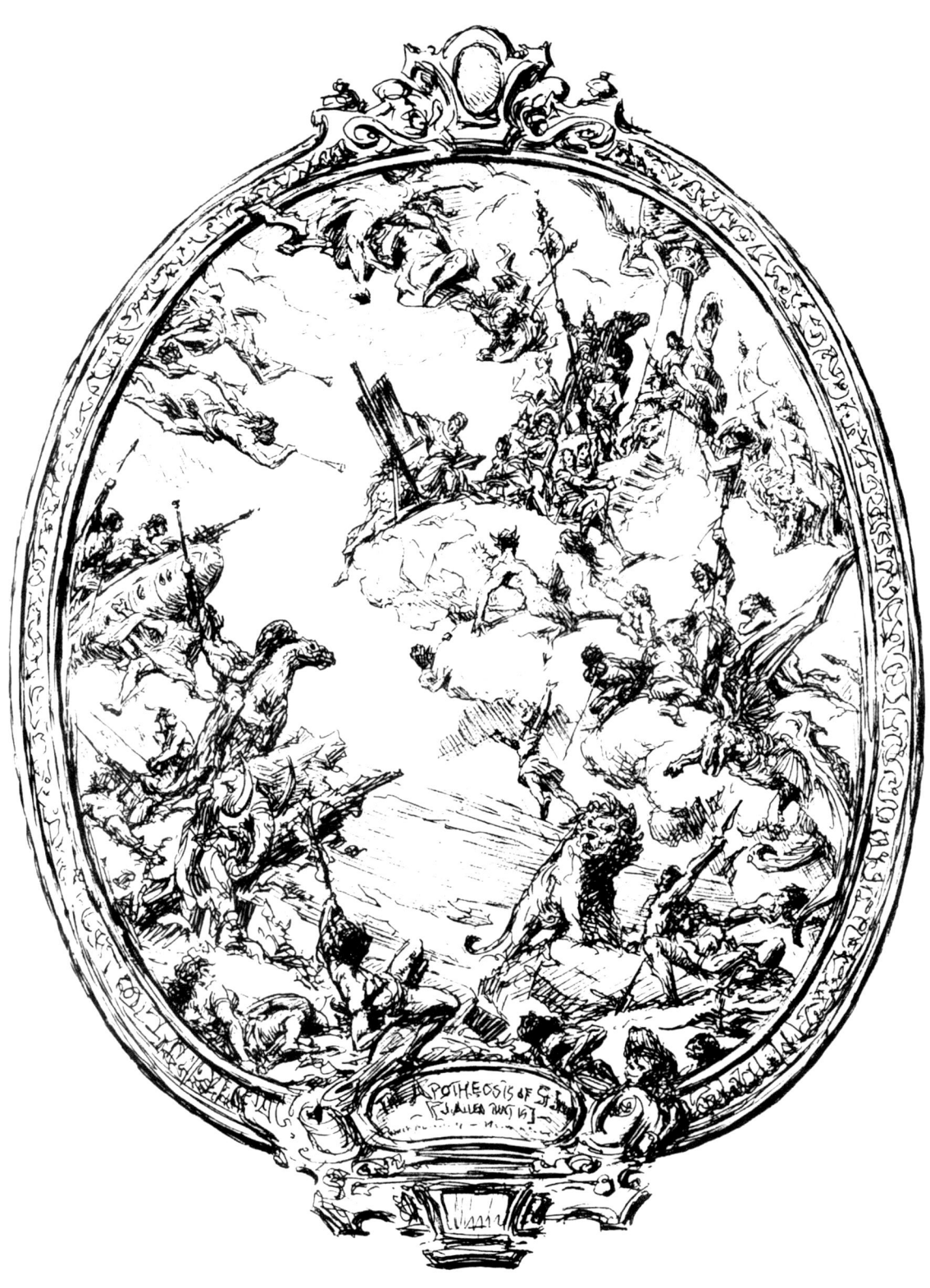

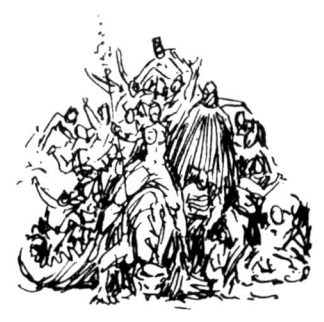

- GROUP IDEA FOR "SORCERY" -

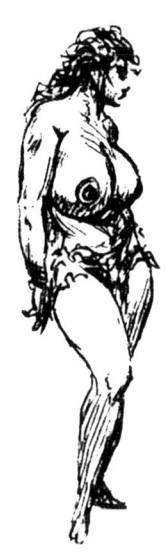

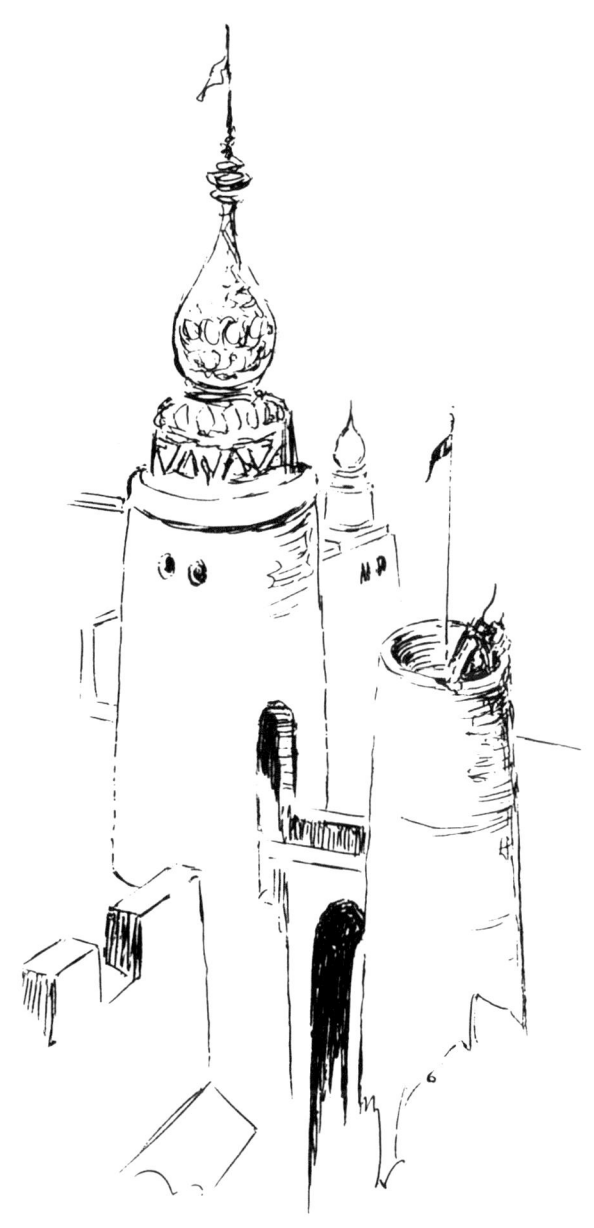

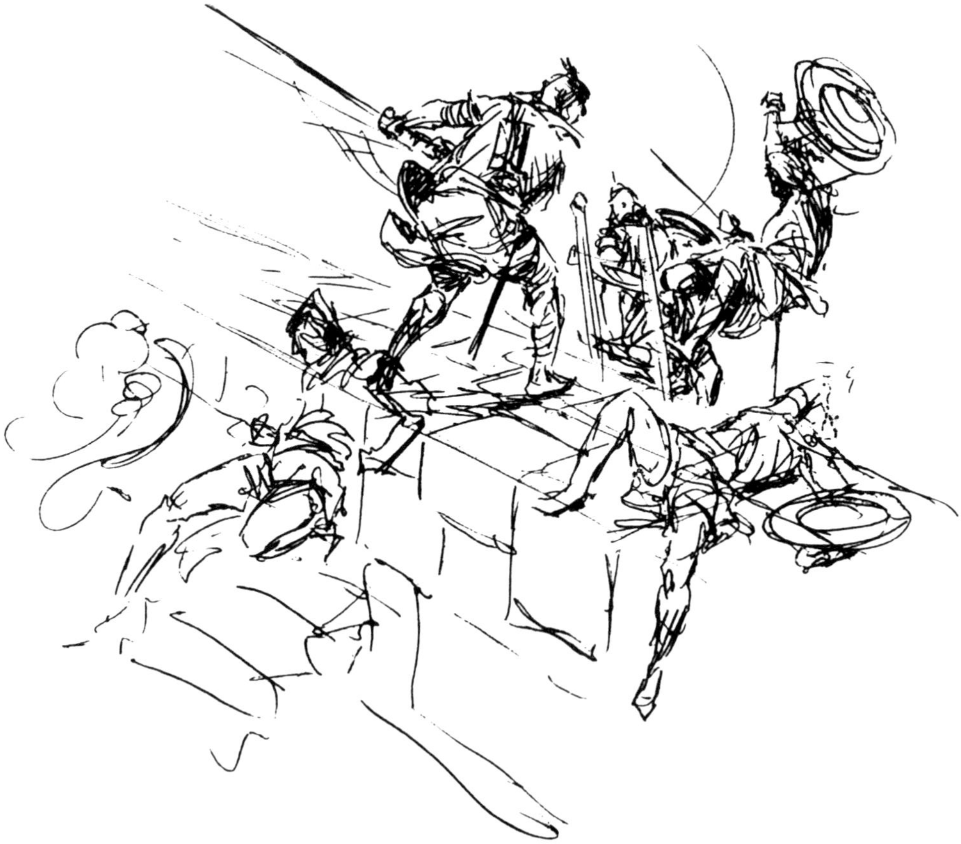

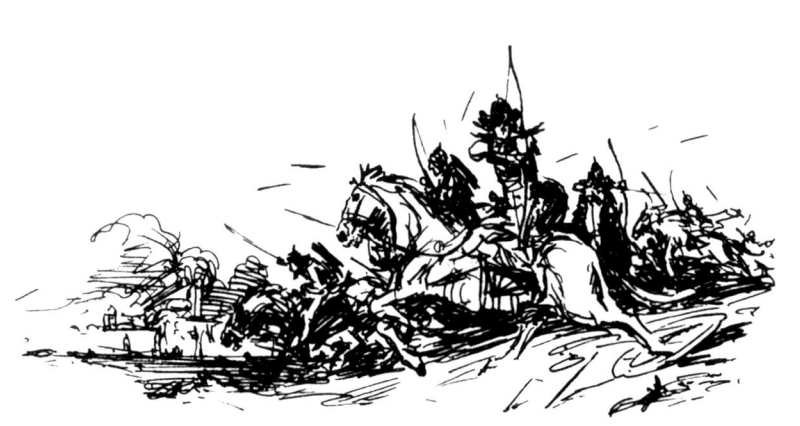

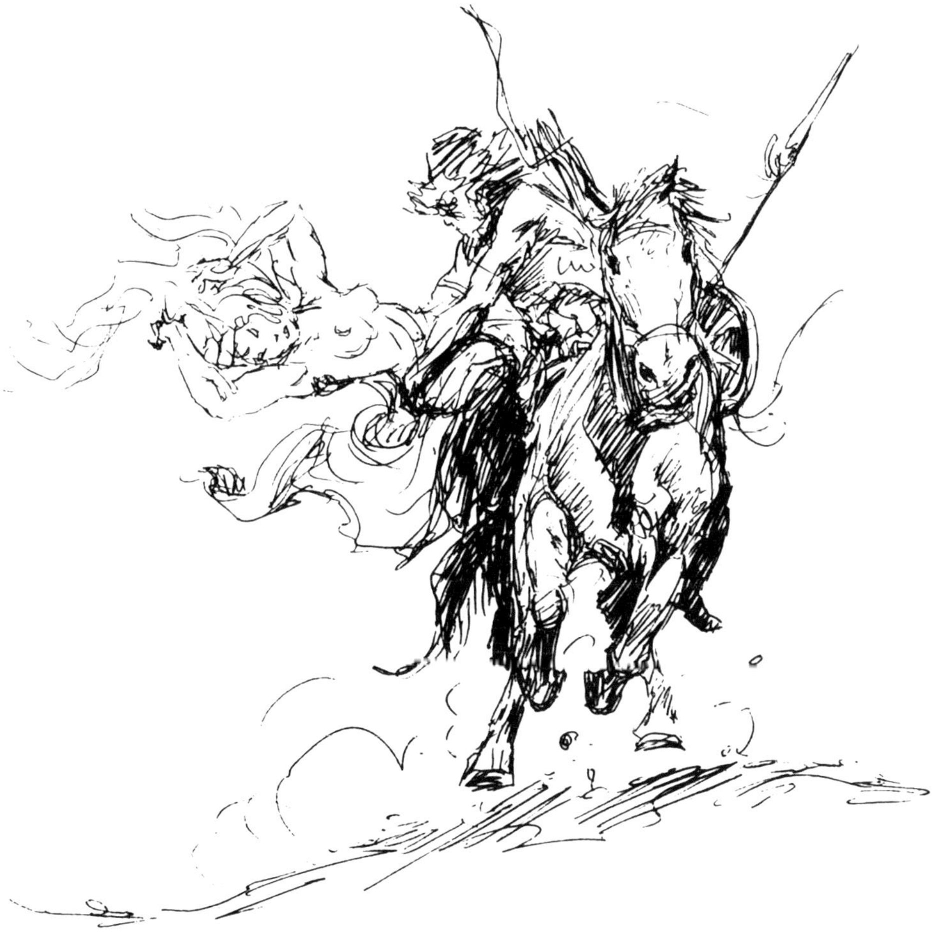

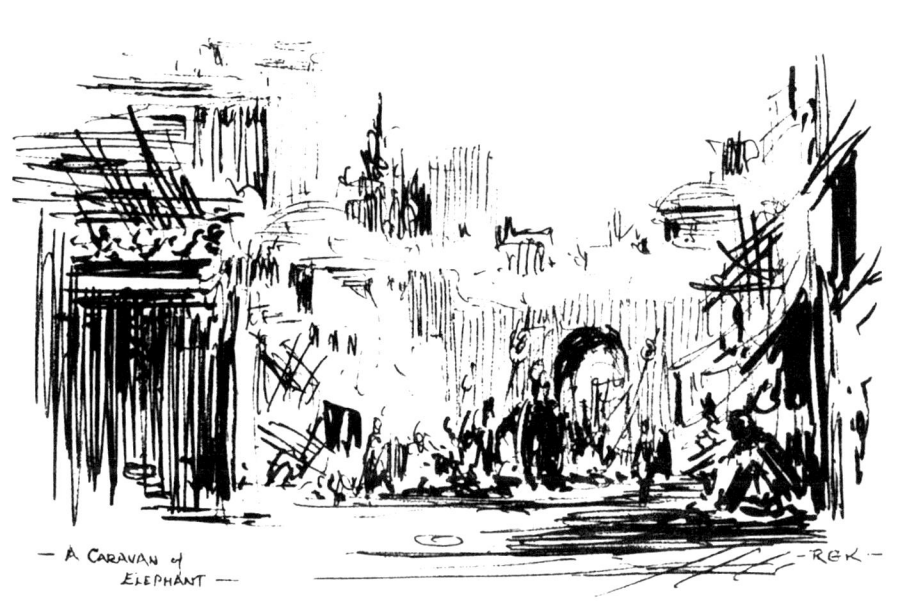

— A CARAVAN of
ELEPHANT —

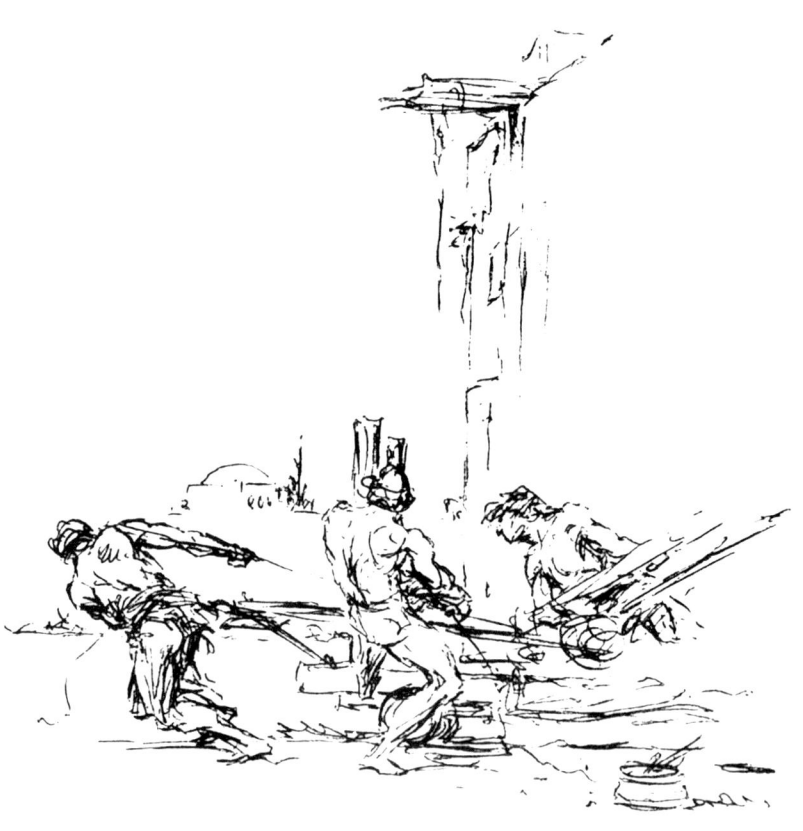

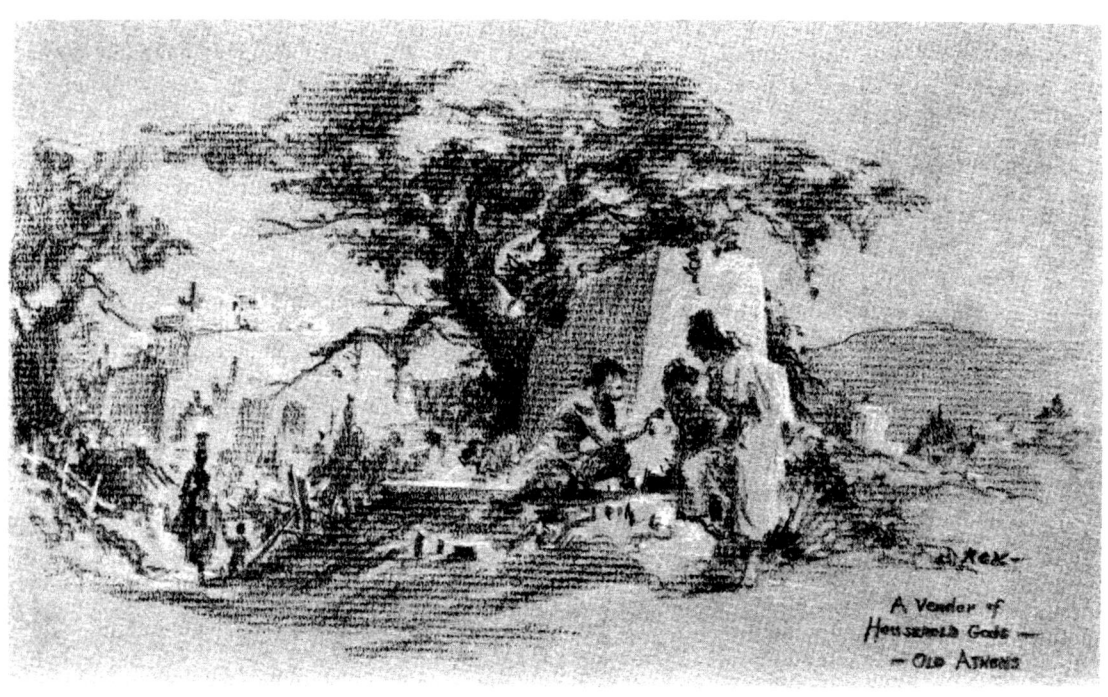

A Vendor of
Household Gods —
— Old Athens

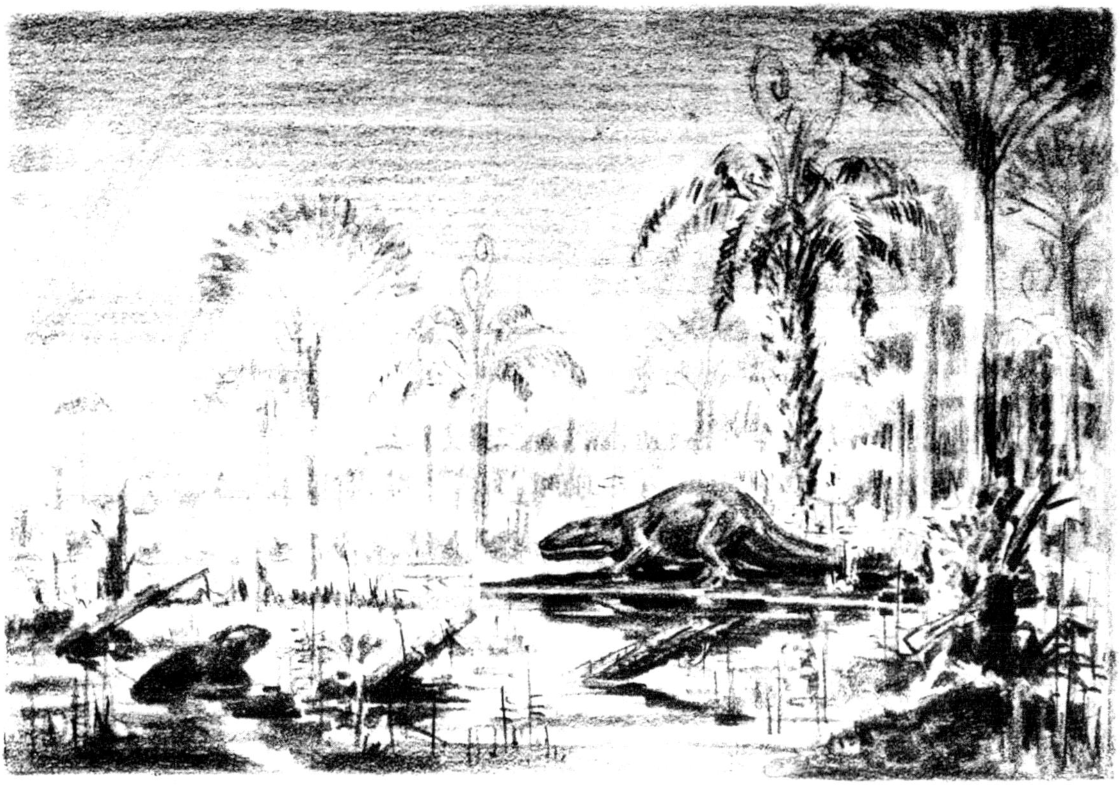

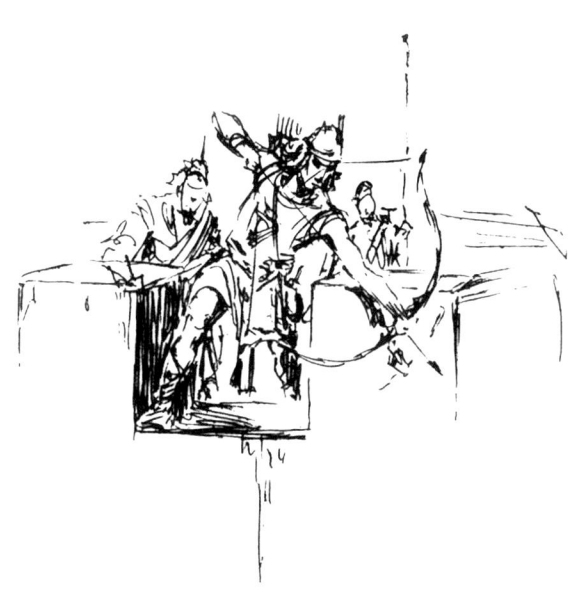

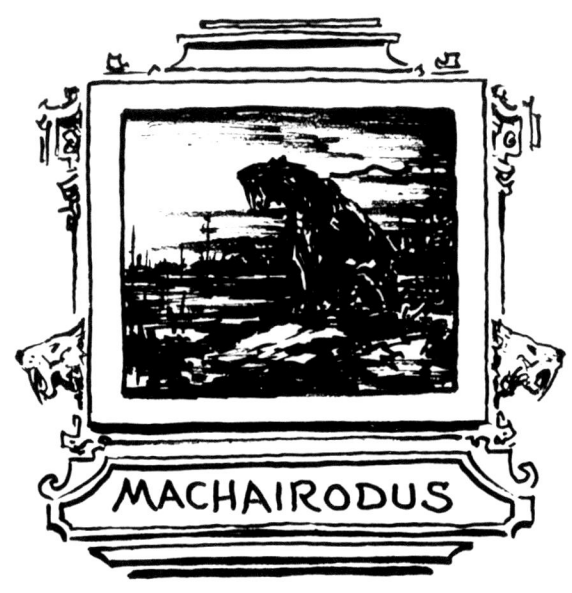

MACHAIRODUS

A BREATH OF HEATHER TANGLES WITH THE GORSE —
THE GREAT ROUND BOULDERS, ETCHED WITH FRETTED SCRUB,
KNIFE VELVET TAPESTRIES ACROSS THE MOVELESS PLAIN:
AFAR AGAINST THE SLOPE OF MIST AND HILL
A CLOUD OF HERON WHEEL VOICELESS TO THEIR COURSE.

GONE NOW TO AMBER AND TO GOLD THE VANISH'D SUN
CUTS SENTINELS FROM PEAK AND DISTANT CRAG —
PALADINS OF LIGHT REBORN FROM HIDDEN TARNS:
AND OVER ALL THAT UPLAND VALLEY, LOST TO TIME,
THE SILENT CASTELAINS OF NIGHT MOVE FORTH AS ONE.

THROWN BACK AS ECHO FROM SOME CLIFFSIDE HIGH
A MAMMOTH CRIES HIS CHALLENGE TO THE NIGHT!
SOFT FROM TAWNY SLUMBER, THE SILKEN CLAWS EXTEND,
THE SABRES FLASH FAREWELL TO DAY — AND, 'ROUSED AT LAST,
HIS SPLENDID HEAD UPLIFTS TO CARVE ITS MAJESTY AGAINST THE SKY!

— R.G.K — (MAY - 1973)

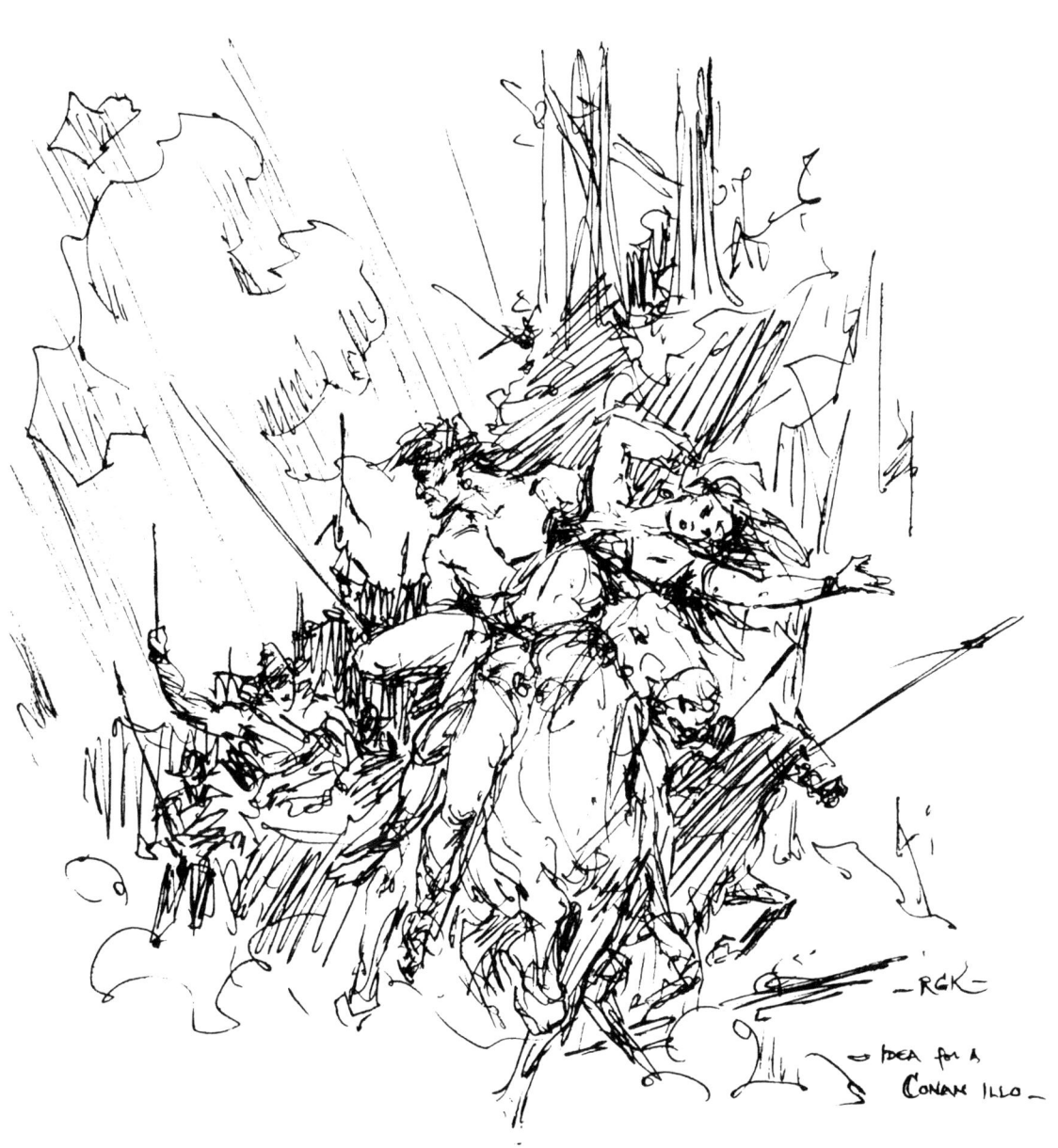

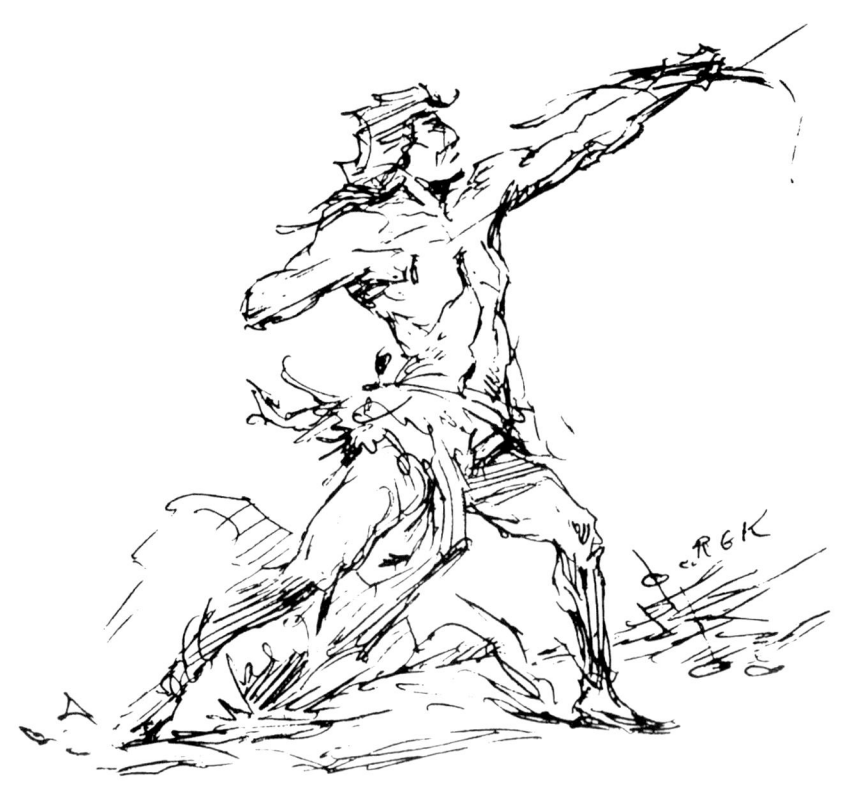

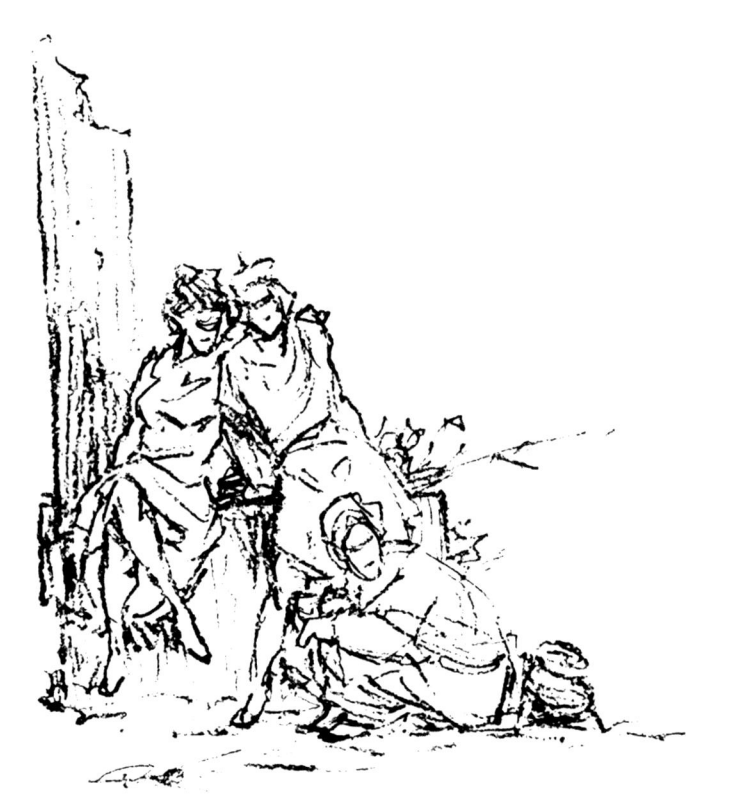

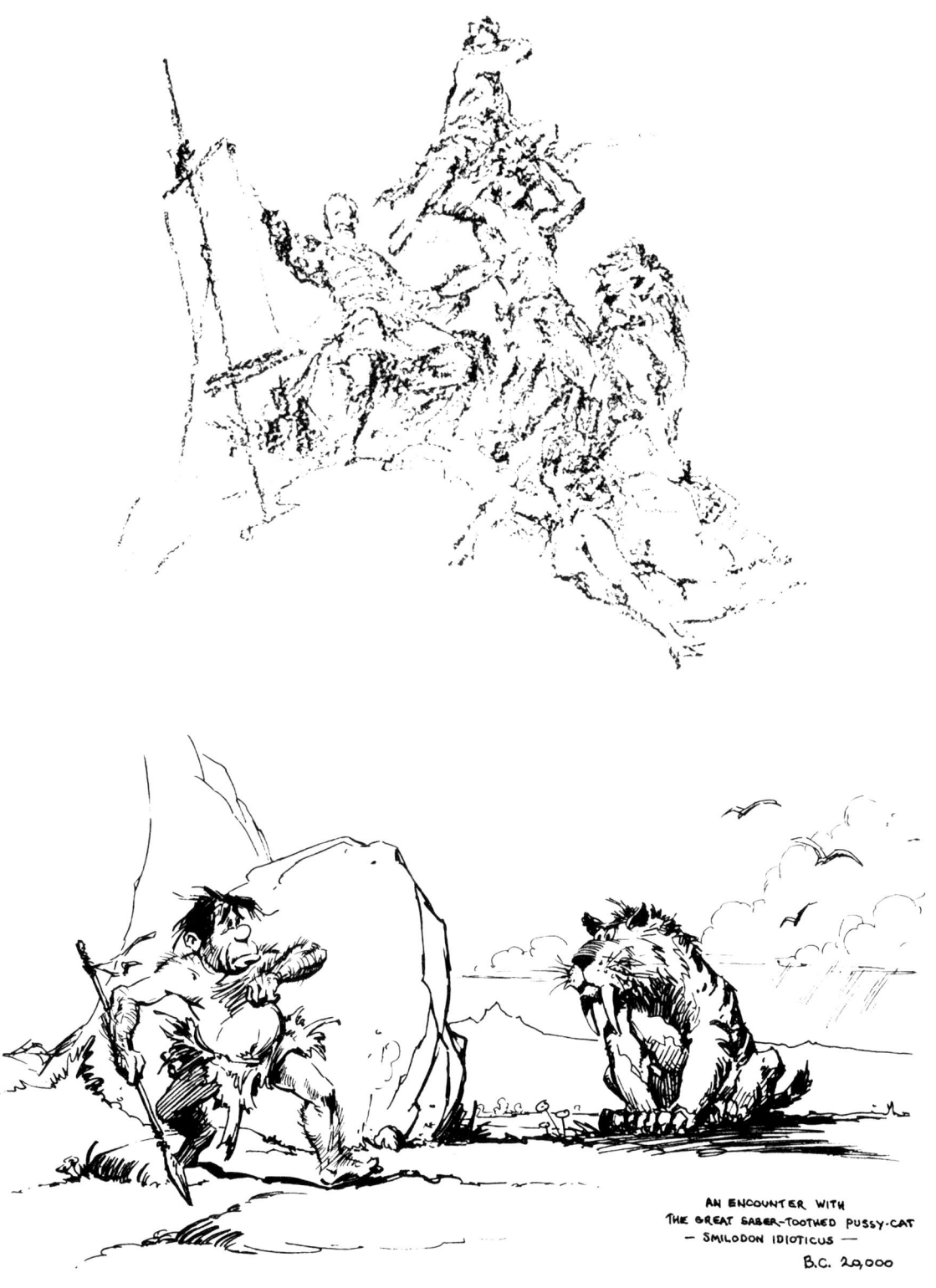

AN ENCOUNTER WITH
THE GREAT SABER-TOOTHED PUSSY-CAT
— SMILODON IDIOTICUS —

B.C. 20,000

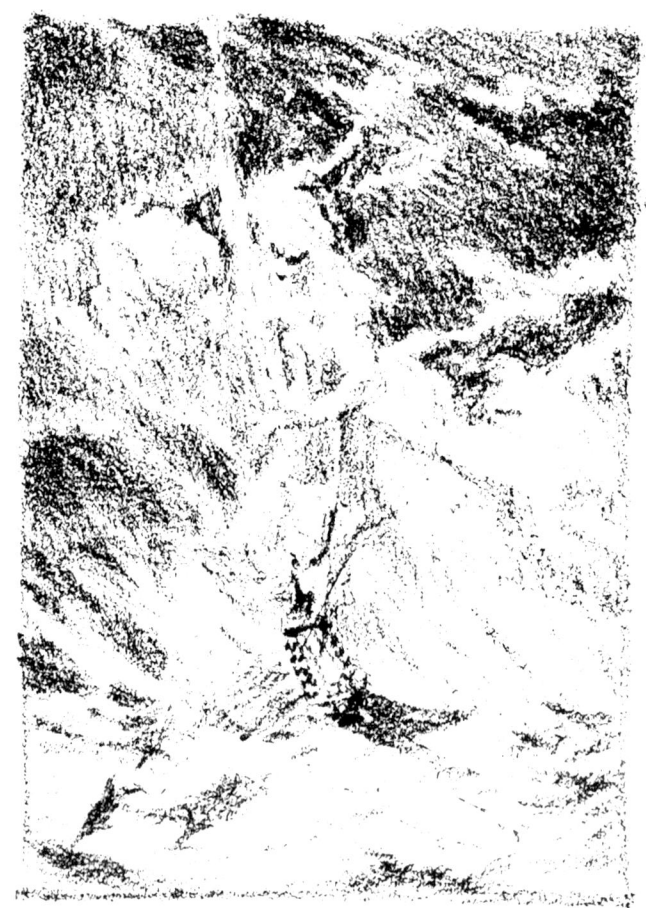

— THE SEA GOD —

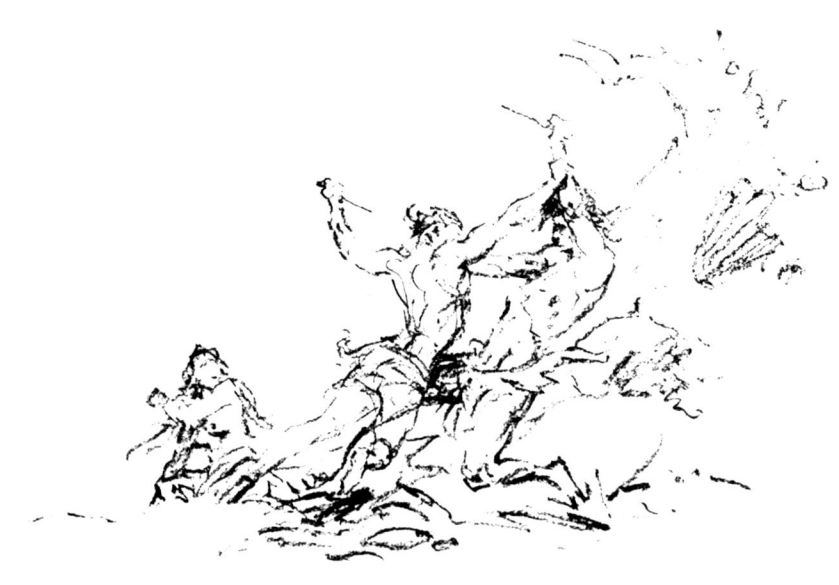

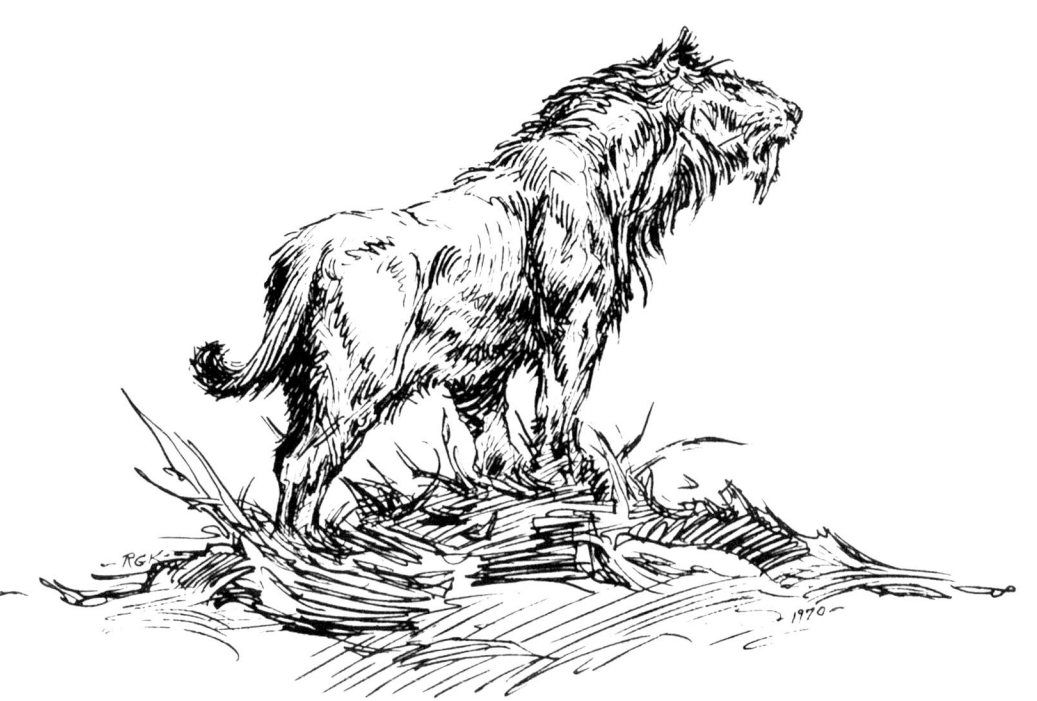

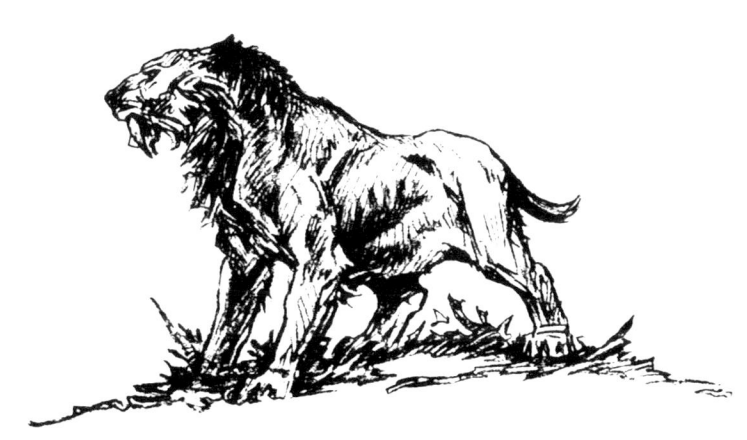

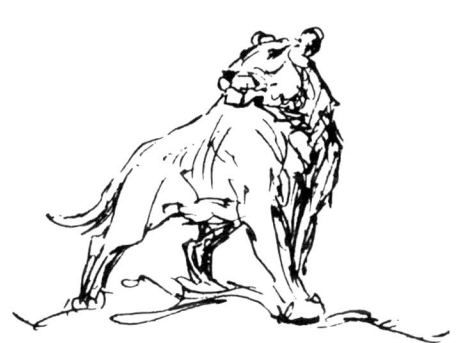

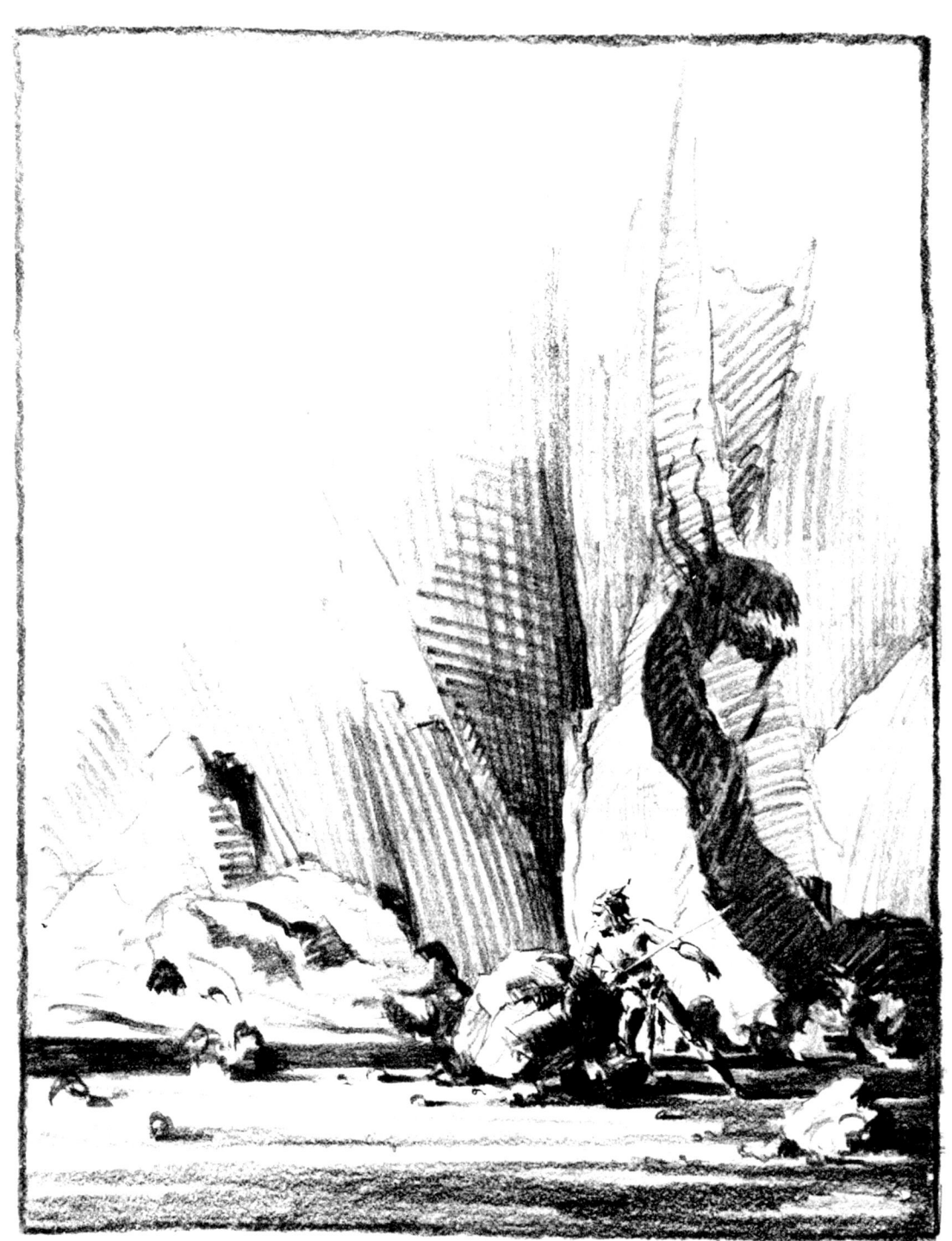

"The Gorge of the Dragon."

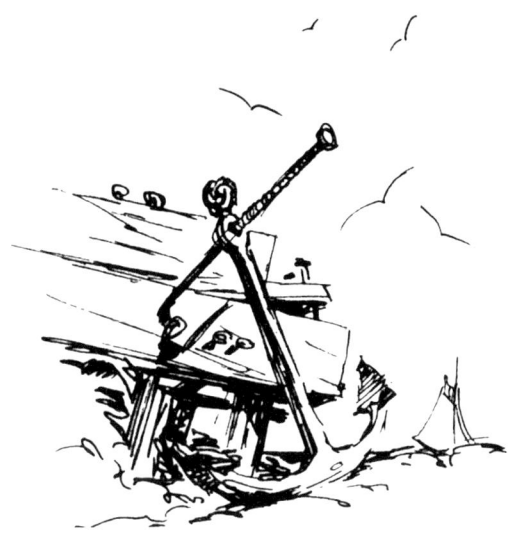

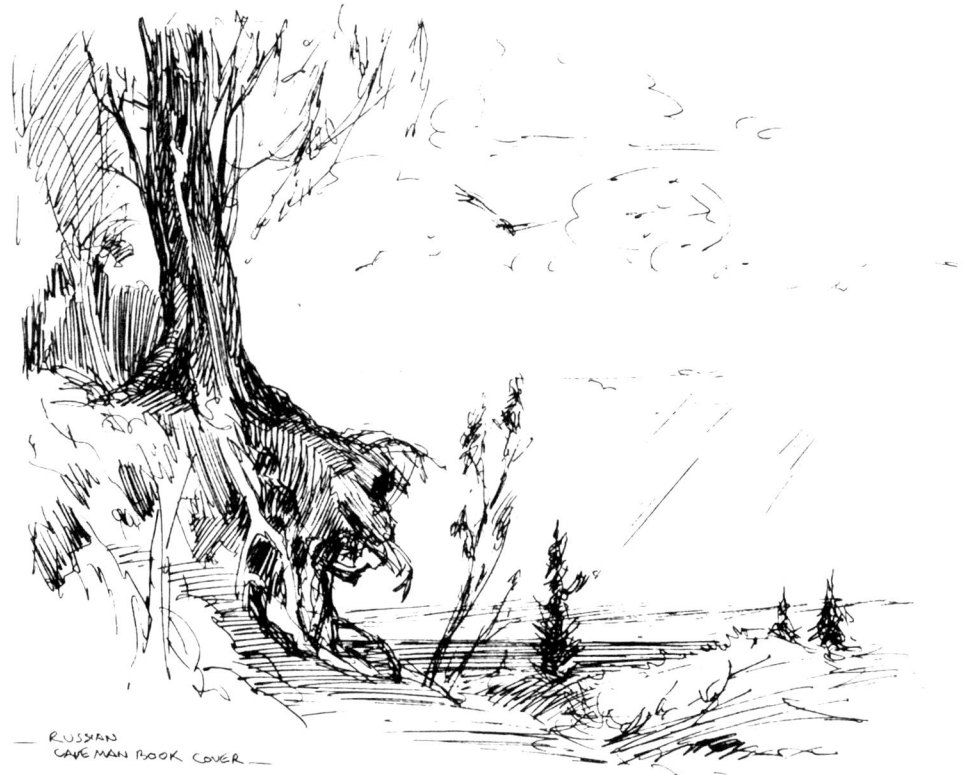

RUSSIAN
CAVEMAN BOOK COVER

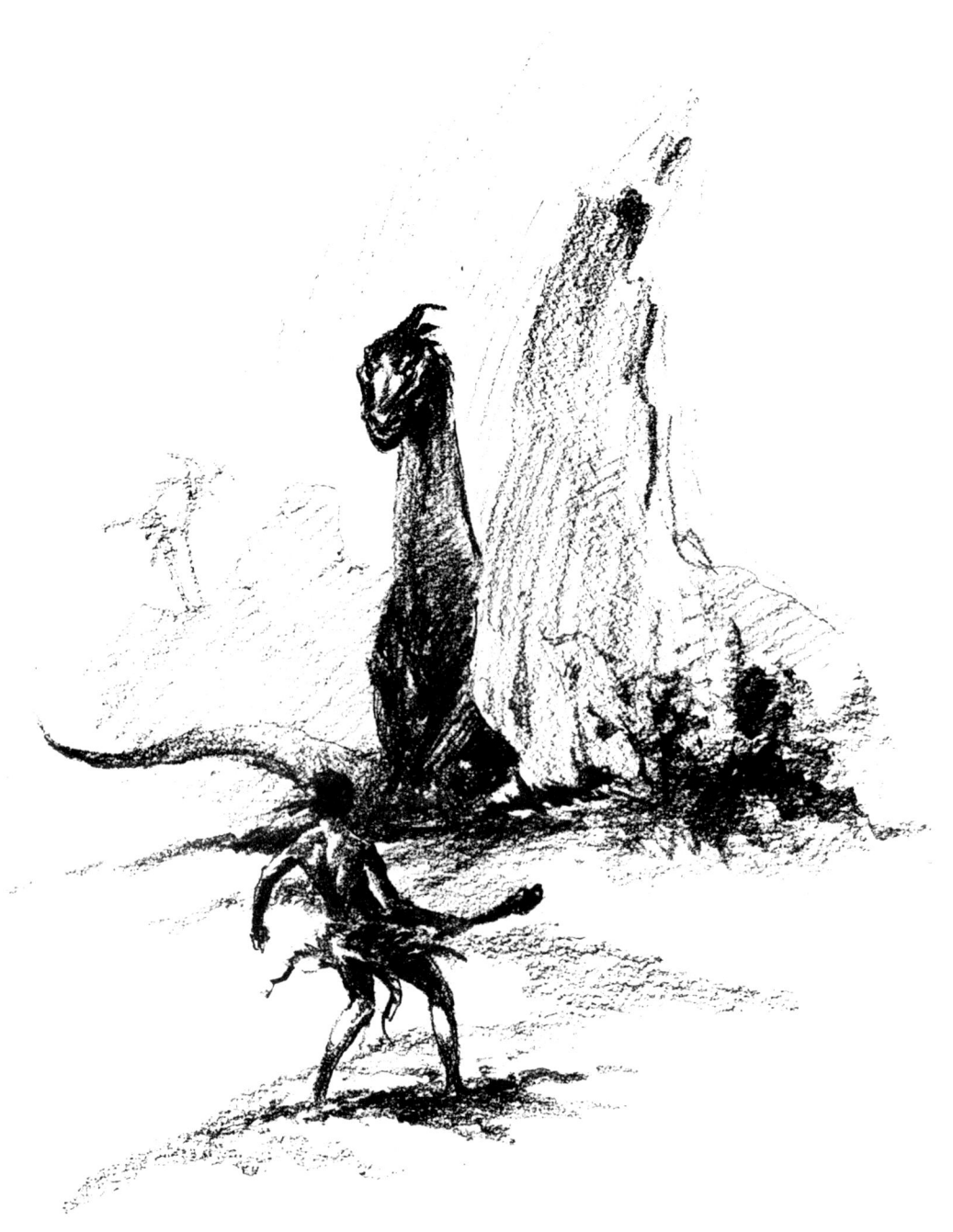

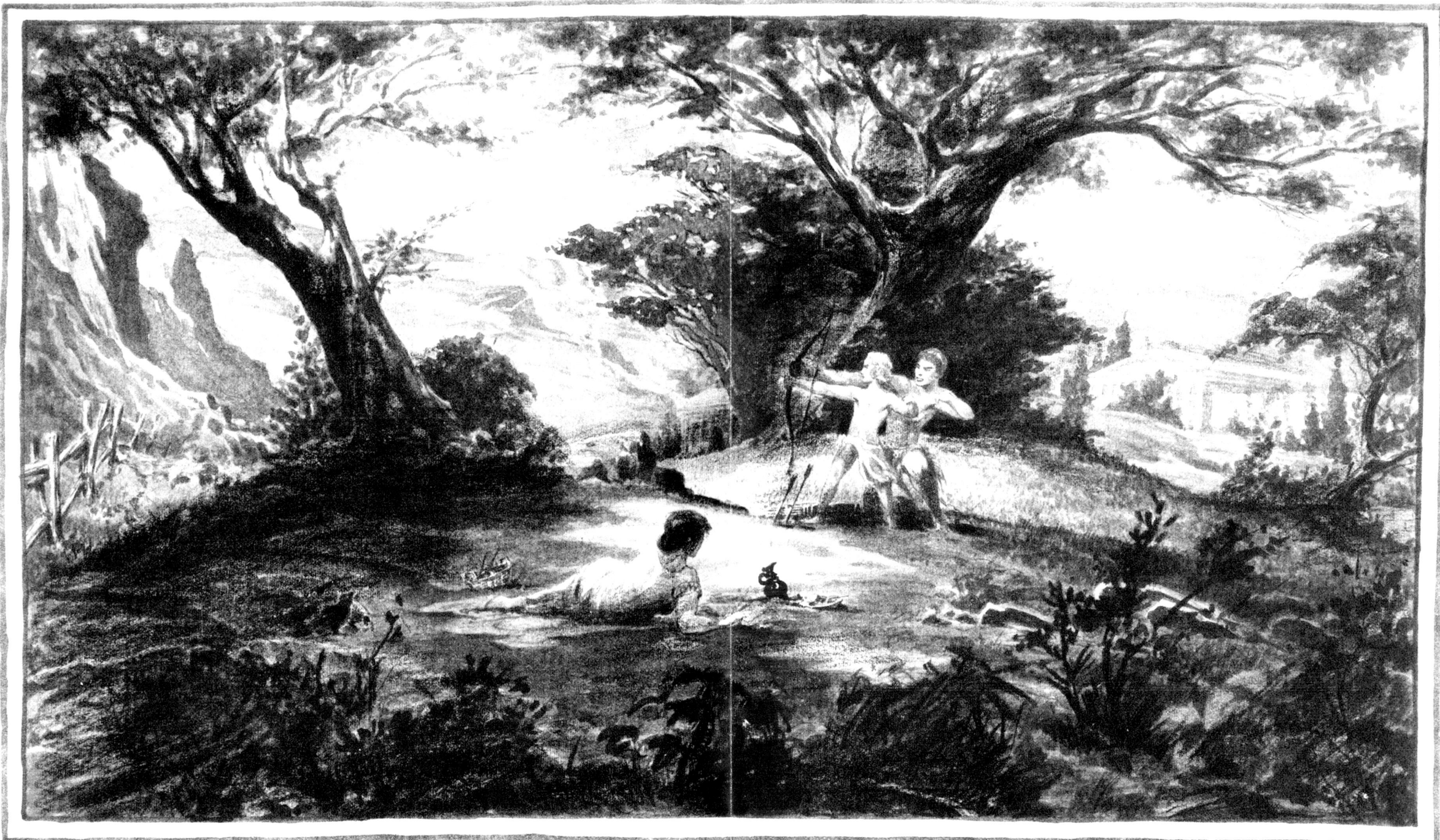

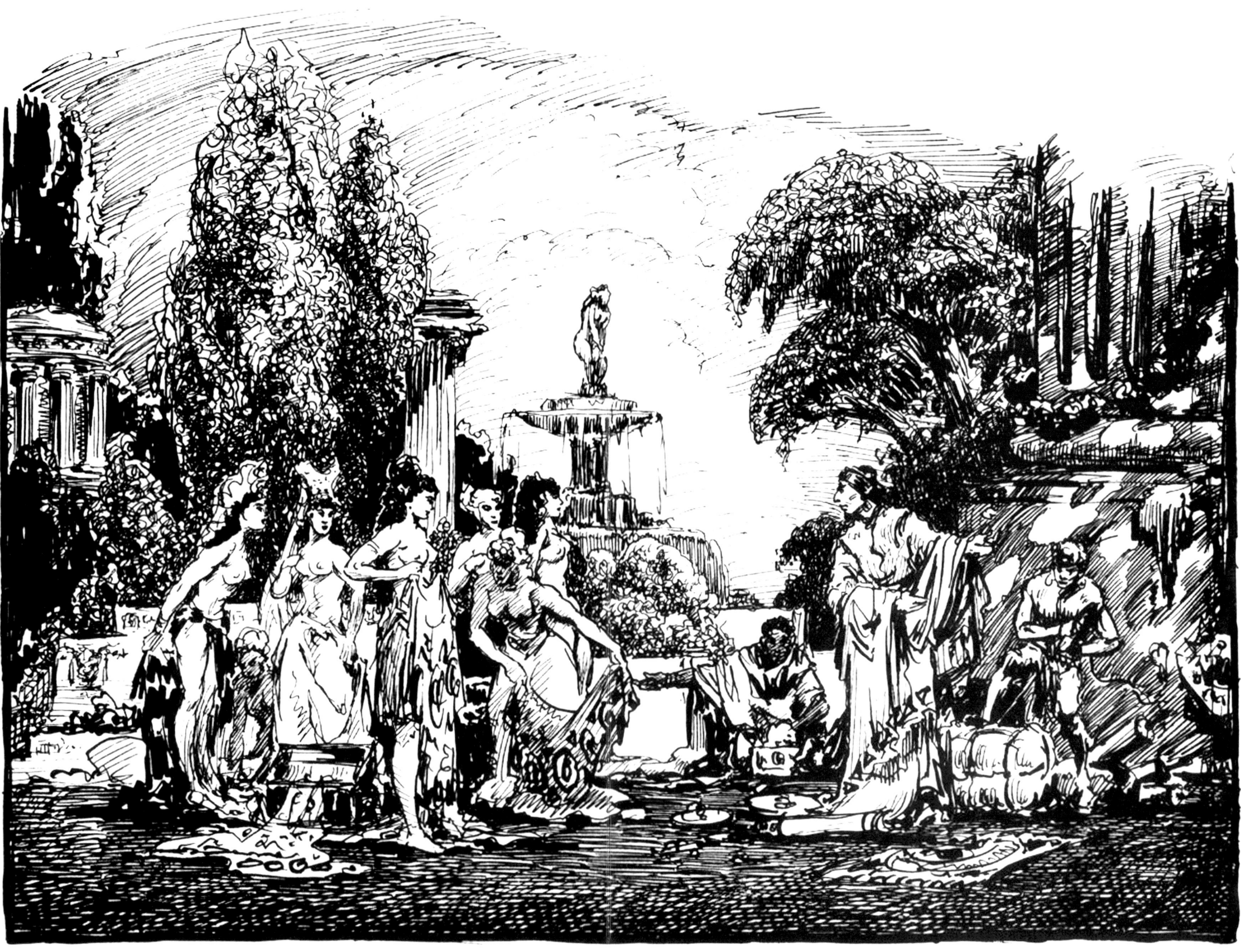

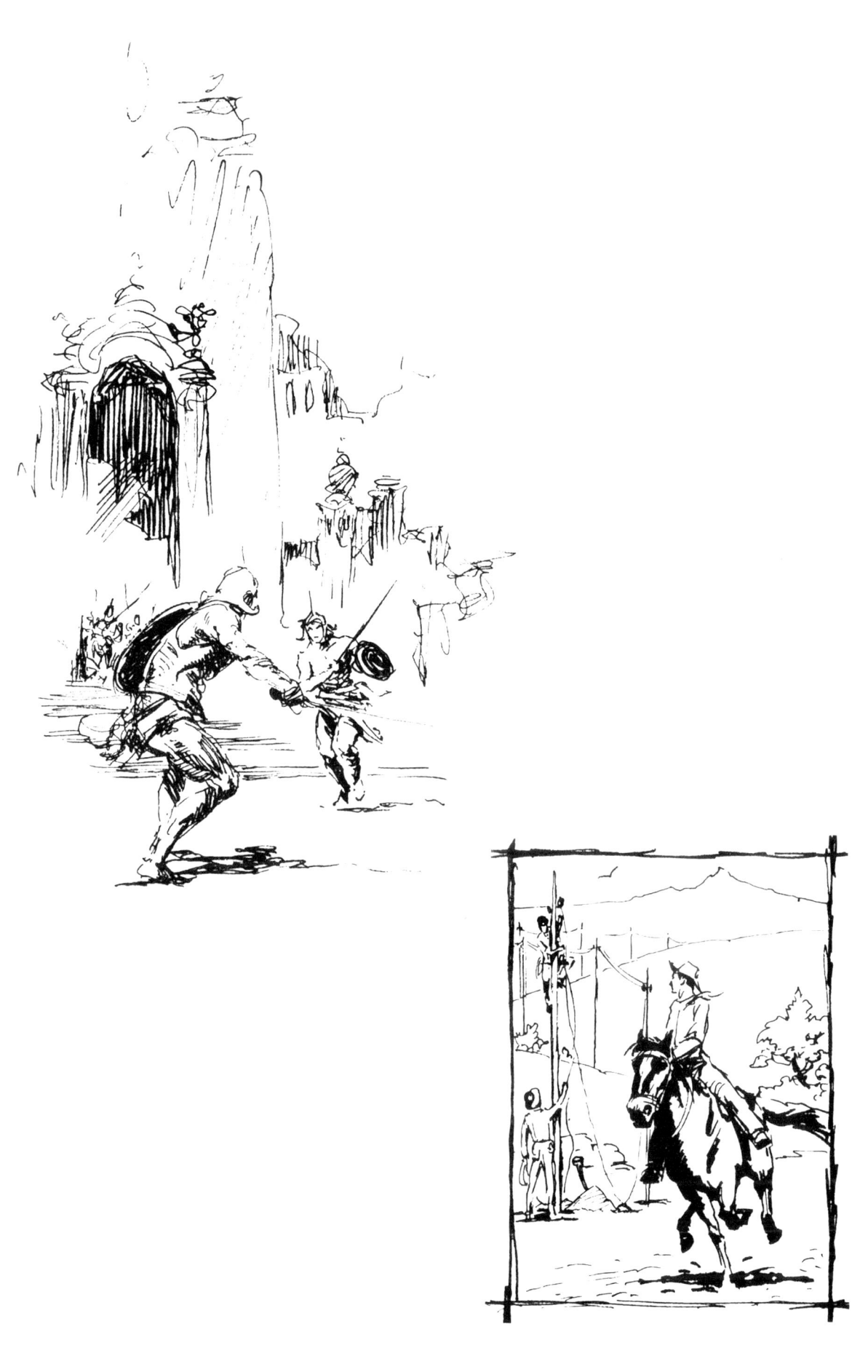

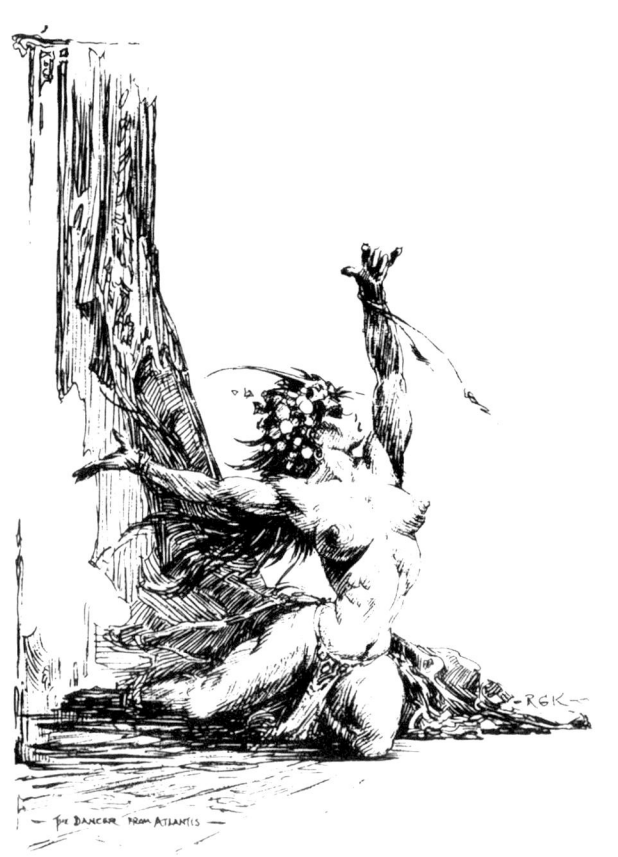

The Dancer from Atlantis

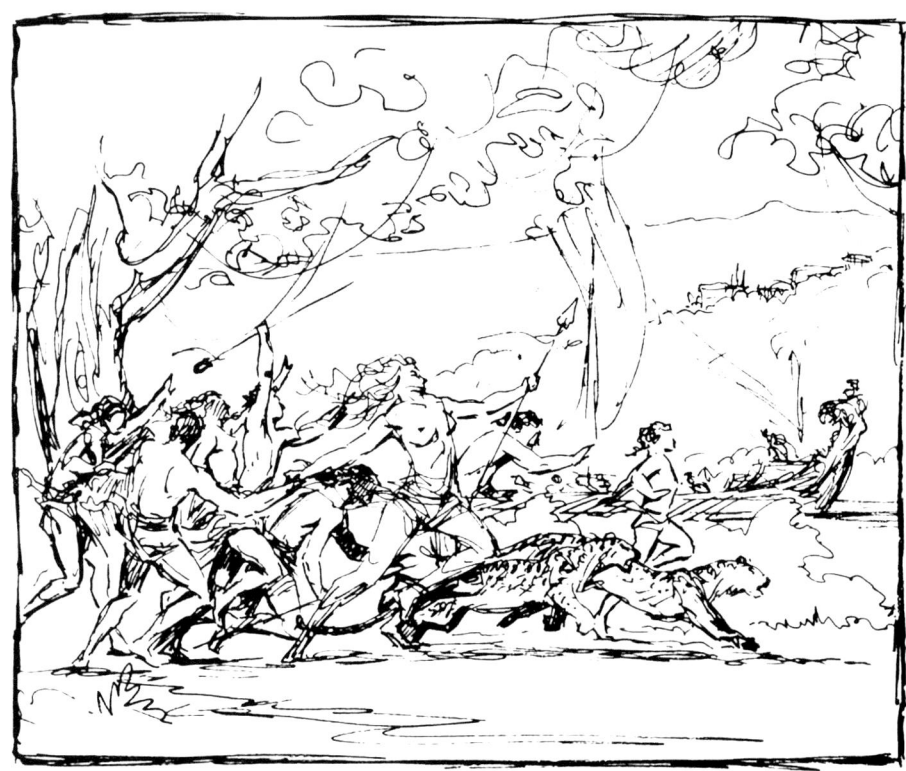

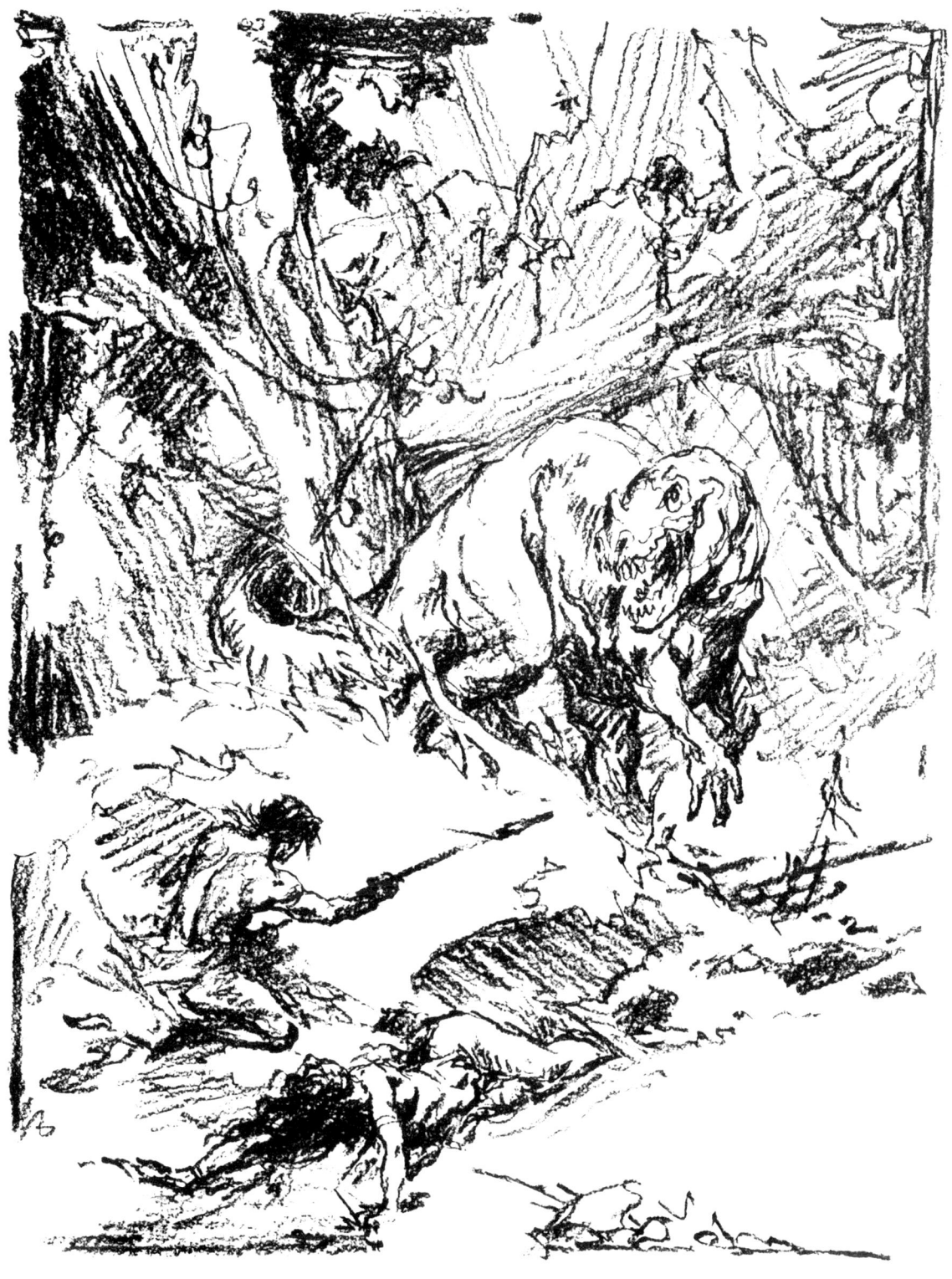

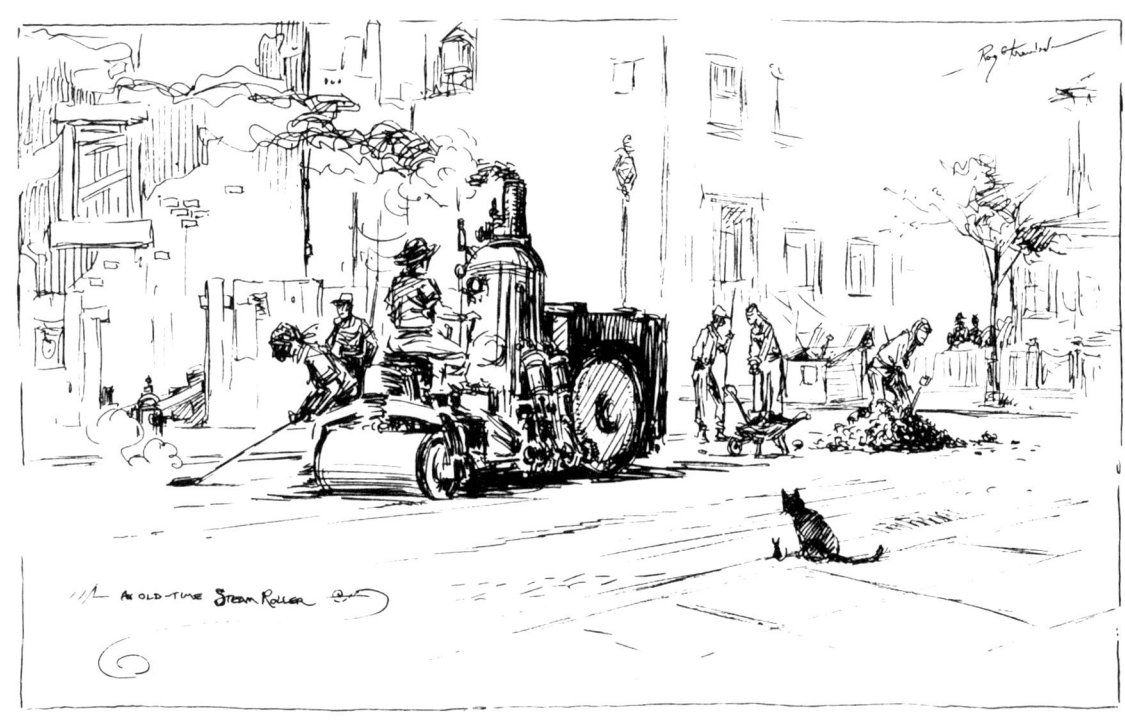

AN OLD-TIME STEAM ROLLER

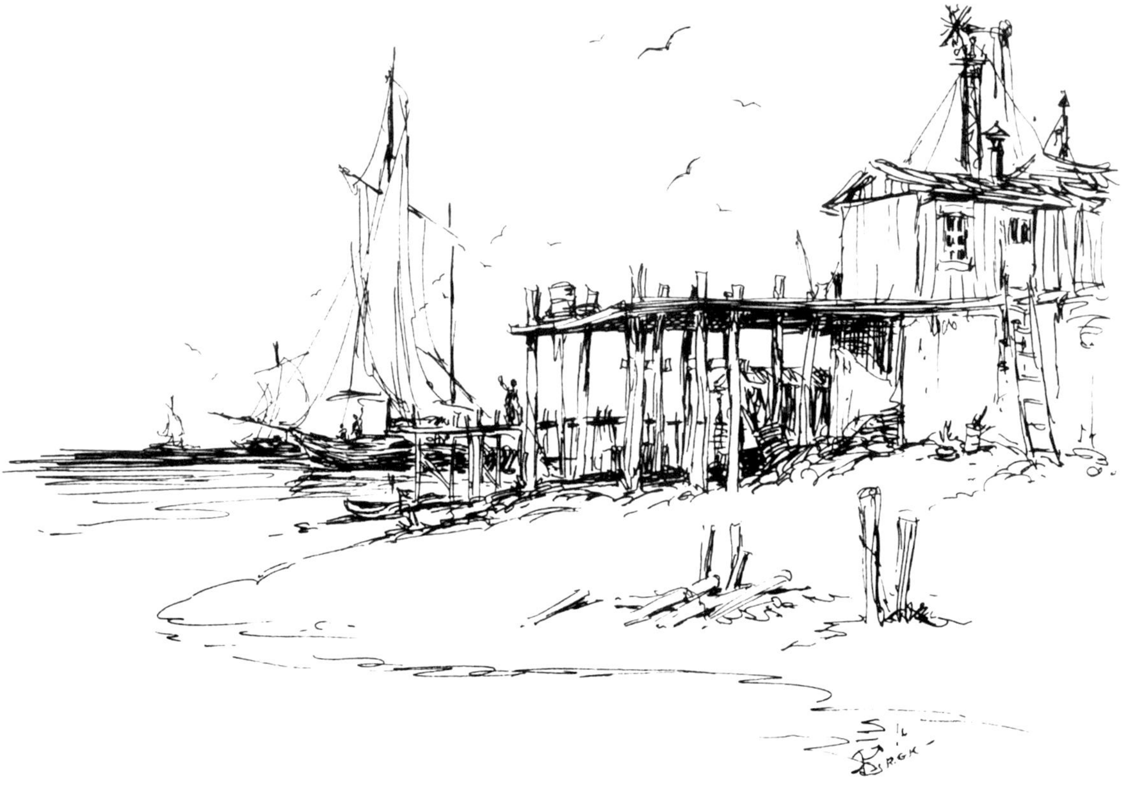

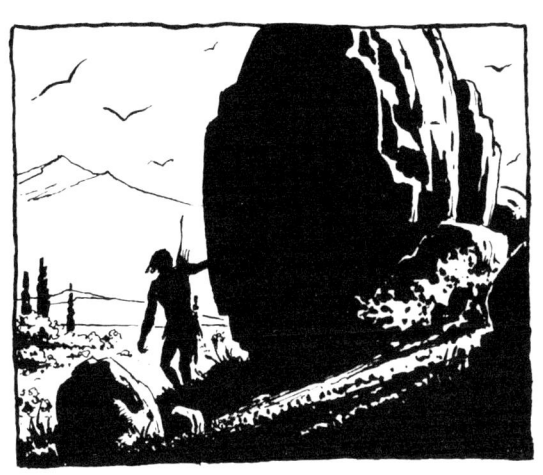

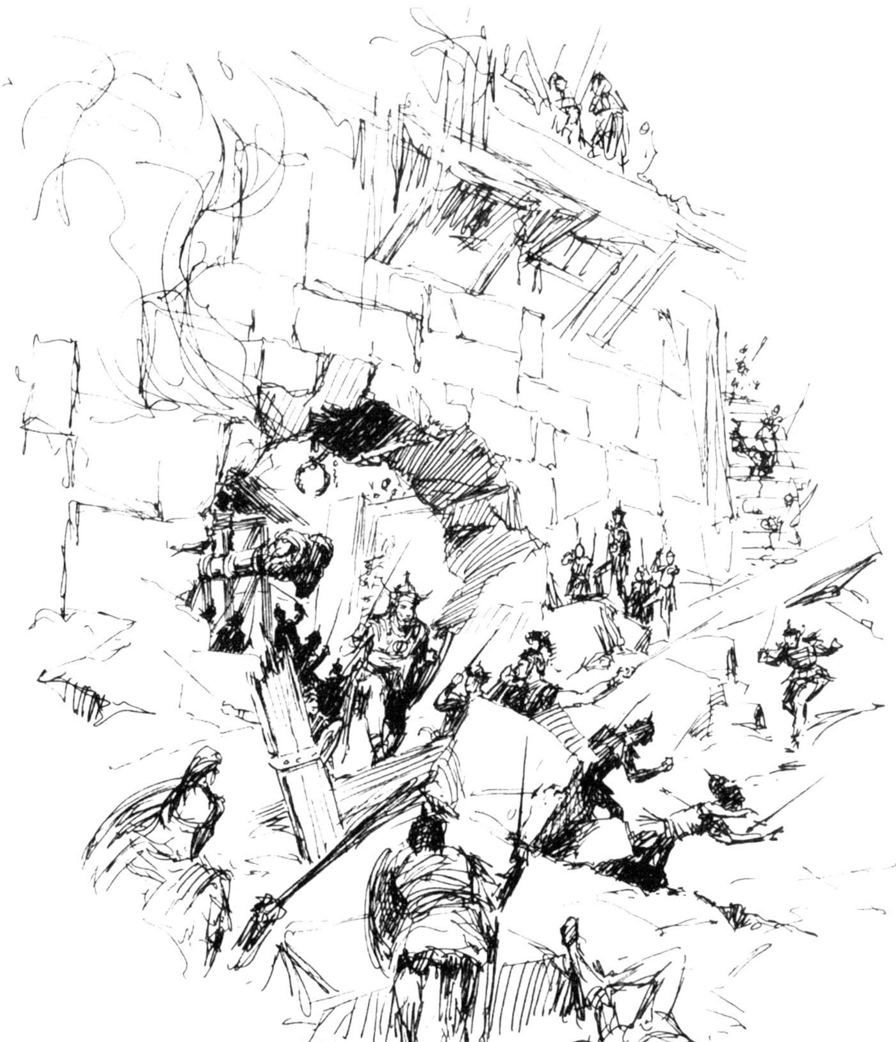

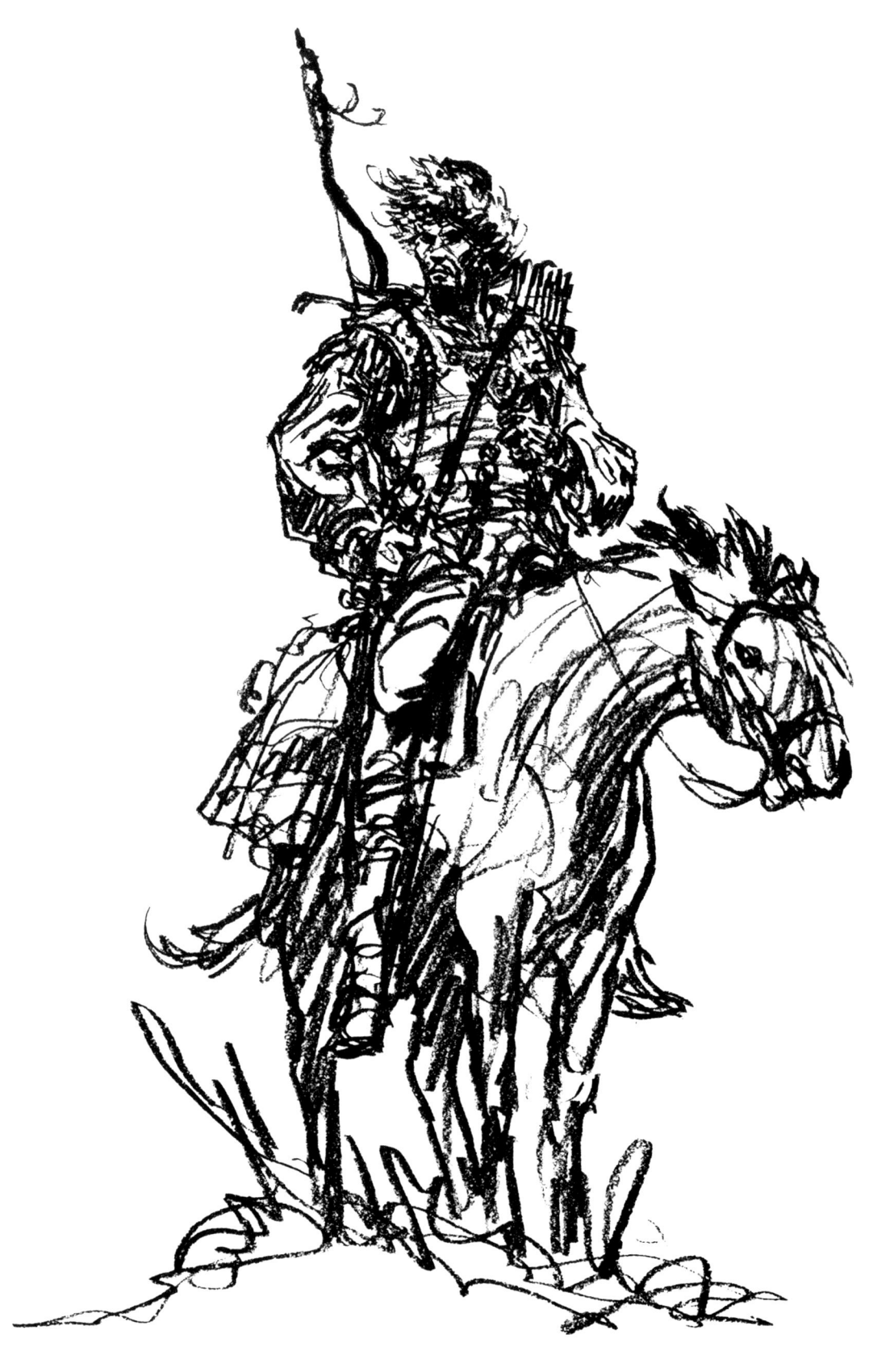

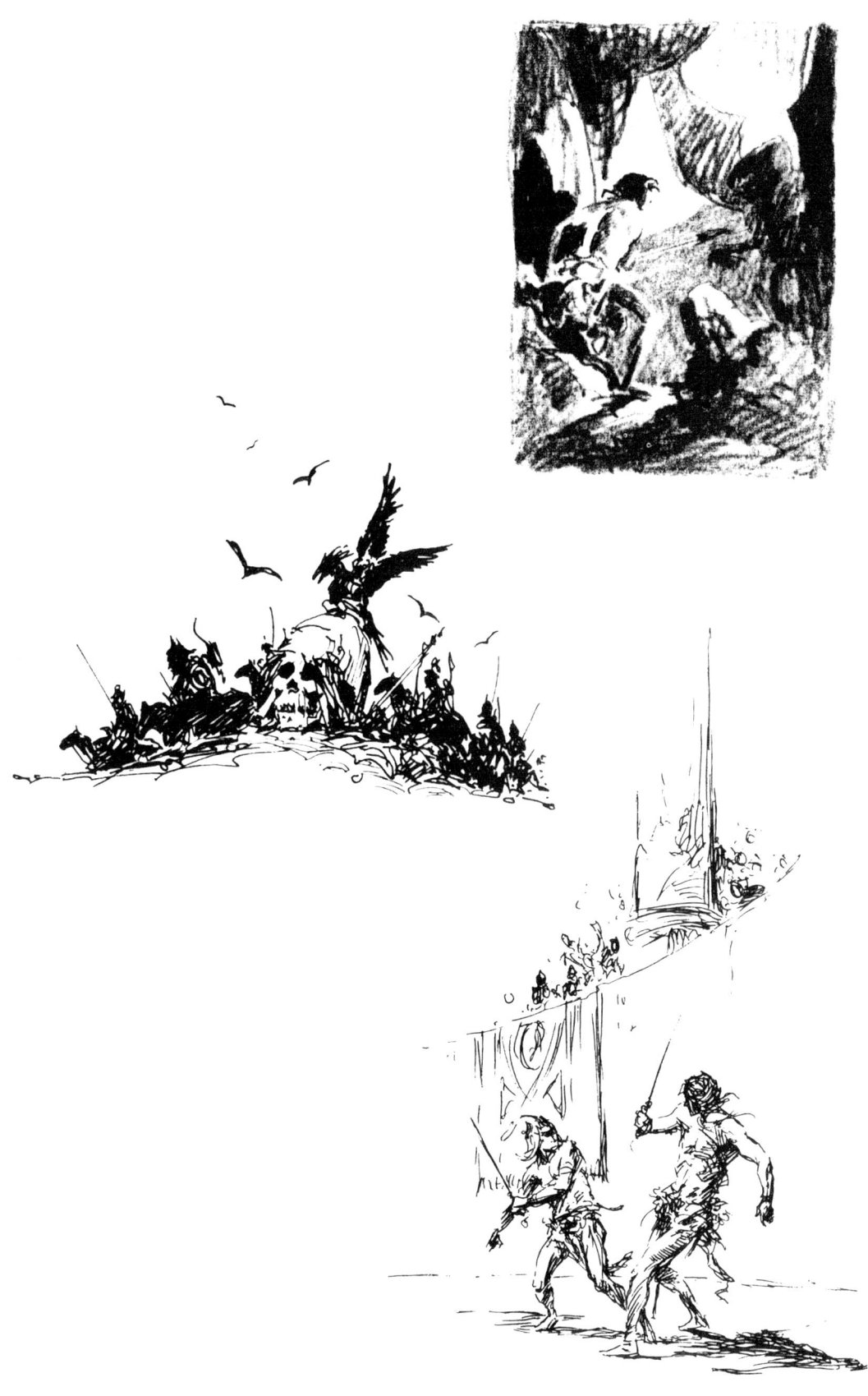

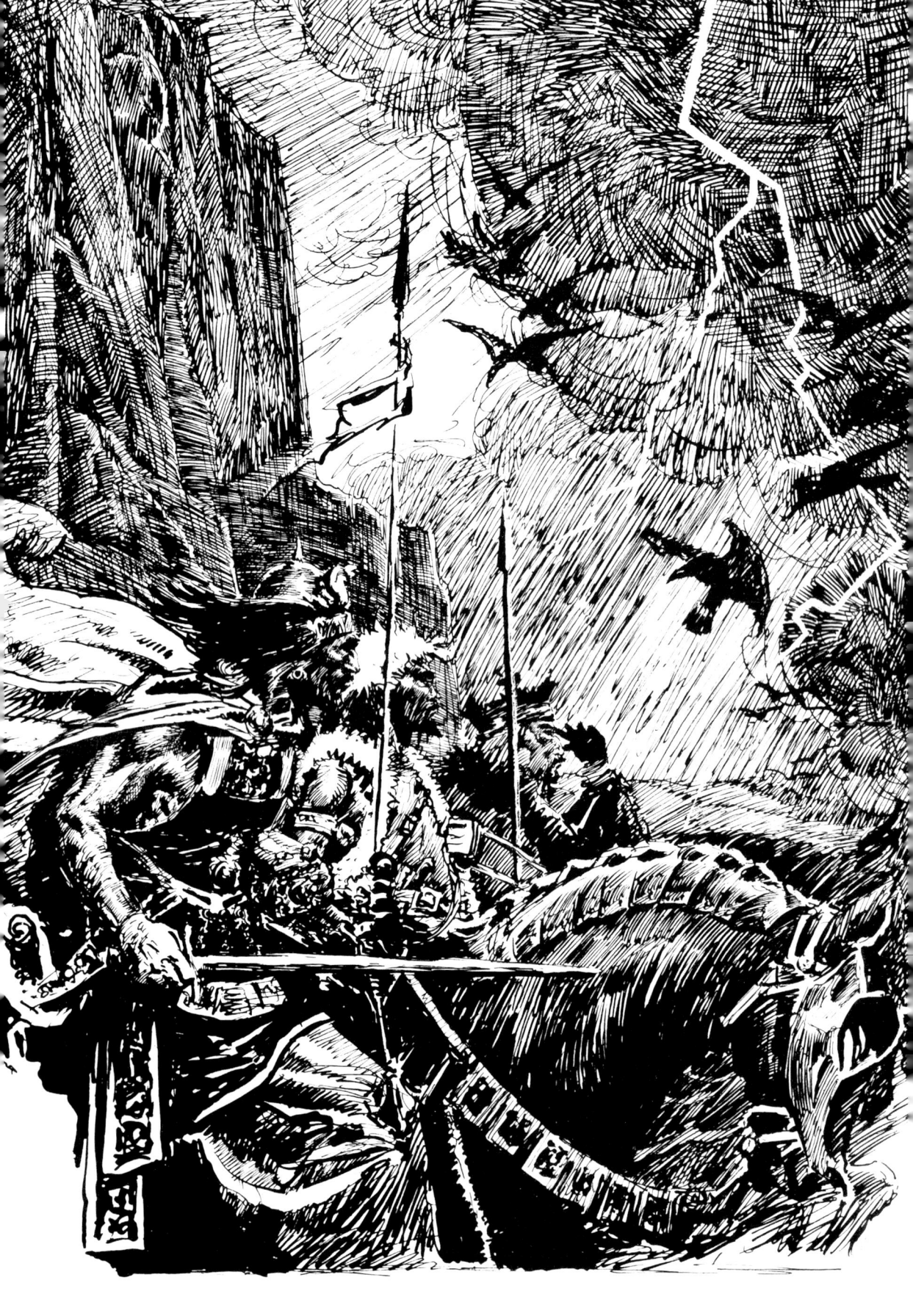

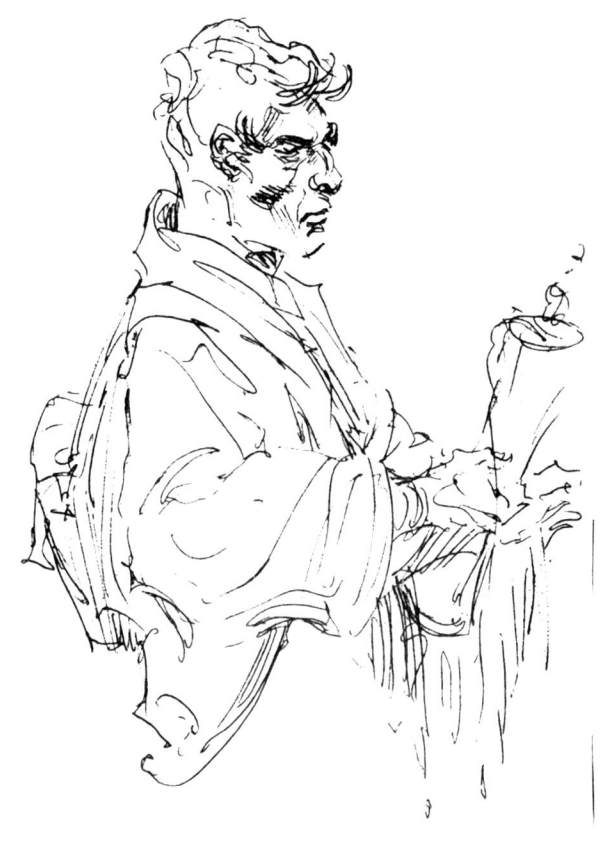

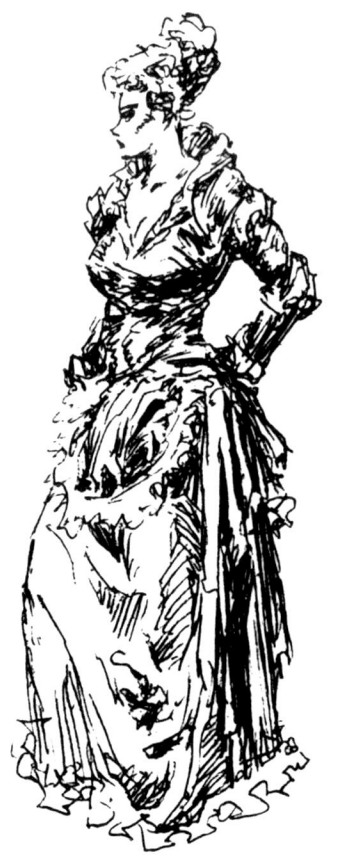

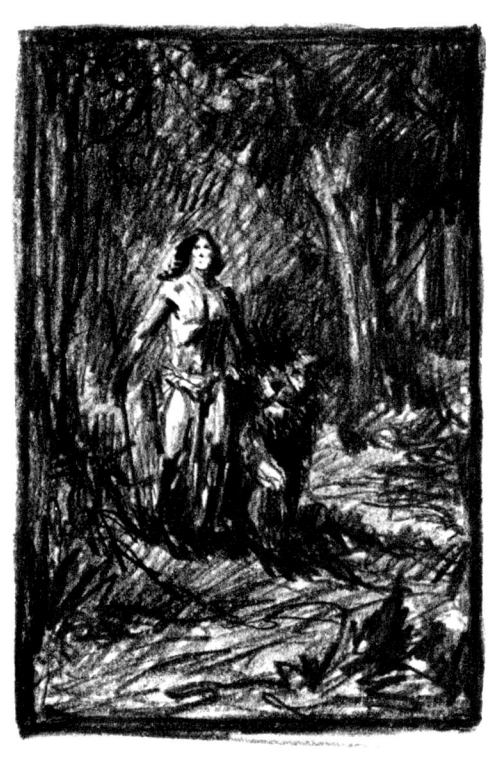

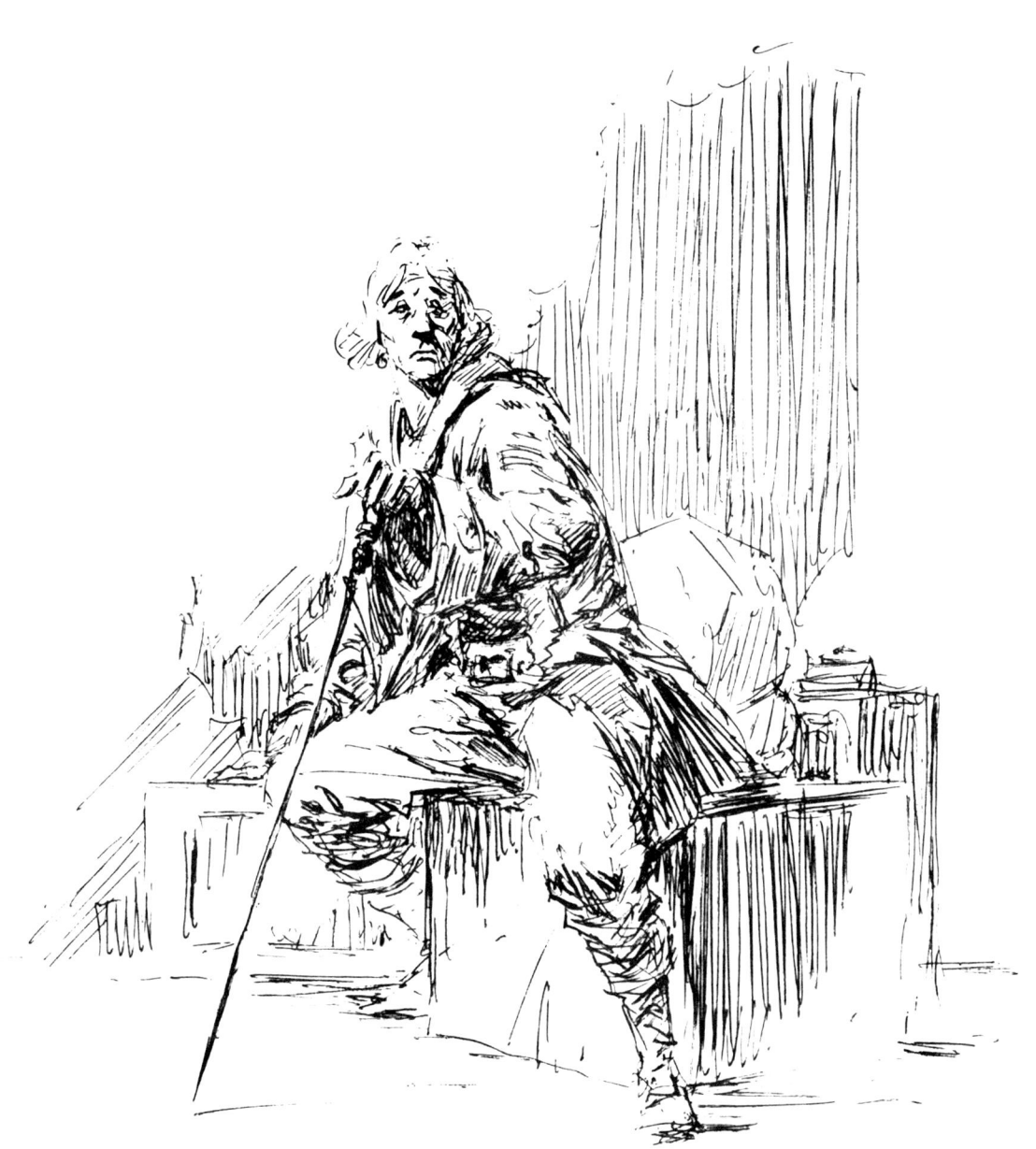

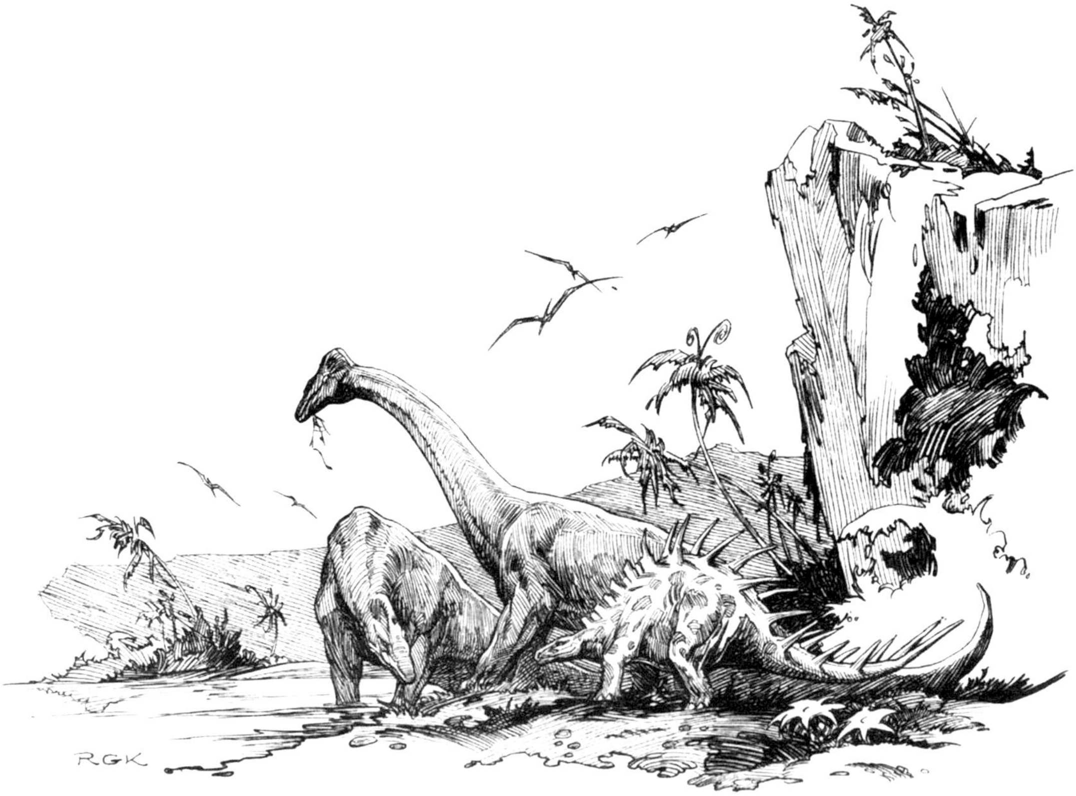
R.G.K.

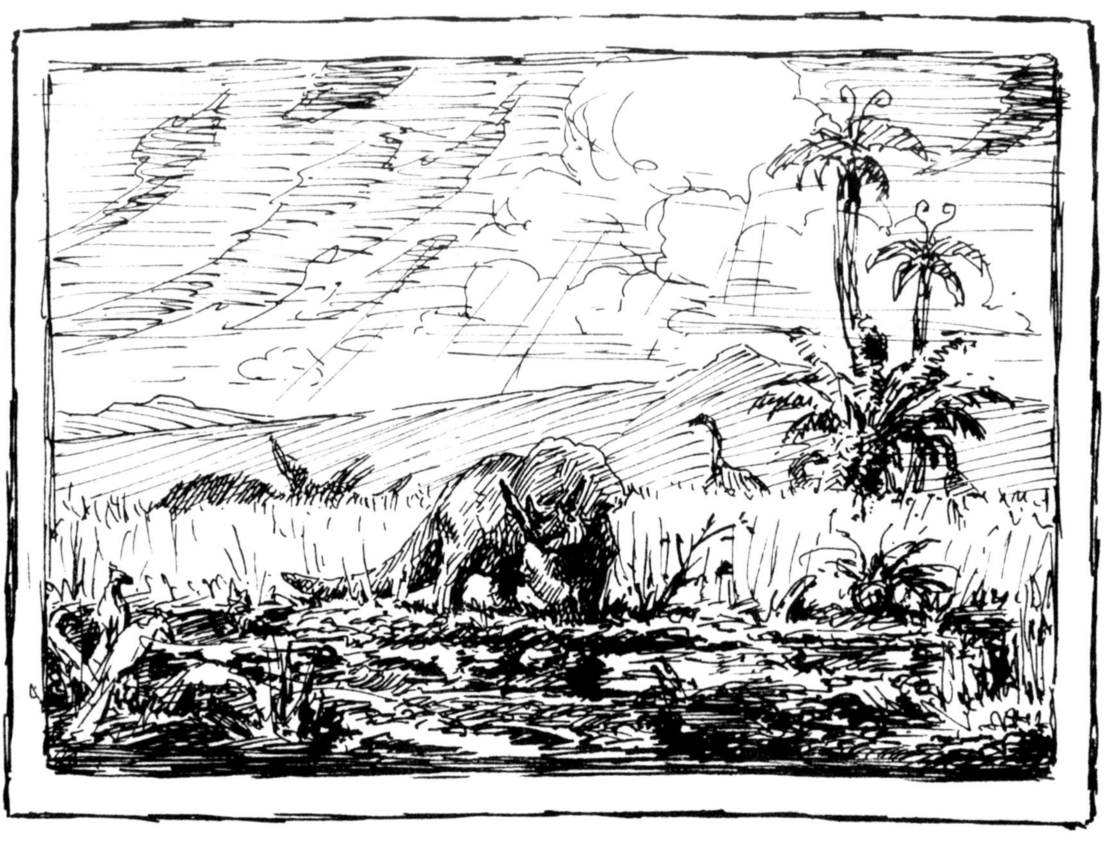

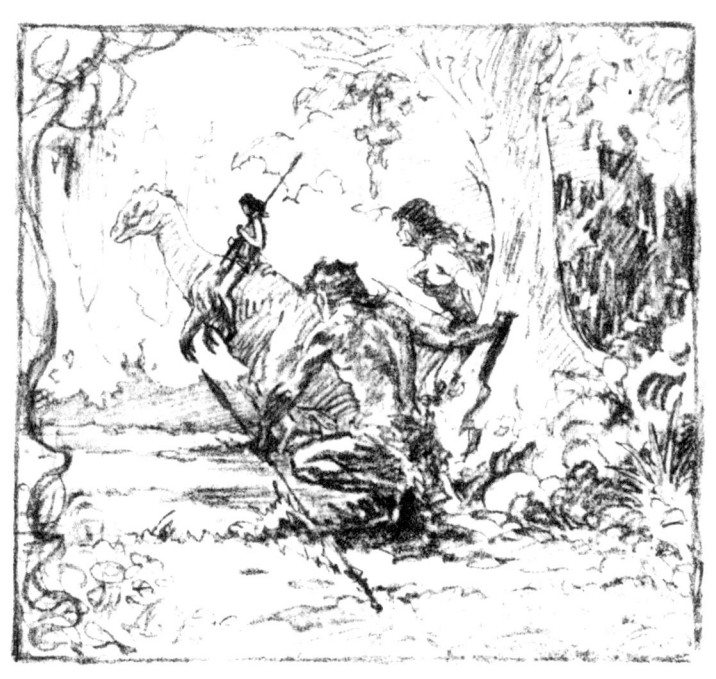

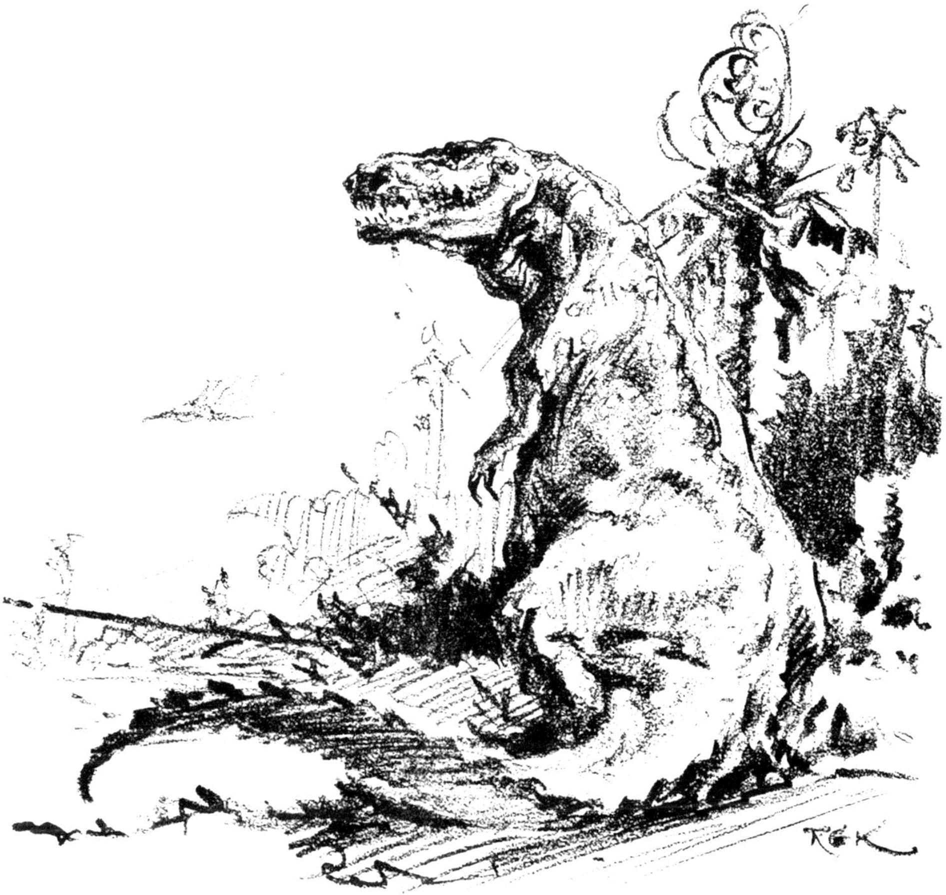

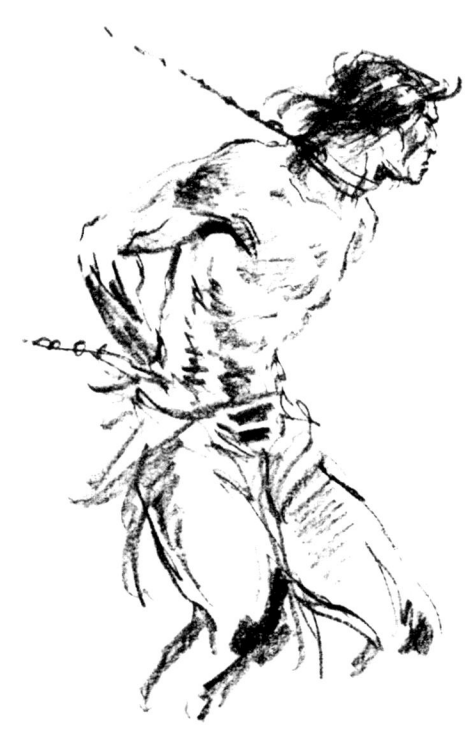

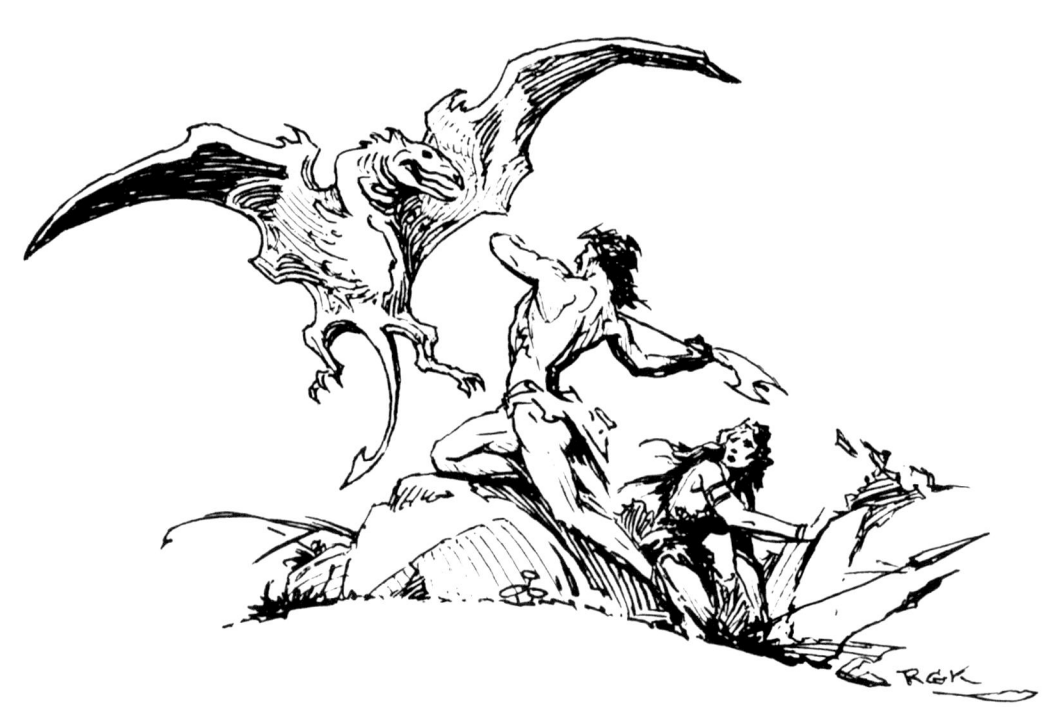

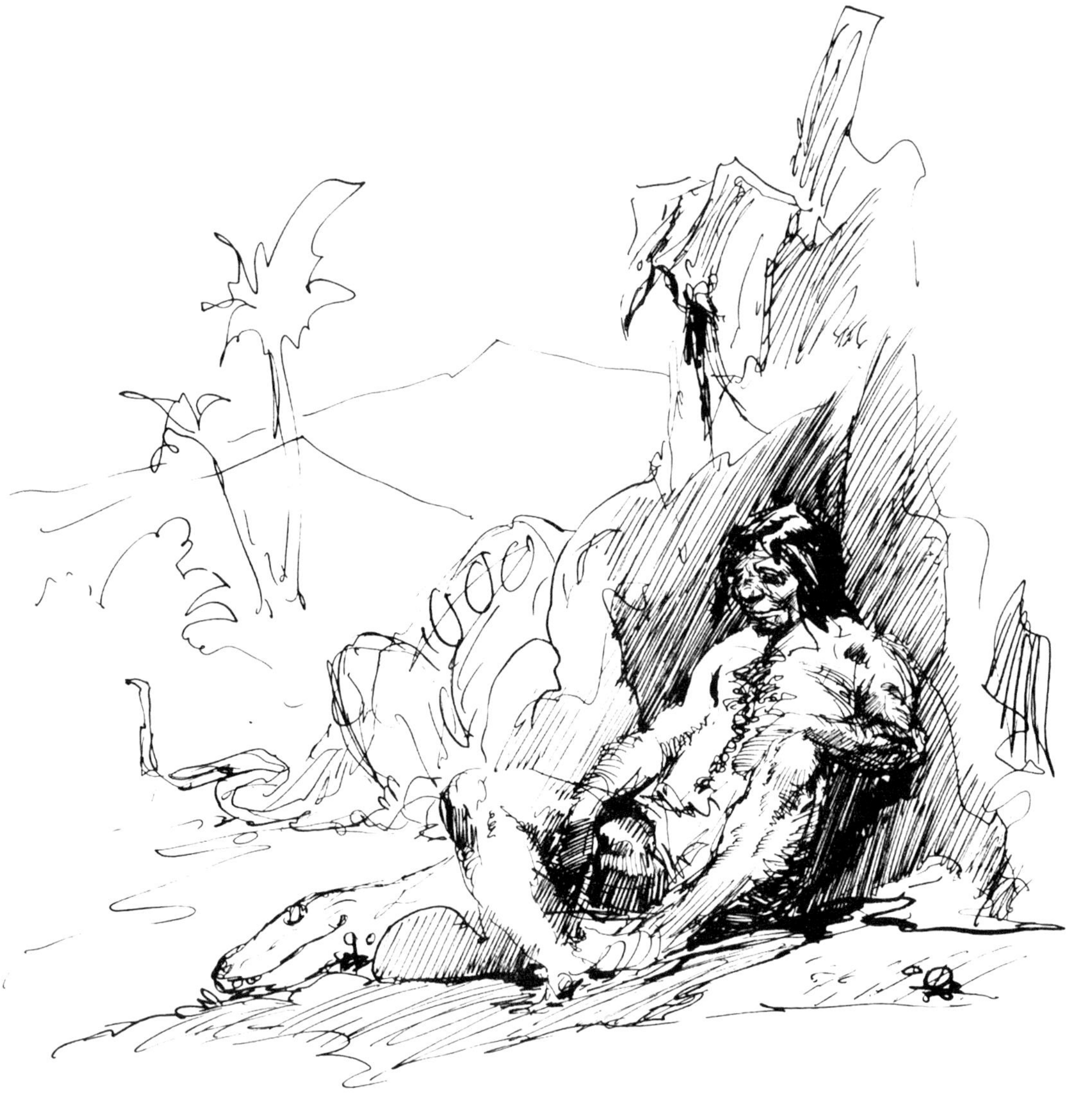

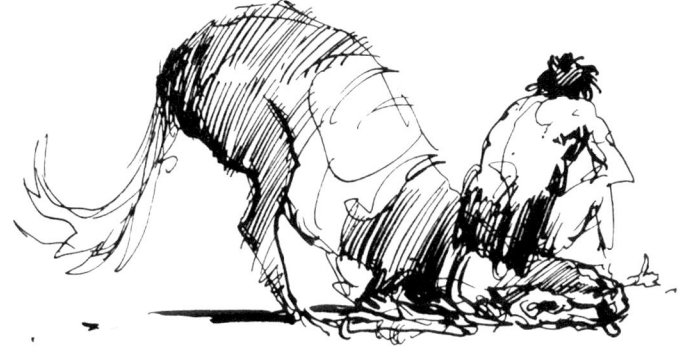

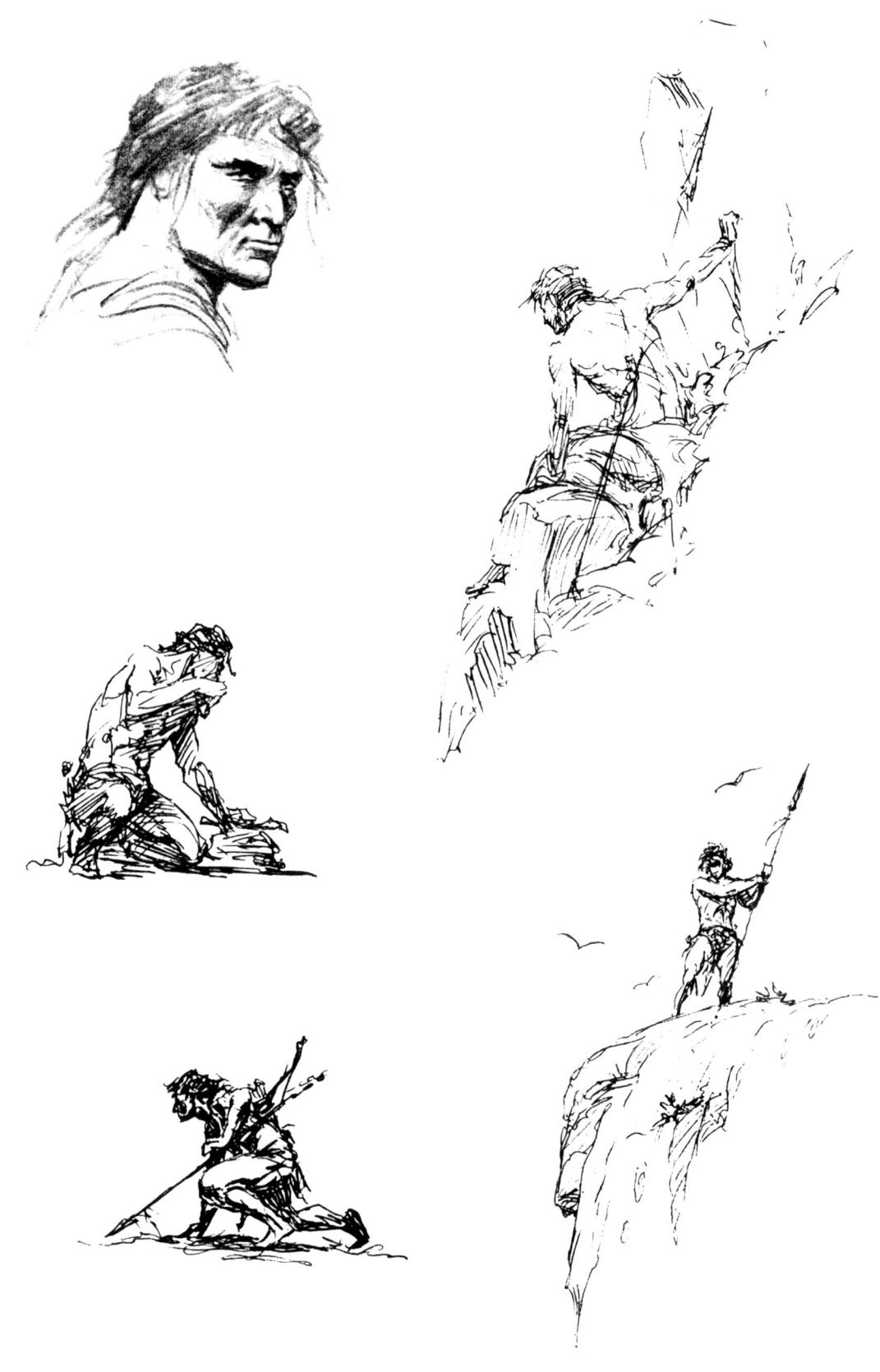

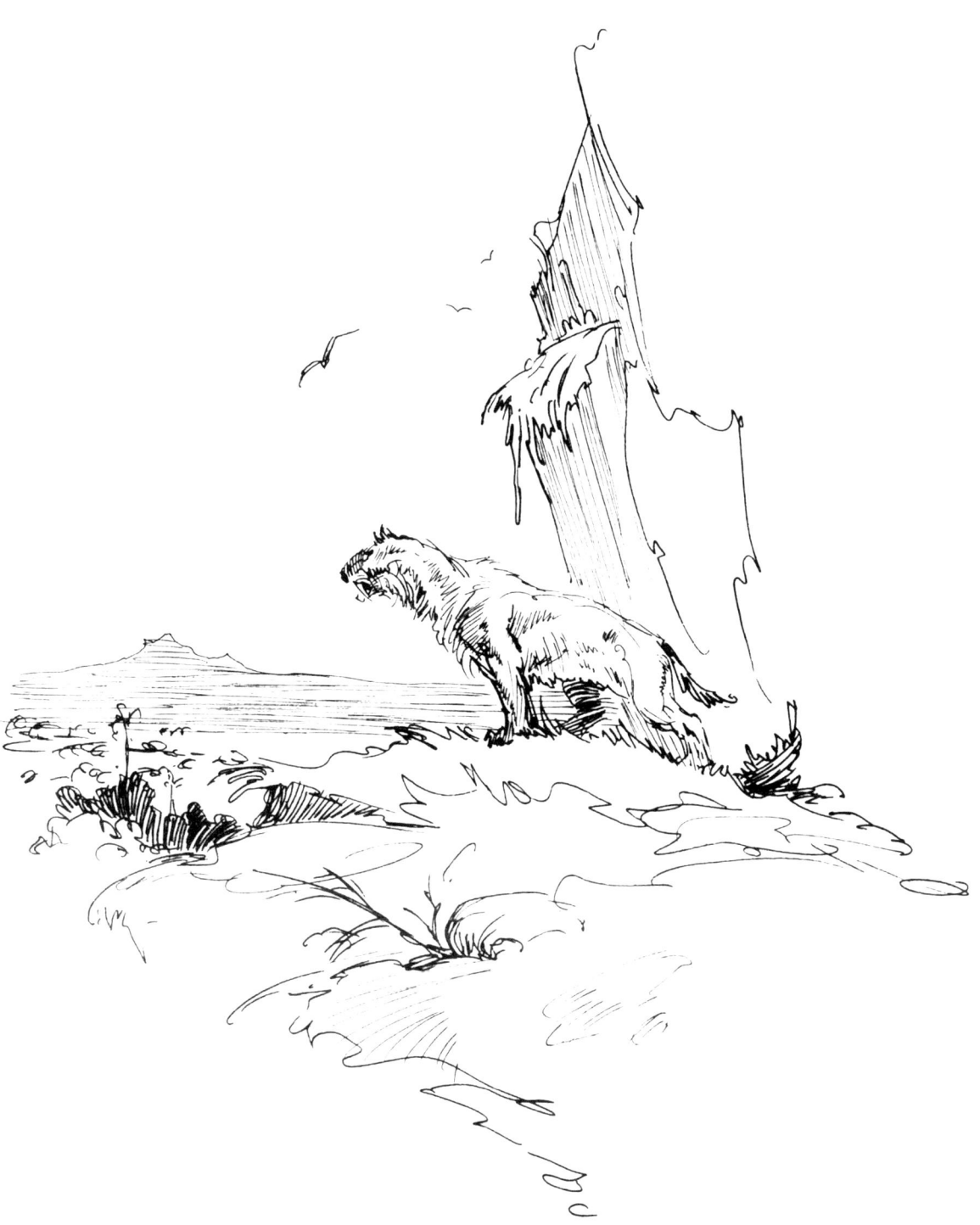

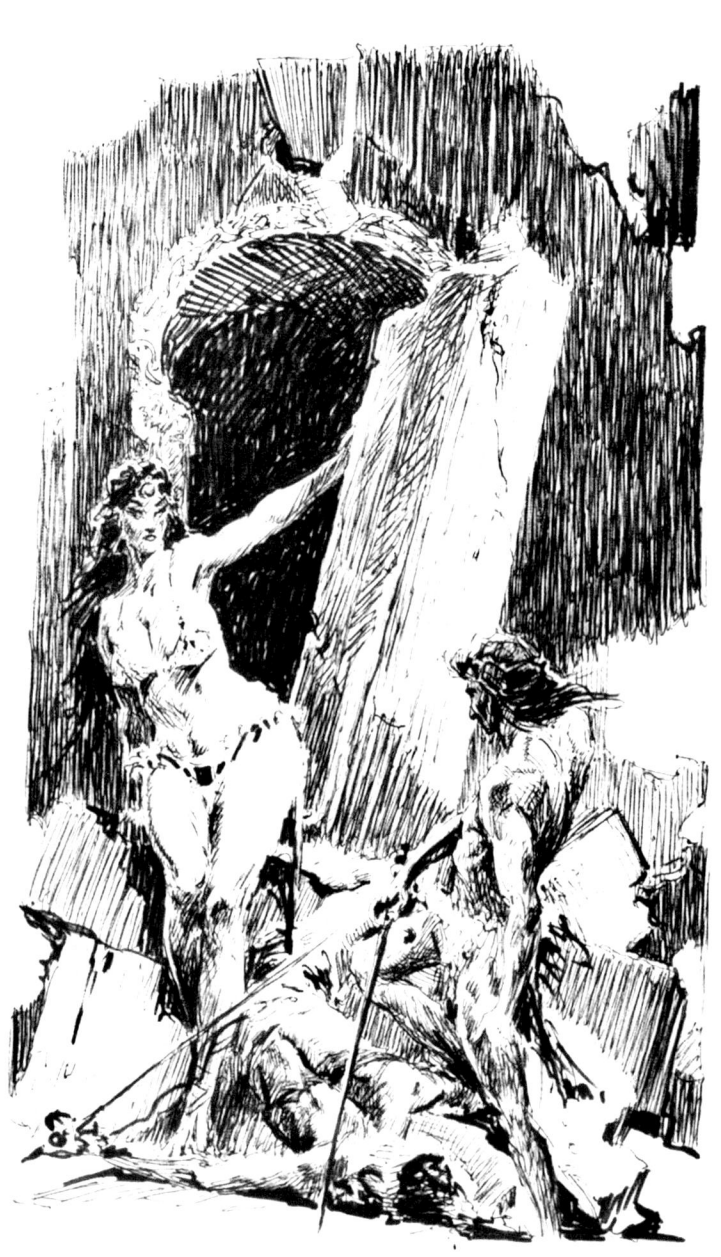

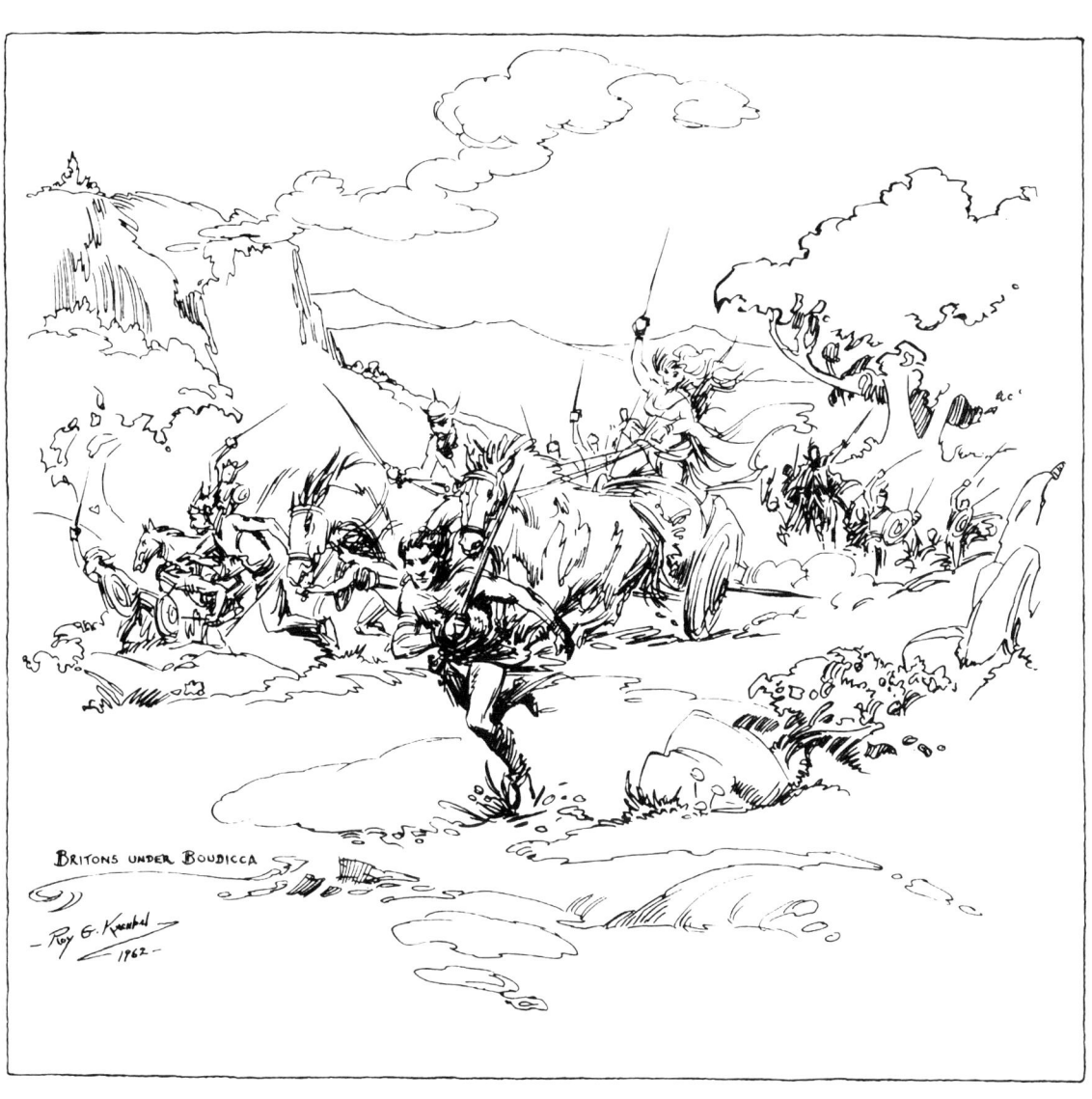

BRITONS UNDER BOUDICCA

Roy G. Krenkel
1962

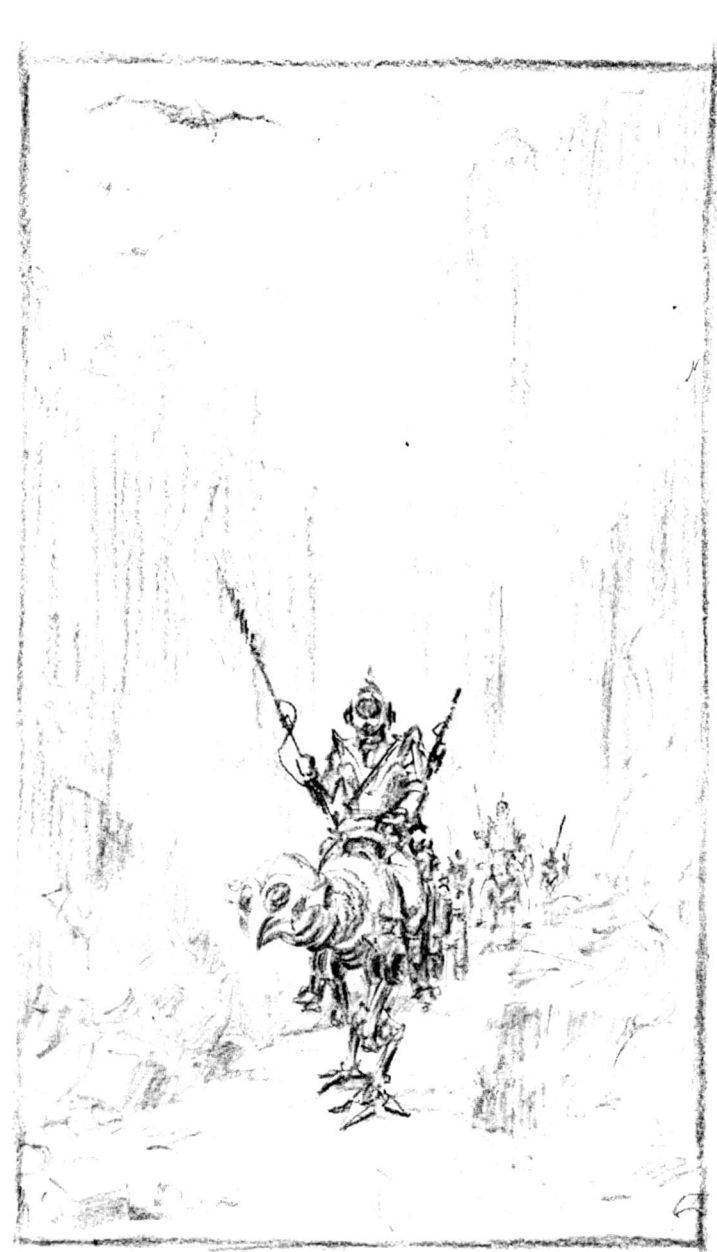

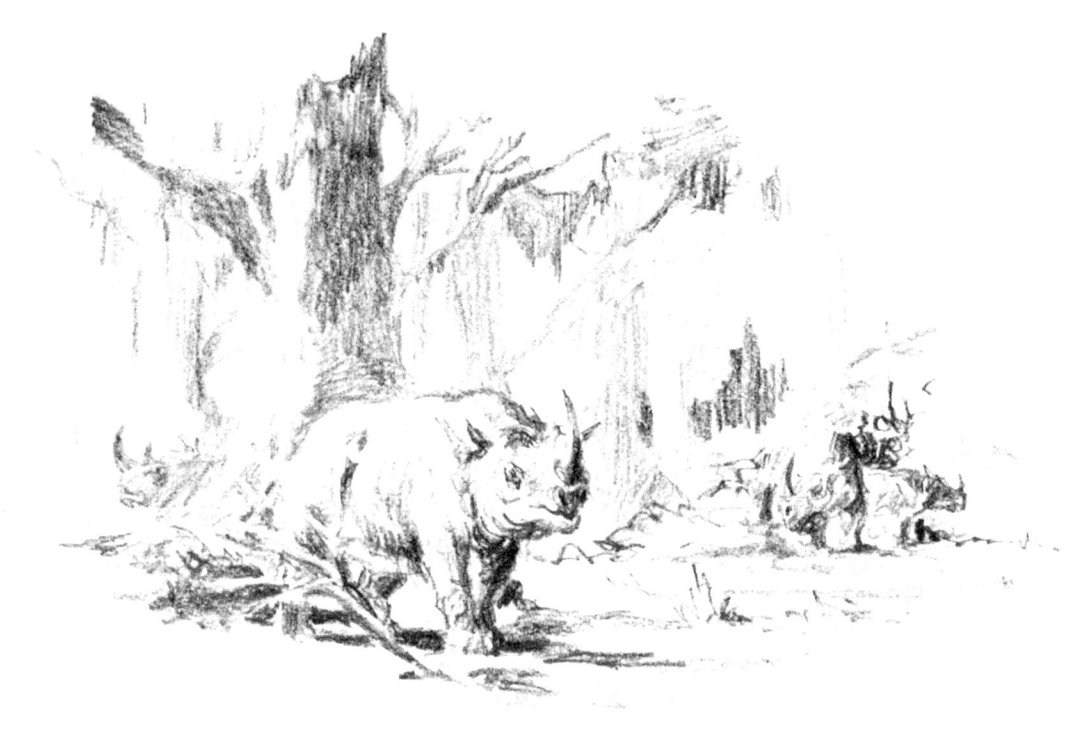

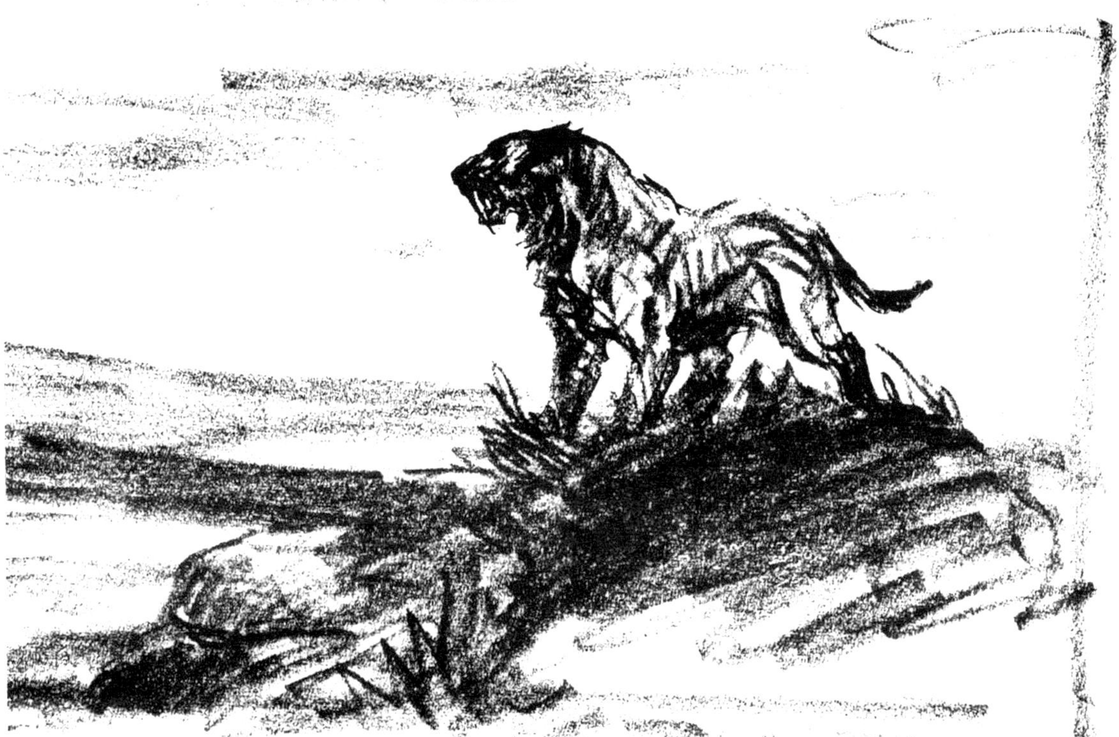

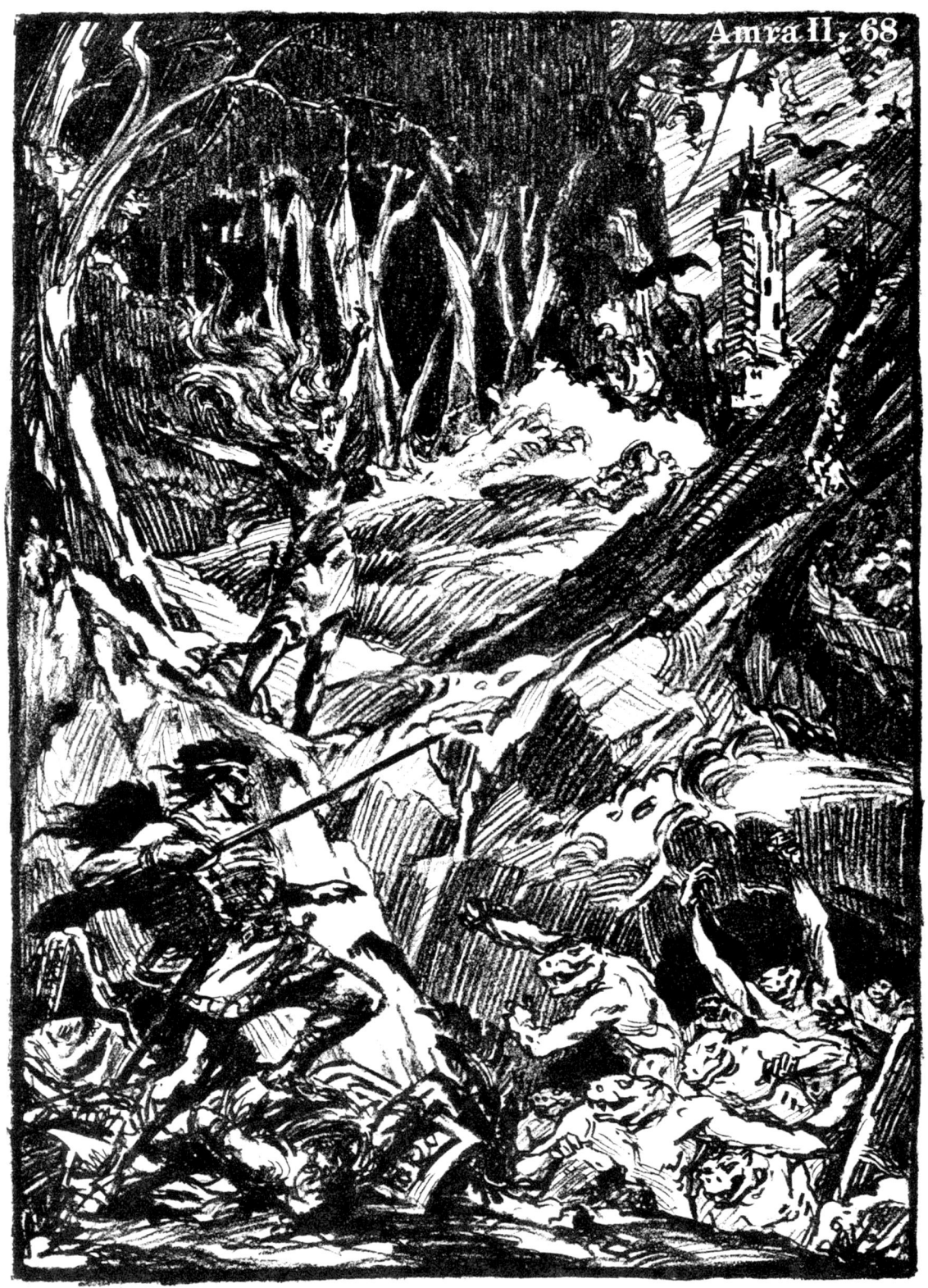

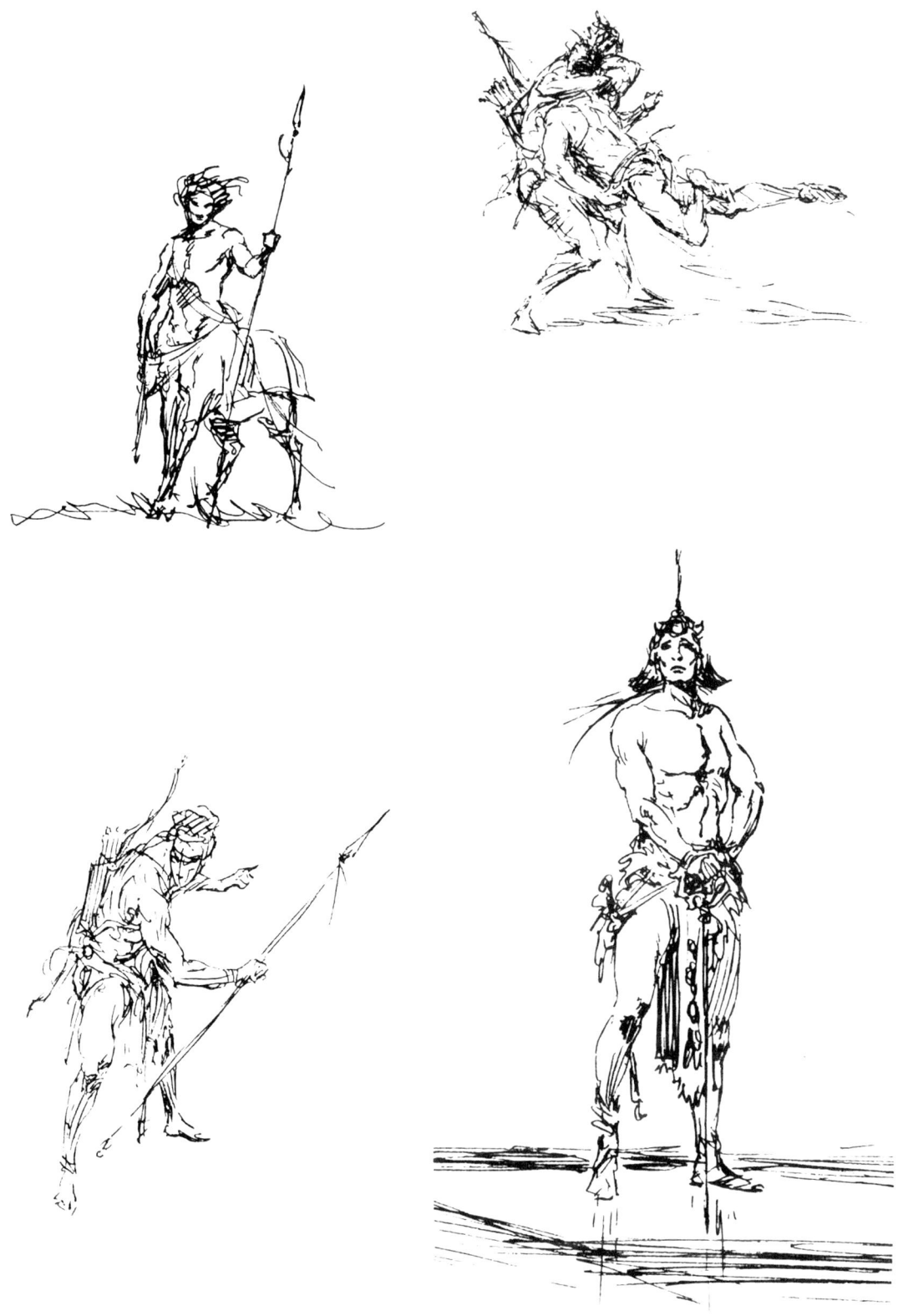

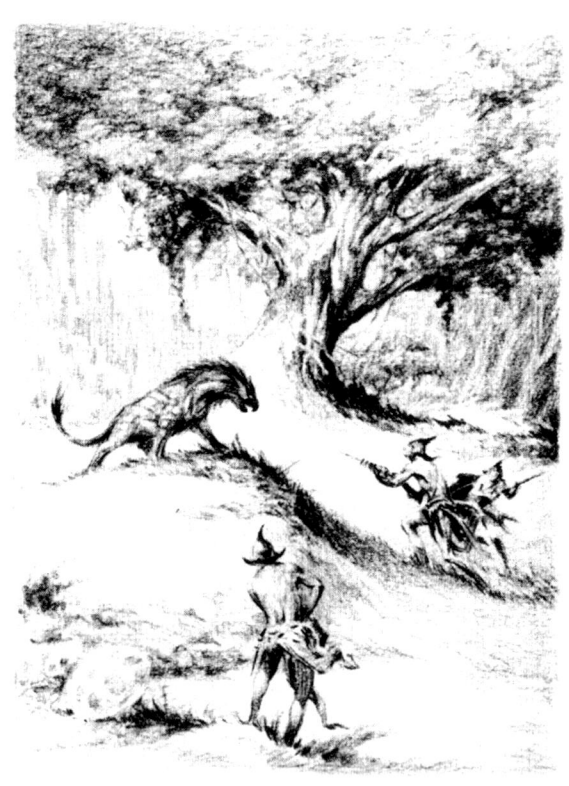

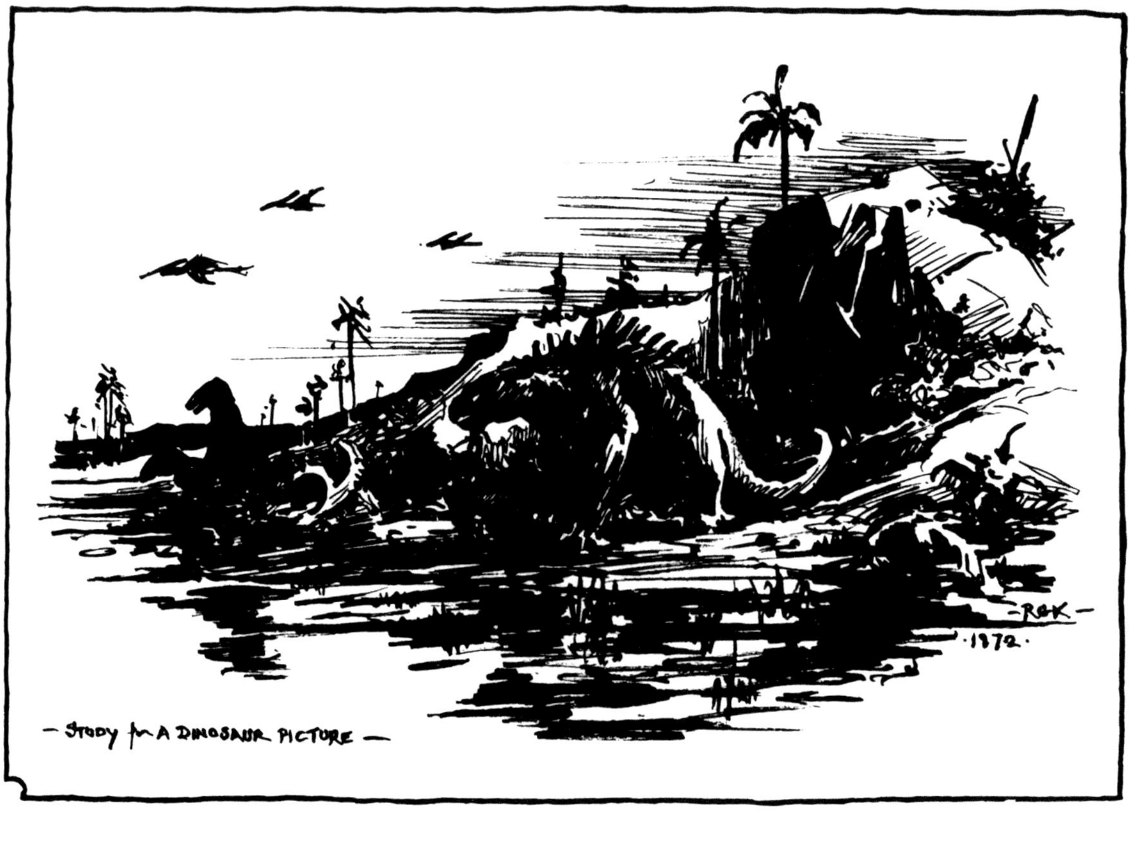

— STUDY for A DINOSAUR PICTURE —

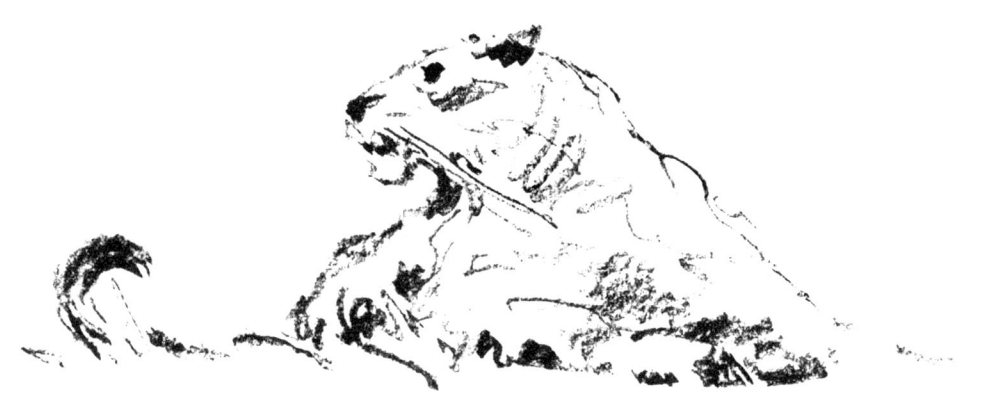

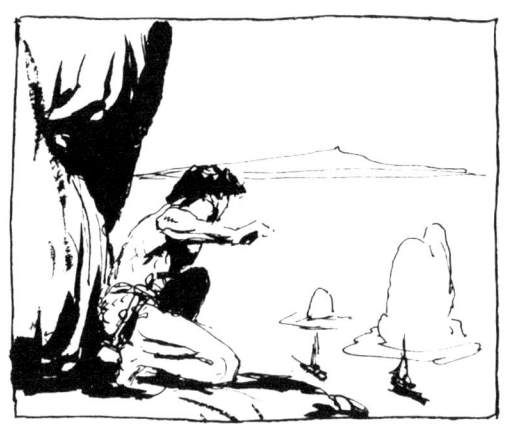

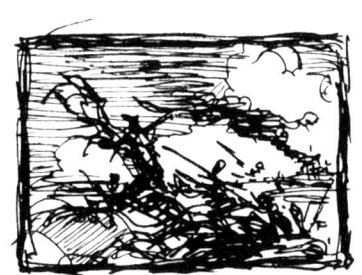

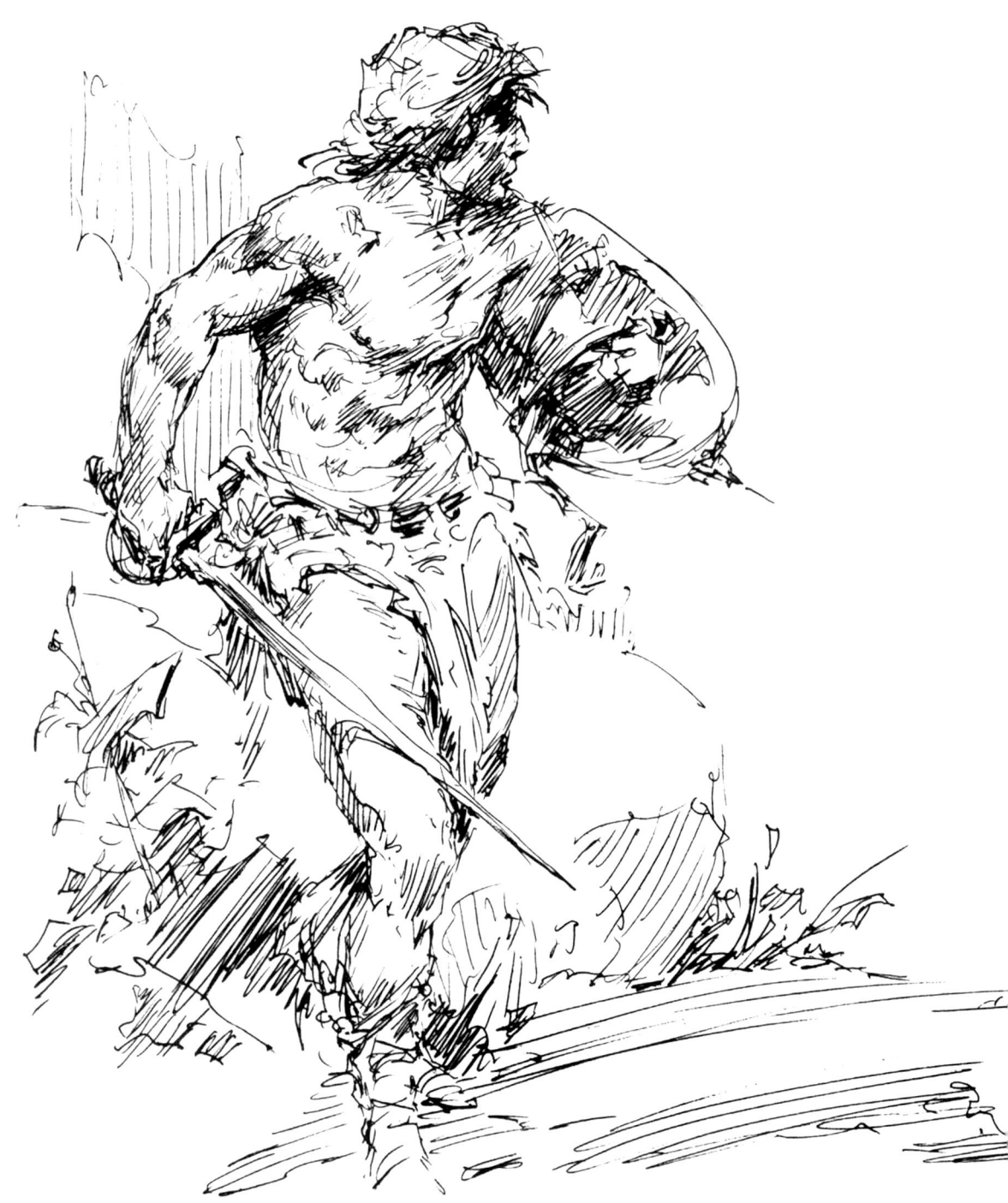

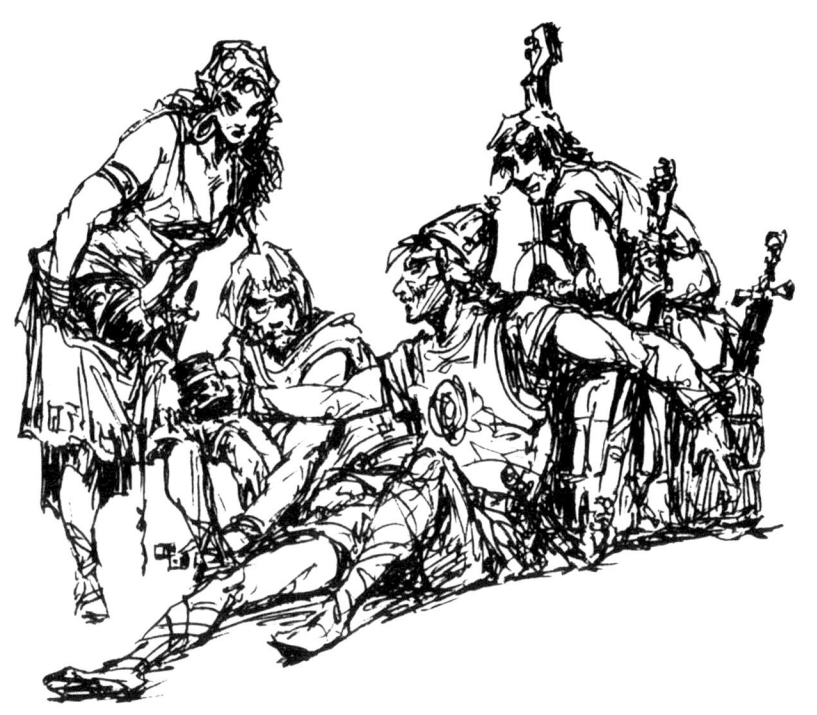

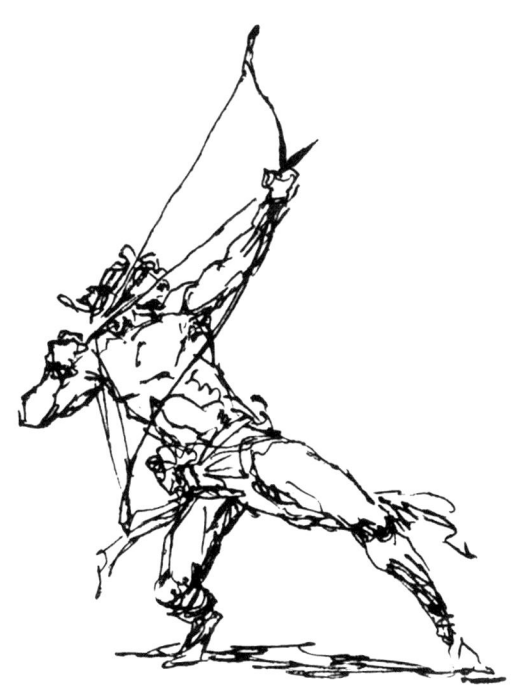

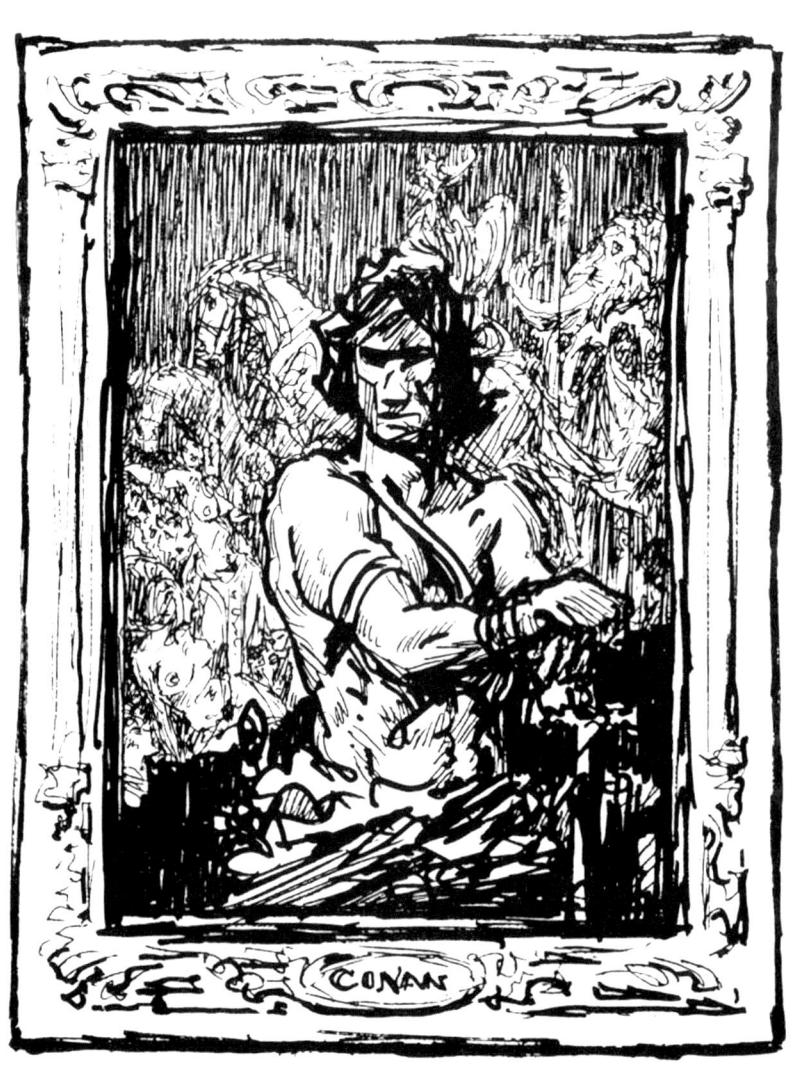

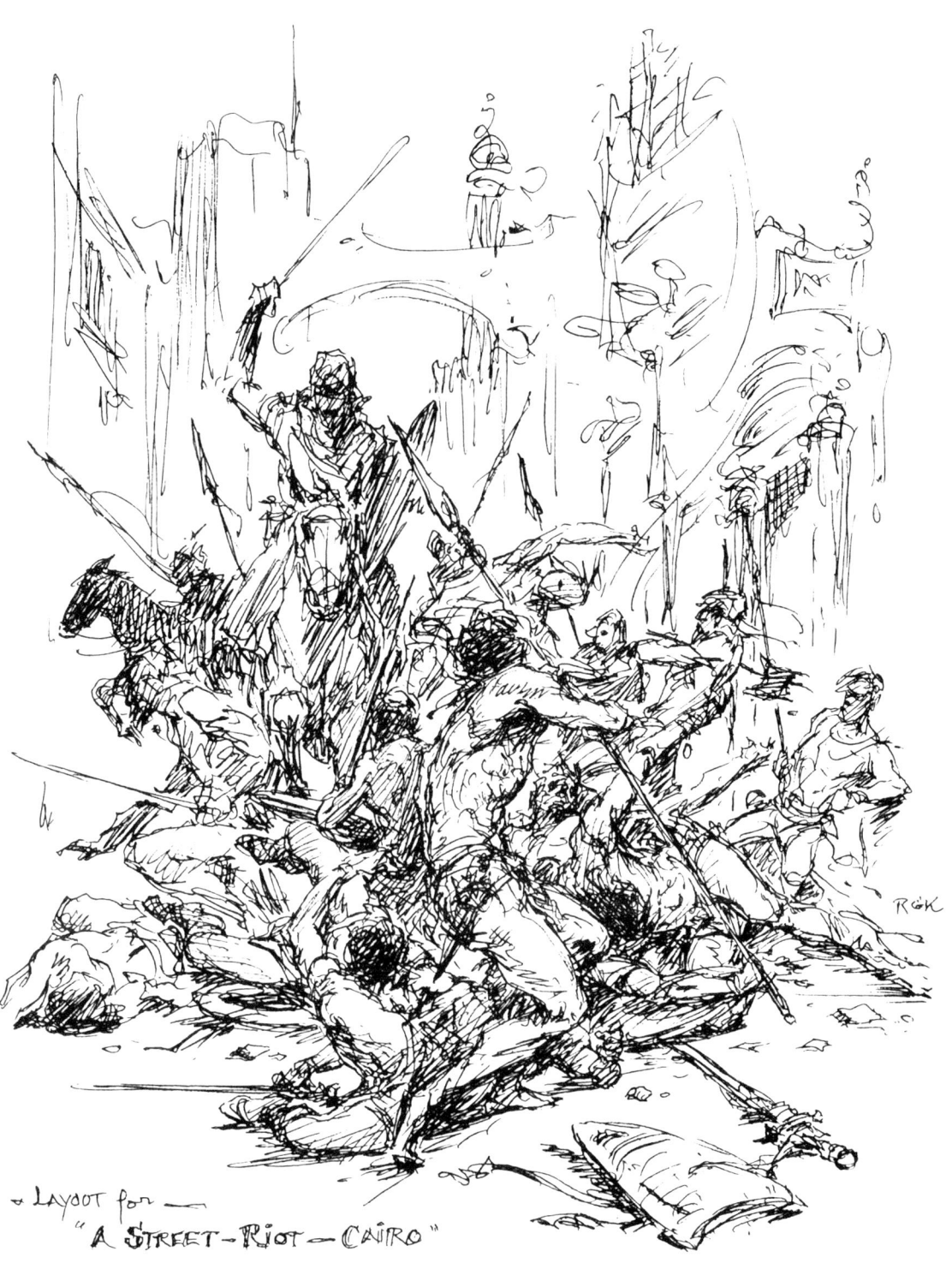

+ Layout for —
"A Street – Riot – Cairo"

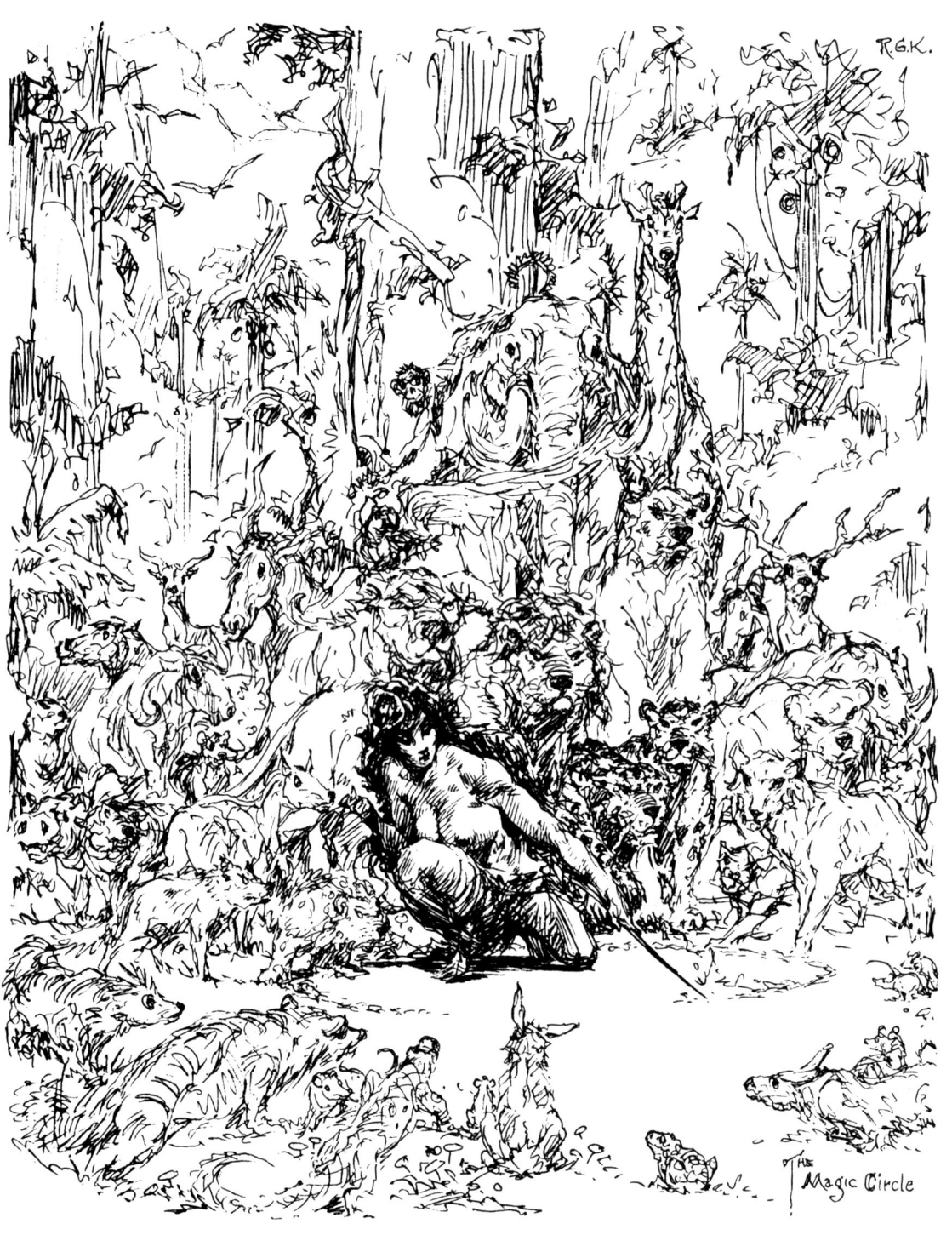

The Magic Circle

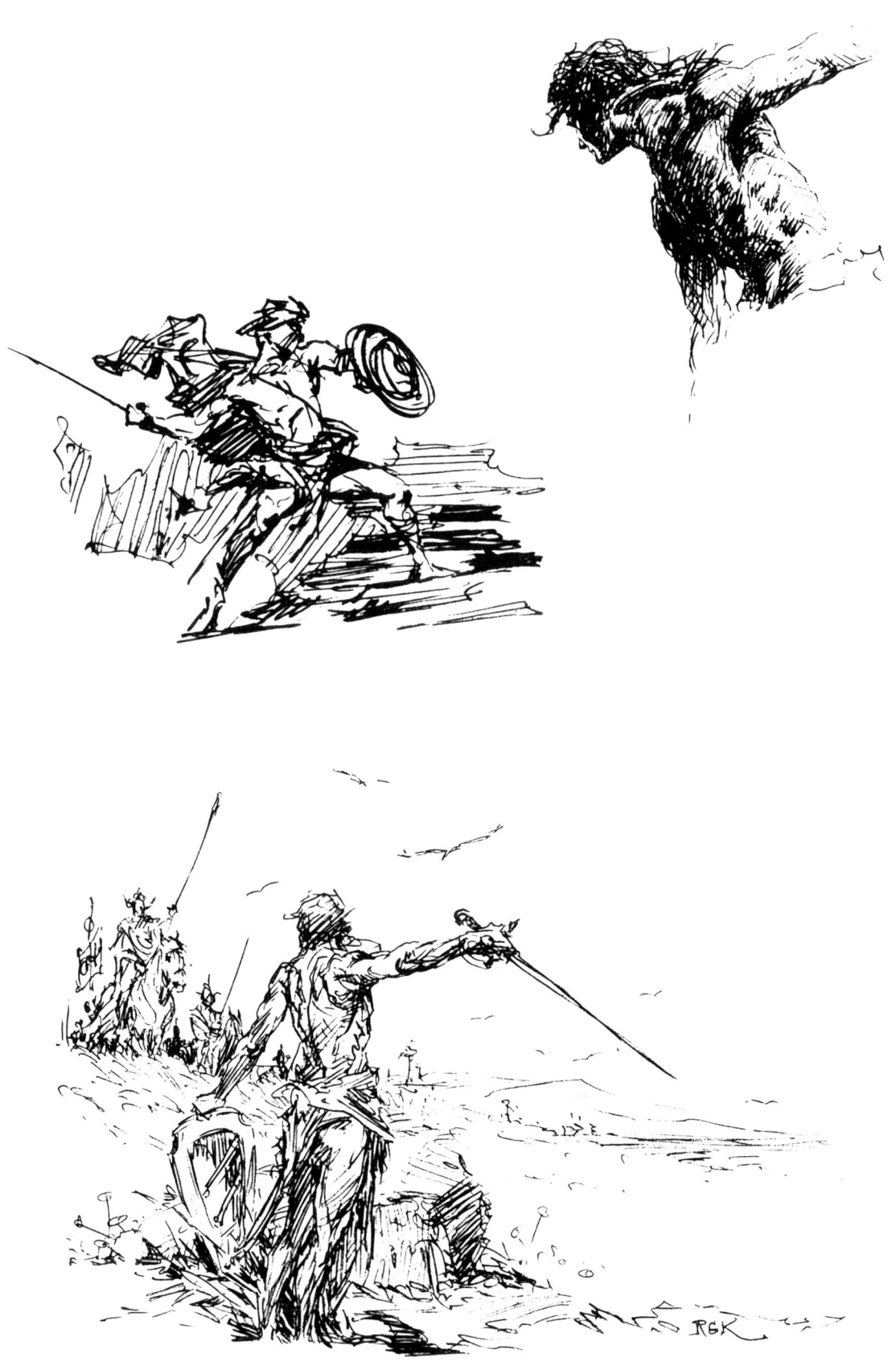

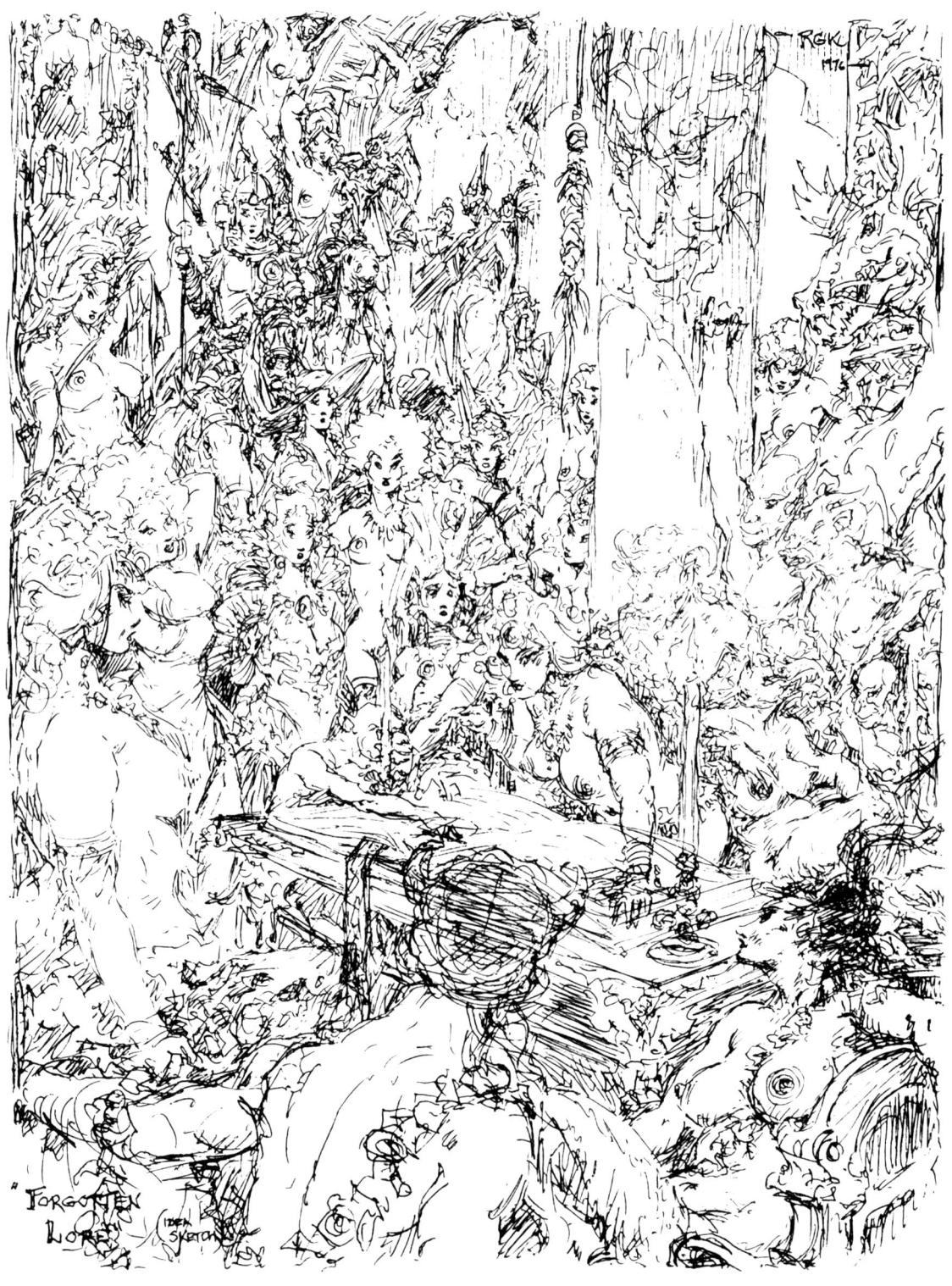

"Forgotten Lore" (Idea Sketch)

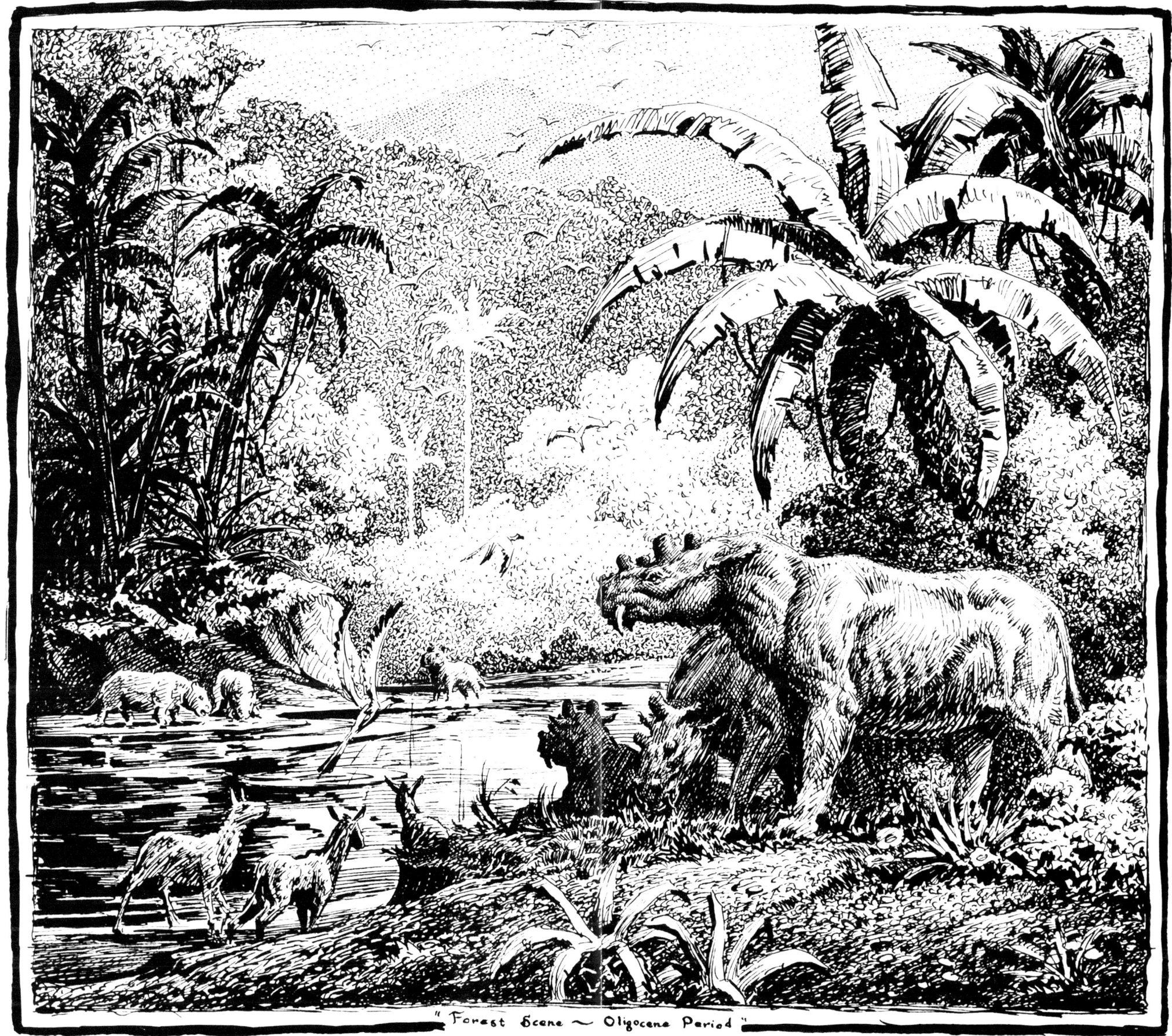

"Forest Scene ~ Oligocene Period"

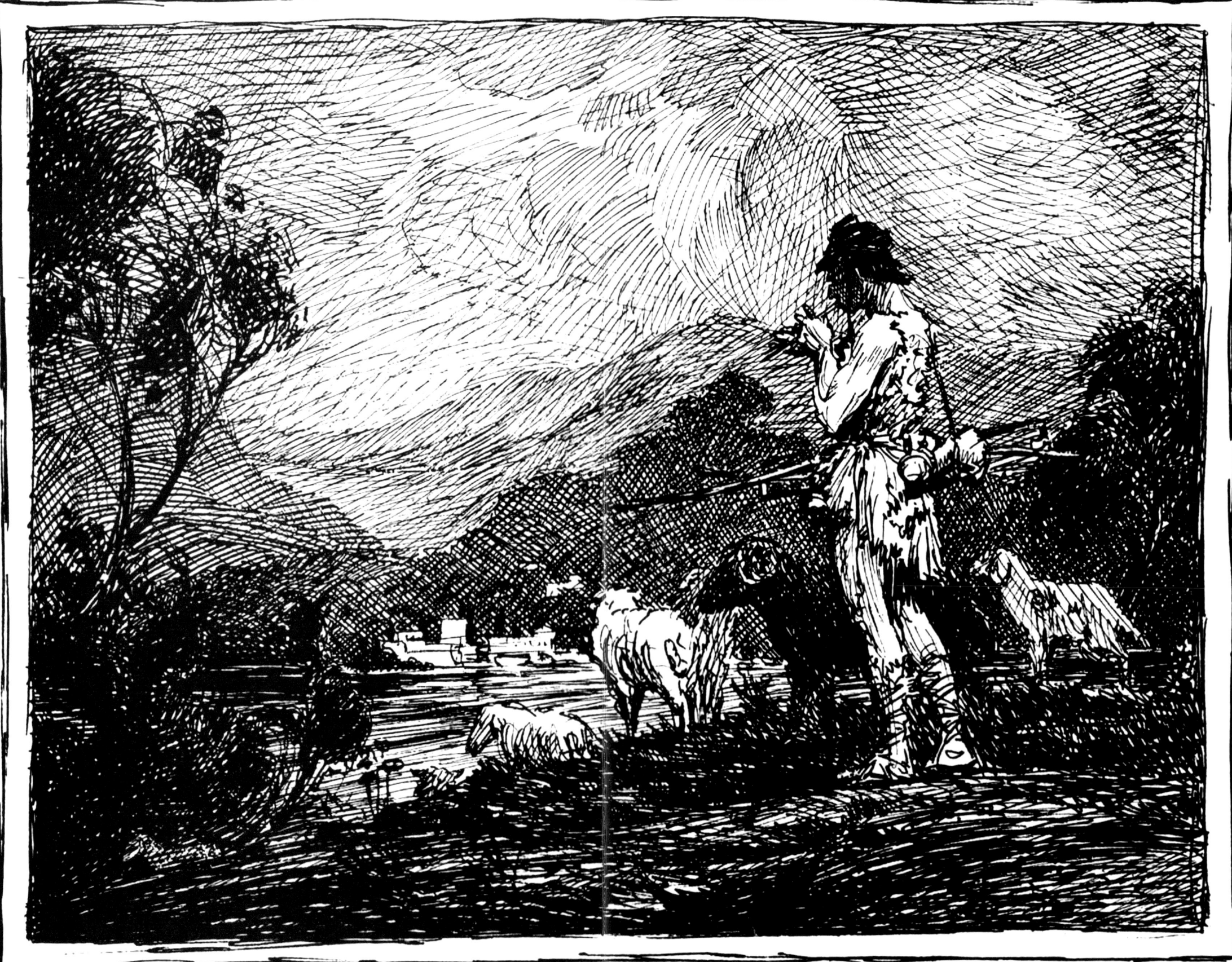

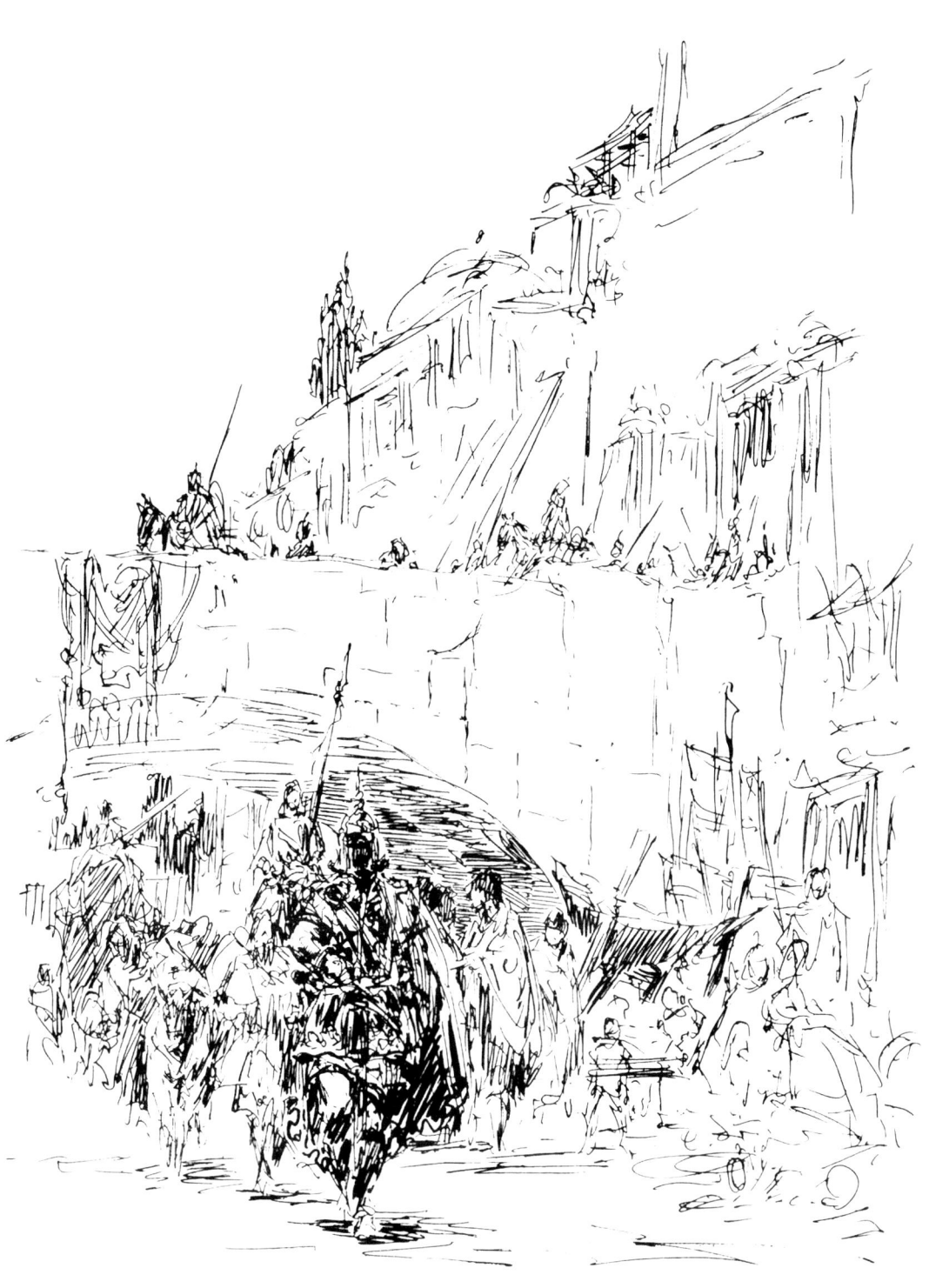

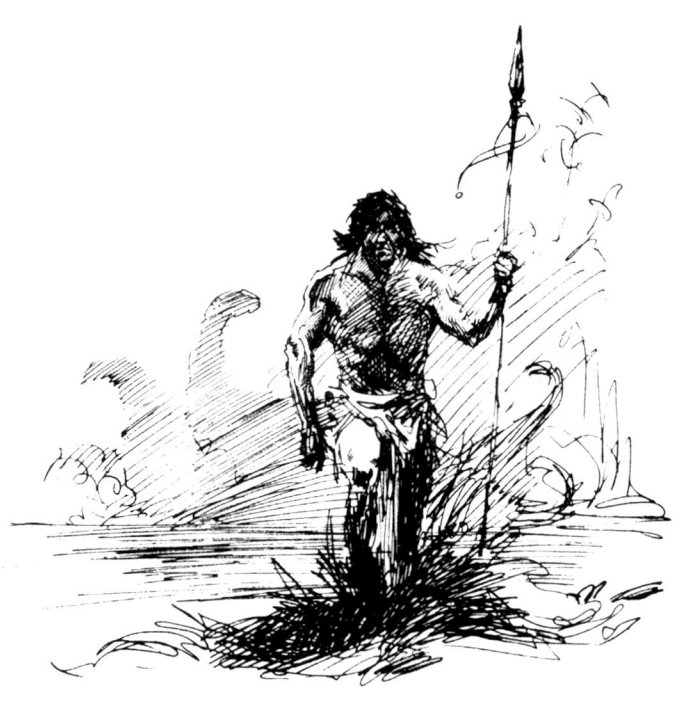

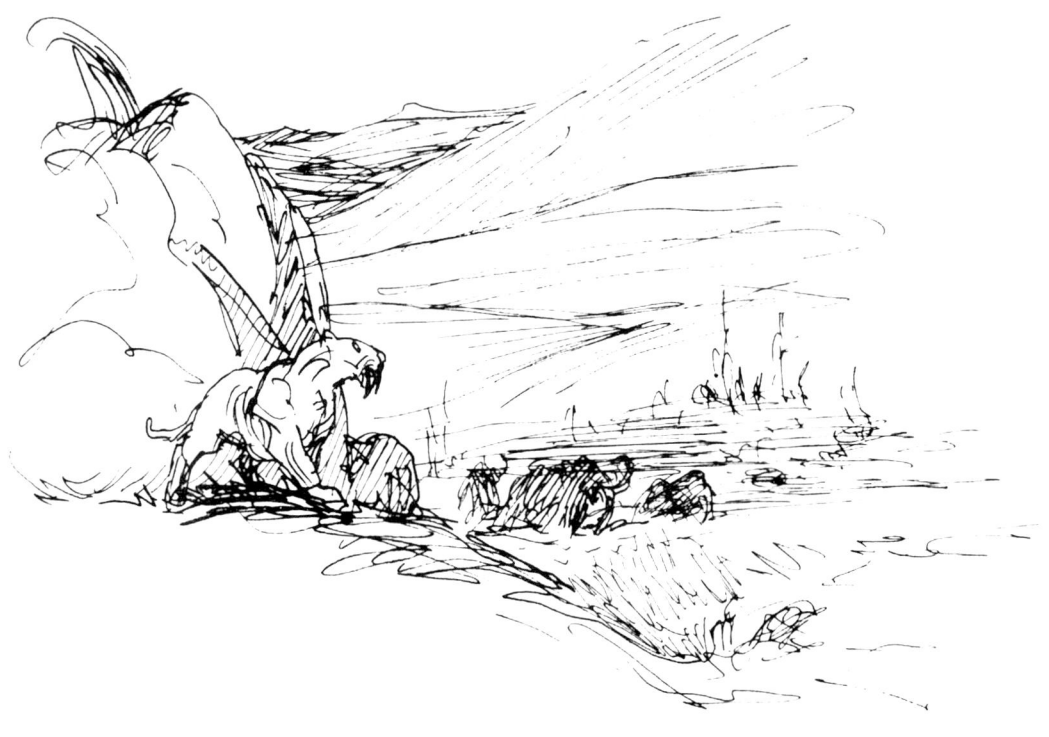

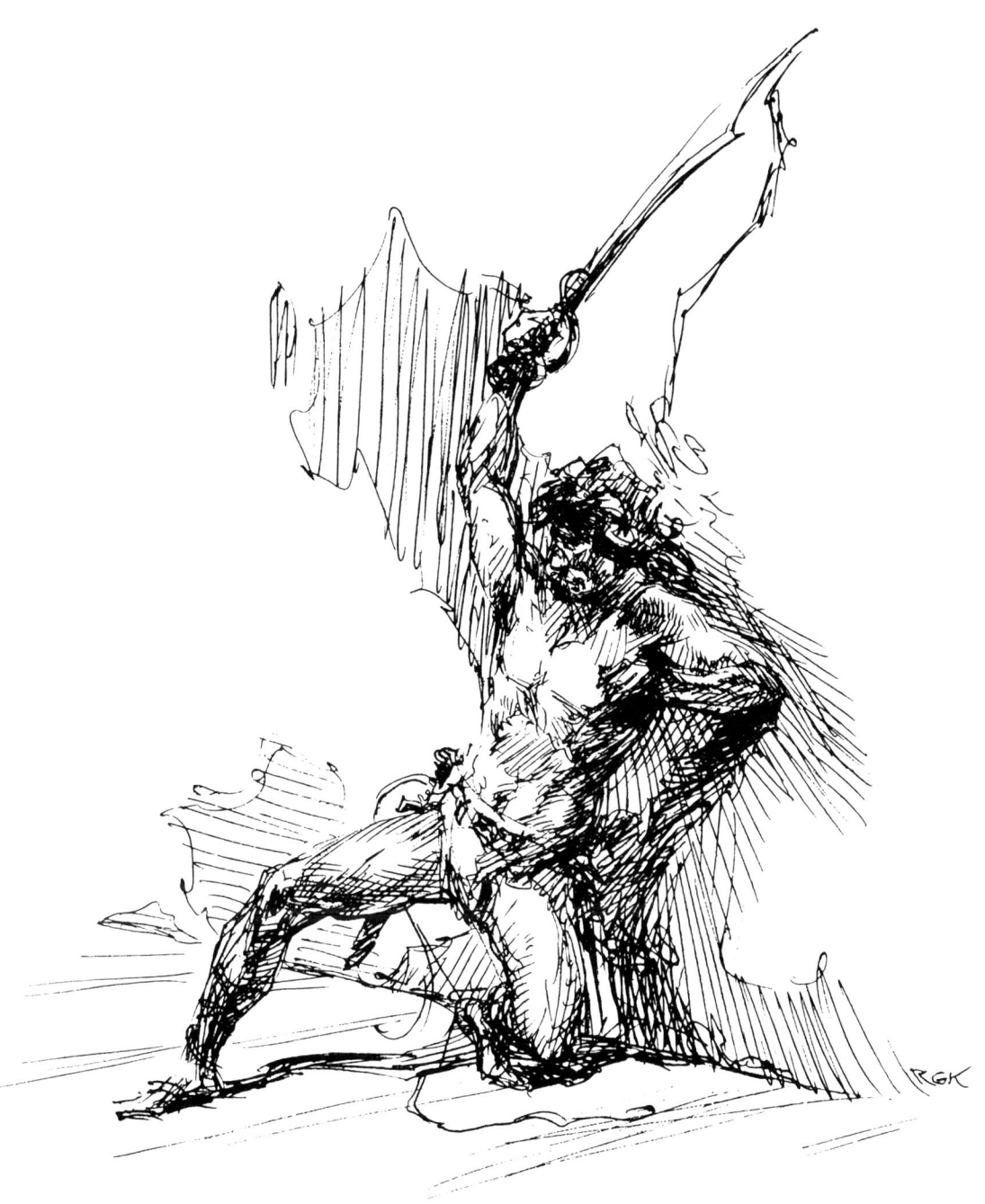

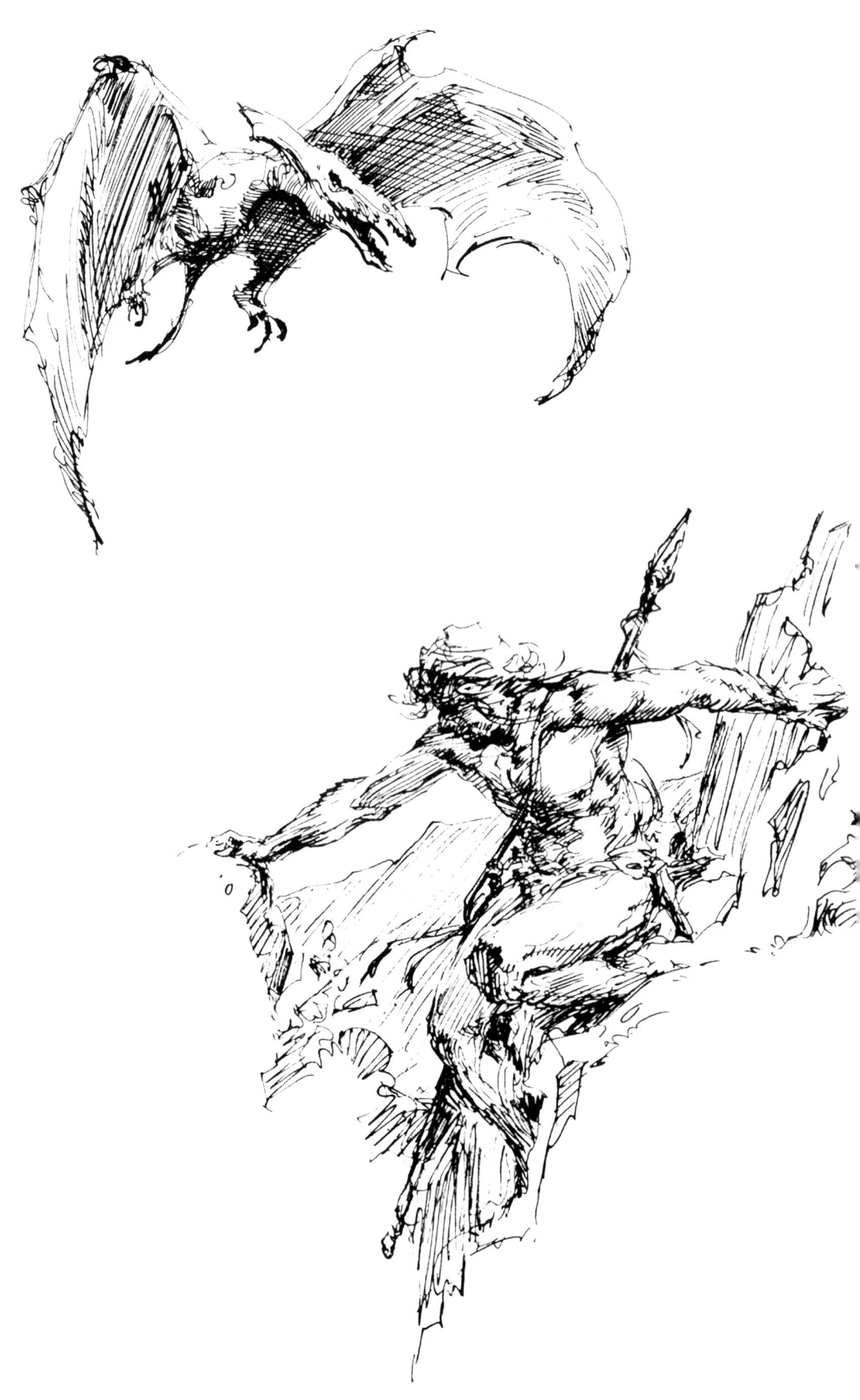

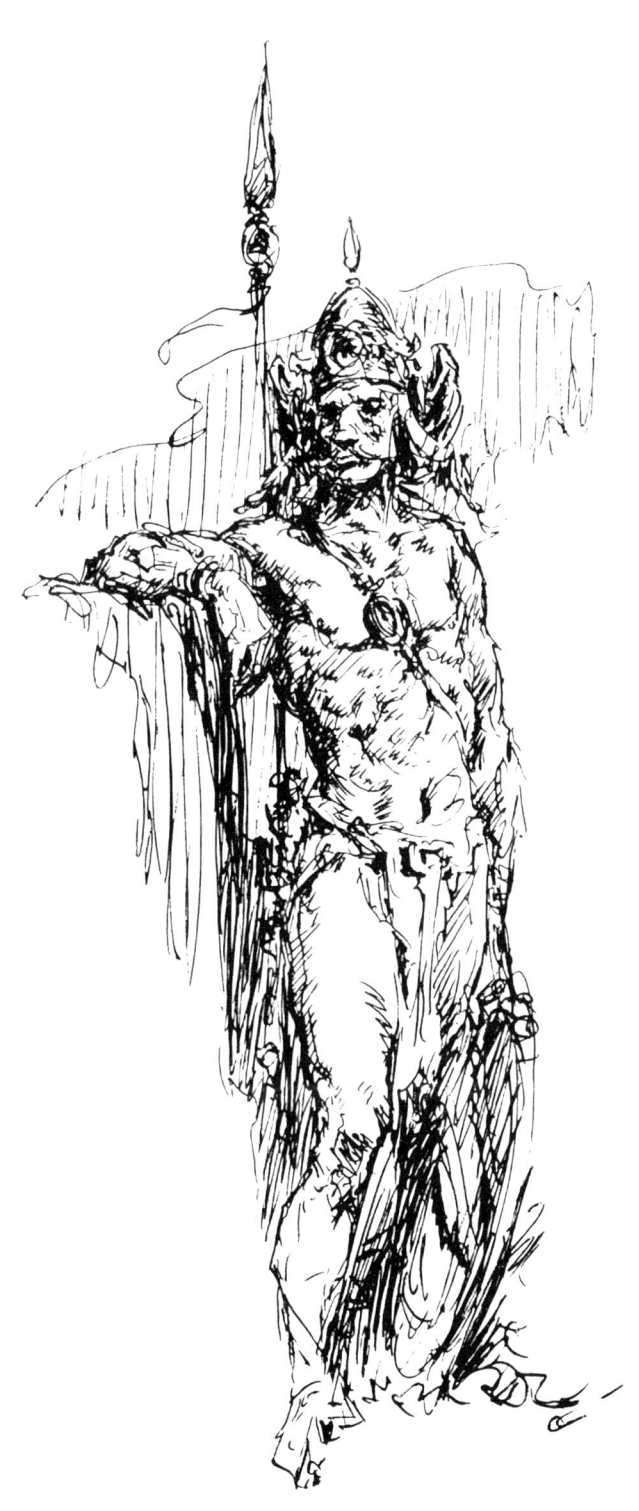

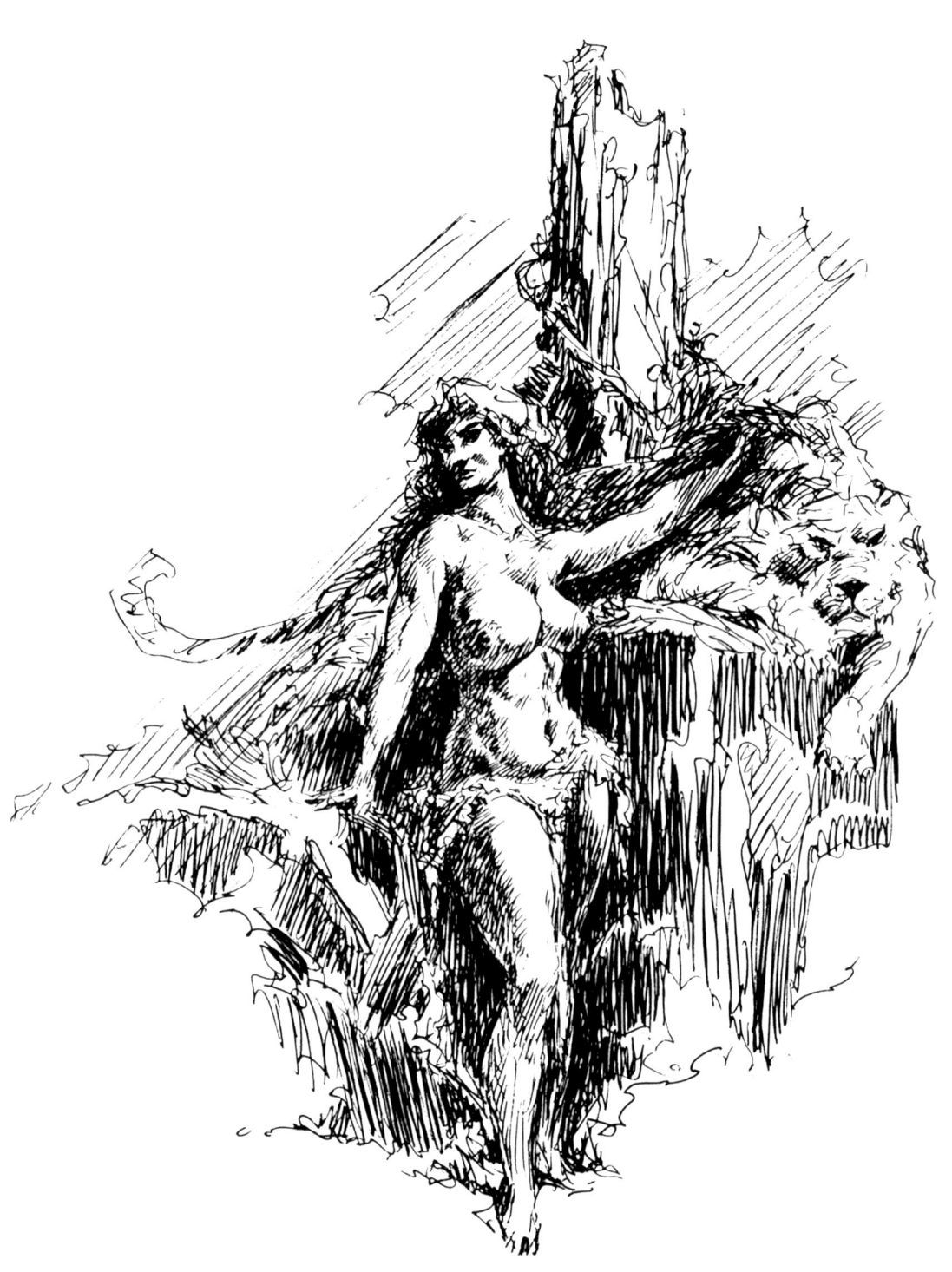

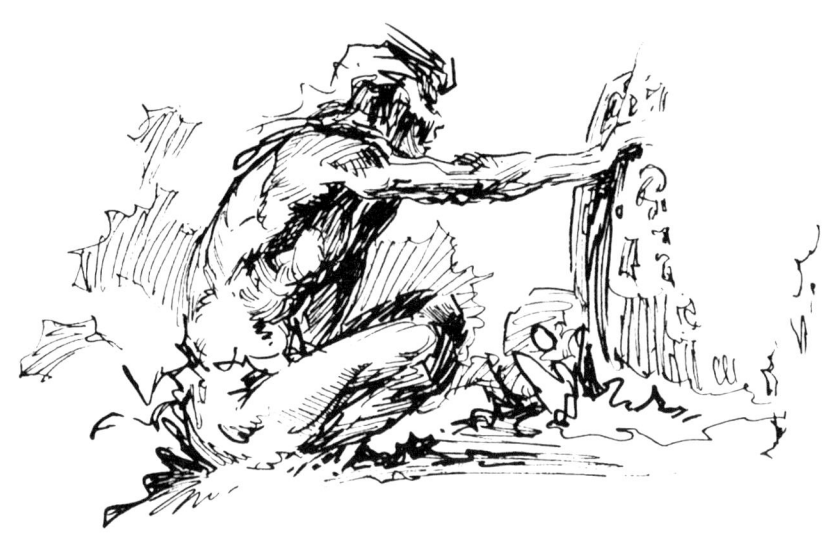

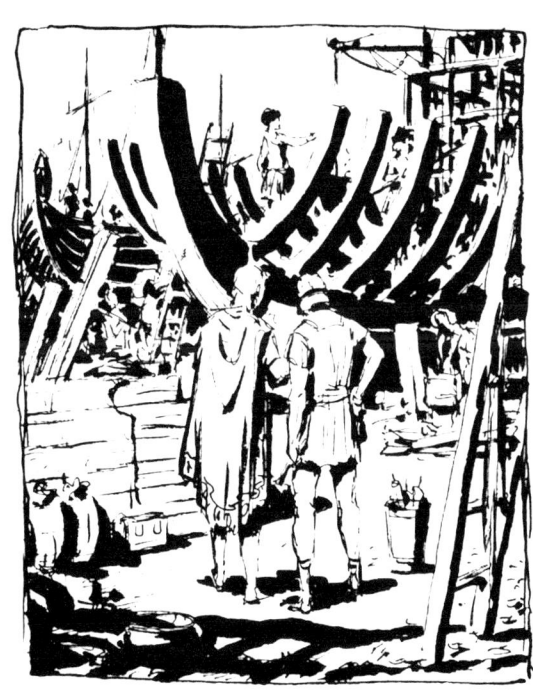

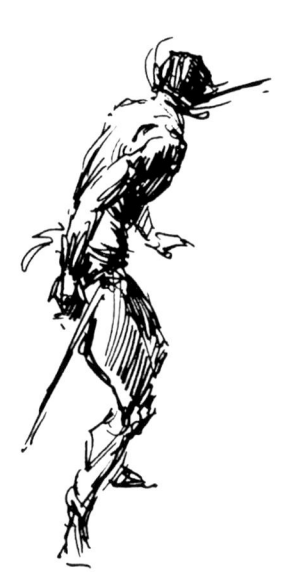

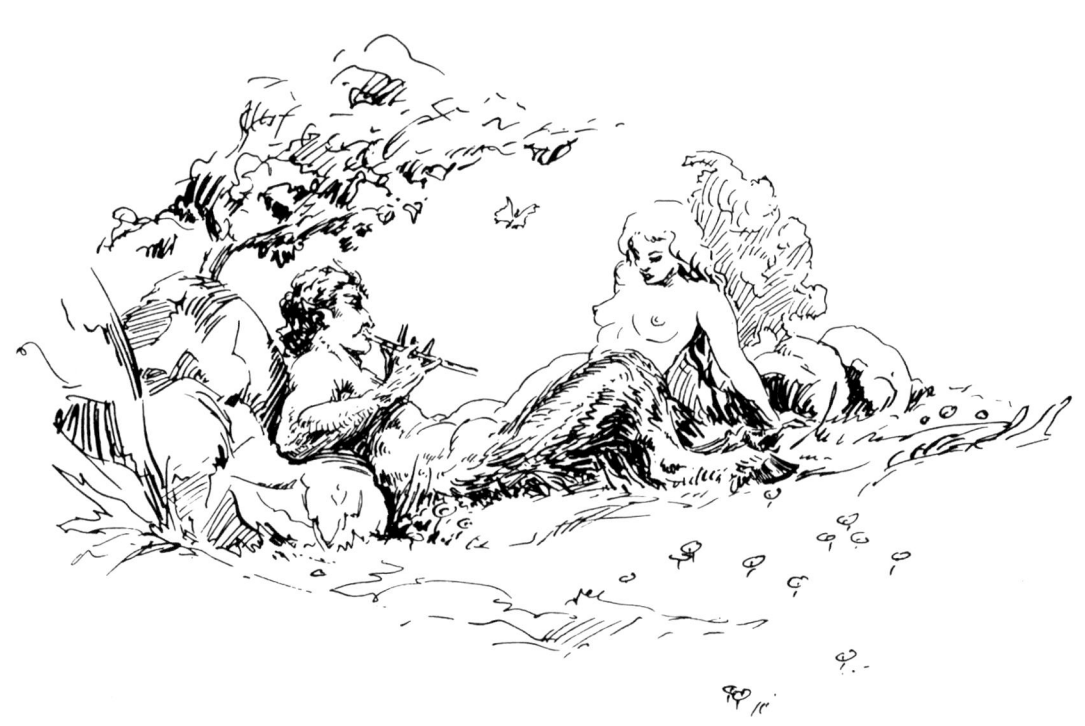

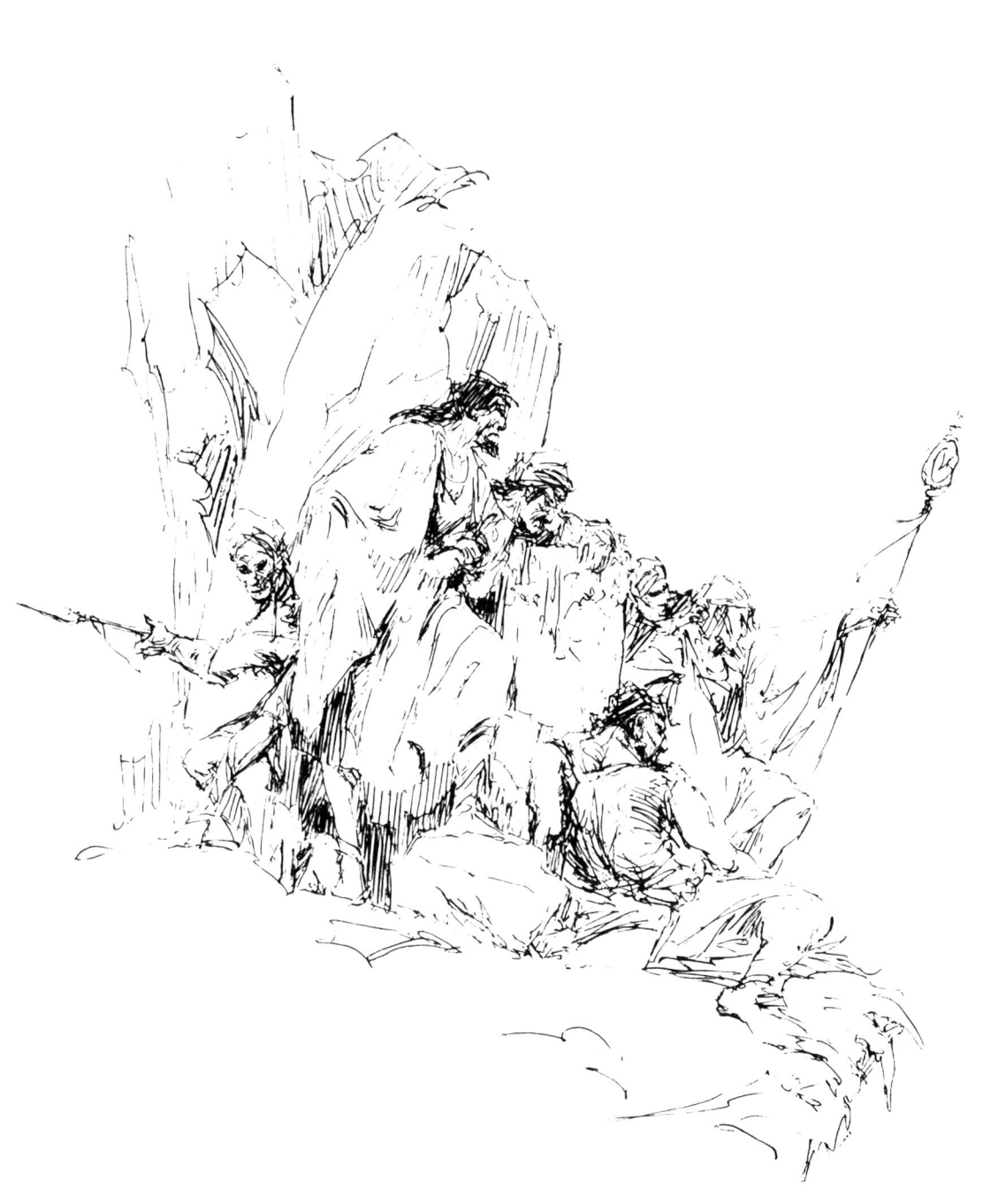

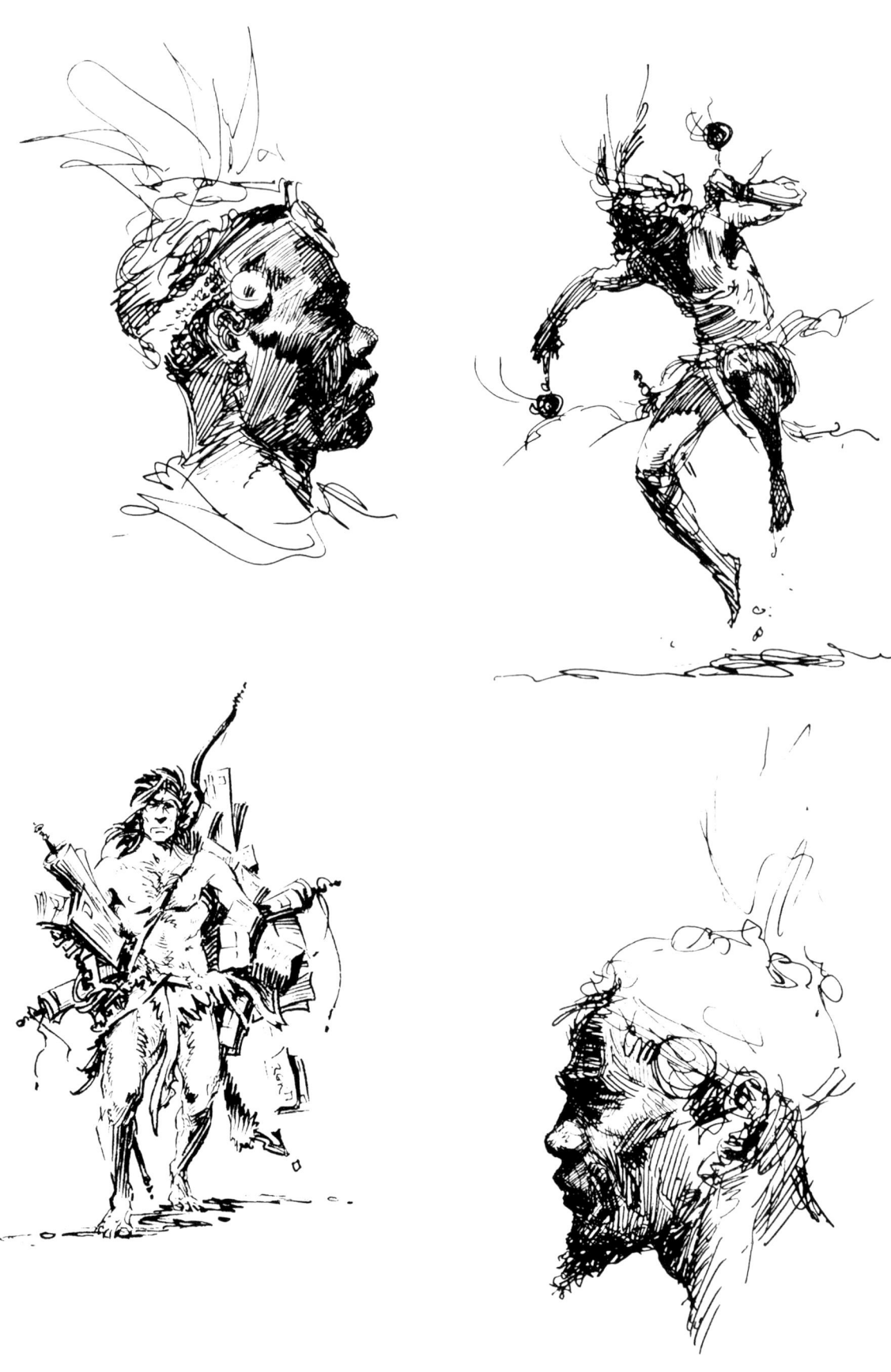

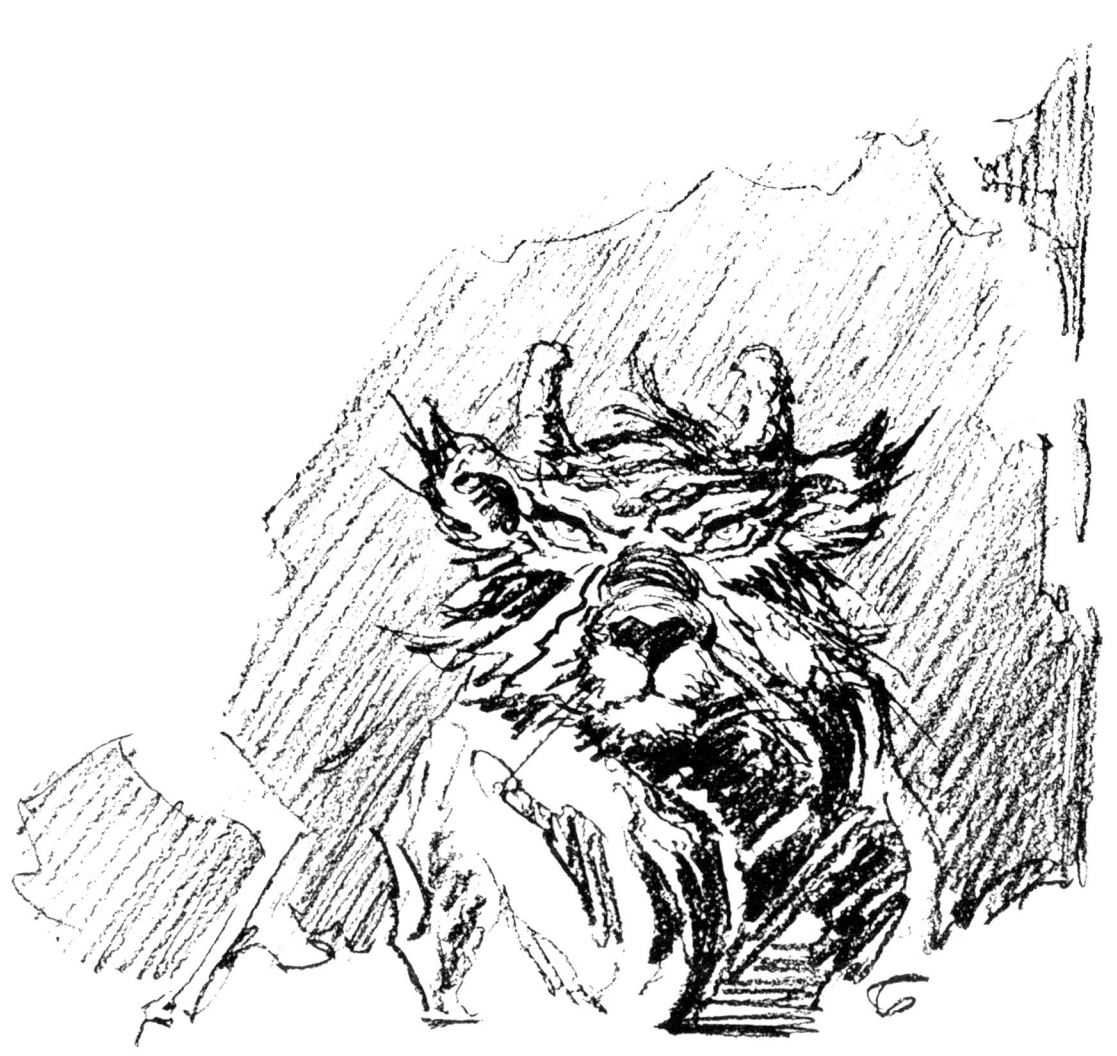

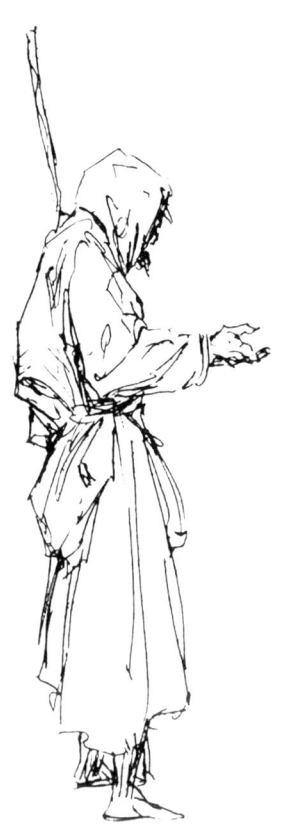

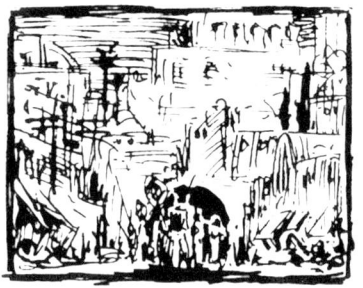

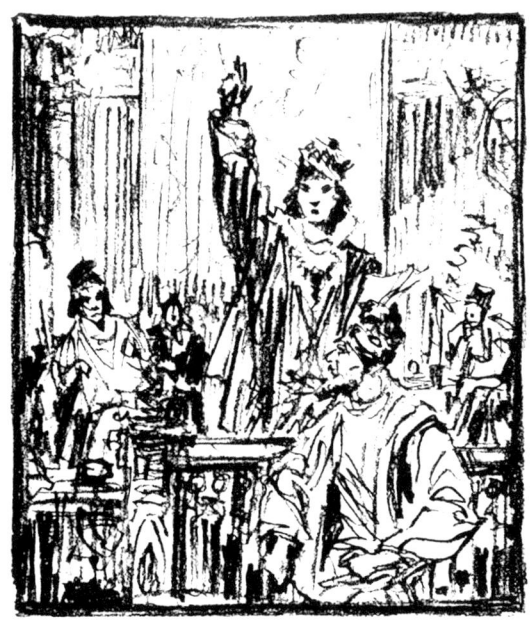

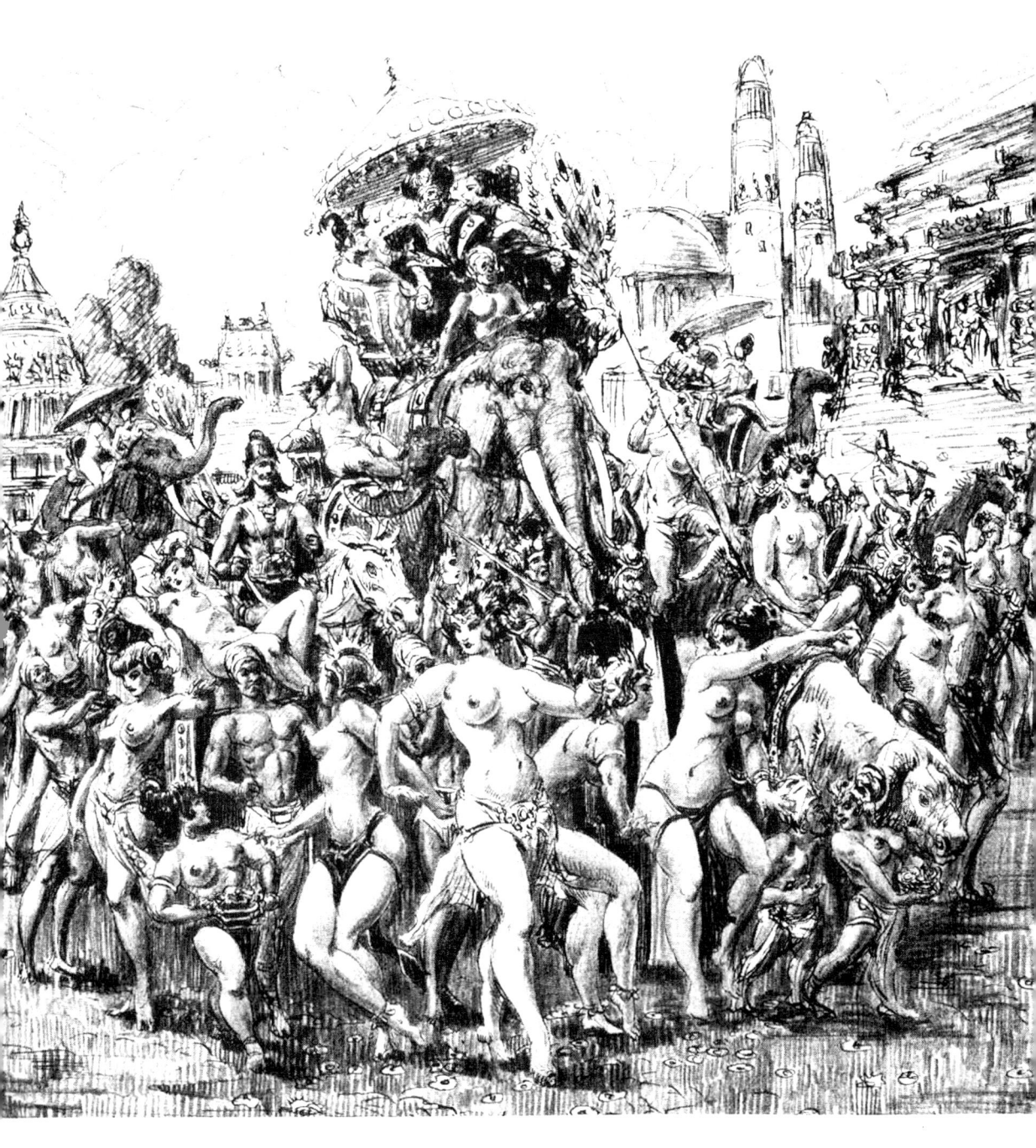

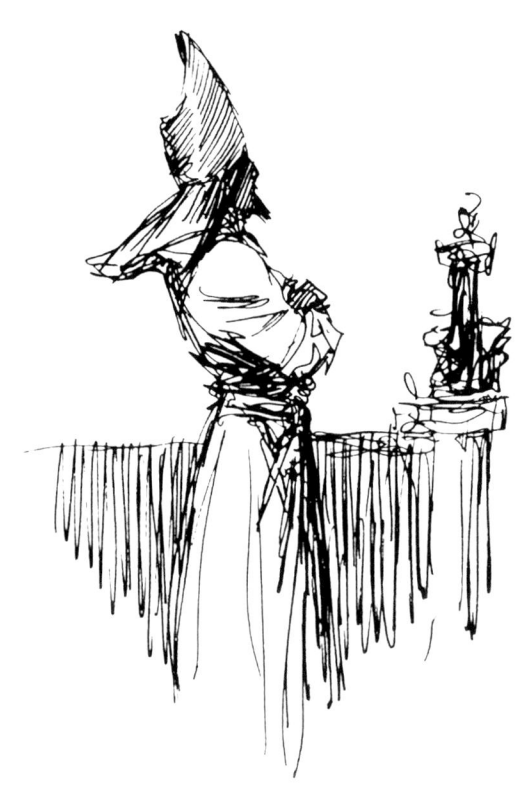

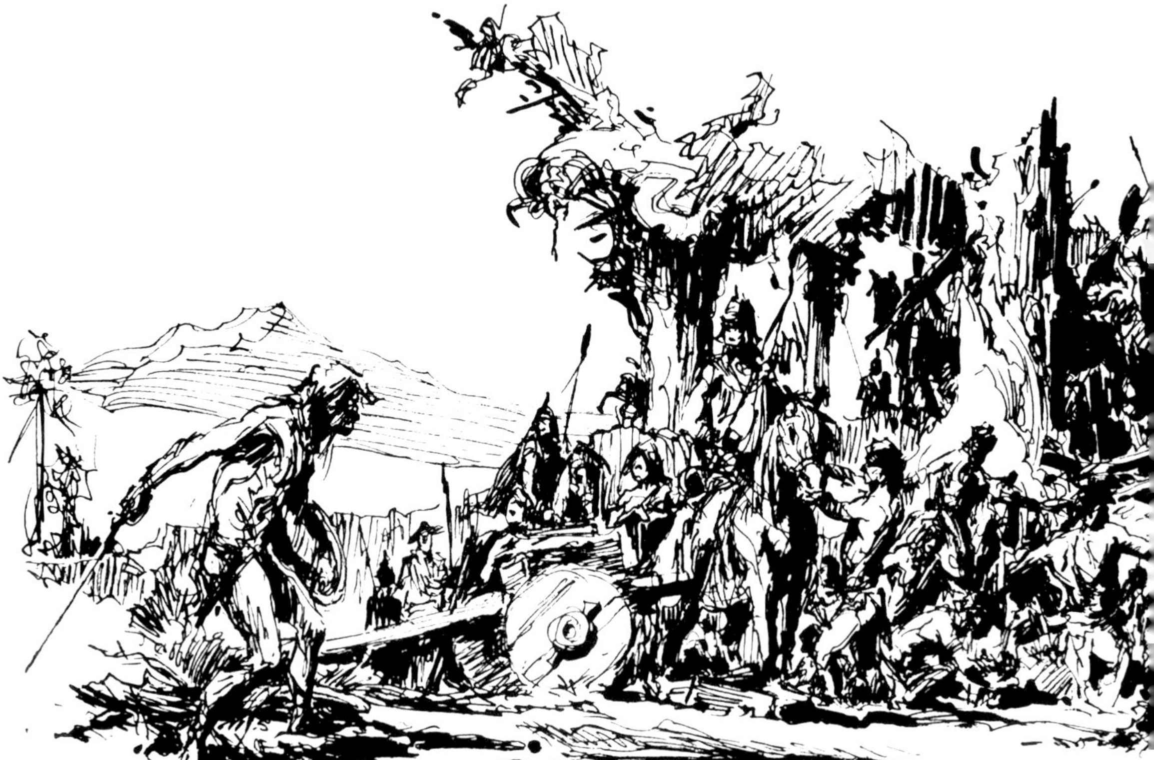

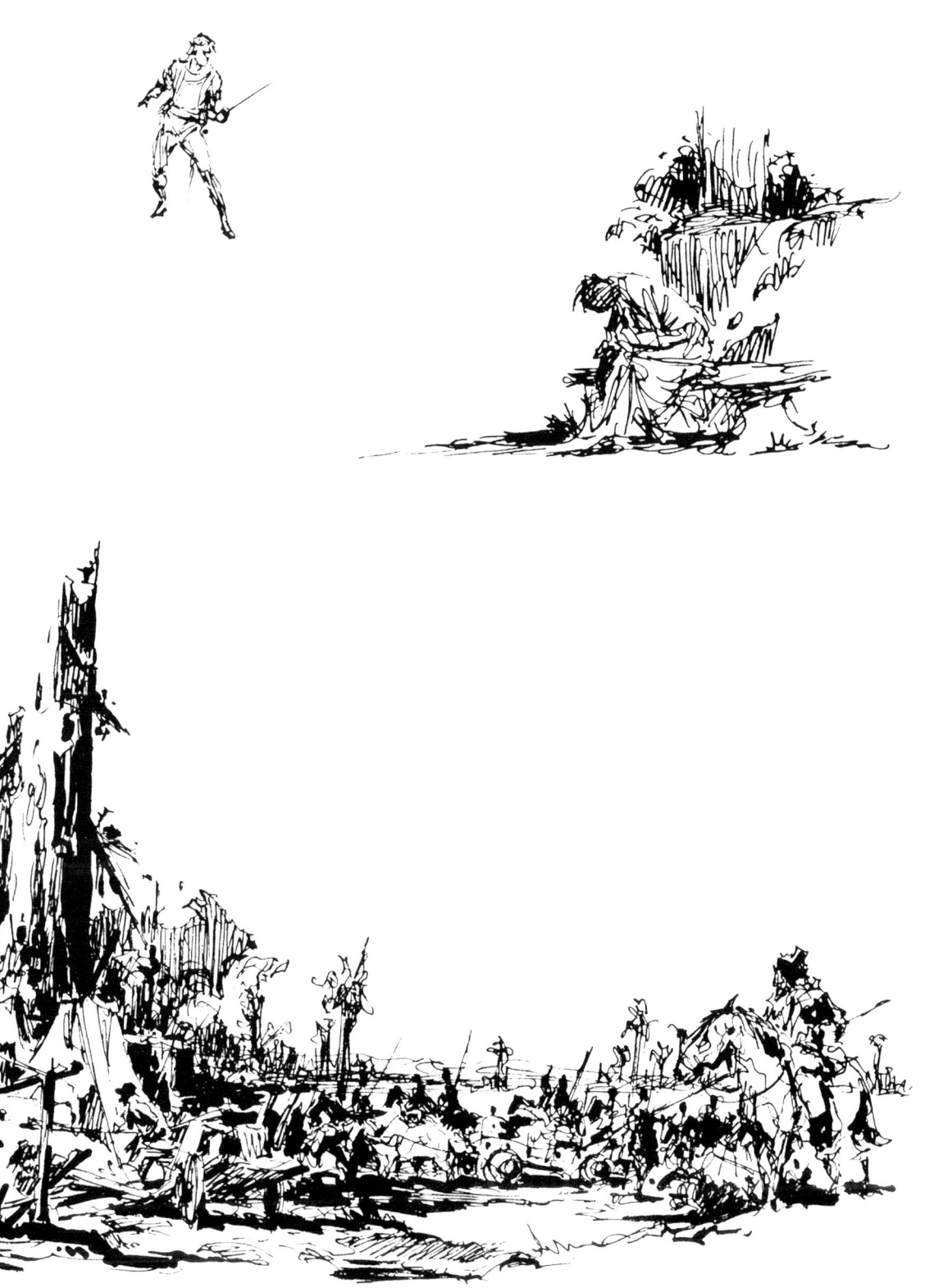

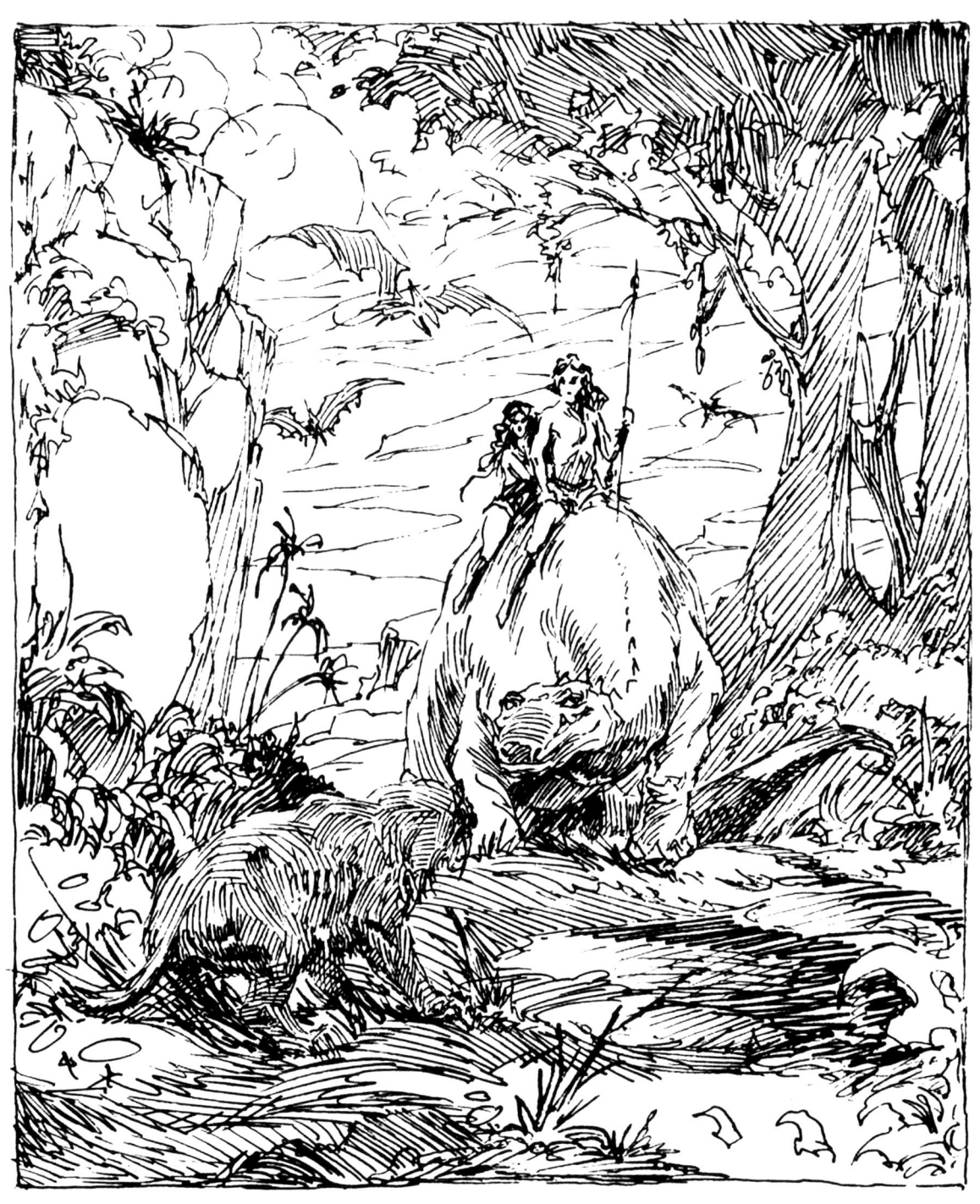